T0256181

HANDBOOK ON TOURISM AND SOCIAL MEDIA

RESEARCH HANDBOOKS IN TOURISM

Series Editor: Robin Nunkoo, *University of Mauritius*

This timely series brings together critical and thought-provoking contributions on key topics and issues in tourism and hospitality research from a range of management and social science perspectives. Comprising specially-commissioned chapters from leading academics these comprehensive *Research Handbooks* feature cutting-edge research and are written with a global readership in mind. Equally useful as reference tools or high-level introductions to specific topics, issues, methods and debates, these *Research Handbooks* will be an essential resource for academic researchers and postgraduate students.

Titles in this series include:

Handbook of Social Tourism
Edited by Anya Diekmann and Scott McCabe

Handbook for Sustainable Tourism Practitioners
The Essential Toolbox
Edited by Anna Spenceley

Handbook on Tourism and Social Media
Edited by Dogan Gursoy and Rahul Pratap Singh Kaurav

Handbook on Tourism and Social Media

Edited by

Dogan Gursoy

Taco Bell Distinguished Professor, School of Hospitality Business Management, Carson College of Business, Washington State University, USA

Rahul Pratap Singh Kaurav

Associate Professor, Fortune Institute of International Business (FIIB), New Delhi, India

RESEARCH HANDBOOKS IN TOURISM

Edward Elgar
PUBLISHING

Cheltenham, UK • Northampton, MA, USA

Published by
Edward Elgar Publishing Limited
The Lypiatts
15 Lansdown Road
Cheltenham
Glos GL50 2JA
UK

Edward Elgar Publishing, Inc.
William Pratt House
9 Dewey Court
Northampton
Massachusetts 01060
USA

A catalogue record for this book
is available from the British Library

This book is available electronically in the **Elgar**online
Geography, Planning and Tourism subject collection
http://dx.doi.org/10.4337/9781800371415

ISBN 978 1 80037 140 8 (cased)
ISBN 978 1 80037 141 5 (eBook)

Printed and bound by CPI Group (UK) Ltd, Croydon, CR0 4YY

Contents

PART III   MARKETING STRATEGIES, CHANNELS, FORMATS

PART IV   TRAVEL BLOGS, USER-GENERATED CONTENT, REVIEWS AND E-WOM

Contributors

Orhan Akova, Istanbul University, Istanbul, Turkey.

Mani Shah Alizadegan, James Cook University, Australia.

Özlem Altun, Faculty of Tourism, Eastern Mediterranean University, TRNC.

Kubra Asan, School of Tourism and Hotel Management, Sinop University, Turkey.

Ozan Atsiz, Yozgat Bozok University, Yozgat, Turkey .

Mehmet Veysi Babayiğit, School of Foreign Languages, Batman University, Turkey.

Prerana Baber, Jiwaji University, Gwalior, India.

Ruth Bamidele, Faculty of Tourism, Eastern Mediterranean University, Turkey.

Cathrine Banga, Faculty of Tourism, Eastern Mediterranean University, Turkey.

Kulvinder Kaur Batth, KC College, India.

Daniel Binder, FH Joanneum, University of Applied Sciences, Graz, Austria.

Evrim Çeltek, Tokat Gaziosmanpaşa University, Turkey.

Heena Chauhan, Amity University, India.

Farah S. Choudhary, The Business School, University of Jammu, India.

Olgun Cicek, University of South Florida, USA.

Ibrahim Cifci, Istanbul University, Istanbul, Turkey.

Merve Aydogan Cifci, Istanbul University, Istanbul, Turkey.

Mehmet Necati Cizrelioğulları, Faculty of Tourism, Cyprus Science University, TRNC.

André F. Durão, Federal University of Pernambuco UFPE, Brazil.

Sheereen Fauzel, Department of Finance and Accounting, University of Mauritius.

Francesc Fusté-Forné, School of Communication and International Relations, Ramon Llull University, Spain.

Sevinc Goktepe, Istanbul University, Istanbul, Turkey.

Pramita Gurjar, Jiwaji University, India.

Dogan Gursoy, School of Hospitality Business Management, Carson College of Business, Washington State University, USA.

Robert Gutounig, FH Joanneum, University of Applied Sciences, Graz, Austria.

Kathryn Hayat, Department of Hospitality & Tourism, University College Birmingham, UK.

Mahmoud M. Hewedi, Department of Hotel Studies, Faculty of Tourism and Hotels, Fayoum University, Egypt.

Komal Kapoor, IMS Ghaziabad, India.

Rahul Pratap Singh Kaurav, Fortune Institute of International Business (FIIB), New Delhi, India.

Hasan Kilic, Faculty of Tourism, Eastern Mediterranean University, Turkey.

Olga Rauhut Kompaniets, Halmstad University, Sweden.

Kuan-Huei Lee, Singapore Institute of Technology, Singapore.

Seungwon (Shawn) Lee, Tourism and Events Management, George Mason University, USA.

Yulin Liu, James Cook University, Australia.

Xander Lub, Nyenrode Business Universiteit Amsterdam, The Netherlands.

Sandra Macher, FH Joanneum, University of Applied Sciences, Graz, Austria.

Giulio Maggiore, Department of Law and Economics, University of Rome, Italy.

Salman Majeed, International center for Hospitality Research and Development, Dedman College of Hospitality, Florida State University, Tallahassee, Florida, USA.

Sarasadat Makian, Urban Planning and Alpine Geography Institute, Grenoble Alpes University, France.

Vittoria Marino, Department of Law, Economics, Management and Quantitative Methods, University of Sannio Benevento, Italy.

Pere Masip, School of Communication and International Relations, Ramon Llull University, Spain.

Brent McKenzie, Department of Marketing and Consumer Studies, Lang School of Business and Economics, University of Guelph, Canada.

Mohamed E.A. Mohamed, School of Hospitality and Tourism Management, Purdue University, USA and Department of Hotel Studies, Faculty of Tourism and Hotels, Fayoum University, Egypt.

Elangkovan Narayanan, Taylor's Business School, Taylor's University Malaysia.

Mert Ogretmenoglu, Istanbul University, Istanbul, Turkey.

Ali Ozturen, Faculty of Tourism, Eastern Mediterranean University, Turkey.

Piyush Pandey, Faculty of Commerce, Banaras Hindu University, Varanasi, India.

Birgit Phillips, Institute of Educational Sciences, University of Graz, Austria and FH Burgenland University of Applied Sciences, Austria.

Letizia Lo Presti, Department of Law and Economics, University of Rome, Italy.

Sonja Radkohl, FH Joanneum, University of Applied Sciences, Graz, Austria.

Haywantee Ramkissoon, College of Business, Law, and Social Sciences, Derby Business School, University of Derby, UK; School of Business and Economics, UiT, The Arctic University of Norway, Norway; College of Business & Economics, Johannesburg Business School, University of Johannesburg, South Africa.

João Romão, Department of International Tourism and Business, Yasuda Women's University, Japan.

Mehmet Altug Sahin, Istanbul University, Istanbul, Turkey.

Kaede Sano, Faculty of Tourism, Wakayama University, Japan.

Nur Syazreema Binte Sazari, Infocomm Technology, Singapore Institute of Technology.

Karina Schaffer, FH Joanneum, University of Applied Sciences, Graz, Austria.

Alka Sharma, The Business School, University of Jammu, India.

Si Shi, Department of Tourism Management, School of Business Administration, Southwestern University of Finance and Economics, China.

Pramendra Singh, Amity University, India.

Heather Skinner, Institute of Place Management, Manchester Metropolitan University, UK.

Susan L. Slocum, Tourism and Events Management, George Mason University, USA.

Verena Tandrayen-Ragoobur, Department of Economics and Statistics, University of Mauritius.

K.S. Thakur, School of Commerce and Business Studies, Jiwaji University, India.

Gozde Turktarhan, University of South Florida, USA.

Gulcin Bilgin Turna, Recep Tayyip Erdogan University, Turkey.

Helena A. Williams, Mohammed VI Polytechnic University, Morocco.

Robert L. Williams Jr, Clarkson University, USA.

Oya Yildirim, Accommodation Management Department, Karataş School of Tourism and Hotel Management, Çukurova University, Turkey.

Medet Yolal, Anadolu University, Eskisehir, Turkey.

Zhengkui Wang, Singapore Institute of Technology, Singapore.

1. Introduction to the *Handbook on Tourism and Social Media*

Rahul Pratap Singh Kaurav and Dogan Gursoy

The rapid development of information technology during the last two decades and the resulting social media development have significantly influenced and reshaped tourism, hospitality and events domains. Even though most of the social media platforms have emerged during the last decade, those social media platforms have become critical mediums for information dissemination and gathering for both consumers and destination marketers and managers. Since consumers heavily use social media and peer-to-peer information sharing platforms as critical sources of information during their decision-making processes, it is not surprising to see that those social media platforms have also become one of the major information sources of information for destination marketers, managers and planners that play important roles in destination policy and strategy development and the dissemination of information related to destination policies and strategies.

The very quick development of information technologies and the rapidly growing speed of information dissemination through the internet have tremendously revolutionized the tourism and hospitality industries. The internet started with the introduction of Web 1.0, and Web 2.0 has led to the emergence of social media environments, which have affected the connectivity of travelers and tourists around the world. Today, travelers gain their knowledge and evaluate destinations through utilizing several information sources, including traditional media, social media and peer-to-peer information sharing websites. Thus, what is being posted and reported in these traditional and non-traditional outlets plays an important role in travelers' destination selection and decision-making process. However, in recent years, the role played by traditional media outlets in the destination selection and decision-making process has been decreasing rapidly, while social media and peer-to-peer information sharing sites have been playing increasingly critical roles. However, the influences of social media and peer-to-peer information sharing sites on tourists' destination selection and decision-making process are very diverse and the components are very complex. Thus, destinations need to pay close attention to how and what type of information is being disseminated through a number of social media mediums and channels, and actively manage those channels in order to positively influence tourists' destination selection and decision-making processes.

It is important for destination managers and marketers to understand that information on social media flows not only from the official destination accounts but also from a large number of independent social media accounts, which serve as both producers and disseminators of information that can influence social media users' destination selection and decision-making processes. While those social media posts can have a great influence on travelers' attitudes and behaviors, they can also influence destination policies, strategies and future plans; since tourism is a highly sensitive and vulnerable industry, information disseminated on social media sites about destinations can significantly influence how social media user view them. Thus, it is critical for destination managers and marketers to pay close attention to the information shared by individuals on social media and peer-to-peer information sharing sites, in order to manage their effects on the destination and on potential visitors to the destination. Because of increasing interest among academic researchers in the increasingly important role of social media in the tourism and travel industry, a good number of studies have reviewed and investigated this relationship.

A quick review of the Web of Science records indicates that the number of papers which examined tourism and social media increased by more than 5000 per cent from 2009 to 2020. According to very recent statistics from the Web of Science, in total 1702 articles have been found by using a search string ["tourism" AND "social media"]. The research growth rate and pattern is indicated in Figure 1.1, which very clearly indicates the increase in academic research, and hence the potential for young and new scholars interested in similar themes. Recent studies report that more than 67 percent of the information travelers use in destination selection and travel decision-making processes is gathered from virtual communities such as social media platforms and blogs. These trends clearly explain why destination managers, marketers, planners, researchers and decision-makers are becoming more interested in understanding the role of social media in tourism and hospitality. These trends can also explain why academia is also more interested in deciphering how in future managers and planners can develop more suitable social media skillsets.

Table 1.1, based on the records of the Web of Science, shows the authors who have written the most papers researching tourism and social media. We selected the authors who have written more than ten academic papers. The list indicates good collaboration opportunities for mid-stage researchers.

The *Handbook on Tourism and Social Media* carefully examines social media issues and challenges raised in the contemporary literature that are faced by destinations in their every-

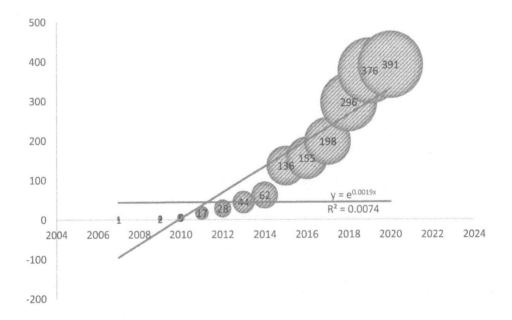

Figure 1.1   *Increasing academic research on tourism and social media*

Table 1.1   *Authors contributing the most research on tourism and social media*

Authors	Records
Law, R.	33
Buhalis, D.	21
Gretzel, U.	12
Vu, H.Q.	10
Xiang, Z.	10

Source: Authors from Web of Science.

day operations. Defining key social media concepts and issues, and exploring the type of impacts they may have on the success of destinations, can enable us to set the stage for a better understanding of the relationships between social media and tourism. Furthermore, examining the current key trends and issues and then focusing on future trends within social media and destinations can provide critical insights for the successful development and implementation of destination social media marketing strategies and activities. The *Handbook on Tourism and Social Media* aims to examine key social media issues and challenges faced by destinations by carefully investigating destination social media practices and academic literature, in order to develop and propose strategies to address those key social media issues and challenges.

Our vision for this *Handbook* is to create an international platform for balanced academic social media research in tourism, with practical applications for destination managers and marketers, to foster synergetic interaction between academia and industry. This *Handbook* includes a collection of conceptual and empirical research chapters, practical case studies and review chapters, written by experts in the field, in order to develop a better understanding of the relationship between tourism and social media. The collection of topics presented in this *Handbook* represents an unprecedented scholarly attempt to cover a large number of both conceptual and practical topics. The contributors to this *Handbook* have provided in-depth coverage of each conceptual and practical topic, so that each chapter can serve as a trusted source of reference which can provide essential knowledge and references on the respective topic for academics and practitioners. It is our strong belief that the topics included in this *Handbook* will appeal to both researchers and practitioners. It is our sincere hope that those chapters will contribute to knowledge and theory of social media utilization in destination marketing and management as distinct, multifaceted fields, approached through the administrative disciplines, the liberal arts and the social sciences. Furthermore, this *Handbook* provides an outlet for innovative studies that can make a significant contribution to the understanding, practice and education of destination social media marketers and managers. We strongly believe that each chapter included in this *Handbook* will make a significant contribution to the dissemination of knowledge, while serving as a unique forum for both industry and academia.

The *Handbook on Tourism and Social Media* addresses cutting-edge social media issues in destination management and marketing. It includes 35 further chapters originating from leading social media scholars in the field. The book is divided into seven thematic parts, each theme exploring social media issues that are critical for destinations.

Part I provides an overview of consumer behaviour and social media and provides definitions of various concepts, and the role of social media in consumer behaviors. It also provides a critical review of factors that are likely to play important roles in consumer behavior and social media.

Part II focuses on effects of social media on destinations and destination management/marketing organizations (DMOs). The chapters in this part show how DMOs have adopted social media in marketing and other management-related models. They also investigate destination image, brand image, and the visit intentions of tourists; and how online tourism communications affect image formation.

Part III examines social media marketing strategies, channels and formats. Social media marketing issues and challenges faced by destinations, and marketing strategies that are appropriate for various destinations, are discussed in these chapters.

Part IV investigates travel blogs, user-generated content, reviews, and electronic word-of-mouth (e-WOM). How user-generated content influences the decisions of other travelers is the main focus. The chapters adopt different methodologies: qualitative, quantitative, sentiment analytics, netnography, and others.

Part V examines the relationships between social media and decision-making by travelers. How social media stimulates the decisions of travelers, different phases, actions and motivations, are explored.

Part VI investigates the effects of social media on culinary and food tourism. Gastronomic events and further gastronomy-related aspects are explored. Chapter 31, specifically, talks about generation Z; while Chapter 32 reconnoiteres a case study on Singapore food tourism.

Part VII provides a critical overview of business performance-related challenges. It especially explores legal aspects and privacy-related issues. How social media supports the development of tourism, hospitality and events, and what Web 2.0 is, are addressed.

We, as editors of the *Handbook on Tourism and Social Media*, acknowledge the fact that we may have left out some critical topics and/or concepts. For the sake of simplicity and functionality we have focused on the topics that are most critical for social media researchers and tourism practitioners. Thus, the topics included in this *Handbook* do not provide complete or exhaustive coverage of the social media topics in tourism. For this, we apologize. Our goal is to simply gather together in one place the most critical social media topics in tourism, in order to create a credible source of information for today's and future researchers and practitioners to use as a point of departure for their research initiatives and business endeavors.

Contributors to this *Handbook* have worked countless hours to provide an in-depth coverage of each conceptual and practical topic, so that each chapter may serve as a trusted source of reference that can provide essential knowledge and references on the respective topic for academics and practitioners. We would like to express our sincere gratitude and thanks to all the contributors who graciously volunteered their time and effort to put this amazing *Handbook* together.

PART I

CONSUMER BEHAVIOUR AND SOCIAL MEDIA

2. Efficacy of social media in influencing consumer adoption intention for tourism decisions

Piyush Pandey

INTRODUCTION

Revolutionary changes in the Internet world and progress in hardware and software technologies to support these changes, starting in the early 2000s, came to be known as Web 2.0. Thereafter, with the concomitant advancements in the mobile technology and mobile Internet, the dynamic dimension of social media took birth. The term 'Web 2.0,' invented by Tim O'Reilly and Dale Dougherty at the O'Reilly Media Web 2.0 Conference, refers to the group of websites that accentuate ease of use, participatory culture, user-generated content and interoperability for the end users. The attributes of social media were enumerated as openness of information, reciprocity, connectivity, cooperation, participation, interactivity, creativity and sharing by Saravana Kumar and Sugandha Lakshmi (Cao et al., 2017). Hu and Liu (2015) declared three basic characters of social media: hypertext, interactive and multimedia.

Web 2.0, along with social media, has a gigantic role to play in tourism because the tourism industry intensifies and is centred on information. Philip C. Wolf, who is the president and chief executive officer of PhoCusWright, a lead consultancy firm in the tourism sector, termed the Web 2.0 applications as Travel 2.0 for the tourism industry (Miguens et al., 2008). Tourists, or the individuals in the process of making tourism-related decisions, have to bear the high risk that is inherent in the experimental characteristics of travel decisions. Travel decisions such as purchases to be made for travel and during travel, hiring of agents, means of commute, etc. encompass a certain degree of risk. In order to minimise risk in making such decisions, an individual must have sufficient and reliable knowledge about various aspects of traveling (Sirakaya and Woodside, 2005). Web 2.0, along with social media, allows tourism consumers to access such information and options for purchase, that in the traditional method could have been given only by intermediaries and agents (Buhalis and Law, 2008).

The majority of the studies that have been conducted on estimating the association between tourism and social media have limited themselves to analysing the role and effects of the inclusion of social media in industrial marketing practices. The studies have analysed social media as an effective marketing tool for businesses and a facilitating media for tourism consumers. Social media assists in shaping the image of the tourists' destinations, and the image of the businesses and agents providing tourism-related services (Milano et al., 2011). However, studies analysing the impact of characteristics of social media platforms on the factor of consumer adoption intention in the case of tourism decisions is sparse (Cao et al., 2017). This chapter attempts to analyse the various elements or characteristics of social media platforms that may have an effect on the intention of the tourism customers to adopt social media, and to study the possible magnitude and direction of effect of such variables or factors on the adoption intention of tourism consumers regarding social media. The chapter also analyses the role of individual heterogeneity in influencing the level of intent of the consumers of tourism to adopt social media.

REVIEW OF LITERATURE

The concept of social media originated in the field of information science, which described social media as a 'communication space' that is a result of social networking services. Various authors have enumerated different platforms as examples of social media. Centred on a review of previous studies, the various social media platforms have been categorised as follows: social networking sites, instant messenger, online encyclopaedias, community networks, content community, microblogging sites, online blogs social review sites, podcasts and online tourist forums (Sigala, 2007; Zeng, 2013; Munar and Jacobsen, 2013; Živković et al., 2014; Cao et al., 2017; Kakkar, 2018).

Tourism is regarded as short-term movement that can be undertaken for a variety of reasons, including sightseeing, adventure, education, culture, profession, and many more. Tourism also encompasses the activities that are undertaken to make travel a success. It has become a business which provides accommodation and supplementary services to tourists. As mentioned by the previous studies, the various types or purpose of tourism have been categorised as follows: sightseeing/entertainment tourism, personal and family concerns tourism, cultural tourism, ecology adventure tourism, professional/work-related tourism, study-related tourism, health-related/medical tourism (Tureac, 2008; Singh, 2011; Arunmozhi and Panneerselvam, 2013; Cao et al., 2017; Dey, 2018).

There are varied categories of social media available under the nexus of Web 2.0 and more are being added each day with improved and innovative features. A number of inherent attributes of social media have been mentioned by previous researchers. According to Gronroos (1984), the quality of a service depends on two factors: the expected service quality, and the actual or perceived service quality. He also categorised the service quality into technical service quality and functional service quality, where the procedural performance of a service is denoted as technical service quality, and the expressive performance of a service refers to the functional quality of a service. As proposed by Chen and Wang (2005) the perception of the service quality of e-commerce services by the network consumers has a direct impact on the buying behaviour of customers:

H1: The perception of consumers about the service quality of social media has a significant effect on consumer adoption intention.

The customer's perception of the services and their participation has an important association with the customer's decision to buy the product or service, to search for the same product or service elsewhere, or to totally postpone the buying decision (Straus et al., 2016). As stated by Dong et al. (2015), an increase in customer participation has an enhancing effect on the perceived service quality. Therefore, with an increase in the level of participation of tourism consumers in social media, their probability of adopting social media for tourism purposes increases (Cao et al., 2017):

H2: The level of participation of consumers in social media has a significant effect on consumer adoption intention.

The process of direct interaction between a user and a social media platform which facilitates communication is referred to as interactivity (Palmer, 2002). According to Teo et al. (2003), interactive marketing strategies such as mobile business circle, SMS website, mobile QR (quick response) code, wireless web, and so on, have a significantly positive impact on the behaviour of consumers. One of the key factors that fosters a sense of belonging in the users is the process of interaction (Rovai, 2002). Therefore, consumers' adoption intention may increase with an increase in the interactivity features of social media (Cao et al., 2017):

H3: The perceived interactivity of social media by the consumers has a significant effect on consumer adoption intention.

As explained by Kaplan and Haenlein (2010), social media platforms are the applications that empower the users to connect to other users, along with connecting to a pool of varied information. Connectedness is one of the basic attributes of Web 2.0-based applications of social media. (Constantinides and Fountain, 2008). Jiao et al. (2013a) put forward that the level of connectivity of social media platforms has a significant impact on trust of the users, as well as on their consumer decision-making:

H4: The perceived connectivity of social media by the consumers has significant effect on consumer adoption intention.

The users of social media tend to share information on social media, and express their likes and dislikes and give their views on the information provided by others. Therefore, the consumers can share their views, their experiences of the quality of products and services, their likes and dislikes, and so on (Constantinides and Fountain, 2008; Kaplan and Haenlein, 2010). Jiao et al. (2013b) put forward that that the users of social media often form a group that behaves like a community, and tend to focus on the discussion of common topics of interest by creation of a circle that is used as a medium to share their feelings, experiences and other information. As social media facilitates sharing, it may have a significantly positive impact on the adoption intention of tourism consumers (Cao et al., 2017):

H5: The perception of consumers regarding sharing in social media has a significant effect on consumer adoption intention.

Being effective refers to the degree or the level of consistency that exists amid the information provided on the social media platforms about various aspects of tourism and the actual experience of the traveller (Cao et al., 2017). Kim et al. (2017) claim that an effective social media platform or page would have a good impact on the trustworthiness of the social media as perceived by the user, and will encourage them to use the provided information in both the cognitive and the affective sense. Schwabe and Prestipino (2005) argued that the quality of travel-related information provided by social media has a direct and positive effect on the travel quality perceived by the consumers:

H6: The perceived information effectiveness of social media by the consumers has a significant effect on consumer adoption intention.

The technology acceptance model (TAM) originally stemmed from the theory of reasoned action (TRA) which was put forward by Ajzen and Fishbein (1980). The theory of reasoned action says that a voluntary action of an individual, or behaviour, can be predicted by the attitude the individual shows towards a behaviour, based on what he perceives to be the beliefs of others regarding the same behaviour. With the help of this theory, Davis (1989) then proposed the TAM, which says that the behavioural intention of an individual can be determined by two primary variables: the perceived ease of use, and the perceived usefulness. Perceived usefulness is explained as the degree of belief of a person towards the personal and professional growth that they may gain by the use of a particular system. Perceived ease of use is explained as the degree of effortlessness that an individual believes would be involved while using a system; it is the perceived extent of freedom from complexities while using a system (Sin et al., 2012; Wirtz and Göttel, 2016). It has been reasoned that perceived usefulness and perceived ease of use may have a significantly positive impact on the consumer's intention to adopt a system (Romero et al., 2011; López et al., 2011; Chung and Koo, 2015):

H7: The perceived ease of use of social media by consumers has a significant effect on consumer adoption intention.

H8: The perceived usefulness of social media by consumers has a significant effect on consumer adoption intention.

Consumer Intention to Adopt Social Media for Tourism Decisions

The majority of the researchers on consumer adoption intention have based their studies wholly on the technology acceptance model (TAM). The theory postulates that usage of a system is governed by the behavioural intentions of the users. Two factors – perceived ease of use and perceived usefulness (also referred to as perceived convenience) – construct the variable 'behavioural intention'. The factor of perceived ease of use, along with external variables, influences the perceived usefulness, whereas perceived convenience is affected by the external variables. Therefore, it has been ascertained that the behavioural intention of the consumers or users towards a new system has a decisive influence on the effective adoption of the technology. In a nutshell, if a consumer is not willing to embrace a specific system or technology, the technology itself cannot be successful in meeting its purpose (Davis, 1989). According to Akman and Mishra (2017), a user's intention to use social media acts as a mediating factor for the consumer's actual use of social media. Therefore, the stronger a consumer's adoption intention of a system, the more effort and time they will put into the use of the system (Cao et al., 2017).

The adoption intention of the consumers for social media depends on the quality of instant user experience and the level of satisfaction derived. Jiao et al. (2013b) studied the effects of specific attributes of social media (participation, interaction, openness of information, connectivity and sharing) on the social media adoption intention of consumers. The results confirmed that the social media characteristics have a significantly positive effect on consumer adoption intention, with 'sharing' having the highest effect, followed by 'interaction', the two most important elements in information searches. Xiang and Gertzel (2010) declare in their study that social media sites form a major portion of the search results when individuals search for travel-related information on various search engines such as Google and Yahoo!. This indicates that the search engines tend to direct the individuals to social media sites when a search for travel information is made. Davis (1989), in his study on the relationship between features of a new system and user intention to adopt the system, states that perceived usefulness of a technology shows significantly high correlation with the current usage of the system as well as with self-predicted future usage. Similarly, perceived ease of use was shown to have a significant positive correlation with current use and future use of the technology. However, perceived usefulness had greater correlation with the usage intention as compared to perceived ease of use.

RESEARCH DESIGN

Design of Questionnaire and Pilot Study

The questionnaire developed for the study consists of two parts. The first part consists of items that measure demographic profile of the respondents, the frequency of their social media usage, the frequency of making travel decisions and the type of tourism undertaken. The second part of the questionnaire consists of questions or items that measure various constructs or variables to be analysed in the study. The questions or items for the constructs have been adopted from standardised questionnaires of previous researches. The consumer adoption intention (*ConAIn*) variable is measured by four items which were adopted from Davis (1989) and Cao et al. (2017). The characteristics of social media is measured by 28 scale items which are divided into 8 sub-scales: the participation (*PART*) scale was adopted from Cermak et al. (1994) and Cao et al. (2017); the interactivity (*INTER*) scale was adopted from Palmer (2002), Jiang and Benbasat (2007) and Cao et al. (2017); the sharing (*SHARE*) scale was adopted from Ennew and Binks (1999) and Cao et al. (2017); the connectivity (*CONN*) scale was adopted from Lee (2005) and Cao et al. (2017); the service quality (*SERVQ*) scale was adopted from Alsajjan and Dennis (2006) and Cao et al. (2017), each consisting of three items; the perceived ease of use (*PerEase*, four items) and perceived usefulness (*PerUse*, five items) scales were adopted from Huang et al. (2012) and Lee and Lehto (2013); and the information effectiveness scale (*INFEFF*, four items) was adopted from Cao et al. (2017). The respondents were required to provide their answers on a scale of 5 (strongly agree) to 1 (strongly disagree), depending on the extent to which a particular item describes them or suits them.

The questionnaire was initially administered to 58 individuals from five different cities in Uttar Pradesh – Varanasi, Lucknow, Noida, Kanpur and Ghazipur – with the help of relatives and friends, in order to test the overall reliability of the questionnaire. Out of the 58 questionnaires, 51 were valid and fully filled questionnaires with a valid rate of 87.93 per cent. The reliability of the items was checked with the help of Cronbach's α examined with SPSS 20. The value of Cronbach's α for the sample of 51 individuals was 0.880, which shows the good consistency and reliability of the whole scale. Thereafter, the questionnaire was further administered.

Table 2.1   *Reliability statistics, KMO and Bartlett's test*

Cronbach's alpha	N of Items
0.970	32
Kaiser–Meyer–Olkin measure of sampling adequacy.	0.902
Approx. chi-square	5570.305
df	496
Sig.	0.000***

Note: *Significant at 0.05 level. **Significant at 0.01 level. ***Significant at 0.001 level.

Sample Selection and Data Collection

The sample for the present study consists of individuals who are residents of Uttar Pradesh and have used social media for making tourism decisions at least once. The questionnaire was distributed to individuals from various cities of Uttar Pradesh. The data was also collected by personal visits to various tourist sites in Uttar Pradesh such as Sarnath, Agra Fort, Kashi Vishwanath Temple, Ganga Ghats, Bada Imambada, Mathura, Iskcon Vrindavan, Ramnagar Fort and Ambedkar Memorial Park. The data was collected by the researcher as well as with the help of friends and relatives resident in the respective cities. A total of 183 questionnaires were administered. with 168 duly filled and valid questionnaires, with a response rate of 91.80 per cent. As the total number of items in the study was 32, the sample size fits the criteria of having a sample size of five times the number of items and a minimum size of 100 participants (Dhall, 2020). The data was collected from December 2019 to March 2020; however, due to successive lockdown periods, data from 31 individuals was collected with the help of Google Forms. The demographic profile of the respondents has been enlisted in Table 2.2.

Reliability and Validity of the Questionnaire

As shown in Table 2.1, the overall reliability of items of the questionnaire was tested with the help of Cronbach's alpha, which has a value of 0.970, showing a good and acceptable reliability of the questionnaire. The Kaiser–Meyer–Olkin (KMO) measure of sampling adequacy has a value of 0.902 and the value of chi-square for Bartlett's test of sphericity shows significance at the 0.001 level, implying the adequacy of the sample, its validity, and that it satisfies the conditions required to conduct factor analysis. Thereafter, for further analysis of data, t-test, one-way ANOVA, factor analysis and multiple regression were applied.

DATA ANALYSIS AND INTERPRETATION

Descriptive Statistics

Types of social media platforms used

The different social media platforms used by the respondents while making a travel decision, and the percentage share of each platform (in descending order) amongst the respondents, are as follows: (1) users of social networking websites (Facebook, Instagram) account for 79.80 per cent of respondents; (2) users of instant messenger (MSN, WhatsApp, Yahoo Messenger, Skype, Facebook Messenger, and so on) and content community (Flickr,

YouTube, SlideShare, and so on), account for 56 per cent of respondents; (3) 44 per cent of respondents use online encyclopaedias (such as Wikipedia); (4) online blogs are used by 40.50 per cent of the respondents; (5) online tourist forums were used by 35.7 per cent of respondents; (6) social review sites (Tripadvisor, Trivago, and so on) had a usage frequency of 27.28 per cent; and (7) the three platforms – community networks (MySpace, Google Plus, Vine, and so on), microblogging sites (Twitter, Pinterest, Digg, and so on) and podcasts – had minimal usage frequency of 20.23 per cent, 9.5 per cent and 2.4 per cent, respectively.

Purpose of travel or type of travel

The type of tourism undertaken by the respondents, or their purpose of tourism, and the percentage share of each tourism purpose (in descending order) amongst the respondents, is as follows: (1) sightseeing/entertainment tourism accounts for 90.5 per cent; (2) cultural tourism accounts for 41.7 per cent; (3) personal and family concerns tourism accounts for 40.5 per cent; (4) ecology/adventure tourism accounts for 31 per cent; (5) study-related tourism accounts for 23.8 per cent; (6) professional/work-related tourism accounts for 19 per cent; and (7) health-related/medical tourism accounts for 7.1 per cent.

Category of information searched

The type or category of information related to travel that the respondents sought from the social media platforms, and the percentage share of each information type (in descending order) is as follows: (1) information about price accounts for 82.1 per cent; (2) accommodation information accounts for 72.60 per cent; (3) other travellers' experience of the same destination and food-related information both account for 65.50 per cent; (4) information about travel routes accounts for 61.90 per cent; (5) Information about scenic spots and weather conditions accounts for 58.30 per cent; (6) information about special products of the place accounts for 44 per cent; (7) information related to travel guides accounts for 42.90 per cent; (8) information about local customs and environment and the entertainment facilities available accounts for 36.9 per cent; and (9) travel agency information and traffic information account for 17.9 per cent and 13.1 per cent, respectively.

Frequency of use of social media and travel activity

The majority of the individuals surveyed in the study, 74.4 per cent, use social media on a day-to-day basis. Among the respondents, 11.9 per cent use social media more than once a week, followed by 6.5 per cent of users who use social media once a week. The percentage share of users using social media once a month was very low, at 4.8 per cent.

Among the respondents of the study, the majority, 44 per cent, undertake travel activities once a year, followed by 35.7 per cent of respondents who opt for travel activities once in six months. The individuals undertaking travel activities once within a period of three months accounted for 10.7 per cent, and the lowest share (9.5 per cent) was of the respondents who undertook travel activities with an interval of more than a year.

Factor Analysis

Based on the items in the questionnaire for the research and the data collected through it, the principal factors that may have an influence on the consumer's intention to adopt social media for tourism purpose were extracted using factor analysis. The method of extraction used

Table 2.2   *Demographic profile of respondents*

Dimension		Number	%
Gender	Male	90	53.6
	Female	78	46.6
Age	18–30	78	46.6
	31–40	35	20.8
	41–50	21	12.5
	51–60	21	12.5
	>60	13	7.7
Education Level	Intermediate	11	6.5
	Graduation	58	34.5
	Postgraduation	60	35.7
	Above graduation	39	23.2
Monthly Income	<₹25 000	76	45.2
	₹25 000–₹50 000	46	27.4
	₹50 000–₹100 000	30	17.9
	>₹100 000	16	9.5
Occupation	Business	12	7.1
	Profession	14	8.3
	Non-government employment	18	10.7
	Employed in government	22	13.1
	Pensioner	10	6.0
	Housewife	12	7.1
	Student	80	47.6
Marital Status	Married	47	28.0
	Unmarried	121	72.0

was principal components analysis (PCA). The factor loadings above 0.5 were considered for selection. Item *PerUse_4* did not load more than the cut-off value of 0.5 on any of the components, and therefore was removed from further analysis. The results of factor analysis confirmed the presence of nine factors. The one factor which measured the extent of intention to adopt was named as consumer adoption intention (*ConAIn*). The other eight factors which measure various characteristics of social media are named as participation (*PART*), interactivity (*INTER*), sharing (*SHARE*), connectivity (*CONN*), service quality (*SERVQ*), perceived ease of use (*PerEase*), perceived usefulness (*PerUse*), and information effectiveness (*INFEFF*) (Table 2.3).

Table 2.3 also reports the Cronbach's α for each construct, along with their average variance extracted and composite reliabilities. (Fornell and Larcker, 1981) The Cronbach's α (CA) and the composite reliability (CR) for each construct are more than 0.70, signifying that the constructs have good reliability and internal consistency (Nunnally, 1978). The average variance extracted (AVE) for every construct is more than 0.50, and majority of the factors loadings are more than 0.70, which indicates that the criteria for convergent validity is met (Hair et al., 2011).

Table 2.3   *Factor analysis (pattern matrix)*

Construct	Item	Factor Loading	CA	CR	AVE
Consumer adoption intention (CAI)	ConAIn_1	0.780	0.762	0.853	0.593
	ConAIn_2	0.704			
	ConAIn_3	0.771			
	ConAIn_4	0.821			
Participation (*PART*)	PART_1	0.592	0.752	0.749	0.502
	PART_2	0.738			
	PART_3	0.782			
Interactivity (*INTER*)	INTER_1	0.900	0.791	0.792	0.572
	INTER_2	0.807			
	INTER_3	0.507			
Sharing (*SHARE*)	SHARE_1	0.737	0.750	0.862	0.674
	SHARE_2	0.853			
	SHARE_3	0.871			
Connectivity (*CONN*)	CONN_1	0.809	0.800	0.846	0.647
	CONN_2	0.857			
	CONN_3	0.744			
Service quality (*SERVQ*)	SERVQ_1	0.709	0.882	0.823	0.609
	SERVQ_2	0.857			
	SERVQ_3	0.769			
Perceived ease of use (PEOU)	PerEase_1	0.861	0.827	0.867	0.622
	PerEase_2	0.727			
	PerEase_3	0.825			
	PerEase_4	0.733			
Perceived usefulness (*PerUse*)	PerUse_1	0.860	0.883	0.882	0.653
	PerUse_2	0.797			
	PerUse_3	0.825			
	PerUse_4	0.250			
	PerUse_5	0.745			
Information effectiveness (*INFEFF*)	INFEFF_1	0.836	0.842	0.860	0.606
	INFEFF_2	0.769			
	INFEFF_3	0.731			
	INFEFF_4	0.775			

Note: Extraction method: principal component analysis. Rotation method: Oblimin with Kaiser normalisation. Rotation converged in 29 iterations.

Analysis of Variance

Gender and marital status

Results of the t-test show that there is a highly significant difference (t (166) = -4.425; p = 0.000) between the males and females regarding consumer adoption intention (CAI). The negative value of the t-test depicts that females have significantly higher adoption intention of social media for tourism purposes as compared to their male counterparts. However, there is no significant difference (t (166) = -0.080; p = 0.937) between married and unmarried individuals regarding adoption intention of social media for tourism.

Age and education

The results of one-way ANOVA depict that CAI differs significantly (F $(4, 163)$ = 2.924; p = 0.023) with regard to the age of the respondents. Hochberg's GT2 post-hoc test was applied as there was significant difference between sample sizes in each group (Field, 2009), which shows that the individuals of age group 31–40 years differ significantly from the age group 41–50, showing that individuals have significantly higher adoption intention as compared to the age group 41–50. There was no significant difference among other age groups. Results reveal that there is no significant difference (F (3, 164) = 2.450; p = 0.065) regarding consumer adoption intention of social media among the various groups based on education level.

Income and occupation
Results of ANOVA show that there exists no significant difference (F (3, 164) = 1.069; p = 0.364) between individuals of different income groups or occupation (F (6, 161) = 1.697; p = 0.125) regarding adoption intention of social media for tourism decisions.

Frequency of using social media and frequency of travel activities
One-way ANOVA was applied in estimating whether a significant difference exists among the various groups of individuals regarding adoption intention when categorised according to the frequency with which they use social media. The same analysis was applied to test for significant difference between groups of customers when categorised according to their frequency of travel activities. The results show that there exists significant difference (F (4, 163) = 2.827; p = 0.027) between groups of frequency of social media usage, regarding their adoption intention. Moreover, there also exists significant difference (F (3, 164) = 3.924; p = 0.010) between different groups of individuals (based on frequency of travel activity) regarding their adoption intention of social media. The post-hoc tests show that individuals using social media platforms daily have significantly higher CAI as compared to individuals using social media platforms once a week. Moreover, the tests also show that individuals who have a travel frequency duration of six months have significantly higher CAI as compared to individuals having travel frequency of more than a year.

Regression Analysis

To analyse the relationship between the features of social media and the adoption intention of consumers, a multiple ordinary least squares (OLS) regression was performed. The eight characteristics of social media were the independent variables in the model and the variable consumer adoption intention was the dependent variable.

Table 2.4 shows the results of the regression analysis along with the collinearity diagnostics. The problem of multicollinearity in the model was tested with the help of variance inflation factor (VIF) and tolerance values. As the value of VIF is less than 10 and greater than 1 for each independent variable, along with the tolerance values for each independent variable being more than 0.1, it can be concluded that the problem of multicollinearity does not exist in the model (Field, 2009).

The F test for the model is significant at the 0.001 level, depicting that the model is highly significant. Moreover, the value of adjusted R-square shows that the independent variables account for approximately 72.7 per cent of variation in the dependent variable.

The result of the regression analysis indicates that all the characteristics of social media, except interaction, have a significant effect on the consumer adoption intention. The positive values of the coefficients show that all the features of social media have a positive effect on

Table 2.4   *Multiple regression and collinearity diagnostics*

Variable	β	Standard error	t	p-value	VIF	Tolerance
Constant	-0.129	0.188	-0.686	0.494		
PART	0.172	0.078	2.205	0.029*	3.515	0.284
INTER	0.136	0.072	1.889	0.061	3.358	0.297
SHARE	0.202	0.096	2.104	0.036*	2.971	0.336
CONN	0.219	0.077	2.844	0.004**	3.816	0.262
SERVQ	0.206	0.076	2.710	0.007**	3.582	0.279
PerEase	0.228	0.086	2.651	0.008**	2.511	0.398
PerUse	0.319	0.104	3.067	0.002**	3.810	0.262
INFEFF	0.300	0.091	3.296	0.001**	2.381	0.419
F-test	56.609					
p-value	0.000					
R	0.860					
R^2	0.740					
Adjusted R^2	0.727					

Note: *Significant at 0.05 level. **Significant at 0.01 level. ***Significant at 0.001 level.

the consumer's adoption intention. Therefore, we reject the null hypotheses H1, H2, H4, H5, H6, H7 and H8. However, we fail to reject the null hypothesis H3.

DISCUSSION

The present study found that the most-used social media platforms among the respondents were social networking websites, followed by instant messenger, online blogs and online encyclopaedias. The least-used platforms were microblogging sites and podcasts. This would provide a base for the providers and owners of such platforms to upgrade their service structure and marketing efforts in the field of online tourism information and services.

The result of the study shows that sightseeing and entertainment forms the biggest reason for undertaking travel activities among the respondents, forming 90.5 per cent of the respondents that undertake travel activities. This is followed by cultural tourism, forming 41.7 per cent of the respondents. This insight would be useful for the tourism industry in the state of Uttar Pradesh in aiming and directing their efforts in tourism destination marketing and promotion of tourism in the state.

The study specifies that the most important information that tourism consumers search for while using a social media platform is information about price or the cost of undertaking a travel activity, followed by accommodation information, and others' experience and food-related information. The least-searched information is about the travel agency and traffic information of the destination. This information can be used by the travel industry in attracting tourism customers by offering a reasonable price structure backed by a wide range of services offered at reasonable prices. This will help in attracting tourism customers from the majority of the income strata. The low information search for travel agencies could mean low trust of tourism customers in the travel agencies. Another reason could be the perception of added cost and complexities in opting for travel agencies. It could also mean that the travel agencies operating in India have a weak online marketing system, and more effort on information promotion and building brands is required. The travel agencies are required to educate the tourism customers about the advantages of opting for their online as well as offline services, and to provide reasonably priced services so as to minimise the prejudice of added cost and complexities of using travel agencies.

According to the results, the female respondents show significantly higher adoption intention as compared to male respondents. As previous studies have suggested that females indulge in social media significantly more than males (Mazman and Usluel, 2011; Jones, 2020), female respondents are therefore more likely to adopt social media for tourism decisions as compared to their male counterparts. The results also show that the level of adoption intention differs significantly between two age groups, with the respondents of age group 31–40 showing significantly higher adoption intention as compared to the respondents of age group 41–50. This can be explained by the fact that people aged over 30 travel more as compared to those aged below 30 ('Travel statistics by age group', 2020). The tourism statistics of India also reveal that people belonging to age group 35–54 years show more tourism activity as compared to other groups (Ministry of Tourism, 2015). However, as the respondents belonging to age group 31–40 years can be expected to be more tech-savvy as compared to the respondents of the group 41–50 years, the respondents of age group 31–40 show more adoption intention towards social media as compared to the other group.

The respondents differ significantly in their level of adoption intention when categorised on the basis of frequency of social media usage and frequency of travel activity. The results show that respondents who use social media daily have higher adoption intention as compared to those who use it once a week. The frequent users of social media can be expected to be well versed in its usage as compared to those who use it less frequently. This may also lead to higher familiarity and awareness among the frequent users about the range of services and opportunities provided by social media platforms, thereby leading to higher adoption intention towards social media for travel decisions. The results imply that the respondents who travel once in six months show higher adoption intention as compared to those who travel once in more than a year. Therefore, higher frequency of travel would affect the adoption intention of respondents, as travel decisions are made frequently and the decision-maker would like to ease the process by adopting the related services provided by social media. However, the respondents who travel once in three months do not show any significant difference. Travel frequency of less than three months could mean that travel is routine for the respondent and they are well informed and decided about the travel activities to be undertaken, and therefore would be less inclined to use the services of social media in making travel decisions.

In a study by Jiao et al. (2013b), the results indicate that trust and perceived enjoyment have a positive impact on consumers' adoption intention of social media, and perceived risk has a negative effect on adoption intention. Moreover, in a study by Ko et al. (2009), the results prove that perceived ease of use, perceived usefulness and perceived enjoyment had a positive effect on perceived value, which in turn positively affects the consumer's adoption intention. In a recent study by Cao et al. (2017), five characteristics of social media – service quality, interactivity, information effectiveness, convenience and participation – have a significant and positive impact on tourism consumers' intention to adopt social media. In relation to this, the results of the present study reveal that seven attributes of social media – participation, sharing, connectivity, service quality, perceived ease of use, perceived usefulness and information effectiveness – have a significant and positive role in determining the tourism consumer's intent to adopt social media for tourism-related decisions. This result could be used as a guide by the social media service providers to enhance the characteristics of social media that are highly desired by the users. Moreover, it would also help the online tourism service providers to employ and utilise those social media outlets that provide the consumers with an excellent quality of the above-mentioned characteristics.

CONCLUSION

The tourism sector has gained a prominent place in the world of information technology. Various tourism services can be accessed online by tourists. Social media platforms have given a major push to the adoption of online sources of information for varied purposes. In this, the present study analysed the effect of the characteristics and quality of social media platforms on the intention of tourism consumers to adopt social media while making a tourism-related decision. The study also examined the role of individual heterogeneity in influencing the intention to adopt social media for tourism decisions. The study was conducted on 168 tourism consumers of Uttar Pradesh. The results reveal that the adoption intention of consumers differs significantly on the basis of gender, age, frequency of social media usage and frequency of travel of the respondents. The study also concludes that seven characteristics of social media – participation, sharing, connectivity, service quality, perceived ease of use, perceived usefulness and information effectiveness – have a significantly positive effect on consumers' adoption intention of social media for tourism decisions.

The study suffers from the following limitations. Only eight characteristics of social media were studied that may impact upon the adoption intention; however, further analysis could be done on various other features of social media. The study was conducted on only 168 participants. A larger sample could provide more robust results. A linear relationship was assumed between characteristics of social media and consumer adoption intention, but a non-linear relationship could also exist. A stuctural relationship could be further analysed among the characteristics of social media and consumer adoption intention.

REFERENCES

Ajzen, I., and Fishbein, M. (1980). *Understanding attitudes and predicting social behavior*. Englewood Cliffs: Prentice-Hall.

Akman, I., and Mishra, A. (2017). Factors influencing consumer intention in social commerce adoption. *Information Technology and People, 30*(2), 1–20.

Alsajjan, B., and Dennis, C. (2006). The impact of trust on acceptance of online banking. *Commercial Distribution, 6,* 27–30.

Arunmozhi, T., and Panneerselvam, A. (2013). Types of tourism in India. *International Journal of Current Research and Academic Review, 1*(1), 84–88.

Buhalis, D., and Law, R. (2008). Progress in information technology and tourism management: 20 years on and 10 years after the Internet – The state of e-tourism research. *Tourism Management, 29*(4), 609–623.

Cao, Q., Yu, B., and Tian , X.-X.T. (2017). The effect of social media on tourism consumer adoption intention: Evidence from Urumqi. *Journal of Accounting and Marketing, 6*(1), 1–10.

Cermak, D.S., File, K.M., and Prince, R.A. (1994). Customer participation in service specification and delivery. *Journal of Applied Business Research, 10,* 90.

Chen, L.F., and Wang, C.M. (2005). Research on the relationship between network behavior and ecommerce service quality. *Consumer Economics*.

Chung, N., and Koo, C. (2015). The use of social media in travel information search. *Telematics and Informatics*, *32*, 215–229.

Constantinides, E., and Fountain, S.J. (2008). Web 2.0: Conceptual foundations and marketing issues. *Journal of Direct, Data and Digital Marketing Practice*, *9*(3), 231–244.

Davis, F.D. (1989). Perceived usefulness, perceived ease of use, and user acceptance of information technology. *MIS Quarterly*, *13*(3), 319–340.

Dey, P. (2018, October 8). What do you travel for – Adventure, wellness, culture or more? Test yourself. Retrieved from *Times of India*: https://timesofindia.indiatimes.com/travel/things-to-do/what-do-you -travel-foradventure-wellness-culture-or-more-test-yourself-/as66071479.cms.

Dhall, P. (2020). Quantitative data analysis. In R.N. Subudhi and S. Mishra (eds), *Methodological issues in management research: Advances, challenges and the way ahead* (pp. 109–125). Bingley: Emerald Publishing.

Dong, B., Sivakumar, K., Evans, K.R., and Zou, S. (2015). Effect of customer participation on service outcomes: The moderating role of participation readiness. *Journal of Service Research*, *18*(2), 160–176.

Ennew, C.T., and Binks, M.R. (1999). Impact of participative service relationships on quality, satisfaction and retention: An exploratory study. *Journal of Business Research*, *46*, 121–132.

Field, A. (2009). *Discovering statistics using SPSS* (3rd edn). London: SAGE Publications.

Fornell, C., and Larcker, D.F. (1981, February). Evaluating structural equation models with unobservable variables and measurement error. *JMR Journal of Marketing Research*, *18*(1), 39–50.

Gronroos, C. (1984). A service quality model and its marketing implications. *European Journal of Marketing*, *18*(4), 38–44.

Hair, J.F., Ringle, C.M., and Sarstedt, M. (2011). PLS-SEM: Indeed a silver bullet. *Journal of Marketing Thoery and Practice*, *19*(2), 139–151.

Hu, X., and Liu, H. (2015). Social media, mining and profiling in. In *The International Encyclopedia of Digital Communication and Society*. John Wiley & Sons.

Huang, Y.-M., Huang, Y.-M., Huang, S.-H., and LinYen-Ting (2012). A ubiquitous English vocabulary learning system: Evidence of active/passive attitudes vs. usefulness/ease-of-use. *Computers and Education*, *58*, 273–282. doi:doi:10.1016/j.compedu.2011.08.008.

Jiang, Z., and Benbasat, I. (2007). Research note – Investigating the influence of the functional mechanisms of online product presentations. *Information Systems Research*, *18*, 454–470.

Jiao, Y.B., Gao, J., and Yang, J. (2013a). Factors influencing consumers' adoption of social media – A theoretical model and its empirical research. *Journal of Shanxi Finance Economics University*, *35*, 43–55.

Jiao, Y., Yang, J., and Xu, S. (2013b). A study of the impact of social media characteristics on customer adoption intention of social media. *International Academic Workshop on Social Science (IAW-SC 2013)* (pp. 1095–1099). Changsha, China: Atlantis Press.

Jones, M. (2020). Studies show women engage on social media more than men. Retrieved from Cox BLUE: https://www.coxblue.com/studies-show-women-engage-on-social-media-more-than-men/.

Kakkar, G. (2018, September 12). What are the different types of social media? Retrieved from Digital Vidya Blog: https://www.digitalvidya.com/blog/category/social-media-marketing/.

Kaplan, A.M., and Haenlein, M. (2010). Users of the world, unite! The challenges and opportunities of social media. *Business Horizons*, *53*, 59–68.

Kim, S.-E., Lee, K.Y., Shin, S.I., and Yang, S.-B. (2017). Effects of tourism information quality in social media on destination image formation: The case of Sina Weibo. *Information and Management*, *54*, 687–702.

Ko, E., Kim, E.Y., and Lee, E.K. (2009). Modeling consumer adoption of mobile shopping for fashion products in Korea. *Psychology and Marketing*, *26*(7), 669–687.

Lee, D.Y., and Lehto, M.R. (2013). User acceptance of YouTube for procedural learning: An extension of the technology acceptance model. *Computers and Education*, *61*, 193–208.

Lee, T. (2005). The impact of perceptions of interactivity on customer trust and transaction intentions in mobile commerce. *Journal of Electronic Commerce Research*, *6*, 165.

López, E.P., Gidumal, J.B., Taño, D.G., and Armas, R.D. (2011). Intentions to use social media in organizing and taking vacation trips. *Computers in Human Behavior, 27*, 640–654.

Mazman, G., and Usluel, Y.K. (2011, April). Gender differences in using social networks. *Turkish Online Journal of Educational Technology, 10*(2), 133–139.

Miguens, J., Baggio, R., and Costa, C. (2008). Social media and tourism destinations: TripAdvisor case study. *IASK ATR2008 Advances in Tourism Research* (pp. 1–6). Aveiro, Portugal.

Milano, R., Baggio, R., and Piattelli, R. (2011). The effects of online social media on tourism websites. *ENTER2011 18th International Conference on Information* (pp. 1–12). Innsbruck, Austria: International Federation fot IT and Travel and Tourism.

Ministry of Tourism (2015). *India tourism statistics.* Government of India.

Munar, A., and Jacobsen, J.K. (2013). Trust and involvement in tourism social media and web-based travel information sources. *Scandinavian Journal of Hospitality and Tourism, 13*(1), 1–19.

Nunnally, J.C. (1978). *Psychometric theory* (2nd edn). New York: McGraw-Hill.

Palmer, J.W. (2002). Web site usability, design, and performance metrics. *Information Systems Research, 13*, 151–167.

Romero, C.L., Constantinides, E., and Alarco'n-del-Amo, M.-d.-C. (2011). Consumer adoption of social networking sites: Implications for theory and practice. *Journal of Research in Interactive Marketing, 5*(23), 170–188.

Rovai, A.P. (2002). Building sense of community at a distance. Retrieved from: http://www.irrodl.org/content/v3.1/rovai.html.

Schwabe, G., and Prestipino, M. (2005). How tourism communities can change travel information quality. *ECIS 2005 Proceedings.* AIS Electronic Library (AISeL).

Sigala, M. (2007). *WEB 2.0 in the tourism industry: A new tourism generation and new e-business models.* Chios, Greece: University of the Aegean.

Sin, S.S., Nor, K.M., and Al-Agaga, A.M. (2012). Factors affecting Malaysian young consumers' online purchase intention in social media websites. *Procedia – Social and Behavioral Sciences, 40*, 326–333.

Singh, I. (2011, May 13). *What is tourism and its types?* Retrieved from India Study Channel: https://www.indiastudychannel.com/resources/140791-What-is-tourism-and-its-types-.aspx.

Sirakaya, E., and Woodside, A.G. (2005). Building and testing theories of decision making by travellers. *Tourism Management, 26*, 815–832.

Straus, L., Robbert, T., and Roth, S. (2016). Customer participation in the customization of services –Effects on satisfaction and behavioral intentions. *Journal of Business and Marketing Management, 1*, 498–517.

Teo, H.-H., Chan, H.-C., Wei, K.-K., and Zhang, Z. (2003). Evaluating information accessibility and community adaptivity features for sustaining virtual learning communities. *International Journal of Human–Computer Studies, 59*, 671–697.

'Travel statistics by age group' (2020). Retrieved from Condor Ferries: https://www.condorferries.co.uk/travel-statistics-by-age-group.

Tureac, C. (2008). Types and forms of tourism. *OECONOMICA*, 92–103.

Wirtz, B.W., and Göttel, V. (2016). Technology acceptance in social media: Review, synthesis and directions for future empirical research. *Journal of Electronic Commerce Research, 17*(2), 97–115.

Xiang, Z., and Gertzel, U. (2010). Role of social media in online travel information search. *Tourism Management, 31*, 179–188.

Zeng, B. (2013). Social media in tourism. *Journal of Tourism and Hospitality, 2*(1), 1–2.

Živković, R., Gajić, J., and Brdar, I. (2014). The impact of social media on tourism. *SINTEZA 2014 E-Business in tourism and hospitality industry* (pp. 758–761). Serbia.

3. Electronic information search and destination satisfaction: a comparison of website and social media pre-trip planning

Susan L. Slocum and Seungwon (Shawn) Lee

INTRODUCTION

The Republic of Belarus has traditionally been a closed country, discouraging visitation by foreigners and earning the status of "Europe's last dictatorship" in the media (Rausing, 2012). Formerly part of the Soviet Union, Belarus as a country is not widely known, resulting in one of the lowest tourist visitation rates in Europe. According the United Nations World Tourism Organization (2019), Belarus received 366 000 non-resident tourists in 2018, which was a 29 percent increase over arrivals in 2017; although mostly likely this figure does not accurately represent visitors from Russia who arrive by automobile. The average length of stay is only four days and the average hotel occupancy rate is a mere 34 percent (National Statistical Committee of the Republic of Belarus, 2017). Belarus suffers from a "the lack of a clear mechanism of attracting domestic and foreign investments in tourism development, as well as by the lack of promotion of the national tourist product on the domestic and foreign market" (Pushkareva and Samusevich, 2017, p. 346).

The natural and cultural resources of Belarus have recently been acknowledged as a viable development path into tourism. The main potentials for tourism in Belarus lie in the beauty and diversity of its nature, its unique historic cultural heritage, and the people themselves: "a very hospitable, diligent and tolerant people" (Slocum and Klitsounova, 2019, p. 67). Since the late 2000s, the government of Belarus has decided to treat tourism as a primary economic sector in order to increase profits from the tourist industry. According to a report by the World Travel and Tourism Council (2017), the tourism sector has had a positive impact on the Belarusian economy and will continue its progress in the future. The direct contribution of travel and tourism to the gross domestic product was $900 million and the total contribution was $2.8 billion in 2016. According to the Ministry of Sport and Tourism, the main types of tourism in Belarus include: ecotourism, religious tourism, agro-ecotourism, battlefield and historical tours, business tourism and medical tourism (Republic of Belarus, 2016).

Much of this recent growth in inbound tourism between 2017 and 2018 is attributed to a new visa-free policy that allows visitors from 74 counties to remain in Belarus for 30 days if they arrive through Minsk International Airport. There are also visa-free regions in Belarus that allow foreigners to travel with a preapproved tour operator for 14 days without a visa. While these regulations have been a boost for international tourism, capitalizing on this opportunity to enhance destination marketing messages and destination exposure are critical if Belarus wants to invest in tourism as an economic development sector. Moreover, the use of social media by visitors could potentially support traditional online marketing (Kaldeen, 2019), if visitors to Belarus have a positive experience and choose to share this experience online. Therefore, understanding overall customer expectations prior to their visit, and how their experiences match these expectations, can provide valuable insight into developing the tourism product, specifically for a country that lacks global recognition as a tourism destination. Therefore, this chapter provides an analysis of the types of pre-trip planning online information media used to research a trip to Belarus, and the resulting satisfaction based on the expectations derived from online media pre-trip planning.

Belarus faces many challenges in transitioning its economy from a centrally controlled, communist model to a transitionary open-market economy. While tourism existed in the former Soviet Union, its focus on domestic, recreational and reward incentives for productive citizens has left it poorly prepared for the international market. Slocum et al. (2020) recognize these tourism transferences as a form of "emerging economies" (p. 208), where tourism infrastructure, entrepreneurship, and tourism-specific marketing strategies did not exist prior to 1991. Therefore, understanding international tourist perspectives of Belarus as a means to grow the economy are essential in supporting a sustainable, diversified and successful tourism industry.

LITERATURE REVIEW

Evolution of Information Technology and Social Media Usage in Tourism

Tourism has been closely connected to the progress of information technology (IT), which was later expanded to information and communication technology (ICT). As early as the 1970s, the tourism industry developed and adopted computer reservation systems (CRSs), followed by global distribution systems (GDSs) in the late 1980s. As many businesses were adopting and growing through the use of Internet technology in the late 1990s, the tourism industry shifted its main distribution and revenue channels to the Internet (Buhalis and Law, 2008). Some of multiple advantages of the ICT-based operational and strategic practices include: faster transactions; current and accurate inventory; worldwide access on inventories; quicker customer response times; and data-driven yield management to maximize revenue. As most of the Internet enhanced tourism management systems support modern database management systems (MDBMs), they also allow tourism businesses to be linked with external stakeholders, specifically customers and suppliers, in secure and direct links (Lee et al., 2016). Further eliminating intermediaries between tourism products and services and their customers has resulted in the birth of many mega online travel agencies (OTAs), and the emergence of digital platforms is changing how travelers research, buy, experience and share travel and tourism (World Bank Group, 2018).

Web-based technology has resulted in two types of Internet-based marketing tools. Pull marketing involves implementing a strategy that draws consumers towards specific products, often classified as marketer-generated content, and includes search engines and organizational websites. Push technology promotes a specific product to a relevant audience and allows customers an opportunity to generate content in response. The most common type of push technology is social media (Goh et al., 2013). Ramseook-Munhurrun et al. (2018) suggest that push factors are more influential in relation to novelty, family relations, escape, prestige and socializing; whereas pull factors have more impact on facilities and infrastructure, accessibility and transportation, key tourist resources, local culture and tradition, and exotic atmosphere.

The importance of social media in tourism has grown, and academic tourism research has addressed emerging trends related to the use of social media in tourism. As the tourism industry embraces the effectiveness of enhanced and improved ICT, customers have also been utilizing social media for their own purposes. Since the middle of the 2000s, social media has positioned itself as a new platform for travel information sources (Xiang and Gretzel, 2010). Social media originally started as a simple tool to connect friends, but is now considered a major e-commerce platform providing access to a vast number of users and the enormous amount of data accumulated through its use. As Fotis et al. (2012) state, social media are mostly used after holidays for experience sharing. The result is an plethora of travel reviews, ratings, pictures, and videos from consumer-generated content (CGC) platforms. Coupled with the ease of searching through the big data that social media generates, it is not surprising that social media has become a primary resource for pre-trip travel planning.

Gretzel et al. (2008) claim that more than three-quarters of United States (US) online consumers have checked online reviews, blogs and other online feedback prior to their travel-related purchase decisions. In turn, various social media channels also play an important role in the marketing of the tourism industry. The role of social media today includes: tourism product and service marketing; updating customer experiences through text and imagery; customer relation management (CRM); and social commerce (for example, groupons and group purchasing). Considering the experiential nature of the service-based tourism industry, dynamic CRM, social commerce and instant access to customers' reviews and demand trends have drastically changed the distribution channels of the tourism industry. They have also affected the power structures in the marketplace, moving market power from marketers to consumers (Yoo and Gretzel, 2016).

Tourist Use of Social Media

There are usually a number of factors that influence the use of social media for travel, and previous studies have identified a number of motivations, including: ego-defensive functions and self-identity (Daugherty et al., 2008); and information acquisition, socio-psychological motives and hedonic benefits (Chung and Buhalis, 2008). Social media platforms must be easy to use, trustworthy and provide useful information related to the topic of research. Social media is often easier for people to access and provides more detailed information about destinations than contacting travel agencies, reading printed material or booking through pre-organized tours (Kaldeen, 2019). Interactive social media can provide up-to-date information, prices, pictures and reviews from past tourists, which increases the perception of trustworthiness (Kaldeen, 2019). Moreover, it has been revealed that social media content, including CGC, is perceived as more trustworthy when compared to official tourism websites, travel agents and mass media advertising (Fotis et al., 2010). There is a strong correlation between perceived level of influence from social media and changes made in holiday travel plans prior to final decision-making, and evidence suggests that technology can empower travelers by facilitating two-way information and interactions (Yu et al., 2014).

Academic researchers and travel industry practitioners show that traveler online behaviors change throughout the trip planning process. Social media is used throughout the travel experience, including during pre-planning, while traveling and after returning home. An increasing number of tourists use social media to plan and research pre-travel options (Vermeulen and Seegers, 2009). According to Think with Google (2016), the top items that travelers look for in their pre-travel research include prices, hotel reviews/pictures/cost/availability, flight length, travel schedules, and activities at a destination. More than 74 percent of travelers use the comments of other consumers when planning trips for pleasure (Gretzel and Yoo, 2008). More travelers than ever use mobile devices for their travel-related activities, as easy access to mobile networks has improved around the world. Travelers can now make real-time informed decisions before and during their trip. Travel industry practitioners (CrowdRiff, 2018) also summarize current trends on social media usage and travel to include: finding directions on social media while travelling; using mobile phones to book hotels or excursions; keeping in touch with family and friends back home; and posting photos and videos on social media to share their experiences. High-quality cameras installed on mobile devices have already replaced traditional cameras due to their convenience and the improving picture and video quality, providing 'immediately ready' images and video clips for social media posting. In turn, the heavy use of mobile devices along with social media networks offers opportunities to connect with travelers before their trips and throughout the entire travel experience in real time (Lee et al., 2016). After the traveler has returned home, they may have already shared many of their travel experiences, and often will reflect on their experiences through social media.

According to Sheraton Hotels and Resorts' StudyLogic, 73 percent of US social network users accessed social media sites at least daily while they were traveling. As expected, travelers between the ages of 25 to 34 accessed social sites most often, with nearly 33 percent using them multiple times in an hour (eMarketer, 2020). Interestingly, men were found to check social networks more often than women, and expressed that not accessing social media sites for several days was much more challenging. Almost 60 percent of respondents, especially men and young adults (ages 25 to 34), considered social media to be a very useful tool to meet people while traveling. In another study by Vision Critical for Wyndham Worldwide's Women on Their Way, Facebook was the top social site for female travelers. The most often-used activities included: sharing photos and video (57 percent); posting status updates or commentary about trips (38 percent); and checking in with family and friends (13 percent). Women tended to used social media the most after a trip (82 percent) and before a trip (55 percent), while the lowest usage occurred during a trip (less than 50 percent) (eMarketer, 2020). The study also found that the top method for accessing social media while traveling was via a laptop (75 percent), compared to 47 percent who used a smartphone, 12 percent who used a netbook, and 8 percent who used a tablet PC. The number of mobile device users surpasses desktop users, and about half of the travelers are comfortable planning, researching and booking their trip using only a mobile device (eMarketer, 2020).

While most studies have focused on the US travel market, Fat Tire Tours (2019) conducted a survey with its global customers on social media usage and vacations. Their study included more than 1500 international travelers and analyzed social media preferences based on the purpose of each social media network service. The study identified various motivations and timings of use. The most common use for Facebook was food and dining research before a trip (47 percent), while 42 percent used it to make decisions about where to visit during the trip. Another popular social media site, Instagram, was used by 38 percent for planning a visit to buildings/architecture/monuments before a trip, compared to 27 percent who used it to make decisions on which buildings/architecture/monuments to visit during the trip. The study also found that:

- 17 percent of the respondents used Twitter for planning experiences, such as concerts and bike riding, before a trip, and 13 percent used it to make similar decisions during a trip;
- 17 percent used Snapchat to plan a visit to buildings/architecture/monuments before a trip, and 10 percent used it to plan experiences during a trip;
- 20 percent used Pinterest to plan a visit to buildings/architecture/monuments before a trip, and 10 percent to make decisions for both visiting buildings/architecture/monuments and food/dining during a trip;
- 15 percent used Reddit in planning to visit buildings/architecture/monuments as well as concerts and bike riding before a trip, while 12 percent percent used it to visit buildings/architecture/monuments during a trip;
- 41 percent used YouTube (video-based CGC social media platform) to plan visits to buildings/architecture/monuments before a trip, and to choose which buildings/architecture/monuments to visit during a trip (30 percent); and
- Yelp and Tripadvisor, while not necessarily social media sites, were mostly used for planning accommodation before a trip (48 percent), and a decision on food/dining during a trip (43 percent).

Social Media Travel Planning in Post-Soviet Countries

Thanks to new opportunities for tourism, propelled by technology-enhanced business models, tourism has grown faster than ever before in emerging and developing economies since 2010 (World Bank Group, 2018). In the meantime, digital platforms have permanently changed the way destinations facilitate tourism, develop products, gather data, access markets and attract visitors. Fotis et al. (2012) studied holiday travelers residing in the former Soviet Union republics and presented usage levels of social media before, during and after their trips. They found that participants were far more likely to use social media after their trip in order to share stories and photos; and during travel, social media usage was primarily used to keep in touch with family and friends. Moreover, they did not find any significant differences in travel-related social media usage based on gender, education level, age, frequency of travel or region of residence. While current findings provide some important insights for understanding social media in tourism, there is still a lack of studies focusing on social media usage in Eastern Europe, both inbound and outbound, including Belarus.

Social Media and Travel Expectations

How social media impacts travelers' trip planning is an important topic for marketers and researchers in the tourism industry (Sigala et al., 2012), as it is important for the industry to understand how social media affects customer expectations and decision-making . Marketing is the primary tool that influences pre-travel expectations, therefore ensuring that marketing materials accurately represent a destination image and showcase authentic experiences can encourage motivation to visit a specific destination (Curtis et al., 2020). Moreover, "Tourists with positive travel experience and high levels of satisfaction with the destination attributes are more likely to revisit the destination" (Ramseook-Munhurrun et al., 2018, p. 844). In turn, these expectations influence a person's motivation for travel. Slocum et al. (2020, p. 157) write: "When tourists have high expectations, they are more willing to search for tour information and learn about a destination's culture and environment and to invest time and other resources to research a journey." Meeting these expectations results in customer satisfaction, and not meeting these expectations can lead to dissatisfaction, which may then be shared on social media sites (Montero and Fernandez-Avilés, 2010). Post-travel social media posts often emphasize whether expectations were met or not.

When using social media, relationships between the message sender and the receiver can influence the perceived quality of the information. Narangajavana Kaosiri et al. (2019) found that tourists' expectations are informed by what they find when researching travel options online. Reviews and feedback from past tourists' experience can have a large effect on travel planning, specifically through the creation of expectations, which in turn lead to motivations and the purchase of travel-related products. In another study, Narangajavana et al. (2017) claim that CGC can be classified into three categories: strong ties (friends and family), weak ties (acquaintances and strangers) and tourism ties (tourism organizations and tourism establishments). They found that CGC influences "tourist expectations and decision making (pre-traveling), perception while having a tourism experience (during and post-traveling), and satisfaction (post-traveling)" (Narangajavana et al., 2019, p. 262). They found that strong-tie sources were more influential in all dimensions of expectations primarily because family and friends are more likely to report opinions and their emotional responses to these experiences. Weak ties were used to gather information relating to the hospitality and attitude of local people, service quality and destination security.

METHODOLOGY AND DATA ANALYSIS

Data were collected around the most popular tourism attraction in Belarus, including Mir Castle, Niasviž Castle, Brest Hero Fortress, Pinsk, Baranovichi, Kobryn, Belavezhskaya Pushcha National Park and Dudutki. Data collection began in January 2020; however, due to the COVID-19 outbreak, data collection ended in March when tourist numbers dwindled. Random sampling was used, and only international visitors were included. Rejection rates were not recorded. In total, 163 surveys were completed.

Surveys were constructed using literature on expectations, motivations and satisfaction (Curtis et al., 2020; Lee et al., 2013). The survey was designed in English and then translated into Russian by a native Belarussian. It was then retranslated back into English by a native Russian speaker to remove idiosyncrasies and to ensure international Russian-speaking tourists would comprehend the meanings. Respondents were offered a choice between an English survey or a Russian survey. Approximately 68 percent of the surveys were completed in Russian.

The questionnaire was designed to ask a number of demographic and sociographic question relating to Belarus as a travel destination, pre-planning electronic media usage, and traveler satisfaction with the destination. Basic demographic questions were asked, as well as travel-related questions, such as group size, primary motivation for visiting, pre-trip electronic media usage, and transportation and accommodation choices. Income information was rarely provided, so this data has been removed from the analysis. All visitor spending information is reported in US dollars based on the currency rates on January 1, 2020.

Twenty nationalities were reported by respondents, which equated to 133 former communist nationalities and 30 non-communist nationalities. Fifty-one percent of the respondents were female, 72 percent were between the ages of 18 and 45, 86 percent held a bachelor degree or higher, 52 percent were not married, and 72 percent did not have children at home. The average travel duration was 12.23 days (range = 1-365) and includes an average group size of five people (range = 1–40). Tourists had visited Belarus, on average, three times before (range = 0–40) and spent approximately $45.50 per day while traveling (range = $10–$95). In-country transportation included: personal car (36.6 percent), public transportation (26.2 percent), organized tour (19.2 percent), rental car (6.4 percent), family/friends (4.7 percent) and taxi (1.7 percent). Accommodation included: budget hotel (29.1 percent), apartment (24.4 percent), friends/family (23.3), bed-and-breakfast/farm stay (12.2 percent), luxury hotel (7.6 percent), camping (5.2 percent), hostel (2.9 percent) and sanatorium (1.7 percent). Nineteen percent traveled to Belarus to experience culture and 19 percent to visit historical sites, as well as 14 percent for business and 24 percent to visit family and friends. Internet sites used for pre-trip research included: Tripadvisor (40.7 percent), Instagram (24.4 percent), Facebook (14.5 percent), Belarus.by (14.0 percent), VK.com (10.5 percent), YouTube/RuTube (9.9 percent), Google (8.7 percent), Belarustravel.by (7.0 percent), Booking.com/Airbnb (6.4 percent), Twitter (2.9 percent), Lonelyplanet.com (2.3 percent), Wikitravel.com (2.3 percent), and other (2.4 percent).

In order to measure travel satisfaction, a number of Likert-scale questions asked respondents to state their level of agreement with certain statements (5 = strongly agree, 1 = strongly disagree) regarding the quality of Belarus attractions, Belarusian culture and food, and intent to return to or to tell family and friends about Belarus as a travel destination (Table 3.1). Using SPSS software, means and frequencies were calculated to provide an overall understanding of tourist satisfaction. Safety and friendliness scored highest, and overall trip satisfaction scored 4.4 out of 5.0.

A correlation analysis was performed to see which types of media were used together in pre-trip planning. Only significant results are reported in Table 3.2. The results show that respondents tended to use social media sites together when pre-trip planning, as shown by the 0.01 significant levels between Facebook and Instagram, Instagram and VK.com, VK.com and YouTube/RuTube. There were also significant correlations at the 0.05 level between Internet site usage, such as the Lonely Planet and Wikitravel sites, and between Belarus.travel and Belarus.by. There is limited data to support a crossover between social media and web-based sites in pre-trip planning, with the exception of Instagram and Belarus.travel.

Media usage by a variety of demographic variables was accessed using MANOVA analysis. In order to understand the difference in media usage by nationality, the independent variable was divided into two categories: former Soviet countries (including Eastern European) and non-former Soviet countries. Using the Wilks' lambda test, it was determined that the number of days traveling was significant at the $p = 0.01$ level, age was significant at the $p = 0.058$ level, and nationality was significant at the $p = 0.078$ level. In order to better understand the relationship between nationality and media usage, binomial regression was used to measure the effects of these variables on the type of media used in pre-trip planning. Initially, a solution could not be achieved because of quasi-complete separation for the Lonely Planet variable. It was removed from the analysis and the results are shown in Table 3.3. Nationality explained approximately 14 percent of the social media usage variance. The only significant variable is the Belarus.travel, which is more popular with non-Soviet visitors. Wikitravel was more

Table 3.1   *Satisfaction descriptive statistics*

	N	Mean	SD
I felt safe in Belarus	155	4.72	0.553
The people of Belarus are friendly	158	4.7	0.547
Belarus is very clean	156	4.69	0.54
I have enjoyed my visit to Belarus	157	4.67	0.524
The food I have eaten in Belarus is good	153	4.64	0.592
I will tell my family and friends to visit Belarus	148	4.59	0.638
Belarus is an interesting place to visit	157	4.57	0.58
Belarus has beautiful nature	153	4.51	0.64
Belarus was good value for the money I spent	152	4.49	0.719
I received good service in Belarus	157	4.47	0.605
I plan to return to Belarus	136	4.44	0.859
Natural areas are well managed	121	4.42	0.68
The historic sites are well preserved	153	4.4	0.781
Belarus has a good selection of restaurants	138	4.4	0.75
Crossing the border and getting a visa was easy	154	4.4	1.050
Getting around Belarus is easy	154	4.38	0.76
Natural areas are easy find	127	4.37	0.733
I feel I had an authentic experience in Belarus	132	4.34	0.836
There is lots to see and do in Belarus	157	4.32	0.734
The culture in Belarus is unique	151	4.26	0.82
It was easy to communicate with people in Belarus	153	4.26	0.916
The local people enjoy engaging with tourists	147	4.22	0.818
I was able to see and do everything I wanted in Belarus	144	4.22	0.832
I wish I had stayed longer in Belarus	140	4.19	0.889
The educational programs at cultural areas are informative	106	4.18	0.826
I now have a better opinion of Belarus than I did before I visited	135	4.16	0.964
The educational programs at natural areas are informative	84	4.1	0.859
The marketing materials I reviewed before my visit accurately describes Belarus	109	3.98	0.923
Overall satisfaction (average of all responses)	163	4.40	0.400
Valid N (listwise)	42		

Table 3.2   *Media correlations*

	Pearson	Sig. (2-tailed)	N
Facebook – Instagram	0.255**	0.001	163
Facebook – Google	0.159*	0.043	163
Twitter – Wikitravel	0.202**	0.010	163
Instagram – VK.com	0.240**	0.002	163
Instagram – YouTube/RuTube	0.166*	0.034	163
Instagram – Belarus.travel	0.156*	0.046	163
VK.com – YouTube/RuTube	0.392**	0.000	163
VK.com – Wikitravel	0.197*	0.012	163
Lonely Planet – Wiki	0.487**	0.000	163
Lonely Planet – Belarus.by	0.158*	0.044	163
Wikitravel – Belarus.by	0.158*	0.044	163
Belarus.travel – Belarus.by	0.413**	0.000	163

Note: ** Correlation is significant at the 0.01 level (2-tailed). * Correlation is significant at the 0.05 level (2-tailed).

Table 3.3   *Media usage by demographics*

	Value	F	Hypothesis df	Error df		Sig.
Days traveling						
Wilks' lambda	0.002	2.339	288.000	853.255		0.000**
Age						
Wilks' lambda	0.390	1.337	60.000	359.657		0.058
Nationality						
Wilks' lambda	0.786	1.722	12.000	76.000		0.078
Media	B	S.E.	Wald	df	Sig.	Exp(B)
Belarus.travel	-1.698	0.827	4.215	1	0.40*	0.183
Wikitravel	-2.659	1.395	3.634	1	0.057	0.070
Instagram	1.165	.689	2.864	1	0.091	3.206

Note: * Significant at the 0.05 level. ** Significant at the 0.01 level.

popular with former Soviet travelers, and Instagram was more popular with non-Soviet travelers, although these results are not significant at the 0.10 level.

Independent sample t-tests were conducted to see if different types of social media influenced satisfaction measures. Each variable was testing for equal variances using the Leven test. Only those that are significant at the $p = 0.10$ level are shown in Table 3.4. Overall satisfaction (the average of all satisfaction measures) was not significantly influenced by pre-trip media usage. It appears that marketer-generated information sources (pull media) were more inclined to generate satisfaction than social media sites (push media).

Because there was some correlation between type of media used and certain satisfaction scale items, a MANOVA was performed on three different independent variables and the 28 satisfaction dependent variables and the overall satisfaction variable. Media were grouped according to Goh et al.'s (2013) push/pull media types. The first analysis assessed the use of social media on all satisfaction scale items (0 = used only social media, 1 = other), the second assessed web-based content on satisfaction (0 = used only web-based media, 1 = other), and the third assessed the use of both social media and web-based content on satisfaction (0 = used both social media and web-based media, 1 = other). Using the Wilks' lambda test, there was not a significant difference in satisfaction by social media usage ($F_{(29,8)} = 0.830$, $p = 0.751$; Wilks' $\Lambda = 0.249$, partial $\eta2 = 0.751$), web-based usage ($F_{(29,8)} = 0.471$, $p = 0.938$; Wilk's $\Lambda = 0.405$, partial $\eta2 = 0.595$), or a combination of both (($F_{(29,8)} = 1.071$, $p = 0.795$; Wilk's $\Lambda = 0.205$, partial $\eta2 = 0.496$).

The next analysis determines pre-trip media usage based on a person's travel motivation using binomial logistic regression for each type of social media. Table 3.5 shows the significant results. Tripadvisor (Chi$^2 = 23.372$, $p = 0.16$, Nagelkerke $R^2 = 0.179$) and Instagram (Chi$^2 = 33.294$, $p = 0.000$, Nagelkerke $R^2 = 2.71$) were the only significant results. The models for Facebook, Twitter, VK.com, YouTube/RuTube were not significant.

Table 3.4   *Independent T-tests*

		t	df	Sig. (2-tailed)	Mean difference	Std. error difference
Tripadvisor	Good food	2.069	151	0.040*	0.197	0.095
Tripadvisor	Clean	2.497	154	0.014*	0.214	0.086
Tripadvisor	Did everything	1.985	142	0.049*	0.276	0.139
Facebook	Marketing	1.938	107	0.055	0.466	0.241
Facebook	Authentic	1.766	130	0.080	0.349	0.197
Instagram	Beautiful nature	2.260	151	0.025*	0.267	0.118
VK.com	Visa process	2.558	152	0.012*	0.679	0.265
YouTube/RuTtube	Historic sites	-2.263	151	0.025*	-0.449	0.198
YouTube/RuTube	Getting around	1.795	152	0.075	0.358	0.199
YouTube/RuTube	Enjoyed visit	1.662	155	0.099	0.222	0.134
Lonely Planet	Marketing	-1.712	107	0.090	-0.798	0.466
Lonely Planet	Visa	2.750	152	0.007**	10.433	0.521
Lonely Planet	Friendly people	1.685	156	0.094	0.464	0.276
Lonely Planet	Stay Longer	-1.808	139	0.073	-0.818	0.452
Wikitravel	Tell family/friends	1.884	146	0.062	0.604	0.321
Wikitravel	Safe	1.744	153	0.083	0.485	0.278
Wikitravel	Did everything	1.775	142	0.078	0.743	0.419
Belarus.by	Tell family/friends	2.161	146	0.033*	0.304	0.141
Belarus.by	Culture education	-2.036	105	0.044*	-0.470	0.231
Belarus.by	Good food	2.002	151	0.047*	0.270	0.135
Belarus.by	Good service	1.965	155	0.051	0.261	0.133
Belarus.by	Getting around	1.740	152	0.084	0.297	0.171
Belarus.by	Clean	2.080	154	0.039*	0.251	0.121
Belarus.by	Communicate	1.998	151	0.047*	0.410	0.205
Belarus.by	Local people	1.954	145	0.053	0.373	0.191
Belarus.travel	Marketing	-1.886	107	0.062	-0.571	0.303
Belarus.travel	Finding nature areas	2.144	125	0.034*	0.510	0.238
Belarus.travel	Restaurants	-1.711	136	0.089	-0.385	0.225
Belarus.travel	Enjoyed visit	-1.717	155	0.088	-0.268	0.156
Belarus.travel	Did everything	-1.953	142	0.053	-0.485	0.248
Google	Visa	-1.734	152	0.085	-0.507	0.293
Google	Authentic	1.860	130	0.065	0.467	0.251
Booking/Airbnb	Nature well managed	-2.170	119	0.032*	-0.609	0.280
Booking/Airbnb	Interesting visit	-1.857	155	0.065	-0.349	0.188

Note: * Significant at the 0.05 level (2-tailed). ** Significant at the 0.01 level (2-tailed).

DISCUSSION

Survey Result

As a destination that remains largely unknown outside former Soviet bloc counties, building a reputation for Belarus as a premier travel destination will require the dissemination of positive information by past visitors. In order for positive experiences to occur, the Belorussia travel industry must meet or exceed visitor expectations (Slocum et al., 2020). Our research shows that visitors to Belarus appear to be highly satisfied with their experiences. Overall satisfaction (an average of all satisfaction measures) scored 4.4 out of 5, with 'I felt safe in

Table 3.5   *Social media usage by travel motivation*

	B	Std. error	Wald	df	Sig.	*Exp(B)*
Tripadvisor – Business	17.265	0.573	906.293	1	0.000	3.176E-8
Triadvisor – Culture	17.003	0.571	888.154	1	0.000	4.129E-8
Tripadvisor – Historic Sites	17.253	0.548	990.596	1	0.000	3.213E-8
Tripadvisor – Special Event	17.254	0.830	432.014	1	0.000	3.211E-8
Tripadvisor – Family/friends	15.457	1.285	144.757	1	0.000	1.936E-7
Instagram – Business	15.101	0.800	356.519	1	0.000	2.767E-7
Instagram – Culture	16.039	0.548	858.008	1	0.000	1.083E-7
Instagram – Historic Site	16.850	0.482	1221.269	1	0.000	4.811E-8
Instagram – Ancestry	18.236	0.920	393.036	1	0.000	1.203E-8

Belarus', 'The people of Belarus are friendly' and 'Belarus is very clean' scoring the highest. Other items of interest include 'I will tell my family and friends to visit Belarus' (4.59) and 'I plan to return to Belarus' (4.44). However, on the low end of the satisfaction scale, 'The marketing materials I reviewed before my visit accurately describes Belarus' (3.98) shows room for improvement in the accurate depiction of Belarus as a travel destination.

This exploratory research shows that electronic media are a significant source for travel information to Belarus. Both push and pull sources were used in pre-travel planning, although visitors were likely to use either marketer-generated content in the form of websites exclusively, or to use social media exclusively. Managing CGC is much harder for destination marketing organizations, and currently social media does not seem to be supporting the pull messages (Kaldeen, 2019). Tripadvisor seemed to be a single source for information, not generally combined with other online platforms, which aligns with the report by Fat Tire Tours (2019). Tripadvisor is more generally used to rate business entities, therefore poor reviews for any one attraction or accommodation property could decrease motivation to visit. Belarus.travel (the official website for the Belarus National Tourism Agency and the Belarus Ministry of Sport and Tourism) and Belarus.by (managed by the BelTA News Agency and simultaneously providing business and investment information for Belarus), appear to be used together. Bealrus.travel has an active Instagram account (as well as Facebook, YouTube and VK.com accounts, although these were not significant in our analysis), which may account for participants' use of both. The Belarus.by website has a more governmental feel and only a Facebook and Instagram presence. It also appears that the use of Wikitravel in partnership with both social media and webpages is common.

While use of only social media, only web-based media, and a combination of both, was not significant, individual platforms did appear to establish expectations that Belarus was able to meet or exceed (Yu et al., 2014). For example, Tripadvisor, which primarily provides reviews, appears to accurately describe good food and cleanliness, and people who used Tripadvisor were more likely to see and do everything they wanted. Facebook provided more accurate marketing and resulted in respondents reporting a more authentic experience. People who use YouTube/RuTube were better able to navigate transportation issues (which can be challenging in Belarus) and were more likely to enjoy their trip. However, Facebook seems to misrepresent the quality of natural and historic sites. According to Fat Tire Tours (2019), YouTube plays an important role in visiting historic sites, so a negative correlation between YouTube users and the quality of historic site could be problematic for Belarus. Overall, web-based marketing sites appear to have a stronger influence on establishing realistic expectations, and were more inclined to see higher satisfaction levels than social media. This contradicts Fotis et al. (2010) and Kaldeen (2019), who claim that social media is perceived as more trustworthy than official tourism websites and mass media advertising.

The primary travel motivation also appears to influence the type of media search practices during pre-trip planning. Business travelers were more likely to use Tripadvisor and Instagram than other forms of social media. The same occurs with travelers motivated by culture and historic sites. Tripadvisor was used by people traveling to experience a special event or to visit family and friends, whereas Instagram was used by diaspora travelers. These results imply that Tripadvisor and Instagram are better equipped to support information-seeking by visitors who already have a primary travel motivation and who are seeking specific experiences. Other social media sites appear to be better suited for people without specific travel motivation, or those who are looking for a more holistic and varied experience, which aligns with the results of the CrowdRiff (2018) study.

Unfortunately, this study did not show a significant difference in the types of media used by a variety of demographic variables, with the exception of age, which corresponds with the results of eMarketer (2020). Moreover, nationality did not predict specific types of media usage, with the exception of Belarus.travel (Fotis et al., 2012). Belarus.travel offers information in English, Russian, Belarusian, Polish. German, Chinese, and Korean, whereas Belarus. by only offers information in English, Russian, Belarusian and Chinese. However, while not significant, it does appear that Instagram is used more by non-former Soviet travelers, whereas Wikitravel is used more by former Soviet travelers. It is apparent that more research is needed into the emerging, and potentially lucrative, post-Soviet outbound market and their media choices.

Implications for Belarus

The results of this study show that Belarus is well positioned to support international tourism in relation to providing quality experiences and satisfying consumers. Overall satisfaction ratings were very positive, and most respondents were likely to tell family and friends about their experience, as well as plan to return to Belarus. Since many travelers choose social media as a means to tell family and friends about their visit, and since this can be classified as a form of strong ties (Narangajavana et al., 2017), this information can be very influential in pre-trip planning for other visitors. Moreover, this study has found a strong relationship between Belarusian websites and visitor satisfaction, specifically in the areas of historical sites and cultural tourism. Therefore, this study highlights the success Belarus has had in developing and meeting tourist expectations.

One aspect of concern is the relatively low score relating to the accuracy of the marketing materials reviewed prior to travel, which aligns with the finding of Pushkareva and Samusevich (2017). Results imply that this mismatch is most evident in Belarus.travel, Belarus.by and Lonely Planet. While this may appear to contradict the findings described in the previous paragraph, it is important to note that websites often provide functional information, such as the best way to reach certain sites, clusters of sites that can be visited together, and specific visa requirements. Social media tends to highlight the quality of an experience and the emotions attached to a person's visit (Narangajavana et al., 2017). This result aligns with Ramseook-Munhurrun et al. (2018). Therefore, Belarus needs to align these marketing messages to more accurately reflect what visitors will actually experience, rather than just the 'how' or 'what' of travel. Facebook seems to present a more realistic perspective, which may be the result of CGC content that explains (and warns) of these realities.

While this study did not separate user-generated content from marketer-generated content in relation to social media (as many tourism operations manage their own social media accounts), Belarus should enhance social media messages, specifically Instagram, to highlight its varied natural, cultural and historic sites, which is supported by the results of the CrowdRiff (2018) study. As Yoo and Gretzel (2016) highlight, "tourism marketers need to fundamentally change their approaches and move from marketing with a sales focus to marketing as an activity that involves the management of conversations." Moreover, the use of social media by business travelers offers an opportunity to increase "bleisure" travel (leisure travel combined with business travel), specifically through Tripadvisor and Instagram. It is recommended that Belarus monitors social media and adapts its marketing messages to align with the positive images highlighted by previous travelers. In other words, user-generated social media content may be well positioned to inform website messages.

Limitations and Future Research

The primary limitation to this research was that it was conducted as the global outbreak of COVID-19 began, which drastically affected inbound tourism to Belarus. As the pandemic spread, there was a noticeable decrease as countries began to close their borders: first a reduction in Chinese travelers, then European travelers, and lastly Eastern European travelers. This resulted in an uneven representation of different nationalities, specifically an over-reliance on Russian, Ukrainian and Polish visitors. While it is recognized that these nationalities (as well as visitors from the Baltic countries of Lithuania, Latvia and Estonia) make up the bulk of Belarus's international market, it is estimated that they are over-represented in this sample. Moreover, the early termination of this research resulted in a low number of responses overall, which limited the types of quantitative analyses that could be performed.

The authors encourage further research relating to nationality and media usage, which has the potential to diversify visitation from emerging outbound travel markets, specifically BRIC countries (Brazil, Russia, India and China). Not only are there different platforms in different countries (such as YouTube and RuTube), but also nationality (and/or culture) could play a role in the selection of social media sites for pre-trip planning. Also, the relationship between motivations for travel and social media usage could inform appropriate online marketing strategies within specific target markets. In this case, ecotourism, religious tourism, agro-ecotourism, battlefield and historical tours, business tourism and medical tourism (Republic of Belarus, 2016) are the primary motivations for travel to Belarus. Outside of the results presented in Table 3.5 (Tripadvisor and Instagram), our study did not find that initial travel motivation influenced social media usage. These types of research could provide valuable target-marketing information for destinations.

Lastly, further research into how media, specifically social media, represent destinations and influence travel expectations can better support destinations as they move from pull-factor marketing into push-factor marketing, or find ways to adequately combine both (Ramseook-Munhurrun et al., 2018). Moreover, the resulting satisfaction with a destination might be measured in relation to user-generated content. While it is recognized that destinations must move towards using both web-based and social media sources, targeted messaging should vary based on the type of media used in destination marketing.

REFERENCES

Buhalis, D. and Law, R. (2008). Progress in information technology and tourism management: Twenty years on and 10 years after the Internet: The state of e-tourism research. *Tourism Management*, 29, 609–623.

Chung, J.Y. and Buhalis, D. (2008). Web 2.0: A study of online travel community, in information and communication technologies in tourism. In P. O'Connor, W. Höpken and U. Gretzel (eds), *Enter* (pp. 70–81). Vienna: Springer Verlag.

CrowdRiff (2018). How travelers use social media for travel (and 5 ways tourism brands can respond). Retrieved April 30, 2020 from https://crowdriff.com/resources/blog/how-travelers-use-social-media -travel.

Curtis, K.R., Bradshaw, M. and Slocum, S.L. (2020). The importance of culinary experiences in destination loyalty. *Journal of Gastronomy and Tourism*, 4(2), 67–79.

Daugherty, T., Eastin, M.S. and Bright, L. (2008). Exploring consumer motivations for creating user-generated content. *Journal of Interactive Advertising*, 8(2), 26–38.

eMarketer (2020). How travelers use social media using the social web before, during and after travel. Retrieved May 5, 2020 from https://www.emarketer.com/Article/How-Travelers-Use-Social-Media/ 1008122.

Fat Tire Tours (2019). New survey reveals how travelers are using social media before and during vacation. Retrieved May 2, 2020 from https://www.fattiretours.com/blog/news/survey-reveals-how -travelers-use-social-media-2018.

Fotis, J.N., Buhalis, D., and Rossides, N. (2012). *Social Media Use and Impact during the Holiday Travel Planning Process* (pp. 13–24). Vienna: Springer-Verlag.

Fotis, J.N., Rossides, N., and Buhalis, D. (2010). Social media impact on leisure travel: The case of the Russian market and the challenges for the Cyprus tourism industry. In *3rd Annual EuroMed Conference of the EuroMed Academy of Business-Conference Readings Book Proceedings-Business Developments Across Countries And Cultures* (pp. 1365–1367). EuroMed Press.

Goh, K.Y., Heng, C.S. and Lin, Z. (2013). Social media brand community and consumer behavior: Quantifying the relative impact of user- and marketer-generated content. *Information Systems Research*, 24(1), 88–107.

Gretzel, U., Kang, M. and Lee, W. (2008). Differences in consumer-generated media adoption and use: A cross-national perspective. *Journal of Hospitality and Leisure Marketing*, 17(1–2), 99–120.

Gretzel, U. and Yoo, K.H. (2008). Use and impact of online travel reviews information and communication technologies in tourism. *Proceedings of the International Information and Communication Technologies in Tourism Conference*, Innsbruck, Austria.

Kaldeen, M. (2019). Factors that trigger the use of social media tools, applications and networks of tourist. *3rd International Conference on Computing and Communications Technologies*, Tamil Nadu, India.

Lee, S., Boshnakova, D. and Goldblatt, J. (2016). *The 21st Century Meeting and Event Technologies: Powerful Tools for Better Planning, Marketing and Evaluation*. Point Pleasant, NJ: Apple Academic Press.

Lee, Y., Chang, C.H. and Chen, Y.S. (2013). The influence of novelty, flexibility, and synergy of package tours on tourist satisfaction: An analysis of structural equation modeling (SEM). *Quality and Quantity*, 47(4), 1869–1882.

Montero, J.M. and Fernandez-Aviles, G. (2010). An alternative to test independence between expectations and disconfirmation versus the positive version of the assimilation theory. An application to the case of cultural/heritage tourism. *International Journal of Management and Information Systems*, 14(4), 7–16.

Narangajavana, Y., Fiol, L.J.C., Tena, M.Á.M., Artola, R.M.R. and García, J.S. (2017). The influence of social media in creating expectations. An empirical study for a tourist destination. *Annals of Tourism Research*, 65, 60–70.

Narangajavana Kaosiri, Y., Callarisa Fiol, L.J., Moliner Tena, M.A., Rodriguez Artola, R.M. and Sanchez Garcia, J. (2019). User-generated content sources in social media: A new approach to explore tourist satisfaction. *Journal of Travel Research*, 58(2), 253–265.

National Statistical Committee of the Republic of Belarus (2017). *Tourism in the Republic of Belarus*. Retrieved November 15, 2019 from http://www.belstat.gov.by/en/ofitsialnaya-statistika/social-sector/ naselenie/turizm/operativnye-dannye_16/tourism-in-the-republic-of-belarus.

Pushkareva, M.A. and Samusevich, D.E. (2017). Problems and prospects of the development of tourism industry in the Republic of Belarus. *International Scientific and Practical Conference of Students and Young Scientists*, Minsk, March 2–3, pp. 346–347.

Ramseook-Munhurrun, P., Naidoo, P., Seebaluck, N.V. and Puttaroo, A. (2018, June). The effects of push and pull travel motivation on tourist experience, tourist satisfaction and loyalty. *8th Advances in Hospitality and Tourism Marketing and Management (AHTMM) Conference*, Bangkok, Thailand.

Rausing, S. (2012, October 7). Belarus: inside Europe's last dictatorship. *Guardian*.

Republic of Belarus (2016). *Belarus' Social and Economic Development Program for 2016–2020 Enacted*. Retrieved April 2, 2019 from http://www.belarus.by/en/government/documents/belarus -social-and-economic-development-program-for-2016-2020-enacted_i_0000050329.html.

Sigala, M., Christou, E. and Gretzel, U. (eds) (2012). *Social Media in Travel, Tourism and Hospitality: Theory, Practice and Cases*. New York: Routledge.

Slocum, S.L., Aidoo, A. and McMahon, K. (2020). *The Business of Sustainable Tourism Development and Management*. London: Routledge.

Slocum, S.L. and Klitsounova, V. (2019). Rethinking tourism in Belarus: The opening of a rural economy. In P. Wiltshier and A. Clarke (eds), *Community-Based Tourism in the Developing World* (pp. 67–80). Abingdon: Routledge.

Slocum, S.L. and Klitsounova, V. (2020). Conclusion. In S.L. Slocum and V. Klitsounova (eds), *Tourism Development in Post-Soviet Nations: From Communism to Capitalism*. Basingstoke: Palgrave Macmillan.

Think with Google (2016). Travel trends 2016. Retrieved May 1, 2020 from https://www.thinkwithgoogle .com/advertising-channels/mobile-marketing/travel-trends-2016-data-consumer-insights/.

United Nations World Tourism Organization (2019). *Yearbook of Tourism Statistics Data Set: Belarus (electronic)*. Retrieved April 2, 2020 from https://www.e-unwto.org/doi/pdf/10.5555/unwtotfb01 12011120142018201907.

Vermeulen, I. and Seegers, D. (2009). Tried and tested: The impact of online hotel reviews on consumer considerations. *Tourism Management*, 30(1), 123–127.

World Bank Group (2018). *Voice of Travelers: Leveraging User-Generated Content for Tourism Development*. Washington DC.

World Travel and Tourism Council (2017). *Travel and Tourism Economic Impact 2017, Belarus*. Oxford: WTCC.

Xiang, Z. and Gretzel, U. (2010). Role of social media in online travel information search. *Tourism Management*, 31, 179–188.

Yoo, K.H. and Gretzel, U. (2016). Web 2.0: New rules for tourism marketing, Travel and Tourism Research Association: Advancing tourism research globally. 26. Retrieved 13 May, 2020 from https:// scholarworks.umass.edu/ttra/2010/Oral/26.

Yu, G., Carlsson, C. and Zou, D. (2014). Exploring the influence of user-generated content factors on the behavioral intentions of travel consumers. *Proceedings of the 25th Australasian Conference on Information Systems*, December 8–10, Auckland, New Zealand: ACIS Publishing.

PART II

DESTINATION AND DMOs

4. Social media adoption among DMOs: a systematic review of academic research

Mani Shah Alizadegan and Yulin Liu

INTRODUCTION

As social media plays an instrumental role in many tourists' decisions of destination choice, destination management/marketing organizations (DMOs) tend to incorporate it as a significant part of marketing strategies. Travel information traditionally came from a restricted range of sources such as tourist boards and travel journals (Grieve, 2013). Nowadays tourists explore alternative sources such as online reviews (Simeon et al., 2017) and travel blogs (Pühringer and Taylor, 2008) to obtain information about a destination. As tourists seek more reliable and diverse sources of information, DMOs have responded to this demand by representing themselves on social networking sites such as Facebook, Tripadvisor and Twitter (Bignéa et al., 2019; Mariani et al., 2016).

Social media has been examined in various aspects in the literature, where some topics have been given more attention, for example, the role of social media in destination image creation and recovery in tourism crisis management (Zhai et al., 2019), and the impact of DMOs' social media activities on perceived destination image (González-Rodríguez et al., 2016). A particular topic favored by academics is how customer reviews (for example, travel blog stories) influence intention to visit a destination (Molinillo et al., 2018; Stylos et al., 2017). DMOs' presence on social media has been examined in numerous tourism studies, but the majority focus on tourist attitudes and behaviors rather than DMOs. DMOs' limited access to resources such as knowledge and technology can hinder effective utilization of social media, causing managerial and communication issues (Law et al., 2014; Zwienenberg et al., 2013). Existing research findings have proposed various solutions and recommendations for DMOs to embrace social media. Through a systematic review of academic research, this chapter aims to curate existing knowledge to answer three questions from DMO practitioners' perspective, namely about the common challenges DMOs encounter when adopting social media, the best social media practices for DMOs, and how to measure the effect of adopting social media.

METHODOLOGY

Terms such as "social media," "user-generated content" and "user engagement" appear multiple times in this chapter. Their definitions have evolved over time and we adopt the following definitions in this study. Based on the intensity of two dimensions, that is, "self-disclosure" and "media richness," Kaplan and Haenlein (2010) construct a typology of social media. For example, collaborative sites such as Wikipedia are low in both dimensions; virtual social worlds such as Second Life are high in both aspects; and social networks such as Facebook and video-sharing communities such as YouTube are at medium levels. User-generated content

(UGC) can be "various forms of media content that are publicly available and created by end-users" (Kaplan and Haenlein, 2010, p. 61). User engagement is "user's state of mind that warrants heightened involvement and results in a personally meaningful benefit" (Di Gangi and Wasko, 2016, p. 56).

In order to critically synthesize the current knowledge base of social media adoption among DMOs, we performed a systematic "integrative review" (Furunes, 2019) of various relevant articles (for example, conceptual, empirical and review studies) published in quality peer-reviewed tourism and hospitality research journals. Considering rigor of research publication, completeness of coverage, and amount of work for this study under a limited budget, other types of literature such as conference papers and book chapters were not included in this systematic review. Similar study designs were employed by recent reviews (e.g., Ahn et al., 2020; Law et al., 2016). The "unique contribution" (Furunes, 2019) of this literature review focuses on creating "added value" in "relevance for real-world applications" (Van Wee and Banister, 2016).

The initial literature search was confined within the 84 (Q1–Q4) academic journals in English listed under the subject category of "Tourism, Leisure and Hospitality Management" on the Scimago Journal Rankings website (SJR, 2016). The search criterion in each journal was set as containing both "social media" and "DMO" anywhere in an article's main body of text to maximize the catch, resulting in an initial pool of 319 articles in early 2018. A total of 268 articles were screened out after three progressive stages of relevance assessment in early 2018, respectively based on article title and abstract (165), introduction and conclusion (89), and full text reading (47). In-depth review was thus conducted on the remaining 51 select articles, which formed the basis of findings. The literature search and review were updated till March 2020 with an additional 20 relevant articles identified. In total 71 articles were reviewed. Centering on the aforementioned three research questions, findings of this study are presented in the following section with overview of knowledge available, examples of real-world cases, and recommendations for practice and research.

FINDINGS

What Social Media Challenges do DMOs Face?

Many DMOs are learning about social media and its applications; however, the majority of them have probably been unable to take full advantage of social media platforms (Zwienenberg et al., 2013). Major social media challenges are the lack of strategy, knowledge or resources, which usually lead to low user engagement on social media. As tourism research has been mostly centering on consumers' views, there is a lack of research on the suppliers' side (Edwards et al., 2017). In addition, DMOs' usage of social media is mostly limited to merely marketing activities that can be carried out on traditional media (Mariani et al., 2016; Munar, 2012). These activities mostly include non-interactive posts or images that lack two-way communication between DMO and end user. In other words, the main benefit of social media, namely direct communication with users, has not been exploited by DMOs. This section provides an overview of relevant issues reported in the articles reviewed.

Despite recently increased social media adoption in DMOs, many of them have failed to create or pursue a clear strategy with feasible goals to achieve. DMOs' understanding of the social media concept is still vague and experimental (Lee and Wicks, 2010; Pabel and Prideaux, 2016), which can affect the effectiveness of DMOs' online activities in various aspects such as communication, UGC utilization and public relations (John, 2017; Schroeder and Pennington-Gray, 2015; Ketter, 2016). Studying the social media activities of Greek DMOs, Perakakis et al. (2016) discovered that their presence was limited to promotional activities on popular platforms such as Facebook and YouTube with a lack of attention to the target groups' needs. Greek DMOs were more concerned about the financial benefits of social media rather than ways to influence the users. Fernández-Cavia et al. (2017) found that destination managers in Spain considered social media as a more participatory tool than official websites; however, most of them lacked a clear communication plan or standardized activities.

Lack of social media strategy hinders effective communication, and consequently DMOs may fail to reach all market segments by providing the right information to the right people. Analyzing Chinese tourism DMOs' micro-blogging, Zhang et al. (2016) discovered that the amount of actual tourism-related information (for example, travel advice, information on tour routes, and online booking service recommendations) was as low as less than one-third of all their posts, which indicates "the lack of professional standards among some China's DMOs" (p. 79). Zhang et al. (2016) also observed that many DMOs were involved "in one-way communication of information" by only providing second-hand information that users could easily find on review websites or via search engines. And DMOs tend to use social media only to inform users about their news or services, with little engagement or persuasive strategy (John, 2017). Hays et al. (2013) point out that DMOs are not yet sufficiently utilizing social media to solve negative comments or criticisms; they either use social media only for marketing purposes or do not focus on customer service when performing other activities; social media should be used to spread fresh and unique information rather than repeating the same knowledge that users can easily gain from DMOs' websites or other sources.

There are studies that have compared user-generated and DMO-generated images of a destination. The primary finding of those studies is that most DMOs have failed to use all the benefits of UGC, by missing the important aspects tourists usually look for in their content (Mak, 2017; Song and Kim, 2016; Stankov et al., 2010; Stepchenkova and Zhan, 2013). By applying UGC in destination image creation, DMOs could eliminate negative comments (Llodrà-Riera et al., 2015), provide an image that stimulates the novelty-seeking behavior of tourists (Song and Kim, 2016), reflect tourists' interests rather than DMOs' interests (Stepchenkova and Zhan, 2013; Woosnam and Aleshinloye, 2013), and present a more trustworthy image (Lange-Faria and Elliot, 2012).

On the other hand, UGC may pose some threats to DMOs' flow of accurate information (Plank, 2016; Pike, 2017). Despite its credibility amongst the internet users, sometimes it may be misleading or less informative (Wang et al., 2017). For instance, it "may create an inflated sense of perceived control over certain risks and as a consequence UGC may encourage increased risk taking" (Plank, 2016, p. 295). Therefore, it has been suggested that DMOs should monitor UGC to identify potential threats. Furthermore, UGC integration is not always beneficial for positive destination image creation, as potential tourists may form their initial destination image based on resources that are out of DMOs' control (Narangajavana Kaosiri et al., 2019).

Lack of resources hinders DMOs' ability to integrate social media successfully. There are two contrary opinions regarding the role of resources in social media adoption in DMOs. Some researchers believe that lack of sufficient resources – whether technological or financial

– can be a challenge to DMOs utilizing social media. For example, DMOs are unable to keep up to date with the latest trends of technology, due to its rapid growth (Pabel and Prideaux, 2016; Zwienenberg et al., 2013) or managers' lack of commitment and knowledge (Milwood et al., 2013; Mariani et al., 2016; Hays et al., 2013). In addition to technological challenges, inadequate financial resources also affect DMOs' ability in adapting information technologies (Pabel and Prideaux, 2016; Stangl et al., 2016). At the same time, some experts consider social media as a more cost-effective marketing tool for destinations with a limited budget (Law et al., 2014; Perakakis et al., 2016). Regardless of which argument is accurate, it is noted in the literature that financial resources and destination managers' awareness about technology are directly related to the level of social media adoption among DMOs.

In summary, most DMOs are using social media merely as a traditional marketing channel, simply as a non-interactive media. This has been caused by DMOs' lack of knowledge, capital or strategy, and a tradition of one-way conversation with customers. The key social media functions such as public relations management and UGC incorporation into digital media strategy have been neglected by DMOs. In the next section, suggestions given in the literature for improving social media presence of DMOs will be synthesized.

How Should DMOs Adopt Social Media?

We synthesize the ways DMOs (should) adopt social media reported in the literature into a hierarchy of seven levels (Figure 4.1).

Managers' conception
Destination managers play a significant role in the process of social media adoption. A major element influencing the social media strategy of a DMO is the attitude of its leadership; once social media has been accepted as a powerful marketing strategy, the whole organization will

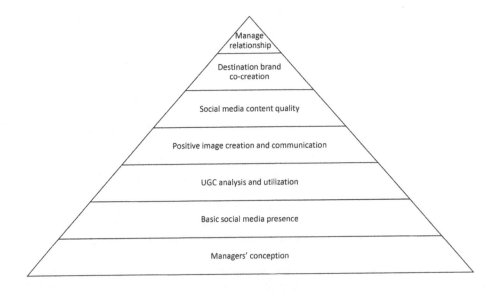

Figure 4.1   Sevens levels of social media adoption in DMOs

promote utilizing it (Hays et al., 2013). Mariani et al. (2016) observed that Italian DMOs used social media in a top-down, DMO-driven manner, rather than a bottom-up, UGC-driven manner. Traditional management structure and managers' lack of social media skills and technology awareness are the major managerial issues that DMOs encounter when using social media (Zeng and Gerritsen, 2014; Mariani et al. 2016).

Milwood et al. (2013) suggest that destination managers who are new to social media should seek assistance from external organizations in the adoption stage. A similar notion is to train managers in how to utilize positive comments to achieve more success, and how to address adverse comments with remedial actions, on Tripadvisor or other social media platforms (Hays et al., 2013). A further action for managers who are familiar with social media is to monitor their efforts and investment to amplify the success of digital marketing activities. In a survey of destination managers, Lee et al. (2013) conclude that during the technology adoption phase, destination managers undergo a mental process which alters their perceptions and attitudes regarding Web 2.0 technology and leads to adopting social media in their organizations.

Basic social media presence

DMOs adopting social media should keep up to date with the users' needs and the industry's best practices to learn from their achievements and mistakes (Hays et al., 2013). A small but effective step for DMOs to facilitate tourists' information acquisition and decision-making process is to provide a link to their social media pages on their websites (Cahyanto and Pennington-Gray, 2015; Li and Wang, 2011). In the basic stages of social media adoption, DMOs should segment users based on their needs, and target each segment differently in marketing in order to secure new markets via social media (Perakakis et al., 2016; Pesonen and Tuohino, 2017). By being present on social media platforms, DMOs can develop a foundation for more advanced activities and benefit from users' participation.

Creating connections with social media influencers can also increase the reach and impacts of DMOs' social media activities. For example, DMOs can offer discounts to influential Twitter accounts sharing their contents (Bokunewicz and Shulman, 2017). Capitalizing on social media influencers can result in powerful influence on tourists' decision-making processes and experience through "passive learning and experiencing" (Seelera et al., 2019, p. 87). This, however, could also have a negative impact on tourists' trust as social media influencers may receive a fee to promote a certain destination (Chatzigeorgiou, 2017; Uchinaka et al., 2019).

UGC analysis and utilization

Nowadays, online reviews have a considerable influence on how consumers search for information and make decisions. Online reviews may help DMOs to understand the problems travelers experience at a destination and then improve services and brand image (Lee and Wicks, 2010). Online reviews must be investigated to find out whether they have a significant impact on potential visitors who consider visiting a destination or not. Marketers can utilize them to broadcast messages that they want travelers to think of when choosing a destination brand (Lim et al., 2012). In food tourism marketing, Lai (2020) suggested that DMOs should monitor user-generated food reviews on social media to adjust promotional activities. Content analysis tools for analyzing reviews can be developed to achieve the best results; by following up UGC with established mechanisms, it is possible to track consumers' perceptions and intentions regarding a destination (Carvão, 2010; Lee et al., 2013; Llodrà-Riera et al.,

2015). For example, using sentiment analysis of online reviews, DMOs can discover the best and worst attributes of a destination through the eyes of tourists. (González-Rodríguez et al., 2016). The main obstacle with user comments and online reviews is that they may be unreliable, as the accounts can be fabricated by competitors or fraudsters. Therefore, DMOs should judge the reviews based on the reviewers' knowledge and the length of their reviews (González-Rodríguez et al., 2016).

Travel blogs are another form of UGC that DMOs can use to increase the efficacy of their online activities. Travel blogs allow travelers to share their opinions and criticize activities or attractions of a destination. Previous research reveal that 70 percent of hospitality businesses used blogs to monitor feedback; however, travel blogs have not yet been completely integrated as a market research tool by DMOs (Pühringer and Taylor, 2008). Some DMOs use blog content on their websites, which is usually limited to positive and promotional material encouraging visits the destination (Banyai and Glover, 2012); notwithstanding, blogs can be used to achieve more valuable data about travelers. From DMOs' point of view, travel blogs are a rich source of information for marketers to understand their target markets.

DMOs can establish their own blogs, where content is created in-house or contracted out to professional bloggers as a supplement to their existing content. This will assist destinations to improve the quality of their social media content and access more accurate information regarding tourists (Mak, 2017). Oliveira and Panyik (2015) analyzed Portugal as a destination and the way that marketing strategies integrated user-generated content. By utilizing online reviews and blogs about Portugal, Visit Portugal identifies the most popular cities, activities and foods within the country to help build its online presence on social media. DMOs can also allow tourists to share their own stories on DMO blogs, because personal stories are easily comprehended and can reach a more diverse demographic (Tussyadiah and Fesenmaier, 2008).

DMOs can connect potential visitors with past visitors who have shared their experiences through the destination's official website, and/or their own travel blogs (Lange-Faria and Elliot, 2012). Each social media platform should be separately examined and used based on its unique characteristics (Garay Tamajón and Cànoves Valiente, 2017). UGC is not only limited to tourist-generated content. Resident-generated content is perceived to be more organic and reliable (Uchinaka et al., 2019). DMOs can collaborate with local residents to promote and strengthen a destination on social media through boosting social bonding of the residents with the destination (Garay, 2019; Chena et al., 2018). This contributes to positive image creation.

Positive image creation and communication
Tourists can go through a process from checking travel blogs to reading online reviews and then using their own social media, to collect opinions to validate the image of a destination (Grieve, 2013). DMOs tend to display a specific image of destination to build its public image, which could be different from visitors' portrayals of the destination in UGC. Comparing the destination image presented by DMOs and visitors' perceived images can help DMOs build on strengths and improve on weaknesses.

Song and Kim (2016) suggested that DMOs and photo sharing platforms (for example, Pinterest) could cooperate to identify the inconsistencies between DMOs' projections and travelers' projections of destinations. Law et al. (2014) went beyond only analyzing photos, and argued that social media should be monitored to rectify destination image in a timely and economic manner. DMOs should also consider including tourist-generated photos in their official websites, to motivate tourists to share memorable photos and engage with the destination, by emphasizing the importance of their contributions to DMOs' online presence (Mak, 2017). Destination managers should ensure that their social media sites are managed professionally to establish a positive image and find out user activities, interests and concerns (Liu et al., 2019). DMOs can incorporate tourists' photos when selecting marketing materials to meet market expectations, particularly when targeting a specific market segment (Deng and Li, 2018).

DMOs should not only try to include the topics and images favored by tourists in their communication, but also provide further relevant information to benefit tourists (Önder and Marchiori, 2017). When dealing with negative or inaccurate tourist perceptions, DMOs should consider tourist perspectives and provide answers to visitors' potential questions (Llodrà-Riera et al., 2015). Furthermore, DMOs can utilize social media in crisis management to build a positive image among the public by timely and efficient responses (Zhai et al., 2019).

Communication with potential visitors via social media is also recommended in the literature (Dedeoğlu et al., 2020; Llodrà-Riera et al., 2015). DMOs should incorporate online review platforms (for example, Tripadvisor), travel-dedicated social media platforms (for example WAYN), focused email marketing, blogs, microblogs, wikis and travelogues in a marketing mix to develop positive word-of-mouth (Stylos et al., 2017). Ketter (2016) suggests creating a destination blog, aimed at influencing travelers' decisions, to gather authentic information. Ideally, these activities should lead to creating a unified destination brand by "wiring a meaningful network of knowledge linked through relevance in their memory" rather than occasional marketing campaigns (Tasci, 2018, p. 156). Micro-films, despite their short duration, can be used for an established destination to "re-position its brand and image successfully" (Shao et al., 2016, p. 449).

Communication between DMOs and tourists must be reciprocal for social media to be effective. DMOs must try to be involved in two-way communications with users instead of merely broadcasting second-hand information (Zhang et al., 2016). DMOs should understand the behavior of tourists and strive to deliver the relevant information that can reach and affect the majority of their target market. The type of content and the quality of users are highly important in delivering a message on Twitter (Bignéa et al., 2019). Social media engagement should not be limited to gaining users' attention for a Facebook post; it should also include replying to comments and providing information about a destination (Gálvez-Rodríguez et al., 2020).

Social media content quality

DMOs' social media content has a profound impact on their audience's desire to travel, and DMOs must ensure their social media content's quality (Koo et al., 2016). DMOs should pay full attention to the quality of their content on social media to provide a positive social media experience for their users (John, 2017). High-quality content not only satisfies the interests of travelers, but also encourages interaction among potential visitors (Koo et al., 2016, p. 1355). Existing offers of a destination and general information about tourism opportunities (for example, shopping centers, hotels) should be present on social media. DMOs could also stimulate public participation by responding to queries and providing lucky draws and contests. It is important for DMOs to involve tourists in content creation for cognitive aspects (one's knowledge) of a destination such as hygiene and safety (Molinillo et al., 2018). This will positively impact the affective image (one's feeling) of a destination.

Information must be realistic and accurate to create realistic expectations among visitors, which will lead to a more positive tourist experience and response on social media (Scholl-Grissemann et al., 2019). Accurate information represents a transparent image of a destination, and visitors can prepare themselves to see the reality at a destination even if social media depicts its unfavorable conditions. Visitors can be willing to accept the imperfections of a destination as long as DMOs' image of the destination is genuine (Scholl-Grissemann et al., 2019).

Co-creation of destination brand

Social media has been considered as an interactive notion, in which users and marketers both create a brand. DMOs can "look on the Internet to find the backbone for a potential destination brand to position tourist destination" (Oliveira and Panyik, 2015, p. 70). DMOs can supply themed content that stimulates the users' sense of curiosity and motivation to share their experiences on the DMOs' official social media accounts (Jiménez-Barreto et al., 2019). The more users participate in the brand creation process, the more interested they will be to share the content on their social networking accounts, subsequently growing the reputation of the destination brand (Oliveira and Panyik, 2015). Storytelling is a powerful strategy to co-create a destination brand. DMOs should tell positive stories about destinations – for example, through promotional videos – on social media to encourage users to share their own positive experiences, monitor their responses, and eventually turn the tourists into brand ambassadors that would consequently decrease the impact of negative comments on a destination (Lund et al., 2019; Moin et al., 2020).

DMOs can collaborate with local experts to establish exclusive social media platforms similar to Tripadvisor's forums (Edwards et al., 2017). DMOs having their own forums are potentially more engaging than DMO-created content on other platforms, since DMOs will have access to more accurate data for their marketing plans. The biggest challenge is to build an interactive platform trusted by visitors. Compared to popular social media platforms such as Facebook and Twitter, DMO-created web pages were found to receive the lowest scores in terms of usefulness for people seeking information about a destination (Llodrà-Riera et al., 2015). DMO-owned platforms must ensure their usability.

Relationship management

"Social media enables users with common interests to communicate with each other and share content. Many organizations believe that having content available on social media is enough; however, they need to engage with social media to understand the audience and create social media content strategically" (Zwienenberg et al., 2013). DMOs must notice that social media has two functionalities: first, as a traditional media form, to spread messages in a cost-effective way; and second, for generating user engagement by communication and personal involvement (Ketter, 2016; Munar, 2012). User engagement can be achieved through ways including but not limited to quizzes, games, polls, and content containing visual content (Mariani et al., 2016), which generate positive electronic word-of-mouth (eWOM) about a destination (Tham et al., 2013).

DMOs should go beyond issues such as promotion and marketing and "take into consideration contextual factors that can influence tourists' experience" (Bulchand-Gidumal et al., 2013, p. 46). Social media presence should be a conscious decision as part of a more comprehensive marketing plan, rather than the global trends; social media marketing should be considered in its own right and not as a part of regular marketing strategies (Pabel and Prideaux, 2016). DMOs must provide a virtual environment in which they can go beyond one-way marketing posts by offering competitive services and creating value for users through direct communications with them (Fernández-Cavia et al., 2017; Xiang et al., 2015).

The usage of virtual worlds such as Second Life in shaping tourists' experience is also discussed in the literature reviewed. This stage is beyond social media, and deserves greater attention in future research. Once virtual worlds become widespread, DMOs will be able to reach a new level of engagement with travelers (Ali and Frew, 2014). Virtual communities can enhance user experience by media specifically chosen for visual appeal, combined with well-written instructions to help tourists navigate their chosen destinations, and enable users to travel and share their experiences without physical travel. Moreover, virtual travel games (for example, Expedia's Around The World In 100 Days) and location-based augmented reality or mixed reality games can be utilized to create interactive tourist experiences (Stylos et al., 2017, p. 26). Virtual experiences can enable DMOs to discover what visitors want to do at a destination, which can potentially increase the positive eWOM (Lee and Wicks, 2010). Nevertheless, the knowledge and acceptance of virtual technology is still low among DMOs, and consequently it requires "high levels of technical support to function effectively" (Lange-Faria and Elliot, 2012, p. 201).

How Could DMOs Measure the Effect of Adopting Social Media?

Measuring the impacts of social media activities is complicated for DMOs as there are multiple factors with various levels of importance. One of the easiest and least precise ways to measure user engagement is to tally the number of page likes or account followers. For example, the number of likes of a DMO's tweets could be related to prediction of tourism demand (Önder and Marchiori, 2017; Yang et al., 2014). France's Tourism Development Agency measures its followers' growth rate, and Tourism Queensland monitors several factors specific to each campaign (Hays et al., 2013). According to Garay Tamajón and Cànoves Valiente (2017), DMOs should analyze each social media platform and their different actors, typologies and components. Users' feedback should be measured by DMOs to evaluate their service quality, tourists' satisfaction and overall experience (John, 2017). Hays et al. (2013) argue that consumer sentiment and engagement are closely connected. If DMOs engage with users on social media, it is possible to measure their experience or feeling about a destination. Philander and Zhong (2016) analyzed sentiment of tweets to measure consumer attitudes. Sentiment analysis is a low-cost and less time-consuming text mining solution compared with traditional marketing research with surveys or focus groups. It can also provide real-time results of marketing campaigns, while traditional methods usually measure after-sales results.

Social media return on investment (ROI) measurement is a controversial notion due to the absence of advanced tools to monitor it. The German National Tourist Board believes that measuring the social media ROI is impossible, as the tourism board is not engaged in commercial activities and consequently is unable to calculate the amount of money made by its activities (Hays et al., 2013). Regional destination managers in Italy were found to use Google Analytics and Blogmeter to measure their social media activities (Mariani et al., 2016). Moreover, the destination managers in Italy considered that measuring the financial benefits of their marketing activities is beyond their capabilities. A set of clearly defined tools for social media measurement among DMOs is lacking, which is partially due to the scarcity of comparable data, as social media managers tend not to share data with competitors.

Destination managers are aware of the importance of social media measurement, although they rarely perform it (Munar, 2012). This may be due to DMOs' traditional role, which is limited to marketing campaigns without analyzing their impacts. It also requires an extensive source of knowledge and skills, and cooperation between various departments such as information technology and marketing. DMOs must discover those factors of social media that should be measured, rather than what can be measured (Morgan et al., 2012). This is a highly important point, as social media is a modern tool, and traditional key performance indicators (KPI) of marketing may no longer be fit for measuring its impacts. Thus, there should be KPIs that are clearly defined and can measure social media effectively, to provide comparable data beyond the number of likes or shares (Zavattaro et al., 2015). In general, social media measurement has yet not been widely discussed in the reviewed literature. More research is needed on this challenging topic for tourism marketers, as it is more than statistics (for example, number of likes of a post) and is directly related to customers' experience and behavior (for example, whether a campaign motivates individuals to visit a destination).

CONCLUSION

The main objective of this literature review was to identify how social media has been adopted by DMOs. Over 70 informative journal articles published in English were identified and reviewed following a systematic approach. The research publications were assessed to identify the challenges DMOs have faced when adopting social media, including lack of strategy, knowledge and resources as well as their ramifications. The most distinct characteristic of social media compared to traditional media is direct engagement with users. For this reason, the recommendations for DMOs' adoption of social media are framed in a seven-level hierarchy, starting from the most basic management conception of social media presence, to more strategic UGC utilization and positive image communication, to the most sophisticated destination brand co-creation and relationship management. DMOs' social media activities should also be measured to increase efficiency and reduce errors. However, only a small number of the articles have addressed this matter.

Multiple areas are identified as in need of further research. Whether effective social media practice has a direct impact on the number of travelers visiting a destination should be investigated. The trustworthiness of popular UGC writers should also be examined, due to the increase of independent social media users' influence, and the benefits they gain when reviewing a destination. Practical measurement of DMOs' social media activities is absent in current literature and needs to be developed to incorporate into KPIs.

This literature review did not cover non-English articles due to the researchers' capacity. Only academic articles in the field of tourism and hospitality research were searched, which could not catch potential insights published, or not published, in other research areas and in non-academic literature. Nevertheless, with a seven-phase hierarchical framework to guide DMOs' strategies for adopting social media, this chapter presents a panorama of up-to-date knowledge on the topic. This panorama provides insights for tourism industry practitioners, educators and academics who wish to bring innovation into their management, teaching and research.

REFERENCES

Ahn, J., Lee, S.L., and Kwon, J. (2020). Impulsive buying in hospitality and tourism journals. *Annals of Tourism Research, 82*, 102764. https://doi.org/10.1016/j.annals.2019.102764.

Ali, A., and Frew, A.J. (2014). ICT and sustainable tourism development: An innovative perspective. *Journal of Hospitality and Tourism Technology, 5*(1), 2–16. https://doi.org/10.1108/jhtt-12-2012 -0034.

Banyai, M., and Glover, T.D. (2012). Evaluating research methods on travel blogs. *Journal of Travel Research, 51*(3), 267–277. https://doi.org/10.1177/0047287511410323.

Bignéa, E., Oltrab, E., and Andreu, L. (2019). Harnessing stakeholder input on Twitter: A case study of short breaks in Spanish tourist cities. *Tourism Management, 71*, 490–450. https://doi.org/10.1016/j .tourman.2018.10.013.

Bokunewicz, J.F., and Shulman, J. (2017). Influencer identification in Twitter networks of destination marketing organizations. *Journal of Hospitality and Tourism Technology, 8*(2), 205–219. https://doi .org/10.1108/jhtt-09-2016-0057.

Bulchand-Gidumal, J., Melian-Gonzalez, S., and Lopez-Valcarcel, B.G. (2013). A social media analysis of the contribution of destinations to client satisfaction with hotels. *International Journal of Hospitality Management, 35*, 44–47. https://doi.org/10.1016/j.ijhm.2013.05.003.

Cahyanto, I., and Pennington-Gray, L. (2015). Communicating hurricane evacuation to tourists: Gender, past experience with hurricanes, and place of residence. *Journal of Travel Research, 54*(3), 329–343. https://doi.org/10.1177/0047287513517418.

Carvão, S. (2010). Embracing user generated content within destination management organizations to gain a competitive insight into visitors' profiles. *Worldwide Hospitality and Tourism Themes, 2*(4), 376–382. https://doi.org/10.1108/17554211011074038.

Chatzigeorgiou, C. (2017). Modelling the impact of social media influencers on behavioural intentions of millennials: The case of tourism in rural areas in Greece. *Journal of Tourism, Heritage and Services Marketing, 3*(2), 25–29. http://doi.org/10.5281/zenodo.1209125.

Chena, N.C., Dwyer, L., and Firth, T. (2018). Residents' place attachment and word-of-mouth behaviours: A tale of two cities. *Journal of Hospitality and Tourism Management, 36*, 1–11. https://doi.org/ 10.1016/j.jhtm.2018.05.001.

Dedeoğlu, B.B., Niekerk, M.v., Küçükergin, K.G., Martino, M.D., and Okumuş, F. (2020). Effect of social media sharing on destination brand awareness and destination quality. *Journal of Vacation Marketing, 26*(1), 33–56. https://doi.org/10.1177/1356766719858644.

Deng, N., and Li, X.R. (2018). Feeling a destination through the "right" photos: A machine learning model for DMOs' photo selection. *Tourism Management, 65*, 267–278. https://doi.org/10.1016/j .tourman.2017.09.010.

Di Gangi, P.M., and Wasko, M.M. (2016). Social media engagement theory: Exploring the influence of user engagement on social media usage. *Journal of Organizational and End User Computing, 28*(2), 53–73. https://doi.org/10.4018/joeuc.2016040104.

Edwards, D., Cheng, M., Wong, I.A., Zhang, J., and Wu, Q. (2017). Ambassadors of knowledge sharing: Co-produced travel information through tourist–local social media exchange. *International Journal of Contemporary Hospitality Management, 29*(2), 690–708. https://doi.org/10.1108/ijchm-10-2015 -0607.

Fernández-Cavia, J., Marchiori, E., Haven-Tang, C., and Cantoni, L. (2017). Online communication in Spanish destination marketing organizations: The view of practitioners. *Journal of Vacation Marketing, 23*(3), 264–273. https://doi.org/10.1177/1356766716640840.

Furunes, T. (2019). Reflections on systematic reviews: moving golden standards? *Scandinavian Journal of Hospitality and Tourism, 19*(3), 227–231. https://doi.org/10.1080/15022250.2019.1584965.

Gálvez-Rodríguez, M.d., Alonso-Cañadas, J., Haro-de-Rosario, A., and Caba-Pérez, C. (2020). Exploring best practices for online engagement via Facebook with local destination management organisations (DMOs) in Europe: A longitudinal analysis. *Tourism Management Perspectives, 34*. https://doi.org/ 10.1016/j.tmp.2020.100636.

Garay, L. (2019). #Visitspain. Breaking down affective and cognitive attributes in the social media construction of the tourist destination image. *Tourism Management Perspectives, 32*. https://doi.org/ 10.1016/j.tmp.2019.100560.

Garay Tamajón, L., and Cànoves Valiente, G. (2017). Barcelona seen through the eyes of TripAdvisor: Actors, typologies and components of destination image in social media platforms. *Current Issues in Tourism, 20*(1), 33–37. https://doi.org/10.1080/13683500.2015.1073229.

González-Rodríguez, M.R., Martínez-Torres, R., and Toral, S. (2016). Post-visit and pre-visit tourist destination image through eWOM sentiment analysis and perceived helpfulness. *International Journal of Contemporary Hospitality Management, 28*(11), 2609–2627. https://doi.org/10.1108/ijchm-02-2015-0057.

Grieve, D. (2013). Validating image in the information age. *Worldwide Hospitality and Tourism Themes, 5*(1), 67–79. https://doi.org/10.1108/17554211311292457.

Hays, S., Page, S.J., and Buhalis, D. (2013). Social media as a destination marketing tool: Its use by national tourism organisations. *Current Issues in Tourism, 16*(3), 211–239. https://doi.org/10.1080/13683500.2012.662215.

Jiménez-Barreto, J., Sthapit, E., Rubio, N., and Campo, S. (2019). Exploring the dimensions of online destination brand experience: Spanish and North American tourists' perspectives. *Tourism Management Perspectives, 31*, 348–360. https://doi.org/10.1016/j.tmp.2019.07.005.

John, S.P. (2017). An analysis of the social media practices for sustainable medical tourism destination marketing. *International Journal of Tourism Policy, 7*(3), 222–249. https://doi.org/10.1504/ijtp.2017.10007956.

Kaplan, A.M., and Haenlein, M. (2010). Users of the world, unite! The challenges and opportunities of social media. *Business Horizons, 53*(1), 59–68. https://doi.org/10.1016/j.bushor.2009.09.003.

Ketter, E. (2016). Destination image restoration on Facebook: The case study of Nepal's Gurkha earthquake. *Journal of Hospitality and Tourism Management, 28*, 66–72. https://doi.org/10.1016/j.jhtm.2016.02.003.

Koo, C., Joun, Y., Han, H., and Chung, N. (2016). A structural model for destination travel intention as a media exposure belief–desire–intention model perspective. *International Journal of Contemporary Hospitality Management, 28*(7), 1338–1360. https://doi.org/10.1108/IJCHM-07-2014-0354.

Lai, I.K.W. (2020). An examination of satisfaction on word of mouth regarding Portuguese foods in Macau: Applying the concept of integrated satisfaction. *Journal of Hospitality and Tourism Management, 43*, 100–110. https://doi.org/10.1016/j.jhtm.2020.02.011.

Lange-Faria, W., and Elliot, S. (2012). Understanding the role of social media in destination marketing. *Tourismos, 7*(1), 193–211.

Law, R., Buhalis, D., and Cobanoglu, C. (2014). Progress on information and communication technologies in hospitality and tourism. *International Journal of Contemporary Hospitality Management, 26*(5), 727–750. https://doi.org/10.1108/ijchm-08-2013-0367.

Law, R., Sun, S., Fong, D.K.C., Fong, L.N.H., and Fu, H. (2016). A systematic review of China's outbound tourism research. *International Journal of Contemporary Hospitality Management, 28*(12), 2654–2674. https://doi.org/10.1108/ijchm-06-2015-0323.

Lee, B.C., Cho, J., and Hwang, D. (2013). An integration of social capital and tourism technology adoption – A case of convention and visitors bureaus. *Tourism and Hospitality Research, 13*(3), 149–165. https://doi.org/10.1177/1467358414522055.

Lee, B.C., and Wicks, B. (2010). Tourism technology training for destination marketing organisations (DMOs): Need-based content development. *Journal of Hospitality Leisure Sport and Tourism, 9*(1), 39–52. https://doi.org/10.3794/johlste.91.241.

Li, X., and Wang, Y. (2011). Measuring the effectiveness of US official state tourism websites. *Journal of Vacation Marketing, 17*(4), 287–302. https://doi.org/10.1177/1356766711423436.

Lim, Y., Chung, Y., and Weaver, P.A. (2012). The impact of social media on destination branding: Consumer-generated videos versus destination marketer-generated videos. *Journal of Vacation Marketing, 18*(3), 197–206. https://doi.org/10.1177/1356766712449366.

Liu, J., Wang, C., Fang, S., and Zhang, T. (2019). Scale development for tourist trust toward a tourism destination. *Tourism Management Perspectives, 31*, 383–397. https://doi.org/10.1016/j.tmp.2019.07.001.

Llodrà-Riera, I., Martínez-Ruiz, M.P., Jiménez-Zarco, A.I., and Izquierdo-Yusta, A. (2015). A multidimensional analysis of the information sources construct and its relevance for destination image formation. *Tourism Management, 48*, 319–328. https://doi.org/10.1016/j.tourman.2014.11.012.

Lund, N.F., Scarles, C., and Cohen, S.A. (2019). The brand value continuum: Countering. *Journal of Travel Research*. https://doi.org/10.1177/0047287519887234.

Mak, A.H. (2017). Online destination image: Comparing national tourism organisation's and tourists' perspectives. *Tourism Management*, *60*, 280–297. https://doi.org/10.1016/j.tourman.2016.12.012.

Mariani, M.M., Felice, M.D., and Mura, M. (2016). Facebook as a destination marketing tool: Evidence from italian regional destination management organizations. *Tourism Management*, *54*, 321–343. https://doi.org/10.1016/j.tourman.2015.12.008.

Milwood, P., Marchiori, E., and Zach, F. (2013). A comparison of social media adoption and use in different countries: The case of the United States and Switzerland. *Journal of Travel and Tourism Marketing*, *30*, 165–168. https://doi.org/10.1080/10548408.2013.751287.

Moin, S. M., Hosany, S., and O'Brien, J. (2020). Storytelling in destination brands' promotional videos. *Tourism Management Perspectives*, 100639. https://doi.org/10.1016/j.tmp.2020.100639.

Molinillo, S., Liébana-Cabanillas, F., Anaya-Sánchez, R., and Buhalis, D. (2018). DMO online platforms: Image and intention to visit. *Tourism Management*, *65*, 116–130. https://doi.org/10.1016/j.tourman.2017.09.021.

Morgan, N., Hastings, E., and Pritchard, A. (2012). Developing a new DMO marketing evaluation framework: The case of Visit Wales. *Journal of Vacation Marketing*, *18*(1), 73–89. https://doi.org/10.1177/1356766711432225.

Munar, A.M. (2012). Social media strategies and destination management. *Scandinavian Journal of Hospitality and Tourism*, *12*(2), 101–120. https://doi.org/10.1080/15022250.2012.679047.

Narangajavana Kaosiri, Y., Callarisa Fiol, L.J., Moliner Tena, M.A., Rodriguez Artola, R.M., and Sanchez Garcia, J. (2019). User-generated content sources in social media: A new approach to explore tourist satisfaction. *Journal of Travel Research*, *58*(2), 253–265. https://doi.org/10.1177/0047287517746014.

Oliveira, E., and Panyik, E. (2015). Content, context and co-creation: Digital challenges in destination branding with references to Portugal as a tourist destination. *Journal of Vacation Marketing*, *21*(1), 53–74. https://doi.org/10.1177/1356766714544235.

Önder, I., and Marchiori, E. (2017). A comparison of pre-visit beliefs and projected visual images of destinations. *Tourism Management Perspectives*, *21*, 42–53. https://doi.org/10.1016/j.tmp.2016.11.003.

Pabel, A., and Prideaux, B. (2016). Social media use in pre-trip planning by tourists visiting a small regional leisure destination. *Journal of Vacation Marketing*, *22*(4), 335–348. https://doi.org/10.1177/1356766715618998.

Perakakis, E., Trihas, N., Mastorakis, G., Kopanakis, I., and Venitourakis, M. (2016). Social media as a marketing tool for Greek destinations. *Tourismos*, *11*(3), 157–181.

Pesonen, J.A., and Tuohino, A. (2017). Activity-based market segmentation of rural well-being tourists: Comparing online information search. *Journal of Vacation Marketing*, *23*(2), 145–158. https://doi.org/10.1177/1356766715610163.

Philander, K., and Zhong, Y. (2016). Twitter sentiment analysis: Capturing sentiment from integrated resort tweets. *International Journal of Hospitality Management*, *55*, 16–24. https://doi.org/10.1016/j.ijhm.2016.02.001.

Pike, S. (2017). Destination positioning and temporality: Tracking relative strengths and weaknesses over time. *Journal of Hospitality and Tourism Management*, *31*, 126–133. https://doi.org/10.1016/j.jhtm.2016.11.005.

Plank, A. (2016). The hidden risk in user-generated content: An investigation of ski tourers' revealed risk-taking behavior on an online outdoor sports platform. *Tourism Management*, *55*, 289–296. https://doi.org/10.1016/j.tourman.2016.02.013.

Pühringer, S., and Taylor, A. (2008). A practitioner's report on blogs as a potential source of destination marketing intelligence. *Journal of Vacation Marketing*, *14*(2), 177–187. https://doi.org/10.1177/1356766707087524.

Scholl-Grissemann, U., Peters, M., and Teichmann, K. (2019). When climate-induced change reaches social media: How realistic travel expectations shape consumers' attitudes toward the destination. *Journal of Travel Research*. https://doi.org/10.1177/0047287519883036.

Schroeder, A., and Pennington-Gray, L. (2015). The role of social media in international tourist's decision making. *Journal of Travel Research*, *54*(5), 584. https://doi.org/10.1177/0047287514528284.

Seelera, S., Lück, M., and Schänzel, H.A. (2019). Exploring the drivers behind experience accumulation – The role of secondary experiences consumed through the eyes of social media influencers. *Journal of Hospitality and Tourism Management, 41*, 80–89. https://doi.org/10.1016/j.jhtm.2019.09.009.

Shao, J., Li, X., Morrison, A.M., and Wu, B. (2016). Social media micro-film marketing by Chinese destinations: The case of Shaoxing. *Tourism Management, 54*, 439–451. https://doi.org/10.1016/j.tourman.2015.12.013.

Simeon, M.I., Buonincontri, P., Cinquegrani, F., and Martone, A. (2017). Exploring tourists' cultural experiences in naples through online reviews. *Journal of Hospitality and Tourism Technology, 8*(2), 220–238. https://doi.org/10.1108/jhtt-10-2016-0067.

SJR (2016). Scimago Journal and Country Rank. Retrieved in November 2017 from https://www.scimagojr.com/journalrank.php?category=1409andyear=2016.

Song, S.G., and Kim, D.Y. (2016). A pictorial analysis of destination images on Pinterest: The case of Tokyo, Kyoto, and Osaka, Japan. *Journal of Travel and Tourism Marketing, 33*(5), 687–701. https://doi.org/10.1080/10548408.2016.1167384.

Stangl, B., Inversini, A., and Schegg, R. (2016). Hotels' dependency on online intermediaries and their chosen distribution channel portfolios: Three country insights. *International Journal of Hospitality Management, 52*, 87–96. https://doi.org/10.1016/j.ijhm.2015.09.015.

Stankov, U., Lazic, L., and Dragicevic, V. (2010). The extent of use of basic Facebook user-generated content by the national tourism organizations in Europe. *European Journal of Tourism Research, 3*(2), 105–113.

Stepchenkova, S., and Zhan, F. (2013). Visual destination images of Peru: Comparative content analysis of DMO and user-generated photography. *Tourism Management, 36*, 590–601. https://doi.org/10.1016/j.tourman.2012.08.006.

Stylos, N., Bellou, V., Andronikidis, A., and Vassiliadis, C.A. (2017). Linking the dots among destination images, place attachment, and revisit intentions: A study among British and Russian tourists. *Tourism Management, 60*, 15–29. https://doi.org/10.1016/j.tourman.2016.11.006.

Tasci, A. D. (2018). Testing the cross-brand and cross-market validity of a consumer-based brand equity (CBBE) model for destination brands. *Tourism Management, 65*, 143–159. https://doi.org/10.1016/j.tourman.2017.09.020.

Tham, A., Croy, G., and Mair, J. (2013). Social media in destination choice: Distinctive electronic word-of-mouth dimensions. *Journal of Travel and Tourism Marketing: Social Media, 30*(1–2), 144–155. https://doi.org/10.1080/10548408.2013.751272.

Tussyadiah, I. P., and Fesenmaier, D.R. (2008). Marketing places through first-person stories – An analysis of Pennsylvania Roadtripper blog. *Journal of Travel and Tourism Marketing, 25*(3–4), 299–311. https://doi.org/10.1080/10548400802508358.

Uchinaka, S., Yoganathan, V., and Osburg, V. (2019). Classifying residents' roles as online place-ambassadors. *Tourism Management, 71*, 137–150. https://doi.org/10.1016/j.tourman.2018.10.008.

Wang, S., Kirillova, K., and Lehto, X. (2017). Reconciling unsatisfying tourism experiences: Message type effectiveness and the role of counterfactual thinking. *Tourism Management, 60*, 233–243. doi: https://doi.org/10.1016/j.tourman.2016.12.008.

van Wee, B. and Banister, D. (2016). How to write a literature review paper? *Transport Reviews, 36*(2), 278–288. https://doi.org/10.1080/01441647.2015.1065456.

Woosnam, K.M., and Aleshinloye, K.D. (2013). Can tourists experience emotional solidarity with residents? Testing Durkheim's model from a new perspective. *Journal of Travel Research, 52*(4), 494–505. https://doi.org/10.1177/0047287512467701.

Xiang, Z., Wang, D., O'Leary, J., and Fesenmaie, D.R. (2015). Adapting to the internet: Trends in travelers' use of the web for trip planning. *Journal of Travel Research, 54*(4), 511–527. https://doi.org/10.1177/0047287514522883.

Yang, Y., Pan, B., and Song, H. (2014). Predicting hotel demand using destination marketing organization's web traffic data. *Journal of Travel Research, 53*(4), 433–447. https://doi.org/10.1177/0047287513500391.

Zavattaro, S.M., Daspit, J. J., and Adams, F.G. (2015). Assessing managerial methods for evaluating place brand equity: A qualitative investigation. *Tourism Management, 47*, 11–21. https://doi.org/10.1016/j.tourman.2014.08.018.

Zeng, B., and Gerritsen, R. (2014). What do we know about social media in tourism? A review. *Tourism Management Perspectives, 10*, 27–36. https://doi.org/10.1016/j.tmp.2014.01.001.

Zhai, X., Zhong, D., and Luo, Q. (2019). Turn it around in crisis communication: An ABM approach. *Annals of Tourism Research, 79*, 102807. https://doi.org/10.1016/j.annals.2019.102807.

Zhang, J., Gui, Y., Wu, B., Morrison, A.M., and Li, C. (2016). Is destination marketing organization microblogging in China delivering? An empirical analysis of information supply against consumer information needs. *Journal of Vacation Marketing, 22*(1), 68–85. https://doi.org/10.1177/1356766715591869.

Zwienenberg, T., Hermann, I., and Barkel, C. (2013). Let's talk destination: Exploring social media (and) marketing strategies for the destination marketing organization. *Tourism Culture and Communication, 13*(1), 61–65. https://doi.org/10.3727/109830413x13769180530729.

5. Understanding online heritage destination image through user-generated content

Ozan Atsiz, Mert Ogretmenoglu and Orhan Akova

INTRODUCTION

The concept of destination image has become an important subject to researchers and destination managers as it has a considerable role in the success of the destination. Different sources of information on the internet enable users to share their feelings, opinions and experiences. Having been shared on social media, content is likely to play an important role in the formation of the destination image. Specifically, in order to provide a successful imaging strategy and destination marketing, heritage attractions need to create and explore the determinants of the destination image.

To date, heritage studies have been conducted within the product and tourist experience framework (e.g. Ung and Vong, 2010; Wang et al., 2010). However, very few studies have paid attention to the online destination image of heritage destinations from the perspective of the tourist. Understanding an insight into nature, and determinants of the online heritage destination image, can help destination managers to create new offerings and strategies for effective destination management. In order to ensure a more comprehensive theoretical framework related to the online destination image of heritage destinations, this chapter aims to clarify the nature and determinants of online heritage destination image using user-generated content (UGC) on a peer-to-peer information sharing platform.

This study aims to reveal the determinants of online heritage destination image. The study examines online reviews of heritage sites posted by visitors who visited heritage attractions in Istanbul, Turkey, where cultural and heritage resources are some of the most important in the world. In order to collect data, Tripadvisor was chosen by the authors due to the availability of a diverse pool of reviews about the Istanbul heritage image. The data were analysed using conventional content analysis. Furthermore, a coding procedure was employed in order to organize the research data and clarify them into meaningful categories.

First, the context of destination image and online destination image is outlined, and the heritage destination is briefly presented. The next section addresses two crucial topics of online destination image: user-generated content, and the role of social media in understanding destination image formation. Then the methodology of the research is introduced, and the obtained results are presented and discussed. The chapter ends with a conclusion section.

CONCEPTUAL BACKGROUND

Online Destination Image

The concept of an image has been addressed for decades in various disciplines, such as marketing, customer behavior, and social and environmental psychology. As a result of this trend, the image has started to be included in the field of tourism (Stepchenkova and Morrison, 2008).

The destination image plays an important role in the success of destination marketing (Tasci and Gartner, 2007). Furthermore, creating and managing an appropriate destination image for countries, regions or cities plays a vital role in marketing strategies and positioning (Echtner and Ritchie, 1993). For this reason, for many years the image of the destination has succeeded in attracting the attention of researchers in the field of tourism (Beerli and Martin, 2004; Stepchenkova and Morrison, 2008).

The history of the studies on the destination image dates back to the 1970s. Hunt (1975) was apparently the first to use the term "destination image," in testing the role of the image in tourism development. Since then, interest in destination image studies of tourism research increased, and much research has been conducted (Hunt, 1975, as cited in Hosany et al., 2006). For example, even between 1973 and 2000, a total of 142 studies had been conducted on the concept of a destination image (Pike, 2002, 2008)

Looking at the literature, there are multiple definitions of the destination image. Despite its common usage, the destination image is used and defined by several authors to mean different things (Lertputtarak, 2012). According to a definition provided by Baloglu and McCleary (1999, p. 870), destination image is "an attitudinal construct consisting of an individual's mental representation of knowledge (beliefs), feelings, and global impression about an object or destination."

For many researchers, the destination image consists of two elements. These elements are called "cognitive and affective" elements. The cognitive (or perceptual), element is someone's "knowledge and beliefs about a destination," while the affective element consists of the feelings of a person about a destination (Stepchenkova and Morrison, 2008).

According to basic consumer behaviour theory, individuals (consumers) make product/ service choice decisions by taking into account the images of diverse brands (Leisen, 2001). Therefore, if the image of a destination is negative and weak, it faces a tough task in terms of attracting visitors. However, a strong and positive image of a destination will probably attract more tourists (Castillo-Villar, 2020). Also, many positive concepts are related with the image of the destination, and there are many studies that have examined the relationship. These studies are shown in Table 5.1.

According to prior research (given in Table 5.1), it is revealed that there are positive relationships between destination image and tourist satisfaction; becoming loyal to that destination, tourists will likely revisit it and, as a behavioral intent, recommend it to others.

The tourism industry has been experiencing a radical change with the emergence of Web 2.0. Web 2.0 applications allow tourists to learn with ease about touristic places and share their experiences, feelings, knowledge and opinions with other tourists. Web 2.0 applications have made it possible to share a large amount of travel-related experiences, and help destinations to have an online destination image (Alrawadieh et al., 2018). Online destination image can be defined as overall feelings about a destination, generated by online sharing of common beliefs, information, thoughts and feelings (Mak, 2017, p. 282).

Table 5.1   Prior research about destination image and its relation with other concepts

Researchers	Relationship	Overall results
Chi and Qu, 2008; Coban, 2012; Jamaludin et al., 2012; Prayag and Ryan, 2012; Tavitiyaman and Qu, 2013; Wang and Hsu, 2010	Destination image and satisfaction	The image of the destination positively and significantly affects the satisfaction of tourists
Coban, 2012; Jamaludin et al., 2012; Kim and Malek, 2017; Kim et al., 2013; Mohamad et al., 2011; Moreira and Iao, 2014; Rajesh, 2013; Song et al., 2013	Destination image and destination loyalty	Destination image positively and significantly affects the destination loyalty of tourist
Cheng and Lu, 2013; Ramseook-Munhurrun and Naidoo, 2015	Destination image and perceived value	The destination image increases the perceived value
Chen and Tsai, 2007; Prayag, 2009; Ramkissoon et al., 2011; Wang and Hsu, 2010	Destination image and behavioral intentions	The destination image has both direct and indirect influences on behavioral intentions

The online destination image attracts attention to topics such as tourist behavior, destination choice, electronic word-of-mouth (eWOM), the success of a destination, and the reputation of a destination (Mak, 2017). Researchers generally examine the online destination image under two categories: perceived (e.g. Sun et al., 2015) and projected (e.g. Govers and Go, 2004). Perceived online destination image is explained as tourists' perception about the tourism products and offerings of a destination. Projected online destination image is "the attributes projected through marketing communications (e.g., NTO websites) that represent the ideal characteristics of tourism products and offerings in a destination" (Mak 2017, pp. 281–282). In this study, we examined the perceived online destination image.

Heritage Destinations

It is well known that people from the past to the present have often preferred coastal destinations with sea, sand and sun elements (Page and Cornell, 2006). However, cultural tourism is one of the fastest-developing sections of the tourism industry (Remoaldo et al., 2014). According to the United Nations Educational, Scientific and Cultural Organization (UNESCO, 2015), destinations with elements such as culture and heritage are expected to develop more rapidly in the tourism industry (UNESCO, 2015, cited in Atsız, 2020).

Cultural tourism is not a new concept. Curiosity about other cultures has been one of the factors affecting travel motivation since ancient times (for example, Grand Tours) (Hausmann, 2007). In previous research related to this topic, the concepts of "cultural tourism," "cultural heritage tourism" and "heritage tourism" are used synonymously by researchers (Wang et al., 2009). Cultural tourism is defined as "visits by people from outside the host community, motivated either entirely or to a certain degree by the cultural offerings and values (aesthetic, historical, etc.) of a particular destination" (Hausmann, 2007, p. 174).

In general, cultural elements are becoming the main component of economic recovery in destinations today, and destinations desire to develop their existing cultural capital to attract foreign visitors to their regions (O'Leary et al., 1998). Tourists visit cultural destinations to see structures from the past to the present, and the lifestyles and cultural values of the local people. In these destinations, tourists travel to increase their knowledge (Goeldner and Ritchie, 2009).

Hausmann (2007) divided culture tourists into four types. The motivation of these four groups to visit cultural areas are different. The priority of the first group (highly motivated people) is culture. Museums, churches, mosques, monuments, temples, cultural landscapes or festivals are important for these travelers, and their main purpose to travel to a destination is culture. On the other hand, purpose of the second group of travelers' is both cultural opportunities and other things such as visiting friends or family, or specific attractions of a city. The main purpose of people in the third group is not to visit cultural destinations: there is another purpose to visit that destination; for example, there may be a business-related reason. However, while visiting that destination, they also visit cultural assets (museums, cultural heritage sites, and so on). Finally, people in the last group visit cultural destinations by chance; for example, a person visiting a museum as a result of rainfall (Hausmann, 2007).

Thus, the purposes and motivations of tourists to visit such cultural destinations are different. In this study, whatever the motivation of the tourists, the cultural destination image of the tourists visiting Istanbul is examined.

The Role of User-Generated Contents on Online Image Formation

In the literature there are many studies conducted on destination image formation (e.g. Baloglu and McCleary, 1999; Camprubí et al., 2013; Chao, 2005; Frias et al., 2008; Ghazali and Cai, 2014; Hung et. al., 2012; Jalilvand, 2017; Jalilvand and Heidari, 2017; Khan et al., 2016; Kim and Chen, 2016; Kim et al., 2017; Kislali et al., 2016; Li et al., 2015; Llodrà-Riera et al., 2015; MacKay and Fesenmaier, 1997; McCartney et al., 2008; Potwarka and Banyai, 2014; Ramkissoon et al., 2009; Santos, 1998; Tseng et al., 2015; Xu and Ye, 2018; Zhang et al., 2018). For instance, Baloglu and McCleary (1999) stated that destination image is created by two significant forces: stimulus factors and personal factors. Personal factors refer to the users' social and psychological characteristics. Conversely, stimulus factors originate from external stimulus, physical objects and previous experience (Baloglu and McCleary, 1999).

Beerli and Martin (2004) divided the attributes or dimensions of the destination image into nine classifications: natural resources; general infrastructure; tourist infrastructure; tourist leisure and recreation; culture, history and art; political and economic factors; natural environment; atmosphere of the place; and social environment. These are the dimensions most considered by researchers on user-generated content (e.g. Alrawadieh et al., 2018; Dwivedi, 2009; Wong and Qi, 2017).

The rapid development of technology has led to the emergence of many internet platforms where users can comment on their travel experiences and holidays, and learn about that destination. The comments made by other users affect the travel decisions of other users. According to Niininen et al. (2007), these resources, which emerged with the internet, have become the primary source not only for consumers but also for businesses. For these reasons, researchers started to benefit from the user-generated content while determining the image of a destination (e.g. Alrawadieh et al., 2018; Dwivedi, 2008; Mak, 2017; Zhou, 2014; Wong and Qi, 2017).

Dwivedi (2008), examined the online image of India, taking into account Beerli and Martin's (2004) nine classifications of the destination image. Her findings showed that, according to visitors, India is good for its natural resources, and its culture, history and art. However, there is much dissatisfaction with the general and tourist infrastructure.

Jani and Hwang (2011) investigated the destination image of Zanzibar (Tanzania). As a result of user content analysis, they determined 13 attractions for this destination. These are: hotel price, hotel quality, hotel location, culture, beach quality, crowded, activities, logistic, weather, nature of people, finance, health and safety.

Zhou (2014) examined online rural tourism destination image of Wuyuan, Jiangxi, China. She designed her work as a qualitative study. She found that the destination image of Wuyuan has two dimensions, cognitive and affective. It was determined by the study that the destination attractions of Wuyuan are divided into three themes: resources, rewards and expected feeling/experience. In addition, nine attractions, including "ecological resources" and cultural and historical heritage, were determined under these three themes.

Marine-Roig and Clavé (2016) examined more than 130 000 useful trip reviews of tourists who visited Catalonia between 2004 and 2014. They obtained considerable results about the destination image of Barcelona via content analysis.

Alrawadieh et al. (2018) examined the online destination image of Istanbul as displayed in travel blogs of Western countries. They found that the online destination image of Istanbul was generally positive. The historical and cultural heritage and touristic infrastructure of Istanbul have been identified as creating its positive image. However, traffic and security have been stated as factors affecting the image negatively.

RESEARCH METHODOLOGY

Research Design

This chaper is designed to examine the dimensions of online heritage destination image using user-generated content (UGC) on a peer-to-peer information sharing platform, Tripadvisor. In order to achieve our purpose, a qualitative case study approach was adopted for the research design. Thus, reviews on Tripadvisor posted on the "Historic Areas of Istanbul" page were examined. This page has a "Certificate of Excellence" by Tripadvisor and gives travelers the opportunity to post their feelings, experiences and perceptions regarding the destination. Furthermore, this is the most widely approach applied to research related to finding out the ideas and feelings of individuals (Creswell, 2009).

Data Collection and Analysis

In 1019, approximately 15 million international tourists visited Istanbul (Istanbul Provincial Directorate of Culture and Tourism, 2020). Therefore, revealing the recent destination image of Istanbul, which is a cultural heritage destination, may be beneficial for both researchers and destination planners. The specific purpose of this study was to assess overall online destination image of Istanbul through reviews posted on Tripadvisor. To achieve this purpose, international tourists' reviews about heritage sites in Istanbul commented on a peer-to-peer information sharing platform were chosen. These reviews (n = 170) were collected from May 1–3, 2020. Due to having more than 10 000 reviews on the "Historic Areas of Istanbul" page, authors imposed some restrictions and only reviews posted from January 1 to December 31, 2019 were selected.

Tripadvisor was chosen due to its supplying a diverse pool of reviews on heritage sites of Istanbul. This website allows tourists to share their feelings and opinions related to service providers and the destination itself. It also enables travelers to come together and interact with each other. Tripadvisor "helps 463 million travellers each month" and has "more than 860 million reviews and opinions of 8.7 million accommodations, restaurants, experiences, airlines, and cruises" (Tripadvisor, 2020). In sum, it gives an opportunity to bring together different travelers online for free, sharing their feelings and views after their actual experience.

During the data collection, reviews written in English by international travelers were selected for the data analysis. Other reviews were not included for the analysis owing to the need to restrict the reviews, because English is a widely used language to communicate to other nations. For data analysis, all collected data were entered into Microsoft Word with demographic profiles of the travelers.

As it systematically evaluates all forms of the symbolical themes of recorded communications, conventional content analysis was used to examine the data. Furthermore, prior research about destination image that conducted content analysis was evaluated (e.g. Alrawadieh et al., 2018; Kladou and Mavragani, 2015). In order to understand the overall online destination image, the coding process in this study was conducted to use a qualitative data analysis software program, Nvivo. This process was carried out separately by the authors in order to provide consistency in the analysis. The authors read and coded all reviews independently, and discussed them until reaching a consensus on exploring the main online destination image themes. The authors explained and categorized the data into meaningful constructs by adopting this process.

As a result of the analysis, 14 main themes emerged for the online destination image of Istanbul as a heritage destination. These representatives of online destination image for heritage destination were listed as: atmosphere of the place, authentic clues, conative component, cultural environment, cultural heritage, food and beverages, functional characteristics, general and tourist infrastructure, history, natural environment, political factor, sense of heritage and history, social environment, and tourist activities.

RESULTS AND DISCUSSION

Reviewers' Profile

As shown in Table 5.2, the majority of reviewers were couples (37 percent), and a minority of them visited the destination for business (6 percent). Nearly all reviews (88 percent) rated Istanbul on Tripadvisor with 5 points, which shows the highest satisfaction level. Moreover, in the same table, it is shown that reviewers visiting Istanbul had come from different parts of the world, such as America (both North and South) (17 percent), Europe (43 percent), Africa (9 percent), and Asia (9 percent). However, more than one-sixth of the reviewers are not specified by their country.

Tripadvisor awards its users "reviewer badges", which are given according to the number of the user's reviews. These badges are listed as New Reviewer, Reviewer, Senior Reviewer, Contributor, Senior Contributor and Top Contributor. Reviewers who have posted more than 50 reviews are regarded as Top Contributors, and others are considered as reviewers who have posted below 50. Top Contributors, who are active users, have a wide range of experience

Table 5.2   *Reviewers' characteristics*

Reviewer	N	%
Traveller type		
Families	40	24
Couples	62	37
Solo	25	15
Friends	30	18
Business	10	6
Rating		
5	147	88
4	16	10
3	4	2
Nationality		
America	28	17
Europe	71	43
Africa	7	4
Asia	15	9
Unspecified	46	28
Total reviews		
0–49	69	35
50–100	24	14
101–200	23	14
201–300	12	7
301–400	5	3
401–500	4	2
501+	40	24

Source: Based on data from Tripadvisor.

of the destination. According to our reviews, the majority of reviewers (65 percent) are well experienced travelers.

Overall Online Destination Image

This study revealed 14 themes related to the overall online heritage destination image of Istanbul. In order to understand the themes, the authors reviewed prior research conducted on various destinations (Echtner and Ritchie, 1991; Sahin and Baloglu, 2011; Huete Alcocer and López Ruiz, 2019). Word frequency, which is shown in Table 5.3, was adopted to analyze the data. According to our findings, reviewers are satisfied by the destination and mention their satisfaction in their reviews as well as in their rating scores, as shown Table 5.2 (147 reviews rated as 5). Furthermore, half of the reviewers recommended the destination to others for having a sense of cultural heritage. For example, R7 stated that "the historical part of Istanbul is a must see for any tourist. Full of history, architecture and stories of rise and fall of empires. Don't forget to visit," and another traveller, R64, stated that, "If you like history, you must see this town. You'll never forget it." From the reviews, it is concluded that Istanbul is seen as a memorable tourist experience for tourists. Concerning a negative image, a few reviews stated that some sellers try to take them into their shops to sell souvenirs. However, although they encountered some bad experiences, they talked positively about their overall experience. For instance, R116 posted, "beware of people helping you as they then want you to go to their shop – mainly carpet sellers," and added, "there are other districts outside of this area worth exploring but if you're limited just go here, it has the main sites you want to see." Therefore, findings from the vast majority of the comments show that overall heritage destination image was positive.

The vast majority of the reviews addressed the cultural heritage of Istanbul. The most referred-to cultural heritage sites are mosques (the Blue Mosque, the Suleymaniye Mosque and the Eyup Sultan Mosque), museums, palaces and the Grand Bazaar. According to Huh and Uysal (2004), cultural and heritage attributes have a significant role in tourist satisfaction. They concluded that the relationship between the cultural environment and satisfaction helps destination planners and marketers in defining tourism strategies to sustain or enhance their competitiveness between destinations. Furthermore, Suhartanto et al. (2018) emphasized that cultural attractions enhance destination image. This finding is therefore an essential factor for online heritage destination image, and accords with other studies carried out on the destination of Istanbul, which concluded that the cultural environment is the most referred-to attribution for the destination image (Alrawadieh et al., 2018; Kladou and Mavragani, 2015; Sahin and Baloglu, 2011). Further to this, factors that relate to the cultural environment, such as history, sense of heritage and history, food and beverage of the destination, cultural heritage and authentic clues, are well-described elements for understanding online heritage destination image. For instance, some reviewers commented in relation to these factors as follows:

Our minds were blown, stepping into an entire different world. (R56)

Tasted and buying the best Turkish delight in the world! Oh and Apple Tea as well. A must! (R87)

We spent three days in Istanbul and its insufficient time to explore and appreciate the grandeur and multi-cultural heritage of this most vibrant, energetic City. (R27)

It is a city of great history, mixed with many culture. European, Asian and Muslim culture. The sultan and Ottoman empire made this city rich of historical area to be visited. (R29)

Cultural attractions are important for both tourists and destinations as they play a major role in the heritage experience of cultural and heritage destinations by creating feelings of experiencing the past and history. Reviewers referred to these attributes of Istanbul as having a feeling of belonging to the destination. According to Timothy (1997), shared heritage attractions and a feeling of belonging to these attractions stimulate tourists to visit the destination. In a study by Huete Alcocer and López Ruiz (2019), they concluded that these attributes help to form the heritage destination image and in planning future tourism marketing strategies.

Reviewers pointed out that they would revisit the destination and recommend potential visitors to visit the destination. They also state that locals and local markets are worth taking time to see. These indicators are considered as conative components in destination image literature (Kladou and Mavragani, 2015). Loyalty is an important indicator of behavioral consequences of tourists at heritage destinations. Using structural equation modelling, Hashemi et al. (2019) pointed out that there is a relationship between revisiting and recommending the destination and destination image. Furthermore, they indicated that the perception of destination image

Table 5.3 *Themes related to the overall online heritage destination image of Istanbul*

		Frequency
Atmosphere of the place	Amazing	11
	Breathtaking	3
	Cosmopolitan	2
	Exciting	2
	Exotic	2
	Full of surprises	2
	Grandeur	7
	Immortality	1
	Impressive	10
	Informative or educative	2
	Lovely	25
	Marvellous	4
	Oriental	1
	Spectacular	16
	The old	11
	Unique	3
	Vibrant	8
Authentic clues	Authenticity	7
	So much to discover	1
	Unique feel	2
Conative component	Must see	9
	Revisiting	2
	Worth seeing (locals and shops)	10
Cultural environment	Architectural monuments	13
	Churches	7
	Cisterns	9
	Forts	1
	Fountain	1
	Galata tower	13
	Grand Bazaar	19
	Gulhane Park	1
	Turkish bath	3
	Hippodrome	4
	mosques	32
	Museums	22
	Old stones on the road	1
	Palaces	23
	Spice bazaar	6
	Sultanahmet square	3
	The Balat	1
	The Roman walls	2
Cultural heritage	Mixed culture	12
	Multicultural heritage	4
	UNESCO	1

		Frequency
Food and beverage	Baklava	1
	Gastronomy	25
	Local markets	3
	Ottoman ice cream	2
	Street food	1
	Teahouses	1
	Turkish Delight	2
	Turkish tea	1
Functional characteristics	Weather and climate	9
	Low prices (food and, beverage, local guide, public transportation and taxi)	9
General and tourist infrastructure	Accessible of attractions	2
	Cafes	8
	Public transportation	11
	Restaurants	11
	Within walking distance	8
History	Clear history	1
	Great history	1
	Historical	32
	Huge history	1
	Rich history	3
	Special history	1
	Two empires	4
Natural environment	Beautiful scenery	1
	Clean	7
	Crowded	7
	Lovely scenery	1
	Traffic	2
Political factor	Safety	7
Sense of heritage and history	Feel like being part of history	4
	Old world experience	1
	Past	1
	Sense of belonging	2
	Stepping into a different world	1
	The ancient with the modern	1
	Traveling through time and history	1
Social environment	Accommodating	1
	Amazing	1
	Friendly	9
	Helpful	6
	Kind	1
Tourist activities	Bosporus tour	7
	Bus tour	4
	Shopping place	7
	Streets	2
	Taksim	5
	Walking	16

Source: Based on data from Tripadvisor.

has a positive effect on the revisit intentions of tourists. In our study, the conative component is one of the most important themes for understanding overall online heritage destination image.

Functional components are described as "directly observable or measurable (e.g. prices or climate)" (Echtner and Ritchie, 1991, p. 40), and reviewers posted about the climate and weather of Istanbul when visiting heritage attractions, and recommended using some services offered by the destination with low prices (food and beverages, local guides, public transportation and taxis). The climate is a significant attribute of a destination that may determine the tourist destination choice decision-making process (Hamilton and Lau, 2005) and destination image (Alrawadieh et al., 2018). For example, R5 pointed out that "going to Istanbul in early May was perfect! Excellent weather for walking and exploring the old town." Moreover, prices are regarded as lower by tourists comparing other destinations. According to Hallmann et al. (2015), prices as a cognitive component of destination image influence destination image, and so are important for choosing a destination.

One of the highlighted findings of this chapter is the atmosphere of the destination, which is described as amazing, breathtaking, cosmopolitan, exciting, exotic, full of surprises, grandeur, immortality, impressive, informative or educative, lovely, marvellous, oriental, spectacular, the old, unique and vibrant. Furthermore, travelers said that local people are accommodating, amazing, friendly, helpful and kind. Social interactions such as being helpful, polite, friendly, hospitable, and so on, are primary attributes that impact the overall tourist experience, and they are important components of the cultural tourist experience of a destination (Cetin and Bilgihan, 2016, p. 144). In his study, Pavesi (2016) investigated the role of social interaction on the destination image formation, and highlighted that positive encounters with locals led to a positive destination image formation. Tourists desire to be comfortable and have a good interaction with locals in order to have a positive experience of the destination (Butler, 1980).

Activities that are carried out at the destination, and general and tourist infrastructure, are the most important factors that impact the destination image (Beerli and Martin, 2004). In this study, both of those are regarded as pivotal attributes for the overall online destination image of Istanbul. For example, R53 mentioned, "Museums, mosques and many markets are all in walking or short public transportation away." and R153 posted, "eat at the restaurants there or take the boats for Bosphorus tours." These attributes are located around the natural environment of Istanbul, and reviewers highlighted that the natural environment is beautiful, with lovely scenery, is clean, is crowded and is full of traffic. Finally, wandering around historical places is safe, and there is no need to be worried about safety. Despite a bad reputation owing to terror attacks in recent years, travelers evaluated Istanbul to be a safe place to visit. According to Donaldson and Ferreira (2009), security perception and risk perception in the minds of the tourists negatively affect the demand for that destination. Potential tourists do not desire to visit such destinations, because of their bad image. In our study, the tourists' perception of Istanbul as safe shows that Istanbul is on its way to being more successful with its positive image.

CONCLUSION

This chapter aims to reveal the determinants of online heritage destination image and examines online reviews of tourists who visited cultural and heritage sites in Istanbul. In order to collect data, Tripadvisor was chosen, and the data were analyzed using conventional content analysis. According to conventional content analysis, 14 themes of online heritage destination image determinants were found. These are: atmosphere of the place, authentic clues, conative component, cultural environment, cultural heritage, food and beverages, functional characteristics, general and tourist infrastructure, history, natural environment, political factor, sense of heritage and history, social environment, and tourist activities.

Istanbul is famous all over the world for its cultural and heritage attractions. Most of them date back to the eras of the Roman, Byzantine and Ottoman empires. Istanbul is also home to places important to three religions, and has a cosmopolitan culture because of its history. Due to the importance of its cultural and heritage attractions, Istanbul has many things to offer heritage tourists. As a heritage destination, it is necessary to understand tourists' views about Istanbul so that destination managers can understand what is needed and what should be done to satisfy tourists, and so that they can create a sustainable destination image. The internet and social media have become a popular platform for tourists to organize and supply information about their travels to a destination. For this reason, their opinions, complaints and reviews about a destination have become a precious information source for destination managers and travel suppliers. Since heritage destinations have gained popularity amongst tourists, heritage destination managers should understand their needs, views and opinions, so that they can create a tempting heritage destination image. We propose that the online heritage destination image determinants we have revealed in this chapter can help these managers to make their destination more sustainable and to create an attractive destination image. The destination managers and travel suppliers who want to be successful should periodically follow and analyze the comments posted by tourists, because tourists' demands and the offers of destinations have been changing dynamically. Further research can focus on the relations between the determinants of online destination image and satisfaction, loyalty and intention to revisit.

REFERENCES

Alrawadieh, Z., Dincer, M.Z., Istanbullu Dincer, F., and Mammadova, P. (2018). Understanding destination image from the perspective of Western travel bloggers: the case of Istanbul. *Journal of culture, tourism and hospitality research*, 12(2), 198–212.

Atsız, O. (2020). Length of stay of tourists in cultural destination. Unpublished PhD thesis. Istanbul: Istanbul University Social Science Institute.

Baloglu, S., and McCleary, K.W. (1999). A model of destination image formation. *Annals of tourism research*, 26(4), 868–897.

Beerli, A., and Martin, J.D. (2004). Factors influencing destination image. *Annals of tourism research*, 31(3), 657–681.

Butler, R.W. (1980). The concept of a tourist area cycle of evolution: implications for management of resources. *Canadian geographer*, 24(1), 5–12.

Camprubí, R., Guia, J., and Comas, J. (2013). The new role of tourists in destination image formation. *Current issues in tourism*, 16(2), 203–209.

Castillo-Villar, F.R. (2020). Destination image restoration through local gastronomy: the rise of Baja Med cuisine in Tijuana. *International journal of culture, tourism and hospitality research*, 14, 507–523.

Cetin, G., and Bilgihan, A. (2016). Components of cultural tourists' experiences in destinations. *Current issues in tourism*, 19(2), 137–154.

Chao, W.Z. (2005). Marketing tools as factors in destination image formation. Unpublished Master's thesis. San Jose State University, California.

Chen, C.F., and Tsai, D. (2007). How destination image and evaluative factors affect behavioral intentions? *Tourism management*, 28(4), 1115–1112.

Cheng, T.M., and Lu, C.C. (2013). Destination image, novelty, hedonics, perceived value, and revisiting behavioral intention for island tourism. *Asia Pacific journal of tourism research*, 18(7), 766–783.

Chi, C.G.Q., and Qu, H. (2008). Examining the structural relationships of destination image, tourist satisfaction and destination loyalty: an integrated approach. *Tourism management*, 29(4), 624–636.

Coban, S. (2012). The effects of the image of destination on tourist satisfaction and loyalty: the case of Cappadocia. *European journal of social sciences*, 29(2), 222–232.

Creswell, J.W. (2009). *Research design: qualitative, quantitative and mixed approaches* (3rd edition). Los Angeles, CA: SAGE.

Donaldson, R., and Ferreira, S. (2009). (Re-) creating urban destination image: opinions of foreign visitors to South Africa on safety and security. *Urban forum*, 20(1), 1–18.

Dwivedi, M. (2009). Online destination image of India: a consumer based perspective. *International journal of contemporary hospitality management*, 21(2), 226–232.

Echtner, C.M., and Ritchie, J.R.B. (1991). The meaning and measurement of destination image. *Journal of tourism studies*, 2(2), 2–12.

Echtner, C.M., and Ritchie, J.R.B. (1993). The measurement of destination image: an empirical assessment. *Journal of travel research*, 31(4), 3–13.

Frias, D.M., Rodriguez, M.A., and Castañeda, J.A. (2008). Internet vs. travel agencies on pre-visit destination image formation: An information processing view. *Tourism management*, 29(1), 163–179.

Ghazali, R.M., and Cai, L. (2014). Social media sites in destination image formation. *Tourism social media: transformations in identity, community and culture,* 18, 73–86.

Goeldner, C.R., and Ritchie, J.R.B. (2009). *Tourism principles, practices, philosophies* (11th edition). John Wiley and Sons.

Govers, R., and Go, F.M. (2004). Projected destination image online: website content analysis of pictures and text. *Information technology and tourism*, 7(2), 73–89.

Hallmann, K., Zehrer, A., and Müller, S. (2015). Perceived destination image: an image model for a winter sports destination and its effect on intention to revisit. *Journal of travel research*, 54(1), 94–106.

Hamilton, J.M., and Lau, M.A. (2005). The role of climate information in tourist destination choice decision making. In S. Gössling and C.M. Hall (eds), *Tourism and global environmental change: ecological, economic, social and political interrelationships* (pp. 1–35). London: Routledge.

Hashemi, S., Kiumarsi, S., Marzuki, A., and Anarestani, B. (2019). Tourist satisfaction and destination loyalty in heritage sites of Shiraz, Iran. In *Experiencing Persian heritage (bridging tourism theory and practice)* (pp. 243–255). Bingley: Emerald.

Hausmann, A. (2007). Cultural tourism: marketing challenges and opportunities for German cultural heritage. *International journal of heritage studies*, 13 (2), 170–184.

Hosany, S., Ekinci, Y., and Uysal, M. (2006). Destination image and destination personality: an application of branding theories to tourism places. *Journal of business research*, 59(5), 638–642.

Huete Alcocer, N., and López Ruiz, V.R. (2019). The role of destination image in tourist satisfaction: the case of a heritage site. *Economic research – Ekonomska istraživanja*, 33(1), 1–18.

Huh, J., and Uysal, M. (2004). Satisfaction with cultural/heritage sites: Virginia historic triangle. *Journal of quality assurance in hospitality and tourism*, 4(3–4), 177–194.

Hung, J.Y., Lin, F.L., Yang, W.G., and Lu, K.S. (2012). Construct the destination image formation model of Macao: the case of Taiwan tourists to Macao. *Tourism and hospitality management*, 18(1), 19–35.

Hunt, J. D. (1975). Image as a factor in tourism development. *Journal of Tavel research*, 13(3), 1–7.

Istanbul Provincial Directorate of Culture and Tourism (2020). Istanbul Turizm Istatistikleri Raporu. Istanbul: Istanbul Provincial Directorate of Culture and Tourism (accessed 1 March 2020).

Jalilvand, M.T. (2017). Word-of-mouth vs. mass media: their contributions to destination image formation. *Anatolia*, 28(2), 151–162.

Jalilvand, M.R., and Heidari, A. (2017). Comparing face-to-face and electronic word-of-mouth in destination image formation. *Information technology and people*, 30(4), 710–735.

Jamaludin, M., Johari, S., Aziz, A., Kayat, K., and Yusof, A. (2012). Examining structural relationship between destination image, tourist satisfaction and destination loyalty. *International journal of independent research and studies*, 1(3), 89–96.

Jani, D., and Hwang, Y.H. (2011). User-generated destination image through weblogs: a comparison of pre-and post-visit images. *Asia Pacific journal of tourism research*, 16(3), 339–356.

Khan, M.J., Chelliah, S., and Haron, M.S. (2016). Medical tourism destination image formation process: a conceptual model. *International journal of healthcare management*, 9(2), 134–143.

Kim, H., and Chen, J.S. (2016). Destination image formation process: a holistic model. *Journal of vacation marketing*, 22(2), 154–166.

Kim, S.E., Lee, K.Y., Shin, S.I., and Yang, S.B. (2017). Effects of tourism information quality in social media on destination image formation: the case of Sina Weibo. *Information and management*, 54(6), 687–702.

Kim, S.H., Holland, S., and Han, H.S. (2013). A structural model for examining how destination image, perceived value, and service quality affect destination loyalty: a case study of Orlando. *International journal of tourism research*, 15(4), 313–328.

Kim, W., and Malek, K. (2017). Effects of self-congruity and destination image on destination loyalty: the role of cultural differences. *Anatolia*, 28(1), 1–13.

Kislali, H., Kavaratzis, M., and Saren, M. (2016). Rethinking destination image formation. *International journal of culture, tourism and hospitality research*, 10(1), 70–80.

Kladou, S., and Mavragani, E. (2015). Assessing destination image: an online marketing approach and the case of TripAdvisor. *Journal of destination marketing and management*, 4(3), 187–193.

Leisen, B. (2001). Image segmentation: the case of a tourism destination. *Journal of services marketing*, 15(1), 49–66.

Lertputtarak, S. (2012). The relationship between destination image, food image, and revisiting Pattaya, Thailand. *International journal of business and management*, 7(5), 111–121.

Li, Y.R., Lin, Y.C., Tsai, P.H., and Wang, Y.Y. (2015). Traveller-generated contents for destination image formation: Mainland China travellers to Taiwan as a case study. *Journal of travel and tourism marketing*, 32(5), 518–533.

Llodrà-Riera, I., Martínez-Ruiz, M.P., Jiménez-Zarco, A.I., and Izquierdo-Yusta, A. (2015). A multidimensional analysis of the information sources construct and its relevance for destination image formation. *Tourism management*, 48, 319–328.

MacKay, K.J., and Fesenmaier, D.R. (1997). Pictorial element of destination in image formation. *Annals of tourism research*, 24(3), 537–565.

Mak, A.H. (2017). Online destination image: comparing national tourism organisation's and tourists' perspectives. *Tourism management*, 60, 280–297.

Marine-Roig, E., and Clavé, S. A. (2016). A detailed method for destination image analysis using user-generated content. *Information technology and tourism*, 15(4), 341–364.

McCartney, G., Butler, R., and Bennett, M. (2008). A strategic use of the communication mix in the destination image-formation process. *Journal of travel research*, 47(2), 183–196.

Mohamad, M., Ali, A.M., and Ab Ghani, N.I. (2011). A structural model of destination image, tourists' satisfaction and destination loyalty. *International journal of business and management studies*, 3(2), 167–177.

Moreira, P., and Iao, C. (2014). A longitudinal study on the factors of destination image, destination attraction and destination loyalty. *Journal of social sciences*, 3(3), 90–112.

Niininen, O., Buhalis, D., and March, R. (2007). Customer empowerment in tourism through consumer centric marketing (CCM). *Qualitative market research: an international journal*, 10(3), 265–281.

O'Leary, J.T., Morrison, A.M., and Alzua, A. (1998). Cultural and heritage tourism: identifying niches for international travelers. *Journal of tourism studies*, 9(2), 2–13.

Page, S.J., and Cornell, J. (2006). *Tourism: a modern synthesis*. Cengage Learning EMEA, Hampshire.

Pavesi, A. (2016). Social interaction and destination image formation. Doctoral dissertation. Hong Kong Polytechnic University.

Pike, S. (2002). Destination image analysis – a review of 142 papers from 1973 to 2000. *Tourism management*, 23(5), 541–549.

Pike, S. (2008). *Destination marketing: an integrated marketing communication approach*. Burlington: MA: Butterworth-Heinemann.

Potwarka, L.R., and Banyai, M. (2014). Autonomous agents and destination image formation of an Olympic Host city: the case of Sochi. *Journal of hospitality marketing and management*, 25(2), 238–258.

Prayag, G. (2009). Tourists' evaluations of destination image, satisfaction, and future behavioral intentions – the case of Mauritius. *Journal of travel and tourism marketing*, 26(8), 836–853.

Prayag, G., and Ryan, C. (2012). Antecedents of tourists' loyalty to Mauritius: the role and influence of destination image, place attachment, personal involvement, and satisfaction. *Journal of travel research*, 51(3), 342–356.

Rajesh, R. (2013). Impact of tourist perceptions, destination image and tourist satisfaction on destination loyalty: a conceptual model. PASOS. *Revista de turismo y patrimonio cultural*, 11(3), 67–78.

Ramkissoon, H., Nunkoo, R., and Gursoy, D. (2009). How consumption values affect destination image formation. In A.G. Woodside, C.H. Megehee and A. Ogle (eds), *Perspectives on cross-cultural, ethnographic, brand image, storytelling, unconscious needs, and hospitality guest research* (pp. 143–168). Bingley: Emerald.

Ramkissoon, H., Uysal, M., and Brown, K. (2011). Relationship between destination image and behavioral intentions of tourists to consume cultural attractions. *Journal of hospitality marketing and management*, 20(5), 575–595.

Ramseook-Munhurrun, P., and Naidoo, P. (2015). Examining the structural relationships of destination image, perceived value, tourist satisfaction and loyalty. *Procedia – Social and behavioral sciences*, 175, 252–259.

Remoaldo, P.C., Vareiro, L., Ribeiro, J.C., and Santos, J. (2014). Does gender affect visiting a world heritage site?, *Visitor studies*, 17(1), 89–106.

Sahin, S., and Baloglu, S. (2011). Brand personality and destination image of Istanbul. *Anatolia – An international journal of tourism and hospitality research*, 22 (1), 69–88.

Santos, J. (1998). The role of tour operators' promotional material in the formation of destination image and consumer expectations: the case of the People's Republic of China. *Journal of vacation marketing*, 4(3), 282–297.

Song, Z., Su, X., and Li, L. (2013). The indirect effects of destination image on destination loyalty intention through tourist satisfaction and perceived value: the bootstrap approach. *Journal of travel and tourism marketing*, 30(4), 386–409.

Stepchenkova, S., and Morrison, A. (2008). Russia's destination image among American pleasure travelers: revisiting Echtner and Ritchie. *Tourism management,* 29, 548–560.

Suhartanto, D., Clemes, M.D., and Wibisono, N. (2018). How experiences with cultural attractions affect destination image and destination loyalty. *Tourism culture and communication*, 18(3), 176–188.

Sun, M., Ryan, C., and Pan, S. (2015). Using Chinese travel blogs to examine perceived destination image: the case of New Zealand. *Journal of travel research*, 54(4), 543–555.

Tasci, A., and Gartner, W. (2007). Destination image and its functional relationships. *Journal of travel research*, 45(4), 413–425.

Tavitiyaman, P., and Qu, H. (2013). Destination image and behavior intention of travelers to Thailand: the moderating effect of perceived risk. *Journal of travel and tourism marketing*, 30(3), 169–185.

Timothy, D.J. (1997). Tourism and the personal heritage experience. *Annals of tourism research*, 24(3), 751–754.

Tripadvisor (2020). http://ir.tripadvisor.com/ (Accessed 15 April 2020).

Tseng, C., Wu, B., Morrison, A.M., Zhang, J., and Chen, Y.C. (2015). Travel blogs on China as a destination image formation agent: a qualitative analysis using Leximancer. *Tourism management*, 46, 347–358.

UNESCO (2015). Policy for the integration of a sustainable development perspective into the processes of the World Heritage Convention. https://whc.unesco.org/en/sustainabledevelopment/. Accessed 20 October 2020

Ung, A., and Vong, T.N. (2010). Tourist experience of heritage tourism in Macau SAR, China. *Journal of heritage tourism*, 5(2), 157–168.

Wang, C.Y., and Hsu, M.K. (2010). The relationships of destination image, satisfaction, and behavioral intentions: an integrated model. *Journal of travel and tourism marketing*, 27(8), 829–843.

Wang, Y.J., Wu, C., and Yuan, J. (2009). The role of integrated marketing communications (IMC) on heritage destination visitations. *Journal of quality assurance in hospitality and tourism*, 10(3), 218–231.

Wang, Y.J., Wu, C., and Yuan, J. (2010). Exploring visitors' experiences and intention to revisit a heritage destination: the case for Lukang, Taiwan. *Journal of quality assurance in hospitality and tourism*, 11(3), 162–178.

Wong, C.U., and Qi, S. (2017). Tracking the evolution of a destination's image by text-mining online reviews–the case of Macau. *Tourism management perspectives*, 23, 19–29.

Xu, H., and Ye, T. (2018). Dynamic destination image formation and change under the effect of various agents: the case of Lijiang, The Capital of Yanyu. *Journal of destination marketing and management*, 7, 131–139.

Zhang, M., Zhang, G.Y., Gursoy, D., and Fu, X.R. (2018). Message framing and regulatory focus effects on destination image formation. *Tourism management*, 69, 397–407.

Zhou, L. (2014). Online rural destination images: tourism and rurality. *Journal of destination marketing and management*, 3(4), 227–240.

6. Online tourism communication in destination image formation

Sarasadat Makian

DESTINATION IMAGE

As more regions of the world develop, the choice of tourist destinations available to consumers continues to expand (Matos et al., 2012). Technological advancements, global media and increased international competition affect how destinations are imagined, perceived and consumed (Frías et al., 2011). To gain a competitive advantage, it is important to create and convey a favorable image to potential tourists in target markets (Di Marino, 2008). Due to its impact on both marketing supply (positioning, promotion) and demand sides (tourist behavior, decision-making), the destination image (DI) is an important issue in successful tourism management, destination marketing and tourism development (Molina et al., 2010). Therefore, developing an image strategy should be a priority for destination management/marketing organizations (DMOs) as a part of their destination marketing's DNA (Stylos et al., 2017).

DI is a form of continual knowledge in which one collects impressions, emotional thoughts, beliefs and prejudices about a destination based on various sources (Kim and Chen, 2016). With a small difference, DI can also be defined as the expression of all objective knowledge, impressions, prejudice, imaginations and emotional thoughts that a person or group will have of a specific place (Jenkins, 1990). DI is a key element in marketing efforts for differentiating a destination (Kislali et al., 2016). It plays an influential role in travelers' decision-making process and, consequently, their travel behaviors (Choi et al., 2007; Huete Alcocer and López Ruiz, 2019). In this regard, the DI is fundamental in the marketing process, as it provides important information on how the place is perceived by the tourist (Ispas and Sargea, 2011). According to Kotler and Gertner (2002), "Images represent a simplification of a larger number of associations and pieces of information connected to a place. They are a product of mind trying to process and pick out essential information from huge amounts of data about a place."

Components and Dimensions

Echtner and Ritchie (1991) proposed three dimensions for developing a DI: attribute–holistic, functional–psychological and common–unique. The attribute–holistic continuum reflects the perceptions of destination attributes. In contrast, the functional–psychological continuum represents the distinction between measurable functional components of a destination and its intangible psychological characteristics. The place's generic common features and unique characteristics are in a third continuum (Baptista and Matos, 2018). DI consists of cognitive, affective and conative components. The cognitive component refers to an individual's perceptions of the characteristics or attributes of a destination (Guzman-Parra et al., 2016), which can be functional, tangible (for example, landscape, cultural attractions) and psychologically abstract (for example, hospitality, atmosphere) (San Martín and Rodríguez del Bosque, 2008).

The image's affective component, on the other hand, represents a person's feelings toward a destination and its emotional responses (Stylidis et al., 2017). Finally, the conative component includes action, which refers to the individual's actual behavior or intention to revisit and recommend the destination to others (Agapito et al., 2013). Beerli and Martin (2004) divide the factors that influence an individual's image of a given destination into nine dimensions: (1) natural resources (for example, weather, beaches, protected nature reserves); (2) general infrastructure (for example, development and quality of roads, airports and ports); (3) tourist infrastructure (for example, hotel and self-catering accommodation); (4) tourist leisure and recreation (for example, theme parks, entertainment and sports activities); (5) culture, history and art (for example, museums, historical buildings, monuments, folklore); (6) political and economic factors (for example, political stability, political tendencies, safety); (7) natural environment (for example, beauty of scenery and attractiveness of cities and towns); (8) social environment (for example, hospitality and friendliness of residents, quality of life); and (9) atmosphere of the place (for example, place with a good reputation, family-oriented destination, exoticism). The selection of attributes (whether specific or more general) largely depends on each destination's attractions, positioning and the objectives of assessing the perceived image.

DESTINATION IMAGE FORMATION

The transmission and development of DI is a continuous process that begins with the projection of images and ends with the reception of these images by target audiences through any appropriate media seeking potential tourists, resulting in the formation of the DI (McCartney et al., 2008). DI can be created before the visit and then modified as more information becomes available or as experience develops (Tan and Chen, 2012). Image formation is the process of constructing a mental representation of a destination using information cues delivered by the image formation agents and selected by an individual (Tasci and Gartner, 2007). Similarly, a tourist destination's perception is derived from information processed by different sources over time. This information is organized into a mental concept that the individual can understand (San Martín and Rodríguez del Bosque, 2008). Tourists initially perceive an organic image that provides a general view of the destination. From their voluntary search for information, tourists perceive induced images issued by tourism agents. These organic and induced images are *a priori* perceived images modified once they arrive at the destination. The tourist will evaluate the DI *in situ* and *a posteriori* based on the image that they had previously perceived during the trip to the destination, resulting in a modified image (Almeida-García et al., 2020).

Two major forces shape the image: stimulus and personal factors. Stimulus factors are those that stem from the external stimulus and physical objects as well as previous experiences. On the other hand, personal factors are the perceiver's characteristics (social and psychological) (Baloglu and McCleary, 1999). Baloglu and McCleary (1999) expanded Gartner's (1993) model and further proposed a DI formation process with three components: personal factors, stimuli factors and DI. Personal factors include psychological variables such as value, motivation, personality, as well as social variables such as age, educational level, marital status, and so on. Information sources and previous experiences are among the stimuli factors (Esu, 2015). The DI formation goes through seven stages: (1) the accumulation of mental images about vacation experiences; (2) the modification of these images by further information; (3) the decision to take a vacation trip; (4) travel to the destination; (5) participation at the destination; (6) returning home; and (7) modification of image based on the vacation experience. DI develops in stages 1, 2 and 7 (Kim and Chen, 2016). The initial image formation stage is the most important phase in the destination selection process, before the trip. Knowing factors influencing this decision will help identify which image can be promoted to which market segment (Baloglu and McCleary, 1999).

Image Formation Agents

Tourist information sources can be considered stimulus factors and image formation agents, contributing to a cognitive image's formation but not its affective counterpart (de la Hoz-Correa and Muñoz-Leiva, 2019). Tasci and Gartner (2007) categorize image formation agents as supply-side or destination (through promotional efforts undertaken by the destination), independent or autonomous (through non-promotional materials which are not related to those promoting the destination), and demand-side or image receivers (through materials originating from tourists' country of origins) (Jamaludin et al., 2013). There is a typology of eight image formation agents relating to the promoter's degree of control and credibility with the target market. The eight domains include: (1) overt induced I agent (referring to traditional advertising forms); (2) overt induced II agent (information received from tour operators); (3) covert induced I agent (second-party endorsement of products through traditional advertising forms); (4) covert induced II agent (second-party endorsement through unbiased reports such as newspaper articles); (5) autonomous agent (news and popular culture); (6) unsolicited organic agent (unsolicited information received from friends and relatives); (7) solicited organic agent (solicited information received from friends and relatives); and (8) organic agent (actual visitation) (Hahm, 2004).

Autonomous image formation agents are more influential in shaping the destination's image than destination-originated information, which is usually not controllable by destination marketers, due to their credibility and the ability to reach mass markets (Xu and Ye, 2018). Organic image formation agents are non-commercial information sources, such as word-of-mouth and actual visitation (Lee et al., 2015). Although tourists are image receptors, they can also participate in image formation as organic agents. Through face-to-face interaction, tourists exchange information, share experiences and give their opinions of the visited destinations (Xu and Ye, 2018). Induced agents are those who conscientiously create and communicate a destination's tourism image (Camprubí et al., 2013). These agents aim to influence tourists' decision-making process by establishing, reinforcing or changing a DI (Xu and Ye, 2018).

INFORMATION SOURCES AND DESTINATION IMAGE

Tourism is an information-intensive industry in which organizations market their products and build relationships with customers by communicating with tourists through various channels (Pan and Fesenmaier, 2006). Once the image has been defined and the dimensions revealed, it is important to understand the factors influencing image formation. The factors influencing the image formation of tourist destinations include information obtained from various sources, and individual characteristics such as travel motivations, personality and values (Almeida-García et al., 2020). Information sources are used as marketing communication tools to reach tourists and positively control the destination's image among target groups (Chetthamrongchai, 2017). The different information sources aim to facilitate the tourist's mental image formation process (Nicoletta and Servidio, 2012).

According to Tasci and Gartner (2007), the role of information sources in DI formation is "constructing a mental representation of a destination based on information cues delivered by the image formation agents and selected by a person." Since the DI is a dynamic concept, Kim and Chen (2016) argue that "DI formation processes are continuous mental progressions in which diverse information sources converge." DI is created by transforming vague partial images into something more complete, using known information (Cherifi et al., 2014). Thus, information is critical in travelers' decision-making and destination selection process. In addition, information gathering and processing are essential stages in the decision-making process, with significant impacts on DI formation, destination selection and on-site decision-making, such as selecting accommodation, transportation, activities and tours (Zhang et al., 2018).

Different types of information influence the DI (Chetthamrongchai, 2017). Historical and contemporary events, media representations, promotional activities and the products marked as "Made in" can contribute to the overall evaluation of a place (Campo and Alvarez, 2014) that appear to be mainly positive based on the mere exposure effect (Jeong et al., 2011). Understanding how visitors obtain information about a destination is important for private and public authorities' marketing and management decisions (Jamaludin et al., 2013), and for selecting effective communication tools and service delivery strategies (Jeong and Holland, 2012).

Different Types of Information Sources in Tourism

There are different categories of information sources for tourists to create an image of a destination. As the spatial dimension of information search, an internal search is the retrieving of knowledge from memory and experience. In contrast, an external search is the gathering of information from the marketplace. External sources include brochures and material published by visitor information centers and tourist boards, articles in specialized journals or magazines, the Internet, TV, word-of-mouth (WOM) by friends and relatives, travel guidebooks, tour guides and travel agents (Tan and Chen, 2012). Information sources are usually classified into organic and induced sources. The organic sources (books, news, movies, actual destination visits) do not have a vested interest in promoting a tourism destination, whereas the induced sources (travel brochures, advertisements, posters, videos and, most recently, the Internet) are means of communicating marketing messages between tourism destination and suppliers, to a selected travel audience. In the absence of actual visitation, tourism DI is formed through induced agents (Pavlović and Belullo, 2007).

According to Beerli and Martin (2004), image formation is based on different secondary information sources, such as induced sources (tourist brochures issued by the destination's public authorities, tour operator brochures, mass-media advertising campaigns, travel agency staff, and the Internet), organic sources (friends and family members who were either requested or volunteered to provide information about a destination), and autonomous sources (guidebooks, news, articles, reports, documentaries and presentations on destinations in the media) (Chetthamrongchai, 2017). Additionally, tourism information sources can be categorized as commercial or non-commercial, and according to whether they were received from personal or impersonal communication (Fodness and Murray, 1997). The information sources include advertising and commercials in the mass media, travel brochures, guidebooks from clubs and welcome centers, and include friends, relatives and personal experiences (Kim et al., 2007).

Internet as a Tourism Information Source

Tourists use external information sources as a starting point for planning their travel (Molina et al., 2010). A negative country image may affect the intention to visit. However, the image is dynamic. It can be revised and modified through the visitation and experience of individuals with the place, or the person's exposure to additional information via external sources (Campo and Alvarez, 2014). The Internet has recently emerged as another valuable tourism destination information source (Nicoletta and Servidio, 2012). Travel-related information is one of the most important types of content on the Internet (Tan and Chen, 2012), and one of the most effective ways for tourists to search for information and to purchase tourism-related products (Pan and Fesenmaier, 2006). Also, most tourism businesses, national tourism and local destination marketing organizations are increasingly using the Internet to disseminate considerable amounts of information (Jacobsen and Munar, 2012). Indeed, internet services influence several aspects of contemporary tourism activities, changing tourists' information-seeking and communication behavior (Nicoletta and Servidio, 2012). In particular, social networks on the Internet play an important role as an information source for potential tourists, allowing them to create a stronger image of a destination through images, interactions and multimedia (Xu and Ye, 2018).

TOURISM COMMUNICATION

Communication is about sending and sharing information and, in doing so, accumulating, creating and advancing knowledge (Blichfeldt, 2017). It is understood as a component of tourism marketing, precisely as one of its operational phases. These strategies are implemented through media aimed at specific audiences with precise objectives (Viallon, 2013). As tourism accounts for a significant portion of most countries' gross domestic product, destinations must communicate effectively in order to improve the economic and social development of their cities and regions (Míguez-González and Fernández-Cavia, 2015). Tourism communication is a strategic tool that combines communication techniques, marketing concepts, available information about the destination to visit, and its hospitality services (Hu et al., 2014). The main goal of DMO activities is designing and implementing marketing communication strategies that match destination resources with market opportunities (Hang Kong et al., 2015). So, tourism destinations can use online communication channels for their promotional activities (Hu et al., 2014). Information and communication technologies (ICTs) make it possible to present a destination's features, products and services to many potential visitors. These technologies help establish and strengthen the brand image and instill the idea of a superior experience in travelers' minds, encouraging them to choose the destination (Baggio et al., 2011). Moreover, online discourses shape a tourism destination's online representation by leveraging what other people think and write about the destination in an online context (Hu et al., 2014).

ONLINE COMMUNICATION IN TOURISM

New ICTs are being developed, transforming the traditional ways of projecting a DI (Camprubí et al., 2013) and changing the information search process (de la Hoz-Correa and Muñoz-Leiva, 2019). The new generation of Web 2.0 tools has revolutionized how DI is projected and how tourists seek and gather information about tourism destinations (Camprubí et al., 2013). These tools enable people to collaborate and share their information with others via the Internet (Kim, S.-E., et al., 2017). Instead of using traditional tour operators or travel agencies, today's travelers prefer to obtain information online using social media platforms and search engines. For this reason, social media platforms such as Facebook, YouTube and Flickr, which are rich in user-generated content (UGC), have gained popularity among online communities of travelers (Roque and Raposo, 2016). DMOs and industry marketing bodies are advised to consider the implications of Web 2.0 and independent consumer-generated content when planning their activities. These provide an alternative information source that some tourists consider more credible and reliable than traditional marketing communications (Lo et al., 2011).

DMOs and industry must compete with a wide range of non-commercial materials posted by tourists, to the extent that these information providers significantly influence tourists' decision-making behavior (Lo et al., 2011). Tourism and destination marketing organizations are aware of these trends. They are trying to explore the opportunities of using tourist-generated content for destination brand positioning purposes (Kim, S.-E., et al., 2017). Furthermore, promotion through various media targets different emotional and cognitive processes of the consumer, which is why the tourism marketing organizations need to understand the impact of various communication channels in order to make high-quality strategic decisions based on promotion development and the information channel selection (Bošković et al., 2010).

Online Destination Image

Tourists can create and share UGC on various social media platforms using Web 2.0 technologies, allowing them to co-construct the image of the destination online (Mak, 2017). Online DI is important for destination management and marketing (Zhou, 2014). Travel-generated content can be shared and consumed at any time and anywhere by geographically dispersed tourists (Mak, 2017). Travel blogs, travel review websites and virtual communities are used as information sources to investigate the online representation of tourism destinations (Hu et al., 2014). The combination of credibility and accessibility makes travel-generated content a powerful way of shaping a destination's online image (Mak, 2017). Tourists increasingly and actively publish personal narratives online, in the form of textual and visual contributions, and rely on UGC to reduce uncertainty when making travel and tourism decisions (Marine-Roig and Anton Clavé, 2015). Online discourses shape an online tourism destination representation (Hu et al., 2014) based on the destination identity and cultural representation perspectives (Zhou, 2014). Online tourism DI is a more dynamic social construction than the traditional projected image found in printed guidebooks and brochures. It is accumulative or generative, as users continuously upload and share photographic representations of the destination, their perceptions and experiences related to it (Hunter, 2016).

Social Media

In recent years, tourism DI has been shaped by multiple information sources and content generated by travelers, suppliers and locals, especially through social media (Marine-Roig and Anton Clavé, 2015). Social media has become one of the most influential marketing tools for companies looking to improve communication with their customers (Kim, S.-E., et al., 2017). Hundreds of millions of people use it on a daily basis all over the world. Social media has rapidly become one of the defining technologies of our time. In 2022, the total number of social media users is expected to reach 3.29 billion users, accounting for 42.3 percent of the world's population (Appel et al., 2020). The interaction between tourism supply and demand is fundamentally influenced and changed by social media. These future opportunities and challenges are significant for DMOs trying to coordinate and market the destination's intangible and intangible tourism products (Bosio et al., 2018). Social media is important in the tourism sector, which strongly relies on electronic systems to distribute its products in the marketplace and communicate with customers. These systems enable destinations to contact visitors at a relatively low cost and with a higher level of effectiveness than more traditional communication tools (Kiráľová and Pavlíčeka, 2015). Social media also greatly impacts how people search for and share information (Kim, S.-E., et al., 2017).

Given the abundance of social media with travel-related content, tourism plays an important role in the emergence and development of social media. Some platforms and applications, such as Tripadvisor, are solely dedicated to tourism and have been widely adopted by travelers. Tourists' expectations of destinations are influenced by these media (Gretzel, 2019). They play a significant role in tourists' choice of destinations (Míguez-González and Fernández-Cavia, 2015). Since marketers can interact directly with tourists on social media, it has become a distinct tourism marketing and communication tool (Kim, S.-E., et al., 2017). Potential travelers can also use social media to collect various multimedia information from different sources and use others' experiences to plan and sometimes enrich their own tourism-related experiences (Roque and Raposo, 2016). Information gathering is possible through blogging, sharing experiences, writing stories that can be published on personal and destination websites, or a social networking site (Kiráľová and Pavlíčeka, 2015). Social media helps travelers organize and share their travel memories and experiences through blogs (for example, Blogger and Twitter), online social networks (for example, Facebook), media sharing websites (for example, Flickr and YouTube), social bookmarking websites (for example, Delicious), (Nezakati et al., 2015), social travel networks (for example, Tripadvisor), podcasting (for example, iTunes), wikis/content-driven communities (for example, Wikipedia) and other ways (Alizadeh and Isa, 2015). Therefore, social media should be considered as a communication tool and an active component in the destination's image formation (Iglesias-Sánchez et al., 2020).

IRAN'S TOURISM AND ITS DESTINATION IMAGE CHALLENGES

Iran is a vast and diverse Middle Eastern country, with a rich diversity of culture, history, heritage, natural attractions and biodiversity (Khodadadi, 2016a). However, it has not completely benefited from its potential (Taghdisi et al., 2015). Iran has 22 World Cultural Heritage sites and two Natural Heritage sites (UNESCO, 2020c), nine biosphere reserves (UNESCO, 2020b), and 14 intangible heritage items (UNESCO, 2020a). In addition, the cities of Rasht for gastronomy, Isfahan and Bandar Abbas for handicrafts and folk arts, and Sanandaj for music have been registered in the UNESCO Creative Cities Network (UNESCO, 2020d).

International tourists visiting Iran are a minimal share, only about 7295 million tourists in 2018 (2.1 percent of world market share) (UNWTO, 2019). Iran's tourism industry has suffered greatly over the past three decades due to several problems, including negative imagery in the tourism-generating markets, political tensions with the West resulting from Iran's nuclear program, and mismanagement (Khodadadi, 2016a). Negative DI is also linked to social conditions and political instability across the Middle East region (Zamani-Farahani and Henderson, 2014). The Iranian government does not consider tourism a priority for its development, as the Iranian economy is based on oil (Khodadadi, 2016a). In Iran's context, inbound tourism poses marketing challenges, and the country has been labeled a 'difficult area' (Butler et al., 2012). Therefore, when it comes to successfully branding Iran, the country faces significant challenges. It is difficult for the country's tourism providers to overcome this powerful negative discourse, as tourism development in Iran is highly dependent on the country's changing political environment (Khodadadi, 2019).

Within the Iranian Ministry of Tourism, external and internal destination marketing activities have not been carried out effectively. However, this is the most important destination management task (Ziyaei et al., 2016). Efforts by small-scale Iranian tourism suppliers to promote their products have failed to reach the target audience. The majority of public and private sector investment is focused on developing and publishing brochures and catalogs and participating in international exhibitions, with little attention paid to recent developments in ICTs, including the Internet (Khodadadi, 2016b). The country's 20-year Development Plan, which was launched in 2005, set a target of 20 million tourists by 2025. Since then, tourism has become a major focus of tourism development in Iran (Jalilvand, 2017). Iran's share of the global market, however, has remained small. During seven months of 2019 (March 21 to October 22), a total of 5 890 952 tourists visited Iran, representing 24 percent growth compared with the same period of the previous year (*Financial Tribune*, 2019). The country's biggest weakness in the global tourism market appears to be a lack of digital marketing, including today's trendiest, reducing its competitiveness (ITN, 2020). The main keys to enhancing tourism growth in Iran are marketing, advertising and using tourism communication tools to achieve some of the Iranian 20-year Development Plan's objectives regarding tourism development and its replacement by the oil industry (Mazidi, 2014).

Iran developed a tourism master plan in cooperation with the United Nations World Tourism Organization (UNWTO) in 2001. It is now attempting to update its tourism master plan (MCTH, 2019). An integrated destination management and marketing framework has yet to be developed and implemented. Iran does not have a comprehensive and targeted tourism marketing plan to improve its image as a tourist destination. The Ministry of Cultural Heritage, Tourism and Handicraft's total credits budget for 2020 increased by 39.10 percent (about 10 percent) compared to the budget for 2019 (*Tehran Times*, 2020). However, it is unknown how much of the budget is allocated to tourism communication. The Marketing and Advertising Bureau of the Ministry of Tourism has increased its activities in recent years, particularly since 2018. Given the importance of tourism's benefits and its potential for development, Iran's national tourism brand was unveiled for the first time in February 2020. This brand is expected to contribute to tourism growth and development (IFPNews, 2020). Another new initiative was the launch of Iran's official tourism website by the Ministry of Cultural Heritage, Tourism and Handicraft in 2018 (https://www.visitiran.ir). However, these measures cannot be taken to justify the ministry's inefficiency in shaping Iran's image.

DISCUSSION AND CONCLUSION

Despite the increase in the Ministry of Tourism's budget, no specific plan has been developed to use this budget to market Iran and create its DI. Besides, on many occasions, the government's decisions and policies have curtailed companies' and individuals' efforts to create Iran's positive image as a tourist destination. Over the years, travel service providers, such as tour operators, hotels and even tour guides, have personally tried to promote Iran's DI by introducing and generating information about Iran on the Internet. Meanwhile, tourists who have already visited Iran have played an important role in improving this image. Via Google, we can find a lot of positive content and information about this destination, which has helped form a positive DI for Iran among potential tourists, despite the media's negative news. This type of UGC is particularly effective in shaping the DI, especially in the case of Iran, where the government has been less involved in this field. The tourism authorities lack the necessary expertise to manage these activities and have sometimes prevented such efforts with their strict laws. In this regard, individuals and the private sector have attempted to shape Iran's DI through online tourism communications.

There are successful examples of these personal attempts. In August 2015, a group of young individuals created the Facebook page "See You in Iran" to counter Iranophobia by allowing people to share their unfiltered narratives about traveling to Iran, to promote a more nuanced understanding of this country (https://seeyouiniran.org). The second successful example was the "Must See Iran" Instagram and Twitter campaign launched in 2014, which asked users to share photos of Iran with the hashtag of the same name. The main goal was to positively portray Iran's tourist destinations (https://www.instagram.com/mustseeiran_insta/). The third one was a fam(familiarization) trip project in 2019, with the hashtag #feeliran and an Instagram page of the same name. It was organized by an Iranian influencer who invited different international bloggers and travel influencers to present the world with a fascinating image of Iran, encouraging foreign tourists to discover it (https://www.instagram.com/feeliran/).

There is no integrated system for monitoring and assessing marketing activities by tourism authorities and service providers in Iran. The Iranian government needs to do tourism marketing research to determine which information about Iran as a destination should be provided to its audience via which social media platform. For example, the ministry's recent statistics are comprehensive, but they do not address how these tourists became acquainted with Iran as a destination. On the other hand, every country has its own social networks, but not necessarily the same ones. A successful destination takes advantage of these online tourism communications. Although social media is considered an important source of tourism information (Kim, S.-E., et al., 2017), the use of social media by the Iranian tourism authorities to promote tourism is limited. Given that Iran currently has a tourism brand, its marketing efforts should be directed towards presenting its real DI. This is the most important aspect of destination marketing, especially for Iran, which has always suffered from a negative image. Consequently, a study of target markets and incoming tourists should determine what type of tourist information appeals to them, and which social media platforms they prefer. In addition, tourism authorities need to consider what tourism communication activities are relevant to each market.

REFERENCES

Agapito, D., Valle, P., and Mendes, J. (2013). The cognitive-affective-conative model of destination image: A confirmatory analysis. *Journal of Travel and Tourism Marketing, 30*(5), 471–481.

Alizadeh, A., and Isa, M.R. (2015). The use of social media in destination marketing: An exploratory study. *Preliminary Communication, 63*(2), 175–192.

Almeida-García, F., Domígunez-Azcue, J., Mercadé-Melé, P., and Pérez-Tapia, G. (2020). Can a destination really change its image? The roles of information sources, motivations, and visits. *Tourism Management Perspectives, 34*, 100662.

Appel, G., Grewal, L., Hadi, R., and Stephen, T.A. (2020). The future of social media in marketing. *Journal of the Academy of Marketing Science, 48*, 79–95.

Baggio, R., Mottironi, C., and Antonioli Corigliano, M. (2011). Technological aspects of public tourism communication in Italy. *Journal of Hospitality and Tourism Technology, 2*(2), 105–119.

Baloglu, S., and McCleary, K. (1999). A model of destination image formation. *Annals of Tourism Research, 26*(4), 868–897.

Baptista, N., and Matos, N. (2018). Analysing destination image from a consumer behaviour perspective. *Marketing and Tourism, 6*(3), 226–236.

Beerli, A., and Martin, J.D. (2004). Factors influencing destination image. *Annals of Tourism Research, 31*(3), 657–681.

Blichfeldt, B.S. (2017). *Strategic Communication in Tourism.* Universitetsparken: Centre for Tourism, Innovation and Culture, University of Southern Denmark.

Bosio, B., Stefanie, H., and Michael, C. (2018). The utilisation of social media marketing in destination management organizations. *6th International OFEL Conference on Governance, Management and Entrepreneurship. New Business Models and Institutional Entrepreneurs: Leading Disruptive Change* (pp. 249–268). Dubrovnik, Croatia.

Bošković, D., Težak, A., and Saftič, D. (2010). Media in collecting information on tourism destinations and sociodemographic characteristics. *Economic Research – Ekonomska Istraživanja, 23*(3), 111–120.

Butler, R., O'Gorman, K.D., and Prentice, R. (2012). Destination appraisal for European cultural tourism to Iran. *International Journal of Tourism Research, 14*(4), 323–338.

Campo, S., and Alvarez, M. (2014). Can tourism promotions influence a country's negative image? An experimental study on Israel's image. *Current Issues in Tourism, 17*(3), 201–219.

Camprubí, R., Guia, J., and Comas, J. (2013). The new role of tourists in destination image formation. *Current Issues in Tourism, 16*(2), 203–209.

Cherifi, B., Smith, A., Maitland, R., and Stevenson, N. (2014). Destination images of non-visitors. *Annals of Tourism Research, 49*, 190–202.

Chetthamrongchai, P. (2017). The influence of travel motivation, information sources and tourism crisis on tourists' destination image. *Journal of Tourism and Hospitality, 6*(2), 1–6. DOI: 10.4172/2167-0269.1000278.

Choi, S., Lehto, X., and Morrison, A. (2007). Destination image representation on the web: Content analysis of Macau travel related website. *Tourism Management, 28*, 118–129.

Di Marino, E. (2008). The strategic dimension of destination image. An analysis of the French Riviera image from the Italian tourists' perceptions. *17th International Tourism and Leisure Symposium*, Barcelona.

Echtner, C.M., and Ritchie, J.R.B. (1991). The meaning and measurement of destination image. *Journal of Tourism Studies, 2*(2), 2–12.

Esu, B. (2015). An analysis of the image of destination Cross River and effect on visitors' future intentions. *Journal of Hospitality and Management Tourism, 6*(7), 80–89.

Financial Tribune (2019, November 18). Iran: Tourist arrivals increase 24% to over 5.8 million. https://financialtribune.com/articles/travel/100806/iran-tourist-arrivals-increase-24-to-over-58-million.

Fodness, D., and Murray, B. (1997). Tourist information search. *Annals of Tourism Research, 24*(3), 503–523.

Frías, D., Rodríguez, M., Alberto Castañeda, J., Sabiote, C., and Buhalis, D. (2011). The formation of a tourist destination's image via information sources: the moderating effect of culture. *International Journal of Tourism Research, 14*(5), 437–450.

Gartner, W. (1993). Image formation process. In M. Uysal and D.R. Fesenmaier (eds), *Communication and Channel Systems in Tourism Marketing* (pp. 191–215). New York: Haworth Press.

Gretzel, U. (2019). The role of social media in creating and addressing overtourism. In R. Dodds and R. Butler (eds), *Overtourism: Issues, Realities and Solutions* (pp. 62–75). Berlin: De Gruyter.

Guzman-Parra, V.F., Vila-Oblitas, J.R., and Maqueda-Lafuente, F. (2016). Exploring the effects of cognitive destination image attributes on tourist satisfaction and destination loyalty: A case study of Málaga, Spain. *Tourism and Management Studies, 12*(1), 67–73.

Hahm, J. (2004). Assessing the impact of movies upon an individual's image formation concerning a given destination. Doctoral dissertation, University of Central Florida.

Hang Kong, W., du Cros, H., and Ee Ong, C. (2015). Tourism destination image development: A lesson from Macau. *International Journal of Tourism Cities, 1*(4), 1–17.

de la Hoz-Correa, A., and Muñoz-Leiva, F. (2019). The role of information sources and image on the intention to visit a medical tourism destination: A cross-cultural analysis. *Journal of Travel and Tourism Marketing, 36*(2), 204–219.

Hu, T., Marchiori, E., Kalbaska, N., and Cantoni, L. (2014). Online representation of Switzerland as a tourism destination: An exploratory research on a Chinese microblogging platform. *Studies in Communication Sciences, 14*, 136–143.

Huete Alcocer, N., and López Ruiz, V. (2019). The role of destination image in tourist satisfaction: The case of a heritage site. *Economic Research – Ekonomska Istraživanja, 33*(1), 2444–2461.

Hunter, W.C. (2016). The social construction of tourism online destination image: A comparative semiotic analysis of the visual representation of Seoul. *Tourism Management, 54*, 221–229.

IFPNews (2020, February 13). Iran unveils national tourism brand. Récupéré sur Iran Front Page News: https://ifpnews.com/iran-unveils-national-tourism-brand.

Iglesias-Sánchez, P., Correia, M., Jambrino-Maldonado, C., and de las Heras-Pedrosa, C. (2020). Instagram as a co-creation space for tourist destination image-building: Algarve and Costa del Sol case studies. *Sustainability, 12*(7), 2793. https://doi.org/10.3390/su12072793.

Ispas, A., and Sargea, R.-A. (2011). Evaluating the image of tourism destinations. The case of the autonomous community of the Canary Islands. *Revista de turism, 12*, 5–12.

ITN (2020, June 10). Iran still not using enough modern tourism marketing tools and lack of digital marketing. Iran Tourism News: https://irantourismnews.com/iran-still-not-using-enough-modern-tourism-marketing-tools-and-lack-of-digital-marketing/.

Jacobsen, J., and Munar, A. (2012). Tourist information search and destination choice in a digital age. *Tourism Management Perspectives, 1*, 39–47.

Jalilvand, M.R. (2017). Word-of-mouth vs. mass media: their contributions to destination image formation. *Anatolia, 28*(2), 151–162.

Jamaludin, M., Aziz, A., Yusof, A., and Idris, N. (2013). Information source influence destination image. *International Journal of Independent Research and Studies, 2*(4), 146–155.

Jenkins, O. (1990). Understanding and measuring tourist destination images. *International Journal of Tourism Research, 1*, 1–15.

Jeong, C., and Holland, S. (2012). Destination image saturation. *Journal of Travel and Tourism Marketing, 29*(6), 501–519.

Jeong, C., Holland, S., Jun, S., and Gibson, H. (2011). Enhancing destination image through travel website information. *International Journal of Tourism Research, 14*(1), 16–27.

Khodadadi, M. (2016a). A new dawn? The Iran nuclear deal and the future of the Iranian tourism industry. *Tourism Management Perspectives, 18*, 6–9.

Khodadadi, M. (2016b). Challenges and opportunities for tourism development in Iran: Perspectives of Iranian tourism suppliers. *Tourism Management Perspectives, 19*, 90–92.

Khodadadi, M. (2019). Challenges of branding Iran: Perspectives of Iranian tourism suppliers. *Tourism Planning and Development, 16*(1), 112–117.

Kim, D.-Y., Lehto, X., and Morrison, A. (2007). Gender differences in online travel information search: Implications for marketing communications on the internet. *Tourism Management, 28*, 423–433.

Kim, H., and Chen, J. (2016). Destination image formation process: A holistic model. *Journal of Vacation Marketing, 22*(2), 154–166.

Kim, S.-E., Lee, K., Shin, S., and Yang, S.-B. (2017). Effects of tourism information quality in social media on destination image formation: The case of Sina Weibo. *Information and Management, 54*(6), 687–702.

Kiráľová, A., and Pavlíčeka, A. (2015). Development of social media strategies in tourism destination. *Procedia – Social and Behavioral Sciences, 175*, 358–366.

Kislali, H., Kavaratzis, M., and Saren, M. (2016). Re-conceptualising destination image formation. *International Journal of Culture, Tourism and Hospitality Research, 10*(1), 70–80.

Kotler, P., and Gertner, D. (2002). Country as brand, product, and beyond: A place marketing and brand management perspective. *Journal of Brand Management, 9*(4–5), 249–261.

Lee, S., Busser, J., and Yang, J. (2015). Exploring the dimensional relationships among image formation agents, destination image, and place attachment from the perspectives of pop star fans. *Journal of Travel and Tourism Marketing, 32*(6), 730–746.

Lo, I.S., McKercher, B., Lo, A., Cheung, C., and Law, R. (2011). Tourism and online photography. *Tourism Management, 32*, 725–731.

Mak, A.H. (2017). Online destination image: Comparing national tourism organisation's and tourists' perspectives. *Tourism Managemen, 60*, 280–297.

Marine-Roig, E., and Anton Clavé, S. (2015). A detailed method for destination image analysis using user-generated content. *Information Technology and Tourism, 15*(4), 341–364.

Matos, N., Mendes, J., and Valle, P. (2012). Revisiting the destination image construct through a conceptual model. *Dos Algarves, 21*, 101–117.

Mazidi, S.F. (2014). A review on effects of advertisements of marketing on tourism industry. *Journal of Management and Accounting Studies, 2*(3), 53–60.

McCartney, G., Butler, R., and Bennett, M. (2008). A strategic use of the communication mix in the destination image-formation process. *Journal of Travel Research, 47*(2), 183–196.

MCTH (2019, November 8). Tehran, WTO discuss master plan to develop tourism in Iran. Ministry of Cultural Heritage, Tourism and Handicrafts: https://www.mcth.ir/english/news/ID/48317.

Míguez-González, M., and Fernández-Cavia, J. (2015). Tourism and online communication: interactivity and social web in official destination websites. *Comunicacion y Sociedad, 28*(4), 17–31.

Molina, A., Gómez, M., and Martín-Consuegra, D. (2010). Tourism marketing information and destination image management. *African Journal of Business Management, 4*(5), 722–728.

Nezakati, H., Amidi, A., Yah Jusoh, Y., Moghadas, S., Abdul Aziz, Y., and Sohrabinezhadtalemi, R. (2015). Review of social media potential on knowledge sharing and collaboration in tourism industry. *Procedia – Social and Behavioral Sciences, 172*, 120–125.

Nicoletta, R., and Servidio, R. (2012). Tourists' opinions and their selection of tourism destination images: An affective and motivational evaluation. *Tourism Management Perspectives, 4*, 19–27.

Pan, B., and Fesenmaier, D. (2006). Online information search vacation planning process. *Annals of Tourism Research, 33*(3), 809–832.

Pavlović, D.K., and Belullo, A. (2007). Internet – An agent of tourism destination image formation: content and correspondence analysis of istria travel related websites. *International Conference on Global Challenges for Competitiveness: Business and Government Perspective* (pp. 541–556). Pula, Croatia: Juraj Dobrila University.

Roque, V., and Raposo, R. (2016). Social media as a communication and marketing tool in tourism: An analysis of online activities from international key player DMO. *Anatolia, 27*(1), 58–70.

San Martín, H., and Rodríguez del Bosque, I. (2008). Exploring the cognitive–affective nature of destination image and the role of psychological factors in its formation. *Tourism Management, 29*(2), 263–277.

Stylidis, D., Shani, A., and Belhassen, Y. (2017). Testing an integrated destination image model across residents and tourists. *Tourism Management, 58*, 184–195.

Stylos, N., Bellou, V., Andronikidis, A., and Vassiliadis, C. (2017). Linking the dots among destination images, place attachment, and revisit intentions: A study among British and Russian tourists. *Tourism Management, 60*, 15–29.

Tan, W.-K., and Chen, T.-H. (2012). The usage of online tourist information sources in tourist information search: an exploratory study. *Service Industries Journal, 32*(3), 451–476.

Taghdisi, A., Varesi, H.R., Ahmadian, M., and Asgari, H. (2015). Identify and analysis the factors affecting development of tourism in rural areas (Case study: Rural areas of Jiroft County). *Journal of Research and Rural Planning, 4*(1), 1–14.

Tasci, A., and Gartner, W. (2007). Destination image and its functional relationships. *Journal of Travel Research, 45*(4), 413–425.

Tehran Times (2020, May 1). Iran raises annual tourism budget by 39%. *Tehran Times*: https://www.tehrantimes.com/news/447385/Iran-raises-annual-tourism-budget-by-39

UNESCO (2020a, June 8). *Intangible Cultural Heritage, Iran*. UNESCO – Intangible Cultural Heritage: https://ich.unesco.org/en/lists?text=&country[]=00105&multinational=3&display1=inscriptionID #tabs.

UNESCO (2020b, June 8). *Biosphere Reserves Directory*. UNESCO – MAB Biosphere Reserves Directory: http://www.unesco.org/mabdb/br/brdir/directory/contact.asp?code=IRA.

UNESCO (2020c, March 25). *Iran (Islamic Republic of) – UNESCO World Heritage Centre*. UNESCO World Heritage Centre: https://whc.unesco.org/en/statesparties/IR.

UNESCO (2020d, June 8). *UNESCO Creative Cities Network – Iran*. UNESCO Creative Cities Network: https://en.unesco.org/creative-cities/creative-cities-map.

UNWTO (2019). *International Tourism Highlights 2019*. UNWTO.

Viallon, P. (2013). La communication touristique, une triple invention. *Mondes du Tourisme, 7*, 2–11.

Xu, H., and Ye, T. (2018). Dynamic destination image formation and change under the effect of various agents: The case of Lijiang, "The Capital of Yanyu." *Journal of Destination Marketing and Management, 7*, 131–139.

Zamani-Farahani, H., and Henderson, J.C. (2014). Community attitudes toward tourists: A study of Iran. *International Journal of Hospitality and Tourism Administration, 15*(4), 354–375.

Zhang, M., Zhang, G.-Y., Gursoy, D., and Fu, X.-R. (2018). Message framing and regulatory focus effects on destination image formation. *Tourism Management, 69*, 397–407.

Zhou, L. (2014). Online rural destination images: Tourism and rurality. *Journal of Destination Marketing and Management, 3*, 227–240.

Ziyaei, M., Abbasi Karjegan, D., Kazemian, G., and Karoobi, M. (2016). Identification and determination of dimensions of tourism management model in Tehran. *Quarterly Journal of Urban Economics and Management, 4*(13), 117–137.

7. Impact of social media-based user-generated content on online reputation of tourist destinations
Komal Kapoor

INTRODUCTION

Social media has not only changed the way people of this world communicate, interact and share, but also how they are approached by marketers of different products and services. In the current connected viral world, consumers have even taken the place of marketers of services that they have experienced, through the contributions they make to the social platforms (Cox et al., 2009). It is critical to first understand what consists of social media and how it has become an important component of digital marketing strategy of an organization. As a part of the integrated marketing communication strategy of an organization, digital marketing methods have evolved from just an email or website hosting to a high level of consumer engagement, to more evolved social media platforms such as Facebook, Instagram, Pinterest, Google+, Twitter, LinkedIn, and so on. The number of consumers on such platforms have increased manifold over the years and today the figure stands at billions (Stepaniuk, 2015).

Such social media platforms have also evolved from just being a source of interaction, to a marketplace and a space for user-generated content for various products and services. In this scenario, services have gained a lot of traction, especially the tourism sector where travellers undertake detailed searches about the destination they are planning to visit. Over the last two decades, exponential growth has been witnessed in both domestic and international tourism that is leading to sharing of the experience, pictures, reviews and ratings by the travellers on social media platforms, along with blogs (Zeng and Gerritsen, 2014). This has created a huge amount of user-generated content that creates a reputation and image of the location that other tourists want to know about before planning their own travel. The real and actual user experiences create a higher level of trust among the potential consumers, as the travel agencies' related content can be misleading and inaccurate. It has been observed that as consumers are connected through the various online platforms they evaluate and review the images and comments posted by actual travellers and even post questions to them to improve their understanding (Xiang and Gretzel, 2010).

The subject of this chapter is thus critical and relevant, as marketers in the travel and tourism business have to understand the impact of social media on consumer perceptions of the destination. It is also important to know the effectiveness and reach of each media platform, along with the consumer usage pattern. This can be achieved better by developing a model of electronic word-of-mouth (eWOM) and its impact on trust creation for a particular destination. Critically, evaluation is also needed of how consumer decision-making is affected by the reviews and user-generated content, so that marketers can use the right inputs for their marketing strategy. In this regard, overtourism and dark tourism are understood and analysed through user-generated content, and are also impacted upon to a large extent by social media communication between consumers. Hence online reputation management of destinations is impacted upon by the social media content and messages.

IMPACT OF SOCIAL MEDIA ON TRAVEL DECISIONS

Social media is playing a pivotal role in tourism and travel destination choice, through the interaction consumers undertake with other travellers from all over the world. Such potential travellers view, read, contribute and develop loyalty towards Facebook pages, travel blogging sites, Instagram Stories describing travel, travel dairies on YouTube, which lead to influencing others towards certain destinations while also creating negative images about others (Leung et al., 2013). Social media exposure and involvement not only creates pre-trip expectations but also influences post-trip satisfaction after travel has happened. Even during travel, consumers tend to post live, real-time stories to keep their audience engaged, which also creates an online image about the travel destination. Consumer-generated content is gaining importance with both researchers and practitioners as many factors require much deeper study: about the ability to trust other travellers, the competence of the travellers, the pressure of social acceptance on content uploading, stimuli acting as consumer brand engagement, and also setting expectations through blog writing (Milano et al., 2011). Such impact also induces the image building that leads to eWOM. The pace and reach of eWOM is greater than the traditional media could ever achieve.

User-generated content (UGC) has become an important source of information not only for travellers but also for travel firms, as it helps in understanding the image that is developing in the consumer world of a destination or even a hotel. The travel decision of consumers to choose one destination over another is highly based on factors linked to differentiation, key attractions, history, culture, food, government rules, own interests and, most importantly, recommendations from family and friends (Lange-Faria and Elliot, 2012). In the connected world of today, all the information pertaining to each travel destination is widely available over the internet, and can be categorized as commercial and UGC. Even when consumers read and analyse the information and marketing undertaken by the commercial bodies promoting the destination, they do not make their final decision until they have read and researched deeply about other travellers' experiences. The commercial organizations consist of the government bodies of the region, travel agencies, hotel and resorts, aviation companies, and so on that are aiming at converting the consumer's attitude positively towards a favoured destination (Hvass and Munar, 2012). These commercial outfits also use technology-based marketing through social media marketing methods but that is a paid content and message for conversion into travel decision. On the contrary, UGC is more neutral, real, actual, genuine and more trustworthy, as it discusses all the aspects of a destination, both negative and positive. But even this cannot be trusted blindly and each traveller has to review and analyse the information created by users to search for the right posts, images, and so on, and to decide what content to trust. Studies indicate that 20 per cent of travellers are influenced by the photographs, videos and comments posted by other travellers on the social networking sites (SNSs), while developing their own expectations, perception, attitude, purchase behaviour and the final decision (Zouganeli et al., 2011).

From the consumer behaviour point of view, social media sites do provide a vast and varied amount of data and content that a consumer filters according to the criteria they have adopted. User-generated content has a critical impact on the learning process of the traveller, motivation to travel, perception of a destination, attitude formation towards travel and also the destination, thus impacting upon the complete consumer decision-making process (Kiráľová and Pavlíčeka, 2015). But these images and reviews may also have a negative impact on the travel decision, which the promoters of that destination cannot control. Many negative ratings and reviews, which cannot be controlled by the marketers of that destination, are converted into negative eWOM for the travel location (Sigala et al., 2012). There is a great need to understand the critical factors leading to success or failure of a travel location based on the social media impact, with the help of a conceptual model that would also provide the desired research direction for the future. Many concerns, such as the trust factor, the efficacy of the social media site, engagement of the consumer, acceptance of the information, seeking of feedback, stages in the consumer decision-making process, would all have to be studied in more detail in trying to gain a deeper understanding.

THE GROWING RELEVANCE OF eWOM AND IMPACT ON TRUST

In a society where trust and credibility are highly based on the source of information, commercial advertising is only leading to creating awareness and visibility among the consumers, as they are resorting to more online sources of content. Above-the-line marketing methods such as advertising, promotions and selling methods focus more on gaining the attention and interest of the consumers, which may not lead to the creation of trust in the product or service (Ayeh et al., 2013). This is more applicable in the case of services, which have to be experienced to be evaluated and trusted. Thus reading and evaluating what other travellers in the tourism industry say about destinations, properties and main attractions provides the desired trust factor of the information, because it does not have commercial value. Consumer interfacing with technology is increasing exponentially, and electronic word-of-mouth is playing a critical role in both positive and negative image formation about destinations, due to the constant engagement of consumers on the SNSs (Ghose et al., 2012). As they are intangible products, their evaluation before the purchase is complex and difficult. eWOM relates to all the online methods of communication adopted by consumers to undertake word-of-mouth linked to their actual experiences. Word-of-mouth can be both negative and positive, as consumers can have both negative and positive experiences from a travel destination that they would like to share. By sharing their experiences, they are providing feedback to the tour operators or hotel management, and even helping other potential customers make informed and correct decisions. eWOM has also gained much importance due to the formation of consumer communities online that aim to disseminate trustworthy information to all their members, to help them make sound decisions. The longevity of such membership not only results in the initial destination decisions but also increases the chances of revisits to the same destination (Wilson et al., 2012).

The relationship between the eWOM and trust about the travel destination can be understood better through certain underlying factors that still have to be analysed. Critical issues include: the source–receiver relationships, variety of channels used, presentation of content, opportunities for information solicitation by others, message retention capabilities, and also the content provider's motivation to disclose the personal level experience to the world (Chung et al., 2015). Studies on this relationship are still in the exploratory stages, and have to build further for different social media platforms and also for different destinations. eWOM be understood not only as showcasing the unique experience of the consumer, but also as developing many marketing opportunities with the destination service providers for a higher level of engagement. eWOM increases the involvement and engagement level of consumers, as people tend to connect socially better and more quickly, which leads to the faster spread of information, but online involvement with a particular brand may be fake, as it may not actually be based on real usage. How far trust and credibility are created with eWOM has to be further researched. A lot of studies have been conducted on the level of trust that is built through the perception and attitude towards the destination website and the aggregating website (such as MakeMyTrip), as it can be completely different for the consumer when compared to offline and traditional marketing channels (Ye et al., 2011).

USER-GENERATED CONTENT VERSUS MARKETER-GENERATED CONTENT

All eWOM and content generation on social media sites is highly dependent on the ability and capability of the user to display and share their experiences which they have gained first-hand. User-generated content (UGC) is the images and reviews that are uploaded on social media sites by travellers from their own experience of travel to certain destinations. These take the forms of pictures, videos, blogs, reviews, ratings and also testimonials (Lu and Stepchenkova, 2015). UGC can be generated during the travel, or post-trip, to share memories with other consumers. To understand the authenticity and efficacy of such UGC, it is important to first understand the motives behind generating content online:

1. General habitual sharing: some consumers are in a habitual mode of sharing with the world what they are doing or undergoing at a particular time. From a human behaviour point of view, it is a basic social need of the consumers to share with their family and friends, as it creates feelings of joy and happiness. Most travel consumers fall into this category, as they are social animals as they lead their lives and also share their connections with others in their online social circle.

2. Social status gratification seeking: many consumers or travellers also fall in the category of status seekers who, through their travel, want to showcase a particular life they are living. Such consumers deliberately seek to for the admiration and liking of others through the interaction taking place on social media sites. These consumers have very high self-esteem that continuously needs pampering and gratification for the satisfaction of the ego. The UGC created by such consumers may be inflated and exaggerated to provide a more pleasant report to the other consumers who may be seeking their opinion leadership.

3. Irritants and terrorist consumers: another category of consumers are the creators of negative eWOM, who tend to share their negative experiences of a travel destination with their social connections, so that they can vent their frustration, along with demotivating other consumers. They are a highly irritated lot, and can destroy the complete image of a destination or a hotel property by their terrorist behaviour over the online platforms, that easily become viral and reach a large number of potential travellers.

For all the above three cases, UGC is highly read, shared and commented upon for the formation of perception and attitude towards a particular travel destination. But UGC is still not regarded as very credible and trustworthy content for taking the final decision, even when it increases the visibility, awareness and preferences towards the destinations. The information processing through such UGC is still not leading to the final travel decision. For example, blogs by travellers do increase the available information and knowledge, but may not necessarily lead to choosing the final travel destination (Abubakar, 2016), as the final choice also largely depends upon the traveller's self-interest, budget, time available, other co-travellers, past experiences, and so on.

The other aspect of content generation is the commercial content which is generated by the marketers involved in these destinations, such as travel agents, hotels, aviation companies, tour operators, and so on. This marketer-generated content has more of a commercial value, by professionally showcasing the destination as among the most preferred ones. Most the studies prove that the content of the marketers is generally misleading, as the images, videos and descriptions are different from the travellers' actual experiences (Filieri and McLeay, 2014). This is a generally held notion, which can be different for different travellers. But it does create awareness, provide information about the details such as tariffs, places to visit, cuisines available, cost of living, and so on, that are beneficial for travellers who are do not have much knowledge of a new place. Hence, marketer-led content needs to be supported by UGC, then the consumers form their final image of the destination (Cantallops and Salvi, 2014).

ONLINE DESTINATION IMAGE MANAGEMENT

Online destination branding through image management relates to the various customer engagement tools used online through both marketer-generated and user-generated content, and how it improves the overall image of the travel destination in the eyes of travellers. Destination branding consists of not only promoting and marketing the actual attractions of the destination, but also trying to develop an emotional connection with the destination through stories, visuals and even history; for example, Paris for romance, Africa for natural wildlife, and so on. Based on the interests of the consumers, such image management would convince the consumers about their travel decisions (Tsao et al., 2015). Online destination image is developed through digital platforms and involvement through social media sites. Consumers search for information related to certain travel destinations that they are planning to visit, or while generally searching. It has been observed that sharing and posting of travel experiences is an important activity that is undertaken during the trip, as well as being a post-trip activity.

Around 52 per cent of travellers help in creating the image of destinations by sharing and posting videos and pictures, which have maximum impact due to the visual appeal of the content. Nearly 25 per cent engage in writing reviews, sharing a news story, liking the photos, and in blog posts about their experiences to convey to others. Also, around 14 per cent of travellers post their check-in status, comment on social media, and tweet about their experience. Through the overall combination of content across the social media platforms, the destination branding takes shape, and is also impacted upon by the marketer-generated content (Bronner and De Hoog, 2011). Coherence in both kinds of content leads to the creation of a more holistic image about the travel destination. Consumers also use a lot of social media while deciding, researching and booking hotels for their travel. Gradually, since 2016, searching in general on

Google has reduced by 70 per cent as consumers prefer to engage with Expedia, Tripadvisor and other such platforms to get more authentic and genuine feedback about a destination. The use of smartphones with apps leads at least 30 per cent of consumers to find hotels and other services through their phones only; 85 per cent of the travellers use their smartphones constantly while travelling, thus increasing the possibility of more engagement with the destination, as people in their circle are able to view and like the travel being undertaken in real time (Abubakar et al., 2017).

A very high number – 92 per cent – of consumers trust 'earned' media which is through word-of-mouth and recommendations provided by their friends and family, as compared to other forms of advertising; 52 per cent of the consumers say they are influenced by the Facebook posts of their friends' photos, which impact upon their own travel decisions. Social media and UGC have also led to a change in their plan to travel, in their destination decision, or even their hotel. Hence social media platforms such as Facebook, Instagram, that are more personal, are having an important influence on travel decisions. Trust in the eWOM recommendations and is also gradually building up, and is expected to increase further in future, based on how consumer engagement is changing (Zainal et al., 2017).

FORMATION OF PERCEPTION TOWARDS TOURIST DESTINATIONS

Each social media blog, review or rating builds upon the perception or imagery about the travel destination that is generalized later. Perception is the image or opinion formed about the travel destination that is based on past experience and content shared by consumers who have already visited. Perception is not only the result of the social media content, but also involves what travellers already know about the travel destination (Ladhari and Michaud, 2015). Perception develops through a three-stage process of selective attention, selective retention and selective perception. The selective attention relates to the user-generated content that the potential consumers pay attention to while reading and viewing on the various social media sites. The normal tendency of the human brain is to only pay attention selectively, while missing out certain aspects that may be important to the person posting the content but not to the reader. In the second stage, the information that has been read would be selectively retained by the consumers based on their interest area and past knowledge (Luo and Zhong, 2015). Retention is also a function of the brain, to only retain limited information while ignoring the rest. Through the lens of this selective attention and selective retention, the final perception is created, which is not just based on user-generated content but also on how the information is processed by the user. This is also impacted upon by the gender of the consumer, other demographics, and psychographic and behavioural variables.

Perception based on the evaluation of social media content is also influenced by the motives behind the travel to be undertaken. Many travellers seek hedonic travel pleasures, whereas others may be seeking more nature tourism or ecotourism for relaxation and mental peace (Mak, 2017). Thus the possibility for the user-generated content to form a perception about the travel destination is also impacted upon by the person's self-interest and motives for visiting the destination. Each SNS also has its perception in the mind of the consumer, such as how Facebook is viewed as compared to Instagram, the engagement level with photographs as compared to a video, and many more such aspects that determine the consumer's buying behaviour for their final decision. Perceptual thresholds are categorically dependent on the existing knowledge of the consumers and how far they trust the other consumers' user-generated content (Pan and Li, 2011). Trust has to be a close function of the perception, not just about the content but also about the person posting the content. Content posted by friends and family has high trust and recommendation value as compared to general blogs and unknown people on social networking sites. Thus the tendency and motivation of travellers needs to be enhanced further so that they regularly and frequently share their travel stories with others. The trend of uploading and sharing is common and gaining momentum, but many travellers are not that social media-savvy, which results in a low level of user-generated content.

IMPACT ON CONSUMER DECISION-MAKING

Social media content about travel destinations and experiences impacts upon overall consumer decision-making in many ways. As part of the overall process, travellers seek to finalize the destination, make a booking for the air tavel and the hotel, seek advice on sightseeing places, activities to be undertaken, cuisines to try, and so on. This takes place pre-trip, during the trip, and also post-trip to gain gratification (Sigala et al., 2012). For information and content related to decisions, travellers regularly use Google searches, and also what others have posted on social media platforms. This is valid to the extent that some travel plans may be triggered by a social media post of others. Each step in the consumer decision-making process is influenced by social media content, in forming an image and also in making the final decision (Lim et al., 2012).

Need Recognition

The need or desire to travel to new unknown places may arise after being influenced by what someone posts on social media, either out of interest or based on the actual visit. This is valid for pleasure-seeking trips such as some adventure vacations, and even some places that entice consumers such as haunted places or sites where some mystery is involved (Chung and Koo, 2015). This need recognition may also be due to personal factors of family and friends that travelling is a regular activity which everyone takes up, in order to take a break from their regular life and routine. But studies have shown that 15 per cent of the need to travel may arise from the social media content posted by others. The consumer behaviour may be influenced by the need to enjoy the destination yourself, or even to showcase a comparison of the various destinations which creates the right motivation for others to consider them. Then it becomes more of an ego-boosting decision, to prove something to the world about one's own capacity to travel abroad.

Information Search

Information posted on social media can act as an important stimulator or source of information when consumers seek more information about travel destinations. SNSs provide information about many destinations that people may have visited. These may fall into the categories of foreign locations, religious trips, tourist 'adventure islands', trekking trips, camping trips, exotic locations such as haunted villages, and so on. Hence, apart from being influenced and attracted to certain destinations, consumers do undertake a lot of research on the internet, via social media platforms such as Facebook communities, YouTube videos about destinations, Tripadvisor, and so on, so that they can be more informed about their choices before finally taking the decision (Mendes-Filho et al., 2018).

Evaluation of Alternatives

Even after being attracted by the social media content posted by other travellers, each consumer undertakes their own evaluation of the travel decision based on the budget, preferences of other family members, time availability, purpose of taking the vacation, and so on (González-Rodríguez et al., 2016). Also, different family members may be attracted to different destinations, based on their own circle of close friends and family that may lead to a scenario of too many options that have to be reviewed for taking the final decision (Ghose et al., 2012). Evaluation of the travel destinations may be a difficult process based on the likes and preferences of all the family members, which may lead to difficulty in attaining a consensus.

Purchase Decision

Based on the evaluation of the travel destination through user-generated content and also the consumer's own review, the final decisions are taken. Even when social media does play a role in influencing the travel decision, personal factors are more critical in the final decision (Filieri and McLeay, 2014). The influence of others may not lead to the right decision, and many consumers have regrets later as their expectations of the destination, based on the recommendations provided by others, are not fulfilled. In this condition, it is critical to understand that the sources of happiness, enjoyment and relaxation are very different for everyone. Hence, decisions should be based on a combination of recommendations by others and one's own preference, so as to achieve maximum satisfaction (Cantallops and Salvi, 2014).

Post-Purchase Evaluation

eWOM plays a critical role in post-travel recommendations and feedback based on both positive and negative evaluations. Most travellers are eager to promote their travel destinations to others as they have had very positive and exciting experiences. But even travellers experiencing dissatisfaction are also very keen to share their feedback, which may be detrimental to the travel destination's future (Tsao et al., 2015). Marketers involved in providing services at the destination need to immediately review the feedback from travellers so that post-trip reviews and WOM can be enhanced for the development of the destination brand (Jalilvand et al., 2012).

Cognitive Dissonance Reduction

Social media also plays a very important role for travellers in the emotional gratification that they receive by sharing their good memories. But negative feelings are also communicated to others to nullify the impact of the bad experiences. Consumers belong to different psychological states of mind and behave differently about their dissatisfaction achieved through travel (Bronner and De Hoog, 2011). Some just withdraw and not share anything, as they feel demotivated to share their experience. Others may be very active in spreading negative WOM, so that they can criticize the destination and also deter others from going there. Similarly, a positive experience would be shared with everyone to communicate how good and pleasant the trip was, which would further motivate others to think about it. In both cases, the emotional and cognitive dissonance in the mind of the traveller is managed through the online content that they generate (Abubakar et al., 2017).

IMPACT ON MARKETING STRATEGY

The understanding gained through analysing the impact of social media and UGC on the choice of travel destination has critical implications for marketers in the travel industry (Költringer and Dickinger, 2015). Marketers can be the agencies promoting the destination, tour operators, hotels and resorts, aviation and other transport companies, restaurants and fast food outlets, and so on. Each one is an important part of the overall supply chain of providing the right kind of infrastructure and services to the travellers that impact upon the content that gets generated online (Zainal et al., 2017). In the era of digital marketing and consumer online communities impacting other consumers, companies also have to modify their marketing methods to improve customer experience, customer satisfaction and also the travellers flow in their favour. Certain key implications are studied below.

Influencer-Based Digital Marketing

Now that the importance of social media and user-generated content has been understood in depth, travel companies need to include influencer-based marketing into their overall pro-motional strategy, which includes: approaching bloggers who have huge followings (Kladou and Mavragani, 2015); regularly undertake social media research on Facebook and Instgram to know about the content being generated for the travel destination, with the help of data analytics: following up current the travellers so that they post their travel stories along with hotel property pictures to enhance the social media presence by posting positive and engaging content during their travel; seek feedback after the trip and motivate travellers to post on their social media platforms for others to see; and many other such strategies that would lead to more positive outcome of the social media methods (Ladhari and Michaud, 2015).

Differentiation Focused Social Media Marketing

Consumers are influenced by the social media campaigns run by companies at the travel des-tination, as they enhance the reach and penetration of the services to the final audience (Pan and Li, 2011). It is very common for potential travellers to search for YouTube videos about the place, read reviews of even unknown people and strangers, ratings for properties given by earlier travellers, autonomous bodies that may be giving neutral evaluations, join community groups online where there are discussions about travel experiences, or even join some forums actively to get to know a place deeply before visiting (Luo and Zhong, 2015). Considering this aspect of consumer decision-making, a more differentiated effort by the travel companies operating in one destination needs to be undertaken so that they all speak the same language. Creating a uniform and consistent image and reputation can help in building the brand equity of the travel destination that can be meaningful for the global consumers irrespective of the country or the culture they belong to. Such success stories have been created by Australia, with the help of its natural wildlife and animal habitats; by the Maldives – romantic and perfect for couples; by India, for its heritage, history and culture (Mak, 2017). Thus it requires an integrated effort of both government and private travel bodies to create the right image over the online platforms so that consumers belonging to any part of the world can have the right impetus for taking their decisions.

ROLE OF SOCIAL MEDIA IN DARK TOURISM

Another very interesting and strange role played by social media is to provide information and entice the interest of travellers to places that are known for something negative or paranormal. This has been termed dark tourism, and builds upon the interest and excitement of the travellers due to the hidden mysteries about the place that builds up a hedonic need to visit and experience it themselves (Sotiriadis, 2017). Sometimes, the incidents related to the dark tourist places are linked to death, tragedy, war, assassinations, ghosts or paranormal activities, that attract people to flock to such places, or less-understood and mysterious locations such as the Bermuda triangle that are visited and read about for the excitement of the unknown. Dark tourism has increased gradually over the years, and today around 900 such place can be located in 112 countries that are regularly visited by tourists, to witness the place themselves and so listen to the actual story that took place there. The travelling reasons and actual decision-making behaviour of such travellers may fall into different categories (Stone, 2013). They may be just plain history buffs who wish to visit the site of battlefields, or maybe the location of the nuclear explosions in Japan, even mysterious places such as the Bermuda Triangle or the sites of the ghostly stories of Bhangarh in India. Categorizing the travellers into different segments based on their dark tourist behaviour can be a future area of research.

An immense amount of data has been generated on the social media sites about the dark tourist spots, which continue to attract visitors for motives including to acquire more knowledge about the place; to analyse what evil has been done in the place's history, such as ethnic cleansing or even nuclear explosions; and also to teach future generations about how the world has evolved (Mowatt and Chancellor, 2011). But it is for the consumer to decide the kind of dark tourist behaviour they wish to showcase online. With the current use of smartphones, many consumers pose smiling pictures with displays of dead bodies, such as the Egyptian mummies, which is considered very bad and inappropriate behaviour. In order to attract attention from their social group by posting novel content, many consumers cross the boundaries of demeaning the reputations of dark tourism spots, which deserve respect. Many videos on YouTube entice consumers to view more, read more and visit the dark tourism places, but the sanctity of the places and the events that took place there need to be maintained while sharing such content on social media platforms (Hooper and Lennon, 2016). Many countries have put certain restrictions on the bad behaviour of dark tourists, to avoid overtourism of such historically important places. Due to a rise in the number of travellers to dark places, the sustainability and natural beauty of the places are also at risk, such as the case of Colosseum in Rome, which is also one of the wonders of the world (Roberts and Stone, 2014).

Social media and the creation of online content influences dark tourism in two ways. First, the social media platforms are creating more awareness and visibility about such places through bloggers writing about them and also travellers sharing their experiences of how they felt at the places of tragedy or death (Isaac and Ashworth, 2011). Through sharing and content uploading on digital platforms, many new dark tourist spots have become very attractive to avid travellers. Hence there has been an increase in the number of travellers to these places, leading to more user-generated content (Miles, 2014). In the second kind of impact, more travellers visiting such places alone, in groups or with families, is leading to overtourism of these places, as they may be harmed by too many people visiting (Biran and Hyde, 2013). Many of these sites are old buildings and broken monuments that have become very delicate with the passage of time. These ruins of the old palaces are at the mercy of the travellers and the manner in which they behave. Thus the damage that is spoiling the nature-tourism quotient of such places is taking place at a rapid pace (Podoshen, 2013). Overtourism is also diminishing the exclusivity and uniqueness attached to the dark tourist places, due to the bad behaviour of people while making videos and taking selfies. For the love of social media contribution, many such places in the world are being both negatively and positively impacted (White and Frew, 2013).

MODEL DEVELOPMENT FOR TRUST AND EFFICACY OF SOCIAL MEDIA

Based on the above analysis and understanding about consumer behaviour in travel destination finalization, as influenced by social media, an academic model can be developed consisting of the various factors that play important roles (Chen et al., 2014). Trust on the social media sites and user-generated content can be evaluated on the basis of the framework in Figure 7.1.

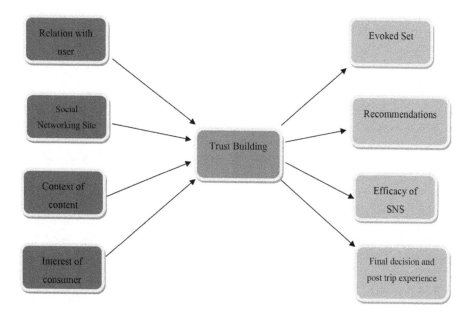

Figure 7.1   Model development

This construct provides a detailed understanding of the determining factors of trust as the outcome of the social media content that is posted by travellers during and post-trip. The main factors recognized to impact upon trust formation are: the relationship of the travellers with the people who are influenced by their social media posts, the social networking site, its content, and the interests of the potential travellers (Narangajavana et al., 2017). These are critical, as a close friend or relative's opinion would be trusted, with the closeness make an impact on the final decision. Similarly, the social media platform also has an important role; it is seen that Instagram has more impact than Facebook, due to the personal nature of the site (Di Pietro et al., 2012). The context of the content, whether in the form of picture, video, review or even a blog, also impacts upon trust among the consumers. These, combined with the actual interest or passion of the potential traveller, would convert into the actual trust that can be formed on the social media platforms.

Based on the trust that is developed, the influence which the UGC of a traveller has on others will have an impact on the decision of the travel destination, along with consideration of the locations each consumer has in mind that they would consider in making their final travel decision (Munar, 2012). Also the trust thus acquired would help in developing recommendations to others through sharing the posts with others in their group. This converts into opinion leadership gained by few consumers that impacts upon the decisions of others. Trust would also help in understanding the efficacy of the SNSs, that is, which social networking site is more trusted and genuine; which would also build future consumers (Sotiriadis, 2017). Marketers would also benefit from knowing the effectiveness of the social media platform while developing their travel marketing strategies for a particular destination to attract the consumers. Finally, the trust that is developed through the user-generated content results in the final decision to travel and in creating memories via post-trip sharing. The model or framework can be effectively used by both marketers and bloggers to create awareness about certain destinations that can attract potential travellers, thus creating a bigger community for the travellers who resort to social media for taking their decisions.

CONCLUSION AND WAY FORWARD

In order to summarize the analysis that has been undertaken in this chapter, certain key aspects need to be revisited that can help understand this phenomenon better. With the growing importance of social media and its impact on consumers of different products and services, knowing about the impact on tourism has become critical with the rise of domestic and international tourism opportunities. As travellers became more mobile, the tendency to regularly interact with their online community has become an important part of their travel experience. This has resulted in a huge amount of user-generated content on the various social networking sites, which is playing an important role in both informing and influencing other potential travellers to choose their next travel destination. But many concerns regarding the trust factor of these sites and the authenticity of the content have been raised, as the data falls into various categories. These have taken the form of pictures, videos, reviews, ratings, blogs, and so on. Also, the online community is vast, where people may not know each other that well, which again leads to concerns about trust and the efficacy of such sites in promoting wrong information. Hence, through the study, certain key factors have been identified that impact upon the trust in these social media sites with respect to the information being provided. The issues of dark tourism and overtourism have also been highlighted with respect to how social media content generates the interest of people in tragic and mysterious places, as information about such places all over the world is widely available. But this is leading to problem of overtourism of these places, with more visitors than they can manage. It also affects the natural balance of these places, with more consumers exhibiting bad tourist behaviour. Hence many concerns have been raised about the negative role that social media plays in dark tourist spots and in the overtourism of popular spots. A framework has been created to understand the impact of social media and user-generated content on travel decisions, that can be studied much more deeply to explore many other areas such as: the effectiveness of each SNS; categorizing consumers into different segments and analysing their travel decisions; creating consumer journey maps of experiences to understand the problems that arise for individual travellers and groups; and in the wake of the current pandemic, how the tourism industry would change, and how far social media reporting would play a role, also needs further investigation. Each subject area aims to bring together many aspects of study, along with providing new areas of research so that the field can continue to grow in the future, as well by evaluating the new issues that need to be discussed.

REFERENCES

Abubakar, A.M. (2016). Does eWOM influence destination trust and travel intention: a medical tourism perspective. *Economic Research – Ekonomska istraživanja, 29*(1), 598–611.

Abubakar, A.M., Ilkan, M., Al-Tal, R.M., and Eluwole, K.K. (2017). eWOM, revisit intention, destination trust and gender. *Journal of Hospitality and Tourism Management, 31*, 220–227.

Ayeh, J.K., Au, N., and Law, R. (2013). 'Do we believe in Tripadvisor?' Examining credibility perceptions and online travelers' attitude toward using user-generated content. *Journal of Travel Research, 52*(4), 437–452.

Biran, A., and Hyde, K.F. (2013). New perspectives on dark tourism. *International Journal of Culture, Tourism and Hospitality Research, 7*(3), 191–198.

Bronner, F., and De Hoog, R. (2011). Vacationers and eWOM: who posts, and why, where, and what? *Journal of Travel Research, 50*(1), 15–26.

Cantallops, A.S., and Salvi, F. (2014). New consumer behavior: a review of research on eWOM and hotels. *International Journal of Hospitality Management, 36*, 41–51.

Chen, Y.C., Shang, R.A., and Li, M.J. (2014). The effects of perceived relevance of travel blogs' content on the behavioral intention to visit a tourist destination. *Computers in Human Behavior, 30*, 787–799.

Chung, N., Han, H., and Koo, C. (2015). Adoption of travel information in user-generated content on social media: the moderating effect of social presence. *Behaviour and Information Technology, 34*(9), 902–919.

Chung, N., and Koo, C. (2015). The use of social media in travel information search. *Telematics and Informatics, 32*(2), 215–229.

Cox, C., Burgess, S., Sellitto, C., and Buultjens, J. (2009). The role of user-generated content in tourists' travel planning behavior. *Journal of Hospitality Marketing and Management, 18*(8), 743–764.

Di Pietro, L., Di Virgilio, F., and Pantano, E. (2012). Social network for the choice of tourist destination: attitude and behavioural intention. *Journal of Hospitality and Tourism Technology, 3*(1), 60–76.

Filieri, R., and McLeay, F. (2014). E-WOM and accommodation: an analysis of the factors that influence travelers' adoption of information from online reviews. *Journal of Travel Research, 53*(1), 44–57.

Ghose, A., Ipeirotis, P.G., and Li, B. (2012). Designing ranking systems for hotels on travel search engines by mining user-generated and crowdsourced content. *Marketing Science, 31*(3), 493–520.

González-Rodríguez, M.R., Martínez-Torres, R., and Toral, S. (2016). Post-visit and pre-visit tourist destination image through eWOM sentiment analysis and perceived helpfulness. *International Journal of Contemporary Hospitality Management, 28*(11), 2609–2627.

Hooper, G., and Lennon, J.J. (eds) (2016). *Dark Tourism: Practice and Interpretation*. Routledge.

Hvass, K.A., and Munar, A.M. (2012). The takeoff of social media in tourism. *Journal of vacation marketing*, *18*(2), 93–103.

Isaac, R.K., and Ashworth, G.J. (2011). Moving from pilgrimage to 'dark' tourism: Leveraging tourism in Palestine. *Tourism Culture and Communication*, *11*(3), 149–164.

Jalilvand, M.R., Samiei, N., Dini, B., and Manzari, P.Y. (2012). Examining the structural relationships of electronic word of mouth, destination image, tourist attitude toward destination and travel intention: an integrated approach. *Journal of Destination Marketing and Management*, *1*(1–2), 134–143.

Kiráľová, A., and Pavlíčeka, A. (2015). Development of social media strategies in tourism destination. *Procedia – Social and Behavioral Sciences*, *175*, 358–366.

Kladou, S., and Mavragani, E. (2015). Assessing destination image: an online marketing approach and the case of Tripadvisor. *Journal of Destination Marketing and Management*, *4*(3), 187–193.

Költringer, C., and Dickinger, A. (2015). Analyzing destination branding and image from online sources: a web content mining approach. *Journal of Business Research*, *68*(9), 1836–1843.

Ladhari, R., and Michaud, M. (2015). eWOM effects on hotel booking intentions, attitudes, trust, and website perceptions. *International Journal of Hospitality Management*, *46*, 36–45.

Lange-Faria, W., and Elliot, S. (2012). Understanding the role of social media in destination marketing. *Tourismos*, *7*(1), 193–211.

Leung, D., Law, R., Van Hoof, H., and Buhalis, D. (2013). Social media in tourism and hospitality: A literature review. *Journal of Travel and Tourism Marketing*, *30*(1–2), 3–22.

Lim, Y., Chung, Y., and Weaver, P.A. (2012). The impact of social media on destination branding: consumer-generated videos versus destination marketer-generated videos. *Journal of Vacation Marketing*, *18*(3), 197–206.

Lu, W., and Stepchenkova, S. (2015). User-generated content as a research mode in tourism and hospitality applications: topics, methods, and software. *Journal of Hospitality Marketing and Management*, *24*(2), 119–154.

Luo, Q., and Zhong, D. (2015). Using social network analysis to explain communication characteristics of travel-related electronic word-of-mouth on social networking sites. *Tourism Management*, *46*, 274–282.

Mak, A.H. (2017). Online destination image: comparing national tourism organisation's and tourists' perspectives. *Tourism Management*, *60*, 280–297.

Mendes-Filho, L., Mills, A.M., Tan, F.B., and Milne, S. (2018). Empowering the traveler: an examination of the impact of user-generated content on travel planning. *Journal of Travel and Tourism Marketing*, *35*(4), 425–436.

Milano, R., Baggio, R., and Piattelli, R. (2011, January). The effects of online social media on tourism websites. In *Information and Communication Technologies in Tourism 2011* (pp. 471–483), Vienna: Springer.

Miles, S. (2014). Battlefield sites as dark tourism attractions: an analysis of experience. *Journal of Heritage Tourism*, *9*(2), 134–147.

Mowatt, R.A., and Chancellor, C.H. (2011). Visiting death and life: dark tourism and slave castles. *Annals of Tourism Research*, *38*(4), 1410–1434.

Munar, A.M. (2012). Social media strategies and destination management. *Scandinavian Journal of Hospitality and Tourism*, *12*(2), 101–120.

Narangajavana, Y., Fiol, L.J.C., Tena, M.Á.M., Artola, R.M.R., and García, J.S. (2017). The influence of social media in creating expectations: an empirical study for a tourist destination. *Annals of Tourism Research*, *65*, 60–70.

Pan, B., and Li, X.R. (2011). The long tail of destination image and online marketing. *Annals of Tourism Research*, *38*(1), 132–152.

Podoshen, J.S. (2013). Dark tourism motivations: simulation, emotional contagion and topographic comparison. *Tourism Management*, *35*, 263–271.

Roberts, C., and Stone, P. (2014). Dark tourism and dark heritage: emergent themes, issues and consequences. In I. Convery, G. Corsane and P. Davis (eds), *Displaced Heritage: Dealing with Disaster and Suffering* (pp. 9–18), Boydell & Brewer.

Sigala, M., Christou, E., and Gretzel, U. (eds) (2012). *Social Media in Travel, Tourism and Hospitality: Theory, Practice and Cases*. Ashgate Publishing.

Sotiriadis, M.D. (2017). Sharing tourism experiences in social media: a literature review and a set of suggested business strategies. *International Journal of Contemporary Hospitality Management, 29*(1), 179–225.

Stepaniuk, K. (2015). The relation between destination image and social media user engagement–theoretical approach. *Procedia – Social and Behavioral Sciences, 213*, 616–621.

Stone, P. (2013). Dark tourism scholarship: a critical review. *International Journal of Culture, Tourism and Hospitality Research, 7*(3), 307–318.

Tsao, W.C., Hsieh, M.T., Shih, L.W., and Lin, T.M. (2015). Compliance with eWOM: the influence of hotel reviews on booking intention from the perspective of consumer conformity. *International Journal of Hospitality Management, 46*, 99–111.

White, L., and Frew, E. (eds) (2013). *Dark Tourism and Place Identity: Managing and Interpreting Dark Places*. London: Routledge.

Wilson, A., Murphy, H., and Fierro, J.C. (2012). Hospitality and travel: the nature and implications of user-generated content. *Cornell Hospitality Quarterly, 53*(3), 220–228.

Xiang, Z., and Gretzel, U. (2010). Role of social media in online travel information search. *Tourism Management, 31*(2), 179–188.

Ye, Q., Law, R., Gu, B., and Chen, W. (2011). The influence of user-generated content on traveler behavior: an empirical investigation on the effects of e-word-of-mouth to hotel online bookings. *Computers in Human behavior, 27*(2), 634–639.

Zainal, N.T.A., Harun, A., and Lily, J. (2017). Examining the mediating effect of attitude towards electronic words-of mouth (eWOM) on the relation between the trust in eWOM source and intention to follow eWOM among Malaysian travellers. *Asia Pacific Management Review, 22*(1), 35–44.

Zeng, B., and Gerritsen, R. (2014). What do we know about social media in tourism? A review. *Tourism Management Perspectives, 10*, 27–36.

Zouganeli, S., Trihas, N., and Antonaki, M. (2011). Social media and tourism: the use of Facebook by the European national tourism organizations. *Tourism Today, 11*, 110–121.

8. DMOs and social media: challenges and strategies to manage them

Mohamed E.A. Mohamed and Mahmoud M. Hewedi

INTRODUCTION

In the digital age, social networking has intensively penetrated daily life in diversified forms, presenting a challenge to those not responding to its rapid adoption. It has become the key platform for consumers to connect and interact with the world. The incredible increase in digital channels has led to a profound change in the marketers' practice. Additionally, this increase has resulted in the creation of online platforms, including social media, which affect consumer behavior and empower consumers to express their opinions freely and openly (Dedeoğlu et al., 2020; Munro and Richards, 2011). Tourism is one of the leading industries that have reacted to social media development (Uşaklı et al., 2017). Over the last two decades, social media has dramatically altered the interactions between visitors and destinations. There is no doubt that future success will depend on catching up with the accelerated developments in using and adapting to new, sophisticated technology. However, the digital arena has brought many changes that have a profound effect on marketing practices, leaving marketing practitioners with many challenges (Hays et al., 2013; Scott et al. 2017).

Social networking and the digital age has become fertile ground for researchers from different backgrounds, resulting in a remarkable number of published research articles and reports in many disciplines, including tourism and hospitality. Although social media adoption has witnessed a growing interest in tourism literature (Xiang and Gretzel, 2010; Gretzel et al., 2006), tourism research on social media use is still limited. Tourism research on social media usage focuses mainly on: (1) tourists' adoption of social media (tourist-generated content); and (2) social media practices and adoption by tourism organizations (Uşaklı et al., 2017). For example, Oh et al. (2004) reviewed 126 marketing articles from four tourism journals and found that more than a third of the reviewed articles (34.4 percent) mainly focused on examining traveler and consumer behavior, demonstrating a rapid advance of consumer behavior research in the discipline, compared to about 20 percent reported by Kotler at al. (1998). Hence, the use of social networking by destination marketing organizations (DMOs) responsible for tourism management and promotion remains mostly unknown (Uşaklı et al., 2017). Studies on how DMOs should adopt and react to social media marketing are limited.

Previous studies have introduced a few attempts to examine DMOs' utilization of social networking to market their destinations. Gonzalo (2012) identified five challenges facing tourism marketers on social media. Hays et al. (2013) later investigated how the ten most visited destinations have adopted social media in their marketing activities. They found that social media usage varies significantly among destinations. Uşaklı et al. (2017) investigated European DMOs' adoption of social networking and found that European DMOs utilize social networking as a traditional marketing tool instead of utilizing it as a consumer service to react to prospective tourist concerns. Harrigan et al. (2017) conducted research to study how customers engage with tourism brands on social networks. In general, previous studies suggest that social media adoption among DMOs remains mostly experimental, and that social media adoption varies from one destination to another.

Considering that the role of DMOs is to market and manage tourism at destinations, and that the nature of tourism marketing is rapidly changing, DMOs must react to these unprecedented changes in the digital environment (Scott et al., 2017; Okazaki and Taylor, 2013). Gretzel et al. (2006) reported that changes in consumer roles and the marketing environment are among the challenges facing destinations. Therefore, DMOs need to implement the appropriate approaches and use acceptable tools and techniques. For example, according to Chan and Guillet (2011), communicating and connecting with users represents a central problem for tourism providers, because ignorance or a late response to tourists' questions on social platforms means a provider displays poor attention to the customers, leading to potential business loss. Therefore, the DMOs that do not optimize social networking lack a significant edge. However, what is more detrimental than not evolving with social media development is using it in a deficient manner.

In response to this issue, this chapter takes a broader perspective to identify and discuss a set of social media challenges facing DMOs. This review connects to previous research and extends and updates the tourism literature by consulting state-of-the-art academic findings and innovative marketing practices in the tourism industry. A related aim is to provide DMOs with possibilities and guidelines to address these challenges and properly manage social media for tourism.

THE ROLE OF DMOs AND SOCIAL MEDIA

The World Tourism Organization identifies a DMO as the institution that brings tourism stakeholders together, including authorities, professionals, partners, and facilities partnerships within the tourism industry, to form a collective vision. The final target of a DMO is to promote and develop the destination via the management and coordination of core activities, including strategic planning, marketing, financing, and developing tourism products (UNWTO, 2010).

As a result of the competition in the tourism market, the DMO role is becoming more prominent in developing a destination and acting as a facilitator and catalyst in tourism development (Roque and Raposo, 2016). The role of the DMO has moved beyond promotion to include other tasks related to destination tourism success in the realm of destination sustainability and competitiveness (Gretzel et al., 2006). It is widely acknowledged that destination management is a crucial mission that maximizes tourist experience value while achieving local benefits. Successful destination administration ensures the destination's operational performance while building a competitive and robust identity (Roque and Raposo, 2016).

According to Mistilis et al. (2014), DMOs need to implement diverse social networking strategies to successfully engage and share with actual and prospective tourists at all stages of their trip, including before, during and after the trip. However, recent studies suggest that the adoption of information technologies and social platforms among DMOs is still low, even according to the top ten best-practice examples (Mistilis et al., 2014). DMOs need to acknowledge that marketing on social networks mainly relates to sharing, engaging, collaborating and interacting, instead of direct promotion and advertising (Shao et al., 2016). Many studies discuss the challenges brought about by the information age, which complicate the role

Table 8.1   Social media challenges facing DMOs

Challenge	Factors
Building an effective social media strategy	Integrating social platforms in marketing activities
	Having a specific and clear strategy for social media
	Identifying the goals for using social networks
	Identifying the target audience
	Choosing social media channels
	Deciding on the effective content
Measuring success in social media	Measuring return on investment (ROI) on social networks
	Identifying the best metrics to determine effectiveness on social media
	Finding new measures of success
Adjusting to reactive marketing management	Power shift to consumer
	Losing control of social media
	Managing customers' expectations
Managing customer engagement	Identifying the optimal ways to engage social media users
	Staying current on social media
	Managing consistency on social media
Adjusting to a changing marketing skill set	The need for advanced skills and capabilities
	Understanding privacy and security issues on social media
	Understanding legal risks on social media
	Protecting intellectual property on social media
Time allocation	Finding time to engage customers
	Finding time to produce high-quality content
	Managing existence across many social media platforms
Managing negative sentiment	Handling negative feedback on social media

of the DMO and cause the disintermediation and reintermediation of tourism distribution and information channels (Munar, 2012). Studies suggest that social media usage is influenced by many situational determinants, highlighting many challenges that face DMOs when dealing with social platforms as marketing tools. We have consulted the literature on social media adoption in general and social media in tourism studies to undertake this review and determine the most critical challenges facing DMOs in social media marketing. Based on this process, we have identified seven main challenges that affect DMOs' adoption of social networks (see Table 8.1). The following sections discuss these challenges and the possible solutions for DMOs to utilize social networking in destination marketing more effectively.

CHALLENGE ONE: BUILDING AN EFFECTIVE SOCIAL MEDIA STRATEGY

Among the numerous challenges facing DMOs, building an integrated social media strategy for marketing is the prime challenge (Paliwal, 2015). Munar (2012) investigated social media adoption among four destinations – Norway, Sweden, Finland and Denmark – and found that only one destination has a specific and precise social media strategy. According to Smarty (2019), 24 percent of social media marketers consider a lack of formal strategy their top challenge on social networks.

To achieve the outcomes intended from social media adoption, it is vital to develop a clear social media strategy that is effective at enhancing visitors' ability to maximize the adoption of social platforms in their information search and holiday-related activities (Pabel and Prideaux, 2016). The destination that fails to invest in social media within a strategic framework will lose opportunities to connect with current and potential visitors (Pabel and Prideaux, 2016). DMOs need answers for different issues of concern, including: how to associate their promotion activities with social networking; who is their target user; why sharing should be in place and with whom; what are the preferred platforms; what comes first, the channels or content; and how to generate content (Usakli et al., 2017). Collecting and incorporating customer feedback is also an issue of concern (Orajärvi, 2015).

Many studies have developed and proposed several approaches and frameworks to build an efficient social media strategy. According to Paliwal (2015), one of the most cited frameworks is proposed by Shields (2017). As shown in Figures 8.1, 8.2 and 8.3, this framework is realistic and straightforward and provides the main principles of building an operative social media management strategy. The Shields's (2017) framework emphasizes five main variables: goal, audience, content, channel and feedback. To construct an effective strategy for social media, the framework proposes that the first task is to decide on marketing goals. It then suggests moving to the other main variables: audience, content, channel and feedback. Based on users' feedback (achieving the strategic goals or not), the framework suggests iterating each variable as necessary (Figure 8.3). According to Shields (2017), the framework order may vary according to the targeted goals. For example, marketers could interchange the order of content and channel, because some businesses may need to identify the content before the channel. In cases where a business needs to interact with customers using images and videos, the content should be determined first, before the channel, because some channels may not fit the content in these formats. Shields (2017) suggested many questions to be answered under each variable of the framework to build a successful social media strategy, and they are as follows:

- Goals: Is the business targeting a new or existing audience? Is it aiming to reinforce the image of the brand or to change it? Is the business plan to use social networking for the short term (that is, launching a new service or product) or the long term (that is, as a tool for communicating the brand with the audience)? Does it search for customer engagement or customer conversation?
- Audience: When determining the social media audience, the organization should consider two fundamental questions: (1) Who is the key audience? and (2) Who is the audience most likely to receive social media messages?
- Content: What is the best content type to generate for the target users? Is it better to use image, text, audio or video? Which format receives higher engagement? How do you create this content? Should the business focus on quality, shareability, or both?
- Channel: Which channels should be utilized for the strategy to maximize its return on investment? Which platform is your audience active on? Should the business go for a platform with a broad audience that now faces a plateau in user growth (i.e., Facebook), or is it better to choose small but fast-growing platforms (i.e., Snapchat)?
- Feedback: How do you react promptly to feedback, and how do you analyze feedback and subsequently build on it? What are the metrics to measure social media feedback? How do you manage excessive or extreme feedback behavior? How do you use feedback to engage customers and build a better relationship with them?

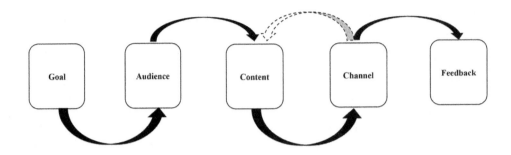

Source: Based on Shields (2017) and Paliwal (2015).

Figure 8.1   Social media strategy framework first phase: getting audience feedback and determining whether the strategy achieved the goals or not

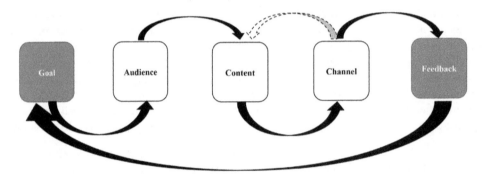

Source: Based on Shields (2017) and Paliwal (2015).

Figure 8.2   Social media strategy framework second phase: in case the strategy achieved its goals then continue building on the achieved results

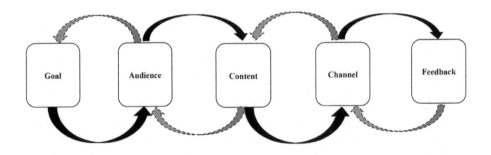

Source: Based on Shields (2017) and Paliwal (2015).

Figure 8.3   Social media strategy framework third phase: in case the strategy has not achieved the goals, make the necessary changes to the strategy variables

CHALLENGE TWO: MEASURING SOCIAL MEDIA SUCCESS

A main challenge businesses face using social networks relates to measuring the ROI, especially in the early phase of implementing social media strategies, or when deciding whether to use social media or not. According to Stelzner (2015), 88 percent of marketers lack awareness of how to measure investment returns on social platforms. Hays et al. (2013) proposed that DMOs are usually required to measure the effectiveness of their activities, suggesting that success on social platforms is often complicated to measure. DMOs are worried about the ROI on money and time, and how it pays off. Marketing via social media requires dealing with an enormous amount of qualitative data which comes with many challenges in its interpretation (Hays et al., 2013). The drivers of the critical value for measuring ROI as it relates to DMOs need to enhance their performance and better integrate social media in their marketing activities (Direction, 2012). Businesses that adopt ROI metrics to evaluate and measure their marketing activities usually gain advantages over their competitors and implement more successful marketing strategies (Direction, 2012).

To date, the metrics used to gauge social media are broad, including measuring engagement (likes or comment statistics), size of the audience (followers), reach (shares), sentiment (consumer feedback), and outcomes (resulting conversations and traffic) (Schetzina, 2010). Hays et al. (2013) specified three common metrics used by DMOs to assess their social media efforts: audience size, consumer engagement level and consumer sentiment. However, they found that most DMOs mainly depend on the audience size (for example, likes and followers on Facebook) and their increase in numbers. Other studies argue that quantitative metrics, such as customer sentiment and interactions, represent more effective ways of measuring ROI on social media because they require more engagement from the users (Hays et al., 2013; Orajärvi, 2015).

Studies suggest that to measure ROI on social networks, marketers need to first determine their goals, which will determine the metrics they should adopt to measure their success (Paliwal, 2015). For instance, in the early stages of social media usage, DMOs may be more concerned with increasing the reach of their brands. The statistics of users following them on their Facebook page might serve as an appropriate criterion. However, when the aim is to affect customer purchasing decisions, the number of followers may not be the right metric, because the number of followers does not represent potential customers (Hays et al., 2013). In his book *How to Measure Digital Marketing*, Flores (2013) suggests five fundamental principles to consider while selecting the metrics to measure ROI:

- The metrics should be consistent with the marketing strategy goals, which must be aligned with the overall strategy of the business. For example, if the DMO's goal is to achieve destination image awareness, measuring the number of likes on Facebook might be a useful metric.
- It should be actionable. An example of action measurement is to measure the "number of shares" to determine the brand reach.
- Limited in number: a large number of metrics might result in more confusion and might be challenging to implement. Thus, it is recommended to use a limited number of metrics.
- Metrics must be standardized. Once they are identified and accepted, it is easier for business partners to understand and follow them.

- Metrics must be simple. The metrics should be simple enough to follow and communicate without being simplistic, which might lead to losing relevant data or information that should be captured.

Finally, according to Gretzel et al. (2006), it is vital for DMOs to find new measures of success in the new digital era. The authors argue that DMOs need to take a leadership role in setting their targets and identifying the right benchmarks to compare the achieved results with, arguing that what constitutes a considerable success for one destination might reflect a weak performance for another.

CHALLENGE THREE: ADJUSTING TO REACTIVE MARKETING MANAGEMENT

As social media gains increased attention, customers acquire more authority and power, compared to a decline in marketers' and institutions' authority (Hofacker and Belanche, 2016). Regarding tourism, DMOs lack full control over the destination brand image. According to Gretzel et al. (2006), Web 2.0 allows the incorporation of the following five functions: representation of information, collaboration, communication, interactivity and transaction.

Social networking resulted in the presence of a massive amount of data created by users, requiring businesses to become reactive and nimble. DMOs are no longer in charge, and Internet accessibility makes it easy for users to continuously provide and demand information at any time and anywhere, while using various devices (Hofacker and Belanche, 2016). Social platforms are increasingly becoming a source of credible travel information because they are becoming the leading media through which tourists share travel-related information (Zeng and Gerritsen, 2014). Visitors are not passively watching the media any more, but are in charge of their pre- and post-trip process. Nowadays, users access content and engage in sharing and creating social media content that becomes more dynamic (Uşaklı et al., 2017). However, most DMOs remain static, losing the opportunity to learn about users through this dynamic interaction (Hays et al., 2013). DMOs usually face challenges with a lack of control and predictability when dealing with customers' behavior on social media (Lepkowska-White, 2017). Additionally, on social networks, customers have higher expectations and consequently they are not easily impressed (Jucan et al., 2013). DMOs also face the challenge of deciphering the real reasons behind users' comments and finding effective ways to react to them (Lepkowska-White, 2017).

Even though social networking content is difficult to control, DMOs can stimulate and monitor destination-related content (Hofacker and Belanche, 2016). Therefore, it is critical for DMOs to continually monitor what the audience is thinking and to collect feedback about destination marketing performance on social media (Moro and Rita, 2018). DMOs need to be actively present in social forums to comprehend how visitor interactions can affect the destination's reputation (Harrigan et al., 2017). DMOs will need to gather information about the social media channels they are utilizing, identify risk areas, develop counteractive plans and communicate them to the marketing staff. DMOs may take advantage of recent big data applications to process user-generated content for enhanced insight and decision-making (Ghani et al., 2019). This data can guide the communication between DMOs and users and help DMOs recognize any risks related to the destination image or reputation on social networks (Hofacker and Belanche, 2016). Dedicating skilled employees to communicate ethically and transparently with visitors and to monitor the online reputation of the destination is crucial to minimize the risks associated with a lack of control over social networks. Social platforms need to be employed as a customer service agent to actively respond to inquiries, criticisms and compliments (Uşaklı et al., 2017). Hence, there is an excellent opportunity to provide visitors with customized information that addresses their preferences and needs, thus building the basis for an open global marketing system that DMOs can use to mitigate the current challenges of tourism marketing (Zeng and Gerritsen, 2014).

CHALLENGE FOUR: MANAGING CUSTOMER ENGAGEMENT

Because visitors utilize social platforms to achieve many necessities, including utilitarian, hedonic, social and affective needs, DMOs need to employ better techniques to enhance travelers' engagement (Dedeoğlu et al., 2020). Some DMOs think that the biggest challenge of social networking relates to the negative feedback the destination might receive on social networks. While this is certainly worth addressing, the biggest challenge is if the DMOs create a social media presence and nobody participates (Boz and Unal, 2011). Most organizations, including DMOs, find it difficult to keep up with a constant online presence and to create relevant and engaging content (Lepkowska-White, 2017). Comments, shares and likes reflect the three common forms of user engagement on social platforms (Kaur et al., 2019). Studies have proven a positive relationship between user engagement on social platforms for a destination and the number of international arrivals to that destination (Uşaklı et al., 2017). In this way, an essential marketing capability is encouraging engagement (Hofacker and Belanche, 2016).

To effectively engage the audience on social networks, DMOs need to incorporate conventional marketing practices online, including customer service and personalized offers as well as approaching social media influencers and getting the benefit of users' innovation and creativity on social media (Hofacker and Belanche, 2016). Additionally, DMOs are required to frequently engage with the user-generated content (Abd-Elaziz et al., 2015) and recognize influential users (Erlandsson et al., 2016). Using interactive content and conversations, DMOs can build one-to-one relationships with users and increase engagement (Direction, 2012). Storytelling is another effective way to engage visitors on social media. Telling stories is about adding personal touches by tapping into the human elements of what makes the destination exceptional. Through sharing the story of the location and its locals and visitors, DMOs can break the monotony in users' feeds while building a sense of trust and loyalty (Lund et al., 2018).

Another way to engage customers is by creating fresh content daily to keep the audience's attention (Orajärvi, 2015). DMOs are required to be active, take part in online conversations and share with the community. They need to engage with the content, be humble about their position on social media, and behave informally when approaching users. It is valuable for DMOs to know whether the discussions on specific topics are hot, and to use them for engagement (Harrigan et al., 2017). According to Chi (2011), social media content should be user-centered, not message-centered. As a result, DMOs need to figure out how to spread their content in a new way to satisfy the customers' needs.

CHALLENGE FIVE: ADJUSTING TO A CHANGING MARKETING SKILL SET

Social media is causing a drastic increase in the complexity of DMOs' responsibilities (Uşaklı et al., 2017). Social media represents a new communication culture that challenges the traditional management structures of DMOs (Gretzel et al., 2006). According to Munar (2012), a lack of technical knowledge and little recognition of the benefits of social media represent a significant challenge for many DMOs. Those in charge of DMOs are required to recognize and understand the different marketing culture on social media and to be aware of the logic of these platforms and the skills needed to succeed on them. Social media requires a new organizational culture that facilitates open leadership and innovation (Munar, 2012). To respond appropriately to real-time interaction and marketing, DMOs need to behave accordingly by using real-time customer service. Additionally, they need to adopt openness, transparency and empowerment with the frontline marketing team (Gonzalo, 2012).

Social media requires proficient technology users. With the increased popularity of three-dimensional (3D) and virtual reality applications, and their use in social media marketing and content, the employees of DMOs need a new marketing skill set to use them effectively (Hofacker and Belanche, 2016). Therefore, the DMOs' social media employees must be carefully selected and should have unique attributes, experience and professional skills to lead the DMO through the ever-changing and dynamic online environment (Jucan et al., 2013). Employees responsible for social media marketing need to be trained and highly skilled in responding effectively to visitors' questions and complaints. They should manage and control negative sentiments before they reach thousands of people (Rugova and Prenaj, 2016). Marketing employees who are responsible for social media must be active and post engaging and high-quality content regularly to stay on the radar of their consumers (Rugova and Prenaj, 2016). This is important to help DMOs create continuous communication with their followers.

Additionally, the results of the social platforms' activities must be measured and controlled to determine and evaluate the effectiveness of the marketing strategy. However, digital data is not simple, clean and ready-to-analyze data. Digital data frequently consists of images, texts and videos. This means that marketers need advanced methodological skills to deal with this data and interpret the results (Hofacker and Belanche, 2016). Thus, DMOs need to hire skilled employees who can deal with specialized software for text mining and the automated extraction of information from pictures and videos.

Moreover, given that social networking raises new issues related to privacy, information security, intellectual property, ethics, and other possible lawful risks, DMO marketers should be highly educated and need to understand and follow carefully the legal rules of information technology before becoming involved in social media practices (Rugova and Prenaj, 2016). The social media team also needs to recognize the security and operational risks of the Internet. Security risks, such as viruses or spyware, represent threats that may lead to many financial risks (Kumar and Somani, 2018). Additionally, social media employees should be aware of intellectual property and media threats, and they should protect third-party rights and avoid publishing any false information or reviews (Rugova and Prenaj, 2016).

CHALLENGE SIX: TIME ALLOCATION

Allocating time for social media work represents a challenge for businesses and organizations (Rana and Kumar, 2016). According to Gonzalo (2014), more than 30 percent of destination marketers consider time management a critical problem on social media. Many DMOs find it challenging to allocate time for customer engagement and constant posting and interaction with visitors (Lepkowska-White, 2017). Promotions, offers and event descriptions need to be continuously updated to remain fresh, and many DMOs find it difficult to allocate enough time to keep up with these updates online (Peters et al., 2013). Additionally, high-quality posts and pictures require time to produce and write; however, DMOs may lack the time or expertise. Extending social media adoption to more than one platform requires more work to ensure consistency and coherency across social media channels (Lepkowska-White, 2017).

Most marketers report that they are always pinched for time to prioritize their efforts on social platforms. Marketers assume they need to spend hours updating their social media accounts to ensure they create an active online presence. However, this is not exactly true (Rana and Kumar, 2016). DMOs need to figure out the optimal posting frequency for targeted audiences, including the best day(s) and the right time(s) in the day to ensure the best audience interaction (Rana and Kumar, 2016). Based on this, DMOs may create an editorial calendar to organize their publications across all of the platforms administered by the organization. Additionally, DMOs should take advantage of social network management tools, such as Facebook scheduler and Hootsuite, to schedule their posts and tweets throughout the day. DMOs use websites such as TweetWhen.com to discover the best days and times to post on Twitter. Additionally, they can get a free summary of their social media activities using services such as Twitter Analytics to help them better organize their work on social media. Time management is a crucial social media challenge. However, being organized, using social media management tools and automating routine tasks are helpful techniques to overcome the challenge (Bhat, 2018).

CHALLENGE SEVEN: MANAGING NEGATIVE SENTIMENTS

Negative sentiments published on social media represent a challenge or at least an annoyance for marketers (Nee, 2016). While social media provides destinations with the chance to build destination awareness and customer loyalty, it involves dangers related to participating in public forums (Llodra-Riera et al., 2015). Social platforms facilitate the spread of customer complaints and negative post-purchase behaviors (Pfeffer et al., 2014). Whenever customers need to express their dissatisfaction with a service or product, they can easily say anything they want on social media platforms. As discussed previously, the lack of control and unpredictability, when faced with customer reactions, makes it difficult for social media marketers to manage online interactions with customers. Studies found that negative comments transfer more easily than positive comments (Tsugawa and Ohsaki, 2015). Additionally, studies have found that an online destination's image depends on the volume (number of comments) and valence (positive versus negative) of the comments shared online on different social platforms. Therefore, DMOs need to develop a clear strategy to deal with negative online comments.

According to Brandt (2013), to manage negative comments, businesses need to identify three variables: the reason (why), the audience (who), and the platform (where). Understanding the audience is significant, because users do not all have the same influence on social media platforms. Negative feedback from influential users can have a severe and damaging effect compared to users with low social media influence. Therefore, DMOs should handle the comments from these users promptly and prevent them from going viral because of their potential adverse effects (Paliwal, 2015). Understanding the reason for the complaint is essential because it helps the company identify the issue and resolve it. If it is a serious and genuine problem, then the company needs to take action to deal with it. Finally, knowing the social media channel of these interactions provides the company with a clear understanding of where it should first address the issue. Having a clear idea about who, where and why can help DMOs identify the best strategy to address negative feedback issues. Studies also suggest some tips that can help DMOs deal effectively with negative sentiments on social media (Paliwal, 2015; Nee, 2016; Baker, 2020):

- Do not ignore negative comments. This will give the dissatisfied customer additional reasons to continue their negative comments. Instead, customer feedback – positive, negative or neutral – should be used to connect with the followers and support the destination's image.
- Choose the best response. This can include apologizing and mortification, explaining the situation, reducing the offensiveness of the event, and taking corrective action.
- Personalize your message. Customers do not want automated replies. Instead, DMOs need to personalize their messages and show empathy when reacting to customer comments.
- Create brand advocates. It is more effective when other consumers support the destination and defend any critique by sharing positive impressions and experiences they have had with the destination.
- Respond on time. Timely responses are important to control negative feedback and to pacify complaining customers.
- Be proactive instead of reactive. DMOs need to appear open and approachable, and keep their eyes and ears open to avoid unfavorable situations.
- Consider another avenue for complaints. DMOs need to publicize the other customers' options to give feedback or complain.

In addition to these guidelines, DMOs need to acquire the appropriate resources and a skilled marketing team who can deal with the negative feedback and implement the appropriate strategies to do so.

CONCLUSION

Social networking has emerged as a cost-effective and a robust tool for global marketing reach. Concerning tourism marketing, social networks are becoming a vital information source for current and potential travelers (Uşaklı et al., 2017). This is easy to understand, because tourism services are usually considered high-risk products that are difficult to judge prior to consumption (Litvin et al., 2008). New information sources (for example, social networks) are increasingly being utilized to reduce the risks associated with tourism decisions (Litvin et al., 2008). However, most DMOs are still in the early stages of experimenting with and identifying how social networks can be utilized for destination marketing (Uşaklı et al., 2017; Hays et al., 2013). Most destination marketers simply move their conventional marketing efforts to social networks instead of harnessing the power of this new technology (Hays et al., 2013). With this research, we identify the main social media challenges for destination marketers and propose several recommendations and guidelines to overcome these challenges, aiming for better adoption of social networks in marketing tourism destinations.

The challenges identified in this review should be considered in light of the increased importance of social networks in the tourism and hospitality domain, specifically as a destination image-building tool. The increased importance of social platforms requires destinations to identify clear and specific strategies in their adoption and implementation of social media marketing, and the metrics they will use to measure the success of these strategies. Additionally, as social media empowers customers to create content and engage with the destination freely, DMOs should recognize the power shift to the consumer and behave accordingly. Instead of using social media to broadcast information, DMOs need to identify the optimal way to engage and interact with tourists before, during and after the trip to establish a long-lasting relationship. Apart from tourist interaction, DMOs should encourage users and followers to propagate positive feelings and opinions among their peers. Being prepared to deal with negative sentiments is more compelling than ever with social media. Thus, DMOs need to develop and identify strategies to promptly handle negative feedback. DMOs need to empower their marketing teams with the skills, time and resources to effectively manage their social media presence. Social media marketing requires advanced skills and capabilities.

DMOs must also address the specific social media challenges of their destinations. According to Hays et al. (2013), DMOs differ in their adaptation of social media, and every destination may face different challenges based on its situation and circumstances. Destinations should encourage research to identify their current position in regard to social media adaptation, and the optimal ways to maximize their opportunities and overcome challenges. Finally, DMOs need to consider that social media is still in the early development stages, particularly for tourism. Continuous evolution will lead to more issues and challenges for marketers. Tourism practitioners and scholars should strive to deal with the aforementioned challenges and be better prepared to tackle new challenges that are sure to come. Cooperation among DMOs and other destination stakeholders is also critical to fully take advantage of social media in destination management.

REFERENCES

Abd-Elaziz, M.E., Aziz, W.M., Khalifa, G.S., and Abdel-Aleem, M. (2015). Determinants of electronic word of mouth (EWOM) influence on hotel customers' purchasing decision. *International Journal of Heritage, Tourism, and Hospitality*, 9(2–2),194–223.

Baker, A. (2020). How brands handle negative comments on social media. Available at https://www.socialpilot.co/blog/negative-comments-social-media (accessed on 20 June 2020).

Bhat, U. (2018). Overcome 7 top social media marketing challenges. Available at https://www.cloohawk.com/blog/overcome-7-top-social-media-marketing-challenges (accessed on 1 July 2020).

Boz, M., and Unal, D. (2011, June). Successful promotion strategy in destination tourism marketing through social media; Queensland, Australia Case. In *Regional Science Conference with International Participation with the Theme Stable Local Development Challenges and Opportunities*, pp. 3–4.

Brandt, M. (2013). How to handle negative brand perceptions on social media. Available at https://www.cmswire.com/cms/customer-experience/how-to-handle-negative-brand-perceptions-on-social-media-022973.php (accessed on 20 June 2020).

Chan, N.L., and Guillet, B.D. (2011). Investigation of social media marketing: how does the hotel industry in Hong Kong perform in marketing on social media websites?. *Journal of Travel and Tourism
Marketing, 28*(4), 345–368.

Chi, H.H. (2011). Interactive digital advertising vs. virtual brand community: exploratory study of user
motivation and social media marketing responses in Taiwan. *Journal of Interactive Advertising, 12*(1),
44–61.

Dedeoğlu, B.B., van Niekerk, M., Küçükergin, K.G., De Martino, M., and Okumuş, F. (2020). Effect
of social media sharing on destination brand awareness and destination quality. *Journal of Vacation
Marketing, 26*(1), 33–56.

Direction, S. (2012). New media needs new marketing: social networking challenges traditional
methods. *Strategic Direction, 28*(6), 24–27.

Erlandsson, F., Bródka, P., Borg, A., and Johnson, H. (2016). Finding influential users in social media
using association rule learning. *Entropy, 18*(5), 164.

Flores, L. (2013). *How to Measure Digital Marketing: Metrics for Assessing Impact and Designing
Success.* London: Palgrave Macmillan.

Ghani, N.A., Hamid, S., Hashem, I.A.T., and Ahmed, E. (2019). Social media big data analytics:
a survey. *Computers in Human Behavior, 101*, 417–428.

Gonzalo, F. (2012). The five challenges of social media management in tourism. Available at
http://fredericgonzalo.com/2012/05/01/the-five-challenges-of-social-mediamanagement- in-tourism/
(accessed on 12 June 2020).

Gonzalo, F. (2014). Social media challenges in destination marketing. Available at https://fredericgonzalo
.com/en/2014/07/31/social-media-challenges-in-destination-marketing/ (accessed on 1 July 2020).

Gretzel, U., Fesenmaier, D.R., Formica, S., and O'Leary, J.T. (2006). Searching for the future: challenges faced by destination marketing organizations. *Journal of Travel Research, 45*(2), 116–126.

Harrigan, P., Evers, U., Miles, M., and Daly, T. (2017). Customer engagement with tourism social media
brands. *Tourism Management, 59*, 597–609.

Hays, S., Page, S.J., and Buhalis, D. (2013). Social media as a destination marketing tool: its use by
national tourism organisations. *Current Issues in Tourism, 16*(3), 211–239.

Hofacker, C.F., and Belanche, D. (2016). Eight social media challenges for marketing managers. *Spanish
Journal of Marketing – ESIC, 20*(2), 73–80. https://www.academia.edu/20766156/How_Marketers
_Are_Using_Social_Media_to_Grow_Their_Businesses_M_A_Y_2_0_1_5.

Jucan, M., Jucan, C., and Rotariu, I. (2013, January). "The social destination": how social media influ-
ences the organisational structure and leadership of DMOs. In *Proceedings of World Academy of
Science, Engineering and Technology*, No. 78, p. 1410. World Academy of Science, Engineering and
Technology (WASET).

Kaur, W., Balakrishnan, V., Rana, O., and Sinniah, A. (2019). Liking, sharing, commenting and reacting
on Facebook: User behaviors' impact on sentiment intensity. *Telematics and Informatics, 39*, 25–36.

Kotler, P., Bowen, J., and Makens, J. (1998). *Marketing for Hospitality and Tourism.* Upper Saddle
River, NJ: Prentice, Hall International.

Kumar, S., and Somani, V. (2018). Social media security risks, cyber threats and risks prevention
and mitigation techniques. *International Journal of Advanced Research in Computer Science and
Management, 4*(4), 125–129.

Lepkowska-White, E. (2017). Exploring the challenges of incorporating social media marketing strategies in the restaurant business. *Journal of Internet Commerce, 16*(3), 323–342.

Litvin, S.W., Goldsmith, R.E., and Pan, B. (2008). Electronic word-of-mouth in hospitality and tourism
management. *Tourism Management, 29*(3), 458–468.

Llodra-Riera, I., Martínez-Ruiz, M.P., Jiménez-Zarco, A.I., and Izquierdo-Yusta, A. (2015). Assessing the
influence of social media on tourists' motivations and image formation of a destination. *International
Journal of Quality and Service Sciences, 7*(4), 458–482.

Lund, N.F., Cohen, S.A., and Scarles, C. (2018). The power of social media storytelling in destination
branding. *Journal of Destination Marketing and Management, 8*, 271–280.

Mistilis, N., Buhalis, D., and Gretzel, U. (2014). Future eDestination marketing: perspective of an
Australian tourism stakeholder network. *Journal of Travel Research, 53*(6), 778–790.

Moro, S., and Rita, P. (2018). Brand strategies in social media in hospitality and tourism. *International
Journal of Contemporary Hospitality Management, 30*(1), 343–364.

Munar, A.M. (2012). Social media strategies and destination management. *Scandinavian Journal of Hospitality and Tourism*, *12*(2), 101–120.

Munro, J. and Richards, B. (2011). "The digital challenge," in Morgan, N., Pritchard, A. and Pride, R. (eds), *Destination Brands*, 3rd edn. Oxford: Butterworth-Heinemann, pp. 141–154.

Nee, I. (2016). *Managing Negative Word-of-Mouth on Social Media Platforms*. Bremen: Springer Gabler Verlag.

Oh, H., Kim, B.Y., and Shin, J.H. (2004). Hospitality and tourism marketing: recent developments in research and future directions. *International Journal of Hospitality Management*, *23*(5), 425–447.

Okazaki, S., and Taylor, C.R. (2013). Social media and international advertising: theoretical challenges and future directions. *International Marketing Review*, *30*(1), 56–71.

Orajärvi, P. (2015). Use of social media as a part of organizations marketing strategy: opportunities, challenges and solutions. Bachelor's thesis, University of Oulu, Finland.

Pabel, A., and Prideaux, B. (2016). Social media use in pre-trip planning by tourists visiting a small regional leisure destination. *Journal of Vacation Marketing*, *22*(4), 335–348.

Paliwal, G. (2015). Social media marketing: opportunities and challenges. Doctoral dissertation, Massachusetts Institute of Technology.

Peters, K., Chen, Y., Kaplan, A.M., Ognibeni, B., and Pauwels, K. (2013). Social media metrics – a framework and guidelines for managing social media. *Journal of interactive marketing*, *27*(4), 281–298.

Pfeffer, J., Zorbach, T., and Carley, K.M. (2014). Understanding online firestorms: negative word-of-mouth dynamics in social media networks. *Journal of Marketing Communications*, *20*(1–2), 117–128.

Rana, K.S., and Kumar, A. (2016). Social media marketing: opportunities and challenges. *Journal of Commerce and Trade*, *11*(1), 45–49.

Roque, V., and Raposo, R. (2016). Social media as a communication and marketing tool in tourism: an analysis of online activities from international key player DMO. *Anatolia*, *27*(1), 58–70.

Rugova, B., and Prenaj, B. (2016). Social media as marketing tool for SMEs: opportunities and challenges. *Academic Journal of Business*, *2*(3), 85–97.

Schetzina, C. (2010). *Introduction to Social Media Analytics*. New York: PhoCusWright.

Scott, P., Scott, T., Stokes, P., Moore, N., Smith, S.M., et al. (2017). The consumer journey in the digital age: the challenges faced by destination and place marketing agencies. *International Journal of Digital Culture and Electronic Tourism*, *2*(1), 28–45.

Shao, J., Li, X., Morrison, A.M., and Wu, B. (2016). Social media micro-film marketing by Chinese destinations: the case of Shaoxing. *Tourism Management*, *54*, 439–451.

Shields, B.R. (2017). *Social Media Management: Persuasion in Networked Culture*. Oxford: Oxford University Press.

Smarty, A. (2019). How to engage customers on social with brand storytelling. Available at https://sproutsocial.com/insights/brand-storytelling/ (accessed on 1 July 2020).

Stelzner, M.A. (2015). How marketers are using social media to grow their businesses. *Social Media Marketing Industry Report*. Available at https://www.tractionwise.com/wp-content/uploads/2021/06/Industry-Report-2021-Final.pdf.

Tsugawa, S., and Ohsaki, H. (2015, November). Negative messages spread rapidly and widely on social media. In *Proceedings of the 2015 ACM on Conference on Online Social Networks*, pp. 151–160.

UNWTO (2010). Survey on destination governance – evaluation report. Madrid: World Tourism Organization

Uşaklı, A., Koç, B., and Sönmez, S. (2017). How "social" are destinations? Examining European DMO social media usage. *Journal of Destination Marketing and Management*, *6*(2), 136–149.

Xiang, Z., and Gretzel, U. (2010). Role of social media in online travel information search. *Tourism Management*, *31*(2), 179–188.

Zeng, B., and Gerritsen, R. (2014). What do we know about social media in tourism? A review. *Tourism Management Perspectives*, *10*, 27–36.

9. Online destination image and user-generated content

Heather Skinner

INTRODUCTION

People travel to visit places for many different reasons, such as for business (Byrne and Skinner, 2007), city breaks (Maitland and Ritchie, 2009), culture and heritage (Smith and Richards, 2012), ecotourism (Boyd and Butler, 1996), health (Connell, 2006) and well-being (Skinner and Soomers, 2019), for voluntary work (Hawkin et al., 2005) and even for sex (Ryan and Kinder, 1996). For many, a vacation quite simply offers the chance to escape from their ordinary everyday life (Williams and Lew, 2015).

What motivates choice of destination, though, tends to be based upon the way a place is portrayed and the image people have of it (Choi et al., 2007). Destination image (DI) comprises the beliefs, ideas and impressions that are formed from an individual's encounters with a range of communications delivered and received across a range of channels (Crompton, 1979). As explained by Tasci and Gartner (2007), 'image formation is defined as a construction of a mental representation of a destination on the basis of information cues delivered by the image formation agents and selected by a person'. Such 'information cues' can be delivered as marketing communications campaigns and materials created by formal 'image formation agents' such as national, regional, or local government agencies, often through an official body such as a destination management organisation (DMO). People can also develop an image of a destination based on the way it is portrayed via informal channels such as in films or television programmes (Skinner, 2016; Williams-Burnett et al., 2016), or in print media (Gabbioneta and De Carlo, 2019), and from friends, family and others offering positive word-of-mouth about a destination from their own experiences (Greaves and Skinner, 2010).

However, 'due to the increasing importance of digital information and its effect on the image formation process ... a rethinking is required into the role of information agents in shaping destination images' (Greaves and Skinner, 2010). According to Kislali et al. (2016) 'the role of the social media and user-generated content in DI formation is an area that needs to be further investigated' as a matter of urgency, yet few studies have been undertaken thus far (Taecharungroj, 2019).

DESTINATION IMAGE FORMATION

The traditional view of destination image formation is that it comprises a number of stages and is formed from an individual's encounters with various clearly differentiated image formation sources (Gartner, 1993; Echtner and Ritchie, 1991; Fakeye and Crompton, 1991; Gunn, 1972). The overall destination image, be that positive or negative (Frias et al., 2007), includes not only the actual knowledge and beliefs an individual has (the cognitive aspect of DI formation) but also the feelings they have about the place (the affective aspect) (Greaves and Skinner, 2010). Tourists visit destinations because of the image they have of them (Kavaratzis, 2005). However, images are rarely developed completely from scratch. Scholars and practitioners must understand what images are already held 'in order to effect any desired changes to the image of the destination in the perceptions of actual and potential visitors' (Greaves and Skinner, 2010). Anholt (2008) therefore stresses that a place's brand image comes first, and that the branding of a place, which concerns the activities undertaken to alter the image as required, comes later.

Although various authors have termed the stages of the DI formation process differently, in general DI formation comprises 'induced images', 'organic images' and 'complex images'. 'Induced images' are from exposure to information about a destination derived from the destination's official marketing and promotional material.

'Organic images' are formed through encounters with less formal sources such as friends, family, film, television, literary works and, increasingly, online and social media (Munar, 2011). Organic information sources also tend be perceived as more unbiased and objective than those sources inducing information, and popular media and social media can project very influential images of a destination (Govers, 2011). Marine-Roig and Clavé (2015) note that not only is user-generated content (UGC) on social media deemed to be trustworthy, but also it can be usefully harnessed for strategic destination marketing and branding. For example, a more developed understanding of the way social media influences destination image formation can be useful to smaller places whose DMOs do not have large promotional budgets, and even more importantly to destinations that have no DMO or formal agencies responsible for their promotion. 'Complex images', the final DI formation stage, are completed following a first-hand visit to the destination.

Gartner (1993) has unpacked the DI formation process into eight possible information sources, each relating to a distinct stage of image formation. Whereas Gunn (1972) originally used the terms 'induced' and 'organic' image, he refers to the final stage, actual visitation to a destination, as 'modified induced'. This chapter uses the terms adopted by Fakeye and Crompton (1991), who similarly refer to the induced and organic stages, but refer to actual visitation as forming a complex image. UGC on social media would appear to fall within the organic information stage, although, as will be explained later in this chapter, the issue of UGC on DI formation is not actually that simple to categorise.

DESTINATION IDENTITY AND IMAGE CREATION

The creation and communication of a desired destination identity is usually seen as a place branding activity that is undertaken from the inside out (Skinner, 2008) by those formally charged with such a task, such as a government agency or DMO. Destination image differs from identity, and is that which is perceived by others externally (Taecharungroj, 2019), from the outside in (Skinner, 2008), formed from all of the induced, formal or official sources, and the organic or informal sources, of information they encounter about a destination. Whilst this distinction is made here, elsewhere 'the branding literature does not always clearly state the distinction between the brand (identity) and its perception (image)' (Merkelsen and Rasmussen, 2016), nor do tourists themselves always distinguish between these constructs (Skinner, 2017). At its heart, place brand identity considers the very essence of what places are (Skinner, 2011): 'an objective thing: it is what the place is actually like' (Taecharungroj, 2019). This identity exists regardless of marketing efforts, although it is also understood that place identity can be created or re-created for branding purposes (Skinner, 2011).

Projected Destination Image

Hunter (2012) explains 'destination image theory … as the generic term for complex relationships between imagery, projected destination image and perceived destination image'. Projected destination image is usually defined as 'the image that is actively and purposively promoted by destination marketers' (Kislali et al., 2020), and 'the strategy of generating a singular and iconic representation of a place or a showcase of ideal features' (Hunter, 2012). This would seem to place such efforts as being from formal induced sources. Kislali et al. (2020) compare the projected image with the perceived image of the destination that is formed in the minds of the promotional campaign's target audiences. However, the term 'projected image' has been broadened to also include the image communicated by organic sources – for example, in film and television, travel writing, and so on – hence the boundaries between formal official induced and informal organic images are becoming increasingly blurred, especially in the online and social media environment.

Moreover, while the DMO or tourism authority continues to be identified as the owner of the destination brand identity creation process in the extant literature, Kavaratzis (2004) has identified a number of elements of the projected destination image over which marketers do and do not actually have control. This lack of control, also identified by Bing et al. (2007) who explored the issue in relation to travel blogging, leads to strong recommendations for DMOs to track what is being posted about a destination across social media (Liu et al., 2015). Kislali et al. (2020) conclude that while the use of social media can help DMOs promote a projected image that contributes to the formal, officially induced image creation of the destination, UGC itself remains related only to the image and not to the identity of a destination, and thus should remain categorised only as a source of organic image.

There do appear to be some challenges to traditional DI formation theory. Govers et al. (2007) believe that, nowadays, 'image formation is no longer a one-way "push" process of mass communication, but a dynamic one of selecting, reflecting, sharing, and experiencing'. Ketter and Avraham (2012) go so far as to contend that UGC and social media are so revolutionary that not only should we consider where they fit with traditional theories, but also we should consider the extent to which these traditional models and theories even remain relevant in this new media landscape. Another issue that suggests traditional models may require rethinking surrounds the posts of social media influencers, which have been 'underexplored in the marketing and branding literature' (Jin and Muqaddam, 2019). Questions here are based on whether such influencers should be categorised as induced or organic sources, with the images they project online and in social media seen as contributing to destination brand identity creation (more traditionally seen only as the role of the DMO or government agency), or whether this type of UGC should remain categorised as relating solely to image creation and not identity (Kislali et al., 2020).

ONLINE AND SOCIAL MEDIA

According to a recent typology, social media are 'not limited to social networks like Facebook but include blogs, business networks, collaborative projects, enterprise social networks, forums, microblogs, photo sharing, product/services reviews, social bookmarking, social gaming, video sharing, and virtual worlds' (Aichner and Jabob, 2015). Xiang and Gretzel (2010) believe that online and social media are 'playing an increasingly important role as information sources for travelers', leading them to predict that UGC 'will challenge the established marketing practices of many tourism businesses and destinations'. However, Schaffer (2015) has recognized that many small and medium-sized tourism businesses lack the skills to engage fully with social media. Moreover, Hays et al.'s (2013) research concluded that there was not even any real consistency in the ways that DMOs use social media. That so much content on social media is generated by its users, 'highlights the need for businesses to know how to effectively respond in an environment where people can speak so freely' (Schaffer, 2015). However, much of the relevant extant literature tends to consider the role and use of online and social media by tourism service providers, rather than focusing on the way tourists themselves use such platforms (Liang et al., 2017).

Over 4.5 billion people globally use the internet. Social media users worldwide have recently been counted to number over 3.8 billion. 'Nearly 60 percent of the world's population is already online, and trends suggest that more than half of the world's total population will use social media by the middle of this year' (Chaffey, 2020).

While various social media platforms, especially visually based platforms such as Instagram and new short-form mobile video sharing platforms such as TikTok, are gaining in popularity, Facebook continues to be the most popular, has the most daily active users, and the highest engagement when considering the amount of time on which users are active (Chaffey, 2020). 'Social media users are now spending an average of 2 hours and 24 minutes per day multinetworking across an average of 8 social networks and messaging apps' (ibid.).

A recent report by Kepios (cited in Chaffey, 2020) based on data obtained as at 25 January 2020 identifies the top 15 social media platforms:

1. Facebook.
2. YouTube.
3. WhatsApp.
4. Facebook Messenger.
5. Weixin / WeChat.
6. Instagram.
7. Douyin / TikTok.
8. QQ.
9. QZone.
10. Sina Weibo.
11. Reddit.
12. Snapchat.
13. Twitter.
14. Pinterest.
15. Kuaishou.

Different platforms have different user demographics, and some are more popular in certain countries than others. This chapter will focus on Facebook, Tripadvisor, Instagram and Twitter, because these are most closely related to the focus of considering destination image in a tourism context in the online and social media environment.

Facebook

Facebook remains highly popular 'and its user base is the most broadly representative of the population as a whole' (Chaffey, 2020), even though is in decline as a social media platform used by young people. Most businesses post on Facebook less than twice each day. Posts that include photographs gain much higher user engagement than posts comprised only of text. Live videos gain even higher engagement rates than still photographs; the next-highest engagement rates are for pre-recorded videos, then posts containing links, with the lowest engagement rates for simple text-based status updates. The highest levels of interaction on Facebook seem to be gained if an organisation posts only once each day, with the best engagement found around midweek at midday (Chaffey, 2020). Facebook has been used successfully as a way to motivate 'customers to participate with organisations and encourage co-creation of customer value' (Hoksbergen and Insch, 2016). However, DMOs, tourism service providers and individuals have the ability to set up Facebook profiles, pages and groups, to post comments, pictures, videos and reviews, and also to share posts from others across a range of profiles, groups and pages. A recent study that examined the photographic images posted across online and social media representing the Holy Saturday celebrations on the Greek island of Corfu (Skinner, 2018) found that many of the same images were shared across a number of Facebook pages and groups, and moreover, because of this, it would be difficult for a potential tourist to establish whether an image originated from a private individual, an individual acting in a professional capacity, from a public sector organisation such as the municipality, or from a tourism service business. This therefore leads to questions as to whether destination identity creation and communication should remain to be seen as a construct owned exclusively by DMOs or other government agencies, especially because the projected destination image in this case was not only overwhelmingly positive, but was also consistent, regardless of the type of person or organisation that was creating the original post.

When negative posts are shared, they can definitely impact on a potential traveller's image of a holiday destination. For example, between 2016 and 2018 across the island of Corfu there were problems when the public rubbish bins were not being emptied and were overflowing. There were many status updates and images shared publicly on Facebook that could be seen by others across the world. A typical example Facebook post from a tourist who had returned from the island states as follows: 'the experience that we had traveling through Corfu town to the airport was something that will stay in my memory for a long time. The mountains of rubbish are far worse than two weeks ago and they stink, you could smell it on the coach.'

This can lead to the formation of a negative destination image of Corfu based upon these organic image formation sources, which, as has already been stated, tend to be considered as more trustworthy than posts from induced sources (Marine-Roig and Clavé, 2015). Potential tourists were posting statuses on resort-based Facebook groups seeking reassurance because they had started to form an unfavourable image of the island; for example: 'can anyone tell me more about the horrendous rubbish issues that I've heard about Corfu having? rats and flies and piles of rubbish all over because their landfill is full', and 'heard people say that Corfu is really dirty, please reassure me'.

Mistreatment of animals, and the high number of free-roaming street dogs and feral cats found in vacation destinations across the Mediterranean, can also help form negative destination images. Tourists post and share photographs and statuses across Facebook about abandoned puppies, dogs, kittens and cats; indeed, animal welfare issues in general receive high levels of engagement when posted on social media. Animal welfare charities also post across these media, and their existence not only contributes to the formation (negative or positive) of others' image of a destination, but also these organizations can raise funds by promoting fundraising events, and raise funds directly through this platform from residents, visitors and indeed from potential visitors (Popescu et al., 2017).

Furthermore, the boundaries are becoming blurred between what is defined as online media and what is defined as social media. For example, a social media user may share a story about a vacation destination across their network that may have been posted in the online version of a newspaper where it may originally have appeared in print; or social media users may use hashtags to join in a conversation on social media during or after the airing of a location-based television programme, which itself may have been viewed when transmitted or even at a later date (sometimes years later) via an online platform such as YouTube (Williams-Burnett et al., 2016). The impact of stories and news articles on destination image formation has been investigated by Gabbioneta and De Carlo (2019). They compare news articles, which they term 'autonomous image formation agents', with 'word-of-mouth and destination experience' posts originating from organic image formation agents, and also with posts from induced agents that comprise the destination's formal promotional material (Gabbioneta and De Carlo, 2019). Interestingly, Gabbioneta and De Carlo categorise blogs as organic information agents, yet all other news media are categorised as autonomous agents even when their content is communicated online. Whilst the 2020 COVID-19 pandemic has generated vast amounts of tourism-related content globally across a wide range of online and social media, returning to Corfu, a widely shared news item, reported in both offline and online press, has informed the world that one of the island's beaches is, at the time of writing, the second-safest in Europe for tourists to visit this year (Corfu Today, 2020). Moreover, online and social media have also reported successful resolution to the rubbish situation, along with the establishment of grassroots recycling points across the island, and the efforts of animal welfare charities and the municipality in dealing with free-roaming animals, including setting up food and water stations in Corfu town during the period of lockdown.

Tripadvisor

Tripadvisor is accessed by around 456 million people each month, and the platform hosts around 660 million travel and place-based reviews. The ethos behind such reviews now dominating the 'reputation economy' is altruistic, with those who post positive or negative reviews stating that they do so in order to assist other travellers with their decision-making. As well as Tripadvisor being perceived as akin to an online guestbook, where guests can write about good and bad experiences at particular accommodation, there are also many forums where actual and potential tourists may discuss various issues about specific resorts and destinations (Kinstler, 2018). When considering destination brand and reputation management, 'places and their stakeholders have a choice: they can either explicitly seek to manage these processes or leave the processes to run their own course' (Hanna and Rowley, 2011), and tripadvisor is one such platform where this course may run. Tripadvisor also takes up causes, such as animal welfare, that impact on destination image; for example, announcing in 2016 that the platform would no longer sell tickets 'for specific tourism experiences where travelers come into physical contact with captive wild animals or endangered species' (Popescu et al., 2017).

Instagram

User 'engagement rates are significantly higher on Instagram compared to Facebook, but there tend to be fewer posts per day' (Chaffey, 2020). The highest engagement rates on Instagram are for 'carousel' posts (posts containing multiple images, including video and still photographs, rather than a single image); and then still images, with the lowest engagement rates for posts containing only a single video. The highest engagement is for posts made midweek between midday and 3 p.m. (Chaffey, 2020).

Whilst selfies are posted across a range of social media, the phenomenon of selfies and other photographs taken at 'Instagrammable' locations can also contribute to destination image formation, as the following examples show. This is in part due to the ability of individuals to geotag the posts and photographs they share on Instagram (and indeed on Facebook) to a specific location or attraction. This can have a direct impact on increasing visitation to places made popular by these social influencers, which can be much more effective in this respect than the induced communications of DMOs. However, the following examples also show that such influence is not without its problems:

- Pavement cafes have been forced to close along Hanoi's famous Train Street, where the single-track trains run perilously close to visiting tourists, due to the influx of so many visitors that the street has become unsafe (Chang, 2019).
- Tenbarge (2019) cites 15 examples of 'destinations Instagram has helped ruin'. As he explains: 'Instagrammers with large followings take pictures at beautiful, previously unheard of or rarely visited locations. People see the likes and the natural beauty and swarm to the streets, parks, cliffs, fields, and more. Sometimes, places end up worse off in the face of new visitors. Sometimes, disasters occur. Of the hot new travel destinations discovered through Instagram, these 15 spots have been ruined, desecrated, or even closed down permanently thanks to a barrage of photo-takers'.

  – Residents of the tree-lined Broadacres area of Houston, Texas, have placed signs asking that no photographs be taken, and warning Instagrammers to stay off their private property.
  – Residents of the picturesque Parisian Rue Crémieux have requested that gates be installed to restrict access from Instagrammers.
  – The colourful Choi Hung public housing development in Hong Kong is also a popular Instagrammable location, but residents are not so keen on being photographed.
  – Photographs of overcrowded narrow streets are affecting the destination image of the Greek island of Santorini.
  – Venice is literally sinking under the weight of the number of visitors it attracts each year.
  – #poppynightmare was used to describe the hordes of visitors who had come to photograph the orange poppies growing at Lake Elsinore, California, where in one week-

end alone, over 66 000 visitors flocked to the town.
–   Even though Bogle Seeds sunflower farm in Ontario, Canada, had started charging people to photograph their sunflower fields, the family finally shut their doors to visitors completely after receiving far too many visitors to cope with.
–   Similarly, while many lavender farmers in England also charge Instagrammers who want to photograph the lavender fields, they are also suffering from overtourism.
–   Instagrammers photographing Delta Lake in Wyoming have been asked to stop geo-tagging the location, with the Jackson Hole Travel and Tourism board issuing posters containing messages such as 'Tag locations responsibly' and 'How many likes is a patch of dead wildflowers worth?'
–   Banff National Park in Canada has had to enforce temporary closures due to the sheer numbers of visitors it has attracted.
–   Horseshoe Bend in the Grand Canyon has had new visitor control measures put in place due to overcrowding from people taking photographs.
–   A Justin Bieber music video that was filmed at Iceland's Fjaðrárgljúfur canyon drew so many visitors that the canyon had to close due to damage being caused to the natural environment. The video had attracted over 448 million online views.
–   Tourists in Yellowstone National Park are at risk when they attempt to get too close to the Park's wildlife in order to get the best possible photographs.
–   People are also literally dying for the perfect photograph, such as the tourist who fell to his death on the mountain pass of Trollstigen in Norway.
–   A widely shared photograph on social media even showed a long line of climbers attempting to reach the summit of Mount Everest. The Chinese government is attempting to limit travelers to only those who have one of the 300 annually issued official climbing permits, but over 8 tons of rubbish was found at the Tibetan base camp that attracts over 40 000 visitors each year.

Twitter

Higher levels of engagement are likely to be gained from multiple rather than single postings on this platform (Chaffey, 2020). However, full engagement in two-way interactivity of tourism businesses and/or DMOs with their target audiences is not highly evident in practice. For example, Twitter is more usually used to deliver one-way information from festival organisers to festivalgoers, and is thus not being used as interactively as it could be (Garay and Pérez, 2017; Sevin, 2013).

Why UGC not TGC?

Wang et al. (2019) do not only suggest that UGC is 'revolutionizing the interaction between users and companies' but also that UGC 'offers great opportunities to zoom in on the multi-faceted dimensionality of destination image'. Whereas in the past consumers were 'passive observers of content', they have now become much more 'active participants who now actually create vast quantities of content' due to the 'paradigm shift in online customer behaviour' (Dolan et al., 2019). However, as has already been discussed, Skinner (2018) found that due to the way users share content across a range of social media platforms, it is becoming increasingly difficult to distinguish between content such as photographs that originally emanates from sources such as government and DMOs, private sector businesses, residents and visitors. Thus, rather than using the term 'tourist-generated content' (TGC), it may be more appropriate to refer to user-generated content (UGC), as this term covers posts made by any destination stakeholder.

While other stakeholder groups including urban planners, architects, local businesses, town and shopping centre managers, retailers and visitors are important (Botschen et al., 2017), unless residents at a minimum accept, and at best take ownership of (Hudak, 2019), a place brand, the strategy may be unsuccessful. Govers (2020) found that 'if done well, imaginative initiatives do not require much marketing at all as they will promote themselves in today's social media landscape'. However, when residents have rejected top-down place branding they may also turn to social media 'to chronicle their own place branding stories instead' (Hudak, 2019).

The term 'internal place branding' has been used to describe the deployment of place branding strategies when these are undertaken by the 'four key publics … visitors, residents and workers, businesspeople and exporters' (Compte-Pujol et al., 2018), identified by Rein et al. (1993). Interestingly, the efforts of these key stakeholder groups are understood as not only 'unruled', but they can also involve 'overwhelming purposive activities' (Zakarevičius and Lionikiaté, 2013). Certain stakeholders can also be classified as 'key influencers who can affect both place brand identity and place brand image' (Rodrigues et al., 2019). Key influencers include both induced 'official sources communicating the place brand identity, including city governments and DMOs', and organic sources such as 'social media, and other unofficial sources such as newspapers, travel writings, television programmes and films featuring particular places' (Rodrigues et al., 2019).

The Role of Social Influencers

Travel bloggers are seen as 'social influencers in destination marketing' (Peralta, 2019), noting two types of influencers: independent and sponsored. Peralta (2019) also distinguishes between the 'projected online' destination image emanating from the DMO, and the 'perceived online' destination image that is shared by tourists. Unlike Skinner's (2018) results from the island of Corfu, Peralta did find differences between the two, with the projected destination image focusing more on diverse natural and cultural attractions, and the perceived destination image being more about the place under investigation, in this case the Phillipines, as a cheap destination that offered fun and beautiful attractions.

The rise of social influencers is now deemed to require a revision to various traditional models related to marketing communications (Jin and Muqaddam, 2019). While Jin and Muqaddam's research explored the notion of the rise of the celebrity influencer on Instagram, the basic ideas proposed in their paper could be seen to transfer to other areas, where social media influence requires further investigation to explore this relatively new phenomenon.

Virtual and Augmented Reality

In a tourism context, any discussion of online and social media should include the way virtual reality (VR) has allowed individuals to actually consume the place product at a distance without ever needing to travel there in person (Giberson et al., 2017): 'The ability for VR to transport people to a new environment in which they are not physically present, but feel as if they are present and immersed, is of great interest to travel marketers who are continuing to develop ways to reproduce destinations and promote a positive destination image' (ibid.).

Augmented reality (AR) technology can enrich the tourist experience while at a destination, through the use of mobile technology, while:

> VR increases the accessibility of destinations, allowing travelers to virtually visit and experience places and activities that are available to the public or unattainable due to financial or physical limitations. VR can remove some of the barriers to travel, including safety, cost and physical capabilities … VR can allow tourists to visit sites that may be too remote, too expensive, too inhospitable, too dangerous, too fragile, or that simply no longer exist. (Giberson et al., 2017)

Many places adopted the use of VR, shared via online and social media, during the COVID-19 pandemic, when travel bans and closures of attractions and destinations affected the global tourism industry.

Dealing with Favourable and Unfavourable UGC

The terms 'overtourism' and 'tourismphobia' grew out of 'unsustainable mass tourism practices and the responses that these have generated amongst academics, practitioners and social movements' (Milano et al., 2019). There are plenty of examples of destinations that have implemented different solutions to these problems:

- Online booking systems at attractions are alleviating the problem of waiting in line, and too many visitors turning up on the chance they may gain admittance.
- There are also promotional measures communicated via online and social media, such as promoting the dispersal of visitors across wider parts of the destination. This involves hosting events and promoting visitor attractions located in less-visited places; promoting visitation during off-peak times through, for example, dynamic pricing; and the use of new technology such as apps that can give real-time information and allow advance bookings to minimise queuing.
- Amsterdam's major selfie attraction, the 'I Amsterdam' sign, was moved to a location outside of the city centre.

The way positive images are shared on social media, especially from events, can offer ideas as to how destination managers may harness these images to aid their destination promotion and branding campaigns.

Crises and Disasters

> In recent years the global tourism industry has experienced many serious crises and disasters including terrorist attacks, political instability, economic recession, bio security threats and natural disasters … The globalization of tourism market [*sic*] is so remarkable that small-scale crises in one part of the world can have a significant impact on other parts of the world. (Maditinos and Vassiliadis, 2008)

All parts of the travel, tourism and hospitality industry and its supply chains have been affected by the unprecedented COVID-19 pandemic. Throughout the many lockdowns across the world that occurred in the latter part of 2019, and especially during the first half of 2020, online and social media were used to share news about closures, health protocols and travel information. Social media was also used widely to facilitate business meetings, which may have longer-term effects on business tourism than can currently be calculated.

SUMMARY AND CONCLUSION

UGC is becoming increasingly important as a source of information about destinations for potential travellers (Liu et al., 2015). Indeed, content on review platforms such as Tripadvisor is seen to help potential tourists 'validate their preconceived images' of a destination (Grieve, 2013). That UGC can indeed contribute to the creation of a place brand identity has already been proposed by Taecharungroj (2019), analysing UGC 'to infer the possible place brand identities of two famous metropolitan areas in Bangkok', and this was the first research to consider both words and images posted on a range of social media in order 'to study place brand identity from UGC'. However, whereas social media, including blogs, are considered to be organic image formation agents, traditional print media have been deemed autonomous agents; yet many individuals now access the news from online sources, whether these are via social media such as Twitter or Facebook or from the news media's own websites or social media. Engagement with news articles transmitted via traditional media is also seen to increase when undertaken on social media. How easy is it, therefore, still to define the boundaries between various image formation agents and image formation sources, especially when a DMO may push out a news story that is picked up and shared by a social media influencer such as a blogger, or when the DMO actually contracts sponsored influencers to share the news content the DMO provides?

Ketter and Avraham (2012) believe that social media have revolutionised communications so much that we may need to consider new theoretical perspectives on the way social media and UGC impact on both destination identity and destination image formation. They also call for marketers to give up some control to social media users not only to distribute content but also to create it. One particular example they offer is of Tourism Australia's 2010 'There's nothing like Australia' campaign. In response to a call for social media users to upload content, over 30 000 items were received that both identified and differentiated Australia as a tourism destination. This content was then included on the place branding campaign's website and used in the campaign's promotional materials. This and other similar examples are evidence of how 'the audience is used to shape the heart of the communication process – the message' (Ketter and Avraham, 2012). The conclusion to this chapter is that scholars and practitioners must further develop our understanding of the way online and social media impacts on traditional models and theories of destination identity and destination image formation and communication. Towards this developed understanding, Figure 9.1 represents the traditional perspective on the formation of destination image (pre-visitation).

In comparison, Figure 9.2 offers a more contemporary perspective addressing the issue of UGC which comes from a broad range of sources, including those that blur the boundaries between organic and induced information sources, and which thus also play a part in projecting a destination image. From this perspective, the destination marketer could project a destination image that includes sponsored or collected and curated UGC, also others share images originating from formal sources.

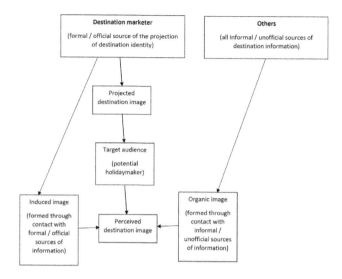

Figure 9.1   *Destination image creation and formation (pre-visitation): the traditional perspective*

Therefore, an understanding of the categorisation of induced and organic image formation sources becomes less relevant than an understanding that all information, whether from formal or informal sources, and whether from traditional or online and social media, all contributes to the projected destination image and thus to the destination image formation in the perception of target audiences.

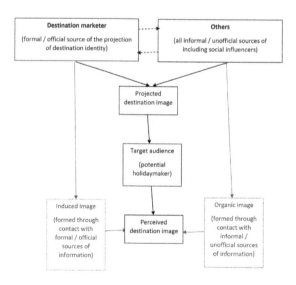

Figure 9.2   *UGC and destination image creation and formation (pre-visitation): a contemporary perspective*

REFERENCES

Aichner, T. and Jabob, F. (2015). Measuring the degree of corporate social media use. *International Journal of Market Research*, *57*(2), 257–276.

Anholt, S. (2008). Editorial. Place branding: Is it marketing, or isn't it? *Place Branding and Public Diplomacy*, *4*(1), 1–6.

Bing, P., McLaurin, T. and Crotts, J.C. (2007). Travel blogs and the implications for destination marketing. *Journal of Travel Research*, *46*(1), 35–45.

Botschen, G., Promberger, J. and Bernhart, J. (2017). Brand-driven identity development of places. *Journal of Place Management and Development*, *10*(2), 152–172. https://doi.org/10.1108/JPMD-07 -2016-0051.

Boyd, S.W. and Butler, R.W. (1996). Managing ecotourism: An opportunity spectrum approach. *Tourism Management*, *17*(8), 557–566.

Byrne, P. and Skinner, H. (2007). International business tourism: Destination Dublin or Destination Ireland? *Journal of Travel and Tourism Marketing*, *22*(3/4), 55–65.

Chaffey, D. (2020). Global social media research summary 2020. Smart Insights, 17 April. https://www .smartinsights.com/social-media-marketing/social-media-strategy/new-global-social-media-research/

Chang, B. (2019). Hanoi shut down its Instagram-famous 'train street' cafes because they were overrun with selfie-taking tourists. Here's how it got to this point. *Business Insider*, 16 October. https://www .businessinsider.com/hanoi-vietnam-shuts-down-instagram-famous-train-street-cafes-2019-10.

Choi, S., Lehto, X.Y. and Morrison, A.M. (2007). Destination image representation on the web: Content analysis of Macau travel related websites. *Tourism Management*, *28*(1), 118–129.

Compte-Pujol, M., de San Eugenio-Vela, J. and Frigola-Reig, J. (2018). Key elements in defining Barcelona's place values: the contribution of residents' perceptions from an internal place branding perspective. *Place Branding and Public Diplomacy*, *14*, 245–259.

Connell, J. (2006). Medical tourism: Sea, sun, sand and … surgery. *Tourism Management*, *27*(6), 1093–1100.

Corfu Today (Η Κέρκυρα Σήμερα) (2020). Corfu: Halikounas one of the safest beaches in Europe (Κέρκυρα: Ο Χαλικούνας στις ασφαλέστερες παραλίες στην Ευρώπη). https://www.kerkyrasimera .gr/κέρκυρα-ο-χαλικούνας-στις-ασφαλέστερες/.

Crompton, J.L. (1979). An assessment of the image of Mexico as a vacation destination and the influence of geographical location upon that image. *Journal of Travel Research*, *17*(4), 18–23.

Dolan, R., Conduit, J., Frethey-Bentham, C., Fahy, J. and Goodman, S. (2019). Social media engagement behavior: A framework for engaging customers through social media content. *European Journal of Marketing*, *53*(10), 2213–2243.

Echtner, C.M. and Ritchie, J.R.B. (1991). The meaning and measurement of destination image. *Journal of Tourism Studies*, *2*(2), 2–12.

Fakeye, P.C. and Crompton, J.L. (1991). Image differences between prospective, first time, and repeat visitors to the Lower Rio Grande Valley. *Journal of Travel Research*, *30*(2), 10–16.

Frias, D.M., Rodriguez, M.A. and Castaneda, J.A. (2007). Internet vs travel agencies on pre-visit destination image formation: An information processing view. *Tourism Management*, *29*(1), 163–179.

Gabbioneta, C. and De Carlo, M. (2019). The role of news articles, prior destination experience, and news involvement in destination image formation. *International Journal of Tourism Research*, *21*(3), 291–301.

Garay, L. and Pérez, S.M. (2017). Understanding the creation of destination images through a festival's Twitter conversation. *International Journal of Event and Festival Management*, *8*, 39–54.

Gartner, W. (1993). Image formation process. *Journal of Travel and Tourism Marketing*, *2*(2/3), 191–216.

Giberson, J., Griffin, T. and Dodds, R. (2017). Virtual reality and tourism: Will the future of travel be virtual? HTMResearch Working Paper No. 2017/1, Ryerson University.

Govers, R. (2011). Guest editorial: From place marketing to place branding and back. *Place Branding and Public Diplomacy*, *7*(4), 227–231.

Govers, R. (2020). Editorial: Imaginative communities and place branding. *Place Branding and Public Diplomacy*, *16*(1), 1–5.

Govers, R., Go, R.M. and Kumar, K. (2007). Virtual destination image, a new measurement approach. *Annals of Tourism Research, 34*(4), 977–997.

Greaves, N. and Skinner, H. (2010). The importance of destination image analysis to UK rural tourism. *Marketing Intelligence and Planning, 28*(4), 486–507.

Grieve, D. (2013). Validating image in the information age. *Worldwide Hospitality and Tourism Themes, 5*, 67–79.

Gunn, C.A. (1972). *Vacationscape: Designing Tourist Regions*. University of Texas.

Hanna, S. and Rowley, J. (2011). Towards a strategic place brand-management model. *Journal of Marketing Management, 27*(5/6), 458–476.

Hawkin, D., Lamoureux, K. and Clemmons, D. (2005). TedQual: VolunTourism as a catalyst for developing the potential of tourism destination (No 7). WTO, Themis Publication.

Hays, S., Page, S.J. and Buhalis, D. (2013). Social media as a destination marketing tool: Its use by national tourism organisations. *Current Issues in Tourism, 16*, 211–239.

Hoksbergen, E. and Insch, A. (2016). Facebook as a platform for co-creating music festival experiences: The case of New Zealand's Rhythm and Vines New Year's Eve festival. *International Journal of Event and Festival Management, 7*, 84–99.

Hudak, K.S. (2019). Resident stories and digital storytelling for participatory place branding. *Place Branding and Public Diplomacy, 15*(2), 97–108.

Hunter, W.C. (2012). Projected destination image: A visual analysis of seoul. *Tourism Geographies, 14*(3), 419–443.

Jin, S.V. and Muqaddam, A. (2019). Product placement 2.0: Do Brands need influencers, or do influencers need brands? *Journal of Brand Management, 26*(5), 522–537.

Kavaratzis, M. (2004). From city marketing to city branding: Toward a theoretical framework for developing city brands. *Place Branding, 1*(1), 58–73.

Kavaratzis, M. (2005). Place branding: A review of trends and conceptual models. *Proceedings of the 38th Academy of Marketing Annual Conference.*

Ketter, E. and Avraham, E. (2012). The social revolution of place marketing: The growing power of users in social media campaigns. *Place Branding and Public Diplomacy, 8*(4), 285–294.

Kinstler, L. (2018). How TripAdvisor changed travel. *The Guardian* 'Long Read', 24 August. https://www.theguardian.com/news/2018/aug/17/how-tripadvisor-changed-travel.

Kislali, H., Kavaratzis, M. and Saren, M. (2016). Rethinking destination image formation. *International Journal of Culture, Tourism and Hospitality Research, 10*(1), 70–80.

Kislali, H., Kavaratzis, M. and Saren, M. (2020). Destination image formation: Towards a holistic approach. *International Journal of Tourism Research, 22*(2), 266–276.

Liang, S., Schuckert, M., Law, R. and Masiero, L. (2017). The relevance of mobile tourism and information technology: An analysis of recent trends and future research directions. *Journal of Travel and Tourism Marketing, 34*(6), 732–748.

Liu, B., Kim, H., and Pennington-Gray, L. (2015). Responding to the bed bug crisis in social media. *International Journal of Hospitality Management, 47*, 76–84.

Maditinos, Z. and Vassiliadis, C. (2008). Crises and disasters in tourism industry: Happen locally – affect globally. *Proceedings of the MIBES Conference 2008.* Technological Institute of Larissa. School of Business and Economics. MIBES E-book, pp. 67–76. mibes.teilar.gr/ebook/ebooks/maditinos_vasiliadis%2067-76.pdf.

Maitland, R. and Ritchie, B.W. (eds) (2009). *City Tourism: National Capital Perspectives*. Wallingford: CABI.

Marine-Roig, E. and Clavé, S.A. (2015). Tourism analytics with massive user-generated content: A case study of Barcelona. *Journal of Destination Marketing and Management, 4*, 162–172.

Merkelsen, H. and Rasmussen, R.K. (2016). Nation branding as an emerging field – An institutionalist perspective. *Place Branding and Public Diplomacy, 12*, 99–109.

Milano, C., Novelli, M. and Cheer, I.M. (2019). Overtourism and tourismphobia: A journey through four decades of tourism development, planning and local concerns. *Tourism Planning and Development, 16*(4), 353–357.

Munar, A.M. (2011). Tourist-created content: Rethinking destination branding. *International Journal of Culture, Tourism and Hospitality Research, 5*(3), 291–305.

Peralta, R.L. (2019). How vlogging promotes a destination image: A narrative analysis of popular travel vlogs about the Philippines. *Place Branding and Public Diplomacy*, *15*(4), 244–256.

Popescu, O., Done, S.G. and Skinner, H. (2017). Corfu PAWS. *Proceedings of the 4th Corfu Symposium on Managing and Marketing Places*, 24–27 April.

Rein, I., Kotler, P. and Haider, D. (1993). *Marketing Places: Attracting Investment, Industry, and Tourism to Cities, States, and Nations*. Free Press.

Rodrigues, C., Skinner, H., Dennis, C. and Melewar, T.C. (2019). Towards a theoretical framework on sensorial place brand identity. *Journal of Place Management and Development*, *13*(33), 273–295.

Ryan, C. and Kinder, R. (1996). Sex, tourism and sex tourism: fulfilling similar needs? *Tourism Management*, *17*(7), 507–518.

Schaffer, V. (2015). Student mentors: aiding tourism businesses to overcome barriers to social media. *Current Issues in Tourism*, *18*, 1022–1031.

Sevin, E. (2013) Places going viral: Twitter usage patterns in destination marketing and place branding. *Journal of Place Management and Development*, *6*, 227–239.

Skinner, H. (2008). The emergence and development of place marketing's confused identity. *Journal of Marketing Management*, *24*(9/10), 915–928.

Skinner, H. (2011). In search of the *genius loci* – The essence of a place brand. *Marketing Review*, *11*(3), 281–292

Skinner, H. (2016). What's occurring? Barry since *Gavin and Stacey*. International Journal of Tourism Research, *18*(3), 251–259.

Skinner, H. (2017). Ήλιος, θάλασσα, άμμος και σεξ: προβλήματα με το ελληνικό μοντέλο μαζικού τουρισμού (Sun, sea, sand and sex: Problems with the mass tourism model) Γεωγραφίες (Geographies), ΤΕΥΧΟΣ 30, ΧΕΙΜΩΝΑΣ, (30, Winter), ΑΦΙΕΡΩΜΑ: ΤΑΥΤΟΤΗΤΑ, ΜΑΡΚΕΤΙΓΚ ΚΑΙ BRANDING ΤΟΠΩΝ (special issue on Identity, Marketing and Branding of places).

Skinner, H. (2018). Who really creates the place brand? Considering the role of user generated content in creating and communicating a place identity. *Communication and Society*, *31*(4), 9–24.

Skinner, H. and Soomers, P. (2019). Spiritual tourism on the island of Corfu: Positive impacts of niche tourism versus the challenges of contested space. *International Journal of Tourism Anthropology*, *7*(10), 21–39.

Smith, M. and Richards, G. (eds) (2012). *Handbook of Cultural Tourism*. Routledge.

Taecharungroj, V. (2019). User-generated place brand identity: harnessing the power of content on social media platforms, *Journal of Place Management and Development*, *12*(1), 39–70.

Tasci, A.D.A. and Gartner, W.C. (2007). Destination image and its functional relationships. *Journal of Travel Research*, *45*(4), 413–425.

Tenbarge, K. (2019). 15 destinations Instagram has helped ruin. Insider, 25 July. https://www.insider.com/travel-destinations-instagram-influencers-ruined-2019-7.

Wang, W., Ying, S., Lyu, J. and Qi, X. (2019). Perceived image study with online data from social media: the case of boutique hotels in China. *Industrial Management and Data Systems*, *119*(5), 950–967.

Williams, S. and Lew, A.A. (2015). *Tourism Geography: Critical Understandings of Place, Space and Experience* (3rd edn). Routledge.

Williams-Burnett, N., Skinner, H. and Fallon, J. (2016). Reality Television Portrayals of Tourists Behaving Badly. *Journal of Travel and Tourism Marketing*, *35*(3), 336–347.

Xiang, Z. and Gretzel, U. (2010). Role of social media in online travel information search. *Tourism Management*, *31*, 179–180.

Zakarevičius, P. and Lionikaité, J. (2013). An initial framework for understanding the concept of internal place branding. *Organizaciju, Vadyba: Sisteminiai Tyrimai*, *67*, 143–160.

10. Social media and tourists' behaviors: post-COVID-19

Salman Majeed and Haywantee Ramkissoon

INTRODUCTION

Tourism experience is intangible, heterogeneous, inseparable, and perishable (IHIP) in its nature (Majeed et al., 2020a) and, thus, is more susceptible to risks, including epidemics, terrorism and natural disasters, which may impact the image of the host destination (Tasci and Gartner, 2007). Limited information on crisis management, risk level and communication channels for help makes tourists more prone to risk while traveling to epidemic-hit destinations (Matyas et al., 2011; Novelli et al., 2018). Due to disease outbreaks in the past – that is, severe acute respiratory syndrome (SARS), Middle East respiratory syndrome coronavirus (MERS-CoV), H1N1, influenza pandemic, foot and mouth disease, Ebola (Novelli et al., 2018) – and recently the novel coronavirus pneumonia (COVID-19) pandemic, the issue of reliable information is of pressing concern for tourists seeking health and well-being.

Social media refers to different applications (apps), such as LinkedIn, Instagram, Twitter, WhatsApp and Facebook, and these play a key role in influencing consumers' behaviors (Dolan et al., 2019; Majeed et al., 2020a; Parra-López et al., 2011; Sotiriadis, 2017). The unprecedented growth of social media is fueled by the rapid development of the internet that has changed tourists' patterns of searching for information and planning their trips (Perez-Vega et al., 2018). Tourists explore online social media to find information when intending to schedule their travel arrangements (Bilgihan et al., 2016). Social media often allows easy access to consult information generated by end-users (Chanchaichujit et al., 2018; Morosan and Bowen, 2018).

Access to social media platforms influences tourists' travel decisions by sharing other tourists' stories, reviews and recommendations (Dolan et al., 2019; Hur et al., 2017; Sotiriadis, 2017). Tourists consider available tourism-related information on social media and share their own evaluations after consulting different tourism offerings at host destinations (Litvin et al., 2008; Perez-Vega et al., 2018). Social media marketing, and information and communication technologies are important tools for information provision (Ramkissoon, forthcoming) and sharing during destination crises and in the post-disaster recovery phase (Austin et al., 2012). Social media helps to develop social relationships between different users, and this in turn could promote social bonding (Ramkissoon, 2015; Ramkissoon et al., 2018) and emotional bonding with unvisited places (Chanchaichujit et al., 2020). It generates a huge volume of information ranging from daily life including entertainment, lifestyle management, product reviews, promoting connections with family and friends, to name a few. Tourists are in search of reliable information as an important factor in their travel-related purchase.

Tourists' travel sharing behaviors can be interpreted with the social influence theory (Kang and Schuett, 2013): people do tend to be socially influenced by others. Munar and Jacobsen (2014) argue that people find a plethora of rich information by interacting with social networks on social media. The latter's popularity can be measured from the fact that approximately 200 million people use Tripadvisor to research destinations and schedule their travel arrangements (Filleri et al., 2015). Tourists' electronic word-of-mouth (eWOM) on social media is an important marketing tool attracting other potential tourists. Tourists' perceived risks of travel, their doubts and negative eWOM decrease, and intentions to visit increase, as the availability of desired information increases (Majeed et al., 2020a).

Researchers and practitioners across different disciplines continue to examine the information load of social media and its impacts on people's behaviors (Oh et al., 2020; Parra-López et al., 2011). The COVID-19 pandemic has shown that people tend to seek further information on social media during crisis. It is perhaps important for researchers to continue focusing on factors that determine tourists' ability to interact with other tourists on social media platforms, to exchange information during destination crises (Gao et al., 2020) such as disease outbreaks, that may ultimately impact their behaviors (Yu et al., 2020).

Given the continued impacts of the global pandemic on the already difficult situation of the tourism and hospitality industry – for example, lack of jobs, low salaries, security threats (Gössling et al., 2020; Sigala, 2020) – it is important to address how social media information sources may assist in promoting the tourism and hospitality industry during and after the pandemic. Further investigation is warranted of factors that determine the ability to use social media information, and how information search using social media platforms impacts tourists' behaviors while considering whether to travel to epidemic-hit destinations. Drawing on extant literature, the objectives of our study are to investigate: (1) factors that determine tourists' ability to use social media information sources; (2) how social media information influences tourists' behaviors; (3) what kind of tourist behaviors are susceptible to the impacts of social media information; and (4) how tourists' perceived risk of epidemics, such as COVID-19, impact their travel-related behaviors.

We develop and propose a conceptual model to integrate the constructs of use of social media information, perceived travel risk of epidemic-hit destinations, anxiety, intentions to visit, and eWOM. The framework is intended to assist researchers to progress this field of study. Our framework is also important for tourism and hospitality stakeholders to better understand tourists' perceptions and behaviors during and after destination crises, in order to devise appropriate strategies for destination competitiveness (Ramkissoon and Nunkoo, 2008, 2012; Ramkissoon and Uysal, 2011; Ramkissoon and Mavondo, 2017). Our study encourages future empirical testing of the proposed theoretical framework.

LITERATURE REVIEW

Social Media Information and Tourism

Social media is a growing widespread global mega trend. The tourism industry is experiencing hyper-growth in the accumulation and dissemination of travel and tourism information on online social media (Xiang et al., 2017; Majeed et al., 2020a). Tourists' use the internet and a variety of information and communication technology (ICT) – for example, mobile phone, laptop, computers (Majeed et al., 2020a) – in their daily lives, and this technology usage trend is carried over to the choice of tourist destination (MacKay and Vogt, 2012; Ramkissoon, 2018a).

Tourists gather information from different sources at all three stages of their travel experience – that is, before, during and after travel – for a successful travel experience (Dolan et al., 2019; Pennington-Gray et al., 2005; Ramkissoon, 2018b). Social media platforms have become a potent marketing tool for successful travel and tourism arrangements (Güçer et al., 2017).

The information gathering trend before travel is fueled by the pressing concerns over individuals' health and well-being. The use of the internet and ICT has promoted tourists' use of social media to gather relevant information for their trips (Parra-López et al., 2011). This online environment has grabbed tourists' attention across the globe, to organize their trips successfully (Sabiote-Ortiz et al., 2016). Tourists interact with others, such as experienced tourists and tourism operators, on social media, and evaluate travel-related information (Litvin et al., 2008). Tourists prefer to consult social media information sources in the planning phase of travel alongside considering other available online travel-related information (Xiang and Gretzel, 2010). Scholars note that the accuracy of tourists' decisions before their travel to host destinations is largely influenced by the reviews and recommendations of other tourists on social media (Güçer et al., 2017; Yang et al., 2019).

Antecedents of Social Media Information Usage

Ma and Chen (2014) proposed the theory of belonging, as well as the intrinsic motivation of altruism, to interpret individuals' motivations for using online social media information. Individuals use online social media information to stay connected to cohesive groups and build relationships by interacting with others (Ma and Chen, 2014). Individuals' desire to use online social media information may be determined by their perceptions (Majeed et al., 2020a), motivations for self-efficacy and enjoyment (Lai and Chen, 2014), negative feelings, self-enhancement and positive feelings (Yoo and Gretzel, 2011). Tourists explore online social media to fulfill their human desires of belongingness, enjoyment, social interaction and well-being during their travel to the host destination (Mkono and Tribe, 2016; Munar and Jacobsen, 2014). Next, we discuss some basic and important parameters that may define tourists' attitudes towards using online social media information for travel-related information.

Prior experience

Tourists attempt to gather relevant information – for example, on tourist attractions, budget, safety measures, among others – before their travel to tourist destinations (Mansfeld, 1992). Tourists' information pre-travel information search behavior reflects tourists' motivations of planned travel arrangements at host tourist destinations (Hyde, 2007). Tourists' prior product knowledge might influence their further information search behaviors and the evaluation of information sources that further lead to shape their behaviors and intentions to visit a destination (Gursoy and McCleary, 2004; Marchiori and Cantoni, 2015).

Tourists rely on their prior information and experience when scheduling trips to familiar destinations or planning to arrange short trips. Tourists' prior knowledge and experience motivate them to continue to explore travel-related information on social media to plan their trips (Lehto et al., 2006) to unfamiliar and distant destinations (Gursoy and Chen, 2000; Gursoy, 2003). Scholars support the notion that prior travel experience impacts tourists' behaviors to gather travel-related information from social media to organize both short and long trips (Kerstetter and Cho, 2004). The cohesion between individuals' self-beliefs and the available information in the online environment confirms individuals' positive attitudes to host destinations (Marchiori and Cantoni, 2015).

Perceived reliability

Consumers' consumption behaviors are based on their emotions and motivations (Majeed et al., 2017b). Individuals' perceptions of a product or service determine their emotions and behaviors (Majeed et al., 2020b). The quality of information that passes through individuals' cognitive filters determines their perception and behaviors (Xue et al., 2020). Scholars across different disciplines acknowledge the fact that tourists also travel across the globe to find optimal health and well-being (Majeed et al., 2017a; Majeed et al., 2018; Majeed and Lu, 2017). However, it is complex to unravel tourists' perceptions, behaviors and preferences for travel-related information that they perceive as reliable to fulfill their goals, for example that contribute to their happiness, satisfaction and improvement in quality of life.

Scholars note that individuals' behaviors are influenced by social interactions with other people (Kang and Schuett, 2013; Ramkissoon et al., 2013). Tourists' preferences for using online social media information are influenced by the credibility of information sources. Tourists' feelings about the truthfulness of information may motivate them to engage and further encourage use of online social media information sources (Kang and Schuett, 2013; Marchiori and Cantoni, 2015; Xiang et al., 2017).

Social media information spreads across different online platforms which allows tourists and tourism service providers to interact with one another (Xiang and Gretzel, 2010). Social media travel content as perceived by tourists may be linked to candid and impartial access to information about potential host destinations (Lo and Yao, 2019; Majeed et al., 2020a). Perceived reliability of social media information impacts tourists' intent for continued use of travel-related information in planning their travel (Ayeh et al., 2013).

Perceived reliability of travel-related information on social media is also linked to the notion of easy accessibility (Saleem et al., 2018). Destinations' tourism information on different online platforms may be considered as reliable information by tourists (Majeed et al., 2020a; Parra-López et al., 2011). Tourists' perceptions of accurate and reliable social media information without the potential threat of financial loss can compel them to visit tourist destinations (Jalilvand et al., 2012). Further understanding of tourists' perceptions of reliable information on social media for their pre-travel and during-travel arrangements may open competitive avenues for destination marketers.

Relationship between Social Media Information and Tourist Behavior

Online social media content is not created by all users of social media (Sun et al., 2014). User-generated content (UGC) on social media is largely developed by about 1 per cent of users that impact the other 99 per cent (Arthur, 2006). UGC or consumer-generated content (CGC) are terms that are sometimes used interchangeably. Consumers' purchasing decision-making is directly influenced by CGC on social media, and this notion corresponds to social influence theories that elaborate people's beliefs, attitudes and behaviors from the perspective of social contagion and social comparison with others (Bilgicer et al., 2015). Thus, social influence intensifies the impact of CGC on potential tourists and determines the positivity or negativity of their behaviors (Mariani et al., 2019).

The next sections present theoretical underpinnings of tourists' behaviors, and how such behaviors vary, to align a coherent flow of contagion and social interaction between users of social media to plan travel-related arrangements.

Anxiety

Social media develops social interaction among people and motivates them to share their opinions, recommendations and reviews to recognize their social influence on one another (Bilgicer et al., 2015). The impacts of social media on people's psychological reactions, such as contagion behaviors, have increased scholars' interests in the field. Scholars note that psychological well-being is directly influenced by the social support (Ramkissoon, 2020) and recognition gained by social media (Bilgicer et al., 2015; Marchiori and Cantoni, 2015; Xiang et al., 2017). Social media users' social influence and comparison with one another might fuel negative self-evaluations, stress and low self-esteem (Nesi and Prinstein, 2015).

Scholars note that there is a direct relationship between social media information use and anxiety, and this relationship grows stronger with the increasing frequency of social media use in everyday life (Vanucci et al., 2017). Anxiety is noted as a subjective feeling of frustration or awkward, uncomfortable, stressful feelings (Hullet and Witte, 2001; McIntyre and Roggenbuck, 1998). People use social media to compare themselves with others, as well as to receive social support for their expressed opinions (Deters and Mehl, 2013) and to feel appreciated (McIntyre and Roggenbuck, 1998). This is considered as the positive aspect of social media that generate users' positive behaviors with social support. Lack of social support or appreciation may lead to anxiety and depression, stress and discomfort, among social media users (Appel et al., 2016; Seabrook et al., 2016; Vandervoort, 1999). With rising concerns about mental health, negative impacts of social media on users' mental well-being need further attention (Kim, 2017).

Tourists find a plethora of information when they explore electronic social platforms to schedule their trips (Majeed et al., 2020a). Given the unknown feeling of the actual tourist experience at the destination (Majeed et al., 2020b), tourists may doubt the reliability of tourism information on social media, feeling that it is risky, and thus become anxious (Dowling and Staelin, 1994).

Given the uncertainties involved in tourism and increasing trend to consult social media information for travel-related information, doubting the reliability of information sources may fuel tourists' anxiety and negatively impact their intentions to visit (Kovačić et al., 2019). Based on the above, hypotheses H1 and H2 are proposed:

Hypothesis H1: Use of social media information has a significantly direct impact on tourists' anxiety.

Hypothesis H2: Anxiety has a significantly direct impact on tourists' intentions to visit.

Intentions to visit and eWOM

Social media allow third-party service providers to interact with tourists and destinations (Ghazali and Cai, 2014). Social media may develop positive imagery of tourist destinations as a result of exchanges of information among third parties, tourists and destination service providers that further lead to positively influence tourists' intentions to visit (Ghazali and Cai,

2014). Good understanding among third parties, tourists and destination service providers exerts a positive influence on tourists' perceived reliability of social media information, which can ultimately lead to favorable intentions to visit destinations (Chen et al., 2014; Duarte and Amaro, 2015).

Destination marketing organizations (DMOs) promote tourism on different online social media and interact with potential tourists in the virtual market (Hristov et al., 2018; Hristov and Ramkissoon, 2016; Naumov et al., 2020; Saleem et al., 2018). Tourists' direct and easy access to online social media information shared by DMOs across different destinations may positively influence their perceived reliability of social media information. Thus, discussion on online social media has geared up the momentum of buying and selling of tourism deals (Cao and Yang, 2016).

Tourists' experience sharing and decision-making behaviors can be divided into personal fulfillment, self-actualization and altruistic motivation notions. Personal fulfillment and self-actualization-oriented tourists spread information among people and develop their recognized image, while altruistic motivation-oriented tourists' views and recommendations attempt to prevent others from making bad decisions about their travel-related arrangements (Munar and Jacobsen, 2014; Yoo and Gretzel, 2011). Tourists with the implied characteristics of personal fulfillment, self-actualization and altruistic motivation influence potential tourists' traveling decisions with their contagion behaviors.

Tourists who are satisfied with travel-related information on social media may visit their intended destinations and spread eWOM (Jalilvend et al., 2012). Scholars document tourists' intentions to visit, which can in turn influence positive eWOM behaviors as a result of reliable travel-related information on social media (Cao and Yang, 2016; Sun et al., 2014; Dewnarain et al., 2019a, 2019b). Perceived reliability of social media information exerts its contagion effect to promote tourists' actual visits and positive eWOM (Majeed et al., 2020a). Likewise, negative perceptions of travel-related information on social media or uncomfortable online browsing experience on social media may deter tourists from their planned and actual visits to tourist destinations, and generate the possibilities of negative eWOM (Jalilvend et al., 2012). Based on the above, the following hypotheses are proposed:

Hypothesis H3: Use of social media information has a significantly direct impact on tourists' intentions to visit.

Hypothesis H4: Use of social media information has a significantly direct impact on tourists' eWOM.

Hypothesis H5: Tourists' intentions to visit exert a significantly direct impact on tourists' eWOM.

The elaboration likelihood model (ELM) states that consumers' perceptions and evaluations of information depend on the shared online content on social media. Tourists' perceptions of reliable and useful online customer-generated content may positively impact their intentions to use social media information to visit destinations (Dedeoğlu et al., 2020). Scholars note that consumers' perceptions of legitimate online social media information reduce the cognitive distance between the evaluation and the consumption process (Dedeoğlu et al., 2020). Tourists' eWOM, which is based on their experience of consulting existing information on social media, may spread contagiously to attract or dissatisfy other tourists from further consulting online travel-related information (Aydin, 2019; Fernandes and Fernandes, 2018). Poor message quality, incomplete responses or negative feedback may create doubt on the reliability of information and deter consumers from continuing to consider consumer-generated content on social media (Sun et al., 2014). Tourists' negative perceptions about social media information, which are shaped by negative eWOM, may exert detrimental impacts on their travel decision to potential destinations (Yoo and Gretzel, 2011). Thus, DMOs consider tourists' eWOM as an important stimulus to spread the notion of reliable information on social media about travel-related content (Hennig-Thurau et al., 2004).

The widespread use of the internet and ICT alongside the unprecedented growth of social media has lubricated the efforts of DMOs in attracting tourists to consult online travel-related content after evaluating other tourists' opinions and recommendations (Majeed et al., 2020a). Tourists often act as agents in disseminating positive destination information (Camprubí et al., 2013). Scholars note that individuals' positive expressions, alongside truthful UGC and CGC on social media, help other individuals to achieve self-actualization, self-realization and social status in parallel to revitalizing their prior experience (Lee and Ma, 2012). UGC and CGC act as eWOM that influences tourists' intentions to use social media information and consumption behaviors (Dedeoğlu et al., 2020). Tourists' behaviors might change due to doubts over the effectiveness and functionality of social media information. Perceived reliability of social media travel information on tourists' prior experience, and positive eWOM of other tourists on different online platforms, may help reduce doubts (Chung and Koo, 2015) and positively influence travel decision-making. We propose the following hypothesis:

Hypothesis H6: Tourists' eWOM has a significantly direct impact on the use of social media information.

Perceived Travel Risk of Epidemic-Hit Destinations, Social Media and Tourist Behavior

Tourists travel across the globe to bring improvement to their health and well-being (Ghosh and Mandal, 2018; Majeed et al., 2019). Tourists' risk perceptions of host destinations determine their intentions to visit (Majeed et al., 2020b, 2018). Tourists may change their intentions to visit, or gather more information, when destinations are perceived as risky or less safe (Chandler, 1991). Destination crises lead to negative impacts on destination credibility (Laws and Prideaux, 2005; Seymour and Moore, 2000). Health crises, such as COVID-19, may create doubts about destinations' health-promising notions and negatively impact tourists' intentions to visit (Gössling et al., 2020; Sigala, 2020). Health crises in the past – such as Ebola, SARS, MERs-CoV – fueled tourists' negative perceptions of destinations' credibility and health-promising notions that consequently discouraged them from visiting epidemic-hit destinations (Novelli et al., 2018; Wilder-Smith, 2006). Perceived risks of terrorism, war, epidemics (Novelli et al., 2018) and a bad environment negatively impact destination image (Wang et al., 2018).

Social media may determine public opinion by generating awareness (Kovačić et al., 2019). ICT and the internet may help to revitalize the tourism and hospitality businesses in destinations hit by pandemics such as COVID-19 (Gretzel et al., 2020). Social media may positively influence tourists' perceptions, anxiety and intentions to visit during and after destination crises (Kovačić et al., 2019; Pennington-Gray et al., 2012). Tourists' intensive use of social media to organize their trips during destination crises may also impact on their eWOM (Pennington-Gray et al., 2012; Shroeder et al., 2013; Sigala, 2011). Scholars note that information shared by word-of-mouth based on prior experience may be considered as quite reliable during destination crises (Pennington-Gray et al., 2012; Sigala, 2011; Xiang and Gretzel, 2010). We propose the following hypotheses based on the above:

Hypothesis H7: Use of social media information has a significantly direct impact on tourists' perceived risk of epidemic-hit destinations.

Hypothesis H8: Tourists' perceived risk of epidemic-hit destinations mediates the relationship between use of social media information and tourists' anxiety.

Hypothesis H9: Tourists' perceived risk of epidemic-hit destinations mediates the relationship between use of social media information and tourists' intentions to visit.

Hypothesis H10: Tourists' perceived risk of epidemic-hit destinations mediates the relationship between use of social media information and tourists' eWOM.

Theoretical Model

Drawing on extant literature, Figure 10.1 shows the theoretical framework of the study describing logical connections among the constructs under investigation. The model proposes that use of social media information exerts a significantly direct impact on tourists' anxiety,

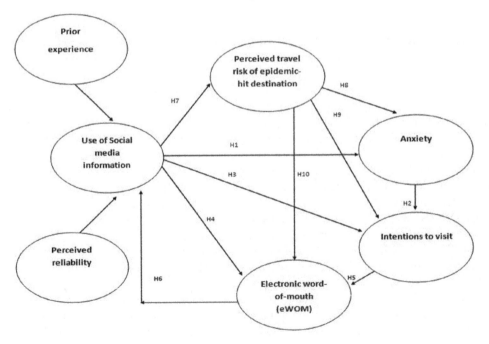

Figure 10.1   Theoretical framework

intentions to visit and eWOM. Tourists' perceived risk of epidemics at host destinations exerts its mediating impact on the relationships between tourists' use of social media information and their anxiety, intentions to visit and eWOM behaviors.

CONCLUSION

This study advances the concept of social media information usage and its impact on tourists' behaviors during epidemics, such as COVID-19. Our study develops and presents a conceptual framework with proposed theoretical links among the use of social media information, perceived risk of epidemic-hit destinations, anxiety, intentions to visit and eWOM. Drawing on extant literature of tourists' perceptions, behaviors and threats of epidemics, such as COVID-19, our study contributes to the existing body of knowledge on the role of social media in tourists' behavioral travel intent in an epidemic context. With a framework supported by theoretical underpinnings, this research points to valuable theoretical and practical implications to promote tourism with social media usage in a time of destination crises.

By developing links between social media information and perceived risk of epidemics at host destinations, this study contributes to existing knowledge to contour the negative impacts of epidemics on tourism with the help of online social media. This study advances the concept of destination image formation during perceived risk of destination crises in the context of epidemics, such as COVID-19, and with the use of social media information. By integrating tourists' anxiety, intentions to visit, and eWOM with social media information and perceived risk of epidemics, this study provides a roadmap for destination marketing organizations to promote tourism using social media during and after the COVID-19 pandemic.

Our study lack empirical evidence, and we encourage researchers to test the proposed theoretical framework. The scope of our model can be extended by including more second-order formative constructs and moderators, such as national culture. Inclusion of more variables into our proposed model will help destination marketers and managers further develop marketing and management tools for tourism destinations impacted by health-related crises, such as the COVID-19 pandemic, with the use of online social media.

REFERENCES

Appel, H., Gerlach, A.L., and Crusius, J. (2016). The interplay between Facebook use, social comparison, envy, and depression. *Current Opinion in Psychology*, *9*, 44–49.

Arthur, C. (2006). What is the 1% rule? Retrieved: https://www.theguardian.com/technology/2006/jul/20/guardianweeklytechnologysection2 (accessed June 19, 2020).

Austin, L., Liu, B.F., and Jin, Y. (2012). How audiences seek out crisis information: exploring the social-mediated crisis communication model. *Journal of Applied Communication Research*, *40*(2), 188–207.

Aydin, G. (2019). Social media engagement and organic post effectiveness: a roadmap for increasing the effectiveness of social media use in hospitality industry. *Journal of Hospitality Marketing and Management*, *29*, 1–21. doi: 10.1080/19368623.2019.1588824.

Ayeh, J.K., Au, N., and Law, R. (2013). Do we believe in Tripadvisor? Examining credibility perceptions and online travelers' attitude toward using user-generated content. *Journal of Travel Research*, *52*(4), 437–452.

Bilgicer, T., Jedidi, K., Lehmann, D.R., and Neslin, S.A. (2015). Social contagion and customer adoption of new sales channels. *Journal of Retailing*, *91*(2), 254–271.

Bilgihan, A., Barreda, A., Okumus, F., and Nusair, K. (2016). Consumer perception of knowledge-sharing in travel-related online social networks. *Tourism Management*, *52*, 287–296.

Camprubí, R., Guia, J., and Comas, J. (2013). The new role of tourists in destination image formation. *Current Issues in Tourism*, *16*(2), 203–209.

Cao, K., and Yang, Z. (2016). A study of e-commerce adoption by tourism websites in China. *Journal of Destination Marketing and Management*, *5*, 283–289.

Chanchaichujit, K., Holmes, K., Dickinson, S., and Ramkissoon, H. (2018). An investigation of how user generated content influences place affect towards an unvisited destination. In *8th Advances in Hospitality and Tourism Marketing and Management (AHTMM) Conference* (p. 213).

Chanchaichujit, K., Holmes, K., Dickinson, S., and Ramkissoon, H. (2020). The role of place affect in forming emotional bonds with unvisited destinations. *CAUTHE 2020: 20: 20 Vision: New Perspectives on the Diversity of Hospitality, Tourism and Events*, 693.

Chandler, J. (1991). How Safe Are Our Airports? *Travel and Leisure*, *21*(5), 94–100.

Chen, Y.C., Shang, R.A., and Li, M.J. (2014). The effects of perceived relevance of travel blogs' content on the behavioral intention to visit a tourist destination, *Computer in Human Behavior*, *30*, 787–799.

Chung, N., and Koo, C. (2015). The use of social media in travel information search. *Telematics and Informatics*, *32*, 215–229.

Dedeoğlu, B.B., Taheri, B., Okumus, F., and Gannon, M. (2020). Understanding the importance that consumers attach to social media sharing (ISMS): scale development and validation. *Tourism Management*, *76*, 103954.

Deters, F.G., and Mehl, M.R. (2013). Does posting Facebook status updates increase or decrease loneliness? An online social networking experiment. *Social Psychological and Personality Science*, *4*(5), 579–586.

Dewnarain, S., Ramkissoon, H., and Mavondo, F. (2019a). Social customer relationship management: an integrated conceptual framework. *Journal of Hospitality Marketing and Management*, *28*(2), 172–188.

Dewnarain, S., Ramkissoon, H., and Mavondo, F. (2019b). Social customer relationship management in the hospitality industry. *Journal of Hospitality*, *1*(1), 1–14.

Dolan, R., Seo, Y., and Kemper, J. (2019). Complaining practices on social media in tourism: a value co-creation and co-destruction perspective. *Tourism Management*, *73*, 35–45.

Duarte, P., and Amaro, S. (2015). An integrative model of consumers' intentions to purchase travel online. *Tourism Management*, *46*, 64–79.

Dowling, G., and Staelin, R. (1994). A model of perceived risk and intended risk-handling activity. *Journal of Consumer Research*, *21* (1), 119–135.

Fernandes, T., and Fernandes, F. (2018). Sharing dissatisfaction online: analyzing the nature and predictors of hotel guests' negative reviews. *Journal of Hospitality Marketing and Management*, *27*, 127–150.

Filieri, R., Alguezaui, S., and McLeay, F. (2015). Why do travelers trust TripAdvisor? Antecedents of trust towards consumer-generated media and its influence on recommendation adoption and word of mouth. *Tourism Management*, *51*, 174–185.

Gao, J., Zheng, P., Jia, Y., Chen, H., Mao, Y., et al. (2020). Mental health problems and social media exposure during COVID-19 outbreak. *Plos One*, *15*(4), e0231924.

Ghazali, R.M., and Cai, L. (2014). Social media sites in destination image formation. In: A.M. Munar and S.L. Gyimóthy Cai (eds), *Tourism Social Media: Transformations in Identity, Community and Culture* (Tourism Social Science Series, Vol. 18). Bingley: Emerald Group Publishing.

Ghosh, T., and Mandal, S. (2018). Medical tourism experience: conceptualization, scale development, and validation. *Journal of Travel Research*, *58*(8), 1–14. doi: 10.1177/0047287518813469.

Gössling, S., Scott, D., and Hall, C.M. (2020). Pandemics, tourism and global change: a rapid assessment of COVID-19. *Journal of Sustainable Tourism*. https://doi.org/10.1080/09669582.2020.1758708.

Gretzel, U., Fuchs, M., Baggio, R., Hoepken, W., Law, R., et al. (2020). e-Tourism beyond COVID-19: a call for transformative research. *Journal of Information Technology and Tourism*, *22*(2), 187–203.

Güçer, E., Bag, C., and Altınay, M. (2017). Consumer behavior in the process of purchasing tourism product in social media. *Journal of Business Research*, *9*(1), 381–402.

Gursoy, D. (2003). Prior product knowledge and its influence on the traveler's information search behavior. *Journal of Hospitality and Leisure Marketing*, *10*(3–4), 113–131.

Gursoy, D., and Chen, J. (2000). Competitive analysis of cross cultural information search behavior. *Tourism Management, 21*(6), 583–590.

Gursoy, D., and McCleary, K.W. (2004). Travelers' prior knowledge and its impact on their information search behavior. *Journal of Hospitality and Tourism Research, 28*(1), 66–94.

Hennig-Thurau, T., Gwinner, K.P., Walsh, G., and Gremler, D.D. (2004). Electronic word of-mouth via consumer-opinion platforms: what motivates consumers to articulate themselves on the internet? *Journal of Interactive Marketing, 18,* 38–52.

Hristov, D., Minocha, S., and Ramkissoon, H. (2018). Transformation of destination leadership networks. *Tourism Management Perspectives, 28,* 239–250.

Hristov, D., and Ramkissoon, H. (2016). Leadership in destination management organisations. *Annals of Tourism Research, 61*(C), 230–234.

Hullett, C., and Witte, K. (2001). Predicting intercultural adaptation and isolation: using the extended parallel process model to test anxiety/ uncertainty management theory. *International Journal of Intercultural Relations, 25*(2), 125–139.

Hur, K., Kim, T.T., Karatepe, O.M., and Lee, G. (2017). An exploration of the factors influencing social media continuance usage and information sharing intentions among Koran travellers. *Tourism Management, 63,* 170–178.

Hyde, K.F. (2007). Contemporary information search strategies of destination-naïve international vacationers. *Journal of Travel and Tourism Marketing, 2*(2/3), 63–76.

Jalilvand, P.M., Samiei, H., Dini, B., and Manzari, Y.P. (2012). Examining the structural relationships of electronic word of mouth, destination image, tourist attitude toward destination and travel intention: An integrated approach. *Journal of Destination Marketing and Management, 1,* 134–143.

Kang, M., and Schuett, M.A. (2013). Determinants of sharing travel experiences in social media. *Journal of Travel and Tourism Marketing, 30*(1), 93–107.

Kerstetter, D., and Cho, M. (2004). Prior knowledge, credibility and information search. *Annals of Tourism Research,* 31, 961–985.

Kim, H.H. (2017). The impact of online social networking on adolescent psychological well-being (WB): a population-level analysis of Korean school aged children. *International Journal of Adolescence and Youth, 22*(3), 364–376.

Kovačić, S., Jovanović, T., Miljković, Đ., Lukić, T., Marković, S.B., et al. (2019). Are Serbian tourists worried? The effect of psychological factors on tourists' behavior based on the perceived risk. *Open Geosci, 11,* 273–287.

Lai, H.-M., and Chen, T.T. (2014). Knowledge sharing in interest online communities: a comparison of posters and lurkers. *Computers in Human Behavior, 35,* 295–306.

Laws, E., and Prideaux, B. (2005). Crisis management: a suggested typology. *Journal of Travel and Tourism Marketing, 19,* 1–8.

Lee, C.S., and Ma, L. (2012). News sharing in social media: the effect of gratifications and prior experience. *Computers in Human Behavior, 28*(2), 331–339.

Lehto, X., Kim, D.Y., and Morrison, A. (2006). The effect of prior destination experience on online information search behavior. *Tourism and Hospitality Research, 6*(2), 160–178.

Litvin, S.W., Goldsmith, R.E., and Pan, B. (2008). Electronic word-of-mouth in hospitality and tourism management. *Tourism Management, 29,* 458–468.

Lo, A.S., and Yao, S.S. (2019). What makes hotel online reviews credible? An investigation of the roles of reviewer expertise, review rating consistency and review valence. *International Journal of Contemporary Hospitality Management, 31*(1), 41–60.

Ma, W.W.K., and Chan, A. (2014). Knowledge sharing and social media: altruism, perceived online attachment motivation, and perceived online relationship commitment. *Computers in Human Behavior, 39,* 51–58.

MacKay, K., and Vogt, C. (2012). Information technology in everyday and vacation contexts. *Annals of Tourism Research, 39*(3), 1380–1401.

Majeed, S., and Lu, C. (2017). Changing preferences, moving places, and third party administrators: a scoping review of medical tourism trends (1990–2016). *Almatourism – Journal of Tourism, Culture, and Territorial Development, 15,* 56–83.

Majeed, S., Lu, C., and Javed, T. (2017a). The journey from an allopathic to natural treatment approach: a scoping review of medical tourism and health systems. *European Journal of Integrative Medicine, 16*, 22–32.

Majeed, S., Lu, C., Majeed, M., and Shahid, M.N. (2018). Health resorts and multi-textured perceptions of international health tourists. *Sustainability, 10*, 1063. doi: 10.3390/su10041063.

Majeed, S., Lu, C., and Usman, M. (2017b). Want to make me emotional? The influence of emotional advertisement on women's consumption behavior. *Frontiers of Business Research in China, 11*, 16. doi: 10.1186/s11782-017-0016-4.

Majeed, S., Majeed, M., and Ajike, M.A. (2019). Dry cupping therapy and wellness management of health travelers. *Traditional Medicine Research, 4*(1), 12–24.

Majeed, S., Zhou, Z., Lu, C., and Ramkissoon, H. (2020a). Online tourism information and tourist behavior: a structural equation modeling analysis based on a self-administered survey. *Frontiers in Psychology, 11*, 599. doi: 10.3389/fpsyg.2020.00599.

Majeed, S., Zhou, Z., and Ramkissoon, H. (2020b). Beauty and elegance: value co-creation in cosmetic surgery tourism. *SAGE Open, April–June*, 1–15. doi: 10.1177/2158244020932538.

Mansfeld, Y. (1992). From motivation to actual travel. *Annals of Tourism Research, 19*(3), 399–419.

Marchiori, E., and Cantoni, L. (2015). The role of prior experience in the perception of a tourism destination in user-generated content. *Destination Marketing and Management, 4*(3), 194–201.

Mariani, M., Ek Styven, M., and Ayeh, J.K. (2019). Using Facebook for travel decision making: an international study of antecedents. *International Journal of Contemporary Hospitality Management, 31*(2), 1021–1044.

Matyas, C.J., Srinivasan, S., Cahyanto, I., Thapa, B., Pennington-Gray, L., and Villegas, J. (2011). Risk perception and evacuation decisions of Florida tourists under hurricane threats: a stated preference analysis. *Natural Hazards, 59*(2), 871–890.

McIntyre, N., and Roggenbuck, J. (1998). Nature/person transactions during an outdoor adventure experience: a multi-phasic analysis. *Journal of Leisure Research, 30*(4), 401–422.

Mkono, M., and Tribe, J. (2016). Beyond reviewing: uncovering the multiple roles of tourism social media users. *Journal of Travel Research, 56*(3), 1–12.

Morosan, C., and Bowen, J.T. (2018). Analytic perspectives on online purchasing in hotels: a review of literature and research directions. *International Journal of Contemporary Hospitality Management, 30*(1), 557–580.

Munar, A.M., and Jacobsen, J.K.S. (2014). Motivations for sharing tourism experiences through social media. *Tourism Management, 43*, 46–54.

Nesi, J., and Prinstein, M.J. (2015). Using social media for social comparison and feedback seeking: gender and popularity moderate associations with depressive symptoms. *Journal of Abnormal Child Psychology, 43*(8), 1427–1438.

Naumov, N., Ramkissoon, H., and Hristov, D. (2020). Tourism planning and development. Distributed leadership in DMOs: a review of the literature and directions for future research. *Tourism Planning and Development*, 1–17.

Novelli, M., Burgess, L.G., Jones, A., and Ritchie, B.W. (2018). 'No Ebola … still doomed' – the Ebola-induced tourism crisis. *Annals of Tourism Research, 70*, 76–87.

Oh, S.-H., Lee, S.Y., and Han, C. (2020). The effects of social media use on preventive behaviours during infectious disease outbreaks: the mediating role of self-relevant emotions and public risk perception. *Health Communication*. doi: 10.1080/10410236.2020.1724639.

Parra-López, E., Bulchand-Gidumal, J., Gutiérrez-Taño, D., and Díaz-Armas, R. (2011). Intentions to use social media in organizing and taking vacation trips. *Computers in Human Behavior, 27*, 640–654.

Pennington-Gray, L., Kaplanidou, K., and Schroeder, A. (2012). Drivers of social media use among African Americans in the event of a crisis. *Natural Hazards*, 1–19. doi:10.1007/s11069-012-0101-0.

Pennington-Gray, L., Reisinger, Y., Kim, J.E., and Thapa, B. (2005). Do US tour operators' brochures educate the tourist on culturally responsible behaviours? A case study of Kenya. *Journal of Vacation Marketing, 11*, 265–284.

Perez-Vega, R., Taheri, B., Farrington, T., and O'Gorman, K. (2018). On being attractive, social and visually appealing in social media: the effects of anthropomorphic tourism brands on Facebook fan pages. *Tourism Management, 66*, 339–347.

Ramkissoon, H. (2015). Authenticity, satisfaction, and place attachment: a conceptual framework for cultural tourism in African island economies. *Development Southern Africa, 32*(3), 292–302.

Ramkissoon, H. (2018a). Hospitality consumers' information search behavior. In *The Routledge Handbook of Hospitality Marketing* (pp. 284–293). Abingdon: Routledge.

Ramkissoon, H. (2018b). Hospitality consumers' decision-making. In *The Routledge Handbook of Hospitality Marketing* (pp. 271–283). Abingdon: Routledge.

Ramkissoon, H. (2020). Place confinement, pro-social, pro-environmental behaviors and residents' wellbeing: a new conceptual framework. *Frontiers in Psychology.* doi: 10.3389/fpsyg.2020.02248.

Ramkissoon, H. (forthcoming). Tourist decision-making. In D. Buhalis (ed.), *Encyclopedia of Tourism Management and Marketing.* Cheltenham, UK and Northampton, MA, USA: Edward Elgar Publishing.

Ramkissoon, H., and Mavondo, F.T. (2017). Proenvironmental behavior: critical link between satisfaction and place attachment in Australia and Canada. *Tourism Analysis, 22*(1), 59–73.

Ramkissoon, H., Mavondo, F., and Uysal, M. (2018). Social involvement and park citizenship as moderators for quality-of-life in a national park. *Journal of Sustainable Tourism, 26*(3), 341–361.

Ramkissoon, H., and Nunkoo, R. (2008). Information search behavior of European tourists visiting Mauritius. *Turizam: međunarodni znanstveno-stručni časopis, 56*(1), 7–21.

Ramkissoon, H., and Nunkoo, R. (2012). More than just biological sex differences: examining the structural relationship between gender identity and information search behavior. *Journal of Hospitality and Tourism Research, 36*(2), 191–215.

Ramkissoon, H., Smith, L.D.G., and Weiler, B. (2013). Testing the dimensionality of place attachment and its relationships with place satisfaction and pro-environmental behaviours: a structural equation modelling approach. *Tourism Management, 36,* 552–566.

Ramkissoon, H., and Uysal, M.S. (2011). The effects of perceived authenticity, information search behaviour, motivation and destination imagery on cultural behavioural intentions of tourists. *Current Issues in Tourism, 14*(6), 537–562.

Sabiote-Ortiz, C.M., Frías-Jamilena, D.M., and Castañeda-García, J.A. (2016). Overall perceived value of a tourism service delivered via different media: a cross-cultural perspective. *Journal of Travel Research, 55,* 34–51.

Saleem, M.A., Yaseen, A., and Wasaya, A. (2018). Drivers of customer loyalty and word of mouth intentions: moderating role of interactional justice. *Journal of Hospitality Marketing and Management 27,* 877–904.

Seabrook, E.M., Kern, M.L., and Rickard, N.S. (2016). Social networking sites, depression, and anxiety: a systematic review. *JMIR Mental Health, 3*(4), e50.

Seymour, M., and Moore, S. (2000). *Effective crisis management: Worldwide principles and practice.* London: Cassell.

Schroeder, A., Pennington-Gray, L., Donohoe, H., and Kiousis, S. (2013). Using social media in times of crisis. *Journal of Travel and Tourism Marketing, Special Issue on Social Media, 30* (1–2), 126–43.

Sigala, M. (2011). Social media and crisis management in tourism: applications and implications for research, *Information Technology and Tourism, 13*(4), 269–283.

Sigala, M. (2020). Tourism and COVID-19: impacts and implication for advancing and resetting industry and research. *Journal of Business Research, 117,* 312–322.

Sotiriadis, M.D. (2017). Sharing tourism experiences in social media: a literature review and a set of suggested business strategies. *International Journal of Contemporary Hospitality Management, 29*(1), 179–225.

Sun, N., Rau, P.P.-L., and Ma, L. (2014). Understanding lurkers in online communities: a literature review. *Computers in Human Behavior, 38,* 110–117.

Tasci, A.D., and Gartner, W.C. (2007). Destination image and its functional relationships. *Journal of Travel Research, 45*(5), 413–425.

Vandervoort, D. (1999). Quality of social support in mental and physical health. *Current Psychology, 18*(2), 205.

Vannucci, A., Flannery, K.M., and Ohannessian, C.M. (2017). Social media use and anxiety in emerging adults. *Journal of Affective Disorders, 207,* 163–166.

Wang, X., Wu, Q., Majeed, S., and Sun, D. (2018). Fujian's industrial eco-efficiency: evaluation based on SBM and the empirical analysis of influencing factors. *Sustainability, 10,* 3333. doi: 10.3390/su10093333.

Wilder-Smith, A. (2006). The severe acute respiratory syndrome: Impact on travel and tourism. *Travel Medicine and Infectious Disease, 4,* 53–60.

Xiang, Z., Du, Q., Ma, Y., and Fan, W. (2017). A comparative analysis of major online review platforms: Implications for social media analytics in hospitality and tourism. *Tourism Management, 58,* 51–65.

Xiang, Z., and Gretzel, U. (2010). Role of social media in online travel information search. *Tourism Management, 31,* 179–88.

Xue, J., Zhou, Z., Zhang, L., and Majeed, S. (2020). Do brand competence and warmth always influence purchase intention? The moderating role of gender. *Frontiers in Psychology, 11,* 248. doi: 10.3389/fpsyg.2020.00248.

Yang, Y., Tan, K. P.-S., Li, X. (Robert) (2019). Antecedents and consequences of home-sharing stays: evidence from a nationwide household tourism survey. *Tourism Management, 70,* 15–28.

Yoo, K.-H., and Gretzel, U. (2011). Influence of personality on travel-related consumer-generated media creation. *Computers in Human Behavior, 27*(2), 609–621.

Yu, M., Li, Z., Yu, Z., He, J., and Zhou, J. (2020). Communication related health crisis on social media: a case of COVID-19 outbreak. *Current Issues in Tourism,* 24(19), 2699–2705.

11. Smart tourism destinations and social media analysis

Gozde Turktarhan and Olgun Cicek

INTRODUCTION

Smart tourism destinations have become more popular and encouraged recently due to digital technology advancements as well as social media usage worldwide. This concept has emerged mainly in the developed tourism destination countries, because of their advanced usage of information technology (IT). The United Nations Educational, Scientific and Cultural Organization (UNESCO) and the European Union (EU) have been announcing these new emerging destinations and recommending other countries to follow. There are competitions taking place among the smart cities regionally as well as globally, and the current trend suggests that more destinations will join the club. The European Capital of Smart Tourism Competition, organized by the EU, is the most comprehensive of these. To be able to compete, candidate cities need to implement their tourism practices in innovative ways in four areas: accessibility, sustainability, digitalization and cultural heritage and creativity (European Commission, 2021). Social media users will follow the trend and use media instruments to get real-time data and to plan their future travels.

According to Tham et al. (2021), there is a persistent perception that social media has a fundamental influence on destination choice and tourists make a choice after collecting information about the destination on social media. According to the results of a study by Internet Marketing Inc., 76 percent of tourists are influenced by holiday photos on social networks (Javed et al., 2020). Also, 52 percent of Facebook users share their holiday experiences to show the places that they visited to their friends (Liu et al., 2019). Studies show that those who love to travel are 44 percent more likely to learn about a new travel brand on Twitter than on the average social media network (Brown, 2017).

SOCIAL MEDIA SITES AND SOCIAL NETWORKS

It is well known that social media platforms such as Instagram, Facebook and YouTube are part of everyday life due to the ubiquitous use of mobile devices that affect people's lives in many ways (Ott and Theunissen, 2015). Out of about 7.2 billion individuals that make up the world population, 3 billion (42 percent) are internet users and slightly more than 2 billion are active social media users (29 percent) (WeareSocial, 2020). The tourism industry in particular benefits significantly from social media through brand awareness and the creation of brand advocacy communities, as well as reaching individual consumers (Creevey and Mehta, 2015). In addition, the frequency of social media usage has influenced every stage of the process, from planning the trip to sharing views during and after travel. This has led to a turning point for the travel industry. According to Google, 70 percent of travelers researched their travel plans using a smartphone, and half of those tourists made their hotel or flight reservation on their smartphone (ThinkwithGoogle, 2016).

Social media, which is effective in destination marketing as well as in many areas, has been a frequently researched subject and will continue to be worthy of research as its effects on the travel industry continue (Chryssoula and Evangelos, 2020). Increasing numbers of travelers who are affected by posts on social media, and plan their travel in line with these posts, is an advantage for destination management organizations (DMOs), as well as a disadvantage (Lange-Faria and Elliot, 2011). Social media plays an important role in many areas of tourism, especially in the process of seeking information and assisting in making decisions, promoting destinations, and focusing on best practices for interacting with tourists. Social media is the most cost-effective tool of advertising available today. Through use of social media only, a company can advertise and market to more than 1,000 people at a price tag below $3.00 USD (Lyfe Marketing, 2021). Should the economy enter a recession where public and government-funded companies see budget cuts, the DMO can remain highly competitive with their marketing strategy through the utilization of social media (Alwis & Andrlic, 2016). According to Pike and Page (2014) there is a steady increase in the number of social media-centric studies conducted by researchers around the world, but there seems to be an unequal adoption and utilization rate among DMOs. Most of the problems faced in social media, such as social scrutiny, community management and measuring an effective return on investment, continue to be faced by DMOs as well.

Instagram is one of the most popular social media platforms. In 2010, it was released to users as a photo sharing and filtering application. Instagram's algorithm calculates how likely someone is to interact with a post, known as a 'score of interest', which ultimately determines the order and frequency in which posts are displayed in the user's feed. The algorithm can be manipulated by attaching 'hashtags' (#) to a visual post. For instance, a picture of a hotel rooftop with the city skyline in the background could be accompanied by the 'hashtags' #Celebration #Birthday. Users will now see the hotel's rooftop post in their feed more frequently and thus will associate this hotel with potential party destinations because the algorithm has grouped the visual of their rooftop with the topics of birthdays and celebrations. The Instagram algorithm also detects interactions among users to understand which content they like to see the most. If a user constantly 'likes' and/or 'comments' on a specific creator's posts, that user will now see more of that specific creator's content in their feed. Thus, the number of likes and comments increased by not only by sharing the images with one's own friends, but also by others sharing them (Uca Ozer et al., 2016). It is a social media site developed especially for use on mobile devices. The ease of use is makes this application attractive, because the navigation bar is understandable and simple (Terttunen, 2017). According to January 2020 data, Instagram ranks sixth among social media, with more than 1 billion users and more than 500 million daily posts worldwide (Aslam, 2020).

SMART CITIES AND SMART TOURISM DESTINATIONS

Smart cities are defined as "living spaces that adopt scalable solutions by using information and communication technologies to increase efficiency, reduce costs and improve the quality of life" (Falconer and Mitchell, 2012, p. 3). In order to make a smart city a more sustainable, livable and productive city, as well as being people-oriented with solutions provided by technology, and having the support of all stakeholders and institutions, there must be transparency and full participation, without violating the confidentiality of ethical rules and personal data.

The features that smart cities must provide are as follows (ISO, 2015):

- Smart cities should be able to provide more convenient and effective services using information technologies for the people living in that city.
- Sensors should provide better city management by utilizing technologies such as radio frequency identification (RFID), cloud services and the Internet of Things.
- It should be able to offer a better living environment.
- It should have more modern industries as well as a greener and human-friendly environment.
- It should have a 'smarter' infrastructure.
- It should have a dynamic and innovative economy.

Smart tourism has been shaped by the changes that have occurred with the internet, population growth, ecological factors, smart technologies and globalization. Another reason for the development of smart tourism is that tourism stakeholders want to understand and evaluate the tourists better in this new smart age, and to offer them better services and more effective tourism experiences (Wang et al., 2016).

Smart tourism is the result of combining the existing tourism online business model with modern information and communication technologies. The basis is the combination of the camera in smartphones, tablets and computers, with technologies such as websites, mobile platforms and the Internet of Things. Other factors are cloud computing, big and open data analysis, and technologies that provide the necessary information and tools before, during and after travel to tourists and users. It is supplemented with simple tools such as microphones and sensors (Kaur and Kaur, 2016).

Population concentration in cities today, energy demand, traffic problems, excessive consumption of natural resources, environmental pollution and economic sustainability concerns, have revealed the need for a more sustainable world. The concept of the smart city emerged as a solution to these problems and aimed to create livable, sustainable, safe and efficient cities while focusing on information and communication technologies (Lazaroiu and Roscia, 2012). The concept of the smart city refers to an environment where technology integrates with the city (Cantuarias-Villessuzanne et al., 2021). Smart cities offer various services to individuals and find solutions to social problems by using information and communication technologies and the internet. Today, smart city applications have become an indispensable element of city administrations. The British Standards Institution (2014) has defined the concept of the smart city. It has the vital technologies that offer sustainability, prosperity and a comprehensive future to citizens with the effective adaptation of physical, digital and human systems to the structural environment (British Standard Institution, 2014, p. 21).

The tourism sector, one of the largest sectors of the world economy, is also affected by these changes in the cities. In line with the use of technological developments at every stage of life, it is apparent that smart applications are increasingly widespread in the tourism sector. In this context, concepts such as smart tourism, smart city, smart hotel and smart transportation are frequently encountered (Buhalis and Amaranggana, 2014). Intelligent tourism applications have facilities such as informing citizens and tourists about the destination, offering food and beverage alternatives, directing them to historical and touristic places to visit, and providing personalized services. Although smart cities focus on the local people, the smart tourism philosophy focuses not only on the local people but also on the experience of tourists. As such, smart tourism focuses on the quality of life, mobility, accessibility and sustainability of local people and tourists (Gretzel et al., 2015).

HOW DO SMART CITIES USE SOCIAL MEDIA?

It is possible to say that the use of social media for businesses has applications in marketing, promotion and reaching larger audiences. Similar functions are known to apply to destinations. There are a few articles on the social media accounts that destinations follow. Such studies are important because they provide an understanding of the network structure of the destinations. Tourism, which is the EU's major socio-economic activity, represents approximately 10 percent of the EU's gross domestic product (GDP). The tourism industry has a significant impact on economic growth and job opportunuties in the EU as well as in many other places. When smart tourism is considered, it is clear that it has an as yet undiscovered and unused potential. Innovation, accessibility and sustainability, which are important elements of smart tourism, are the future of tourism, and the EU has formed a commission in this field. The task of this commission is to keep European tourism ahead of the curve within the scope of smart tourism (European Capital of Smart Tourism, 2020).

Malaga and Gothenburg are the 2020 European Capitals of Smart Tourism. Besides these cities, four cities were also recognized with 2020 European Smart Tourism Awards for their outstanding achievements in the initiative's four categories. These cities are Gothenburg in the category of sustainability, Breda in the category of accessibility, Ljubljana on the category of digitalization and Karlsruhe in the category of cultural heritage and creativity.

When the official Instagram accounts of these five cities, the smart tourism destinations of 2020 throughout Europe, are examined within the framework of four basic research questions, a wide variety of results are encountered. This basic research is adapted from the questions Park et al. (2016) and Dogra and Kale (2020) adopted. Accordingly, by focusing on the following questions, the Instagram pages of five smart tourism destinations in Europe were examined:

- Q1: How many followers do the smart tourism destinations' Instagram accounts have?
- Q2: How many accounts are followed by smart tourism destinations' Instagram accounts?
- Q3: How many posts do the smart tourism destinations' Instagram accounts have?
- Q4: What is the profile of accounts followed by smart tourism destinations?

The official Instagram accounts of the cities selected as the smart tourism destinations by the European Commission were determined in June 2020 (see Gemeente Breda, n.d.; Göteborg/ Gothenburg, n.d.; Ljubljana, n.d.; Málaga Ciudad Genial, n.d.; Visit Karlsruhe, n.d.). The accuracy of the accounts has been confirmed on the official websites of those smart cities. Then, the number of posts shared by these accounts, the number of followers and the number of accounts followed, and the profile of the accounts were determined. In addition, hashtags followed by smart destinations are also used as data. Since the Instagram accounts of smart cities are not private accounts, anyone can follow them. For this reason, we focused on the profile of the pages followed, not the follower profile. Each account followed by smart tourism destinations was examined individually, and the profile of these accounts was determined based on the explanation in the bio section of their Instagram profile page.

Table 11.1   *Basic information of the Instagram accounts of smart cities*

City, country	Category	Name of account	Followers	Followed by	Posts	Language of posts
Gothenburg, Sweden	Capital/ Sustainability	goteborgcom	51 000	557	1 564	Swedish, English
Malaga, Spain	Capital	malagatourismo	50 100	223	1 428	Spanish
Ljubljana, Slovenia	Digitalization	visitljubljana	36 700	1042	1 765	English
Karlsruhe, Germany	Cultural heritage and Creativity	visitkarlsruhe	8 743	495	943	German
Breda, Netherlands	Accessibility	gemeente_breda	8 168	267	120	Dutch

Source: Based on data from Instagram (June 7, 2020).

As a result, it is seen in Table 11.1 that the numbers of followers and posts are similar when the official Instagram accounts of Gothenburg and Malaga, one of the smart tourism capitals, are examined. However, although the posts on the Gothenburg account are both local and English, the posts on the Malaga account are only in Spanish. In addition, Karlsruhe and Breda accounts are posted in the local language, not in English. On the other hand, Ljubljana posts on its Instagram account only in English, not in Slovenian, the official language.

According to another striking result, when the Instagram accounts followed by smart tourism destinations were examined using content analysis, it was determined that there was a wide variety of profiles. Table 11.2 provides information on these profiles. According to Table 12.2, the most common profile type followed by the Instagram account of each smart tourism destination is individual profiles. These are followed by restaurants and photographers. Another noteworthy result is that very few accounts are followed based on accessibility, digitalization, sustainability, cultural heritage and creativity, which are among the elements of smart tourism. Only Ljubljana and Breda follow non-governmental organizations that work on sustainability.

DISCUSSION

Based on the above literature review and analysis it can be stated that social media tools play crucial roles in marketing and promoting destinations as well as in developing smart tourism destinations by providing real-time data, innovation, accessibility and sustainability for the future of tourism. As a social media tool, Instagram was analyzed closely for the purpose of this study. The results are promising and show that there is a direct relationship between the customer choice of a destination via the social media tool, as well as the promotion of the destination through the same social media tools.

The content analysis indicates that among the smart tourism destinations in Europe, Gothenburg has the most followers on Instagram and Breda has the least. Ljubljana shares the most posts, while Malaga shares the least. When the language used is examined, it is seen that only Gothenburg and Ljubljana share posts in English. Malaga, Karlsruhe and Breda's Instagram accounts use local languages; Gothenburg uses not only English but also the local language. Also, when the accounts that Europe's smart tourism destinations follow on Instagram are classified according to their types, it is seen that there are various account profiles, ranging from politicians to activity pages, from individual accounts to airline compa-

Table 11.2   *The profiles of the accounts followed by smart cities' Instagram accounts*

Account type	Gothenburg	Malaga	Ljubljana	Karlsruhe	Breda	Total
Airline company	-	9	-	-	-	9
Art gallery	-	12	-	-	-	9
Artist	22	-	-	50	8	80
Blogger	45	-	-	67	24	136
Chef	-	-	36	-	-	36
Entertainment	17	12	1	72	-	102
Hotel		22	-	-	-	22
Individual	210	64	552	48	60	934
LMS	-	-	-	-	2	2
Local wine producer	-	-	-	18	-	18
Non-governmental organizations (NGOs)	-	-	6	-	5	11
Other city's account	-	12	-	22	-	34
Photographer	78	28	69	67	32	274
Politician	12	-	6	-	-	18
Press	-	-	75	29	18	122
Public body	19	9	24	-	12	64
Real estate	-	-	-	-	6	6
Restaurant	154	38	123	122	68	505
Shopping	-	-	6	-	-	6
Sports team	-	-	9	-	-	9
Tourist guide	-	-	21	-	-	21
Travel agency	-	17	46	-	32	95
Traveler	-	-	68	-	-	68
Total	557	206	907	495	235	

Source: Based on data from Instagram (June 7, 2020).

nies, from distance education systems to tourism businesses. Individual accounts, which are the most frequently followed account type among all smart tourism destinations, are followed most by Ljubljana. Restaurants accounts and photographers' accounts come right after the individual Instagram accounts. Another remarkable result is that among the accounts followed by the Instagram accounts of smart tourism destinations, there are no official accounts related to the EU, sustainability and accessibility. In today's world, while there are many Instagram accounts on accessibility, sustainability, digitalization, cultural heritage and creativity, it is seen that these accounts are not followed by smart tourism destinations. Social media plays a very important role in today's life. It is a web-based online tool that enables people to discover and learn new information, share ideas, and interact with new people and organizations. The concept of reality is ever-changing and social media platforms have blurred those lines evermore. It has changed the way people live their lives, rapidly increased the rate of communication, even shifted social priorities. Although social media represents a very narrow scope of inter-institutional relations of smart tourism destinations, it deserves more credit than it is given as a conduit of judgement. The requisition of 'friends', a yearning to be 'liked', accumulating a 'following', all these nuances of social media influence the users' perception and thus influence the users' decision-making processes.

Social networks have developed targeted ad solutions that allow businesses to reach their potential customers based on the profile of the user. Social networks also have unique access to the most personal information of their users like their hobbies, interests, places frequently visited, and so on. Social media allows people to interact in ways we could never have previously imagined. It is quite easy to catch up on someone's life through a simple message on the computer or mobile phone, even email. Social media enables communication for not only one's personal life, but also for business life.

Finally, it is a fact that smart tourism destinations are getting more popular and are being encouraged, due to digital technology advancements as well as social media usage worldwide. This trend will boost the number of smart tourism cities from the marketing and promotion perspective on the supply side, as a competitive advantage, and the usage of social media tools from the consumer perspective on the demand side, globally.

REFERENCES

Alwis, A.C., and Andrlic, B. (2016). Social media in destination marketing. *International Journal of Management and Applied Science*, *2*(4), 121–125.

Aslam, S. (2020, February 10). Instagram by the numbers: stats, demographics and fun facts. Retrieved July 1, 2020, from Omnicore: https://www.omnicoreagency.com/instagram-statistics/.

British Standards Institution (2014). *Smart City Framework – Guide to Establish Strategies for Smart Cities and Communuties*. London: British Standards Institution.

Brown, R. (2017, January 18). The impact of social media on travel inspiration. Retrieved June 6, 2020, from Olapic: https://www.olapic.com/resources/the-impact-of-social-media-on-travel -inspiration_blog-p1aw-f1tr-v1th-t1sm/.

Buhalis, D., and Amaranggana, A. (2014). Smart tourism destinations. In Z. Xiang and I. Tussyadiah (eds), *Information and Communication Technologies in Tourism* (pp. 553–564). Cham: Springer International Publishing.

Cantuarias-Villessuzanne, C., Weigel, R., and Blain, J. (2021). Clustering of European smart cities to understand the cities' sustainability strategies. *Sustainability*, *12*(2). https://doi.org/10.3390/su13020513.

Chryssoula, C., and Evangelos, C. (2020). Adoption of social media as distribution channels in tourism marketing: a qualitative analysis of consumers' experiences. *Journal of Tourism, Heritage and Services Marketing*, *6*(1), 25–32.

Creevey, D., and Mehta, G. (2015). Investigating the use of social media tools by destination marketing organisations. In *11th Annual Tourism and Hospitality Research in Ireland Conference (THRIC)* (pp. 15–35). Ireland: Letterkenny Institute of Technology.

Dogra, J., and Kale, S. (2020). Network analysis of destination management organization smart tourism ecosystem (STE) for e-branding and marketing of tourism destinations. In C. Ramos, C. Almedia, and P. Fernandes (eds), *Handbook of Research on Social Media Applications for the Tourism and Hospitality Sector* (pp. 3–17). Hershey, PA: IGI Global.

European Capital of Smart Tourism (2020, January 20). About, European Capital of Smart Tourism. Retrieved April 26, 2020, from European Capital of Smart Tourism: https://smarttourismcapital.eu/about/.

European Commission (2021). EU launches European Capital of Smart Tourism 2022 competition. https://ec.europa.eu/growth/content/eu-launches-european-capital-smart-tourism-2022-competition _en.

Falconer, G., and Mitchell, S. (2012). *Smart City Framework*. San Jose, CA: Cisco Internet Solutions Group.

Gemeente Breda [@gemeente_breda] (n.d.). Posts [Instagram profile]. Accessed June 7, 2020, https://www.instagram.com/gemeente_breda/.

Göteborg/Gothenburg [@goteborgcom] (n.d.). Posts [Instagram profile]. Accessed June 7, 2020, https://www.instagram.com/goteborgcom/.

Gretzel, U., Koo, C., Sigala, M., and Xiang, Z. (2015). Special issue on smart tourism: convergence of information technologies, experiences, and theories. *Electronic Markets*, *25*(3), 175–177.

ISO (2015, January 20). *Smart cities Preliminary Report 2014*. Retrieved July 2, 2020, from ISO: https://www.iso.org/files/live/sites/isoorg/files/developing_standards/docs/en/smart_cities_report-jtc1.pdf.

Javed, M., Tučková, Z., and Jibril, A.B. (2020). The role of social media on tourists' behavior: an empirical analysis of millennials from the Czech Republic. *Sustainability, 12*(18), https://doi.org/10.3390/su12187735.

Kaur, K., and Kaur, R. (2016). Internet of Things to promote tourism: an insight into smart tourism. *International Journal of Recent Trends in Engineering and Research, 2* (4), 357–361.

Lange-Faria, W., and Elliot, S. (2011). Understanding the role of social media in destination marketing. *Tourismos, 7* (1), 193–211.

Lazaroiu, G.C., and Roscia, M. (2012). Definition methodology for the smart cities model. *Energy, 47* (1), 326–332.

Liu, H., Wu, L., and Li, X. (2019). Social media envy: how experience sharing on social networking sites drives millennials' aspirational tourism consumption. *Journal of Travel Research, 58* (3), 355–369.

Ljubljana [@visitljubljana] (n.d.). Posts [Instagram profile]. Accessed June 7, 2020, https://www.instagram.com/visitljubljana/.

Málaga Ciudad Genial [@malagaturismo]. (n.d.). Posts [Instagram profile]. Accessed June 7, 2020, https://www.instagram.com/malagaturismo/.

Ott, L., and Theunissen, P. (2015). Reputations at risk: engagement during social media crises. *Public Relations Review, 41* (1), 97–102.

Park, J.H., Lee, C., Yoo, C., and Nam, Y. (2016). An analysis of the utilization of Facebook by local Korean governments for tourism development and the network of smart tourism ecosystem. *International Journal of Information Management, 36*(6), 1320–1327.

Pike, S., and Page, S.J. (2014). Destination marketing organizations and destination marketing: a narrative analysis of the literature. *Tourism Management, 41*(2), 202–227.

Terttunen, A. (2017). The influence of Instagram on consumers' travel planning and destination choice. Unpublished Master thesis, Haaga Heiki University of Applied Sciences, Helsinki.

Tham, A., Mair, J., and Croy, G. (2021). Social media influence on tourists' destination choice: importance of context. *Tourism Recreation Research, 45*(2), 161–175.

ThinkwithGoogle (2016, July 15). How the travel research process plays out in time to make a plan moments. Retrieved May 25, 2020, from Think with Google: https://www.thinkwithgoogle.com/consumer-insights/travel-research-process-make-a-plan-moments/.

Uca Ozer, S., Albayrak, A., and Guduk, T. (2016). Edirne iline özgü gastronomi kültürünün pazarlanmasında sosyal medyanın rolü [The role of social media in the marketing of Edirne city-specific gastronomy culture]. *Uluslararası Sosyal ve Ekonomik Bilimler Dergisi, 6*(2), 71–80.

Visit Karlsruhe [@visitkarlsruhe] (n.d.). Posts [Instagram profile]. Accessed June 7, 2020, https://www.instagram.com/visitkarlsruhe/.

Wang, X., Li, X., Zhen, F., and Zhang, J.H. (2016). How smart is your tourist attraction? Measuring tourist preferences of smart tourism attractions via a FCEM-AHP and IPA approach. *Tourism Management, 54*(3), 309–320.

WeareSocial (2020, January 10). *Digital in 2019*. Retrieved May 20, 2020, from We Are Social: https://wearesocial.com/global-digital-report-2019.

PART III

MARKETING STRATEGIES, CHANNELS, FORMATS

12. The impact of social media and information technology on service quality and guest satisfaction in the hospitality industry

Elangkovan Narayanan

INTRODUCTION

Improvement in service quality on an operational level can bring about immediate positive responses from guests in a restaurant (Cohen and Olsen, 2013). Moreover, the introduction of certain policies in the hospitality industries emphasizes service quality to increase guest loyalty and ultimately leads to guest satisfaction. Apart from this, many other leading experts on service quality management back the fact that the two variables indeed complement each other and are correlated (Connolly and Lee, 2006). However, with the advent of the twenty-first century the focus of most industries in the world has turned to information technology (Connolly and Sigala, 2001). As the economy recovers from the global recession, competition seems to be on the rise, and thus the race to secure more market share and attract the most guests is increasing (Dominici and Guzzo, 2010). This has been especially true in the hospitality industry, which is on its way to becoming the largest and the fastest-growing industry in the world by 2022 (Fantazy et al., 2010).

Some regions around the world, especially the Middle East, Central Asia and South East Asia, seem to be hotspots for tourism activity in the coming years. Countries such as Qatar have announced that they will be looking forward to opening approximately 500 hotels by 2020 which will also cater to the FIFA football World Cup of 2022 (Hung and Chen, 2013). On the other hand, Starwood, one of the largest hotel groups in the world with up to nine different brands, has announced that it will be opening almost 32 properties throughout South East Asia by 2021. In addition to this Dubai was looking to increase its market share and attract more global clientele by 2020 for the World Expo (Jayawardena et al., 2013). The race to meet their objectives has become increasingly difficult as ways to maximize revenue look bleak and minimizing cost is becoming an ordeal. As a result, a shift towards information technology provides a short-term as well as a long-term answer (Jayawardena et al., 2013). Thus, on the global scale, information technology appears to be playing a crucial role in the operations and management for hospitality. Furthermore, the uncertainty of the ecological environment has forced hospitality organizations to be dependent on information technology.

PROBLEM STATEMENT

Studies have shown that guest satisfaction leads to an increase in revenue. Revenue is expected to increase with the usage of social media and information technology in the hospitality industry (Lee, 2013). However, it has been reported (Liat et al., 2014), that budget allocations for information technology development for hotels were only 0.9 per cent, which indicates that the hospitality industry is lacking in the application of social media and information technology. Research on service quality and guest satisfaction is scarce; however, social media and information technology play a mediating role in the relationship between the two variables. Social media and information technology usage has become an important factor when it correlates to guest satisfaction (Chathoth, 2007; Kandampully and Suhartanto, 2000; Shanka and Taylor, 2003; Torres and Kline, 2006; Skogland and Siguaw, 2004). Today's guests are becoming more technology-friendly and more receptive to change. Thus the current trend is for guests to demand higher standards of service quality via social media and information technology (Cobanoglu et al., 2011). This article also explores that social media and information technology could develop a strategic tool to improve market analysis and detect new markets for the hotel industry.

There is no doubt that, even despite low investment in information technology, there has been a significant increase in the market share of certain companies and providers that focus on information technology (Kim and Ham, 2006). Several studies have shown that customer satisfaction leads directly to an increase in revenue for organizations, especially for those that have focused more on information technology (Lee, 2013). Thus, there are significant indicators suggesting that information technology has a place in this relationship. However, there is still reluctance within the hospitality industry to fully adopt technological advances and adapt to guests' changing requirements. It has taken a long while for hotels to realize the true potential of property management systems, and they are still struggling to understand the significance of Wi-Fi for guests. This chapter intends to explore the importance of social media technology in the hospitality industry to provide service quality and guest satisfaction.

GUEST SATISFACTION

Customer satisfaction is basically defined as the customer's attitude and mindset that is created by comparing their expectations of the product before the purchase to the value or satisfaction they gain after they receive it (Oliver, 1980). Customer satisfaction is also defined by Kotler (2000, p. 36) as a customer's experienced emotions of content or discontent when the predicted performance of a product is compared with the real expectation. It is also regarded as a combined result of psychological reactions, evaluation and perception towards the usage experience of the good or service, whether tangible or in tangible. Guest satisfaction and customer satisfaction are the same in academic and professional circles. The customer is considered to be satisfied when, after purchase, the quality obtained is greater than the expected quality (Kotler et al., 2003). This scenario is the objective of every hospitality firm. Zeithaml et al. (2006) postulated that there is a direct and positive relationship of customer satisfaction and customer loyalty. Numerous studies have been carried out on the links and relationships between customer satisfaction, customer loyalty and service quality (Skogland and Siguaw, 2004; Yee et al., 2009).

It has been debated that even providing high-quality service does not guarantee customer retention (Kotler et al., 2003; Reid and Bojanic, 2009; Zeithaml et al., 2006). There could be numerous reasons that can lead to customer retention besides high-quality service. One factor could be that the customer likes the travel experience and explores different areas instead of sticking with one. This mindset means that even if a customer returns to a same hotel, they might still want to try a new place. This leaves a window open for other hotels to attract customers through different deals and packages.

However, Yee et al. (2009) found that service quality has a significant and direct impact on customer satisfaction, and that the relationship between customer satisfaction and loyalty is also significantly high. Skogland and Siguaw (2004) stated that satisfied guests have the highest ratio of returning and showing loyalty.

Zeithaml et al. (2006) talk about the fact that customer expectations of a service are dependent on several factors that come together to form a complex consensus about it. Moreover, it is also said that apart from the above factors, word-of-mouth is a strong factor that affects the expectations of guests at a hotel. People today tend to trust their friends' and family's viewpoint of a certain product more than adverts, because it is based on experience. One reason for this is probably the increased number of false advertisements by hotels. When reality does not meet their expectations, disappointment and frustration set in, which leads to customer dissatisfaction.

SOCIAL MEDIA AND INFORMATION TECHNOLOGY

The adoption of information technology in the hospitality industry started around the early 1970s (Collins and Cobanoglu, 2008; Erdem et al., 2009; Kasavana and Cahill, 2007; Sammons, 2000). The adoption of technology became an absolute necessity for operational management in the hospitality industry, in terms of managing accommodation, food and beverages, recreation, and so on (Piccoli and Torchio, 2006). The new trend of technological advancements made processes comparatively faster, if not considerably faster. The overall transformation in technology has taken place throughout the hospitality industry in terms of operations and guest services (Lee et al., 2003).

Guest-oriented technological amenities are mostly adopted to improve performance and for the ease hotel employees, as well as to meet the ever-changing needs for guest satisfaction. The technological amenities found inside the room are present to provide a convenient, safe and comfortable ambience for the guest, and include the following: mini-bars, electronic locks and safes, alarm clocks, desktop computers, entertainment systems, climate control systems, and fire alarms and security systems (Collins and Cobanoglu, 2008). Information technology is an important factor when it comes to guest satisfaction and is vital for success in the long run not only for the hospitality industry but also in many other industries (Chathoth, 2007; Kandampully and Suhartanto, 2000; Shanka and Taylor, 2003; Torres and Kline, 2006). Skogland and Siguaw (2004).

The trend is for today's guests to become more technology-friendly and more receptive to changes in social media. These changes have also triggered them to desire higher standards of quality, and thus technology must step in to fill the gap (Cobanoglu et al., 2011). Another factor is the fact that today an average person carries around two to three devices when travelling, and thus hotels must provide a strong and easily available Wi-Fi connection. This is often not the case, as many hotels just provide one login per room and have other inconvenient zones to use Wi-Fi. As a result, the needs of the guests are not met (Williams, 1997).

As the clientele of the hospitality industry changes to include Generation Y, guest expectations also change in accordance with their habits. Generation Y are tech-savvy and very active on social media networks, thus it is crucial to exploit this technological avenue by training staff and adjusting company's attitude to put emphasis on these factors. Social networking online has become the fastest and most effective way to spread word-of-mouth and has quickly replaced the face-to-face approach. With the rise of social networking it is vital to monitor it thoroughly as well to respond to queries and complaints (Šerić et al., 2014).

The number of people who carry smartphones today compared to two decades ago has considerably increased, and they ahve become a modern necessity for social communications. It is no surprise that recently hoteliers have started to shift their interest to capitalizing on the increased social media usage through smartphones (Sun and Kim, 2013). Mobile check-in and check-out is the latest innovation in this line, and has gained in popularity. Hotels have introduced applications via smartphones that allow guests to check in easily. By removing the front desk from the check-in procedure, a lot of time is saved and thus customers are satisfied; it has been shown through studies that a waiting time of more than five minutes at the front desk can cause guest dissatisfaction and a negative effect on service quality (Singh and Kasavana, 2005). In addition to this, Generation Y also prefer self-service; thus, the trend of automated check-in/check-out kiosks is also on the rise (Papathanassis and Buhalis, 2007). They provide swift service, and the long wait at the front desk can be avoided, giving the guest an opportunity to save time and feel at ease with the least hassle and enjoy the comfort of their room.

SERVICE QUALITY

The recipe for success in the hospitality industry is always benchmarked against service quality. In general, service quality enhances guest satisfaction. Without doubt, service quality is the benchmark for the hospitality industry to be competitive, thus guest satisfaction is always dependent on how hospitality industries provide the best-quality service (Oh and Park, 1999; Nadiri and Hussain, 2005). The relationship between both variables – service quality and customer satisfaction – has been the focus of attention of many scholars. According to Parasuraman et al., service quality can be defined as the experience of customer service, with comparisons between what they receive and what is in their mind before the actual experience (Parasuraman et al., 1988). Additionally, perceived service quality has been characterized as customers' opinion or mentality in relation to the quality and predominance of the service generally (Zeithaml, 1988). It has been agreed upon by many researchers that the concept of service quality has been defined in many possible ways and has many dimensions, although it appears there has been no conclusion yet reached on how many ways and dimensions there are (Lehtinen and Lehtinen, 1982; Gronroos, 1984; Parasuraman et al., 1985, 1988).

Quality of service is usually measured by the SERVQUAL model, which was created by Parasuraman et al. (1985, 1988). There are five dimensions of quality service that can be measured by 22 items constituting this SERVQUAL model. The five dimensions of service quality are as follows:

- Tangibility (physical facilities, equipment and employees' appearance).
- Reliability (the ability to perform what is promised accurately).
- Responsiveness (speedy service and willingness to help the customers).
- Assurance (knowledge, courtesy of employees, their ability to convey trust and confidence).
- Empathy (the individualized attention and caring the firm offers to its customers).

Customer satisfaction is the opinion of the customer that they felt pleasure after consuming the product or service (Oliver, 1997). If we look at previous studies conducted on this matter, they imply that service quality is one of the principal resons for customer satisfaction. The relationship between them is positive, which shows that the higher the quality of the service, the higher the level of satisfaction for the customer. Explorations on quality services and customer satisfaction in different countries in various research areas have been conducted: Caruana (2002) looked into banking services in Malta; Kang and James (2004) explored mobile phone services in Korea; Tsoukatos and Rand (2006) examined insurance services in Greece; Hsu (2008) investigated online retail services in Taiwan; Bai et al. (2008) researched hotel websites in China; Wang and Hing (2009) looked into tourist destination in China); and Huang et al. (2010) explored tour guide services in Shanghai.

Even though analysts by and large concur with the multidimensionality of the service quality concept, just a couple of observational studies have reported connections between service quality dimensions and consumer loyalty. Studies on customers in the United States have noticed that in full service restaurants, four elements had a major impact on customer satisfaction, namely: food quality, reliability, price and responsiveness (Andaleeb and Conway, 2006). Mohammad and Alhamadani (2011) stated that five service quality dimensions – empathy, tangibles, reliability, responsiveness and assurance – had a significant influence on customer satisfaction in commercial banks in Jordan. In a study of the Hong Kong hotel industry, these elements were found to have a primary effect on customer satisfaction. Those elements were related to quality of the rooms, value, service staff quality, amenities, business services and, especially, security (Choi and Chu, 2001). According to Fah and Kandasamy (2011) the five dimensions of service quality, along with ecological design, had noteworthy associations with guest satisfaction in the Malaysian hotel industry.

Everyone's point of view about service quality can be different, as it varies from person to person in terms of their perception of the service and the way it is communicated (Cronin and Taylor, 1992; Oliver, 1993; Zeithaml et al., 1993).

There is no doubt that today the tertiary and service sectors are trying continuously to improve the quality of their service and to achieve maximum customer satisfaction through service delivery (Biswas and Seetharam, 2007). This is particularly true for the hotel industry, where the first objective of hotels is to identify guest expectations and understand them so that they may be able to anticipate and comprehend future changes or shifts. As a result of being able to pinpoint guest expectations, hotels will find it easy to fulfill them and make sure their guests are content with the service, thus achieving guest satisfaction, which is the number one priority in every hotel. Through continued guest satisfaction, guest loyalty follows, and this increases the number of repeat customers, which brings higher revenues in the short and long run.

METHODOLOGY

The research reported here focuses on a qualitative method. The reason for this is that the research questions constructed require different methods to be used for the effective collection of data. Thus, interviews were used to provide in-depth analysis of the respondents' replies, to justify the study. This allows the researcher to effectively obtain feedback from potential guests as well as hospitality providers. The interviews were conducted as part of the qualitative research to obtain data from managers and directors of various four- and five-star hotels in Subang Jaya and Kuala Lumpur Malaysia.

Seven interviews in total were conducted. Two were done with a director of finance of a five-star hotel in Subang Jaya. The remaining two were done with the front office, and three were with the human resource managers, of a four-star property in Kuala Lumpur. These managers were chosen because they hold important positions and possess in-depth operational knowledge as they function as decision-makers.

Interview Design

The interviews can be classified as semi-structured. The questions were formed in a such way that they target problems and barriers regarding technology change and adaption in the hospitality industry. The interviewees were people in a position of some decision-making power who influence technological changes in their hotel. The interviews were conducted through different channels. The preferred method was to conduct the interview face-to-face. Three of the managers were met personally to conduct a face-to-face interview. In some cases, the data was collected via email, whereby a template was sent that had to be answered. The responding emails with the answers were then received and the data was recorded. This method was efficient and effective since it took less time and we were able to gather information in written form and could keep a record. Four respondents replied to the email with the attached questions as they could not attend face-to-face interviews; however, prior to emailing them, telephone interview were conducted with feedback sent over email.

The following questions were posted to the managers to obtain feedback for the study:

1. How do you think technology has changed the industry today and what has its effect been?
2. How important do you think technology is when it comes to improving service quality and guest satisfaction?
3. Despite the benefits technology provides, it is still one of the departments with the least investments within the hospitality industry. Why do you think that is so?
4. What policies or practices do you look to when coming up with innovations or integrating new technology?
5. How do you think technology can help in the future?

Data Analysis

The qualitative analysis was conducted based on the questions posted to the relevant managers from four- and five-star hotels situated in Klang Valley. Table 12.1 indicates the findings from the interview conducted with seven managers. All seven managers provided similar feedback regarding the variables tested on social media and technology usage, service quality and guest satisfaction.

From the analysis in Table 12.1, the qualitative data clearly indicates the emergence of the social media and technology usage in the hospitality industry. Further analysis was conducted to determine shortfalls of the present study, and further recommendations to be made from the analysis (Table 12.2).

Based on the summary of findings, the effect of technology in the hotel industry is clearly significant; the application of technology is generally welcomed, with only very limited draw-

Table 12.1   *Qualitative results from the interview conducted in four- and five-star hotels in Klang Valley*

Interview questions	Feedback from respondents
How do you think technology has changed the industry today and what has its effect been?	The respondents hold a strong belief that technology has a significant impact in the hospitality industry. The respondents believe that it has had a positive effect, and has helped the hospitality industry to cater to guests' needs swiftly and effectively. However, one respondent did state that technology can be disadvantageous in certain cases. Upon further inquiry, he stated that in some cases technology is not accepted well and does not fit well into the system of the hotel. Thus, the timing and implementation procedure should be right, or else technological implementations can have an undesirable effect.
How important do you think technology is when it comes to improving service quality and guest satisfaction?	The responses received were varied. Three agree that technology is important and improves service quality and guest satisfaction. However, one respondent maintained that it hinders guest satisfaction and service quality at times because the element of true hospitality and face-to-face interaction is lost. This might be true when we observe people of an older age group who prefer elements of the hotel to stay consistent, and feel more comfortable with environments that they have been used to. In conclusion, technology's effect may vary among age groups and preferences, but overall it does have a strong impact.
Despite the benefits technology provides it is still one of the departments receiving the least investment within the hospitality industry. Why do you think that is so?	The overall response revolves around several factors that might hinder a manager or a director from adopting new technologies: convergence, time, cost, risk and fear. These factors lead managers/directors to delay this process or look for other avenues for solutions.
What policies or practices do you look to when coming up with innovations or integrating new technology?	Upon interviewing all seven respondents, it was obvious that in most cases no specific plan or policy is in place to encourage the perception of technology as an answer to problems. Some respondents adhere to certain plans; however, they vary from case to case, and mostly rely on what comes in from the parent company or headquarters. The technology discussion is not considered a part of any meeting, daily weekly agenda or any other sort of discussion.
How do you think technology can help in the future?	The respondents have a strong belief that technology will play an important role and carries great significance for the survival of the industry. The emergence of Generation Y as the next major market cannot be ignored, and will demand the industry to be more tech-savvy than it is.

backs. This result strongly resembles the findings based on the previous work done by Saura et al. (2014). The result regarding service quality and guest satisfaction suggested a positive relationship for technology with both the variables; however, a slight negative perception was registered among the older patrons to four- and five-star hotels, with similar findings from Saleem and Sarfraz (2014). One of the biggest challenges faced by the hotel industry in applying technology for its operations is the cost. Many of these hotels are sceptical about technological investment and more reliant on human service. Hotels often claim that humans provide the best form of service to satisfy guests. This has led to a lack of research into technological advancement among four- and five-star hotels. Based on the findings, hotels are still lacking in technological development and are not ready to provide the best quality of services for guests; likewise, academic institutions are more concerned with research development. The findings are similar to a study conducted by Li et al. (2008) on technology advancement and learning in hospitality management; however, the findings for this study also indicated a strong preference among Generation Y for the implementation of technology and social media. This can

Table 12.2   *Summary of findings*

Qualitative questions	Findings
Effect of technology on industry	Significant effect
	Largely positive
	Limited drawbacks
Effect on service quality and guest satisfaction	Positive effect and relationship with both variables
	Older age groups have negative relationship
Reason for low investment in technology	Convergence issues
	Time
	Cost
	Risk
	Fear
Policies for research and technological development	No fixed policies
	Technology given second priority
	Majority upgrades from headquarters
Future of technology	Strong due to Generation Y's emergence

be expected to be the trend for the future of hospitality operations, and a necessity in order to achieve service quality and guest satisfaction.

CONCLUSION AND RECOMMENDATIONS

The main focus of the study was to develop a superior understanding and comprehension of the many ways in which technology impacts upon service quality and customer satisfaction in the hospitality industry. The research questions were constructed keeping two parties in mind that will be directly or indirectly affected: the consumers or guests, and the hotel providers.

The analysis for the study proved that today's guests have become technologically savvy; that they carry numerous devices to work, for communication and for entertainment purposes. These devices are usually connected to social networks. Thus, hotels must be aware of guests who are knowledgeable and demanding. Hotels should be ready to provide complementary technologically advanced services and support to improve their overall service quality. One of the variables for this study includes the availability of not just Wi-Fi but also high-speed internet connectivity. Moreover, increased usage of mobile phones has provided easy access information for room check-ins and keyless entry to rooms. This directly improves the efficiency of the guest check-in process.

Furthermore, the impact of technology was again highlighted when people used sites online to rate and book hotels; in fact, guests now prefer this method rather than physical or telephone bookings. This demonstrates that the service quality of reservations and bookings has improved, causing an increase in service quality and guest satisfaction, since guests can access faster and acquire better promotions and packages.

The interviews conducted were designed to obtain a better understanding of whether hospitality professionals throughout the industry do understand the significance of information technology on service quality and customer satisfaction, but fail to implement it due to challenging cost constraints. We were able to determine that many perceive high cost as an issue. The industry itself struggles to control its costs. Although technology provides a solution, it turns out to be too costly in the short run, even if it is going to lower costs in the long run.

Furthermore, the initial set-up takes time and disrupts operations due to initial fixes and adjustments, which also give rise to increased risks and fears of implementing new technology. This also results in convergence issues which can lead firms to exploring other options that require less hassle.

The overall trend seen in the analysis was that guests were increasingly inclined towards choosing technology options; they are considered to be a rising market in the current scenario, and a dominant presence in the future of the hospitality industry. This gives rise to certain practices and trends that might be beneficial for the hospitality industry to adopt.

It is crucial for the industry to provide more technologically friendly solutions to target this market towards the new generation of guests which is going to become the highest spending segment in the hospitality sector (Lee, 2013). As a result, the focus should shift to Generation Y as they will become the next market for the hospitality industry. They were found to be tech-savvy, and appreciative of swiftness and convenience in service. Generation Y seem to be the upcoming highest spenders on travel out of all generations, as they look to travelling in order to live intangible experiences instead of acquiring tangible products. Similarly, social networking should be used more by hotels to advertise themselves and create a complete online profile that is interactive and responsive, thus establishing themselves as proactive. Moreover, loyalty programmes need to be revamped as the guests of today ask for more for less, and are still at a stage where they are trying out a few different brands and developing their loyalties (Sharma, 2015).

As people become more aware of their surroundings, they have realized that being green and eco-friendly is an important factor. Generation Y look for hotel providers who care for the environment and are not just their for-profit motives. Green hospitality also provides solutions through technologically advanced means such as solar panels, laundry practices, and waste and energy management systems (Manaktola, 2009). This will provide a complete mesh of technology and green hospitality that will increase service quality and guest satisfaction.

The hospitality industry is now faced with new challenges in terms of cost in developing new technology. The application of new technology is expected to increase room rates and the costs of other utilities which will escalate the rates for accommodation for guests resulting in higher rates for accommodation that will not be available to everyone. Thus, many will be deprived of such experiences and guest satisfaction may suffer. This was proven by this study as well, where almost half of the sample said that it is not affordable. As a result, further research into ways of making technology affordable will be useful for the hospitality industry, and hospitality industries in the Klang Valley should be creative in providing cost-effective technology operations that could cater to guests in providing effective service quality and guest satisfaction.

REFERENCES

Andaleeb, S.S., and Conway, C. (2006). Customer satisfaction in the restaurant industry: an examination of the transaction-specific model. *Journal of Services Marketing, 20*, 3–11.

Bai, B., Law, R., and Wen, I. (2008). The impact of website quality on customer satisfaction and purchase intentions: evidence from Chinese online visitors. *International Journal of Hospitality Management, 27*, 391–402. https://doi.org/10.1016/j.ijhm.2007.10.008.

Biswas, A.K., and Seetharam, K.E. (2007). Achieving water security for Asia. *International Journal of Water Resources Development, 24*(1), 145–176.

Caruana, A. (2002). Service loyalty: the effects of service quality and the mediating role of customer satisfaction. *European Journal of Marketing*, *36*(7/8), 811–828.

Chathoth, P. (2007). The impact of information technology on hotel operations, service management and transaction costs: a conceptual framework for full-service hotel firms. *International Journal of Hospitality Management*, *26*(2), 395–408. doi:10.1016/j.ijhm.2006.03.004.

Choi, T.Y., and Chu, R. (2001). Determinants of hotel guests' satisfaction and repeat patronage in the Hong Kong hotel industry. *International Journal of Hospitality Management*, *20*(3), 277–297.

Cobanoglu, C., Berezina, K., Kasavana, M., and Erdem, M. (2011). The impact of technology amenities on hotel guest overall satisfaction. *Journal of Quality Assurance in Hospitality and Tourism*, *12*(4), 272–288. doi:10.1080/1528008x.2011.541842.

Cohen, J., and Olsen, K. (2013). The impacts of complementary information technology resources on the service-profit chain and competitive performance of South African hospitality firms. *International Journal of Hospitality Management*, *34*, 245–254. doi:10.1016/j.ijhm.2013.04.005.

Collins, G.R., and Cobanoglu, C. (2008). *Hospitality Information Technology: Learning How to Use It*, 6th edn. Dubuque, IA: Kendall/Hunt Publishing Company.

Connolly, D., and Sigala, M. (2001). Major trends and IT issues facing the hospitality industry in the new economy: a review of the 5th Annual Pan-European Hospitality Technology Exhibition and Conference (EURHOTEC 2000). *International Journal of Tourism Research*, *3*(4), 325–327. doi:10.1002/jtr.308.

Cronin Jr, J.J., and Taylor, S. (1992). Measuring service quality: a reexamination and extension. *Journal of Marketing*, *56*, 55–68.

Dominici, G., and Guzzo, R. (2010). Customer satisfaction in the hotel industry: a case study from Sicily. *International Journal of Marketing Studies*, *2*(2). doi:10.5539/ijms.v2n2p3.

Erdem, M., Schrier, T., and Brewer, P. (2009). Guest empowerment technologies: tools that give hotel guests personal control over their stay in a hotel. *Bottomline*, *24*(3), 17–19.

Fah, L.K., and Kandasamy, S. (2011). an investigation of service quality and customer satisfaction among hotels in Langkawi. *International Conference on Management (ICM 2011) Proceedings 2011-056-168*, Conference Master Resources.

Fantazy, K., Kumar, V., and Kumar, U. (2010). Supply management practices and performance in the Canadian hospitality industry. *International Journal of Hospitality Management*, *29*(4), 685–693. doi:10.1016/j.ijhm.2010.02.001.

Gronroos, C. (1984). A service quality model and its marketing implications. *European Journal of Marketing*, *18*, 36–44.

Hsu, S. (2008). Creating a learning management system to support instruction. *Communications of the ACM*, *51*(4), 59–63.

Hung, L., and Chen, C. (2013). A study of customer care and satisfaction towards hotel service quality. *IJECRM*, *7*(3/4), 161. doi:10.1504/ijecrm.2013.060710.

Jayawardena, C., Pollard, A., Chort, V., Choi, C., and Kibicho, W. (2013). Trends and sustainability in the Canadian tourism and hospitality industry. *WW Hospitality Tourism Themes*, *5*(2), 132–150. doi:10.1108/17554211311314164.

Kandampully, J., and Suhartanto, D. (2000). Customer loyalty in the hotel industry: the role of customer satisfaction and image. *International Journal of Contemporary Hospitality Management*, *12*(6), 346–351.

Kang, G.D., and James, J. (2004). Service quality dimensions: An examination of Gronroos's service quality model. *Managing Service Quality*, 14(4), 266–277. doi:10.1108/ 09604520410546806.

Kasavana, M.L. and Cahill, J.J. (2007). *Mananging Technology in the Hospitality Industry*, 4th edn. New Delhi: New Age International Publishers.

Kim, W., and Ham, S. (2006). The impact of information technology implementation on service quality in the hotel industry. *Information Technology in Hospitality*, *4*(4), 143–151. doi:10.3727/154595306779868430.

Kotler, P. (2000). *Marketing Management. The Millennium Edition*. Upper Saddle River, NJ: Prentice Hall.

Kotler, P., Bowen, J.T., and Makens, C.J. (2003). *Marketing for Hospitality and Tourism*. Harlow, UK: Prentice Hall.

Lee, L. (2013). Hospitality industry web-based self-service technology adoption model: a cross-cultural perspective. *Journal of Hospitality and Tourism Research*. doi:10.1177/1096348013495695.

Lee, S., Barker, S., and Kandampully, J. (2003). Technology, service quality, and customer loyalty in hotels: Australian managerial perspectives. *Managing Service Quality, 13*(5), 423–432. doi:10.1108/09604520310495886.

Lehtinen, U., and Lehtinen, J.R. (1982). A study of quality dimensions. *Service Management Institute, 5*, 25–32.

Li, X., Lee, H., and Law, J.L. (2008) 2008. Self-Selection and Information Role of Online Product Reviews. *Information Systems Research, 19*(4), 1–47.

Liat, C., Mansori, S., and Huei, C. (2014). The associations between service quality, corporate image, customer satisfaction, and loyalty: evidence from the Malaysian hotel industry. *Journal of Hospitality Marketing and Management, 23*(3), 314–326. doi:10.1080/19368623.2013.796867.

Manaktola, A. (2009). The impact of quality practices on customer satisfaction and business results: product versus service organizations. *Journal of Quality Management, 6*(1), 5–27. doi:10.1016/s1084-8568(01)00026-8.

Mohammad, A., and Alhamadani, S. (2011). Service quality perspectives and customer satisfaction in commercial banks working in Jordan. *Middle Eastern Finance and Economics, 14*(2), 60–72.

Nadiri, H., and Hussain, K. (2005). Diagnosing the zone of tolerance for hotel services. *Managing Service Quality: An International Journal, 15*(3), 259–277.

Oh, H., and Park, K. (1999). Service quality, customer satisfaction, and customer value: a holistic perspective. *International Journal of Hospitality Management, 18*(1), 67–82. doi:10.1016/s0278-4319(98)00047-4.

Oliver, L. (1980). A cognitive model of the antecedents and consequences of satisfaction decisions. *Journal of Marketing Research, 17*, 460–469.

Oliver, Richard L. (1981). Measurement and evaluation of satisfaction processes in retail settings. *Journal of Retailing, 57*, 95–48.

Oliver, R.L. (1993). Cognitive, affective, and attribute bases of the satisfaction response. *Journal of Consumer Research, 20*, 418–430. http://dx.doi.org/10.1086/209358.

Oliver, R.L. (1997). *Satisfaction: A Behavioral Perspective on the Customer*. New York: J.W.E. Sharpe.

Papathanassis, A., and Buhalis, D. (2007). Exploring the information and communication technologies revolution and visioning the future of tourism, travel and hospitality industries, 6th e-Tourism Futures Forum: ICT Revolutionising Tourism 26–27 March 2007, Guildford. *International Journal of Tourism Research, 9*(5), 385–387. doi:10.1002/jtr.624.

Parasuraman, A., Zeithaml, V.A., and Berry, L.L. (1985). A conceptual model of service quality and its implications for future research. *Journal of Marketing, 49*(4), 41–50.

Parasuraman, A., Zeithaml, V.A., and Berry, L.L. (1988). SERVQUAL: a multiple-item scale for measuring consumer perceptions of service quality. *Journal of Retailing, 64*, 12–40.

Piccoli, G., and Torchio, P. (2006). The strategic value of information: a manager's guide to profiting from information. *Cornel Hospitality Report, 7*(6), 1–10.

Reid, R.D., and Bojanic, D.C. (2009). *Hospitality Marketing Management*, 4th edn. Hoboken, NJ: Wiley.

Saleem, H., and Sarfraz, N. (2014). The impact of service quality on customer satisfaction, customer loyalty and brand image: evidence from hotel industry of Pakistan. *IOSR Journal of Business and Management, 16*(1), 117–122.

Sammons, D. (2000). Assessing active learning in the hospitality learners model. *Journal of Hospitality and Tourism Education, 28*(1), 1–12.

Saura, I.G., Ruiz Molina, M.E., and Berenguer Contrí, G. (2014). Retail innovativeness: importance of ICT and impact on consumer behaviour. In F. Musso and E. Druica (eds) *Handbook of Research on Retailer Consumer Relationship Development* (pp. 384–403). Hershey, PA: IGI Global.

Šerić, M., Saura, I.G., and Molina, M.E.R. (2014). How can integrated marketing communications and advanced technology influence the creation of customer-based brand equity? Evidence from the hospitality industry. *Journal of Hospitality Management, 39*(4), 144–156.

Shanka, T., and Taylor, R. (2003). An investigation into the perceived importance of service and facility attributes of hotel satisfaction. *Journal of Quality Assurance in Hospitality and Tourism, 3–4*(4), 119–134.

Sharma, R. (2015). Effect of celebrity endorsements on brand quality perceptions & brand loyalty – a comparative study of luxury & non luxury brands in India. *AIMA Journal of Management & Research*, 9(4), 1–13.

Singh, A., and Kasavana, M. (2005). The impact of information technology on future management of lodging operations: a Delphi study to predict key technological events in 2007 and 2027. *Tourism and Hospitality Research*, 6(1), 24–37. doi:10.1057/palgrave.thr.6040042.

Skogland, I., and Siguaw, J.A. (2004). Are your satisfied customers loyal? *Cornell Hotel and Restaurant Administration Quarterly*, 45(3), 221–234.

Sun, K., and Kim, D. (2013). Does customer satisfaction increase firm performance? An application of American Customer Satisfaction Index (ACSI). *International Journal of Hospitality Management*, 35, 68–77. doi:10.1016/j.ijhm.2013.05.008.

Torres, E., and Kline, S.F. (2006). From customer satisfaction to delight: a model for the hotel industry. *International Journal of Contemporary Hospitality Management*, 18(4), 290–301.

Tsoukatos, E., and Rand, G.K. (2006). Path analysis of perceived service quality, satisfaction and loyalty in Greek insurance. *Managing Service Quality: An International Journal*, 16(5), 501–519.

Yee, R.W.Y, Yeung, A.C.L., and Cheng, T.C.E. (2009). An empirical study of employee loyalty, service quality and firm performance in the service industry. *International Journal of Production Economics*, 124(1), 109–120.

Wang, Y., and Hing, L. (2009). Service quality, customer satisfaction and behaviour intentions: evidence from China's telecommunication industry. *Journal of Service Marketing*, 4(6), 50–60.

Zeithaml, V.A. (1988). Consumer perceptions of price, quality, and value: a means–end model and synthesis of evidence. *Journal of Marketing*, 52, 2–22.

Zeithaml, V.A., Berry, L.L., and Parasuraman, A. (1993). The nature and determinants of customer expectation of service. *Journal of the Academy of Marketing Science*, 21, 1–12.

Zeithaml, V.A., Bitner, M.J., and Gremler, D.D. (2006). *Services Marketing: Integrating Customer Focus Across the Firm*, 4th edn. New York: McGraw-Hill.

13. Leveraging social media to enhance customer value in tourism and hospitality

Robert Gutounig, Birgit Phillips, Sonja Radkohl, Sandra Macher, Karina Schaffer and Daniel Binder

INTRODUCTION

Information and communication technologies (ICTs) have greatly changed the role of the guest in tourism. With the rise of the World Wide Web, a neutral network was established with every user being a sender and receiver at the same time (Christakis and Fowler, 2009). Social media has again enhanced these possibilities by enabling people to connect directly and to find new networks. Social media has also substantially changed the way individuals and businesses interact online by allowing for a two-way communication between tourists and tourism service providers (Leung et al., 2013). This greatly influences the way tourists plan, spend or look back at their holidays, and has led to mobile social tourism, for example by enabling user-generated content (UGC) on social media for tourism activities (Hew et al., 2017). With the rise of social networks (for example, Facebook, Twitter, Instagram, Pinterest, Snapchat) and review platforms (for example, Tripadvisor, Google Reviews, Yelp), the passive consumer has become an active participant who shares and creates content, as well as influencing opinions; the so-called "prosumer" (Fine et al., 2017). This has led to the co-creation of tourist experiences, often facilitated by social media. Travelling itself is a social activity, and therefore social media are very much used by tourists and companies to share travel information via UGC or co-creation (Fry, 2019; Lindgren, 2017; Xiang, 2018). For tourist destinations, it is consequently becoming more and more important to monitor closely the tourist's digital customer journey.

But what does this development mean for tourist service providers? It is widely accepted that social media have partly shifted the control from destination managers and tourist service providers to consumers. On the one hand, this has brought risks (for example, negative reviews). On the other hand, this has opened up opportunities for enhanced customer value creation. Customer value, which has long been a central concept in marketing, is defined as the benefits customers subjectively perceive by achieving their goals and purposes when using a service or product (Woodruff, 1997). A number of tourist service providers have already made use of this dialogic structure to (co-)create customer value. Social media, by their very nature, offer numerous possibilities to exploit this potential.

This chapter explores the changes this shift has brought about, with a special focus on the role of social media in the digital customer journey during the attendance phase, and the potential for co-creating experiences with the tourist destinations. In addition, we assess the role of technology in this co-creation process, and then go on to point out the relevance of strategic planning and leadership for the implementation of the aforementioned processes.

THE CUSTOMER JOURNEY IN TOURISM

Although customer experiences have become an increasingly important topic of research, they are difficult to quantify. To overcome this challenge, tourism scholars have turned to frameworks and theories from non-tourism contexts to understand the multifaceted nature of tourist experiences, such as those related to the customer journey and touchpoints (Prayag et al., 2020). Thus, customer journey mapping has become an established practice in the tourism industry, and can be a powerful tool to provide insight into the customer experience (Stienmetz et al., 2020). Customer journey maps are used to visualize customer touchpoints and to manage them more effectively, in order to optimize the experiences along the whole customer journey (Kalbach, 2016). For example, one way to illuminate the tourist customer journey is the three-phase model, which divides the tourist experience into pre-stay, attendance (during-stay) and post-stay phases (Radde, 2017). Every contact point and interaction a guest has with a company during these phases is called a "touchpoint," and a distinction must be made between physical and digital touchpoints. Physical touchpoints are situations or moments with "real-life" contact, such as an encounter with receptionists; whereas digital touchpoints range from classic advertising and online marketing measures to rating portals and social media interventions (Brunner, 2019; Hahn, 2018; Radde, 2017).

It is important to mention that the process of mapping should start before customer needs arise, and continue beyond the purchase of the product or the travel. Touchpoints along the way may differ, and the customer journey will be different for different customers; it always depends on the context, and every company can create its own customer journey map based on its target group (Brandão and Wolfram, 2018). Two of the most significant benefits companies receive by using the customer journey model for mapping are that they learn how to better engage and interact with their customers, and that a more sophisticated target-group orientation can generate savings on communication costs (Brunner, 2019).

Although the relevant literature features mainly linear customer journey map models (Brunner, 2019), a circular illustration is more practice-oriented, as it shows that the journey does not end (Radde, 2017). Based on the existing literature, we have outlined an example of a customer journey in the hospitality industry (see Figure 13.1). This model is divided into 12 steps that customers pass through on their journeys. This customer journey is roughly divided into three overarching phases. The pre-stay phase consists of five steps and starts with the inspiration (1) and information (2) phases, where customers become aware of a destination or the need for a holiday through digital touchpoints, such as social media and TV, or through physical touchpoints, such as word-of-mouth or travel agencies. The evaluation (3) and decision (4) phases also take place before the actual journey. After gathering information, guests compare different offers and decide on a hotel. Common digital touchpoints in these stages include websites, blogs and review platforms, while physical touchpoints are mostly travel agencies. In the pre-sales phase (5), guests may be offered additional suitable products and services via email or personal letters, which can be booked for the stay.

The second overarching phase, attendance, encompasses the steps during the actual journey, starting with the outward journey (6) and the check-in phase (7). In these steps, the guests are already on the way to the hotel and may come into contact with digital touchpoints such as Google Maps and check-in services, although check-in may still be done traditionally with receptionist staff. The next step, the stay phase (8), is the most important step for this chapter and includes attractions, sights and employees. The most common digital touchpoints here are

Figure 13.1   Example of a customer journey in the hospitality industry

social media, a destination app and virtual reality (VR), which will be discussed later. While most social media studies are focused on the tourist's research phase (Leung et al., 2013), the present chapter focuses on the digital touchpoints in this attendance phase. The check-out (9) and homeward journey (10) phases include physical touchpoints, such as receptionist staff and feedback forms, and digital touchpoints, such as online reviews and Google Maps.

The final overarching phase, post-stay, consists of two steps: after-sales (11), where guests may evaluate the trip on review platforms and social media; and customer retention (12), where the hotel attempts to maintain contact with customers through various loyalty programs and digital (email) or physical (personal) newsletters.

SOCIAL MEDIA IN TOURISM DURING THE ATTENDANCE PHASE

The Relevance of Social Media Reviews

The impact of social media on the tourism industry has been staggering. UGC, often in the form of reviews written by tourists themselves, has a significant impact on tourists' decisions. Tourists engage with social networking platforms to find inspiration for an upcoming holiday, to share experiences of particular accommodation, a destination or activity, during and after the trip, and to build and maintain relationships. It is hardly surprising that content created by other users is seen as much more trustworthy and accurate than content created by companies, as UGC is understood to be neutral and without a sales purpose (Dedeoğlu et al., 2020; Oliveira et al., 2019). Content posted by tourists' contacts with strong social ties, such as family or friends, tends to affect opinions the most, while content posted by weak social ties (for example, casual acquaintances) is mainly used to find information (Luo and Zhong, 2015). The closer an individual is, the more likely people are to try to adopt their behavior (Kang and Schuett, 2013), "particularly if they perceive these experiences as being positive, enjoyable, aspirational and/or worthy of appreciation" (Dedeoğlu et al., 2020). This sort of content is expected to represent reality, which shapes tourist expectations prior to the trip and implies another challenge for tourism businesses, as the content the businesses produce themselves is perceived as less trustworthy (Narangajavana et al., 2017; Sedera et al., 2017).

Reviews are often shared during the attendance and the post-stay phase. In their reviews, tourists focus on both internal factors (for example, cleanliness, staff friendliness) and external factors (for example, location) of a tourist location or business. Friendly and well-trained staff members can help to create a positive image that results in a positive review, while the opposite often results in negative reviews (Barreda and Bilgihan, 2013; Fine et al., 2017). Studies show that negative reviews have a much greater impact than positive ones (Zhao et al., 2015), in that they negatively influence overall ratings on review platforms, such as Tripadvisor or Booking.com, which correlates with business performance. It is, therefore, crucial for tourism service providers to respond quickly to such negative reviews, in order to mitigate the negative effects they have on their business (Sotiriadis, 2017).

User Motivation to Post Travel Experiences on Social Media

One area of inquiry that researchers have turned to is the question of what motivates or inhibits tourists to post content on social media. Perceived enjoyment, altruism factors, perceived ease of use, reciprocity, habit, personal fulfillment and belief in integrity (of a company/experience) are among the most important factors that make people want to share their touristic experiences, while security and privacy issues keep users from posting content online. In addition, economic rewards (for example, incentives, bonus points, discounts, giveaways) decrease the motivation to post content online, as users feel an obligation to post content they otherwise might not have shared (Bakshi et al., 2019; Bilgihan et al., 2016; Oliveira et al., 2019). Furthermore, the tourist's own social media environment is crucial to keep users active on social media. Rewards, such as shares, comments and likes, have a high motivational impact on sharing further information (Bilgihan et al., 2016).

Social Media Use During the Attendance Phase

Content shared immediately (that is, during the attendance phase) shows spontaneous emotions, which can help companies gain insight into honest, unaltered tourist experiences (Park et al., 2020). Users often tend to use hashtags to describe a certain experience, or geotags to specify their location. These socio-technological features of platforms can be very useful for businesses and researchers in trying to find postings describing certain experiences (Shin and Xiang, 2020). Looking at travel paths and patterns might help to form new cooperations with related businesses and create travel packages with activities that meet traveler needs (Vu et al., 2020). In addition, since content posted during a trip has a significant impact on the expectations of future tourists, expectation management is a key aspect of businesses' communication strategies. One possible method for managing expectations is to find relevant influencers posting about related topics (Ferreira et al., 2020; Sedera et al., 2017); although the general impact of content created by influencers is disputed (Guerreiro et al., 2019). Furthermore, companies should use review platforms and social media to interact with users, give feedback and generally show appreciation for active users in order to reward their effort and to keep them engaged (Bakshi et al., 2019). Today, many businesses spend most of their marketing budgets on the "consider" and "buy" stages, but Hudson and Thal (2013) suggest that the "evaluation" and "enjoy–advocate–bond" stages, including the attendance stage, deserve more consideration. Content shared while on a trip has a significant influence on future tourists who are planning their own trips, and should therefore be considered as more important (Hudson and Thal, 2013).

With regard to content formats, pictures and videos are considered the most important formats for the attendance phase, as they are believed to be accurate, authentic and to depict "physical evidence" of an experience. They often show relationships or document trips, and are therefore perceived as sensational and aesthetic (Conti and Cassel, 2020; Conti and Lexhagen, 2020). When analyzing pictures or videos, metadata (for example, captions, geotags, hashtags) are useful, as they provide context (Shin and Xiang, 2020).

With regard to pictures, two trends have emerged. First, some tourists feel pressure to take pictures and engage in the actual activity at the same time; they miss the real activity, because they have to take a picture. The second trend involves tourists searching for "instagrammable" places, always on the lookout for the best picture (Siegel et al., 2019; Walsh et al., 2019). The first trend could be a possibility for brands to offer "detox" experiences to help tourists reconnect with authentic offerings. For example, the "anti-hashtag" campaign by the Tourist Board in Vienna asked visitors to not use their cameras and social media. Results were positive, indicating a need for "detox" experiences. The second trend might encourage destinations to focus on their Instagram strategy, such as by asking photographers to take over their account for a while and to share their pictures, thus offering an authentic glance at a destination (Thelander and Cassinger, 2017).

POTENTIAL TECHNOLOGY OPTIONS FOR ENHANCING CO-CREATION WITH SOCIAL MEDIA

Generally speaking, ICT applications in tourism are not only gaining prevalence, but are also becoming more user-centered and thus fostering a strategic approach to co-creating valuable customer experiences (Buhalis and Leung, 2018). Easily available technologies (for example, action cameras such as GoPro) have led to extensive documentation and sharing of tourist experiences on social media (Pencarelli, 2019). Tourist destinations themselves have put great emphasis on making use of technological advances. These efforts, which are also referred to as "smart tourism," leverage data processing to generate value (Gretzel et al., 2015). In order to promote both the provision of the necessary infrastructure and the development of relevant technologies, China, for example, has published guidance documents for smart tourism development (Ye et al., 2020). Technologies applied in this context include the Internet of Things (IoT), mobile applications, location-based services, geotag services, virtual reality (VR), augmented reality (AR) and social media (Ye et al., 2020).

The use of VR to market tourism experiences has risen sharply in recent years, and this trend is bound to continue. VR technologies will play an increasingly important role in the future. VR-based apps (for example, Orbulus, the Travel World VR App), or VR technologies built into social media platforms (for example, Facebook's Virtual Selfie Stick) (Hollebeek et al., 2020) offer a try-before-you-buy experience. Travel agents and companies can promote their destinations, accommodation, cruise liners and travel services by taking their potential customers through 360-degree videos and giving them a taste of the travel experience.

In addition to VR, which allows guests to see a virtual world through VR glasses, there are other forms of "realities." Augmented reality involves the extension of the real world with virtual elements (virtuality overlapping reality), and mixed reality (MR) mixes the real and the virtual world and offers more interaction possibilities than, for example, AR. On the other hand, there is also reality overlapping virtuality, the so-called augmented virtuality (AV), which plays a role in virtual environments, but is beyond the scope of this chapter (Flavián et al., 2019).

The generic terms for these forms are "extended reality" or "cross-reality." Cross-reality, which was ranked as one of the most fascinating trends of 2019 (Faber, 2019), includes VR, AR and MR. Examples of cross-reality include marker-based AR, such as QR (quick-response) codes. Cranmer et al. recommend that tourism managers explore opportunities to integrate AR into marketing materials to provide additional information in a more engaging and informative format (Cranmer et al., 2020). Another example of cross-reality during the attendance phase is the usage of VR devices during a wine-tasting session or at an art gallery. Visitors could use AR glasses to see digital information (history, opinions, and so on) when looking at the piece of art. Besides the Virtual Selfie Stick on Facebook, there are other combinations of AR and social media. After visiting the gallery (post-stay), customers could rate the paintings and gallery services on their smartphones and share their opinions and photographs on social networks. The art gallery might also stage a contest of 360-degree videos uploaded on the social platform YouTube (Flavián et al., 2019). One of the most famous existing examples of mixed reality in Germany is the TimerideVR in Cologne, Munich, Berlin, Frankfurt and Dresden, which offers the possibility to experience virtual time travel to former worlds of the cities. For this virtual city tour, the visitors take a seat in a real replica of a historical means of transport; which in Cologne, for example, is an old tram (Timeride, 2020).

The relentless progress of information technology and its wide acceptance both in the consumer market and the industry over the last 20 years have generated enormous amounts of data. The analysis of this data has yielded new information which has served as the basis for tourism design and development activities. Particularly with regard to smart tourism, data is one of the most important tools for the generation of new business models and industry-wide innovations in travel and tourism (Xiang and Fesenmaier, 2017). Within smart tourism research, data generated through social media is of particular importance for the development of smart tourism applications and has been widely researched (Ye et al., 2020). With the help of advanced analytics tools and technical infrastructure, so-called "big data" can be analyzed in order to find hidden patterns or themes (Mirzaalian and Halpenny, 2019). This customer data is particularly important for determining customer needs and preferences in order to design personalized experiences (Rasoolimanesh et al., 2019). Based on the analysis of large data sets, systems for forecasting tourism demand seem promising (Li et al., 2020; Ye et al., 2020).

However, big data analysis is fraught with challenges and unresolved issues. For tourism providers, one such challenge is to harmonize the wide range of data forms that are generated by different "tagging" approaches used by social media platforms, in an effort to create useful recommendations tailored to specific contexts (Wong et al., 2017). Another barrier for smart tourism applications is the issue of privacy, especially in the context of smart tourism and with regard to location-based services. Although big data is highly useful for tourism operators, without stringent privacy laws and regulations, customers remain vulnerable (Xiang and Fesenmaier, 2017). Despite their vulnerability, recent research points towards the "privacy paradox," which states that most social media users are still willing to share personal information despite privacy concerns (Hew et al., 2017; Ioannou et al., 2020). With the introduction of the General Data Protection Regulation (GDPR), the European Union has resolved some of the most pressing privacy concerns and established one of the most stringent privacy laws in the world, with other regions of the world already following this path (Milner-Smith and Silkin, 2019).

CO-CREATION IN TOURISM

In the context of a service-dominant logic, consumers always play an important part in the process of value creation, as they have to accept the offered value proposition (Ye et al., 2020). The internet and social media platforms have become catalysts of change, which have not only influenced the way companies and consumers interact, but have also fundamentally changed both how and by whom tourism products, services and experiences are designed, created and consumed (Neuhofer, 2016). The prosumer is not only consuming experiences, but also plays an active role in the creation of experiences (Fine et al., 2017; Neuhofer et al., 2014). Generally, touristic services are becoming more consumer-centric, personalized and contextualized (Buhalis and Sinarta, 2019). Prahalad and Ramaswamy (2004) recognized this change and introduced the concept of co-creation. Co-creation refers to the interaction between suppliers, consumers and consumer communities for the purpose of joint value creation. Customers are actively involved in the generation of experiences. In other words, experiences are not only generated by tourism providers, but are co-created with customers.

In addition to the emergence of digital technologies, the increasing need for personalization of services is a major reason for the emergence of co-creation. Guests have different identities and cultural backgrounds, which service providers must consider individually, and services are becoming increasingly interchangeable, so personalization is the key to differentiation (Sugathan and Ranjan, 2019). The emergence of co-creation also has sociological roots and is based on changed tourist behavior, attitudes and motivation. Instead of just being passive sightseers, tourists today increasingly want to be actively involved (physically, cognitively or intellectually) and explore destinations in a multisensory way. Active participation means that tourists not only observe but also interact, actively learn and apply knowledge (Eraqi, 2011).

The concept of co-creation is useful in all phases of the customer journey: before, during and after the stay. For example, before the trip, guests can be involved in co-creating value by generating ideas (Campos et al., 2018); during the trip by using an AR app as an interactive personal travel guide with which they can create their own individual sightseeing tour (Cranmer et al., 2020); and after the trip by sharing experiences and memories with the virtual community on social media channels (Campos et al., 2018).

Binkhorst and Den Dekker (2009) emphasize the role of digital technologies as an important element in co-creating experiences by enabling tourists and providers to network across multiple platforms. This includes technologies that can be used in all phases of travel, such as websites, mobile devices and apps, mobile travel guides, virtual living environments or technology-enhanced hotel rooms (Neuhofer et al., 2013). For example, the Qbic Design Hotels allow their guests to change the room color according to their mood (Sugathan and Ranjan, 2019). Another example of virtual co-creation is VisitBritain's LoveUK mobile app, which lists the top 100 locations or attractions in the United Kingdom based on Facebook check-ins. Travel suggestions made by tourists co-create value by determining the "must-see" places in a destination through their collective behavior and preferences (Neuhofer et al., 2012). This example shows that instead of controlling and defining popular websites, VisitBritain puts its travel suggestions in the hands of customers who, through their collective behavior, determine the places in a destination that other tourists must visit (Neuhofer, 2016).

Research has shown a positive relationship between the degree of co-creation and tourist satisfaction. In a recent study, Sugathan and Ranjan (2019) examined the effects of co-creation on the tourist experience. The results show that co-creation improves the customer experience on-site and can have a strong influence on the revisit intention. The higher the level of co-creation, the higher the tourist's intention to visit the destination again (Sugathan and Ranjan, 2019). Similarly, Buonincontri et al. (2017) explored the influence of co-creation on tourist satisfaction in Nepal. They confirmed their hypotheses that co-creation has a strong positive influence on tourist satisfaction, the level of expenditure within the destination and the feeling of happiness (Buonincontri et al., 2017). These results are consistent with earlier studies (Grissemann and Stokburger-Sauer, 2012) which showed that social media by their very nature offer significant potential for creating customized experiences in tourism, which can enable real-time communication in order to solve problems of tourists (for example, when booking a flight) (Buhalis and Sinarta, 2019).

However, for social media to be truly effective, timely reactions from operators are mandatory. In this context, the concept of "nowness" is worth mentioning. This concept suggests that brands strive to ensure that services are personalized, based on specific needs and preferences at that particular moment (Buhalis and Sinarta, 2019). These real-time conversations are often enabled through the use of hashtags (for example, of brand names such as #BritishAirways) or direct mentions (for example, by directly addressing a brand account on Twitter @British_Airways) (Buhalis and Sinarta, 2019).

THE IMPORTANCE OF DIGITAL LEADERSHIP AND STRATEGIC APPROACHES

When new technologies or value-creating methodologies are adopted, it is essential to consider the underlying strategy. In this context, leadership plays a crucial role, and leadership qualities or general "digital mastery" (Westerman et al., 2014) might be required to integrate new technologies or services into a company environment. Zhu (2015) suggests that "digital-minded leadership," which is capable of transforming organizations, consists of three determining elements: (1) thoughtfulness, that is, the ability to create a digital vision, build trust or inspire others to change; (2) transcendence, which means the ability to create something new out of something that already exists, to initiate a fundamental cultural change and also to recognize the right moment to do so; and (3) transdisciplinarity: since the hyper-networked digital world offers some highly complex challenges that cannot be solved with disciplinary knowledge alone, people who can break down functional silos to understand the big picture are needed. Spencer et al. (2012) found that leadership was the most significant driver for technology adoption for small owner-managed travel firms. Such companies are characterized not solely through their investment in technology or human resources, but mostly through their investment in time, tenacity and leadership (Westerman et al., 2014). This distinctive characteristic makes them successful even when new technologies or services emerge.

With regard to creating digital content or services, an in-depth understanding of concepts such as the customer journey can help organizations become fully customer-oriented. The discipline of content strategy (Halvorson and Rach, 2012) has assembled a wide-ranging tool set for the user-centric development of web content on digital channels, including social media. This involves conducting user research in order to find out where and how the target group communicates, which enables tourism providers to select the right channel or platform to interact with the customers. A strategic approach should ensure that "the right content gets to the right audiences in the right context" (Bailie, 2019, p. 121). Based on a strategic plan and design, tactical measures, such as the use of UGC for co-creation through active community management, can be implemented (Tuten, 2017).

CONCLUSION

The advent of social media has had a significant impact on the tourism industry in offering unprecedented opportunities, and at the same time giving rise to challenges for creating customer value. This chapter has critically examined this changing media landscape and highlighted strategies for successfully dealing with it. By adopting the customer journey model, tourism organizations and companies are able to better understand the digital customer journey and the influence of social media on their own services. The chapter has also stressed the importance of linking physical and digital touchpoints when designing customer experiences. In order to unleash the full potential of social media for the tourist experience, it is crucial to focus more attention on the attendance phase. Since tourists believe that UGC is accurate, authentic and depicts "physical evidence" of an experience, it can play a central role not only for selecting destinations but also during the tourist's stay. This, in turn, means that content produced by providers themselves is perceived as less trustworthy. Co-creation is a suitable framework to tackle the challenges of the shifting landscape in new media and technology. It enables direct dialogue with the customers, and customer integration into the process of value creation. It is also recommended to use the co-creation approach to integrate new technology trends into an organization. With the many technological possibilities offered today and in the future, it must not be forgotten that a key to their successful integration into the business lies in a strategic approach. All the activities undertaken must be in line with a strategic approach in order to lead to success.

REFERENCES

Bailie, R.A. (2019). Bringing clarity to content strategy. *Technical Communication, 66*(2), 121–124.

Bakshi, S., Dogra, N., and Gupta, A. (2019). What motivates posting online travel reviews? Integrating gratifications with technological acceptance factors. *Tourism and Hospitality Management, 25*(2), 335–354. https://doi.org/10.20867/thm.25.2.5.

Barreda, A., and Bilgihan, A. (2013). An analysis of user-generated content for hotel experiences. *Journal of Hospitality and Tourism Technology, 4*(3), 263–280. https://doi.org/10.1108/JHTT-01-2013-0001.

Bilgihan, A., Barreda, A., Okumus, F., and Nusair, K. (2016). Consumer perception of knowledge-sharing in travel-related online social networks. *Tourism Management, 52*, 287–296. https://doi.org/10.1016/j.tourman.2015.07.002.

Binkhorst, E., and Den Dekker, T. (2009). Agenda for co-creation tourism experience research. *Journal of Hospitality Marketing and Management, 18*(2–3), 311–327. https://doi.org/10.1080/19368620802594193.

Brandão, T. K., and Wolfram, G. (2018). *Digital Connection. Die bessere Customer Journey mit smarten Technologien – Strategie und Praxisbeispiele.* Springer Fachmedien Wiesbaden. https://link.springer.com/book/10.1007/978-3-658-18759-0.

Brunner, M. (2019). *Customer Journey 4.0.* Independently published.

Buhalis, D., and Leung, R. (2018). Smart hospitality – Interconnectivity and interoperability towards an ecosystem. *International Journal of Hospitality Management, 71*, 41–50. https://doi.org/10.1016/j.ijhm.2017.11.011.

Buhalis, D., and Sinarta, Y. (2019). Real-time co-creation and nowness service: Lessons from tourism and hospitality. *Journal of Travel and Tourism Marketing, 36*(5), 563–582. https://doi.org/10.1080/10548408.2019.1592059.

Buonincontri, P., Morvillo, A., Okumus, F., and van Niekerk, M. (2017). Managing the experience co-creation process in tourism destinations: Empirical findings from Naples. *Tourism Management, 62*, 264–277. https://doi.org/10.1016/j.tourman.2017.04.014.

Campos, A.C., Mendes, J., Valle, P.O. do, and Scott, N. (2018). Co-creation of tourist experiences: A literature review. *Current Issues in Tourism, 21*(4), 369–400. https://doi.org/10.1080/13683500.2015.1081158.

Christakis, N.A., and Fowler, J.H. (2009). *Connected: The Surprising Power of Our Social Networks and How They Shape Our Lives.* HarperPress.

Conti, E., and Cassel, S.H. (2020). Liminality in nature-based tourism experiences as mediated through social media. *Tourism Geographies, 22*(2), 413–432. https://doi.org/10.1080/14616688.2019.1648544.

Conti, E., and Lexhagen, M. (2020). Instagramming nature-based tourism experiences: A netnographic study of online photography and value creation. *Tourism Management Perspectives, 34*, 100650.

Cranmer, E.E., tom Dieck, M.C., and Fountoulaki, P. (2020). Exploring the value of augmented reality for tourism. *Tourism Management Perspectives, 35*, 100672. https://doi.org/10.1016/j.tmp.2020.100672.

Dedeoğlu, B.B., Taheri, B., Okumus, F., and Gannon, M. (2020). Understanding the importance that consumers attach to social media sharing (ISMS): Scale development and validation. *Tourism Management, 76*, 103954. https://doi.org/10.1016/j.tourman.2019.103954.

Eraqi, M.I. (2011). Co-creation and the new marketing mix as an innovative approach for enhancing tourism industry competitiveness in Egypt. *International Journal of Services and Operations Management, 8*(1), 76. https://doi.org/10.1504/IJSOM.2011.037441.

Faber, M. (2019, March 18). Virtual Reality im Tourismus: Use Cases and 12 Trends für 2019 [Virtual reality in tourism: Use cases and 12 trends for 2019] *Tourismuszukunft* [Tourism Future (Blog)]. https://www.tourismuszukunft.de/2019/03/virtual-reality-im-tourismus/.

Ferreira, M.M., Loureiro, S.M.C., and Pereira, H.G. (2020). Communication tools in the customer's journey: Application to the tourism sector. In E. Li, S.M.C. Loureiro and H.R. Kaufmann (eds), *Exploring the Power of Electronic Word-of-Mouth in the Services Industry* (pp. 288–316), Advances in Marketing, Customer Relationship Management, and E-Services, Vol. 6. IGI Global. https://doi.org/10.4018/978-1-5225-8575-6.ch016.

Fine, M.B., Gironda, J., and Petrescu, M. (2017). Prosumer motivations for electronic word-of-mouth communication behaviors. *Journal of Hospitality and Tourism Technology, 8*(2), 280–295. https://doi.org/10.1108/JHTT-09-2016-0048.

Flavián, C., Ibáñez-Sánchez, S., and Orús, C. (2019). The impact of virtual, augmented and mixed reality technologies on the customer experience. *Journal of Business Research, 100*, 547–560. https://doi.org/10.1016/j.jbusres.2018.10.050.

Fry, H. (2019). *Hello World: Being Human in the Age of Algorithms*. W.W. Norton & Company.

Gretzel, U., Reino, S., Kopera, S., and Koo, C. (2015). Smart tourism challenges. *Journal of Tourism, 16*(1), 41–47.

Grissemann, U.S., and Stokburger-Sauer, N.E. (2012). Customer co-creation of travel services: The role of company support and customer satisfaction with the co-creation performance. *Tourism Management, 33*(6), 1483–1492. https://doi.org/10.1016/j.tourman.2012.02.002.

Guerreiro, C., Viegas, M., and Guerreiro, M. (2019). Social networks and digital influencers: Their role in customer decision journey in tourism. *Journal of Spatial and Organizational Dynamics, 7*(3), 240–260.

Hahn, C. (2018, October 4). Hotellerie Entlang Der Customer Journey. [Hotel business along the customer journey.] Gchhotelgroup.com. https://www.gchhotelgroup.com/de/newsroom/blog/customer_journey/3258?rel=/de/newsroom.

Halvorson, K., and Rach, M. (2012). *Content Strategy for the Web* (2nd edition). New Riders.

Hew, J.-J., Tan, G.W.-H., Lin, B., and Ooi, K.-B. (2017). Generating travel-related contents through mobile social tourism: Does privacy paradox persist? *Telematics and Informatics, 34*(7), 914–935. https://doi.org/10.1016/j.tele.2017.04.001.

Hollebeek, L.D., Clark, M. K., Andreassen, T.W., Sigurdsson, V., and Smith, D. (2020). Virtual reality through the customer journey: Framework and propositions. *Journal of Retailing and Consumer Services, 55*, 102056.

Hudson, S., and Thal, K. (2013). The impact of social media on the consumer decision process: Implications for tourism marketing. *Journal of Travel and Tourism Marketing, 30*(1–2), 156–160. https://doi.org/10.1080/10548408.2013.751276.

Ioannou, A., Tussyadiah, I., and Lu, Y. (2020). Privacy concerns and disclosure of biometric and behavioral data for travel. *International Journal of Information Management, 54*, 102122. https://doi.org/10.1016/j.ijinfomgt.2020.102122.

Kalbach, J. (2016). *Mapping Experiences: A Complete Guide to Creating Value through Journeys, Blueprints, and Diagrams*. O'Reilly Media.

Kang, M., and Schuett, M.A. (2013). Determinants of sharing travel experiences in social media. *Journal of Travel and Tourism Marketing, 30*(1–2), 93–107. https://doi.org/10.1080/10548408.2013.751237.

Leung, D., Law, R., Hoof, H. van, and Buhalis, D. (2013). Social media in tourism and hospitality: A literature review. *Journal of Travel and Tourism Marketing, 30*(1–2), 3–22. https://doi.org/10.1080/10548408.2013.750919.

Li, H., Hu, M., and Li, G. (2020). Forecasting tourism demand with multisource big data. *Annals of Tourism Research, 83*(3), 102912. https://doi.org/10.1016/j.annals.2020.102912.

Lindgren, S. (2017). *Digital Media and Society*. SAGE.

Luo, Q., and Zhong, D. (2015). Using social network analysis to explain communication characteristics of travel-related electronic word-of-mouth on social networking sites. *Tourism Management, 46*, 274–282. https://doi.org/10.1016/j.tourman.2014.07.007.

Milner-Smith, A., and Silkin, L. (2019). The impact of the GDPR outside the EU. *Ius Laboris*. https://theword.iuslaboris.com/hrlaw/whats-new/the-impact-of-the-gdpr-outside-the-eu.

Mirzaalian, F., and Halpenny, E. (2019). Social media analytics in hospitality and tourism: A systematic literature review and future trends. *Journal of Hospitality and Tourism Technology, 10*(4), 764–790. https://doi.org/10.1108/JHTT-08-2018-0078.

Narangajavana, Y., Fiol, L.J.C., Tena, M.Á.M., Artola, R.M.R., and García, J.S. (2017). The influence of social media in creating expectations. An empirical study for a tourist destination. *Annals of Tourism Research, 65*, 60–70.

Neuhofer, B. (2016). An exploration of the technology enhanced tourist experience. *European Journal of Tourism Research, 12*, 220–223.

Neuhofer, B., Buhalis, D., and Ladkin, A. (2012). Conceptualising technology enhanced destination experiences. *Journal of Destination Marketing and Management, 1*(1), 36–46. https://doi.org/10.1016/j.jdmm.2012.08.001.

Neuhofer, B., Buhalis, D., and Ladkin, A. (2013). Experiences, co-creation and technology: A conceptual approach to enhance tourism experiences. *CAUTHE 2013: Tourism and Global Change: On the Edge of Something Big*, Lincoln University, Christchurch, NZ, 546–555.

Neuhofer, B., Buhalis, D., and Ladkin, A. (2014). A typology of technology-enhanced tourism experiences. *International Journal of Tourism Research*, 16(4), 340–350. https://doi.org/10.1002/jtr.1958.

Oliveira, T., Araujo, B., and Tam, C. (2019). Why do people share their travel experiences on social media? *Tourism Management*, 78, 104041. https://doi.org/10.1016/j.tourman.2019.104041.

Park, S.B., Kim, J., Lee, Y.K., and Ok, C.M. (2020). Visualizing theme park visitors' emotions using social media analytics and geospatial analytics. *Tourism Management*, 80, 104127. https://doi.org/10.1016/j.tourman.2020.104127.

Pencarelli, T. (2019). The digital revolution in the travel and tourism industry. *Information Technology and Tourism*. https://doi.org/10.1007/s40558-019-00160-3.

Prahalad, C.K., and Ramaswamy, V. (2004). Co-creation experiences: The next practice in value creation. *Journal of Interactive Marketing*, 18(3), 5–14. https://doi.org/10.1002/dir.20015.

Prayag, G., Spector, S., and Finsterwalder, J. (2020). Customer experience in tourism. In S.K. Dixit (ed.), *The Routledge Handbook of Tourism Experience Management and Marketing* (Vol. 1, pp. 67–76). Routledge.

Radde, B. (2017). *Digital Guest Experience: Tools to Help Hotels to Manage and Optimize the Digital Guest Experience*. Tredition.

Rasoolimanesh, S.M., Law, R., Buhalis, D., and Cobanoglu, C. (2019). Development and trend of information and communication technologies in hospitality and tourism. *Journal of Hospitality and Tourism Technology*, 10(4), 481–488. https://doi.org/10.1108/JHTT-11-2019-143.

Sedera, D., Lokuge, S., Atapattu, M., and Gretzel, U. (2017). Likes – The key to my happiness: The moderating effect of social influence on travel experience. *Information and Management*, 54(6), 825–836. https://doi.org/10.1016/j.im.2017.04.003.

Shin, S., and Xiang, Z. (2020). Social media-induced tourism: A conceptual framework. *E-Review of Tourism Research*, 17(4), 581–591.

Siegel, L.A., Tussyadiah, I., and Scarles, C. (2019). Does social media help or hurt destinations? A qualitative case study. *E-Review of Tourism Research*, 17(4), 571–580. https://journals.tdl.org/ertr/index.php/ertr/article/view/541.

Sotiriadis, M.D. (2017). Sharing tourism experiences in social media: A literature review and a set of suggested business strategies. *International Journal of Contemporary Hospitality Management*, 29(1), 179–225. https://doi.org/10.1108/IJCHM-05-2016-0300.

Spencer, A.J., Buhalis, D., and Moital, M. (2012). A hierarchical model of technology adoption for small owner-managed travel firms: An organizational decision-making and leadership perspective. *Tourism Management*, 33(5), 1195–1208.

Stienmetz, J., Kim, J., Xiang, Z., and Fesenmaier, D.R. (2020). Managing the structure of tourism experiences: Foundations for tourism design. *Journal of Destination Marketing and Management*, 100408. https://doi.org/10.1016/j.jdmm.2019.100408.

Sugathan, P., and Ranjan, K.R. (2019). Co-creating the tourism experience. *Journal of Business Research*, 100, 207–217. https://doi.org/10.1016/j.jbusres.2019.03.032.

Thelander, A., and Cassinger, C. (2017). Brand new images? Implications of Instagram photography for place branding. *Media and Communication*, 5(4), 6–14.

Timeride (2020). TimerideVR. https://timeride.de/timeride-vr-startseite/ueber-uns/.

Tuten, T.L. (2017). *Social media marketing* (3rd edition). SAGE.

Vu, H.Q., Li, G., and Law, R. (2020). Cross-country analysis of tourist activities based on venue-referenced social media data. *Journal of Travel Research*, 59(1), 90–106. https://doi.org/10.1177/0047287518820194.

Walsh, M.J., Johns, R., and Dale, N.F. (2019). The social media tourist gaze: Social media photography and its disruption at the zoo. *Information Technology and Tourism*, 21(3), 391–412.

Westerman, G., Bonnet, D., and McAfee, A. (2014). *Leading digital: Turning technology into business transformation*. Harvard Business Review Press.

Wong, E., Law, R., and Li, G. (2017). Reviewing geotagging research in tourism. In R. Schegg and B. Stangl (eds), *Information and Communication Technologies in Tourism 2017* (pp. 43–58). Springer.

Woodruff, R.B. (1997). Customer value: The next source for competitive advantage. *Journal of the Academy of Marketing Science*, *25*(2), 139. https://doi.org/10.1007/BF02894350.

Xiang, Z. (2018). From digitization to the age of acceleration: On information technology and tourism. *Tourism Management Perspectives*, *25*, 147–150. https://doi.org/10.1016/j.tmp.2017.11.023.

Xiang, Z., and Fesenmaier, D.R. (2017). Big data analytics, tourism design and smart tourism. In Z. Xiang and D.R. Fesenmaier (eds), *Analytics in Smart Tourism Design* (pp. 299–307). Springer.

Ye, B.H., Ye, H., and Law, R. (2020). Systematic review of smart tourism research. *Sustainability*, *12*(8), 3401. https://doi.org/10.3390/su12083401.

Zhao, X.R., Wang, L., Guo, X., and Law, R. (2015). The influence of online reviews to online hotel booking intentions. *International Journal of Contemporary Hospitality Management*, *27*(6), 1343–1364. https://doi.org/10.1108/IJCHM-12-2013-0542.

Zhu, P. (2015). *Digital Master: Debunk the Myths of Enterprise Digital Maturity*. Lulu Press.

14. Social media relationship marketing for tourism: key antecedents and outcomes

Si Shi

INTRODUCTION

With the growing popularity of social media in recent years, many tourism companies have recognized its the potential as a competitive tool to connect with their customers and help them to achieve better business performance (Hew et al., 2018). With respect to this increasingly popular phenomena of business implications in social networking sites (SNSs), Faase et al. (2011) pointed out that companies should not only focus on adopting new information technologies, but rather they should focus on "company-specific strategy for creating customer involvement and building stronger customer relationships" (p. 9) in SNS applications. The prevalent use of the brand page as a form of business enhancement in SNSs represents one of the most potentially transformative impacts of information and communication technologies on tourism business. The brand page is a popular product of social media that allows tourism companies to create their own profiles in social media platforms and provides tourism companies with a platform to engage with their customers. On brand pages, customers can engage in conversations with parties such as the company and the community members. Such interactions are facilitated on the brand page through functions which allow customers to leave comments, forward messages, click "likes," engage in discussions, and so on (Zhang et al., 2013).

Studies indicate that brand pages enable tourism companies to engage with their customers in a more efficient and relevant manner (Liu et al., 2017), as well as to build and maintain better relationships with current and potential customers (Rishika et al., 2013). From the customers' standpoint, evidence suggests that followers of brand pages tend to be more open to receiving tourism companies' promotional information, and may also develop a deeper emotional attachment to the brand than non-followers (Dholakia and Durham, 2010). The study of the factors influencing the relationship development between brand pages and customer attitudes and behaviors is emerging as an important topic in the field of tourism (Wang and Fesenmaier, 2004). However, although tourism companies now recognize the significance of brand pages for improving performance and boosting business opportunities, the key factors that contribute to success in this area remain unclear. Theoretical frameworks are needed to promote a better understanding of brand page features and to examine how they contribute to customers' attitudes and behaviors. To shed light on the above issues, this chapter draws upon the commitment–trust theory of relationship marketing (Morgan and Hunt, 1994) to develop a deeper understanding of the key antecedents and outcomes of customer relationship marketing on the brand pages of tourism companies.

A FRAMEWORK OF TOURISM SOCIAL MEDIA MARKETING

Overview of Social Media Marketing

Social media (also called social networking sites), such as MySpace, Facebook, Twitter and Microblog provide a new form of web services that support effective communication and information exchange with others (Lu and Hsiao, 2010). The concept of "social networking" is built on person-to-person connections and includes exchanges or interactions across a group of individuals (Ellison, 2007). Person-to-person interactions may consist of a group of users, customers or employees who form a social network based on their social relationships (Chen, 2013). These networks confine how resources flow and circulate among them, and how these individuals are connected to each other (Haythornthwaite, 2005). Social media marketing consists of the following characteristics: (1) it is based on connections among users; (2) it allows users to establish relationships with others; and (3) it facilitates the exchange of user-generated content.

The brand page (also known as the fan page) is a popular example of a tourism company's profile on social media. A brand page is usually designed for companies to directly post brand-related information to subscribing users for brand promotion (Cvijikj and Michahelles, 2011a). The conversations on the brand page can be categorized into the following three ways: company to customer, customer to company, and customer to customer (de Vries et al., 2012). Harnessing the power of connected customers, the brand page provides a great opportunity for tourism companies to improve their business performance (Gu and Wang, 2012). However, there are still many managerial problems associated with the operations of brand pages on social media, including that strategic planning is not well formulated, and that what customers really value from their interactions on the brand page is not well known. Regarding the relationship marketing strategies of the brand page on social media, Askool and Nakata (2011) stated that a customer-centric model should be considered as the main component, and companies should focus more on customers and relationships with them rather than on products or services.

The Commitment–Trust Theory of Relationship Marketing

Morgan and Hunt (1994) developed the commitment–trust theory (CTT) to study the relational exchanges in relationship marketing. Commitment and trust are theorized to play key mediating roles in establishing, developing and maintaining the relationships between concerned parties. Morgan and Hunt (1994) posit commitment and trust as central elements in relationship marketing, for several reasons. First, a high level of commitment and trust encourages investment from exchange partners to achieve mutual benefits. Second, commitment and trust prevent business partners from being attracted by short-term benefits. Third, they guarantee trading parties will engage in fewer opportunistic behaviors.

The CTT contains a model called the key mediating variable (KMV) model, which proposes that commitment and trust serve as mediators between five antecedents and five outcomes of relationship marketing. Figure 14.1 shows the theoretical framework of the CTT, which includes three sets of model components: relationship antecedents, relationship mediators and relationship outcomes. Relationship antecedents include model constructs of relationship termination costs, relationship benefits, shared values, communications and opportunistic behav-

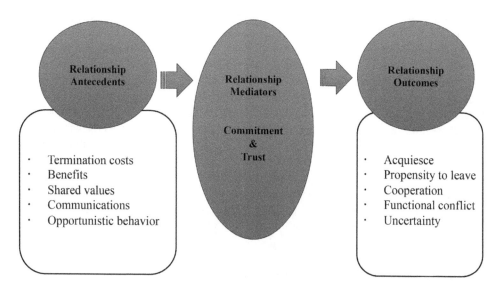

Figure 14.1   The commitment–trust theory of relationship marketing

ior. Relationship mediators include model constructs of commitment and trust. Relationship outcomes include model constructs of acquiescence, propensity to leave, cooperation, functional conflict and uncertainty.

RELATIONSHIP ANTECEDENTS OF TOURISM SOCIAL MEDIA MARKETING

Relationship Antecedents of Commitment and Trust

Morgan and Hunt (1994) originally propose five relationship antecedents in the commitment–trust theory: relationship termination cost, relationship benefits, shared values, communication and opportunistic behavior. According to Morgan and Hunt (1994), relationship termination cost refers to the "switching cost" that one party will suffer if seeking an alternative business partner. Relationship benefits refer to the mutual benefits that both parties generate in the business relationship. Shared value is the common belief that both parties share about their goals, behaviors and regulations in a business relationship. Communication refers to the exchanging of timely and valuable information between trading partners. Lastly, opportunistic behavior refers to the behavior of one partner for self-interest maximization, especially in short-term relationships.

The above five original factors of relationship antecedents have been proven to have great power in predicting commitment and trust between trading parties in business partnerships (e.g., Goo and Huang, 2008; Wu et al., 2012). However, these constructs may have a limited insight in explaining customers' commitment and trust towards the brand page, because such commitment and trust in this case are considered to be unilateral. This chapter proposes customer values based on the customer value theory to explain the causes of customer commitment, trust and relationship outcomes towards the brand page of tourism companies. First, for the brand pages of tourism companies, customers' commitment and trust towards the brand page are considered as unilateral. Therefore, applying the commitment–trust theory in this context requires modifications to account for possible differences of this one-directional commitment and trust, and to accommodate the nature of the brand page. Second, in traditional exchange relationships, Morgan and Hunt (1994) explain that shared values would impact the development of mutual commitment and trust. In the social media context, studies suggest that understanding what customers really value is the first and most vital step in building successful customer relationships (e.g., Baird and Parasnis, 2011). Faase et al. (2011) also suggest that companies should center on customers and deliver tangible values to customers in online social communities. Therefore, we include customer values based on the customer value theory to explain customer commitment, trust and relationship outcomes towards the brand page of tourism companies.

Customer Values as Key Antecedents of Relationship Marketing

Studies on customer decision-making have evolved from an initial focus solely based on cognitive factors to include intrinsic factors such as hedonic and esthetic perceptions (Kim et al., 2007). Following this stream of directive research, the customer value theory is developed to explain why consumers make the choices they do, based on different value perceptions, such as functional, social and conditional values (Sheth et al., 1991). These value dimensions consider different aspects of customer perceptions, and they make different contributions in different choice situations (Chang and Weng, 2012). Woodcock et al. (2011) also point out that although many tourism companies today recognize the importance of using social media to connect with customers, most of them fail to understand what customers really value.

There are five key customer values: functional value, conditional value, social value, emotional value and epistemic value (Sheth et al., 1991). These multiple values make different contributions to customers' attitudes and behaviors in different situations. Along with the development of this theory, many scholars have pointed out that some of these values (functional value, conditional value, social value, emotional value and epistemic value) are interrelated, and there is no well-accepted measure for how to quantify these values (Sweeney and Soutar, 2001). With respect to these issues, Sweeney and Soutar (2001) designed an instrument called PERVAL to quantify the measure of customer values. They conducted reliability and validity assessment tests for the PERVAL, and refined the original five values into three major ones: functional, social and emotional values. According to Sweeney and Soutar (2001), functional value includes aspects of quality and value-for-money, and it derives from the perceived performance and monetary value of products or service. It is traditionally recognized as the principal driver of a customer's value perception. Social value refers to the perceived benefits of enhancing customers' social well-being and social relationships. Emotional value is the perceived utility derived from the inner feelings or affective states that a product or service generates.

In the social media context, these three customer values (functional, social and emotional values) are widely employed to understand customers' attitudes and behaviors. For example, Kim et al. (2011) investigated customers' intention to buy digital items in SNSs, and confirmed that both emotional and social values have positive effects on customers' purchase intention. The study of Wang and Fesenmaier (2004) confirmed that users' perceptions of functional, social and hedonic values all positively influence their participation in an online community. Gummerus et al. (2012) find that both social and emotional values could improve customers' satisfaction with a brand community, while emotional value further increases customers' loyalty.

Although much research focuses generally on these three customer values, Kim et al. (2011) point out that it is important to gain a full understanding of the content of each customer value in a specific context. By doing so, we can provide deeper explanations of what actually leads to a perception of increased value in each of these customer values. Woodruff (1997) suggests a hierarchical structure to study a higher order of these customer values that is based on their structural properties. This approach articulates customer values to be operated at the top level of the hierarchy and provide the contextual frame for various customer experiences (Mathwick et al., 2001). Following this doctrine, we propose the key subconstructs under each customer value dimension in the context of tourism social media marketing, as shown in Figure 14.2.

"Functional value" is defined as "the utility derived from the product due to the reduction of its perceived short term and longer term costs, or from the perceived quality and expected performance of the product" (Sweeney and Soutar, 2001, p. 211). In the context of tourism social media marketing, functional value refers to the utility derived from the brand page for presenting high-quality content and providing superior rewards. We have identified three constructs that can be used to quantify the model construct of functional value: information quality, product-related learning and economic benefit. Information quality measures the overall perceived value of information posted on a brand page. Since customers tend to seek benefits from the timely updated and extensive information in online environments (Dholakia et al., 2009), a tourism brand page with high-quality information would be regarded as a valuable resource for customers (Lin, 2008). Such a perception of quality forms the major source for customers to gain more tourism product knowledge on the brand page. A high quality of information can enhance customers' confidence in a brand page since it implies that the brand page does not make inaccurate and false statements (Cvijikj and Michahelles, 2011b; Hsiao

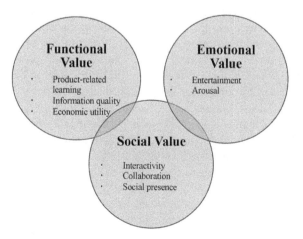

Figure 14.2   *Key customer values of tourism social media marketing*

et al., 2010). Moreover, it is expected that a high quality of information on a brand page can result in customers staying with the brand page in order to continue receiving this high-quality information (Gummerus et al., 2012). Product-related learning measures the tourism brand page's functional value in providing customers with tourism product-related knowledge. Many customers participate in tourism social media in order to learn more about specific tourism products. For tourism companies, the product-related information that they post on brand pages is not only for promotional purposes, but also for the enhancement of customers' product knowledge (Pentina et al., 2013b). This information can help customers become more familiar with the company's tourism products and services (Pentina et al., 2013b). Through this learning process, customers may perceive that the brand page can offer professional advice on their product selection, and they may thus develop trust towards the brand page. Moreover, customers who have acquired knowledge and achieved learning goals via a tourism social media brand page are more likely to remain engaged in the community for continuing knowledge enhancement and to help others (Dholakia et al., 2004). Economic benefit refers to the economic value that customers obtain from brand pages by means of receiving coupons, gaining discounts, getting better services, participating in raffles, and so on. Tourism companies may constantly offer monetary rewards to customers on the brand page as a form of incentive that stimulates customers' participation and loyalty (Vorvoreanu, 2009). In addition to monetary rewards, tourism companies can also offer economic benefits to customers by providing them with better services and faster responses on the brand page (Gummerus et al., 2012). Ba (2001) suggested that users' confidence in a community is largely based on an economic calculation. When customers receive economic benefits from a brand page, they may develop a positive attitude towards it, because this event generates the brand page's ability to create added value for them (Yen et al., 2011). Providing economic benefits to customers on the brand page is one way to show that the tourism company takes care of customers' interests (Muk, 2013).

"Social value" is defined as "the utility derived from the product's ability to enhance social self-concept" (Sweeney and Soutar, 2001, p. 211). In the context of tourism social media marketing, social value refers to the utility derived from the brand page's ability to enhance customers' social relationships and social self-concept on the brand page. We have identified three constructs for measuring the model construct of social value: interactivity, collaboration and social presence. Interactivity on the brand page refers to customers' social interactions with the tourism company and other members of a brand page. On the brand page, customers can interact with others by replying to their posts, forwarding their posts, directly chatting with them, and so on. Powell (2009) suggests that the interaction and communication on social media brand pages allow customers to establish their social ties with other members, which could further foster trust relationships between them. Lin and Lu (2011) indicate that one way to gain trust on the brand page is to develop a platform that allows customers to communicate and interact with each other. Dholakia et al. (2004) indicate that social interactions with other members in a virtual community could enhance customers' sense of belonging and commitment. Such interactions generated over time would strengthen customers' emotional attachment, and help them develop a stronger social identity among other members (Kim et al., 2008). Collaboration is another aspect of social value that refers to the exchange of help and support among followers on the tourism brand page. Customers may collaborate with each other on the brand page by helping with travel issues, exchanging valuable information, contributing to tourism product development, and so on (Lin and Lu, 2011). Such a collaboration effort and member support may make customers feel a sense of belonging, which could further foster relationships among social media members (Hsiao and Chiou, 2012). Users' collaborations may also increase familiarity and closeness among them (Ng, 2013). The familiarity and closeness developed among social media members could further enhance their trust in the tourism company's brand community, because users perceive the good intentions offered by other users. In addition, collaboration on the tourism brand page enhances social ties among customers. Strong social ties would form a solid foundation of attachment to a social media brand page (Cvijikj and Michahelles, 2013). Social presence is recognized as one of the key features of social media (Chen, 2013; Xu et al., 2012). The technology characteristics of social media brand pages make users feel a higher level of social presence, because it facilitates them to experience others as being psychologically present through close and frequent contacts (Xu et al., 2012). Social media brand pages could further facilitate social presence by creating a community in which customers feel a sense of human warmth (Dholakia et al., 2004). The presence of social values may also help improve customers' confidence in the tourism company's brand page because it reduces uncertainty during their participation and engagement in online communities (Lancastre and Lages, 2006). In the meantime, the social warmth promoted by social presence could help customers develop an emotional attachment to the tourism company, and thus further elevate their commitment (Xu et al., 2012).

"Emotional value" is defined as "the utility derived from the feelings or affective states that a product generates" (Sweeney and Soutar, 2001, p. 211). In the context of tourism social media marketing, emotional value refers to the utility derived from the inner-feelings or affective state that a brand page generates. We have identified two constructs for measuring the model construct of emotional value: entertainment and arousal. Entertainment is the intrinsic fun and enjoyment that customers experience when engaging with a tourism brand page (Gummerus et al., 2012). Elements of entertainment may derive from the information posted on the brand page, or from the activities initiated by the brand page (Nambisan and Baron, 2007). The entertaining contents could contribute to customers' happiness, and such feelings could enhance customers' positive feelings toward that brand page. According to Pentina et al. (2013b), positive feelings of engagement generate a positive attitude towards building trust in social media. In addition, Chen (2013) finds that individuals who enjoy using social media exhibit a stronger intention to continue their use. Kim et al. (2013) also suggest that users who experience pleasure and fun when engaging with technology would be intrinsically motivated toward a higher level of engagement and continuance intention. Since the tourism brand page is built on social media which focuses heavily on hedonic elements, entertainment should be regarded as one of the major emotional experiences that are provided to users. Arousal refers to the perceived stimulation, excitement or curiosity generated by engaging in absorbing interactions on a tourism brand page (Gupta and Kim, 2007). Kim and Stoel (2004) show that when users feel cheerful about a website, they tend to trust that particular website more. On the brand page, a high level of arousal would encourage more frequent participating behaviors, which would lead to a high level of social capital. Relationships among users become more solid when there is greater social capital involved in an online community. Arousal would also help to enhance customers' affective states and, in turn, would encourage them to continue following a tourism brand page. On the brand page, emotional value can be derived from customers' feelings of being aroused and excited about receiving information and participating in related activities (Gummerus et al., 2012). This could help strengthen customers' feelings about the tourism brand page, and thus could help them to develop a deeper attachment to it (Westerlund et al., 2009).

RELATIONSHIP MEDIATORS OF TOURISM SOCIAL MEDIA MARKETING

Commitment as a Key Relationship Mediator

Commitment is considered as one of the most critical issues in the customer relationship and customer behavior literature (Garbarino and Johnson, 1999). Good customer relationships cannot be built effectively without a solid foundation of commitment (Fullerton, 2005; Hocutt, 1998). In traditional exchange relationships, commitment is generally defined as "an enduring desire to maintain a valuable relationship" (Moorman et al., 1992, p. 316). Such a commitment is built upon the mutual benefits that the trading partners receive by maintaining their business relationship. In the tourism literature, customers' commitment to companies is viewed as a precursor of brand loyalty and is built through providing superior benefits and promoting companies' values (Nusair et al., 2011).

On the social media brand page, commitment refers to a customer's strong attachment and emotional bonds with a brand page. Commitment to a brand page can be built upon superior values derived from the regular posts on the brand page, as well as customers' engagement with the brand page (Hsu et al., 2010). Commitment is also considered as central to gain the understanding of user attachment and behaviors in the SNS and brand community literature. Jang et al. (2008) confirm that brand communities' characteristics, such as information quality and interaction intensity, would affect customer commitment and brand loyalty. As such, commitment could also contribute to a set of targeted favorable outcomes of customer relationships, such as loyalty (Cater and Zabkar, 2009), retention (Gustafsson et al., 2005) and co-production intention (Gruen et al., 2000). A high level of commitment to a brand page is believed to be associated with customers' loyalty to a brand (Zhang et al., 2013).

Commitment to a social media brand page consists of two constructs: affective commitment and cognitive commitment. The affective commitment is an emotional factor that is based mainly on customers' emotional involvement and feelings (Wirtz et al., 2013). It is mainly based on customers' perceptions of a sense of belonging, and feelings of being cared for (Gustafsson et al., 2005). Cognitive commitment is a more rational and utility-based factor which relies on the benefits that a customer receives from the relationship (Gustafsson et al., 2005). It has been reported that cognitive commitment is largely determined by the continuing benefits that are delivered to customers (Royo-Vela and Casamassima, 2011).

Trust as a Key Relationship Mediator

Trust is considered as another important factor for business success in many different disciplines, such as knowledge sharing (Chow and Chan, 2008), social networks (Grabner-Kräuter, 2009) and e-commerce (McKnight et al., 2002). Morgan and Hunt (1994, p. 23) define trust in traditional business relationships as "existing when one party has confidence in an exchange partner's reliability and integrity." They consider "gaining confidence" as a key factor in trust between two trading parties, and that this confidence is based on certain qualities of a trustworthy party, such as consistency, honesty and fairness.

In the social media context, it is suggested that trust could already be developed before a customer actually consumes the products or services of a company (Mukherjee and Nath, 2007). The major characteristic of social media brand pages is the dissemination of brand information to customers (Cvijikj and Michahelles, 2011b). The information allows customers to better assess the quality of the brand page (for example, its honesty and integrity). Therefore, brand page trust may be largely based on the brand page's information quality, such as its accuracy, reliability and objectivity (Grabner-Kräuter, 2009). On the other hand, customers' interpersonal trust on the brand page may be based on their identification with others. The trustworthiness (for example, honesty, integrity, benevolence) of brand page members can also be transferred to the brand page, and therefore can help customers to build stronger confidence on the brand page (Lankton and McKnight, 2011; Ng, 2013). As Westerlund et al. (2009) indicate, trust in social networking communities can be understood in the context of interpersonal relationships, that is, trust between members in the community.

Therefore, trust in the tourism social media brand page can be categorized into two dimensions: information-based trust and identification-based trust. Information-based trust represents customers' trust in the information that posted on the brand page, including information from companies and from other customers. Identification-based trust represents customers' trust in other members on the brand page, which is based on the trustworthiness of other customers.

RELATIONSHIP OUTCOMES OF TOURISM SOCIAL MEDIA MARKETING

Relationship Durability

In the tourism social media context, relationship durability refers to the likelihood that customers will continue being followers of a brand page of the tourism company. As long as customers do not terminate their relationships with the brand page, their future procurements can be encouraged through the brand page's marketing activities (Pentina et al., 2013a). This relationship durability is essential to brand page success, because once the relationship is terminated none of the other outcomes can be accomplished (Wang, 2013). As Algesheimer et al. (2005) stated, membership duration in an online brand community is considered as one of the most essential customer relationship outcomes. Moreover, studies have confirmed that customers' intention to continue as a member in the brand community has a positive impact on their loyalty intentions toward the company of the brand community (Brodie et al., 2013). As such, customers' willingness to continue their relationship with the brand page would also enhance their loyalty to the company of the brand page. Wang (2013) further confirmed the importance of customers' relationship durability as it contributes to customers' willingness to participate on the brand page.

Electronic Word-of-Mouth

Electronic word-of-mouth (eWOM) refers to non-commercial online interpersonal communication among individuals (Cheung and Lee, 2012). The brand page in social media provides a platform for users to spread eWOM about tourism companies faster and more easily among their connected friends (Brown et al., 2007). Therefore, tourism companies are increasingly exploring the potential of brand pages that could promote the awareness of their brands using eWOM practices (de Vries et al., 2012). The extant literature recognize that user-generated content and information exchange on the brand page are rich sources to create eWOM marketing effects (Cvijikj and Michahelles, 2013; Jansen et al., 2009). Good customer relationships on the brand page are solid foundations for motivating customers to spread positive eWOM to their connected friends (Jansen et al., 2009). The spreading of eWOM would also help other customers make better-informed tourism-related purchasing decisions (Zheng et al., 2013). In the meantime, tourism companies of brand pages can also attract potential customers through positive eWOM generated by existing consumers (Stephen and Toubia, 2010). Zheng et al. (2013) suggest that the credibility of the company should be enhanced through brand page activities in order to encourage more helpful eWOM communications.

Continued Interaction

Continued interaction refers to the behavioral intentions of customers to continue engaging and interacting with the tourism company of a brand page. On the brand page, customers can provide feedback and suggestions to tourism companies through various channels, such as posting comments and sending private messages (de Vries et al., 2012). Customers' continued interactions with the tourism company are considered essential for business success, because customers' feedback and opinions would help to improve the products and services of a company (Nambisan and Baron, 2009). Customers' interaction with the tourism company, in terms of suggesting new ideas and opinions, is an important outcome of customer relationships in online social media. Such interactions indicate that customers care about the development of a company. On the social media brand page, many tourism companies often organize activities, as an attempt to encourage customers to interact directly with them (Cvijikj and Michahelles, 2013). Through close and constant interactions on the brand page, tourism companies believe that they can learn more about customers' needs and thus could improve their products and services accordingly.

Functional Conflict

Functional conflict is another important factor in customer retention (Skarmeas, 2006). Functional conflict provides a "medium through which problems can be aired and solutions arrived at" (Morgan and Hunt, 1994, p. 26) in the future. Conflict and disagreements between tourism companies and customers are inevitable. However, through the platforms of social media brand pages, they can be resolved much more quickly and effectively (Subrahmanyam et al., 2008). When a tourism company and a customer achieve a mutually satisfying conflict resolution through communications and interactions on a brand page, this situation is often referred to as functional conflict (Harris et al., 2008). Social media platforms bring tourism companies closer to their customers, and brand pages activities are helpful in resolving conflicts between tourism companies and customers. On the brand page, tourism companies also consider the harmonious resolution of conflicts with customers as an important aspect of e-marketing success. As explained by Lee et al. (2013), when customers experience or observe how a company satisfactorily resolves conflicts on the brand page, they would develop stronger confidence in that company.

CONCLUDING REMARKS

In the digital age, it is important for tourism companies to build and manage strategic plans for sustaining a successful social media brand page in order to motivate and enhance the sustainable and continued participation and engagement of customers. For this purpose, the activities on the brand page need to be designed with a view to supporting customers in the long term, and to guarantee that the customer values which are important to users will be satisfied. Since customers are concerned about the value provided by brand pages, managers need to make an effort to create and promote desirable value elements for followers. In particular, this chapter suggest that functional, social and emotional value perceptions have significant impacts on customers' commitment to, and trust in, brand pages. Moreover, the motivations of one's commitment are centered on social and emotional values, which surpass the importance of functional value in brand pages. In other words, although social media brand pages are initially designed to promote brand-related information to subscribers, tourism companies should deploy more aggressive strategies to increase their perceived social and emotional values. However, functional value should also be provided, because it serves as a basis for customers to develop confidence in the brand page.

In order to improve functional value, managers of brand pages need to focus on improving the quality of the information they post, and to enhance customers' knowledge about the products and services provided by the company. Also, monetary rewards are required in order to encourage customers' perceived functional value. To encourage the perception of social value, brand page managers need to facilitate interactions and collaborations between customers by organizing discussions and activities related to tourism products and services. Facilitating customers' sense of social presence is another important aspect of social value on the brand page. In order to increase customers' perceptions of emotional value, entertaining and stimulating content is needed to enhance their feelings about the brand page. If customers find reading the content or participating in conversations on the brand page enjoyable and stimulating, they will be more likely to develop deeper commitment and trust.

In addition, this chapter helps tourism companies to understand the main relationship outcomes of customers' commitment to, and trust in, social media brand pages. This will help to identify the outcomes considered most desirable, so as to target these when developing strategies. As discussed in this chapter, customers' commitment to and trust in brand pages contribute to the durability of their relationship, intention to transmit by word-of-mouth, intention to continue the interaction, and levels of functional conflict. These insights are useful to tourism companies not only in maintaining relationships with current customers and followers of their brand page, but also in attracting new and potential customers.

REFERENCES

Algesheimer, R., Dholakia, U.M., and Herrmann, A. (2005). The social influence of brand community: Evidence from European car clubs. *Journal of Marketing, 69*(3), 19–34.

Askool, S., and Nakata, K. (2011). A conceptual model for acceptance of social CRM systems based on a scoping study. *AI and society, 26*(3), 205–220.

Ba, S. (2001). Establishing online trust through a community responsibility system. *Decision Support Systems, 31*(3), 323–336.

Baird, CH., and Parasnis, G. (2011). From social media to social customer relationship management. *Strategy and Leadership, 39*(5), 30–37.

Brodie, R.J., Ilic, A., Juric, B., and Hollebeek, L. (2013). Consumer engagement in a virtual brand community: An exploratory analysis. *Journal of Business Research, 66*(1), 105–114.

Brown, J., Broderick, A.J., and Lee, N. (2007). Word of mouth communication within online communities: Conceptualizing the online social network. *Journal of Interactive Marketing, 21*(3), 2–20.

Cater, B., and Zabkar, V. (2009). Antecedents and consequences of commitment in marketing research services: The client's perspective. *Industrial Marketing Management, 38*(7), 785–797.

Chang, W.-L., and Weng, S.-S. (2012). Revisiting customer value by forecasting e-service usage. *Journal of Computer Information Systems, 52*(3), 41–49.

Chen, R. (2013). Member use of social networking sites – An empirical examination. *Decision Support Systems, 54*(3), 1219–1227.

Cheung, C.M.K., and Lee, M. K. O. (2012). What drives consumers to spread electronic word of mouth in online consumer-opinion platforms. *Decision Support Systems, 53*(1), 218–225.

Chow, W.S., and Chan, L.S. (2008). Social network, social trust and shared goals in organizational knowledge sharing. *Information and Management, 45*(7), 458–465.

Cvijikj, I.P., and Michahelles, F. (2011a). A case study of the effects of moderator posts within a Facebook brand page. *Social Informatics, 69*(1), 161–170.

Cvijikj, I.P., and Michahelles, F. (2011b). Understanding social media marketing: A case study on topics, categories and sentiment on a Facebook brand page. *Proceedings of the 15th International Academic MindTrek Conference: Envisioning Future Media Environments, Tampere, Finland*, 175–182.

Cvijikj, I.P., and Michahelles, F. (2013). Understanding the user generated content and interactions on a Facebook brand page. *International Journal of Social and Humanistic Computing, 2*(1), 118–140.

de Vries, L., Gensler, S., and Leeflang, P.S. (2012). Popularity of brand posts on brand fan pages: An investigation of the effects of social media marketing. *Journal of Interactive Marketing, 26*(2), 83–91.

Dholakia, U.M., Bagozzi, R.P., and Pearo, L.K. (2004). A social influence model of consumer participation in network- and small-group-based virtual communities. *International Journal of Research in Marketing, 21*(3), 241–263.

Dholakia, U.M., Blazevic, V., Wiertz, C., and Algesheimer, R. (2009). Communal service delivery: How customers benefit from participation in firm-hosted virtual P3 communities. *Journal of Service Research, 12*(2), 208–226.

Dholakia, U.M., and Durham, E. (2010). One café chain's Facebook experiment. *Harvard Business Review, 88*(3), 26.

Ellison, N.B. (2007). Social network sites: Definition, history, and scholarship. *Journal of Computer-Mediated Communication, 13*(1), 210–230.

Faase, R., Helms, R., and Spruit, M. (2011). Web 2.0 in the CRM domain: Defining social CRM. *International Journal of Electronic Customer Relationship Management, 5*(1), 1–22.

Fullerton, G. (2005). How commitment both enables and undermines marketing relationships. *European Journal of Marketing, 39*(11/12), 1372–1388.

Garbarino, E., and Johnson, M.S. (1999). The different roles of satisfaction, trust, and commitment in customer relationships. *Journal of Marketing, 63*(2), 70–87.

Goo, J., and Huang, C.D. (2008). Facilitating relational governance through service level agreements in IT outsourcing: An application of the commitment–trust theory. *Decision Support Systems, 46*(1), 216–232.

Grabner-Kräuter, S. (2009). Web 2.0 social networks: the role of trust. *Journal of Business Ethics, 90*(4), 505–522.

Gruen, T.W., Summers, J.O., and Acito, F. (2000). Relationship marketing activities, commitment, and membership behaviors in professional associations. *Journal of Marketing*, *64*(3), 34–49.

Gu, C., and Wang, S. (2012). Empirical study on social media marketing based on Sina Microblog. *Proceedings of International Conference on Business Computing and Global Informatization, Shanghai University, Shanghai, China*, 537–540.

Gummerus, J., Liljander, V., Weman, E., and Pihlström, M. (2012). Customer engagement in a Facebook brand community. *Management Research Review*, *35*(9), 857–877.

Gupta, S., and Kim, H.W. (2007). Developing the commitment to virtual community: The balanced effects of cognition and affect. *Information Resources Management Journal*, *20*(1), 28–45.

Gustafsson, A., Johnson, M.D., and Roos, I. (2005). The effects of customer satisfaction, relationship commitment dimensions, and triggers on customer retention. *Journal of Marketing*, *69*(4), 210–218.

Harris, L.C., Ogbonna, E., and Goode, M.M.H. (2008). Intra-functional conflict: an investigation of antecedent factors in marketing functions. *European Journal of Marketing*, *42*(3/4), 453–476.

Haythornthwaite, C. (2005). Social networks and Internet connectivity effects. *Information, Community and Society*, *8*(2), 125–147.

Hew, J.J., Leong, L.Y., Tan, W.H., Lee, V.H., and Ooi, K.B. (2018). Mobile social tourism shopping: A dual-stage analysis of a multi-mediation model. *Tourism Management*, *66*, 121–139.

Hocutt, M.A. (1998). Relationship dissolution model: antecedents of relationship commitment and the likelihood of dissolving a relationship. *International Journal of Service Industry Management*, *9*(2), 189–200.

Hsiao, C.-C., and Chiou, J.-S. (2012). The effect of social capital on community loyalty in a virtual community: Test of a tripartite-process model. *Decision Support Systems*, *54*(1), 750–757.

Hsiao, K.-L., Lin, J. C.-C., Wang, X.-Y., Lu, H.-P., and Yu, H. (2010). Antecedents and consequences of trust in online product recommendations: An empirical study in social shopping. *Online Information Review*, *34*(6), 935–953.

Hsu, C.L., Liu, C.C., and Lee, Y.D. (2010). Effect of commitment and trust towards micro-blogs on consumer behavioral intention: A relationship marketing perspective. *International Journal of Electronic Business*, *8*(4), 292–303.

Jang, H., Olfman, L., Ko, I., Koh, J., and Kim, K. (2008). The influence of on-line brand community characteristics on community commitment and brand loyalty. *International Journal of Electronic Commerce*, *12*(3), 57–80.

Jansen, B.J., Zhang, M., Sobel, K., and Chowdury, A. (2009). Twitter power: Tweets as electronic word of mouth. *Journal of the American Society for Information Science and Technology*, *60*(11), 2169–2188.

Kim, H.-W., Gupta, S., and Koh, J. (2011). Investigating the intention to purchase digital items in social networking communities: A customer value perspective. *Information and Management*, *48*(6), 228–234.

Kim, H.W., Chan, H.C., and Gupta, S. (2007). Value-based adoption of mobile internet: An empirical investigation. *Decision Support Systems*, *43*(1), 111–126.

Kim, J.W., Choi, J., Qualls, W., and Han, K. (2008). It takes a marketplace community to raise brand commitment: The role of online communities. *Journal of Marketing Management*, *24*(3–4), 409–431.

Kim, S., and Stoel, L. (2004). Dimensional hierarchy of retail website quality. *Information and Management*, *41*(5), 619–633.

Kim, Y.H., Kim, D.J., and Wachter, K. (2013). A study of mobile user engagement (MoEN): Engagement motivations, perceived value, satisfaction, and continued engagement intention. *Decision Support Systems*, *56*, 361–370.

Lancastre, A., and Lages, L.F. (2006). The relationship between buyer and a B2B e-marketplace: Cooperation determinants in an electronic market context. *Industrial Marketing Management*, *35*(6), 774–789.

Lankton, N.K., and McKnight, D.H. (2011). What does it mean to trust Facebook? Examining technology and interpersonal trust beliefs. *ACM SiGMiS Database*, *42*(2), 32–54.

Lee, T.R., Lin, J.H., Liao, L.W.C., and Yeh, T.H. (2013). Managing the positive and negative characteristics of enterprise microblog to attract user to take action through the perspective of behavioural response. *International Journal of Management and Enterprise Development*, *12*(4), 363–384.

Lin, H.-F. (2008). Determinants of successful virtual communities: Contributions from system characteristics and social factors. *Information and Management, 45*(8), 522–527.

Lin, K.-Y., and Lu, H.-P. (2011). Intention to continue using Facebook fan pages from the perspective of social capital theory. *Cyberpsychology, Behavior, and Social Networking, 14*(10), 565–570.

Liu, C.-L., Yang, H.-W., and Song, W.-G. (2017). Effects of service convenience on consumer trust, commitment and behavioral intention in social commerce service: Focusing on the eating out consumers in China. *Journal of Tourism and Leisure Research, 29*(10), 463–482.

Lu, H.-P., and Hsiao, K.-L. (2010). The influence of extro/introversion on the intention to pay for social networking sites. *Information and Management, 47*(3), 150–157.

Mathwick, C., Malhotra, N., and Rigdon, E. (2001). Experiential value: Conceptualization, measurement and application in the catalog and Internet shopping environment. *Journal of Retailing, 77*(1), 39–56.

McKnight, D.H., Choudhury, V., and Kacmar, C. (2002). Developing and validating trust measures for e-commerce: An integrative typology. *Information Systems Research, 13*(3), 334–359.

Moorman, C., Zaltman, G., and Deshpande, R. (1992). Relationships between providers and users of market research: The dynamics of trust within and between organizations. *Journal of Marketing Research, 29*(3), 314–328.

Morgan, R.M., and Hunt, S.D. (1994). The commitment–trust theory of relationship marketing. *Journal of Marketing, 58*(3), 20–38.

Muk, A. (2013). What factors influence millennials to like brand pages? *Journal of Marketing Analytics, 1*(3), 127–137.

Mukherjee, A., and Nath, P. (2007). Role of electronic trust in online retailing: A re-examination of the commitment–trust theory. *European Journal of Marketing, 41*(9/10), 1173–1202.

Nambisan, S., and Baron, R.A. (2007). Interactions in virtual customer environments: Implications for product support and customer relationship management. *Journal of Interactive Marketing, 21*(2), 42–62.

Nambisan, S., and Baron, R.A. (2009). Virtual customer environments: Testing a model of voluntary participation in value co-creation activities. *Journal of Product Innovation Management, 26*(4), 388–406.

Ng, C.S.-P. (2013). Intention to purchase on social commerce websites across cultures: A cross-regional study. *Information and Management, 50*(8), 609–620.

Nusair, K.K., Parsa, H.G., and Cobanoglu, C. (2011). Building a model of commitment for Generation Y: An empirical study on e-travel retailers. *Tourism Management, 32*(4), 833–843.

Pentina, I., Gammoh, B.S., Zhang, L., and Mallin, M. (2013a). Drivers and outcomes of brand relationship quality in the context of online social networks. *International Journal of Electronic Commerce, 17*(3), 63–86.

Pentina, I., Zhang, L., and Basmanova, O. (2013b). Antecedents and consequences of trust in a social media brand: A cross-cultural study of Twitter. *Computers in Human Behavior, 29*(4), 1546–1555.

Powell, J. (2009). *33 Million people in the room: How to create, influence, and run a successful business with social networking.* Upper Saddle River, NJ: Pearson.

Rishika, R., Kumar, A., Janakiraman, R., and Bezawada, R. (2013). The effect of customers' social media participation on customer visit frequency and profitability: An empirical investigation. *Information Systems Research, 24*(1), 108–127.

Royo-Vela, M., and Casamassima, P. (2011). The influence of belonging to virtual brand communities on consumers' affective commitment, satisfaction and word-of-mouth advertising: The ZARA case. *Online Information Review, 35*(4), 517–542.

Sheth, J.N., Newman, B.I., and Gross, B.L. (1991). Why we buy what we buy: a theory of consumption values. *Journal of Business Research, 22*(2), 159–170.

Skarmeas, D. (2006). The role of functional conflict in international buyer–seller relationships: Implications for industrial exporters. *Industrial Marketing Management, 35*(5), 567–575.

Stephen, A.T., and Toubia, O. (2010). Deriving value from social commerce networks. *Journal of Marketing Research, 47*(2), 215–228.

Subrahmanyam, K., Reich, S.M., Waechter, N., and Espinoza, G. (2008). Online and offline social networks: Use of social networking sites by emerging adults. *Journal of Applied Developmental Psychology, 29*(6), 420–433.

Sweeney, J.C., and Soutar, G.N. (2001). Consumer perceived value: The development of a multiple item scale. *Journal of Retailing, 77*(2), 203–220.

Vorvoreanu, M. (2009). Perceptions of corporations on Facebook: An analysis of Facebook social norms. *Journal of New Communications Research, 4*(1), 67–86.

Wang, S.-M. (2013). Exploring the factors influencing the usage intention of Facebook fan page – A preliminary study. *Proceedings of The 19th Americas Conference on Information Systems, Chicago, Illinois*, 15–17.

Wang, Y., and Fesenmaier, D.R. (2004). Towards understanding members' general participation in and active contribution to an online travel community. *Tourism Management, 25*(6), 709–722.

Westerlund, M., Rajala, R., Nykänen, K., and Järvensivu, T. (2009). Trust and commitment in social networking – Lessons learned from two empirical studies. Paper presented at the the 25th IMP Conference, Marseille, France.

Wirtz, J., Den Ambtman, A., Bloemer, J., Horváth, C., Ramaseshan, B., et al. (2013). Managing brands and customer engagement in online brand communities. *Journal of Service Management, 24*(3), 223–244.

Woodcock, N., Green, A., and Starkey, M. (2011). Social CRM as a business strategy. *Journal of Database Marketing and Customer Strategy Management, 18*(1), 50–64.

Woodruff, R.B. (1997). Customer value: the next source for competitive advantage. *Journal of the Academy of Marketing Science, 25*(2), 139–153.

Wu, M.Y., Weng, Y.C., and Huang, I.C. (2012). A study of supply chain partnerships based on the commitment–trust theory. *Asia Pacific Journal of Marketing and Logistics, 24*(4), 9–9.

Xu, C., Ryan, S., Prybutok, V., and Wen, C. (2012). It is not for fun: An examination of social network site usage. *Information and Management, 49*(5), 210–217.

Yen, H.R., Hsu, S.H.-Y., and Huang, C.-Y. (2011). Good soldiers on the Web: Understanding the drivers of participation in online communities of consumption. *International Journal of Electronic Commerce, 15*(4), 89–120.

Zhang, K.Z., Lee, M.K., and Feng, F. (2013). Enterprise Microblog as a new marketing strategy for companies: Enterprise Microblog commitment and brand loyalty. Paper presented at the Pacific Asia Conference on Information Systems, Jeju Island, Korea.

Zheng, X., Zhu, S., and Lin, Z. (2013). Capturing the essence of word-of-mouth for social commerce: Assessing the quality of online e-commerce reviews by a semi-supervised approach. *Decision Support Systems, 56*(1), 211–222.

15. The transformative role of social media in the business-to-business tourism distribution channel

Kathryn Hayat

INTRODUCTION

The tourism industry has evolved in tandem with web-enabled technologies to be a global industry that uses global distribution systems (GDSs) to manage flight, hotel and attraction ticket bookings, amongst other tourism products. Often these changes have been reactive, as the benefits of these technologies have been clear from the outset. As a result, the structure of the tourism industry has seen a significant shift to online travel agents, and other online intermediaries who can offer the same or better service in an online environment. The influence of technology on business practices, and arguably the industry as a whole, is often referred to as e-tourism, which Buhalis (2003) defined as the digitisation of all the processes and value chains in the tourism industry (amongst others) that enable organisations to maximise their efficiency and effectiveness. Following these initial technological developments, online communities and social networks evolved, and as technology progressed to Web 2.0 and interactive technology, a mass expansion of the social web resulted in a diverse range of social media platforms to facilitate tourism marketing. The ability of users to generate content and to interact freely in a new, dynamic internet environment resulted in a surge in weblogs, interest-based communities and other user-generated content. The most widespread adoption as a result of Web 2.0 technologies was by social media networks and communities such as the globally popular Facebook, Instagram and Twitter, as well as nation-specific social media networks such as Renren in China and VK in Russian-speaking countries. Indeed, as a result of Web 2.0 technologies, and significantly that of social media, a website is often seen as no longer sufficient (Howison et al., 2015), and from some perspectives as a redundant tool, based on the abundance of information being disseminated online (Hua et al., 2017). There is a wide body of research into the role of social media in tourism marketing distribution channel that identifies it as a route to market from business to consumer (B2C) (Leung et al., 2013), destination to consumer (Hua et al., 2017), and even business to consumer through the guise of a consumer (Roth-Cohen and Lahav, 2019), the last of these raising some significant ethical issues. This wide-ranging research focus has been encapsulated in the development of the Travel 2.0 concept, where customers share experiences and emotions at every moment of travel consumption (Elki et al., 2017) through a range of media, including images and videos, reviews and travel blogs. This concept, and the focus of research, clearly identifies a shift in tourism marketing practices from mass message marketing broadcasting (Munar et al., 2013), to consumers advocating marketing messages in a much more personalised way (Oklobdzija and Popesku, 2017) through user-generated content on social media networks and mobile applications.

However, there is a distinct lack of research into how this shift in tourism marketing practices is reflected in business-to-business (B2B) marketing. This form of marketing is also known in the tourism industry as trade marketing or sales marketing, and given the significant impact that the internet in general has had on business practices (Oklobdzija and Popesku, 2017), this lack is perplexing. Moreover, in general business there is a scarcity of research (Diba et al., 2019), with the focus often leaning towards business to consumer (B2C) social media marketing, rather than exploring the potential nuances of B2B marketing. Where research does exist, Schulze (2013, cited in Habibi et al., 2015) identified that the three most common uses of social media for B2B marketing are: posting content on a company blog; building relationships with bloggers, community moderators and social influencers; and uploading content to social sharing sites. These all reflect the general merits of Web 2.0 that B2C marketing employs and enjoys. There are clear benefits of using social media for B2B marketing, and Miller et al. (2018) identified these from a general business perspective. The authors identify that the use of social media is gaining popularity, surpassed only by email marketing, and the benefits are perceived as being multiple. They include:

- increase brand awareness;
- increase customer engagement;
- promote products and services;
- build customer advocacy/loyalty;
- increase lead generation;
- gather insight into customers;
- provide customer support.

SOCIAL MEDIA FOR B2B TOURISM MARKETING

Where there is some consensus on the benefits of using social media in B2B marketing, there is an opportunity to explore the uses of social media in B2B tourism marketing. There is some recent interest in this area (Kumar et al., 2020), which is gaining attention as a significant tool to mediate B2B marketing. The significance of the benefits of social media for the tourism industry cannot be overlooked. Whilst tourist purchase patterns and behaviours have evolved, as a result of Web 2.0 technologies, to more direct booking of tourism products (ABTA, 2018, 2019; Ting, 2019) and the use of virtual communities (Roth-Cohen and Lahav, 2019), the high-street travel agent still has a strong presence. Indeed, the collapse of the British travel group Thomas Cook Group PLC in 2019 was quickly followed by the purchase of almost all Thomas Cook retail shops by a competitor (Keeley, 2019). Big players dominate the B2B market and include tour operators, accommodation suppliers and bed banks, airline seat wholesalers, attraction ticket retailers and resort transfer suppliers, amongst smaller, more niche providers. In Europe, the TUI group dominates the market (Mintel, 2019), although it is worth noting the impact that these traditional operators have faced with a more recent Web 2.0 advancement: the sharing economy and major players such as Airbnb and Uber. Therefore, understanding social media marketing of trade products seems a critical element of this aspect of the tourism industry at a critical time for the industry. Historically, tourism products from airlines, accommodation, attractions, and so on, would have been marketed to the travel trade through a range of traditional marketing methods. These methods included trade flyers/

leaflets, shop window display materials, in-person product training, and fax and email product updates (such as special offers). These were all (and often still are, with the exception of fax), commonplace not only as sales methods, but also as ways to make and manage long-term relationships with trade customers and all parts of the wider tourism marketing distribution channel. This exemplifies why B2B marketing has a significant role to play in tourism marketing, as it provides channels for product updates, sales promotions and relationship management, amongst others. Often, these methods are successful because tourism distribution channels frequently include the reselling of a product on a commission basis. This distribution channel is referred to as B2B2C (business to business to consumer), and is a common structure in Europe, for example (Reino et al., 2016). To illustrate this, consider an example where the hotel chain 'sells' rooms to the travel agent, with the hope that they will then 'sell on' to the customer in a package. This provides the hotel chain with an additional marketing distribution channel to the customer, and often functions alongside a direct distribution channel where the customer books directly with the hotel, such as via a website, a mobile application or through a social media page. Where commission is involved in the marketing and sales of a product, the personal marketing that B2B brings can be vitally important, as it provides a competitive advantage over companies that are selling a similar product. Morrison (2019, p. 425) refers to these as travel trade inducements, which typically involve some type of commission paid to travel agencies, or a discount offered on services and facilities within the destination. This would be a preferential and therefore a competitive rate. These travel trade inducements are often referred to as recognition programmes, which are a form of promotion that recognises travel trade companies for a positive sales history. This aspect of B2B marketing is little researched, and whilst there are studies that focus on distribution channels in tourism, they often focus on B2C marketing or destination marketing; for the latter, online B2B marketing is well established amongst destination management organisations (DMOs) (Estêvão et al., 2013), as often the cost of traditional forms of B2B marketing and sales outweigh the returns.

Fountoulaki et al. (2015) identified the range of distribution channels in tourism and focused on how the impact of technology has changed distribution. However, the research only focused on customer-facing technology and trade distribution via content management systems and XML feeds; the information about a product (hotel, flight, attraction, and so on) that would feed into another website where a booking would take place. Relationship sales and B2B marketing is omitted from this research, and from the authors' model of 'structure of tourism distribution channels in the future' (ibid.). The need for customer relationship management (CRM) within B2B tourism marketing has been highlighted by Tuzunkan (2018), who focused on the use of CRM systems in the Turkish tourism sector. However, again this research overlooks the wider features of B2B relationship management and marketing.

Alongside a paucity of research into this aspect of traditional B2B tourism marketing, there is also a lack of research into B2B marketing via social media. Although anecdotally these platforms are known about within the industry, there is no research to fully understand how these social media accounts are used, the benefits or drawbacks, or indeed any conclusions about how they can best be used. The general societal shift towards advocacy and persuasive and adaptable two-way communication (Oklobdzija and Popesku, 2017) means that B2B marketing and sales, and the management of these relationships, should embrace the general characteristics of social media. This is important, as B2B customers would be accustomed to this in their personal use of social media. Indeed, Nath et al. (2019) clearly state that the lines between internal (B2B) and external (B2C) stakeholders are blurred when it comes to social media, and this suggests that relationship management needs to engage with social media alongside traditional marketing and sales methods, as otherwise efforts become counterproductive.

Alongside the widespread use of social media platforms to promote tourism products through business pages, accounts and sponsored/paid adverts by tourism businesses to market to consumers (B2C), there is a niche area of social media whereby new forms of B2B or tourism trade marketing is taking place. There are significant examples of B2B marketing where this is the case, such as the well-established Facebook group Travel Gossip (https://www.facebook.com/groups/TravelGossipUK/), which at over ten years old claims to be 'the largest and most active and online community for the UK travel industry' (Travel Gossip, 2017). At the time of writing in December 2020 the group had 21 292 members and over 7000 posts in the previous 28 days. There are also examples where B2B marketing has been embraced and therefore company control is high. For example, the Facebook page Airport Gurus (https://www.facebook.com/airportgurus/) is a trade-facing social media account run by Birmingham Airport (UK) and following its launch in 2012, it had over 2000 likes by December 2020.

These two examples sit amongst countless others that include closed Facebook groups, Twitter feeds, Pinterest boards and Instagram and Snapchat accounts (the latter two often being private) that are all used for B2B tourism social media marketing. Interestingly, these social media platforms still utilise the known features of B2C social media marketing, such as personalisation, instant information and customisable products (Oklobdzija and Popesku, 2017), and relationship management (Howison et al., 2015; Kumar et al., 2020), but for a different audience. These are used in a way that demonstrates the credibility of social media platforms as sources of valuable criticisms and recommendations, just like the consumer to consumer (C2C) Travel 2.0 counterpart accounts. The result is B2B social media displaying characteristics familiar to users of social media for personal use. The little research into the transformative role of social media on B2B trade tourism marketing, by Howison et al. (2015), identified how marketing from tourism operators to consumers utilised groups and pages on social media platforms such as Facebook as a significant marketing tool. Indeed, Kumar et al. (2020) concisely state that the benefits of digital channels are often restricted by a range of operational (and organisational) cultural barriers. These barriers are clearly reflected in Taiminen and Karjaluoto's (2015) classification of digital marketing channels, where social media is identified as providing a two-way communication with low company control. This element of control could be considered as significant in contributing to operational and organisational barriers in using social media, and is a clear area where the industry can direct the use of social media for B2B marketing purposes.

TRANSFORMATIVE ROLE OF SOCIAL MEDIA

The role of social media in the B2B marketing of tourism can be split into two main areas – ephemeral social media and community-based marketing – and it is suggested that these can provide multiple benefits to all areas of the industry through tactics such as instant marketing and storification.

Ephemeral Social Media

Evolutions in social media technology, and the creation of apps such as Snapchat, forced a significant move in the way social media is used. This has seen social media content move away from nostalgia and memory-based content (such as the social media timeline, photo albums on Facebook, and the Instagram grid), to short-lived posts of mixed content (image, video and text) that often disappear after being viewed. This ephemeral content can be highly engaging, and as Anderson (2015) states, Snapchat was quickly adopted by teenagers when released, who were attracted to this different style of content. Subsequently, established social media platforms added functionality for ephemeral content shortly afterwards, to facilitate this change in social media use and remain competitive, with WhatsApp status, Facebook story and Instagram story features all disappearing after 24 hours, offering both ephemeral and permanent content. This content is exciting because of its short duration, and can often encourage regular viewing of accounts so as not to miss posts, something that can be easily reflected in the various data available on average daily time spent on a mobile phone. Furthermore, this content can be very reactive to changes in the business and wider social environment. Social media provides a new platform for ephemeral content, and this is a stark contrast to traditional B2B marketing methods, which are often quite static or unreactive. The benefits of short-lived story content can provide a new way to promote flash sales or other special promotions, or sales incentives, in a way not seen in the tourism industry before, and add another layer to the tourism marketing distribution channel.

Community-Based Marketing

Social media networks can provide an additional platform for B2B marketing to take place by utilising existing groups and pages, and by creating new groups and pages to suit a specific need. The ever-popular social media network, Facebook, has capitalised on the function of private and public groups and pages that facilitate people with a common interest networking on demand. Just like consumer-generated websites (and social media) can be seen as playing an increasingly important role in tourist travel planning (Nath et al., 2019), so these B2B social media accounts can be and are increasingly important as a trade selling tool, and to influence travel planning decisions at a travel agent or intermediary level. As Buhalis et al. (2017) state, interaction and engagement are two key attributes to competitiveness, and the high levels of interaction and engagement in these social media groups and pages facilitate this for 24 hours a day, 365 days of the year. Importantly, the consumer is still an active participant in the communication process (Happ and Ivaneso-Horvath, 2018) just as in B2C or C2C marketing. The ways in which B2B marketing take place in these social media networks are multiple, and include some of the following opportunities for B2B marketing:

- Sales promotions.
- Questions and answers.
- News and announcements.
- Event promotion.
- Social messages (quiz, games, GIFs).
- Complaints.
- Recommendations.

- Competitions and trade incentives.
- Reviews.

This broad range of uses of social media pages and groups offers some replication of traditional B2B marketing methods, but also provides new opportunities to enhance the tourism distribution channel, and facilitates the development of new B2B relationships, or the strengthening of existing ones. Furthermore, the use of these pages and groups without working-hours restrictions means that tourism businesses can be much more efficient in responding to posts, which is especially important where reviews and complaints are concerned.

THE NEAR FUTURE AND EVOLVING TRANSFORMATIONS

As we have seen, evolutions in social media such as short-lived stories on Snapchat are quickly embraced and adopted by competing social medias, and these evolutions are continuous. It can be assumed that the near future and evolving transformations of social media will follow this trend. Therefore, it is important to explore how B2B marketing could exploit these trends and use them to complement existing tourism marketing distribution channels. There are two key areas that are currently mostly limited to use in B2C and C2C social media – snackable video content and social media influencers – but there are opportunities to explore both for B2B purposes.

Snackable Video Content

Video content is not new, with YouTube leading the Web 2.0 revolution from as early as 2005, and it is still a globally popular social media network today. However, as with other evolutions in social media, TikTok is one example of how the social media landscape has been disrupted. The main difference here is in how users engage with video content, moving away from long, detailed videos to snackable video content and stories, all within a 60-second restriction. TikTok has firmly created a place in the social media landscape for song-and-dance based challenges, as well as lip-syncing, which all form the premise of the social media app, alongside the use of hashtags (although these are considered less significant compared to the video content itself). Therefore, this concept of snackable video content provides numerous opportunities for B2B tourism marketing, and in two key areas of B2B marketing: relationship management and product marketing. Time-restricted content can be centrally created, but with mobile phone proficiencies ever competing with professional equipment the opportunities for reactive content to be produced by suppliers and agents are endless. This means that the industry can build new B2B relationships and nourish existing ones through regular video content, that can be shared easily and can reflect some of common usages of B2B tourism social media identified in Figure 15.1. Furthermore, whilst traditional marketing of products still has a place in the tourism marketing distribution channel, short-lived video of products such as hotels, attractions and aircraft can be used as a method to capture interest and gain attention from buyers and suppliers alike.

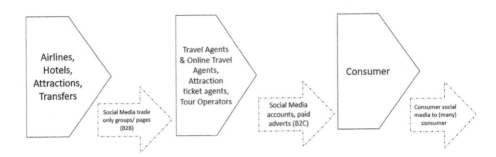

Figure 15.1   B2B social media marketing through the tourism distribution channel

Social Media Influencers

Social media influencers are now well established in many marketing distribution channels, and some brands are almost completely reliant on influencers for marketing. This is especially the case for brands that target Millennials and Generation Z, who are often seen as the most receptive to influencer marketing (Gutfreund, 2016). Whilst there are some examples of B2B marketing via social media influencers, in general this distribution channel is late to the game, considering the global explosion of influencer B2C marketing as a tool for relationship-building with brands. The social media influencer provides another way to create or strengthen relationships between buyers and suppliers, and this is because it utilises the most powerful aspect of influencer marketing, which is trust. Whilst big industry players can replicate the big celebrity names used in celebrity endorsement campaigns, or international marketing campaigns (for example, Arnold Schwarzenegger featuring in the California Tourism commercial 'California Calling'; or Jennifer Aniston, Cristiano Ronaldo or Shah Rukh Khan in various Emirates promotions) and use mega- or macro-influencers, the role of micro- or nano-influencers should not be overlooked. Rather than trying to reach audiences in the millions, tourism social media can reach smaller, more targeted audiences using influencers for niche B2B marketing. Furthermore, these influencers can be a mixture of interest-specific and industry-specific, but also provide a platform for influencers of the trade, and support a contemporary version of the trade sales and account manager roles that exist in the industry and who traditionally facilitate a large proportion of the B2B marketing function.

CONCLUSION

The role of social media in the marketing of tourism is significant enough that it should be embraced by B2B marketing, in the same way as it has been in B2C marketing. As a disruptive force, it can enhance the tourism distribution channel and facilitate the functions of B2B marketing, which still play an important role in tourism marketing. By exploiting the technological evolutions in social media, the tourism industry can maximise distribution channels and enhance marketing practice. Social media might be seen as disrupting a well-established distribution channel, and therefore raise issues of power and control in the organisation and operations of marketing, but the opportunities only supplement the traditional marketing practices of tourism suppliers and agents. Social media provides multiple platforms for advocacy to allow B2B marketing to move away from pushing a marketing message towards encouraging collaborative marketing and message sharing. Importantly, the broad landscape of social media means that it is easy to differentiate marketing aims, and target markets through different platforms. How the marketing distribution channel may look as a result of continued adoption of social media is displayed in Figure 15.1. It is clearly identified in the distribution channel how social media for B2B is assimilated within the broader use of social media platforms by B2C and customer-to-customer (C2C) channels, forming a social media ecosystem for tourism marketing.

REFERENCES

ABTA (2018). Holiday Habits Report. https://www.abta.com/sites/default/files/2018-10/Holiday %20Habits%20Report%202018%20011018.pdf.

ABTA (2019). Holiday Habits Report. https://www.abta.com/system/files/media/uploads/ABTA %20Holiday%20Habits%20Report%202019.pdf.

Anderson, K. Elson (2015). Getting Acquainted with Social Networks and Apps: Snapchat and the Rise of Ephemeral Communication, *Library Hi Tech News*, Vol. 32(10), pp. 6–10. http://dx.doi.org/10 .1108/LHTN-11-2015-0076.

Buhalis, D. (2003). *eTourism: Information Technology for Strategic Tourism Management* (Pearson/ Financial Times/Prentice Hall).

Buhalis, D., Kavoura, A. and Cooper, C. (2017). Social Media and User-Generated Content for Marketing Tourism Experiences, *Tourismos*, Vol. 12(3), pp. x–xvi.

Diba, H., Vella, J.M. and Abratt, R. (2019). Social Media Influence on the B2B Buying Process, *Journal of Business and Industrial Marketing*, Vol. 34(7), pp. 1482–1496. https://doi.org/10.1108/JBIM-12 -2018-0403.

Elki, A. Abubakar, Ilkan, A.M., Kolawole, M. and Lasisi, T.T. (2017). The Impact of Travel 2.0 on Travelers Booking and Reservation Behaviors, *Business Perspectives and Research*, Vol. 5(2), pp. 124–136. https://doi.org/10.1177%2F2278533717692909.

Estêvão, J.V., Carneiro, M.J and Teixeira, L. (2013). Improving the Tourism Experience by Empowering Visitors, in Kozak, M., Andreu, L., Gnoth, J., Lebe, S.S and Fyall, A. (eds), *Tourism Marketing: On Both Sides of the Counter* (Cambridge Scholars Publishing).

Fountoulaki, M., Leue, C.M. and Jung, T. (2015). Distribution Channels for Travel and Tourism: The Case of Crete, in Tussyadiah, I. and Inverini, A. (eds), *Information and Communication Technologies in Tourism* (Springer International Publishing).

Gutfreund, J. (2016). Move Over, Millennials: Generation Z is Changing the Consumer Landscape, *Journal of Brand Strategy*, Vol. 5(3), pp. 245–249.

Habibi, F., Hamilton, C.A., Valos, M.J. and Callaghan, M. (2015). E-Marketing Orientation and Social Media Implementation in B2B Marketing, *European Business Review*, Vol. 27(6), pp. 638–655. https://doi.org/10.1108/EBR-03-2015-0026.

Happ, E. and Ivaneso-Horvath, Z. (2018). Digital Tourism is the Challenge of Future – A New Approach to Tourism, *Knowledge, Horizons, Economics* Vol. 10(2), pp. 9–16.

Howison, S., Finger, G. and Hauschka, C. (2015). Insights into the Web Presence, Online Marketing, and the Use of Social Media by Tourism Operators in Dunedin, New Zealand, *Anatolia – An International Journal of Tourism and Hospitality Research*, Vol. 26(2), pp. 269–283. https://doi.org/10.1080/ 13032917.2014.940357.

Hua, L.Y., Ramayah, T., Ping, T.A. and Jun-Hwa, C. (2017). Social Media as a Tool to Help Select Tourism Destinations: The Case of Malaysia, *Information Systems Management*, Vol. 34(3), pp. 265–279. https://doi.org/10.1080/10580530.2017.1330004.

Keeley, A. (2019). Hays Travel to Acquire Entire Thomas Cook Retail Estate. https://www.travelweekly .co.uk/articles/345886/hays-travel-to-acquire-entire-thomas-cook-retail-estate.

Kumar, B., Sharma, A., Vatavwala, S. and Kumar, P. (2020). Digital Mediation in Business-to-Business Marketing: A Bibliometric Analysis, *Industrial Marketing Management*, Vol. 85, pp. 126–140. https://doi.org/10.1016/j.indmarman.2019.10.002.

Leung, D., Law, R., van Hoof, H. and Buhalis, D. (2013). Social Media in Tourism and Hospitality: A Literature Review, *Journal of Travel and Tourism Marketing*, Vol. 30(1–2), pp. 3–22. https://doi.org/10.1080/10548408.2013.750919.

Miller, R.K., Washington, K.D. and Richard K. Miller & Associates (2018). *Business-to-Business Marketing 2018–2019* (RKMA Market Research Handbook Series).

Mintel (2019). The European Leisure Travel Industry – December 2019. https://reports-mintel-com .ucbirmingham.idm.oclc.org/display/924562/.

Morrison, A.M. (2019). *Marketing and Managing Tourism Destinations* (Routledge)

Munar, A.M., Liping, C. and Gyimothy, S. (2013). *Tourism Social Media: Transformation in Identity, Community and Culture* (Emerald Publishing).

Nath, A., Saha, P. and Salehi-Sangari, E. (2019). Blurring the Borders between B2B and B2C: A Model of Antecedents behind Usage of Social Media for Travel Planning, *Journal of Business and Industrial Marketing*, Vol. 34(7). pp. 1468–1481. https://doi.org/10.1108/JBIM-11-2018-0329.

Oklobdzija, S.D and Popesku, J.R. (2017). The Link Between Digital Media and Making Travel Choices, *Marketing*, Vol. 48(2), pp. 75–85. https://doi.org/10.5937/markt1702075o.

Reino, S., Alzua-Sorzabal, A. and Baggio, R. (2016). Adopting Interoperability Solutions for Online Tourism Distribution: An Evaluation Framework. *Journal of Hospitality and Tourism Technology*, Vol. 7(1), pp. 2–15. https://doi.org/10.1108/JHTT-08-2014-0034.

Roth-Cohen, O. and Lahav, T. (2019). Going Undercover: Online Domestic Tourism Marketing Communication in Closed and Open Facebook Groups, *Journal of Vacation Marketing*, Vol. 24(3), pp. 349–362.

Taiminen, H. and Karjaluoto, H. (2015). The Usage of Digital Marketing Channels in SMEs. *Journal of Small Business and Enterprise Development*, 22(4), pp. 633–651. https://doi.org/10.1108/JSBED-05 -2013-0073.

Ting, D. (2019). Who's Really Winning the Direct Booking Wars Between Hotels and Online Travel Agencies?   https://skift.com/2019/03/04/whos-really-winning-the-direct-booking-wars-between -hotels-and-online-travel-agencies/.

Travel Gossip (2017). Travel Gossip Group. http://www.travelgossip.co.uk/facebook-group/.

Tuzunkan, D. (2018). Customer Relationship Management in Business to Business Marketing: Example of Tourism Sector, *GeoJournal of Tourism and Geosites*, Vol. 22(2), pp. 329–338. https://doi.org/10 .30892/gtg.22204-291.

16. How social media transformed tourism marketing: a case study of Lund, Sweden

Olga Rauhut Kompaniets

INTRODUCTION

The global digitalization and instantaneous development of communication technologies, internet and social media have revolutionized the tourism sector not only from the destination marketing organization's (DMO) perspective, but also from the tourist's point of view (Buhalis and Law, 2008; Xiang and Gretzel, 2010; Chung and Koo, 2015; Li, S.C.H., et al., 2017; Yoo et al., 2017). Social media brought smartness into tourism marketing (Jovicic, 2016; Li, Y., et al., 2017; Gretzel, 2018a; Rauhut Kompaniets, 2018), by changing tourists' behavior in terms of collecting and exchanging travel information and experiences (Chung and Koo, 2015), the communication strategies of DMOs, and the role of stakeholders in tourism marketing (Kavaratzis and Hatch, 2013; McComb et al., 2017).

A significant transformation has occurred between local tourism organizations and various destination stakeholders, on the one hand, and residents on the other hand. Before this transformation DMOs, using top-down tourism marketing strategies, had full control over marketing activities, for example visitor attraction, place marketing and branding, and communications (Mariani et al., 2016; Insch and Stuart, 2015; Yang and Wang, 2015; Eshuis et al., 2014). Tourism marketing content creation and promotion, however, are increasingly becoming more independent of local DMOs, and more inclusive in terms of their focus on tourists and citizens (Lalicic and Önder, 2018; Gretzel, 2018a; Munar, 2012). Bottom-up approaches can be seen to exert greater control than ever before over tourism marketing activities (Hudson et al., 2017; Rauhut Kompaniets, 2018). The development of social media technologies changed the role of tourists from consumers of destination products to content creators (Uşaklı et al., 2019; Oliveira and Panyik, 2015; Chung and Koo, 2015). The era of passive package-tour consumers appears now as an historical oddity; today's tourists are smart, demanding and knowledgeable, and willing to manage their travel itinerary by themselves (Rauhut Kompaniets, 2018; Yoo et al., 2017; Jovicic, 2016). Thus, success in relation to tourist attraction is now dependent on the ability of places and destinations to use social media in their tourism marketing activities (Xiang et al., 2008; Li, Y., et al., 2017). Moreover, social media delivers the opportunity, for residents, not just to influence the tourism marketing strategy of local DMOs but even to oppose local government where dissatisfaction arises with their marketing actions (Nunkoo et al., 2013).

In 2016, some residents of Lund, a city at the southern tip of Sweden, reacted against the dismantling of the tourism city brand by the local DMO, by creating the social media residents' association Destination Lund Sweden (DL). The residents' reaction when demanding an increase in tourism flows has been surveyed in previous research (Andriotis and Vaughan, 2003; Zhang et al., 2006; Kavaratzis, 2012; Braun et al., 2013; McComb et al., 2017). The conclusion is that to succeed in tourism marketing, DMOs have to take into consideration the residents' point of view as "place ambassadors" (Giles et al., 2013; Kavaratzis and Hatch, 2013; Braun et al., 2010; Messley et al., 2010; Zenker and Petersen, 2010).

The introduction of modern social media platforms has increased the number of available arenas for collaboration between place stakeholders, as well as their active participation in the tourism marketing process. This is a prerequisite for successful tourism marketing (Huang et al., 2017; Jovicic, 2016). By introducing free and downloadable material for smartphones and tablets (maps, guides, films and useful links), Destination Lund Sweden has directly intervened in the tourism marketing process through its active presence on social media, creating direct interaction with stakeholders (Destination Lund på svenska, n.d.). The municipal tourism office, which wants tourists to visit it and purchase printed products, displays a very negative attitude towards Destination Lund Sweden (Interview-1, 2017a). Although the local DMO has increased its suite of digital products and its presence on social media, its focus is still on Lund's surrounding countryside (Visit Lund, 2020).

This chapter discusses the role of social media and citizen initiatives in tourism marketing. The city of Lund in southern Sweden, with a rich cultural history, is used as a case study. Two research questions were formulated: (1) In what way(s) has social media transformed tourism marketing? (2) What key factors have contributed to the success of Destination Lund Sweden?

SOCIAL MEDIA DEVELOPMENT AND TOURISM MARKETING GOVERNANCE

Two parallel and inter-related processes with great impact on tourism marketing have occurred over recent decades. One relates to the development of social media, while the other relates to the issue of the control of the tourism marketing activities process, thus problematizing the question of whether tourism marketing is a top-down or bottom-up process.

Tourism Marketing and Social Media

Tourism marketing is tightly connected to the place marketing process whereby local government uses it as an instrument of place positioning and development (Lichrou et al., 2010). Tourism development can thus be seen as an attempt to increase place attractiveness for both external and internal stakeholders (Stylidis et al., 2014; Reiser and Crispin, 2009), where places are considered as the central element of tourism products (Költringer and Dickinger, 2015; Blichfeldt, 2005).

Social media, however, has undeniably changed tourism marketing (Pan and Crotts, 2016; Hays et al., 2013), moving the main focus from tourism products to people, as such tourists, visitors, stakeholders and, in particular, residents (Sazhina and Shafranskaya, 2017; Braun et al., 2013). Increasing competition across the global tourism market has put pressure on DMOs to activate their social media presence not just in terms of visitor attraction and tourism destination promotion (Uşaklı et al., 2019; Mariani et al., 2016), but also as a strategic tourism marketing tool (Hays et al., 2013; Munar, 2012).

Communicational marketing strategies and traditional promotion tools have been rapidly replaced by digital communication strategies and promotion tools (Dijkmans et al., 2015). The growing influence of social media has emerged as a tourism marketing communication strategy, giving destinations the opportunity to exert "global reach" at relatively low cost (Uşaklı et al., 2019). Furthermore, social media brought two-way communications into tourism marketing relations with stakeholders, employing interaction, participation and transparency of information (Oliveira and Panyik, 2015; Hvass and Munar, 2012), where stakeholders do not just give feedback on the activities of DMOs, but also communicate, influence and co-create their tourism destination marketing activities (Jamhawi and Hajahjah, 2017; Sazhina and Shafranskaya, 2017). For tourism to be successfully marketed, stable and balanced relationships between stakeholders and tourism organizations are necessary (Zhang et al., 2006).

Moreover, social media is characterized by bottom-up content production, the steady flow of content transformation and the richest online information contribution; while DMOs are passive in their adoption of new technology and limited by their continued top-down approach (Li, S.C.H., et al., 2017; Mariani et al., 2016; Költringer and Dickinger, 2015; Davidson and Keup, 2014; Wöber and Gretzel, 2000).

In recent years, the impact of social media has emerged as an area of research interest in the tourism sector, particularly with regard to marketing (Mariani, 2020; Choudhury and Mohanty, 2018; Roque and Raposo, 2016; Pan and Crotts, 2016; Chung and Koo, 2015; Hvass and Munar, 2012). Much of the research on the use of social media in tourism marketing has focused on three major areas: (1) tourist-generated content, with a focus on how tourists use social media platforms for searching and creating tourism-related information (Uşaklı et al., 2019; Yoo et al., 2017; Jovicic, 2016; Oliveira and Panyik, 2015; Chung and Koo, 2015); (2) DMO-generated content, with a focus on how tourism organizations use social media for tourist attraction and destination marketing purposes (Mariani, 2020; Choudhury and Mohanty, 2018; Gretzel, 2018b; Lund et al., 2018; Mariani et al., 2016; Roque and Raposo, 2016; Yang and Wang, 2015; Hays et al., 2013; Munar, 2012); and (3) top-down resident engagement campaigns created by DMOs with a view to activating locals in relation to tourism marketing (Mariani et al., 2016; Davidson and Keup, 2014; Stylidis et al., 2014). As such, local residents' use of social media and their bottom-up influence on the tourism marketing activities of DMOs remains an underexplored topic in this research field.

Top-Down, Bottom-Up and the Role of Residents in Tourism Marketing

Historically, tourism and place marketing has viewed local residents primarily as consumers of the place in which they live, and as the bearers of attitudes such as satisfaction, consumer loyalty to the place, place attachment, purpose of staying and place attractiveness (Rauhut Kompaniets, 2018; Insch and Florek, 2008; Zenker and Petersen, 2010; Zenker and Rütter, 2014). Viewing the tourism sector as a community industry (Nunkoo et al., 2013; Kavaratzis, 2012; Blichfeldt, 2005), however, sees a significant role shift, where residents form one of the main stakeholders' group actively creating and influencing the success of tourism destination marketing (Hereźniak, 2017; Sazhina and Shafranskaya, 2017; Rauhut Kompaniets and Rauhut, 2016; Stylidis et al., 2014; Giles et al., 2013; Kavaratzis, 2012; Hankinson, 2004).

While previous research indicates that residents play a significant role in tourism marketing and branding (Rauhut Kompaniets, 2018; Insch and Stuart, 2015; Eshuis et al., 2014; Braun et al., 2013; Kavaratzis, 2012), it suggests also that they played little if any role in the implementation of tourism marketing strategies (Compte-Pujol et al., 2018). The top-down approach remains dominant in tourism marketing, as DMOs are part of the local political administration (Rauhut and Rauhut Kompaniets, 2020; Insch and Stuart, 2015; Braun et al., 2013). As a more controllable and politically beneficial process, top-down tourism marketing strategies ignore the importance of residents as citizens and place ambassadors, excluding them from place and tourism marketing (Rauhut Kompaniets, 2018; Eshuis et al., 2014; Insch and Florek, 2008). Moreover, this highlights the one-sided image of the place, deemed more favorable and comfortable by the local DMOs, while the residents' view of the place is viewed as irrelevant (Braun et al., 2013; Kavaratzis, 2012). This leads, almost inevitably, to disagreement and to resident opposition to the DMOs' tourism marketing policy, expressed through the generation of bottom-up tourism marketing and branding activities (Rauhut Kompaniets, 2018; Insch and Florek, 2008; Kavaratzis, 2012).

The bottom-up perspective thus becomes a key factor in any successful tourism marketing strategy (Jamhawi and Hajahjah, 2017; Simpson and Siguaw, 2008), while negative results in respect of residents' disengagement and a top-down approach to tourism marketing activities lead to the de-branding of destinations, conflicts and anti-tourist movements, which also have to be taken into consideration (Insch and Stuart, 2015; Kavaratzis, 2012). Social media provides a useful medium through which bottom-up initiatives can enable residents not just to raise their voice against top-down tourism policy, but also to oppose the tourism strategies of DMOs deemed to be dismantling a destination brand (Rauhut Kompaniets, 2018).

Much of the research in the residents' engagement in tourism marketing activities field, however, is focused on the fact that DMOs are actively using social media in their tourism marketing strategies and engaging locals as active participants and supporters in these activities (Sazhina and Shafranskaya, 2017; Dijkmans et al., 2015). Taking into consideration the challenges faced by DMOs in terms of the adaption of social media tools to tourism marketing strategy, it is not enough just to create social media profiles. Their active, creative use is obligatory (Gretzel, 2018b). Clearly, there are situations where the active use of social media is not effectively utilized by local DMOs. Moreover, situations also occur where residents are happy to be involved in, and to help with, tourism marketing information and activities, but the local DMO does not want such help and nor does it favor the creation of such activities. This is clearly the case in Lund (Rauhut Kompaniets, 2018).

METHODOLOGICAL CONSIDERATIONS

This study is based upon case study methodology (Yin, 1990), participant observation (Bowen, 2002) and the "participant-as-observer" role in particular (Gold, 1958), as well as the use of internet sources, primary and secondary literature, and official documentation. Burgess (1984) highlights the potential value of using the "participant-as-observer" role: the advantage is that the researcher can apply observations together with theoretical insights, and generate recommendations for further research (Bowen, 2002; Burgess, 1984). Yin (1990) also mentions a number of opportunities in connection with participant observation, such as the observer as "insider" rather than as an external person, enabling them to access the events, meetings and communities that are normally out of reach to the traditional research investigation process.

During the course of the participant observations, a series of informal conversational interviews (ICIs) took place, to maximize the understanding of conducting observations (see Appendix). As an unplanned, unforeseen and even spontaneous interaction between an observant and a respondent, the ICI is the most open-ended interview form when while talking; the respondent does not even think of the conversation as an interview (Rubin and Babbie, 2011; Robson, 2002). The disadvantage with this methodology is that the participant-as-observer can be biased in their views (Yin, 1990). However, as Holme and Solvang (2010) conclude, there is no truly unbiased and objective research in social science in a normative sense.

THE CITY OF LUND AND TOURISM MARKETING

Lund is the twelfth-largest city in Sweden, with c. 120 000 inhabitants (Statistics Sweden, 2019), located at the southernmost tip of Sweden in the region of Scania (in Swedish: Skåne). Considered as one of the oldest cities in Scandinavia (Cinthio, 2018), Lund played a significant role as a religious, administrative and commercial center in the Nordic countries until the Danish reformation (Carelli, 2012). Today Lund combines this heritage and culture-based attractiveness with an economy based around modern technology and innovations, and buttressed by high-level political access. Lund University is a top-100 world university, the city is a research and development (R&D) innovation cluster for biotech and information technology (IT) solutions, and also hosts the European research center ESS (Oredsson, 2012; Wetterberg, 2017) while a United Nations (UN) Security Council meeting took place in Lund in early 2018 (Nord, 2018). Recognizing the historical and religious importance of the city, Pope Francis chose Lund as the place for the 500-year celebration of the Protestant Reformation in 2016, where in Lund the Catholic Church and the Lutheran World Federation were finally reconciled (Hitchen, 2018).

Besides its cultural and historical importance, the city of Lund has a developed infrastructure with regular inland railway and bus traffic, and easy access to two airports: Copenhagen airport is located just 50 minutes away by train, while the regional airport at Malmö airport also has good bus connections to the city. In addition, there are numerous ferry connections between Scania and Central Europe. Despite most of the ingredients needed for successful tourism promotion as a cultural-historical destination, Lund is a city suffering from undertourism. It remains a sleepy academic village where nothing really ever happens. In an era of smart tourism and social media, Lund thus remains undiscovered, as the municipal tourism office appears uninterested in promoting Lund's history and culture (Lindberg, 2018). According to the UN World Tourism Organization (UNWTO), historical and cultural tourism activities are included in the definition of cultural tourism, as:

> A type of tourism activity in which the visitor's essential motivation is to learn, discover, experience and consume the tangible and intangible cultural attractions/products in a tourism destination. These attractions/products relate to a set of distinctive material, intellectual, spiritual and emotional features of a society that encompasses arts and architecture, historical and cultural heritage, culinary heritage, literature, music, creative industries and the living cultures with their lifestyles, value systems, beliefs and traditions. (UNWTO, 2017, par. 4)

Despite international tourism media recommending Lund and the southern region of Sweden as a destination with a magnificent cultural and historical heritage, and as a gastronomic experience (Abend, 2016; Wergeland, 2017), the municipal tourism office is happy to provide tourists with information about the countryside outside Lund, but not the sights of Lund city itself (Visit Lund, 2020). Given that DMOs in Sweden are part of local public administration, with highly politicized and controlled activities (Rauhut and Rauhut Kompaniets, 2020), it is perhaps not so strange after all. A content analysis of the homepages of 75 municipalities in northern Sweden showed that most of them promote their destinations as places to visit, by focusing on their beautiful surrounding countryside rather than finding any unique, city-specific, selling points (Rauhut Kompaniets and Rauhut, 2013). Moreover, municipal DMOs tend to function reactively by copying the strategies of their neighbors and then gaining acceptance from the municipal government. As such, an explanation for why Lund's DMO promotes the surrounding countryside but not the unique selling points of the city itself becomes rather obvious, and relates to the pro forma process of simple benchmarking in respect of the neighboring municipalities with "beautiful countryside" (Rauhut Kompaniets, 2018).

Obviously, the city of Lund is struggling with what can be termed undertourism, when business in the historical city center is unprofitable not just in terms of local retailers and cafes, but also for the local galleries and souvenir shops. Without tourists and visitors, local residents cannot fulfill all the requirements for the profitability of the city center; but they can raise their voice and oppose the dismantling of the city's tourism brand. That is what happened during the late autumn of 2016.

A BOTTOM-UP REACTION

The Facebook group "You know that you are from Lund if …" (Du vet att du är ifrån Lund om …, n.d.), where almost 20 000 residents and people connected with Lund discuss common problems and share images and stories of the city, became the place where the residents' initiative was born. During the late autumn of 2016, five private residents of Lund discussed on Facebook the city's problem related to the lack of tourists, the absence of city promotion as a tourist destination, the fact that the official Lund brand excludes its cultural history, and that the local DMO ignores the need for a tourism marketing strategy. After this discussion, the new Facebook community established a non-profit Lund tourist association with the aim of better highlighting the great cultural history of the city, in an effort to attract more tourists and create opportunities for new jobs and business growth in the city. Residents decided to use social media as a platform for their volunteer project. After the first offline meeting in January 2017, the unofficial Lund tourist association had a name: Destination Lund Sweden (DL). Today the DL community is a third-sector non-profit organization, with volunteer members, working without a budget, and which has not spent a single krone on any activity (Rauhut Kompaniets, 2018; Kniivilä, 2017; Rumpf, 2017; Stierna, 2017). DL consists of 12 active members, it has 170 members of Lund's tourist association, more than 3500 Facebook followers (including both English and Swedish pages), more than 1150 followers on Instagram, and active readers of the blog posts from 68 countries.

Social media has changed the tourist information searching process: formerly, tourists were prepared to receive a published travel guide and information from the tour operator; now social media does the work. If there is no interesting and eye-catching information available, the city as a destination simply does not exist. That was exactly the case with Lund, as very limited tourist information was available. So DL began its activity with the creation of accounts on social media platforms such as Facebook and Instagram. The next step was to write short but informative stories about Lund's culture and history. Since DL was focusing not just on international tourists but also on locals interested in their own history, two Facebook pages are active with information in English and in Swedish.

The tourists' and visitors' maps were created in Google Maps where all the sights of Lund together with practical information (ATMs, toilets, bike stations, and so on) were marked as pop-up windows with a short story behind them, and the homepage address, opening hours, and so on. The map is free of charge (as is everything produced by DL) and functions on every electronic platform device (Destination Lund Sweden, 2017a). The rapidly growing number of downloads shows the importance of this work, and interest in the place from target groups. Identifying unique selling points of Lund and attracting different target groups are the two main ideas behind the DL community.

DL works actively on guide brochures, the downloadable PDF guides describe different routes and events, historical persons and buildings, in short stories with attached images embedded in a digital map. Almost 20 different brochures are already available for tourists (Destination Lund Sweden, 2020).

One of the first offline activities, in August 2017, was a guided bicycle tour around the battlefield site of the Battle of Lund (1676), with a map and brochure made by DL. As a newcomer association existing just on social media, DL expected to get ten, or a maximum of 15, participants; 50 persons came to the meeting point with their bikes, excited to spend about six hours with DL (Rauhut Kompaniets, 2018; Destination Lund Sweden, 2017b). This tour became a great success. In June 2018, the Swedish nationwide tourist association (STF Sydvästra Skåne Lokalavdelning, 2018) evaluated the tour as excellent and unique for Sweden.

Social media networks are important communication tools, where anybody can find new contacts by sharing common interests and ideas. A journalist from a Siberian TV channel contacted DL via Instagram and offered the opportunity to showcase the city to a Russian TV audience (almost 2 million viewers, plus social media channels), free of charge. This cooperation resulted in two 15 minute films in Russian, covering the history and culture of Lund, broadcast on the travel program *Tour Insider* and still available on YouTube (*Tour Insider*, 2017a, 2017b). If Russian bus tour-operators formerly planned just a short stopover in Lund, from summer 2018 their stay was extended to two full days due to increased demand (Aksenova, 2018). Russian tourists posted many positive reviews on social media, which led to a further growth of interest in exploring the city of Lund (Interview-5, 2018c). Even in 2020, DL continues to receive positive reviews in relation to these two travel films.

DL contacted the local DMO for a meeting to discuss potential future cooperation. Voluntary help in terms of city marketing and promotion was offered. The DMO's tourism director, however, explained to DL that they were not willing to use any DL material and could not talk about any kind of cooperation; the advice received was to dissolve DL and stop all the unofficial activities: only the DMO, they claimed, has the right to engage in tourism activities in the city (Interview-1, 2017a). City residents wanted to become more deeply involved and fully engaged in the tourism marketing of Lund, without desiring to compete with the DMO, but ended up in the situation where their voluntary work was viewed as a threat to the local DMO (Rauhut Kompaniets, 2018). Furthermore, in less than a year, a group of residents working on a voluntary basis had managed to outperform the local DMO with all its full-time employees and budget.

During the following year (Interview-2, 2017b; Interview-3, 2018a), DL began to cooperate with other third-sector organizations, and this cooperation is ongoing. Receiving positive feedback on what they do, DL gladly provides anybody with tourist information on the cultural history of Lund, and helps others to arrange events and meetings. Lundaspelen is one such event; the world's largest indoor handball tournament for youth players has taken place in

Lund for more than 40 years. More than 10 000 persons come to Lund during the tournament period, including participants, team staff and accompanying families; everybody is keen to know more about the city and DL helps with the information dissemination process, with the social media products particularly appreciated (Interview-4, 2018b). While the third-sector organizations are happy to cooperate with each other, the official tourism organizations are not. The Church of Sweden, for instance, does not accept Lund cathedral, the second most visited church in Sweden, as a tourist attraction (Interview-6, 2018d).

Historical storytelling makes the local history of Lund even more colorful. Officially it was known that in archives of the Versailles museum in France there is a portrait of the Swedish King Karl XII, which was painted in Lund. The most fascinating with this portrait is that Karl XII did not like it and cut the portrait with a knife immediately after it was painted. The painting was repaired by the artist, but the scar remained. Shortly after that, Karl XII presented the destroyed portrait to the French king. What happened to the painting afterwards is unknown. DL wrote to the Versailles museum and asked about the portrait. In their reply to DL's enquiry, Versailles sent photos of the painting and re-counted the story behind it. This story relates to an important period in Lund's history, as Karl XII resided in Lund for two years and made it the de facto capital of the Swedish empire (Pileby, 2018).

Growing interest in DL's activities, an increasing number of followers across social media, positive reviews from residents, local third-sector actors and journalists, thus combined to provide the necessary energy to continue the social media cultural historical initiative.

DISCUSSION AND CONCLUSION

During the autumn of 2019, the municipal government decided to transfer the local DMO from municipal public administration control into a joint stock company owned by the municipality, with a focus on organizing conferences and meetings (Lunds kommun, 2019). The rationale behind why the local DMO decided to reposition itself towards the B2B market is unclear, but it is obvious that attracting tourists was simply not on its agenda.

The COVID-19 outbreak during the spring of 2020 allowed DL to continue with its volunteer activities focused on domestic tourism, while DMO and the tourist center remained closed from mid-April to mid-June. DL has grown in popularity among the local population, who are dissatisfied with the very limited information written by the local DMO's social media staff; even the news sites of Lund have begun to question the quality of the DMO's tourism marketing strategy (Interview-8, 2020b). DL began a new tourism marketing campaign on social media with "Hemester Lund" ("Staycation Lund"), where it published tips for a summer staycation in Lund. Using the hashtag #hemesterlund, locals publish on their social media accounts stories about their favorite places in Lund. More and more residents of Lund are now following the campaign, local businesses also joined in, as have residents in other parts of the Scania region. New cooperation opportunities are increasing: among other things, for instance, DL has now joined the International Greeters Association (Interview-7, 2020a).

Destination Lund Sweden is a volunteer-based social media initiative run by the residents of Lund. It was initially established because of the dissatisfaction with the local DMO's tourism marketing approach. As Lund's DMO is a part of the municipal administration, tourism marketing activities are not the result of a professional marketing strategy, but rather are reflective of politically based decisions. Using a top-down strategy, the local DMO tries to show its interest in residents, which in reality increases the residents' social media reaction to the dismantling of the city's brand as a cultural historical destination. It is clear that social media has revolutionized traditional tourism marketing, enabling the residents to act in a bottom-up manner even against the direct wishes of the local DMO where they perceive this to be necessary in creating a new place development strategy for Lund as a tourism destination (Rauhut Kompaniets, 2018).

This chapter discusses the role of social media and citizens' initiatives in tourism marketing, with two research questions initially formulated and which can now be directly addressed, as follows. First, social media has radically transformed tourism marketing, especially in its communication aspect, turning the traditional one-way channel of fully controlled (by DMOs) communication into a network of multiple-channeled communications, where the role of tourists and residents has changed from that of simple consumers of tourism products (places) to that of its active co-creators. Indeed, residents are now considered the main participants in all stages of tourism marketing and branding process.

Second, some key factors contributing to the success of Destination Lund Sweden can now be identified. One such factor relates to the fact that tourists have become "smart," that is, they demand digital and social media-based information. This finding should be seen in light of the fact that many DMOs are rather conservative in the sense of their exposure to new technologies. A second success factor is that several local associations and organizations related to the tourism and hospitality sector have noticed the products of Destination Lund and have subsequently sought collaboration. Lastly, the local tourism office opposes both smart tourism and the involvement of other stakeholders in the place marketing of Lund. As previous research has shown, when stakeholders actually feel locked out of the tourism marketing of a city, the city marketing will become inefficient and unsuccessful. The politically controlled, top-down tourist marketing strategy of Lund appears to be losing ground to a stakeholder-based, bottom-up marketing process. Top-down tourism marketing can, as such, be seen as something of a reminder of the pre-social media era marketing campaigns dominated by the complete absence of IT and social media.

A general conclusion here is that social media, as bottom-up communication platforms, has built the core of the tourism marketing strategy for places and destinations, by transforming tourism marketing not just from the tourists' own perspectives and that of the DMOs, but also from the residents' perspective. Social media puts locals at the center of the tourism marketing strategy, not as mere consumers but rather as creators and influencers. Tourism and place marketing research, considering the tourism sector as a community industry, emphasizes the significant role played by residents in the tourism marketing process (Sazhina and Shafranskaya, 2017; Stylidis et al., 2014). Residents are motivated, active creators of these tourism marketing and branding activities, not a passive group accepting the old top-down approach (Nunkoo et al., 2013; Kavaratzis, 2012). Previous research has also highlighted the issue of resident opposition to local politicians in regards to tourist-related attraction and development questions (Andriotis and Vaughan, 2003; Zhang et al., 2006; Kavaratzis, 2012; Braun et al., 2013; McComb et al., 2017). The actions of the residents of the city of Lund provide further confirmation of this observed trend.

Further research could discuss the consequences of the top-down approach in tourism marketing, while the need for closer collaboration between local DMOs and resident initiative groups should also be explored, as well as the issue of social media as a bottom-up strategic communication channel for resident actions, and resident social media activism. Furthermore, future research could also usefully investigate the theory and practice of participant-oriented and even resident-oriented social media approaches in tourism marketing. From the DMOs' perspective, the effective use of social media in tourism marketing is surely also required.

REFERENCES

Abend, L. (2016, January 7). No. 9: Skane. Sweden. Nordic cuisine's next big thing. 52 places to go 2016. *New York Times*. https://www.nytimes.com/interactive/2016/01/07/travel/places-to-visit.html.

Aksenova, E. (2018, July 4). The romantic travel in Scandinavia. Tourists' forum of TTV. http://forum .tourtrans.ru/topic/20640-romanticheskoe-puteshestvie-po-sadam-i-parkam-skandinavii-ot-30042018 -g/?page=8.

Andriotis, K., and Vaughan, R.D. (2003). Urban residents' attitudes toward tourism development: the case of Crete. *Journal of Travel Research*, *42*, 172–185. https://doi.org/10.1177/0047287503257488.

Blichfeldt, B.S. (2005). Unmanageable place brands? *Place Branding*, *1*(4), 388–401. https://doi.org/10 .1057/palgrave.pb.5990036.

Bowen, D. (2002). Research through participant observation in tourism: a creative solution to the measurement of consumer satisfaction/dissatisfaction (CS/D) among tourists. *Journal of Travel Research*, *41*(1), 4–14. https://doi.org/10.1177/004728750204141001002.

Braun, E., Kavaratzis, M., and Zenker, S. (2010, August 19–23). My city – my brand: The role of residents in place branding. Paper presentatied at the 50th European Regional Science Association (ERSA) Congress, Jönköping, Sweden.

Braun, E., Kavaratzis, M., and Zenker, S. (2013). My city – my brand: the different roles of residents in place branding. *Journal of Place Management and Development*, *6*(1), 18–28. https://doi.org/10.1108/ 17538331311306087.

Buhalis, D., and Law, R. (2008). Progress in information technology and tourism management: 20 years on and 10 years after the Internet – the state of etourism research. *Tourism Management*, *29*(4), 609–623. https://doi.org/10.1016/j.tourman.2008.01.005.

Burgess, R.G. (1984). *In the Field: An Introduction to Field Research*. Unwin Hyman.

Carelli, P. (2012). *Lunds Historia, Vol. 1. Medeltiden 990–1536*. Historiska Media.

Choudhury, R., and Mohanty, P. (2018). Strategic use of social media in tourism marketing: a comparative analysis of official tourism boards. *Atna Journal of Tourism Studies*, *13*(2), 41–56. https://doi .org/10.12727/ajts.20.4.

Chung, N., and Koo, C. (2015). The use of social media in travel information search. *Telematics and Informatics*, *32*, 215–229. https://doi.org/10.1016/j.tele.2014.08.005.

Cinthio, M. (2018). Lund från Första Början. In M. Cinthio and A. Ödman (eds), *Vägar mot Lund*. Historiska Media.

Compte-Pujol, M., San Eugenio-Vela, J., and Frigola-Reig, J. (2018). Key elements in defining Barcelona's place values: the contribution of residents' perceptions from an internal place branding perspective. *Place Branding and Public Diplomacy*, *14*(4), 245–259. https://doi.org/10.1057/s41254 -017-0081-7.

Davidson, R., and Keup, M. (2014). The use of web 2.0 as a marketing tool by European convention bureaux. *Scandinavian Journal of Hospitality and Tourism*, *14*(3), 234–254. https://doi.org/10.1080/ 15022250.2014.946232.

Destination Lund på svenska. (n.d.). *Home* [Facebook page]. Retrieved May 10, 2020, from https://www .facebook.com/SvenskaDestinationLund/.

Destination Lund Sweden (2017a). *Tourists' and Visitors' Map of Lund*. http://bit.ly/turistkarta.

Destination Lund Sweden (2017b). *Tourists' Brochure and Map, Biking Tour 'Battle of Lund'*. https:// drive.google.com/file/d/0B9-doBOg2L1NTmczbXBSS3Vsd2M/view.

Destination Lund Sweden (2020). Tourists' brochures. http://bit.ly/turistbroschyrer.

Du vet att du är ifrån Lund om… (n.d.). Home [Facebook page]. Retrieved May 10, 2020, from https:// www.facebook.com/groups/Du.vet.du.ar.ifran.Lund/about/.

Dijkmans, C., Kerkhof, P., and Beukeboom, C.J. (2015). A stage to engage: social media use and corporate reputation. *Tourism Management*, *47*, 58–67. https://doi.org/10.1016/j.tourman.2014.09.005.

Eshuis, J., Klijn, E.-H., and Braun, E. (2014). Place marketing and citizen participation: branding as strategy to address the emotional dimension of policy making? *International Review of Administrative Sciences*, *80*(1), 151–171. https://doi.org/10.1177/0020852313513872.

Giles, E., Bosworth, G., and Willett, J. (2013). The role of local perceptions in the marketing of rural areas. *Journal of Destination Marketing and Management*, *2*(1), 4–13. https://doi.org/10.1016/j.jdmm .2012.11.004.

Gold, R.L. (1958). Roles in sociological field observations. *Social Forces*, *36*(3), 217–223.

Gretzel, U. (2018a). From smart destinations to smart tourism regions. *Journal of Regional Research*, *42*, 171–184.

Gretzel, U. (2018b). Tourism and social media. In C. Cooper, W. Gartner, N. Scott and S. Volo (eds), *The SAGE Handbook of Tourism Management* (Vol. 2, pp. 415–432). SAGE.

Hankinson, G. (2004). Relational network brands: towards a conceptual model of place brands. *Journal of Vacation Marketing*, *10*(2), 109–121. https://doi.org/10.1177/135676670401000202.

Hays, S., Page, S.J., and Buhalis, D. (2013). Social media as a destination marketing tool: its use by national tourism organisations. *Current Issues in Tourism*, *16*(3), 211–239, https://doi.org/10.1080/ 13683500.2012.662215.

Hereźniak, M. (2017). Place branding and citizen involvement: participatory approach to building and managing city brands. *International Studies. Interdisciplinary Political and Cultural Journal*, *19*(1), 129–142. https://doi.org/10.1515/ipcj-2017-0008.

Hitchen, P. (2018, April 4). Sweden's Lund cathedral to host first Catholic Mass since Reformation. *Vatican News*. https://www.vaticannews.va/en/church/news/2018-04/lund-cathedral-catholic-mass -ecumenical-lutheran.html.

Holme, I.M., and Solvang, B.K. (2010). *Forskningsmetodik*. Studentlitteratur.

Huang, C.D., Goo, J., Nam, K., and Yoo, C.W. (2017). Smart tourism technologies in travel planning: The role of exploration and exploitation. *Information and Management*, *54*(6), 757–770. https://doi .org/10.1016/j.im.2016.11.010.

Hudson, S., Cárdenas, D., Meng, F., and Thal, K. (2017). Building a place brand from the bottom up: a case study from the United States. *Journal of Vacation Marketing*, *23*(4), 365–377. https://doi.org/ 10.1177/1356766716649228.

Hvass, K.A., and Munar, A.M. (2012). The takeoff of social media in tourism. *Journal of Vacation Marketing*, *18*(2), 93–103. https://doi.org/10.1177/1356766711435978.

Insch, A. and Florek, M. (2008). A great place to live, work and play: conceptualising place satisfaction in the case of a city's residents. *Journal of Place Management and Development*, *1*(2), 138–149. https://doi.org/10.1108/17538330810889970.

Insch, A., and Stuart, M. (2015). Understanding resident city brand disengagement. *Journal of Place Management and Development*, *8*(3), 172–186. https://doi.org/10.1108/JPMD-06-2015-0016.

Jamhawi, M.M., and Hajahjah, Z.A. (2017). A bottom-up approach for cultural tourism management in the Old City of As-Salt, Jordan. *Journal of Cultural Heritage Management and Sustainable Development*, *7*(1), 91–106. https://doi.org/10.1108/JCHMSD-07-2015-0027.

Jovicic, D.Z. (2016). Key issues in the conceptualization of tourism destinations. *Tourism Geographies*, *18*(4), 445–457. https://doi.org/10.1080/14616688.2016.1183144.

Kavaratzis, M. (2012). From "necessary evil" to necessity: stakeholders' involvement in place branding. *Journal of Place Management and Development*, *5*(1), 7–19. https://doi.org/10.1108/ 17538331211209013.

Kavaratzis, M., and Hatch, M. J. (2013). The dynamic place brands: an identity-based approach to place branding theory. *Marketing Theory*, *13*(1), 69–86. https://doi.org/10.1177/1470593112467268.

Kniivilä, K. (2017, October 17). Hennes film ska locka ryska turister till Lund. *Sydsvenskan*. https://www .sydsvenskan.se/2017-10-17/hennes-film-ska-locka-ryska-turister-till-lund.

Költringer, C., and Dickinger, A. (2015). Analysing destination branding and image from online sources: a web content mining approach. *Journal of Business Research*, *68*(9), 1836–1843. https://doi.org/10 .1016/j.jbusres.2015.01.011.

Lalicic, L., and Önder, I. (2018). Residents' involvement in urban tourism planning: opportunities from a smart city perspective. *Sustainability*, *10*(6), 1852–1867. https://doi.org/10.3390/su10061852.

Li, S.C.H., Robinson, P., and Oriade, A. (2017). Destination marketing: the use of technology since the millennium. *Journal of Destination Marketing and Management, 6*, 95–102. https://doi.org/10.1016/j.jdmm.2017.04.008.

Li, Y., Hu, C., Huang, C., and Duan, L. (2017). The concept of smart tourism in the context of tourism information services. *Tourism Management, 58*, 293–300. https://doi.org/10.1016/j.tourman.2016.03.014.

Lichrou, M., O'Malley, L., and Patterson, M. (2010). Narratives of a tourism destination: local particularities and their implications for place marketing and branding. *Place Branding and Public Diplomacy, 6*(2), 134–144. https://doi.org/10.1057/pb.2010.10.

Lindberg, C. (2018, October 03). Vi måste berätta om allt fint vi har. *Hallå Lund.*

Lund, N.F., Cohen, S.A., and Scarles, C. (2018). The power of social media storytelling in destination branding. *Journal of Destination Marketing and Management, 8*, 271–280. https://doi.org/10.1016/j.jdmm.2017.05.003.

Lunds kommun. (2019, December 4). Lunds kommun bildar destinationsbolag. Press release. http://www.mynewsdesk.com/se/lund/pressreleases/lunds-kommun-bildar-destinationsbolag-2950021.

Mariani, M. (2020). Web 2.0 and destination marketing: current trends and future directions. *Sustainability; Basel, 12*(9). https://doi.org/10.3390/su12093771.

Mariani, M., Di Felice, M., and Mura, M. (2016). Facebook as a destination marketing tool: evidence from Italian regional destination management organizations. *Tourism Management, 54*, 321–343. https://doi.org/10.1016/j.tourman.2015.12.008.

McComb, E.J., Boyd, S., and Boluk, K. (2017). Stakeholder collaboration: a means to the success of rural tourism destinations? A critical evaluation of the existence of stakeholder collaboration within the Mournes, Northern Ireland. *Tourism and Hospitality Research, 17*(3), 286–297. https://doi.org/10.1177/1467358415583738.

Messley, L., Dessein, J., and Lauwers, L. (2010). Regional identity in rural development: three case studies of regional branding. *APSTRACT, 4*(3–4), 19–24. https://doi.org/10.19041/Apstract/2010/3-4/3.

Munar, A.M. (2012). Social media strategies and destination management. *Scandinavian Journal of Hospitality and Tourism, 12*(2), 101–120. https://doi.org/10.1080/15022250.2012.679047.

Nord, S. (2018, April 20). Säkerhetsrådet på plats i Lund. SVT Nyheter. https://www.svt.se/nyheter/lokalt/skane/nu-har-fn-s-sakerhetsrad-rullat-over-oresundsbron.

Nunkoo, R., Smith, S.L.J., and Ramkissoon, H. (2013). Residents' attitudes to tourism: a longitudinal study of 140 articles from 1984 to 2010. *Journal of Sustainable Tourism, 21*(1), 5–25. https://doi.org/10.1080/09669582.2012.673621.

Oliveira, E., and Panyik, E. (2015). Content, context and co-creation: digital challenges in destination branding with references to Portugal as a tourist destination. *Journal of Vacation Marketing, 21*(1), 53–74. https://doi.org/10.1177/1356766714544235.

Oredsson, S. (2012). *Lunds Historia. Modern Tid 1862–2010* (Vol. 3). Historiska Media.

Pan, B., and Crotts, J. C. (2016). Theoretical models of social media, marketing implications, and future research directions. In E. Christou, M. Sigala, and U. Gretzel (eds), *Social Media in Travel, Tourism and Hospitality: Theory, Practice and Cases* (pp. 84–95). Routledge.

Pileby, J. (2018, July 31). Unik trasig tavla återfunnen i Versailles. *Lokaltidningen Lund.*

Rauhut, D., and Rauhut Kompaniets, O. (2020). How to measure the impact of place marketing activities: a methodological discussion. *Geografisk Tidsskrift – Danish Journal of Geography, 120*(1), 67–78. https://doi.org/10.1080/00167223.2020.1767669.

Rauhut Kompaniets, O. (2018). A "bottom-up" place marketing initiative: Destination Lund Sweden. In L.A.N. Dioko (ed.), *Proceedings of the 3rd Annual Conference of the International Place Branding Association (IPBA)* (pp. 132–142). Institute for Tourism Studies, Macao, China.

Rauhut Kompaniets, O., and Rauhut, D. (2013). The place marketing concept of rural municipalities in Northern Sweden: a content analysis of the municipals' homepages. *Romanian Journal of Regional Science, 7*(2), 11–36.

Rauhut Kompaniets, O., and Rauhut, D. (2016). Why marketing of cities and rural areas differ: a theoretical discussion. *Romanian Journal of Regional Science, 10*(1), 23–40.

Reiser, D., and Crispin, S. (2009). Local perception of the reimagining process. *Journal of Place Management and Development, 2*(2), 109–124.

Robson, C. (2002). *Real World Research*. Blackwell.

Roque, V., and Raposo, R. (2016). Social media as a communication and marketing tool in tourism: an analysis of online activities from international key player DMO. *Anatolia, 27*(1), 58–70, https://doi.org/10.1080/13032917.2015.1083209.

Rubin, A., and Babbie, E.R. (2011). *Research Methods for Social Work*, 8th edition. Brooks/Cole Cengage Learning.

Rumpf, K. (2017, August 16). De vill öka stadens turism med historia. *Hallå Lund*.

Sazhina, A., and Shafranskaya, I. (2017). Residents' attitudes towards place marketing: tourism marketing focus. *Almatourism, 8*(7). https://doi.org/10.6092/issn.2036-5195/6775.

Simpson, P.M., and Siguaw, J.A. (2008). Destination word of mouth. The role of traveler type, residents, and identity salience. *Journal of Travel Research, 47*(2), 167–182. https://doi.org/10.1177/0047287508321198.

Statistics Sweden (2019, December 31). Folkmängd, topp 50. https://www.scb.se/hitta-statistik/statistik-efter-amne/befolkning/befolkningens-sammansattning/befolkningsstatistik/pong/tabell-och-diagram/topplistor-kommuner/folkmangd-topp-50/.

STF Sydvästra Skåne Lokalavdelning (2018, June 17). Cykelutfärd "Slaget vid Lund 1676" – lördag 16 juni 2018. [Image with link attached.] Facebook. https://www.facebook.com/stfsydvastraskane/posts/2051742671819868.

Stierna, J. (2017, August 10). En miljon turister är målet. *Skånska Dagbladet*.

Stylidis, D., Biran, A., Sit, J., and Szivas, E.M. (2014). Residents' support for tourism development: the role of residents' place image and perceived tourism impacts. *Tourism Management, 45*, 260–274. https://doi.org/10.1016/j.tourman.2014.05.006.

Tour Insider [10kanal] (2017a, November 16). *Tour insider. Lund. Part 1* [Video]. YouTube. https://www.youtube.com/watch?v=ubP2BecHl5Q&feature=player_embedded&list=PLzacB5WFwQPlmKTFQz_JgiGyY0mH4Ii09.

Tour Insider [10kanal] (2017b, November 23). *Tour insider. Lund. Part 2* [Video]. YouTube. https://www.youtube.com/watch?v=2yGylqGg6Ok.

UNWTO (2017). Tourism and culture. World Tourism Organization (UNWTO). https://www.unwto.org/tourism-and-culture.

Uşaklı, A., Koç, B., and Sönmez, S. (2019). Social media usage among top European DMOs. In N. Kozak, and M. Kozak (eds), *Tourist Destination Management: Instruments, Products, and Case Studies* (pp. 1–14). Springer Nature. https://doi.org/10.1007/978-3-030-16981-7_1.

Visit Lund (2020). The official homepage of Visit Lund. https://visitlund.se/.

Wergeland, M. (2017, August 4). A guide to Sweden's charming, relaxed southernmost county: Skåne. Vogue. https://www.vogue.com/article/skane-county-scania-sweden-travel-guide?mbid=social_facebook.

Wetterberg, G. (2017). *Skånes Historia. Vol. 3, 1720–2015*. Bonniers förlag.

Wöber, K., and Gretzel, U. (2000). Tourism managers' adoption of marketing decision support systems. *Journal of Travel Research, 39*(2), 172–181. https://doi.org/10.1177/004728750003900207.

Xiang, Z., and Gretzel, U. (2010). Role of social media in online travel information search. *Tourism Management, 31*, 179–188. https://doi.org/10.1016/j.tourman.2009.02.016.

Xiang, Z., Wöber, K., and Fesenmaier, D.R. (2008). Representation of the online tourism domain in search engines. *Journal of Travel Research, 47*(2), 137–150. https://doi.org/10.1177/0047287508321193.

Yang, X., and Wang, D. (2015). The exploration of social media marketing strategies of destination marketing organizations in China. *Journal of China Tourism Research, 11*(2), 166–185. https://doi.org/10.1080/19388160.2015.1017071.

Yin, R.K. (1990). *Case Study Research*. Sage.

Yoo, C.W., Goo, J., Huang, C.D., Namn, K., and Woo, M. (2017). Improving travel decision support satisfaction with smart tourism technologies: a framework of tourist elaboration likelihood and self-efficacy. *Technological forecasting and Social Change, 123*, 330–342.

Zenker, S., and Petersen, S. (2010, August 19–23). Resident-city identification: Translating the customer relationship management approach into place marketing theory. Paper presented at the 50th European Regional Science Association (ERSA) Congress, Jönköping, Sweden.

Zenker, S., and Rütter, N. (2014). Is satisfaction the key? The role of citizen satisfaction, place attachment and place brand attitude on positive citizenship behaviour. *Cities*, *38*, 11–17. https://doi.org/10.1016/j.cities.2013.12.009.

Zhang, J., Inbakaran, R.J., and Jackson, M.S. (2006). Understanding community attitudes towards tourism and host–guest interaction in the urban–rural border region. *Tourism Geographies*, *8*(2), 182–204. https://doi.org/10.1080/14616680600585455.

APPENDIX: INFORMAL CONVERSATIONAL INTERVIEWS

An informal conversational interview is where one takes an opportunity that arises to have a (usually short) chat with someone in the research setting about anything that seems relevant. As these interviews are spontaneous, they are not recorded (as getting out the recorder, asking permission etc., would likely remove the spontaneous and informal interaction), but a detailed note of the interaction is written down as soon as possible afterwards (Rubin and Babbie, 2011). In this study, eight such informal conversational interviews took place.

Interview-1 (2017a, November 9). Meeting between DL and Lund's municipality's Deputy Director of one devision.

Interview-2 (2017b, December 17). Meeting with a non-profit association in memorial to Johan Henrik Thomander.

Interview-3 (2018a, February 7). Meeting with a third-sector organization working for the preservation of archaeological findings.

Interview-4 (2018b, May 18). The 'breakfast meeting' with a manager.

Interview-5 (2018c, June 2). Meeting with a guide from DL.

Interview-6 (2018d, August 31). Meeting between DL and Church of Sweden.

Interview-7 (2020a, February 6). A meeting with one of the coordinators of International Greeters Association (IGA).

Interview-8 (2020b, June 5). A meeting with an editor of a news portal.

PART IV

TRAVEL BLOGS,
USER-GENERATED CONTENT,
REVIEWS AND E-WOM

17. Online hospitality and the collaborative paradigm of communication: a conceptual understanding of collaborative platform peer-to-peer interaction experiences

André F. Durão and Xander Lub

INTRODUCTION

Currently, there are over 4 billion users connected to the internet. This number represents a 53 per cent penetration rate of the world's population and is expected to increase, based on a 1052 per cent increase since the year 2000 (Digital, 2018). In one internet minute, 38 million messages are exchanged on WhatsApp, 18 million text messages are sent, 174 000 users scroll down on Instagram, and there are 973 000 Facebook logins (Digital Information World, 2018). People are intensely interacting and communicating with each other, using a variety of online platforms and media.

Even before impacting upon organisations, online social networks and media were and still are a component of the everyday life of the individual/consumer, and significantly influence how people communicate, relate and consume (Molz, 2012; Matos et al., 2016; Sigala and Gretzel, 2018). Peer-to-peer online interactions could therefore be considered as one of the pivotal elements of contemporary human relationships on a daily basis, and consequently impact upon all areas, including hospitality. According to Sigala (2016), the exchange of information and interactions are essential aspects of tourism and hospitality experiences and, as a result, are strongly affected by technological changes and trends.

Specifically regarding hospitality, new technologies and online social networking platforms are creating hybrid spaces of interaction, providing new ways of relating to distance and redefining who counts as a 'friend' or 'stranger' (Molz, 2012, p. 215). Over approximately the past two decades, the discussion on hospitality field theory development was proposed and conducted by recognised researchers (Lashley, 2000; Lashley et al., 2007; Molz and Gibson, 2007; Brotherton and Wood, 2007; Lashley, 2008; Morrison and O'Gorman, 2008; Molz, 2012; Lugosi, 2014; Molz, 2014; Lashley, 2017).

Recently, Lynch et al. (2011) invited researchers to develop hospitality theory critically, and in an interdisciplinary manner. They proposed a research agenda that addresses specific gaps and novel areas that require further debate and theorizing. In this chapter, we address one of these novel areas, namely hospitality and virtuality. As Lynch et al. (2011, p. 15) point out:

As social relations are increasingly conducted in mediated formats, hospitality provides a useful lens through which to explore the way humans interact with each other in virtual spaces and with new technologies in physical spaces. To date, surprisingly little research has applied a hospitality perspective to these emerging phenomena. Those authors who do engage the metaphor of hospitality in this context, however, reveal that bringing hospitality to bear on studies of human–machine interactions, online social networking, and virtual communities enables us to ask important questions about belonging, exclusion, power, and identity. (Lynch et al., 2011, p. 15)

Since then, hospitality research on this matter has remained scarce, although the need for its discussion increases exponentially each year, along with the rise in information and technology adoption. In addition, there is an emergence of new forms of interaction, communication and consumption, particularly in online social networks.

This study's main aim is to emphasise the hospitality perspective regarding online peer-to-peer interactions conceptually. Furthermore, as inspired by Lynch et al. (2011), it aims to further develop theoretical arguments, as suggested by Lashley and Morrison (2003) and Molz and Gibson (2007). The studies of Molz (2012), Dredge and Gyimóthy (2017) and Lashley (2017) will introduce the collaborative paradigm of an online communication approach (Gulbrandsen and Just, 2011) to elucidate hospitable online interactions on collaborative platforms.

This study's premise will focus on collaborative platforms, such as Airbnb, CouchSurfing and HomeExchange's online peer-to-peer (host-to-guest) interactions. These are observed on what Dredge and Gyimóthy (2017) define as a collaborative economy platform, which can occur on a digital platform peer-to-peer network. In addition, it adds value by providing the context and forum for transactions. It connects travellers worldwide, rendering it conceivable to welcome each other into their homes, and is crucial in enabling new arrangements of collaboration and exchange (Molz, 2014; Forno and Garibaldi, 2015). Airbnb presently has over 5 million listings in more than 191 countries, and has intermediated over 300 million guest arrivals in the last decade (Airbnb, 2018). The Couchsurfing website states that the platform is a global community of 14 million people in more than 200 000 cities (Couchsurfing, 2018). HomeExchange has over 65 000 homes in 150 countries (HomeExchange, 2018). These could be considered as relevant examples of the collaborative economy and consumption.

Collaborative consumption is based on the reinvention of traditional market behaviours, by increasing the value of access for a fee or other compensation, as an alternative mode of consumption, as opposed to property (Belk, 2014; Bardhi and Eckhardt 2012; Belk and Llamas, 2011; Belk, 2010). In this case, ownership is no longer the consumer's ultimate desire (Chen, 2009).

In addition, online peer-to-peer interactions and the sharing of personal experiences may allow individuals to create and maintain social connections with each other. Participating in collaborative consumption is an opportunity to develop meaningful social connections and authentic experiences in guest–guest relations and exchanges (Botsman and Rodgers, 2011; Tussyadiah, 2015; Pesonen and Tussyadiah, 2017).

These intermediated interaction approaches include relevant questions, such as how consumers interpret hospitality in the collaborative environment when they are interacting online, and how and when they engage in and perceive hospitable actions through communication and its implications on their experience. We believe that hospitable actions can be performed online through communication. By considering hospitality collaborative platforms, such as Airbnb, Couchsurfing and HomeExchange, the essential component of perceived experience occurs mainly before and during accommodation.

This is a new contribution to the hospitality literature, since it focuses on peer-to-peer interactions within the online environment, and it considers the possibility of the performance and perception of online hospitable actions of both parties. This occurs essentially before and during the accommodation, which will be pivotal to a uniquely perceived hospitality experience.

In order to present answers, this chapter relies on the collaborative paradigm of online communication, which is an ongoing process determined by more collective, opened and recursive terms, and a peer-to-peer relational approach (Gulbrandsen and Just, 2011). This theory introduces a new approach to hospitality and is directly related to how people mainly interact nowadays. It is a good fit for understanding hospitable actions/behaviour occurring in online environments, and most importantly on hospitality collaborative platforms.

By approaching hospitality, collaborative consumption, the collaborative paradigm of online communication, and online peer-to-peer meaningful/authentic interaction constructs, this study aims to contribute to the literature by proposing a conceptual understanding of online hospitality. It also aims to understand the potential experiences based on perceived peer-to-peer collaborative consumption interactions.

Thus, we present the concept of online hospitality as: a collaborative communication form of engagement between peers – host and guest – conducted on a collaborative platform, mainly before and during accommodation, where truthful and genuine information regarding who, what, where, and for how much are provided and exchanged by both parties through multimedia, to make them perceive and feel a safe, satisfying and authentic online host and hosting experience.

The literature review will be presented to explain the theoretical propositions on this concept by: (1) situating online hospitality into hospitality theory; (2) presenting the collaborative paradigm of online communication by relating it to hospitality and online peer-to-peer interaction on collaborative consumption; (3) describing possible peers' perceptions of online hospitality actions and its implications on satisfying and authentic interaction experiences; (4) presenting final discussions, implications for the hospitality industry, and future research opportunities.

SITUATING ONLINE HOSPITALITY

The emergence of the internet has drastically transformed the way individuals interact and communicate with one another, as well as changing the relationship between consumers and organisations to the same extent (Sigala and Gretzel, 2018). Moreover, enabling a practically instantaneous and uninterrupted form of interaction enables the consumer to be a greater protagonist, for example providing online collaborative settings for hospitality transactions between individuals.

Discussions on hospitality theory evolution and its definition have been developed for years. Lugosi (2014) also noted the complexity of hospitality conceptualisation, and welcomed complementary intellectual perspectives. Prior to explaining the collaborative paradigm of online communication, we will situate online hospitality into the past and present publications in the area, establishing some notable conceptual boundaries. These include private/domestic and commercial domains, as well as reciprocal and commercial motives for hosting.

Our peer-to-peer approach corroborates Molz's (2014, p. 4) argument that, 'Moments of hospitality are not confined to the hotels, restaurants, in-flight service, or guided tours that constitute the hospitality industry. Hospitality seeps into the crevices of public and private life'. The exchange of public and private personal information and items between individuals is one of the core values of collaborative consumption (Belk, 2007, 2010, 2014; Botsman and

Rodgers, 2011; Belk and Llamas, 2011; Cheng and Jin, 2019). Traditional 'offline' welcoming actions between individuals currently also occur on and are adapted to online collaborative platforms, such as Airbnb, Couchsurfing and HomeExchange.

The notion of the private/domestic domain in hospitality was introduced by Lashley (2000). The research stated that interactions occur on an individual/private level and not in the traditional commercial hospitality industry. This allows individuals to perform hospitality roles in their homes, which could be perceived as a more genuine and authentic experience of hospitality (Lashley, 2000; Lashley et al., 2007; Lashley, 2017).

Non-genuine and inauthentic hospitality experiences and/or actions have also been discussed as characteristics of a commercial setting (Slattery, 2002; Ritzer, 2004), whereby 'commercial' should essentially be understood by the following example: a hotel's service provision that is compulsory to be paid for by consumers. This organisation–guest consumption relation, however, has already been confronted and thus broadened. According to Lashley (2000), it is labelled the 'commercial/industrial domain'.

Telfer (2004) argues that an inhospitable commercial setting could be mitigated by individuals who naturally possess hospitable personalities and behaviour, and on an individual level provide a true hospitable experience. For Lashley and Morrison (2003), actions related to the private/domestic domain are inherent to commercial settings, arguing that successful hosts engage with consumers on a personal and emotional level, and the greater the quality of emotion they experience, the more satisfied and loyal consumers will be (Lashley, 2017).

Lugosi (2008, 2009) presented two articles relating commercial settings to hospitable spaces and moments. First, he investigated the production of the hospitable experience between consumers in commercial hospitable spaces, by presenting three types: 'The offer of food, drink, shelter, and entertainment within commercial transactions, the offer of hospitality as a means of achieving social or political goals, and meta-hospitality – temporary states of being that are different from the rational manifestations of hospitality' (Lugosi, 2008, p. 139). The author described those differences to explain that hospitable moments could be experienced by consumers in commercial settings.

In 2009, Lugosi examined the interrelation of social and commercial hospitality forms by executing an ethnographic study at a queer bar, focusing on guests' experience and guest–guest transactions. He highlighted subjective elements of its perception, as well as demonstrating a broader and more complex hospitality perspective to understand it as a process of 'ongoing relationships between individuals in and through spaces' (Lugosi, 2009, p. 409).

Although there remain questions and beliefs regarding the possibility of hospitality actions in commercial places, both philosophical and empirical counter-arguments have already demonstrated the possibility of genuine and true actions even in exchange for a monetary value or other compensation, such as the practice of collaborative consumption. Therefore, we note that online hospitality can be located in the intersection between the domestic/private and commercial/industrial domains, illustrated in Figure 17.1.

In his most recent research, Lashley (2017) resumed working on a compilation of a set of six host motivations for offering hospitality to guests, from researchers from different study fields (Heal, 1984; Nouwen, 1998; Telfer, 2004 and O'Gorman, 2007). He named this a 'continuum of hospitality' (Lashley, 2017, p. 4), where the extremes are represented by ulterior motives hospitality and altruistic hospitality. Ulterior motives hospitality is where the host ultimately expects gains and benefits from guests' favourable impressions of their services, such as accommodation, food, drink. Altruistic hospitality is where hospitality is an act of genuine

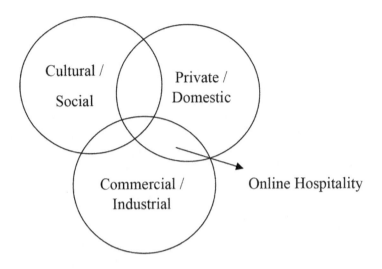

Source: Adapted from Lashley (2000).

Figure 17.1　The domains of hospitality

generosity, benevolence and willingness to please the guest, and not expecting anything in return.

Towards the continuum's centre, containing hospitality is presented, which is derived from a sense of the close monitoring of a stranger or enemy. The following concept of redistributive hospitality is where an individual who has more shares who have less expecting no payment, return, or reciprocity; however, the host status is a result of the sharing action. The two centre levels of this representation are commercial and reciprocal hospitality. The former implicates a mandatory financial transaction in exchange for hosting, considering both possible entrepreneurial and hospitable actions. The latter 'involves hospitality being offered within a context whereby hosts become guests and guests become hosts, at different times' (Lashley, 2017, p. 5). Online hospitality is located between commercial and reciprocal hospitality purposes/ motivations, as depicted in Figure 17.2. It takes place in an online commercial setting.

Ulterior motives hospitality	Containing hospitality	Commercial hospitality	**ONLINE HOSPITALITY**	Reciprocal hospitality	Redistributive hospitality	Altruistic hospitality

Source: Adapted from Lashley (2017, pp. 220–232).

Figure 17.2　A continuum of hospitality

The internet has enabled the emergence of new business models and consumption forms in all areas, including hospitality. The associated benefits are strongly focused on the consumer and the relationship between individuals. Collaborative consumption, Airbnb, CouchSurfing and HomeExchange are some of its most notable results. They can be related to private/domestic and commercial domains, and commercial and reciprocal motivations for hosting.

Belk (2014, p. 1597) introduces a collaborative consumption definition that interrelates a sense of the private and the commercial, which is 'people coordinating the acquisition and distribution of a resource for a fee or other compensation'. This access to a resource is not as altruistic as sharing, but could feature economic exchange and reciprocity (Belk, 2010).

Airbnb provides an online setting in which individuals can engage in private interactions and communications to offer their home or a room to others at a cost. Interaction and communication commences by presenting personal profiles, where the host and the guest can minutely introduce themselves, their lifestyle values, and offer their home/room/neighbourhood information, payment and domestic usufruct rules. In addition, they are able to access the third parties' perception of all of these aspects, as well as their past behaviour as a host and/or guest.

CouchSurfing and HomeExchange have similar procedures, except for their payment procedures to obtain accommodation. The requirement is that a consumer must pay a fee to present a personal profile and to access the accommodation to exchange (HomeExchange). This also requires a verified profile, which enables a safer interaction, which could lead to more accommodation acceptance (Couchsurfing). The cost approach of these two collaborative platforms is aimed at saving expense when compared to the traditional hospitality service. Moreover, the three collaborative platforms provide an online space for private and detailed interactions and communications between peers.

Reflecting on the collaborative economy and tourism, Dredge and Gyimóthy (2015) emphasise the individual protagonist and argue that feedback tools, such as evaluation comments and performance ratings, could lead to genuine and authentic peer-to-peer relations.

We consider that the hospitable roles and actions on a collaborative platform are performed online mainly before and during accommodation. An array of communication forms of interactions on Airbnb, Couchsurfing and HomeExchange will be engaged with by peers. This also applies to other social media, such as WhatsApp, Instagram and Facebook, once the transaction is complete. This online communication engagement is an essential component of the experience and is where hospitable actions should be performed.

For Yannopoulo et al. (2013), opportunities for digitally transparent offers and comparability of prices benefit consumers, and can provide genuine cross-cultural encounters in return. In this chapter, we consider the host and the guest as the 'consumers': thus, both benefit from the exchange of information.

We therefore present the first theoretical proposition:

Online hospitality is essentially a peer-to-peer interaction, where hospitable actions are considered as exchanges of true and private information between peers, conducted on (and are adapted to) online platforms. This occurs mainly before and during accommodation and is driven by reciprocal and commercial motivations to provide a safe and authentic experience.

This exchange of information originates from online interactions and, assuming that those interactions or hospitable roles and actions take place on online media platforms, we consider it as a communicational form of engagement. We will present the collaborative paradigm of an online communication concept hereafter by relating it to hospitality and online peer-to-peer interactions on collaborative consumption.

THE COLLABORATIVE PARADIGM OF ONLINE COMMUNICATION

In order to explain that online communication is required to be located between some essential ideas of communication and, simultaneously, an unexplored type thereof, Gulbrandsen and Just (2011) presented a processual and collaborative approach. To locate their theoretical approach in past theory, Gulbrandsen and Just (2011) cited Scolari's (2009) online communication continuity–discontinuity axis. At one end of the axis, studies that understand online communication as another normal form of communication are located. At the other extreme, those considering it as a new communicative paradigm, and for which new theories and analytical tools must be developed, are located (Scolari, 2009).

The continuity approach applies traditional communication theory to online interaction, such as rhetorical theory, which considers online communication as a form to directly persuade an audience with classical forms of appeals, such as in online debates and mailing lists in political communication (Marshall, 2004; Scolari, 2009). At the discontinuity axis, there is, for example, computer-mediated discourse analysis that demonstrates the need for new methods to understand online communication. Currently, the major focus is only on text interactions (Herring, 2004). This axis is represented by studies that usually take existing theories and try to fit them to new practices of online communication (Gimmler, 2001; Dean, 2003).

Diverting from opposing axes views, Gulbrandsen and Just (2011, p. 1096) argue that the field of online communication needs to reconnect with some elementary ideas of communication and, simultaneously, to discontinue other modes of thought. Therefore, they define online communication as processual and collaborative. The processual approach is a movement from the sender to the receiver, a traditional view of communication. However, collaborative communication is the newest element presented by the authors, who described its key, distinct features: negotiable and uncontrolled, time-space free, hypertextual, hyper-public and two-way mass communication. We consider that those features could be located to explain collaborative platform interactions/hospitableness roles and actions as a communication form of engagement.

The first feature relies on easy access by internet users, which produces content communication. There is no further control over the receiving information moment. It can be stored, deleted, replicated and edited. It is an 'in-the-making' process (Harrison and Barthel, 2009; Gulbrandsen and Just, 2011). As far as is negotiable and uncontrolled, individuals interested in collaborative platforms offerings, such as hosts or guests, should freely fill in a personal profile describing who they are, where they are from, their values, lifestyle, what they are offering, and at what cost or compensation. Airbnb, CouchSurfing and HomeExchange platforms constantly encourage and negotiate with their consumers to store and edit information to present the most detailed profile possible, by both sides. In addition, it encourages the use of the evaluation tools to provide information regarding the latest hosting and guest experience, including the interaction between individuals involved. Peers involved do not have control over the information produced and published about each other.

Second, online communication can be performed at any time and anywhere, and is not dependent or defined by offline time and space. Therefore, it is not a traditional linear sequence of communication, but a permanent state of information exchange (McKenna and Bragh, 2000; Gulbrandsen and Just, 2011). Time-space freedom is inherent to internet inter-actions and communication. People throughout the world can access collaborative platforms at any time. One of the valuable criteria for online communication, for example, is the time response rate. Quick and detailed answers are expected from both parties. Rapid responses could be perceived as a thoughful, caring behaviour.

The third feature is characterised by the convergence of multimedia content, such as graph-ics, photos, audio and video content, that is exchanged between individuals. It is a hypertext mode that encourages active communication consumption (Hoffman and Novack, 1996). A hypertextual characteristic is also one of most distinguishing forms of online communi-cation. It is a form of multimedia. It is no longer only text or face-to-face communication. Online face-to-face or 'eface-to-face' interactions mean the presentation of information by a set of media. At Airbnb, Couchsurfing and HomeExchange, individuals can access the text about and images of themselves and their homes. The possibility of information exchange by other media, besides text and images, is vast: such as audio and video through, for example, WhatsApp, YouTube and Instagram.

The hyper-public characteristic represents more people having faster access to more com-munication produced by various sources, extending it to the public sphere, and facilitating free participation in public debates (Gerhards and Schäfer, 2010; Scammel, 2000). We con-sider part of the hyper-public characteristic as being suitable to the collaborative platforms' interaction, as far as more people having faster access to more content produced by others is concerned. However, the public element is constrained mostly to those who have a profile. To be able to fully interact and exchange information, individuals must sign into the platforms. It is common to perceive newcomers as having little profile information about themselves and null collaborative consumption experience.

Two-way mass communication is when one interacts directly with a few and indirectly with many (Napoli, 2010). Gulbrandsen and Just (2011) argue that two-way mass communication is one of the most important online communication features. Once a person signs into a collabo-rative platform, fills in its profile, completes deals and has interaction and hosting experience, almost every step is registered on the evaluation comments by both the host and the guest. One interacting and hosting experience once posted/registered, along with one's profile informa-tion, could result in others easily accessing and replicating it.

The collaborative aspect of Gulbrandsen and Just (2011) addresses a limited view of the communicative process as an individual transmission act, and as a one-way sender–receiver movement. They note that actual social interaction is not constituted of individuals' actions between specific and fixed individuals, but as a sum of the interrelations between many in a permanent flow of information exchange (Abbott, 2010).

Presenting collaboration as an explanatory concept, the interaction's meaning is perceived as a co-created experience and does not lie with the individual. Interactions are shared, changeable, and rely on communicative processes for their existence (Gulbrandsen and Just, 2011, p. 1103). This should be observed and explained as a collective and open-ended process (Engeli, 2000; Deuze, 2006). Individuals who engage in tourism collaborative consumption are responsible for generating value as protagonists and actively participating in it (Forno and Garibaldi, 2015). Therefore, the meaning of online hospitality actions and roles is co-created and perceived by individuals' interactions on collaborative platforms. Information is provided, accessed, exchanged and interpreted by multiple parts.

Thus, we present the second theoretical preposition:

Online hospitality is a multimedia online communicational form of engagement, where hospitableness roles and actions are performed by peers in a permanent flow of information exchange, based on collaboration. This is understood as a co-created, collective and open-ended process.

How peers could perceive online hospitable actions and their implications for authentic and meaningful interaction experiences will be addressed below.

PEER-TO-PEER SATISFYING AND AUTHENTIC COLLABORATIVE INTERACTIONS

Engaging in collaborative consumption is essentially defined as to stray from the standard and traditional organisation–consumer approach. Essentially, it is made possible and driven by the internet through collaborative platforms. The experience of peer-to-peer collaborative consumption interaction is expected to be satisfying, but also authentic and meaningful. Regarding online hospitality, economic elements, authenticity's constructivist perspective and online social bonds development are the core elements of consumers' overall perceived meaningfulness experience.

When Belk (2014) argues that collaborative consumption is organised by individuals who exchange and distribute resources for a fee or other compensation, it is important to reflect on not only a possible mandatory monetary value (Airbnb reservation cost, Couchsurfing profile verifications and HomeExchange profile subscription fees). However, it important to also reflect on how compensation could be broadly perceived and described, which will allow this new approach of consumption experience to materialise. We could even slightly adapt Belk's (2014) concept, considering that the collaborative transaction is organised by peers and majorly involves a monetary element, with perceived economic savings. It could also involve other compensation, and state these as inherent and intertwined elements of collaborative consumption.

Despite some noticeable research emphasis on other aspects of collaborative consumption (Molz, 2014; Hamari et al., 2015; Cheng and Jin, 2019), the economic aspect of it appears to be relevant in a similar manner. In collaborative platforms, we consider it as a part of the overall consumer's hospitality online experience perception, and it could be involved as literal worth spent or money earned, or as cost saving sense or perception.

Low cost from the guest's perspective, and earning income from the host's perspective, are perceived as collaborative consumption drivers and peer-to-peer accommodation advantages (Botsman and Rogers, 2011; Bardhi and Eckhardt, 2012; Kohda and Matsuda, 2013; Guttentag, 2015; Tussyadiah, 2015; Lampinen and Chesire, 2016; Pesonen and Tussyadiah, 2017). Initially, the global crisis in 2008 boosted and changed consumers' values regarding spending habits (Gansky, 2010). In conjunction with this, information technology innovations made possible more convenient forms of exchange and collaboration between individuals by decreasing costs (Grit and Lynch, 2011; Mosedale, 2012).

When engaging in online hospitality, individuals are also seeking financial advantages. On Airbnb, home profiles are indicated with an overnight stay cost. Hosts have to pay a platform service tax. On HomeExchange, a fee payment is mandatory to have and access a profile. Couchsurfing customers also have to pay a fee for their profile to be verified. Therefore, satisfaction in financial advantages originates from perceived true online interactions and the exchange of information before accommodation. This relates the perceived benefits of price fairness, income gain or cost saving to what is offered, who is offering, and who is willing to take up the offer. It is therefore a combination of monetary and non-monetary elements. Authenticity is one of the non-monetary elements perceived.

Online hospitality, as noted previously, is a communication form of engagement, performed by hospitable actions between individuals on collaborative platforms. It is a multimedia communication experience. Authenticity thus originates from the perception of the online interaction experience. According to Wang (1999), there are three types of authenticity approaches in tourism experience: objectivist, constructivist/symbolic and existential. We consider authenticity in online hospitality as a social construction process: 'By constructive authenticity, it is meant the result of social construction, not an objectively measurable quality of what is being visited. Things appear authentic not because they are inherently authentic but because they are constructed as such in terms of points of view, beliefs, perspectives, or powers' (Wang, 1999, p. 351).

Following Wang's idea, for Cohen (1988) and Salamone (1997), authenticity is relative, negotiable and context-determined. Literature discussions on this matter are mainly related to offline and on-site experiences. Collaborative consumption interactions also occur on online platforms. An online hospitality experience is a previous phase to the accommodation itself.

Collaborative consumers will engage in online interaction and perceive it as authentic when they perceive proximity between what is published online, and what it is in reality, as well as the interpretation of what could be an actual offline hosting experience. Airbnb, Couchsurfing and HomeExchange provide tools to develop this social construction approach. Individuals' profiles with personal and value details, the accommodation's description and images, third parties' post-experience objective and subjective evaluations, and 'eface-to-face' communication are valid examples of this. Therefore, authenticity is an interpretation of the online interaction between peers, corroborating Wang's (1999) argument that it is a result of how individuals perceive phenomena from their own perspectives and interpretations.

Another relevant non-monetary element is the social connections perspective. According to Forno and Garibaldi (2015), collaborative consumption provides a high-level personalisation experience. The experience of peer-to-peer interactions and its implications permit participants to develop and maintain social connections with each other (Tussyadiah, 2015). By making possible digital connections between tourists through information and communication technologies, such as online platforms, a relationship of mutual trust among strangers is developed (Mosedale, 2012). As indicated above, collaborative consumers can evaluate each other and establish pre- and post-travel social connections, rendering it a relevant incentive to deliver a good overall experience in order to develop an online and offline trustworthiness and reputation (Botsman and Rogers, 2011; Tussyadiah, 2015).

Thus, we present the third theoretical preposition:

Online hospitality is perceived as being satisfying and authentic through previous per-ceived monetary benefits, socially constructed interactions and online social connections development.

DISCUSSION

This chapter is the first to present the collaborative perspective online communication approach in relation to explaining hospitable roles and action between peers on collaborative platforms. As noted, this is a unique contribution to the hospitality literature, since it focuses on peer-to-peer interactions in the online environment, and also considers the possibility of performance and the perception of online hospitable actions of both parties before and during accommodation. Most importantly, the collaborative paradigm of online communication is a theory that introduces a new perspective to hospitality, which is directly related to how people mainly interact nowadays. It fits perfectly in understanding hospitable actions/performance conducted in the online environment and, specifically, on hospitality collaborative platforms. Hospitality, hospitable actions and interactions in a collaborative online environment should be viewed as forms of multimedia communication between individuals.

By interweaving hospitality, collaborative consumption and collaborative online communication theoretical constructs, we have proposed an online hospitality concept: a collaborative communication form of engagement between peers – hosts and guests – conducted on a collaborative platform. This occurs mainly before and during accommodation, where truthful and genuine information about who, what, where and for how much are provided and exchanged by both parties through multimedia to enable them to perceive and feel a safe, satisfying and authentic online host and hosting experience. This answers questions such as how consumers make sense of hospitality in the collaborative environment when they are interacting online, and how and when they engage in and perceive hospitable actions through communication, and its implications on their experience.

Three theoretical prepositions were presented to respond to those questions:

Online hospitality is essentially a peer-to-peer interaction in which hospitable actions are considered as an exchange of true and private information between peers conducted on and adapted to online platforms. This occurs mainly before and during accommodation and is driven by reciprocal and commercial motivations to provide a safe and authentic experience.

Online hospitality is a multimedia online communicational form of engagement where hospitableness roles and actions are performed by peers in a permanent flow of information exchange, based on collaboration. This is understood as a co-created, collective and an open-ended process.

Online hospitality is perceived as satisfying and authentic through previous perceived monetary benefits, socially constructed interactions and online social connections' development.

This theoretical study opens up empirical avenues for future research, which must first focus on providing empirical evidence of the online hospitality concept by inquiring into Airbnb, Couchsurfing and HomeExchange consumers regarding their perceptions of their hosting and host experiences. Besides online interviews, methodologically speaking, online approaches such as sentiment analysis, data mining from profile descriptions and consumers' evaluations are recommended. Furthermore, it is important to understand the effect of multimedia online communication on perceived hospitable actions before and during accommodation. It is also important to do the same for social connections development, and the manner in which media such as Skype, WhatsApp and Instagram are used to communicate and provide truthful and genuine information. Finally, we propose further investigations of the role of authenticity in consumers' perceptions of authenticity in online collaborative platforms.

It is also possible to reflect on practical implications for the hospitality industry from this theoretical proposal. The online hospitality approach is about the perception of meaningful experience through multimedia communication, and has the potential to allow the effects of the new business models to influence the traditional ones. Traditional hospitality organisations must plan and design their interaction and communication strategies to an increasingly particular and individualised level, to the extent that an organisation is perceived as a 'person'. In addition, more than accommodation in 'old' online travel agencies and their booking and peer review mechanisms, such as Booking.com, Hotels.com, Tripadvisor, they have to open their own multi-communication channels to provide and develop permanent, collective, co-created, open-ended and transparent interactions.

REFERENCES

Abbott, A. (2010). *Chaos of Disciplines*. Chicago, IL: University of Chicago Press.

Airbnb (2018, 3 September). Fast facts. Retrieved from https://press.airbnb.com/fast-facts/

Bardhi, F., Eckhardt, M. (2012). Access-based consumption: the case of car-sharing. *Journal of Consumer Research, 39*(March), 881–898. https://doi.org/10.1086/666376.

Belk, R. (2007). Why not share rather than own? *Annals of the American Academy of Political and Social Science, 611*(1), 126–140. https://doi.org/10.1177/0002716206298483

Belk, R. (2010). Sharing. *Journal of Consumer Research, 36*(February), 715–734.

Belk, R. (2014). You are what you can access: sharing and collaborative consumption online. *Journal of Business Research, 67(8)*, 1595–1600.

Belk, R., Llamas, R. (2011). The nature and effects of sharing in consumer behavior. In D. Glen Mick, S. Petigrew, C. Pechmann, J.J. Ozanne (eds), *Transformative Consumer Research for Personal and Collective Well-Being* (pp. 625–646). New York: Routledge.

Botsman, R., Rogers, R. (2011). *What's Mine is Yours: The Rise of Collaborative Consumption*. New York: Harper Business.

Brotherton, B., Wood, R.C. (2007). Key themes in hospitality management. In R.C. Wood, B. Brotherton (eds), *The SAGE Handbook of Hospitality Management* (pp. 35–61). London: SAGE.

Chen, Y. (2009). Possession and access: consumer desires and value perceptions regarding contemporary art collection and exhibit visits. *Journal of Consumer Research, 35*(6), 925–940. https://doi.org/10.1086/593699.

Cheng, M., Jin, X. (2019). What do Airbnb users care about? An analysis of online review comments. *International Journal of Hospitality Management, 76*(April), 58–70. https://doi.org/10.1016/j.ijhm.2018.04.004.

Cohen, E. (1988). Authenticity and commodization in tourism. *Annals of Tourism Research, 15*, 371–386.

Couchsurfing (2018, 26 September). About us. Retrieved from http://www.couchsurfing.com/about/about-us/.

Dean, J. (2003). Why the net is not a public sphere. *Constellations, 10*(1), 95–112. https://doi.org/10.1111/1467-8675.00315.

Deuze, M. (2006). Participation, remediation, bricolage: considering principal components of a digital culture. *Information Society, 22*(2), 63–75.

Digital (2018, 9 April). Retrieved from https://wearesocial.com/blog/2018/01/global-digital-report -2018.

Digital Information World (2018, 22 May). This is what happens in an internet minute in 2018. Retrieved from https://www.digitalinformationworld.com/2018/05/infographic-internet-minute-2018.html.

Dredge, D., Gyimóthy, S. (2015). The collaborative economy and tourism: critical perspectives, questionable claims, and silenced voices. *Tourism Recreation Research, 40*(3), 286–302. https://doi.org/ 10.1080/02508281.2015.1086076.

Dredge, D., Gyimóthy, S. (2017). Collaborative economy and tourism. In D. Dredge, S. Guimóthy (eds), *Collaborative Economy and Tourism: Perspectives, Politics, and Prospects* (1st edn, pp. 1–12). New York: Springer.

Engeli, M. (2000). *Digital Stories: The Poetics of Communication*. Basel, Switzerland: Springer Science & Business Media.

Forno, F., Garibaldi, R. (2015). Sharing economy in travel and tourism: the case of home-swapping in Italy. *Journal of Quality Assurance in Hospitality and Tourism, 16*(2), 202–220. https://doi.org/10 .1080/1528008X.2015.1013409.

Gansky, L. (2010). *The Mesh: Why the Future of Business is Sharing*. New York: Portfolio Penguin.

Gerhards, J., Schäfer, M.S. (2010). Is the internet a better public sphere? Comparing old and new media in the USA and Germany. *New Media and Society, 12*(1), 143–160. https://doi.org/10.1177/ 1461444809341444.

Gimmler, A. (2001) Deliberative democracy, the public sphere, and the internet. *Philosophy and Social Criticism, 27*(4), 21–39. https://doi.org/10.1177/019145370102700402.

Grit, A., Lynch, P. (2011). An analysis of the development of home exchange organisations. *Research in Hospitality Management, 1*(1), 19–24. https://doi.org/10.1080/22243534.2011.11828271.

Gulbrandsen, I.T., Just, S.N. (2011). The collaborative paradigm: towards an invitational and participatory concept of online communication. *Media, Culture and Society, 33*(7), 1095–1108. https://doi.org/ 10.1177/0163443711416066.

Guttentag, D. (2015). Airbnb: disruptive innovation and the rise of an informal tourism accommodation sector. *Current Issues in Tourism, 18*(12), 1192–1217. https://doi.org/10.1080/13683500.2013 .827159.

Hamari, J., Sjoklint, M., Ukkonen, A. (2015). The sharing economy: why people participate in collaborative consumption. *Journal of the Association for Information Science and Technology, 67*(9), 2047–2059. https://doi.org/10.1002/asi.23552.

Harrison, T.M., Barthel, B. (2009). Wielding new media in Web 2.0: exploring the history of engagement with the collaborative construction of media products. *New Media and Society, 11*(1–2), 155–178. https://doi.org/10.1177/1461444808099580.

Heal, F. (1984) The idea of hospitality in early modern England, *Past and Present, 102*(1), 66–93.

Herring, S.C. (2004). Online communication: through the lens of discourse. In M. Consalvo, N. Baym, J. Hunsinger, K.B. Jensen, J. Logie, M. Murero, L.R. Shade (eds), *Internet Research Annual* (pp. 65–76). New York: Peter Lang. http://ella.slis.indiana.edu/~herring/ira.2004.pdf.

Hoffman, D.L., Novak, T.P. (1996). Marketing in hypermedia environment foundations: conceptual foundations. *Journal of Marketing, 60*(3), 50–68. https://doi.org/10.2307/1251841.

HomeExchange (2018, 26 September). Front page. Retrieved from https://www.homeexchange.com/en/.

Kohda, Y., Matsuda, K. (2013). How do sharing service providers create value? In *Proceedings of the Second Asian Conference on Information System (ACIS 2013)*, 31 October – 2 November, Phuket, Thailand.

Lampinen, A., Cheshire, C. (2016). Hosting via Airbnb: motivations and financial assurances in monetized network hospitality. *Proceedings of the 2016 CHI Conference on Human Factors in Computing Systems* (pp. 1669–1680). https://doi.org/10.1145/2858036.2858092.

Lashley, C. (2000). In search of hospitality: towards a theoretical framework. *International Journal of Hospitality Management, 19*(1), 3–15. https://doi.org/10.1016/S0278-4319(99)00035-3.

Lashley, C. (2008). Studying hospitality: insights from social sciences. *Scandinavian Journal of Hospitality and Tourism, 8*(1), 69–84.

Lashley, C. (ed.) (2017). *Routledge Handbook of Hospitality Studies*. Abingdon: Routledge.

Lashley, C., Lynch, P., Morrison, A. (eds) (2007). *Hospitality: A Social Lens*. Oxford: Elsevier.

Lashley, C., Morrison, A. (2003). Hospitality as a 'commercial friendship'. *Hospitality Review*, *6*(3), 31–36.

Lugosi, P. (2008). Hospitality spaces, hospitable moments: consumer encounters and affective experiences in commercial settings. *Journal of Foodservice*, *19*(2), 139–149.

Lugosi, P. (2009). The production of hospitable space: commercial propositions and consumer co-creation in a bar operation. *Space and Culture*, *12*(4), 396–411.

Lugosi, P. (2014). Hospitality and organizations: enchantment, entrenchment, and reconfiguration. *Hospitality and Society*, *4*(1), 75-92. doi: 10.1386/hosp.4.1.75_1.

Lynch, P., Molz, J.G., Mcintosh, A., Lugosi, P. (2011). Theorizing hospitality. *Hospitality and Society*, *1*(1), 3–24. https://doi.org/10.1386/hosp.1.1.3.

Marshall, J. (2004). Governance, structure, and existence: authenticity, rhetoric, race, and gender on an internet mailing list. *Proceedings of the Australian Electronic Governance Conference*. https://opus.lib.uts.edu.au/bitstream/10453/7722/1/2004001034.pdf.

Matos, B.G., Barbosa, M.D.L.D.A., Matos, M.B. de A. (2016). Consumo colaborativo e relacional no contexto do turismo: a proposição de um modelo entre a sociabilidade e a hospitalidade em rede. *RevistaHospitalidade*, *13*(1), 218–241.

McKenna, K.Y.A., Bragh, J.A. (2000). Plan 9 from cyberspace: the implications of the internet for personality and social psychology. *Personality and Social Psychology Review*, *4*(1), 57–75. https://doi.org/10.1207/S15327957PSPR0401_6

Molz, J.G. (2012). CouchSurfing and network hospitality: 'It's not just about the furniture.' *Hospitality and Society*, *1*(3), 215–225. https://doi.org/10.1386/hosp.1.3.215_2.

Molz, J.G. (2014). Toward a network hospitality. *First Monday, 19*(3), 1–16. doi: http://dx.doi.org/10.5210/fm.v19i3.4854.

Molz, J.G., Gibson, S. (eds) (2007). *Mobilizing Hospitality: The Ethics of Social Relations in a Mobile World*. New York: Routledge.

Mosedale, J. (2012). Diverse economies and alternative economic practices in tourism. In *The Critical Turn in Tourism Studies* (pp. 236–249) New York: Routledge.

Morrison, A., O'Gorman, K. (2008). Hospitality studies and hospitality management: a symbiotic relationship. *International Journal of Hospitality Management, 27*(2), 214–221.

Napoli, P.M. (2010). Revisiting 'mass communication' and the 'work' of the audience in the new media environment. *Media, Culture and Society*, *32*(3), 505–516. https://doi.org/10.1177/0163443710361658.

Nouwen, H. (1998). *Reaching Out: A Special Edition of the Spiritual Classic including Beyond the Mirror*, London: Fount / HarperCollins.

O'Gorman, K.D. (2007). The hospitality phenomenon: philosophical enlightenment? *International Journal of Culture, Tourism and Hospitality Research*, *1*, 189–202.

Pesonen, J., Tussyadiah, I. (2017). Peer-to-peer accommodation: drivers and user profiles. In D. Dredge, S. Gyimóthy (eds), *Collaborative Economy and Tourism. Perspectives, Politics, Policies and Prospects* (pp. 285–303). Springer. http://www.springer.com/gp/book/9783319517971.

Ritzer, G. (2004). *The McDonaldization of Society*, rev. New Century edn. London: SAGE.

Salamone, F.A. (1997). Authenticity in tourism: the San Angel Inns. *Annals of Tourism Research, 24*(2), 305–321.

Scammell, M. (2000). The internet and civic engagement: the age of the citizen-consumer. *Political Communication, 17*(3), 351–355. https://doi.org/10.1080/10584600050178951.

Scolari, C.A. (2009). Mapping conversations about new media: the theoretical field of digital communication. *New Media and Society*, *11*(6), 943–964.

Sigala, M. (2016). Learning with the market: a market approach and framework for developing social entrepreneurship in tourism and hospitality. *International Journal of Contemporary Hospitality Management, 28*(6), 1245–1286.

Sigala, M., Gretzel, U. (2018). Introduction. In M. Sigala, U. Gretzel (eds), *Advances in Social Media for Travel, Tourism, and Hospitality. New Perspectives, Practices, and Cases* (pp. 1–5). New York: Routledge.

Slattery, P. (2002). Finding the hospitality industry Part I: in search of hospitality. *Journal of Hospitality, Leisure, Sport and Tourism Education*, *1*(1), 19–28. https://doi.org/10.3794/johlste.11.7.

Telfer, E. (2004). A filosofia da 'hospitabilidade'. In C. Lashley, A. Morrison (eds). *Em busca da hospitalidade: perspectivas para um mundo globalizado* (pp. 53–78). São Paulo: Manole.

Tussyadiah, I.P. (2015). An exploratory study on drivers and deterrents of collaborative consumption in travel. In I. Tussyadiah, A. Inversini, A. (eds), *Information and Communication Technologies in Tourism 2015* (pp. 817–830). Lugano. https://doi.org/10.1007/978-3-319-14343-9_59.

Wang, N. (1999). Rethinking authenticity, in tourism experience. *Annals of Tourism Research, 26*(2), 349–370.

Yannopoulou, N., Moufahim, M., Bian, X. (2013). User-generated brands and social media: Couchsurfing and Airbnb. *Contemporary Management Research, 9*(1), 85–90.

18. Opinion mining or sentiment analysis of online reviews in tourism
Evrim Çeltek

INTRODUCTION

With the explosive growth of social media (that is, reviews, forum discussions, blogs and social networks) on the web, individuals and organizations are increasingly using public opinions for their decision-making. However, finding and monitoring opinion sites on the web and distilling the information remains an enormous task because of the proliferation of diverse sites. Each site typically contains a huge volume of opinionated text that is not always easily deciphered in long forum postings and blogs. Thus, the average human reader will have difficulty identifying relevant sites and accurately summarizing the information and opinions contained in them. Moreover, it is also known that human analysis of text information is subject to considerable biases; for example, people often pay greater attention to opinions that are consistent with their preferences. People also have difficulty, owing to their mental and physical limitations, producing consistent results when the amount of information to be processed is large. Automated opinion mining and summarization systems are thus needed, as subjective biases and mental limitations can be overcome with an objective sentiment analysis system.

Sentiment analysis or opinion mining is the computational study of people's opinions, appraisals, attitudes and emotions toward entities, individuals, issues, events, topics and their attributes. The task is technically challenging and practically very useful. For example, businesses always want to find public or consumer opinions about their products and services. Potential customers also want to know the opinions of existing users before they use a service or purchase a product.

Today, there are numerous social media sites on the internet containing written data on customer opinions and experiences on products and services, and the number is increasing continuously. This medium, which globalizes the customer opinions, is a new media increasing the interaction of businesses with their customers that warrants further study. Also, new media provides ample written data for customer relations management to analyse. Therefore, business firms should follow the blogs, social media, reviews and forum discussions to find out about the impression of their products and services on their customers, which they should consider as an important source of data that needs to be analysed.

Sentiment analysis about customer reviews is built on the premise that information provided through text (for example, a review) is either subjective (that is, opinionated) or objective (that is, factual). Consumer reviews and social media posts often reflect happiness, frustration, disappointment, delight and other feelings. Tapping into these large volumes of subjective electronic word-of-mouth (e-WOM) is of great value to tourism organizations and businesses which seek to improve customer management and business profitability.

SENTIMENT ANALYSIS (OPINION MINING)

Sentiment analysis is a field of study that analyses people's opinions, evaluations, attitudes and emotions towards assets, individuals, problems, events, issues and qualities (Kirilenko et al., 2018) and feelings from written language (Liu, 2017), which is also called opinion mining (Medhat et al., 2014; Baykara and Gürtürk, 2017; Alsaqer and Sasi, 2017). Sentiment analysis uses natural language processing (NLP), text analysis and computational techniques to automate the extraction or classification of sentiment from sentiment reviews (Hussein, 2018). Besides being one of the most active research fields in NLP, it also has wide coverage in data mining, web mining and text mining fields (Liu, 2017; Baykara and Gürtürk, 2017). According to Onan and Korukoğlu (2016), sentiment analysis is a field of research aiming to extract subjective information such as opinions, emotions and attitudes specified by the author in the text by using computer science methods. In addition to sentiment analysis, the academic world also uses the term 'opinion mining' (Karaoğlan et al., 2019). In summary, sentiment analysis is the process of automatically detecting and interpreting the emotion expressed by the text using computer technologies. In other words, sentiment analysis is a set of methods that tries to analyse the emotions of people or masses in any text by various methods.

Sentiment analysis uses the texts written by users as input and tries to identify whether the emotions are positive, negative or neutral, and also whether the users' current emotional state is happy or sad in relation to the topic they are talking about (Afzaal and Usman, 2015; Aytekin, 2011). From this point of view, sentiment analysis can be helpful for businesses, such as if it is necessary to do preliminary market research for a new product to be placed on the market, or whether a decision to be taken for a community will cause them to react positively or negatively, or whether people will decide to watch a movie according to previous comments made (Şeker, 2016).

The importance of sentiment analysis has increased significantly with the development of social media such as reviews, forum discussions, blogs, microblogs, twitter and social networks (Alsaqer and Sasi, 2017). Sentiment analysis systems are applied in almost all business and social areas. Sentiment analysis helps to learn what customers love and think about brands, products and services (Baykara and Gürtürk, 2017), which in particular when concerning customer reviews is built on the basis that the information provided through the text is either subjective or objective. Subjective reviews are based on opinions, personal feelings, beliefs and judgements about assets or events. On the other hand, objective reviews are based on facts, evidence and measurable observations (Alaei et al., 2019).

Sentiment analysis involves text processing, which aims to determine the class of the given text as emotion. The first studies on sentiment analysis were referred as sentimental polarity, which aims to classify the given text as positive, negative and neutral. Today, analysis can be made indicating different emotional states. In order to encode the emotional states, the class tagging approach, such as labelling each text with a single emotion on the dataset or tagging multiple emotions in the texts, is widely used (Şeker, 2016).

In general, sentiment analysis or opinion mining is used to perform the following functions (Şeker, 2016; Serrano-Guerrero et al., 2015; Kaynar et al., 2016):

- The sentiment or opinion classification: this is based on the idea of expressing an opinion about a case in a document or text, and measuring the emotion towards the subject from the opinion owner. It tries to find out whether a given sentence is positive, negative or neutral.

- Subjectivity classification: this is generally used to determine whether a sentence is subjective or not. A successful subjectivity classification provides a better sentiment classification. This process is seen as a more difficult process than separating positive, negative and neutral sentences.
- Summarizing opinions: this is about removing the main subject from the document and the emotion in its content. It provides a short expression of a large number of ideas or a long idea text, such as extracting key phrases or classifying them according to the product or the perspective of the author.
- Extraction of comparative ideas: this is used to determine which concept the text compares in what way, and the relative positions of the concepts according to this comparison in any given ideas where two or more products or concepts are compared.
- Obtaining an opinion: this is the extraction of documents indicating an opinion with the query. In such systems, two types of point calculations should be made: points of relevance versus query and opinion points about the query, both of which are often used to determine the level of documents.
- Finding sarcasm and irony: this is aimed at finding phrases containing sarcasm and irony. This task is one of the most complex areas in sentiment analysis, especially since there are disagreements among researchers on how to define mockery and irony.
- Undesirable opinion scanning: this is used to detect the situation of writing maliciously. Fraudulent and misleading (spam) message detection attempts to identify opinions and comments with untrustworthy content that distort the message in favour or against a particular segment, company or product.
- Genre and author identification: this is aimed at finding the author who rewrites the genre and text.

To summarize, sentiment analysis is a subdiscipline of NLP, and it is a science that works to determine the views, feelings, thoughts and attitudes in the content (Afzaal and Usman, 2015). Although they differ slightly from each other, it is also expressed in the literature with the following titles: 'opinion mining', 'opinion extraction', 'sentiment mining', 'subjectivity analysis', 'affect analysis', 'emotion analysis', 'review mining'. All these topics have recently been gathered under the umbrella of sentiment analysis, and the lebel of 'sentiment analysis' has been adopted in the sector (Karaoğlan et al., 2019).

SENTIMENT ANALYSIS LEVELS

Sentiment analysis studies are generally carried out at five levels, namely document, sentence, aspect-based, concept and comparative sentiment analysis (Medhat et al., 2014; Patil and Yalagi, 2016; Balaji et al., 2017; Katrekar, 2005; Özyurt and Akçayol, 2018).

Document-Level Sentiment Analysis

In sentiment analysis at the document level, a comment or a review article stating an opinon is classified as positive or negative as a whole (Hemmatian and Sohrabi, 2019). All of the first studies in the field of sentiment analysis are classification studies at the document level. In a document in which opinions are expressed, some sentences may have positive polarity, that is the feeling and assessment that the sentence brings in mind or is associated with; and some other sentences may have negative polarity (Gupta et al., 2015; Liu and Zhang, 2012). Also, document-level sentiment analysis is a method that classifies all thoughts in a document as negative or positive. For example, in a product review, the system checks all the words and outputs a negative or positive value as a result. This form of analysis is not suitable for documents comparing multiple products or situations, because when more than one situation or product comparison is made in the document, more than one result should be obtained. However, this method yields only one result (Medhat et al., 2014; Patil and Yalagi, 2016; Balaji et al., 2017; Katrekar, 2005; Özyurt and Akçayol, 2018).

Sentence-Level Sentiment Analysis

In sentence-level sentiment analysis, the document is taken at a lower level, namely sentences. This type of analysis aims to determine the sentiment polarity (positive/negative/neutral) of each sentence (Hemmatian and Sohrabi, 2019). Due to this characteristic, it is also qualified as a subjectivity analysis. Subjectivity analysis is a previous step to sentiment analysis, and if the sentence does not contain subjectivity, it is labelled as neutral and the sentiment analysis process is not carried out. However, many texts contain implicit subjectivity even though they are apparently objective, due to the flexibility of the language (Özyurt and Akçayol, 2018). In this case, the sentiment in the sentence is labelled as positive or negative (Liu and Zhang, 2012). The issue of double (negative/positive) or triple (negative/positive/neutral) classification is one of the subjects that researchers cannot agree on at the sentence level as well as at the document level (Medhat et al., 2014; Patil and Yalagi, 2016; Balaji et al., 2017; Katrekar, 2005; Özyurt and Akçayol, 2018).

Aspect-Based (Aspect-Level) Sentiment Analysis

Sentiment classification at the document level and sentence level causes the goals of the sentiment expressions to remain uncertain. The fact that the comment made on an entity in the sentiment classification at the document and sentence level is classified as positive does not mean that the author gives a positive opinion about all the properties of that entity (Hemmatian and Sohrabi, 2019). For example, if an author made a positive comment about four attributes of an entity, and a negative comment about three attributes, that comment is classified as positive at the document level. There is a significant loss of information here. The author commented negatively about three characteristics of the entity, but this information has not been revealed. The most comprehensive information about a comment is the information about which properties of the entity are regarded as positive and which properties are negative. This is what is done in aspect-based sentiment analysis studies. The properties of the entity, which is the target of the sentiment expression, are determined. This process is called aspect extraction (Özyurt and Akçayol, 2018). Sentiment polarity classification methods used in aspect-based sentiment analysis are mostly similar to document-level sentiment polarity classification methods. Aspect-level sentiment analysis can produce a summary of the sentiments about different aspects of the desired entity. The important thing here is to determine the target and scope of the sentiment expression and to perform the aspect extraction correctly (Medhat et al., 2014; Patil and Yalagi, 2016; Balaji et al., 2017; Katrekar, 2005; Özyurt and Akçayol, 2018; Liu and Zhang, 2012).

Concept-Level Sentiment Analysis

Concept-level sentiment analysis is based on the extraction of conceptual information about emotions and sentiments related to natural language, and thus allows for a comparatively finely detailed sentiment analysis. Conceptual approaches focus on semantic analysis of the text and analyse concepts that do not express any emotions clearly. Emotion labels are assigned to conduct sentiment analysis at the concept level, and natural language processing and machine learning techniques are combined to analyse conceptual-level interpretations. Machine learning and dictionary-based approaches are used together in sentiment analysis at the concept level (Hemmatian and Sohrabi, 2019).

Comparative Level of Sentiment Analysis

In many cases, users do not give direct opinions about a product, but instead can use expressions that compare the product or service; for example, 'Hotel x is superior to hotel y'. In this case, the purpose of the sentiment analysis system is to identify sentences containing comparative opinions and to subtract the preferred entity (or entities) in each opinion. One of the leading articles on comparative sentiment analysis is by Jindal and Liu (2006, cited in Feldman, 2013), which revealed that 98 per cent of comparative views can be covered using relatively few words.

METHODS IN SENTIMENT ANALYSIS

The two most common approaches used in the sentiment analysis technique are dictionary-based and machine learning-based approaches, which are applied to reveal what emotion the author writes about, by analysing the text data (Akın and Şimşek, 2018a, 2018b). In recent years, hybrid methods have been used as the third method.

Machine Learning-Based Methods

The machine learning approach is based on machine learning algorithms that use syntactic and/or linguistic features (Can and Alataş, 2017). In the machine learning-based approach, the focus is on deciding the emotion with algorithms developed by defining an attribute for each word or syllable (Akın and Şimşek, 2018a, 2018b). While sentiment analysis is carried out with methods based on machine learning, the classification model is created by applying an emotion pole labelled data set to one of the machine learning algorithms (decision trees, support vector machines, artificial neural networks, K-nearest neighbours, Naïve Bayes, and so on), which is then used to classify new samples. The data set related to the sentiment analysis is represented by using linguistic features (Onan and Korukoğlu, 2016). Machine learning algorithms are the tools that analyse the sentiment states of the texts by training the textual data with the previously prepared training data set without emotional dictionaries. One of the main difficulties in using machine learning algorithms is that the data to be used to train algorithms must be classified individually by a human (Kearney and Liu, 2014). The methods based on machine learning are examined under three basic classes, namely supervised, semi-supervised and unsupervised methods (Onan and Korukoğlu, 2016).

Supervised learning methods
There is a need for labelled data sets to be used for training and testing in supervised learning. Different learning algorithms are trained using the training data set, and then their performances are measured on the test data set. The content with unknown polarity is subjected to the learned model and sentiment classification is performed (Hemmatian and Sohrabi, 2019; Can and Alataş, 2017). In order for these methods to work properly, the data set used for training must be large enough. The most basic study in the supervised learning method is the research done by Pang et al. (2002, as cited in Onan and Korukoğlu, 2016). In this study, support vector machines, Naïve Bayes and maximum entropy classifiers were applied on the 'Movie Review' dataset containing movie reviews to determine whether the comments about the movies are positive or negative (Onan and Korukoğlu, 2016). Labelled data in supervised learning train the algorithm on how to label the data. For example, for the algorithm to understand that comment about a hotel is positive, if there are 'like, excellent' expressions in it, the algorithm should be guided as perceiving this comment as positive. Among non-probabilistic classifiers widely used in supervised learning methods, neural network, support vector machine (SVM), K-nearest neighbours, decision tree and rule-based methods; and among probabilistic classifiers, Naïve Bayes, Bayesian network and maximum entropy methods (Hemmatian and Sohrabi, 2019).

Semi-supervised learning methods
Semi-supervised learning is used in learning problems where a small amount of labelled data is combined with a large amount of unlabelled data. In semi-supervised learning, the amount of unlabelled data is huge and a small amount of labelled data is used for training purposes (Kızılkaya, 2018). In sentiment classification, semi-supervised learning methods are used to eliminate the field-transfer problem and classify texts that express opinions in different languages. The field-transfer problem is that a classifier trained in a field has significantly reduced performance when used to classify a data set for a different field (Onan and Korukoğlu, 2016). Traditional classifiers use only labelled data (feature/label pairs) to train. However, labelled samples are often difficult, expensive or time-consuming as this requires experienced people. Besides, labelling a scenario requires strong field knowledge when analysing comments. Semi-supervised learning solves this problem by using large amounts of unlabelled data along with a small amount of labelled data to create better classifiers. Semi-supervised learning approaches require less human effort and provide higher accuracy, so they are of great interest in the field of sentiment analysis (Hemmatian and Sohrabi, 2019). One of the most basic studies on semi-supervised learning methods in sentiment classification is that conducted by Aue and Gamon (2002, as cited in Onan and Korukoğlu, 2016). In this study, the effectiveness of different strategies for classifier training was investigated in areas where there is not enough labelled data. 'Movie', 'Book', 'Product Support Services' and 'Knowledge Base' data sets were used in the study (Onan and Korukoğlu, 2016). In semi-supervised learning methods, self-training, co-training, multi-view learning, graph-based methods and generative model are widely used (Hemmatian and Sohrabi, 2019).

Unsupervised learning methods
Unsupervised learning methods are used to eliminate the problem of field addiction. In the unsupervised learning method, the sentiment dictionary is given as preliminary information to determine the sentiment pole. Creating field-independent sentiment dictionaries is less costly

than creating a field-specific corpus (Onan and Korukoğlu, 2016). In unsupervised learning methods, the algorithm is not trained, but the algorithm itself is expected to learn. This learning is based on similarities or differences between the data. Unsupervised learning methods are generally used for clustering (Aydin et al., 2018). Labelling of data is not done in unsupervised learning. The aim is for relationships in the data set to be learned without labelling and marking (Kızılkaya, 2018). One of the most basic studies in the field of unsupervised learning is the work carried out by Turney and Littman (2002, as cited in Onan and Korukoğlu, 2016). In this study, the classification of a particular document as positive or negative is based on the sentiment aspects of the markers and adjectives included in the document. In determining the emotional aspects, seven are positive ('good', 'nice', 'excellent', 'positive', 'fortunate', 'correct', 'superior) and seven are negative ('bad', 'nasty', 'poor', 'unfortunate', 'wrong', 'inferior'): a total of 14 words were taken into account. The sentiment direction of any word in the text is calculated by subtracting the relationship from the seven positive words mentioned, from the relationship to the seven negative words (Onan and Korukoğlu, 2016). Clustering methods such as hierarchical clustering (agglomerative algorithms and divisive algorithms), partitioning clustering (K-means and fuzzy C-means) are used in unsupervised learning (Aydın et al., 2018).

Lexicon-Based Methods

Lexicon based methods are semi-controlled methods, which aim to determine the sentiment of the texts according to the sentiment dictionaries previously prepared (Aydın et al., 2018; Akın and Şimşek, 2018a, 2018b). Lexicon based methods are examined under two basic classes: dictionary-based approaches and corpus-based approaches. While determining the sentiment pole of the text with dictionary-based approaches, a calculation based on the semantic orientations of the words and sentences in the text is performed. In corpus-based approaches, sentiment pole is determined by using statistical or semantic methods (Onan and Korukoğlu, 2016). The basic logic in lexicon-based sentiment analysis is to perform sentiment analysis using a semantic dictionary database that expresses sentiment. The sentiment status of the texts can be determined according to these dictionaries. Ready-made databases can be used for this, as well as a corpus created by the person themself. In the lexicon-based method, the words in the texts expressing feelings and emotions are evaluated with a predetermined sentiment score. Scores are given not only to words but also to emojis, which means visual characters. These sentiment scores range from -5 to +5 and the total score value determines whether the sentence or text contains positive or negative emotions and feelings. The score value of each word in the sentence or text is written and summed: if the resulting value is greater than 0, the sentence has a positive sentiment; and if it is less than 0, the sentence contains a negative sentiment. A sentence with a total score of 0 is considered neutral. It is said that these sentences do not contain expressions of sentiment (Kızılkaya, 2018; Akın and Şimşek,2018a). For example, words such as 'success', 'trust', 'perseverance', 'determination, 'profit' are included in the positive sentiment dictionary, and the texts of these words are labelled in the positive category. Similarly, words such as 'bankruptcy', 'loss', 'resignation' are found in the negative sentiment dictionary because they express negativity. and the texts containing these words are labelled accordingly (Atan and Çınar, 2019).

Dictionary-based approach

It is common to use the dictionary method to compile sentiments. This method is based on the bootstrapping technique, since the lexicons mainly contain synonym lists. The procedure in this method is as follows. First, to create a small set, several sentiment words which have a positive or negative semantic orientation are identified manually (Yousefpour et al. 2014). Then the algorithm helps grow this collection by searching the WORD NET corporation and other online dictionaries to find synonyms and antonyms. This process continues until no new words can be detected (Hemmatian and Sohrabi, 2019; Kızılkaya, 2018). When the process is finished, manual control is made by correcting and debugging the errors (Can and Alataş, 2017).

Corpus-based approach

Since the dictionary-based method is labour-intensive, corpus-based methods have been developed. The word 'corpus' means keeping large amounts of text collections electronically in the computer environment. Based on the corpus, there is a logic of the combination of content-specific words. In the corpus-based method, the words related to the content are brought together and a very large corpus is created. The words expressing sentiment in the text are compared with the patterns in the list in this collection. Corpus-based methods can be statistical or semantic (Kızılkaya, 2018). The statistical method uses statistics to find adjectives in a corpus. It is possible to use all the documents in the directory as a corpus for dictionary construction on the web. If the created corpus is not big enough, the searched word may not be in the corpus. Statistics are used at this stage. The frequency polarity of the searched word is checked. Whether the word is in the positive or negative pole can be determined by the frequencies of the words used with that word. For example, if the word occurs more frequently among positive texts, its polarity will be positive, and if it is included more frequently among negative texts, its polarity is negative. If the frequencies are equal, then it is called neutral for the word. Words with similar opinions are often together in the corpus, so if the two words often come together, they will probably have the same feeling. Therefore, whether an unknown word is negative or positive can also be found by calculating the pole with the word it contains (Kızılkaya, 2018). The semantic approach gives sentiment values directly and is based on different calculation principles of similarity between words. These principles give similar sentiment values for emotionally close words. The semantic approach is used to create a data dictionary model for the definition of verbs, nouns and adjectives (Can and Alataş, 2017).

Hybrid-Based Methods

Lexicon-based sentiment analysis methods are frequently applied in sentiment classification due to their high scalability. However, machine learning includes many effective algorithms for the classification problem. The simple structure of machine learning algorithms, and a structure that is partially easily adaptable to sentiment classification applications in different fields, make machine learning an important research area for sentiment analysis (Medhat et al., 2014). In order to take advantage of the two methods, mixed analysis is carried out. In hybrid approaches, approaches based on lexicon and machine learning can work in parallel to calculate two sentiment polarities. Results obtained from the lexicon and machine learning methods are then combined to provide a final sentiment polarity. It is also possible to design a sentiment analysis model by including both lexicon and machine learning methods at different stages of the model (Alaei et al., 2019).

ADVANTAGES OF SENTIMENT ANALYSIS IN TOURISM

People make use of the feelings and thoughts of others who have already made the same decision on where to go on vacation or which hotel to stay at. The most practical way to learn about other people's feelings and thoughts is to analyse the posts made on social media. This is where sentiment analysis may be utilized, since it helps to analyse huge amounts of data automatically. Therefore, by going through a series of comments and reviews, the decision process for all parties, that is, for individuals as prospective buyers and sellers, will be shorter.

Sentiment analysis applied in tourism has an important effect on the development of tourism and businesses, because sentiment analysis can be used to examine texts with opinions and emotions presented by tourists (Gao et al., 2015). Thus, it is possible to find out what the tourists who experience the services provided by tourism companies think and feel about these products and services.

Sentiment analysis can be very useful and effective in identifying negative trends that occur online for destinations, restaurants, museums and hotels, so tourism businesses can be more effective (proactive) and they can handle customer complaints more smoothly. Sentiment analysis can also help managers identify solutions. By analysing the sentiments of customer reviews of competing restaurants and hotels, the competitiveness and weaknesses of the business can be determined (Ma et al., 2018).

Sentiment analysis can provide foresight to managers in the tourism industry to enrich their perspectives. It is an objective feedback mechanism for all businesses that are open to development and change. Besides, considering the level reached by social media platforms, sentiment analysis also provides valuable data on an individual scale. In general terms, application areas and advantages of sentiment analysis in the tourism sector today and in the future can be listed as follows:

- Determining the most correct reaction in line with customer reviews for touristic products and services, managing customer relations effectively and creating correct and healthy feedback to the relevant departments. Product quality also increases with sentiment analysis. Market research teams can better measure consumer needs and preferences. Product development ideas can also be taken from target customers with sentiment analysis.
- Giving the opportunity to monitor the change of emotion perceptions on the time axis in all digital platforms for target assets (hotel, travel agency, airline business, destination, tourism services, countries, and so on).
- Developing appropriate dialogue systems according to the emotional state of the users.
- Providing a healthier foresight opportunity to consumers, producers and investors with the correct determination of the impact created by customer reviews.
- Real-time automatic sentiment analysis on Twitter, Instagram, YouTube, Facebook pages and groups with developing technologies. During a particular situation such as an instant event on social media (for example, a negative complaint about the brand or business on social media at a festival event), or situations related to an angry customer, sentiment anal-

ysis can be used in real time to identify critical information, because it is essential to make quick decisions and intervene accordingly in such cases.

- Determining customers' feelings and thoughts (categorizing texts into positive, negative or neutral categories) related to tourism services in consumer reviews on social media.
- Giving the opportunity to reveal whether consumers are satisfied with a product or service, in product and service reviews. Satisfied or dissatisfied customers can be identified.
- Measuring the impact of the consumer's response to the advertising campaign of a business or a new service, or to the latest business news on social media.
- Minimizing manpower and achieving clearer results by automating companies' business processes and extracting meaningful information. Since most of the world's data (80 per cent) – that is, emails, chats, social media, comments, surveys and articles – is unstructured data, it is very difficult to understand and analyse it. Sentiment analysis helps businesses process large amounts of data efficiently and cost-effectively (Pervan, 2020), and is free from human error.
- Helping business websites with chatbots recognize and respond to the customer's mood. For example, sentiment analysis can determine when a conversation should be directed to a human representative so that necessary actions can be taken (whoson. com, 2020).

CHALLENGES OF SENTIMENT ANALYSIS IN TOURISM

While conducting sentiment analysis in the tourism sector, researchers generally encounter some difficult situations due to language differences, data insufficiency and noisy data. The difficulties encountered in sentiment analysis are as follows.

The basis of automatic sentiment analysis is the use of large data sets. In order to use the sentiment analysis system and take action, it is necessary to have a large data source and volume. When there is not enough data to feed the system, it is inevitable for the model to make an incorrect evaluation. (Pervan, 2020; Hussein, 2018).

Since sentiment analysis aims to extract meaning from subjective texts, the texts created can be written in everyday spoken language or without paying attention to grammar rules. Also, texts can contain metaphorical and sarcastic expressions. Sentiment analysis systems are unable to distinguish metaphorical and sarcastic expressions. Besides, data capacity is limited in defining various human emotions such as anxiety and fear (Aytekin, 2011; Pervan, 2020). Automated systems cannot distinguish sarcasm from intimate text, and cannot always accurately analyse the specific contextual meaning of a word (Aytekin, 2011; Katrekar, 2005).

The raw material of sentiment analysis is the language used. For this reason, it is extremely important for the success of the analysis that the researcher knows in detail the language that they are analysing. Multilingual texts are one of the challenging situations. While it is possible to reach a lot of data and research especially in the English language, the number of resources in other languages is very low. Each language has its own sentence structure, emotional words and metaphoric expressions, which require different sentiment analysis models. In multilingual texts, it is necessary to determine the language of the text and develop a language-appropriate model (Pervan, 2020).

Uses such as 'lol' in text or abbreviations of words create difficulties in interpretation (Aytekin, 2011; Katrekar, 2005). Especially, Twitter data contains many abbreviations. Therefore, the pre-processing of this data is time-consuming (Ravi and Ravi, 2015).

Classifying mixed opinions might be challenging. For example, in reviews like 'I liked the quality of the room, but the room is too small' (Katrekar, 2005) or 'I surprised my wife on her birthday with a tour of Italy and she just freaked out!', it is hard to classify the opinion as positive or negative because they are mixed. The computer software that performs the sentiment analysis may evaluate the concept of 'freaked out' in a negative sense, or it may confuse the classification of this concept as positive or negative.

Noisy texts (those with spelling or grammatical errors, missing or problematic punctuation, and slang words) are a big challenge for most sentiment analysis systems since it takes a long time to convert this raw data into structured data (Feldman, 2013).

Since many alternative names for a product are explicitly stated in the same document and between documents, there occur problems in distinguishing them (Feldman, 2013).

EXAMPLES OF SENTIMENT ANALYSIS OF ONLINE REVIEWS IN TOURISM

In this section, the role of sentiment analysis in the tourism sector is analysed by referring to various applications of it in the field. The studies shared in this section used different methods to analyse the data they had. As discussed previously, they included the dictionary-based approach, the corpus-based approach, the machine learning approach. In some studies, mixed methods were also used.

To begin with, there are a number of studies that utilized the dictionary-based approach. In a study by Gonzalez et al. (2016), shared views (400 comments) about the city of Barcelona on an eWOM website (www.ciao.co.uk) were analysed. The results revealed no extreme polar views (very negative, very positive) about the subcategories related to the city of Barcelona (hotels, restaurants, tourist attractions and nightlife). In another study, Geetha et al. (2017) researched the relationship between customer feelings and customer ratings for hotels (hotels in the budget category and the premium category) in online reviews in India, but the number of the comments analysed was not specified. According to the results, consistency was found between the customer scores in the budget category hotels and real customer feelings. Compared to premium hotels, it was concluded that managers of budget category hotels need to improve staff performance and hotel services. In a study on hotels, He et al. (2017) analysed 11 043 English online user reviews collected from the Tripadvisor.com website for 58 hotels (three-, four-, five-star) in four major cities in China (Beijing, Shanghai, Guangzhou and Shenzhen). The reviews included both structured information (overall rating score and specific rating scores) and unstructured information (titles and text review content), which were later analysed in terms of positivity and negativity in 33 categories. The results revealed that 'satisfied' customers expressed satisfaction in food, location, rooms, service, staff and lounge categories. On the other hand, 'extremely dissatisfied' customers expressed dissatisfaction in rooms, food, check-in, service and staff categories. Another study using Tripadvisor reviews was carried out by Ma et al. (2018). They reviewed the Tripadvisor reviews of a fine-dining restaurant called Spice Temple in Sydney. This restaurant was particularly chosen because it is one of the top three restaurants specializing in Chinese cuisine. They analysed 212 comments on the Tripadvisor website . The results revealed positive and negative status of the restaurant reviews, and the words most frequently mentioned in the comments. Park et al. (2020) reviewed 3313 reviews of the top ten five-star hotels in Korea with the most reviews on the tripadvisor.com website, as a rich source for reviews. Sentiment analysis was done in nine categories (room environment, service, basic facility, dining, location, auxiliary facility, furniture and appliances, bathroom, and price). A comparison of hotels was made according to positive and negative comments in these nine categories. In another study, Philander and Zhong (2016) examined 31 550 tweets about hotels in Las Vegas, and the research revealed which hotels received the most positive comments. The last study using the dictionary-based approach discussed here was carried out by Misopoulos et al. (2014). In this study, 67 953 English tweets about four airline companies were analysed, and the results revealed positive and negative comments on these four businesses.

As for the studies in which the machine learning method was utilized, a variety of examples can be shared here. To begin with, Kim et al. (2017) applied sentiment analysis to a total of 19 835 reviews collected from the website www.virtualtourist.com to analyse tourist reviews about Paris. The comments are grouped into 14 categories. According to the research results, the comments made in the transportation category turned out to be negative. In another study, Capriello et al. (2013) reviewed the comments on rural tourism businesses in Australia, Italy, England and the United States of America (USA) on the tripadvisor.com website. In the research, 800 comments were analysed, and the results revealed that positive and negative comments differ between countries in the categories of weather, appearance, entertainment, geographical location, animals, bugs, people, beverages, geographical features, and activities. Based on the results, the researchers provided suggestions to the rural tourism businesses about which subjects should be taken into consideration. In their study, Gascón et al. (2016) examined 240 customer reviews of four hotels in Barcelona on booking.com and tripadvisor.com with sentiment analysis. The results of the research showed that the majority of the comments made were positive. In another study on hotels, Martin et al. (2018) reviewed English reviews (9640 reviews) for hotels on the island of Tenerife on the booking.com and tripadvisor.com websites. In the research, the words most frequently mentioned in the positive and negative comments were revealed. Guo et al. (2017) also reviewed 266 544 online reviews from 25 670 hotels in 16 countries on the tripadvisor.com website. The words most frequently mentioned in the comments were determined in the research, and 25 categories were found by examining the subjects of positive and negative comments. The emerging issues were then compared according to the star rating of the hotels. As a rich source of information, blogs are also used in some studies. For example, Chiu et al. (2015) reviewed 1364 reviews of 15 hotels from the two largest Chinese blogs in Taiwan, Yahoo Blogs (http://tw.blog.yahoo.com/) and Wretch (http://www.wretch.cc/blog/). With the positive and negative comments obtained, hotels were compared in seven categories (hotel image, services, price/value, food and beverages, room, amenities, location). In another study using research sites as the source of information, Kang et al. (2012) collected 70 000 English reviews from restaurant research sites. The results revealed the negativity and positivity of these comments. The last study utilizing the machine learning method to be shared here was again on hotels: Xiang et al. (2015) reviewed 60 648 customer reviews of hotels in 100 USA cities on expedia.com. The research identified the most frequently mentioned words in the comments.

In some other studies in the field, it is seen that more than one method was used to analyse the data. For instance, Ren and Hong (2017) conducted a subject-based sentiment analysis on 2000 customer reviews on Ctrip (www.ctrip.com) which related to four- and five-star hotels in ten popular Chinese destinations. Comments in different languages were translated into English and analysed. Emotions in positive and negative comments, such as complaints about crowds in some tourist areas, are grouped by topics (management, scenery, price, and suggestions). For the analysis in this study, machine learning methods and topic-based sentiment analysis were used. In another study, Claster et al. (2010) analysed 70 570 800 English tweets to gain knowledge regarding tourist sentiments on the travel resort destination of Cancun in the Yucatan Peninsula of Mexico, by using hybrid-based methods. The results revealed positive and negative status of the tweets by month, and in which months the most tweets were sent.

CONCLUSION

Sentiment analysis can be very useful and effective in identifying negative trends that occur online for destinations, restaurants, museums and hotels, so tourism businesses can be more effective (proactive) and they can handle customer complaints more smoothly. Sentiment analysis can also help managers identify solutions. By analysing the sentiment of customer reviews of competing restaurants and hotels, the competitiveness and weaknesses of the business can be determined (Ma et al., 2018). Sentiment analysis allows customers' feelings and thoughts to be determined (categorizing texts into positive, negative or neutral categories) related to tourism services in online reviews on social media.

As seen in the studies mentioned above, the studies utilizing sentiment analysis are mostly related to hotels. The reviews and comments analysed were in English, and tripadvisor.com was the most preferred source of data to be analysed. The studies aimed to measure the performance algorithms used in sentiment analysis. The majority of them, however, did not reveal in-depth information about tourism.

In future sentiment analysis studies, reviews on different tourism sectors (such as travel agencies, countries) and different social media sites should also be examined. In addition, methodologically, future studies could make more in-depth comparisons among widely used sentiment analysis tools and evaluate their suitability in hospitality and tourism research.

REFERENCES

Afzaal, M. and Usman, M. (2015, October). A novel framework for aspect-based opinion classification for tourist places. In *2015 Tenth International Conference on Digital Information Management (ICDIM)* (pp. 1–9). IEEE.

Akın, B.K. and Şimşek, U.T.G. (2018a). Adaptif öğrenme sözlüğü temelli duygu analiz algoritması önerisi. *Bilişim Teknolojileri Dergisi*, 11(3), 245–253.

Akın, B., and Şimşek, U.T.G. (2018b). Sosyal medya analitiği ile değer yaratma: duygu analizi ile geleceğe yönelim. *Mehmet Akif Ersoy Üniversitesi İktisadi ve İdari Bilimler Fakültesi Dergisi*, 5(3), 797–811.

Alaei, A.R., Becken, S. and Stantic, B. (2019). Sentiment analysis in tourism: capitalizing on big data. *Journal of Travel Research*, 58(2), 175–191.

Alsaqer, A.F. and Sasi, S. (2017, July). Movie review summarization and sentiment analysis using rapidminer. In 2017 *International Conference on Networks and Advances in Computational Technologies (NetACT)* (pp. 329–335). IEEE.

Atan, S. and Çınar, Y. (2019). Borsa İstanbul'da finansal haberler ile piyasa değeri ilişkisinin metin madenciliği ve duygu (sentiment) analizi ile incelenmesi. *Ankara Üniversitesi SBF Dergisi*, 74(1), 1–34.

Aydın, İ., Salur, M.U. and Başkaya, F. (2018). Duygu analizi için çoklu populasyon tabanlı parçacık sürü optimizasyonu. *Türkiye Bilişim Vakfı Bilgisayar Bilimleri ve Mühendisliği Dergisi*, 11(1), 52–64.

Aytekin, Ç. (2011). Müşteri İlişkileri Yönetimi İçin Bloglar Üzerinde Fikir Madenciliği, Yayınlanmamış Doktora Tezi, Marmara Üniversitesi Sosyal Bilimler Enstitüsü İletişim Bilimleri Anabilim Dalı Bilişim Programı.

Balaji, P., Nagaraju, O. and Haritha, D. (2017, March). Levels of sentiment analysis and its challenges: a literature review. In 2017 *International Conference on Big Data Analytics and Computational Intelligence (ICBDAC)* (pp. 436–439). IEEE.

Baykara, M. and Gürtürk, U. (2017). Sosyal medya paylaşımlarının duygu analizi yöntemiyle sınıflandırılması. In *Proceedings of 2. International Conference on Computer Science and Engineering* (pp. 911–916). Retrieved from http://web.firat.edu.tr/ mbaykara/ubmk3.pdf.

Can, Ü. and Alataş, B. (2017). Review of sentiment analysis and opinion mining algorithms. *International Journal of Pure and Applied Sciences*, 3(1), 75–111.

Capriello, A., Mason, P.R., Davis, B. and Crotts, J.C. (2013). Farm tourism experiences in travel reviews: a cross-comparison of three alternative methods for data analysis. *Journal of Business Research*, 66(6), 778–785.

Chiu, C., Chiu, N.H., Sung, R.J. and Hsieh, P.Y. (2015). Opinion mining of hotel customer-generated contents in Chinese weblogs. *Current Issues in Tourism*, 18(5), 477–495.

Claster, W.B., Dinh, Q.H. and Cooper, M. (2010). Naïve Bayes and unsupervised artificial neural nets for Cancun tourism social media data analysis. In *Proceedings of the Second World Congress on Nature and Biologically Inspired Computing*, (pp. 158–163). New York: IEEE.

Feldman, R. (2013). Techniques and applications for sentiment analysis. *Communications of the ACM*, 56(4), 82–89.

Gao, S., Hao, J. and Fu, Y. (2015, June). The application and comparison of web services for sentiment analysis in tourism. In *2015 12th International Conference on Service Systems and Service Management (ICSSSM)* (pp. 1–6). IEEE.

Gascón, J., Bernal, P., Román, E., González, M., Giménez, G., et al. (2016). Sentiment analysis as a qualitative methodology to analyze social media: study case of tourism. *1st International Symposium on Qualitative Research* / CIAIQ2016, 5.

Geetha, M., Singha, P. and Sinha, S. (2017). Relationship between customer sentiment and online customer ratings for hotels – an empirical analysis. *Tourism Management*, 61, 43–54.

González-Rodríguez, M.R., Martínez-Torres, R. and Toral, S. (2016). Post-visit and pre-visit tourist destination image through eWOM sentiment analysis and perceived helpfulness. *International Journal of Contemporary Hospitality Management*, 28(11), 2609–2627.

Guo, Y., Barnes, S.J. and Jia, Q. (2017). Mining meaning from online ratings and reviews: tourist satisfaction analysis using latent dirichlet allocation. *Tourism Management*, 59, 467–483.

Gupta, E., Rathee, G., Kumar, P. and Chauhan, D.S. (2015). Mood swing analyser: a dynamic sentiment detection approach. *Proceedings of the National Academy of Sciences, India Section A: Physical Sciences*, 85(1), 149–157.

He, W., Tian, X., Tao, R., Zhang, W., Yan, G. and Akula, V. (2017), Application of social media analytics: a case of analyzing online hotel reviews. *Online Information Review*, 41(7), 921–935. https://doi.org/10.1108/OIR-07-2016-0201.

Hemmatian, F. and Sohrabi, M.K. (2019). A survey on classification techniques for opinion mining and sentiment analysis. *Artificial Intelligence Review*, 52, 1495–1545. https://doi.org/10.1007/s10462-017-9599-6.

Hussein, D.M.E.D.M. (2018). A survey on sentiment analysis challenges. *Journal of King Saud University – Engineering Sciences*, 30(4), 330–338.

Kang, H., Yoo, S.J. and Han, D. (2012). Senti-lexicon and improved naïve Bayes algorithms for sentiment analysis of restaurant reviews. *Expert Systems with Applications*, 39(5), 6000–6010.

Karaoğlan, K.M., Temizkan, V. and Fındık, O. (2019). Sentiment analysis for hotel reviews with recurrent neural network architecture. *International Conference on Advanced Technologies, Computer Engineering and Science (ICATCES 2019)*, 26–28 April, Alanya, Turkey.

Katrekar, A. (2005). *An Introduction to Sentiment Analysis.* GlobalLogic. https://www.globallogic.com/wp-content/uploads/2014/10/Introduction-to-Sentiment-Analysis.pdf.

Kaynar, O., Yıldız, M., Görmez, Y. and Albayrak, A. (2016). Makine öğrenmesi yöntemleri ile Duygu Analizi. In *International Artificial Intelligence and Data Processing Symposium (IDAP'16)* (pp. 17–18).

Kearney, C. and Liu, S. (2014). Textual sentiment in finance: a survey of methods and models. *International Review of Financial Analysis*, 33, 171–185.

Kim, K., Park, O.J., Yun, S. and Yun, H. (2017). What makes tourists feel negatively about tourism destinations? Application of hybrid text mining methodology to smart destination management. *Technological Forecasting and Social Change*, 123, 362–369.

Kirilenko, A.P., Stepchenkova, S.O., Kim, H. and Li, X. (2018). Automated sentiment analysis in tourism: comparison of approaches. *Journal of Travel Research*, 57(8), 1012–1025.

Kızılkaya, Y.M. (2018) Duygu Analizi Ve Sosyal Medya Alanında Uygulama. Uludağ Üniversitesi Sosyal Bilimler Enstitüsü Ekonometri Anabilim Dalı İstatistik Bilim Dalı Doktora Tezi.

Liu, B. and Zhang, L. (2012). A survey of opinion mining and sentiment analysis. In C. Aggarwal and C. Zhai (eds), *Mining Text Data* (pp. 415–463). Boston, MA: Springer.

Liu, B. (2017). Many facets of sentiment analysis. In E. Cambria, D. Das, S. Bandyopadhyay and A. Feraco (eds), *A Practical Guide to Sentiment Analysis* (pp. 11–39). Cham: Springer International Publishing AG.

Ma, E., Cheng, M. and Hsiao, A. (2018). Sentiment analysis – a review and agenda for future research in hospitality contexts. *International Journal of Contemporary Hospitality Management*, 30(11), 3287–3308.

Martín, C.A., Torres, J.M., Aguilar, R.M. and Diaz, S. (2018). Using deep learning to predict sentiments: case study in tourism. *Complexity*, 2018, 1–9.

Medhat, W., Hassan, A. and Korashy, H. (2014). Sentiment analysis algorithms and applications: a survey. *Ain Shams Engineering Journal*, 5(4), 1093–1113.

Misopoulos, F., Mitic, M., Kapoulas, A. and Karapiperis, C. (2014). Uncovering customer service experiences with Twitter: the case of airline industry. *Management Decision*, 52(4), 705–723.

Onan, A. and Korukoğlu, S. (2016). Makine öğrenmesi yöntemlerinin görüş madenciliğinde kullanılması üzerine bir literatür araştırması. *Pamukkale University Journal of Engineering Sciences*, 22(2), 111–122.

Özyurt, B. and Akçayol, M.A. (2018). Fikir madenciliği ve duygu analizi, yaklaşımlar, yöntemler üzerine bir araştırma. *S.Ü. Mühendislik. Bilim ve Teknoloji. Dergisi*, 6(4), 668–693.

Park, S., Kwak, M. and Choi, J. (2020). Comparing competitive advantages of hotel services using opinion mining of online customer reviews: a study focusing on 5-star hotels in Seoul, Korea. *ICIC Express Letters, Part B: Applications*, 11(8), 1–7.

Patil, P. and Yalagi, P. (2016). Sentiment analysis levels and techniques: a survey. *International Journal of Innovations in Engineering and Technology (IJIET)*, 1(6), 523–528.

Pervan, N. (2020). Duygu analizi neden önemli? Retrieved from https://www.sisasoft.com.tr/duygu -analizi-neden-onemli/.

Philander, K. and Zhong, Y. (2016). Twitter sentiment analysis: capturing sentiment from integrated resort tweets. *International Journal of Hospitality Management*, 55(2016), 16–24.

Ravi, K. and Ravi, V. (2015). A survey on opinion mining and sentiment analysis: tasks, approaches and applications. *Knowledge-Based Systems*, 89, 14–46.

Ren, G. and Hong, T. (2017). Investigating online destination images using a topic-based sentiment analysis approach. *Sustainability*, 9(10), 1765.

Serrano-Guerrero, J., Olivas, J.A., Romero, F.P. and Herrera-Viedma, E. (2015). Sentiment analysis: a review and comparative analysis of web services. *Information Sciences*, 311(2015), 18–38.

Şeker, S.E. (2016). Duygu Analizi (Sentimental analysis). *YBS Ansiklopedi*, 3(3), 21–26.

whoson.com (2020). Top ten benefits of sentiment analysis. Retrieved from https://www.whoson.com/ customer-service/top-ten-benefits-of-sentiment-analysis/.

Yousefpour, A., Ibrahim, R., Hamed, H.N.A. and Hajmohammadi, M.S. (2014). A comparative study on sentiment analysis. *Advances in Environmental Biology*, 8(13), 53–69.

Xiang, Z., Schwartz, Z., Gerdes Jr, J.H. and Uysal, M. (2015). What can big data and text analytics tell us about hotel guest experience and satisfaction? *International Journal of Hospitality Management*, 44, 120–130.

19. Digital communication tools and tourism engagement: instant CRM strategies through instant messaging apps

Letizia Lo Presti, Giulio Maggiore and Vittoria Marino

INTRODUCTION

With the advent of the internet, tourism has undergone a profound transformation that has made it essential for operators in the sector to rethink their methods of communicating the tourist offer. With the intensification of the use of social media before, during and after the travel experience, the engagement of the tourist is amplified. In particular, today we are witnessing a metamorphosis of social media, from a simple tool for sharing experiences in the peer group, to real digital engagement platforms used by public and private organizations to communicate in real time with their customers (Marino and Lo Presti, 2019a, 2019b, 2018). These trends for some years now have been changing the way people relate to customers, also imposing a change in the ways and methods of interacting with and engaging tourists (Taheri et al., 2019; Buhalis and Law, 2008), something which up until a few years ago was implemented through the more traditional direct marketing channels such as emails, newsletters, telephone contact, and so on.

Furthermore, today the opportunities offered by these new communication channels require a rethinking of customer relationship management (CRM) strategies towards the so-called social customer relationship management (SCRM) (Dewnarain et al., 2019; Trainor et al., 2014), and an adaptation of the tactics in the function of marketing objectives and customer typology. While literature delves into the tourism engagement construct as a lever to improve the tourist experience in a certain destination (Huang and Choi, 2019; Rasoolimanesh et al., 2019; Rather et al., 2019), to date the literature has done little to investigate the role of instant messaging apps in the tourism and hospitality sector as new touchpoints capable of contributing to the co-creation of value and generating a lasting relationship with the customer. In particular, since these apps are based on chatline conversations aimed at promoting customer engagement (today an increasingly important aspect of the tourist experience), tourist engagement can be thought of as a factor that stimulates satisfaction and consequently actions of active participation regarding the destination or the accommodation (word-of-mouth, comments on social networks, sharing of one's own tourist experience, and so on). In this unprecedented framework, this work investigates whether and how instant messaging apps elicit responses from the customer who interacts with an organization in the tourism and hospitality sector (measured through the degree of engagement and satisfaction). In fact, knowing the effectiveness of these new touchpoints in terms of engagement and satisfaction has important managerial implications, since it allows the identification of actions for improvement in the use of these new communication channels in the light of an integrated approach to marketing communication that can assist the CRM manager in their relationship strategies.

BACKGROUND

Customer Engagement and Satisfaction

Tourism engagement can be included within customer engagement studies, a topic widely discussed in many areas of study including psychology, marketing and organization (So et al., 2014). In all these fields, the concept of engagement has taken on different shades of meaning, adapting itself to the field of study. On the whole, engagement is considered to be a mental state that implies the activation of a cognitive and emotional process. In this sense, customer engagement is expressed through three dimensions: a cognitive, an affective and, finally, a behavioural dimension (Pansari and Kumar, 2017; Vivek et al., 2012; Brodie et al., 2011). Used above all with the diffusion of social media, the concept of engagement has been enriched with a new perspective, that is, the interaction between organizations and consumers on platforms used for participation between the parties involved (Hollebeek et al., 2014). In this regard, some authors speak of engagement platforms as the place where an exchange of information and services is activated which co-creates value among its components and determines satisfaction for the actors involved in the exchange (Breidbach and Brodie, 2017; Jaakkola and Alexander, 2014). By virtue of the countless opportunities offered by technological innovation and the possibility of using tourist services even on smartphones, it is plausible that the integration between the tourist offer and the way it is used is now customer-oriented and guided. In these increasingly 'conversational' markets, tourist engagement is therefore crucial today. In the tourism sector, the concept of engagement has become important because it is considered a driver of the tourist experience (Rather, 2020). Rather et al. (2019) explore the antecedents and consequences of tourism engagement in India. Among the main antecedents, the authors identify authenticity and the link with the territory. The results also reveal a positive effect of customer engagement on customer loyalty, trust and value co-creation. Huang and Choi (2019), on the other hand, have developed a multidimensional scale to measure tourism engagement. The authors have identified in the social interaction, in the interaction with the service provider, in the relationship and in the specific activities related to the involvement of the tourist, the main dimensions for measuring the destination experience and thus segmenting the tourists. In this regard, Rasoolimanesh et al. (2019) demonstrate the link between tourism engagement, satisfaction and loyalty. Previously, customer engagement was studied in the context of service-dominant logic (Hollebeek et al., 2019) and the implications for customer relationship management were identified. Kumar et al. (2019), in studying customer engagement in services, noted the importance of the perception of experience on satisfaction as a driver of consumer engagement beyond purchasing (Brodie et al., 2011). Therefore, giving due consideration to the experience when managing the service seems to be decisive for triggering satisfaction and engagement activities. A consumer who is engaged with a destination develops a more favourable attitude and is therefore more interested in reliving that experience.

Customer engagement literature defines satisfaction and involvement as two interrelated concepts. For Bowden (2009a, 2009b), customer engagement is a 'psychological process' in which cognitive and emotional aspects play different roles in the process that leads to customer satisfaction and, subsequently, to their continued use of the service. From a theoretical point of view, for Bowden (2009a), cognitive involvement is only the beginning of a process which, if further developed and promoted, could lead to something that goes beyond purchasing and which involves the affective and behavioural sphere, thus decreeing a longer-lasting relationship.

Furthermore, the literature demonstrates the mediating role of satisfaction between customer engagement and loyalty (Deng et al., 2010; Bowden, 2009a, 2009b). For Bravo et al. (2019), for example, this means that the satisfied tourist, during their website activities, will be induced to activate a series of proactive and purposeful behaviours (which he calls customer engagement behaviour), which are therefore beneficial for the tourist destination or organization. As part of online travel marketing, Willems et al. (2019) asked themselves what role the presentation of the destination information in the various media has on the presentation of travel destinations during the pre-purchase process; and they noted how interaction and active participation (for example, through virtual reality) intensifies the interest of potential visitors and increases the probability of purchase. The merit of this study was to demonstrate the importance of activities preparatory to the purchase (pre-purchase), and therefore initial to the customer journey. Previous studies have confirmed satisfaction with the services offered as one of the main factors influencing the customer's intention to engage in value creation (Dovaliene et al., 2015; Kim et al., 2015). Therefore understanding the role of engagement during the tourist experience through the use of dedicated services can help to understand which strategies to activate in the context of relationship marketing activities.

The Digital Engagement Platforms

Social media websites are revolutionizing the way companies and consumers interact. Their massive diffusion, and the possibility of interacting directly and effectively in a two-way communication process, offer companies, public institutions and non-profit organizations new ways to manage the relationship with their main stakeholders: consumers, citizens and customers. In particular, instant messaging applications, including Facebook Messenger, WhatsApp, Telegram and WeChat, are today among the most frequently used communication channels, especially among young people and professionals, thanks above all to the fact that they are free and allow smartphones fast and easy access to social networks. Nevertheless, only recently the most popular instant messaging applications in Europe and Italy have started to open their doors to the business world. In confirmation of this, many companies are investing in mobile instant messaging today because, as Antony Ayes, chief executive officer of Spherix, a well-known investment company in cutting-edge technologies, declares: 'instant messaging is evolving from simple social conversations to business related conversations and ... messaging apps are increasingly becoming a second home screen' (*New York Times*, 2019).

Conversations with human interaction (person-to-person) are still little considered in this area of marketing, although there is an established habit among small and medium-sized enterprises to use instant messaging as a support for customer assistance, for bookings and for sending promotions (Marino and Lo Presti, 2019a, 2019b, 2018).

The rapid metamorphosis of these interactive platforms towards e-commerce platforms has stimulated research towards understanding the potential of conversations as a push towards the propensity to buy and sell in an increasingly service-oriented context. Mostly, the articles that talk about the use of social networks in business refer to the concept of social commerce (electronic commerce through social media). This is plausible, given that social networks such as Facebook, Instagram and WhatsApp, which were mostly channels for socialization, have now become 'virtual villages' where you can find the exposure and promotion of brands. Only in recent years has it been possible to find a definition of conversation-based business that refers to the instant messaging channel as a lever for the promotion and marketing of products (Messina, 2015). Rather than places for commerce, however, these 'digital engagement platforms' (Marino and Lo Presti, 2019b) are more a 'front office', where the first contact with customers takes place and where it is possible to interact with customers through customer relationship management activities. Social media and smartphones have transformed the relationship between companies and customers, thus inducing companies to propose relationship management strategies that would go beyond mere commercial transactions (Hollebeek et al., 2014).

While the consulting and managerial field has already seized the opportunities offered by instant messaging, scientific research in the tourism sector focuses its attention mainly on the traditional use of social media, while completely neglecting the role now assumed by instantaneous messaging apps as places of contact with the potential tourist, despite the fact that companies from the tourism and hospitality sector have recently started to interact with consumers using the mobile instant messaging (MIM) apps; integrating them, among other things, in their communication activities.

Marketing literature, however, has shown over the years a slow and timid shift from the characteristics of the channel (what social media can offer in terms of sharing) to the potential of the channel, and above all to the role of conversation in the choosing processes of potential buyers. Some studies have tried to detect the importance of instant messaging in the process of peer group interaction or in business dealings with an organization. Oghuma et al. (2016), for example, find that the perception of utility and ease of use are the main factors that influence the use of MIM apps. Marino and Lo Presti (2018) talk about 'mobile instant messaging engagement', with reference to post-technological acceptance behaviour that leads consumers to use instant messaging apps and to maintain the relationship for as long as possible. This behaviour, the result of motivational drives (of a hedonic, utilitarian or social nature) and psycho-social attitudes (of an affective, cognitive and conative nature) is a generator of satisfaction and an activator of a medium- to long-term relationship.

However, despite these results, little is known about the role of digital engagement platforms in the tourism and hospitality systems on the level of engagement and satisfaction of the digital tourist. In this chapter we aim to explore this relationship in the context of the use of instant messaging apps. Knowing whether and how these new channels work helps in adapting CRM strategies to the real needs of customers, and in developing new engagement activities.

Social Customer Relationship Management

CRM, defined as a 'set of customer-oriented activities supported by organizational strategy and technology, designed to improve customer interaction in order to build customer loyalty and increase profits over time' (Padmavathy et al., 2012, p. 247), with the advent of social media has undergone a profound change over recent years. In fact, it has gone from being a strategy to create relationships with customers in order to encourage the purchase of products and services, to becoming more and more a platform for the promotion of relationships of an exclusively interactional nature with customers, and intended to stimulate engagement and participation, known as social customer relationship management (SCRM) or CRM 2.0 (Dewnarain et al., 2019). This evolution of CRM is particularly true in the field of tourism and hospitality, very often with a customer service-orientated approach and therefore based on interaction as a constituent element of the effectiveness of its organizational performance. In particular, it is important for hospitality practitioners to acquire specific skills and competencies regarding the use of the new communication channels, in order to adequately respond to the opportunities offered by the metamorphosis of social media and maximize performance. To explain the link between CRM and hotel performance, Mohammed and Rashid (2012) identified four behavioural dimensions of CRM: consumer orientation, corporate skills, knowledge management and the use of technology in the social media context. On this last point, many authors (Dewnarain et al., 2019) have tried to demonstrate how social media does not replicate traditional CRM systems, but creates opportunities for small, medium-sized and large enterprises through processes of exchange of relational information between businesses and consumers, or in the communication that ensues among the peer group (Diffley and McCole, 2015; Harrigan et al., 2017). Other authors have taken time to investigate which aspects firms should give more importance to. Technical skills and those related to the management of privacy and transparency seem to be the most important (Di Gangi and Wasko, 2016). With regard to the latter, Keinänen and Kuivalainen (2015) clarify the important role played by the characteristics, attitudes and habits of the employee when adopting social media in business. This is obviously linked to the idea of the perception of utility and effectiveness that determines the adoption of a new technology (Keinänen and Kuivalainen, 2015; Davis, 1989). In line with the school of thought that supports the importance of managerial and personal skills and abilities for the management of social media (Wang et al., 2017) is the contribution of Bolat et al. (2016), who in investigating the use of mobile social media in business-to-business (B2B) marketing found that social skills are important for overcoming the advancement of disruptive technologies, and transforming what can be considered as external challenges into opportunities for businesses and customers. In the same vein, Wang et al. (2017) discover that organizational social media capabilities are dependent on a firm's technological capabilities which allow them to recognize and respond quickly to environmental changes. The authors therefore identify a social media capability maturity model on four levels (technological, operational, managerial and strategic) which progressively transforms social media's technological capability into a dynamic organizational capability. Although the literature on the use of social networks in businesses recognizes the importance of social platforms aimed at customer interaction, and identifies the skills of employees and the company's predisposition towards technological innovation as the key factors for the success of these channels, the role of conversation in interaction processes, when it is conveyed through these new ways of using social media, is not yet clear. In addition, the marketing literature has little explored the potential of conversational marketing through the new digital engagement platforms; if it is known how to use these properly, they can become a direct channel to the customer. Furthermore, the issue of the role played by social media in activating CRM activities through engagement is a topic not yet fully discussed in the studies on the tourism and hospitality sector (Dewnarain et al., 2019).

METHODOLOGY

An online survey was conducted to find out how instant messaging is used in the tourism and hospitality sector. Of 261 consumers who stated that they had used instant messaging with an organization, 90 said they had used this tool with a company that operates in the tourism and hospitality sector. The questionnaire collected the opinions of consumers regarding their level of engagement and their level of satisfaction. Finally, descriptive information was collected from the sample. The contribution of Vivek et al. (2012) was used to detect the degree of engagement, while the Wang et al. (2004) scale was adapted to measure satisfaction. A seven-point Likert scale was used to measure the judgement (from 1 = completely disagree, to 7 = completely agree). The scales have a Cronbach's α coefficient above 0.80. Finally, information was collected regarding type of instant messaging app, direction of contact (if contacted by the customer, 1; if contacted by the company, 0) and the purpose of the contact. Since the construct of customer engagement was measured in its three dimensions (cognitive, affective and behavioural), the degree of engagement (engagement index) was calculated as the arithmetic mean of the value of each dimension divided by the number of dimensions. The degree of satisfaction (satisfaction index) was calculated as the arithmetic mean of the items representative of the construct.

The Sample

The sample consisted of an equal number of men and women (46 per cent and 54 per cent, respectively), mostly young adults (70 per cent) under the age of 36, with a high school diploma (44 per cent) or a degree (53 per cent). Of these, 46 per cent declared they were in work, while 42 per cent were university students.

Ninety-seven per cent of the sample interviewed usually used WhatsApp to interact with an organization; 59 per cent said they also used Messenger; and 12 per cent of the interviewees said they used other instant messaging apps together with WhatsApp, such as Telegram, Wechat and Google Talk. Seventy-two per cent of respondents said they had contacted an organization through an instant messaging app, while 28 per cent had been contacted directly by an organization in the tourism and/or hospitality sector.

RESULTS

It is the customer who usually takes the initiative in using instant messaging to contact the organization (72 per cent), while only 28 per cent were contacted directly by the organization that operates in the hospitality or tourism sector. In fact, the results of the literature analysis suggest that very often the use of instant messaging by customers is determined by their perception of practicality and ease of use (Marino and Lo Presti, 2019b). In addition, the 'proximity' of the channel (WhatsApp, for example, is an application used daily in private life as well as in the workplace) facilitates the intention to continue using the instant messaging app if the contact experience is positive and satisfactory (Marino and Lo Presti, 2018). The customer in fact uses tools that are practical, fast and less expensive, and these features are well in line with instant messaging apps. Below is an analysis of the level of satisfaction and engagement in the use of instant messaging with businesses and organizations for the tourism and hospitality sector based on CRM activities.

Customer Relationship Management Activities on Instant Messaging Apps

Observing the degree of engagement relative to the purposes for which the customer contacted or was contacted by an organization in the tourism and hospitality sector, we analysed

Table 19.1   Degree of customer engagement and satisfaction during interaction with an instant messaging application

	Degree of engagement (%)		Degree of satisfaction (%)	
Goals of the conversation	Low	High	Low	High
	(47%)	(53%)	(29%)	(71%)
Updating on new products/services	0.39	0.61	0.22	0.78
Providing more information and assistance to the customer	0.43	0.57	0.27	0.73
Sending promotions	0.53	0.47	0.29	0.71
Participation in an event	0.46	0.54	0.24	0.76
Express an evaluation	0.45	0.55	0.41	0.59
Sending updates on a product/service	0.59	0.41	0.23	0.77
Request/complete a reservation	0.47	0.53	0.38	0.63

Note: High engagement, >3.5; low engagement, ≤3.5; High satisfaction, >3.5; low satisfaction, ≤3.5. The percentage is calculated on the actual number of customers who declared using messaging for that purpose.

the relationship between the goals of the conversation and the impact produced in terms of engagement and satisfaction (Table 19.1). The interviewees could indicate more than one option; therefore, more activities could have been undertaken by the same interviewee.

Overall, the majority of goals are linked to the following activities: provide customer assistance, sending promotions, participation in an event and requesting and completing a booking.

Table 19.1 shows that the satisfaction level is higher than the engagement level (71 per cent versus 53 per cent). This means that instant messaging applications are able to respond to customer needs effectively, but still struggle to create truly engaging and participatory relationships.

Looking at the goals for using the applications, it can be seen that there are some CRM activities that can encourage both engagement and satisfaction in a particularly significant way: these being updating on new products/services (61 per cent high engagement and 78 per cent high satisfaction) and providing more information and assistance to the customer (57 per cent high engagement and 73 per cent high satisfaction). A common element in these two activities is the proactive role played by the customer, who takes the initiative to find an answer to their immediate need both in the first contact phase with the company and in the post-purchase phase. The client's proactivity is also evident with reference to participation in an event, where we can find high levels of engagement (54.1 per cent) and satisfaction (75.7 per cent).

On the other hand, where the customer is the object or recipient of information (sending updates on a product/service) and the firm's promotional initiatives (sending promotions), the level of satisfaction is still high, proving that the message sent reaches its goal (high levels of satisfaction, equal to 77 per cent and 71 per cent, respectively); but the majority of users reveal lower than average engagement (users who declare low engagement are 59 per cent and 53 per cent, respectively). This shows that although the applications can be valid tools for corporate communication campaigns, if there is no spontaneous user activation this translates into less engagement. Finally, it should be noted that the activities that give the least user satisfaction are those concerning expressing an evaluation and requesting/completing a booking. In the first case, it is probable that the lower satisfaction is due to the low amount of effort required of the user, who does not perceive any value in this activity. In the second case, however, the problem may be related to the relative inadequacy of the tool when performing activities characterized by a high level of complexity.

Digital tourist profiles

By crossing the two variables just analysed, that is the level of satisfaction (high, ≥3.5; low, <3.5) and the level of declared engagement (high, ≥3.5; low, <3.5) we obtain four types of digital tourist:

- Transitories (low engagement, low satisfaction). They have declared that they feel neither engaged nor particularly satisfied when using the instant messaging app with the tourism organization (19 tourists, 21 per cent). In particular, these tourists used the app to ask for information and assistance, to complete a booking and when the organization sent them promotions via chat. Given their level of engagement and satisfaction, these customers may be discouraged from continuing to use this touchpoint to contact the organization, and for this reason they have been labelled 'transitory customers'.
- Delighted (high engagement, high satisfaction). They are the majority of respondents. These customers said they were satisfied and felt engaged during the chat with the tourism organization (41 tourists, 45.6 per cent). These customers could become loyal customers if the instant messaging app were used as a relational channel and not just as a simple information channel. If their level of engagement is not kept high, or if the level of satisfaction is lowered, these customers could be disillusioned or retreat towards more 'pragmatic' or 'opportunistic' behaviour without any interest in activities that extend the life cycle of the relationship.
- Pragmatics (low engagement, high satisfaction). They are users who have shown themselves satisfied with using instant messaging with the organization despite not feeling particularly engaged during the chat (22 tourists, 24 per cent). Because of their keenness on the result, they have been called pragmatic clients. If the performance is not kept high, these customers could become transitory customers.
- Disappointed (high engagement, low satisfaction). They are the minority (eight tourists, 9 per cent). They are users who, though feeling engaged while using the messaging app with the organization, were not particularly satisfied with the performance obtained. For their disillusioned expectations they have been labelled as disappointed customers. These customers could turn into delighted customers if the tourism organization were more committed during the process of service delivery; otherwise, these customers might only use the app occasionally and therefore behave like temporary customers.

Table 19.2 illustrates the number of activities carried out by customers with reference to their degree of satisfaction/engagement. Furthermore, since these customer relationship management activities are activated during the customer journey – considered for practicality in a three-phase path: pre-purchase, purchase, post-purchase – they illustrate the activation of the contact phase.

In particular, as can be seen from Table 19.2 many of these customer relationship management activities fall into the post-purchase phases, therefore they are decisive for establishing a lasting relationship with the customer. From Table 19.2, we can include the activities update on new products/services and send promotions in the pre-purchase activities. The request/complete a reservation activity belong to the purchase phase. Finally, sending product/service

Table 19.2   *Main activities based on engagement/satisfaction*

| Digital tourists | Pre-purchase activities | | Purchase phase | Post-purchase activities | | | |
	Updating on new product/ service (%)	Sending promotions (%)	Request/ complete a reservation (%)	Sending updates on a product/ service (%)	Providing more info and assistance (%)	Participation in an event (%)	Express an evaluation (%)
Transitories	16	37	37	21	37	32	26
Pragmatics	23	41	36	14	14	32	23
Disappointed	25	50	63	0	50	38	50
Delighted	29	34	29	17	46	42	20

Note: Users could choose more than one option.

news, product/service assistance, attending an event and expressing an evaluation were considered to be post-purchase activities.

Delighted customers are those who used instant messaging more than other tourists in many activities during all phases of the customer journey, favouring an approach that is attentive to the quality and continuity of the relationship. This attention was manifested both in the initial stages (updates on products/services) (29 per cent) and in the final stages of the customer journey (assistance and participation in events) (46 per cent).

The disappointed customers, on the other hand, used little instant messaging with tourism organizations, focusing mainly on the service booking phase, with unsatisfactory results (63 per cent), especially when compared with the expectations generated by the strong initial involvement. The pragmatics, less involved in the relational opportunities of the medium, focused above all on the possibility of obtaining immediate benefits connected to functionalities capable of satisfying their needs (to use promotions, 41 per cent or ask/complete a reservation, 36 per cent). Finally, transitory customers mostly used all forms of contact with the organizations without becoming engaged, and so maintained a limited level of satisfaction.

Those who are satisfied and engaged used instant messaging for many more activities than those who are only satisfied or only engaged. This means that the activities that trigger engagement are not sufficient to create 'potential customers'; therefore operators working with instant social networks must also be able to respond to customer needs in terms of the effectiveness and efficiency that the instant messaging service offers. This suggests that they must implement actions that are related to the customer's actual needs and capable of activating user engagement. Some activities are considered especially urgent, since many of these (for example, the activity of requesting/completing a reservation of a room in a hotel), are the precursors of the effective contact that the organization will have with the customer/tourist and are consequently a first presentation of the image of the organization in the eyes of potential customers. Therefore, they are fundamental to laying the foundations of a long-lasting relationship based on engagement beyond purchasing (Brodie et al., 2011).

Strategies and tactics for instant CRM
Table 19.3 illustrates the strategies and tactics that can be used to improve the tourist relationship through instant messaging apps. With transitory customers it will be necessary to adopt a reactive strategy that can minimize the inefficiencies perceived by the customer. Since the customer is particularly unhappy in all phases of the customer journey (Table 19.3) it will be

Table 19.3   *Instant CRM strategies and activities that should be implemented to improve
the relationship with the customer*

Digital tourists	Pre-purchase activities	Purchase phase	Post-purchase activities	Marketing strategy
Transitories	Timeliness and personalization of information	Customize assistance	Give an immediate advantage	Reactive
Pragmatics	-	Enhance the role of the customer	Effective communication	Engage
Disappointed	Finalize engagement	Efficiency of services	-	Proactive
Delighted	-	-	Retain the customer	Advocate

necessary, in the pre-purchase phase, to give a speedy and personalized response to the request for information. During the purchase phase, show that you know how to listen to the customer and their requests. Finally, in the post-purchase phase, CRM activities should be orientated towards returning an immediate advantage. In particular, it is necessary to immediately intercept the real interests of the customer, avoiding a superficial approach which will inevitably depress any effective engagement and the final satisfaction. However, these are subjects who are probably not very familiar with the medium, and therefore it is essential to encourage them to overcome the initial prejudice that leads them to an attitude of scepticism towards the real potential of this tool.

With pragmatic customers, given their low engagement in the purchase and post-purchase phases, it will be appropriate to enhance the role of the customer as a co-actor in the process of providing the service during the online chat with the organization. For this reason, it will be crucial to communicate effectively, showing friendliness and proactivity during the interaction. Since these customers could become delighted customers, it is appropriate to invest in employee training to acquire what Trainor et al. (2014) call social skills. It is essential to push users to overcome a too-speculative approach, so that they learn to appreciate a long-term relationship capable of generating longer-lasting benefits.

With disappointed customers, it will be necessary to adopt a proactive strategy aimed at increasing the perception of satisfaction during the services received in chat from the tourism organization through greater effectiveness in the service delivery phase. In this case, it is necessary to take advantage of the opportunities deriving from a high level of engagement which, as the literature confirms (Marino and Lo Presti, 2018), has the effect of producing an increase in expectations but can contribute to increasing the satisfaction levels of the customer provided that they become an active part of the value co-creation process. In the absence of this element, the relationship with the customer can enter an involutionary phase which leads to a progressive disengagement.

With delighted customers it will be necessary to try to retain them with strategies that can support the relationship in the long term. In effect, these are activities related to loyalty programmes and purchase incentives. Furthermore, the sense of belonging that develops thanks to high levels of engagement and satisfaction can be the basis for fuelling advocacy strategies (Mattiacci and Pastore, 2013) that could enhance their role within the relationship.

DISCUSSION AND CONCLUSIONS

This research shows that where push logic prevails (activated, for example, by sending promotions, or updates on products and services), there is a tendency for less customer engagement. In the presence of a pull logic, which stimulates the interaction of the consumer and leaves to them the initiative of starting the conversation (as, for example, when information and assistance services are provided 'on demand', and when participation in an event is asked for), there is greater engagement and also greater satisfaction. Thus, instant messaging apps provide support for social CRM activities, becoming another important touchpoint for intercepting and interacting with the customer. Nevertheless, research shows that not all activities have the same effect on digital tourists in terms of high engagement and high satisfaction. For example, when the messaging app is used to request an evaluation of the service provided, you risk obtaining a less positive reaction in terms of satisfaction, probably because the customer perceives this request as too invasive. A higher level of dissatisfaction is also recorded among users who use instant messaging to complete a booking, probably due to the objective difficulties in completing a procedure that involves greater psychological stress.

Furthermore, research shows that an engaged customer is not always a satisfied customer, and vice versa. In fact, it may happen that an effective customer activation generates very high expectations, which could clash with the actual ability of the company to ensure adequate performance, fuelling a feeling of dissatisfaction and disappointment. On the contrary, instant messaging can respond effectively to specific customer needs, guaranteeing good satisfaction, even without being capable of developing a relationship of real engagement. This second situation, which is obviously preferable to the first, can however result in a loss of opportunity where the inability to create a lasting relationship with the customer leads to a 'speculative' approach that prevents the activation of co-creation of value. Although it is therefore not possible to affirm a clear correlation between engagement and customer satisfaction with reference to the individual act of purchase, the need to activate a virtuous circuit between these two dimensions can be hypothesized to ensure the maximization of lifetime value. This aspect, however, requires further study in the context of specific research, which goes beyond the objective of this chapter.

In addition, this research highlights the importance of activating new social skills and specialized abilities to tackle the new skills that an advanced use of instant messaging applications requires from operators of tourist services. These skills, which the literature calls 'dynamic organizational capabilities' (Wang et al., 2017), are necessary for the implementation of those operational tactics that improve the levels of engagement and satisfaction of digital tourists, and which in this research have been found to be speediness and personalization of information, enhancement of the customer's role, efficiency of the service and effective communication.

With a view to a new consumer vision – the so-called 'social consumer' who performs their 'customer journey' by collaborating with the company – instant messaging apps are a suitable tool for keeping in touch with the consumer and maintaining their loyalty, but they are also a tool that allows more flexibility at reduced costs (Lo Presti et al., 2020). The speed with which messages can be exchanged, their wide diffusion and zero cost, and their level of 'proximity' are some of the main factors favourable to their use.

This study underlines the appropriateness of obtaining valid suggestions on a topic of interest for the academic and managerial fields. Two lines of research seem particularly promising. The first could be focused on the business perspective; the second should aim to further knowledge on the effect of social CRM activities on real company performance. In view of an integrated communication, it is important to measure the degree of effectiveness of these activities, compared to other direct marketing activities that are planned in business strategies. It would therefore be useful, in a logic of integrated communication plans, to verify the weight of these activities against the more traditional ones, in order to adequately allocate the budget available for marketing expenses. On an academic level, this research contributes further knowledge on the phenomenon of the metamorphosis of social media towards a commercial dimension that has been little explored in this sector to date. In addition, precisely in this area, this study demonstrates the importance of two axes in the customer relationship – engagement and satisfaction – as measurements of this channel's effectiveness. In the future, research should go as far as measuring the effect of these two constructs on post-purchase activities such as loyalty, word-of-mouth, and the intention to continue using these channels to contact the customer.

REFERENCES

Bolat E., Kooli K. Wright L.T. (2016). Businesses and mobile social media capability. Journal of Business and Industrial Marketing, 31(8), 971–981.

Bowden, J. (2009a). The process of customer engagement: a conceptual framework. *Journal of Marketing Theory and Practice*, 17(1), 63–74.

Bowden, J. (2009b). Customer engagement: a framework for assessing customer–brand relationships: the case of the restaurant industry. *Journal of Hospitality Marketing & Management*, 18(6), 574–596.

Bravo, R., Catalán, S., Pina, J.M. (2019). Intergenerational differences in customer engagement behaviours: An analysis of social tourism websites. *International Journal of Tourism Research, 22*(2), 182–191.

Breidbach, C.F., Brodie, R.J. (2017). Engagement platforms in the sharing economy: conceptual foundations and research directions. *Journal of Service Theory and Practice*, 27(4), 761–777.

Brodie, R.J., Hollebeek, L.D., Juric, B., Ilic, A. (2011). Customer engagement: conceptual domain, fundamental propositions, and implications for research. *Journal of Service Research*, 14(3), 252–271.

Buhalis, D., Law, R. (2008). Progress in information technology and tourism management: 20 years on and 10 years after the Internet – the state of eTourism research. *Tourism Management*, 29(4), 609–623.

Davis, F.D. (1989). Perceived usefulness, perceived ease of use, and user acceptance of information technology. *MIS Quarterly*, 13(3), 319–340.

Deng, Z., Lu, Y., Wei, K.K., Zhang, J. (2010). Understanding customer satisfaction and loyalty: an empirical study of mobile instant messages in China. *International Journal of Information Management*, 30(4), 289–300.

Dewnarain, S., Ramkissoon, H., Mavondo, F. (2019). Social customer relationship management in the hospitality industry. *Journal of Hospitality*, 1(1), 1–14.

Diffley, S., McCole, P. (2015). Extending customer relationship management into a social context. *Service Industries Journal*, 35(11) 591–610.

Di Gangi P.M., Wasko M.M. (2016). Social media engagement theory: exploring the influence of user engagement on social media usage. *Journal of Organizational and End User Computing (JOEUC)*, 28(2), 53–73.

Dovaliene, A., Masiulyte, A., Piligrimine, Z. (2015). The relations between customer engagement, perceived value and satisfaction: the case of mobile applications. *Procedia – Social and Behavioral Sciences*, 213, 659–664.

Harrigan, P., Evers, U., Miles, M., Daly, T. (2017). Customer engagement with tourism social media brands. *Tourism Management*, 59(C), 597–609.

Hollebeek, L., Glynn, M.S., Brodie, R.J. (2014). Consumer brand engagement in social media: conceptualisation, scale development and validation. *Journal of Interactive Marketing*, 28(2), 149–165.

Hollebeek, L.D., Srivastava, R.K., Chen, T. (2019). SD logic–informed customer engagement: integrative framework, revised fundamental propositions, and application to CRM. *Journal of the Academy of Marketing Science*, *47*(1), 161–185.

Huang, S., Choi, C.H.S. (2019). Developing and validating a multidimensional tourist engagement scale (TES). *Service Industries Journal*, *39*(7–8),1–29.

Jaakkola, E., Alexander, M. (2014). The role of customer engagement behaviour in value co-creation: a service system perspective. *Journal of Service Research*, *17*(3), 247–261.

Keinänen H., Kuivalainen O. (2015). Antecedents of social media B2B use in industrial marketing context: customers' view. *Journal of Business and Industrial Marketing*, *30*(6), 711–722.

Kim, S. J., Wang, R.J.H., Malrhouse, E.C. (2015). The effects of adopting and using a brand's mobile application on customers' subsequent purchase behavior. *Journal of Interactive Marketing*, *31*, 28–41.

Kumar, V., Rajan, B., Gupta, S., Dalla Pozza, I. (2019). Customer engagement in service. *Journal of the Academy of Marketing Science*, *47*(1),138–160.

Lo Presti, L., Maggiore, G., Marino, V. (2020). Mobile chat servitization in the customer journey: from social capability to social suitability. *TQM Journal*, *32*(6), 1139–1158.

Marino, V., Lo Presti, L. (2018). Engagement, satisfaction and customer behavior-based CRM performance: and empirical study of mobile instant messaging. *Journal of Service Theory and Practice*, *28*(5), 682–707.

Marino, V., Lo Presti, L. (2019a). Stay in touch! New insights into end-user attitudes towards engagement platforms. *Journal of Consumer Marketing*, *36*(6), 772–783.

Marino, V., Lo Presti, L. (2019b). Disruptive marketing communication for customer engagement: the new frontiers of mobile instant messaging. *International Journal on Media Management*, *21*(1), 3–23.

Mattiacci, A., Pastore, A. (2013). *Marketing: il management orientato al mercato*. Milano, Hoepli.

Messina, C. (2015). Conversational commerce. Retrieved from https://medium.com/chris-messina/conversational-commerce-92e0bccfc3ff.

Mohammed, A.A., Rashid, B. (2012). Customer relationship management (CRM) in hotel industry: a framework proposal on the relationship among CRM dimensions, marketing capabilities, and hotel performance. *International Review of Management and Marketing*, 2(4), 220–230.

New York Times (2019, December 11). Spherix highlights size of multi-billion dollar mobile messaging sector. Retrived from http://markets.on.nytimes.com.

Oghuma, A.P., Libaque-Saenz, C.F., Wong, S.F., & Chang, Y. (2016). An expectation–confirmation model of continuance intention to use mobile instant messaging. *Telematics and Informatics*, *33*(1), 34–47.

Padmavathy, C., Balaji, M.S., Sivakumar, V.J. (2012). Measuring effectiveness of customer relationship management in Indian retail banks. *International Journal of Bank Marketing*, *30*(4), 246–266.

Pansari, A., Kumar, V. (2017). Customer engagement: the construct, antecedents, and consequences. *Journal of Academy of Marketing Science*, *45*(3), 294–311.

Rasoolimanesh, S.M., Noor, S.M., Schuberth, F., Jaafar, M. (2019). Investigating the effects of tourist engagement on satisfaction and loyalty, *Service Industries Journal*, *39*(7–8), 559–574.

Rather, R.A. (2020) Customer experience and engagement in tourism destinations: the experiential marketing perspective, *Journal of Travel and Tourism Marketing*, *37*(1), 15–32.

Rather, R.A. Hollebeek, L.D., Islam, J.U. (2019). Tourism based customer engagement: the construct, antecedents, and consequences, *Service Industries Journal*, *39*(7–8), 519–540.

So, K.F., King, C., Sparks, B., Wang, Y. (2014). The role of customer engagement in building consumer loyalty to tourism brands. *Journal of Travel Research*, *55*(1), 64–78.

Taheri, B., Hosany, S., Altinay, L. (2019). Consumer engagement in the tourism industry: new trends and implications for research, *Service Industries Journal*, *39*(7–8), 463–468.

Trainor, K.J., Andzulis, J.M., Rapp, A., Agnihotri, R. (2014). Social media technology usage and customer relationship performance: a capabilities-based examination of social CRM. *Journal of Business Research*, *67*(6), 1201–1208.

Vivek, S.D., Beatty, S.E., Morgan, R.M. (2012). Customer engagement: exploring customer relationships beyond purchase. *Journal of Marketing Theory and Practice*, *20*(2), 122–146.

Wang Y., Po L.H., Chi R., Yang Y. (2004). An integrated framework for customer value and customer-relationship-management performance: a customer-based perspective from China. *Managing Service Quality: An International Journal*, *14*(2–3), 169–182.

Wang, Y., Rod, M., Ji, S., Deng, Q. (2017). Social media capability in B2B marketing: toward a definition and a research model. *Journal of Business and Industrial Marketing*, *32*(8), 1125–1135.

Willems, K., Brengman, M., Van Kerrebroeck, H. (2019). The impact of representation media on customer engagement in tourism marketing among millennials. *European Journal of Marketing*, *53*(9), 1988–2017.

20. Digitization of word-of-mouth

Kulvinder Kaur Batth

INTRODUCTION

Word-of-mouth advertising is a platform where the consumer is central. A platform which allows consumers to share their experiences, opinions, perceptions and attitudes. Digitization of word-of-mouth has not only expanded its scope but also broadened the approach into a far more intensive advertising strategy. It is a collaboration with an existing marketing trend known as experiential marketing. Marketing strategies aim at providing a memorable and enriched experience to consumers, whether it is a vacation tour, a resort, a restaurant or a product. Experiential marketing sounds more realistic and truthful, and has a story-telling approach. Moreover, consumers do not associate word-of-mouth with marketing gimmicks or promotional propaganda, but see it as a genuine effort toward sharing personal experiences. Word-of-mouth marketing is a positive and well-accepted trend. It provides a set of information that works well with the different trends in the field of advertising, and a forum which completes the consumer's research toward a product or a service.

Apparently, over time, consumers developed a perception that products endorsed by the celebrities were not actually used by them, leading to a sense of discontent and distrust. Consumers developed an impression that these celebrities avoid actual usage of the products in their real lives, and only act as brand endorsers for purely monetary incentives. Further, they felt that the marketing companies were only interested in more sales and profits.

Evolution of Digital Word-of-Mouth Advertising

Over a period, as the digital landscape unfolded, several spaces widened, creating platforms for consumers to share product reviews with their fellow consumers. This developed a positive sentiment among the masses and the trend snowballed. It further flourished among a large number of internet and social media users, who grabbed this opportunity. A large number of people started sharing their ideas and product experiences on these open platforms. The sharing of ideas initially began with few review statements and photos, and then expanded to videos and recommendations.

It became an opportunity for companies to capitalize upon and increase their profits. Marketers encouraged consumers to share, comment and post about their product or service experiences on various social media platforms. Additionally, the opportunity attracted many consumers due to financial incentives. Several brands created pages on social media platforms to engage and involve their consumers through different ways and means, and publicized these pages to gain momentum.

The word-of-mouth advertising on the internet became popular, and companies thought of capitalizing more in this area by luring their customers with rewards for product or service referrals. The rewards were distributed through cashback, offers, discounts, free gifts, coupons and many more such innovative gestures.

WORD-OF-MOUTH PUBLICITY

Word-of-mouth publicity is a combination of emotions, attributes and recommendations. It can also be termed an experiential approach. In an experiential approach, consumers share their experiences with others through different modes. The approach is popular across different demographics and socio-economic backgrounds, and across geographic boundaries.

Word-of-mouth publicity is also termed 'new age' marketing. Traditional buying decisions were based on gathering information about the products or services from family members, friends or sometimes acquaintances. The method was limited in approach, as often the prospective buyers could not gather all the required information to complete their buying process. On the contrary, the world of the internet was limitless. The online platform catered to all the needs of prospective buyers in the form of information concerning products and services. Consumers gather all the required information within a fraction of a second, with the click of a button. More so, the information is not limited to known sources. The most prominent example of word-of-mouth publicity is the research which prospective buyers do while reading the reviews on the online websites. These reviews aid customers in analysing their buying decisions, considering the positive as well as negative aspects. Word-of-mouth publicity thus is more associated with the promotion of products by consumers, and for consumers.

Evolution of Word-of-Mouth Publicity

Word-of-mouth publicity is also termed consumer-generated advertising. Since it is initiated by consumers, prospective buyers do not associate it with monetary gains and consider it to be a more genuine approach (Campbell et al., 2014). Also, for consumers, it is much easier to connect with a fellow consumer, rather than believing in celebrities or models. Word-of-mouth publicity evolved from the product discussions and forums that initially began for the exchange of information, and slowly evolved as systematic platforms for consumers to share their experiences. Numerous brands – such as Dove, Nestlé, Cadbury, Airtel, and so on – have capitalized upon word-of-mouth in their advertising campaigns.

The idea appeared unexpectedly profitable to many companies, especially e-commerce giants. Therefore, it was incorporated in their selling strategies by encouraging consumers to write reviews for the products. Several brands, such as Amazon, have focused on affiliate marketing programmes, a strategy that is a win–win for companies and consumers. Consumers are rewarded for their product recommendations, referrals and write-ups. Thus, based on the views or referrals of particular products or services, consumers are rewarded with cash or vouchers. Moreover, in these promotions the consumers offer a coupon code, shared by the company, to the prospective buyers, which ultimately becomes a win–win for all parties.

Word-of-Mouth Publicity versus Celebrity Endorsement

Word-of-mouth publicity is more connective, relative to the prospective buyers. The promoters of word-of-mouth publicity are considered as the actual users of the product and thus their experiences add a lot of value in the consumers' buying decisions. Celebrity endorsement, though widely popular, lacks the same associations and perceptions of reality in its promotion, from the perspective of consumers. On one hand, celebrity endorsement attracts attention and engages the audience; whereas on the other hand it draws resentment from the audience. The audience feels that the endorsers never actually use the products they endorse. These advertisements are considered as purely profit-making gimmicks. In contrast, word-of-mouth publicity is deemed a genuine approach that attempts to make a connection with the audience.

Celebrities are paid large sums for their product or the service endorsements. Mostly, they have fixed contracts lasting a set period of time with the brands for product endorsements. Celebrity endorsements have been considered to be powerful, to the extent that people start associating the product with the celebrity. These advertisements are impactful, effective and noticeable. The established brands have the habit of using extensive marketing strategies using celebrities to reach out to their customers.

Celebrity endorsements are much more impactful, especially with children and young adults. Celebrities have huge fan followings, especially among children and young people, who tend to follow their favourite celebrities in terms of their choices, personality or lifestyles. This is so to such an extent that these youngsters follow their favourite celebrities as role models in terms of outfits, grooming, make-up, accessories, lifestyle, and so on. The celebrity ads are watched more, and lead to high viewing figures among the audience. These advertisements are more noticed, and therefore they carry high retention value.

In contrast, word-of-mouth publicity is effective and impactful in its approach. Also, there is a greater element of trust, confidence and association, which adds value. As a result, big brands have introduced the monetary element to word-of-mouth publicity to make the most of it.

Association with E-Commerce

In e-commerce, reviews have evolved, grasped a large amount of space, and have a significant impact on potential buyers in their decision-making process. E-commerce platforms have emerged as the stage for the word-of-mouth publicity. These platforms have witnessed immense scope for open communication networks. They have supported and created business-to-business (B2B), business-to-customer (B2C), customer-to-business (C2B) and customer-to-customer (C2C) levels. The C2C platforms have emerged as networking spaces, which have garnered open discussions, brainstorming and supplied many research inputs.

Word-of-mouth publicity has been transformed in the C2C platform: a platform where customers can engage with their prospective counterparts, by sharing user-specific product-related reviews, and experiences concerning products and services, which they have bought and used themselves.

It is a platform where customers can learn about the hands-on experiences of their counterparts, and these are considered trustworthy and reliable as the reviews are neither paid-for nor sponsored. The customers feel that whatever is written about the products or services is genuine and not a marketing gimmick. These reviews are taken seriously and customers base their decisions on these reviews.

Over time, many companies have started capitalizing on these platforms. The customers are encouraged to refer the products or services to their friends or family members, and in return both parties receive a discount or cash back from the company.

E-commerce has extended to accommodate word-of-mouth publicity by officially designing a space and promoting the reviews. Advertising is seen as only focusing on positive aspects and inflated claims, while word-of-mouth publicity on the other hand provides a discussion on both positive and negative aspects. Thus, the open-ended discussion is an unbiased and fair approach for prospective buyers to make a decision.

Transformation of Word-of-Mouth Platforms

Over a time, as the new advertising trends evolved, word-of-mouth publicity also expanded. The transformation of the word-of-mouth publicity from local to global has been miraculous. No one could ever have imagined that this platform would emerge and expand so widely. The jump from local to global has been extraordinary and unimaginable. Word-of-mouth publicity has evolved and transformed from verbal expressions, to written communication which is shared, liked and commented about on various platforms. The broader online landscape has captured the essence of word-of-mouth publicity, whether it is social media, e-commerce portals, search engines, emails, videos, blogging platforms, influencers, and so on.

The online world and marketing companies have been successfully using affiliate marketing programmes. The biggest secret of success for these famous programmes has been attributed to the power of word-of-mouth publicity. Word-of-mouth publicity adds value, especially when provided by the influencers, the popular bloggers, YouTubers, Instagrammers and many other people trending on the social media platforms.

The suggestions of these influencers, or their recommendations, play a large role in increasing the sales and reach of the products and services. These famous bloggers and bloggers have millions of followers, subscribers and viewers who consistently watch, share, post or comment on their updates.

The influencers have wide reach and impact among their audiences. They are the ones to whom the consumers connect and associate with most strongly. Their product recommendations make a much larger impact than those of celebrity endorsements. Influencers opt for affiliate marketing programmes and promote products or services. These products and services are ones which they themselves use in their videos. The videos both send a message, and have a profit motive. Influencers rule over a surprisingly large number of markets through their fan bases in the form of subscribers and followers. Influencers have become stars on social media platforms, and their fan bases have been widening day by day. The combined effect of suggestions and recommendations given in the videos is reflected in the consumer's decision-making process.

Soft Appeal vis-à-vis Word-of-Mouth

Hard appeal and soft appeal are the two categories of popular advertising. Compared to hard appeal, soft appeal is considerably more in use, and widely effective. Word-of-mouth publicity uses soft appeal. In the time of the coronavirus pandemic, fear, anxiety, panic and a sense of urgency have grown. The psychology of hoarding due to uncertainty has emerged. Due to this situation, buying motives are filled with fear, anxiety, necessity, urgency and, even more so, there is a focus on hygiene. The bulk buying and huge demand has led to price rises for products and services, leaving a situation of stock-outs and enormous panic.

Interestingly, word-of-mouth publicity, whether positive or negative, has a strong impact, as evident in buying behaviour, especially when led by rumours. Further, it has gained a large amount of authority due to the widening landscape of interactive platforms.

Numerous examples in the past have showcased how the emotions of fear, anxiety or panic can turn the tide for the best of brands with a history of market stability. For example, a small rumour about ICICI bank in India going bankrupt led to large queues outside every branch of the bank in the country, leading to a large amount of uncertainty and fear among the public. Nestlé also faced a similar problem when the fear spread of its products being adulterated; information snowballed from friends to family members to relatives, acquaintances, and so on. As a result, a product that people had enjoyed since their childhood was suddenly taken off the shelves, showcasing the strong impactful approach of word-of-mouth publicity. The impact was so powerful and long-lasting that it took around two years for consumers to revive their good memories and welcome the product back into their lives. Word-of-mouth is sharp, concise and has an instant cause-and-effect relationship, which is directly quantifiable in the sales of the product.

Virtual Word-of-Mouth Publicity

The virtual world has overpowered the physical world, whether for businesses, professionals or people's personal lives. The constant pestering and interventions in the digital spaces have become the 'new normal' trend. Our lives from dawn to dusk are constantly revolving around these digital platforms. Further, these platforms have silently intervened and acquired an immense space in our lives. The presence and participation on these platforms have no demographic, geographic or social boundaries.

The virtual platforms are the spaces which help companies, all the stakeholders and especially the prospective consumers to voice their opinions in a fair and unbiased manner. Customers share their insights, views and perspectives concerning the products and services. The word-of-mouth platform incorporates paid and unpaid forms of communication. It generates a great sense of trust and faith in the minds of the audience. Word-of-mouth publicity has led to the incorporation of customers' opinions and ideas.

The digital platforms gave birth to virtual communities, bringing like-minded people closer together to share their opinions and perceptions. The virtual communities evolved and extended their reach across the masses. They emerged as strong helping hand in developing a sense of community. Moreover, virtual brand communities play a significant role in creating and building brand satisfaction among prospective customers. Not every brand has realized and recognized the power of virtual brand communities. Certain brands have showcased greater participation in the virtual brand communities, compared to others which have either ignored or undermined the power of such forums. When the active participation of the brands compared to non-active participation in the virtual brand communities, it depicted a significant difference. The story of the brand Zara could be an example for illustration (Royo-Vela and Casamassima, 2011). Different communities of brands exist across several social media platforms; Facebook is an example, with its pages and communities. These communities create a sense of belonging and ownership, as people with similar interests join together on a virtual platform and share their issues as well as their experiences.

THE PANDEMIC

The coronavirus pandemic has presented enormous challenges for individuals, sectors and countries. It has impacted upon both products and services. The virus led to an enormous shifting of attention towards health, hygiene and protection. The word of mouth publicity by doctors has been via various platforms, whether news channels or advertisements, or other platforms focused on the importance of hygiene, protection and care. Topical advertisements have resulted in a surge in sales, and corresponding price rises of sanitizers, masks and a range of hygiene-related products.

Whether it is social media or any other platform, the attention is largely focused toward soaps, hand-washing campaigns, liquid cleaners, cleaning agents and sanitizers. Sanitizers and all types of germ cleaners have become an important part of all marketing strategies. Every other advertisement is vocal about health and hygiene-related aspects. Similarly, on social media platforms, health and hygiene have surpassed all other selling points. The continuous push toward sanitizers is seen in every other sanitizer advertisement. The word-of-mouth publicity generally is also more focused towards hygiene, cleanliness, handwashing, disinfectants, floor cleaners, and so on. This scenario has made sanitizers the most necessary product, especially in a country such as India, where it was formerly deemed a sophisticated product, not used by the masses.

Companies selling handwash or soaps or cleaning agents have been capitalizing through their topical advertisements and making mass appeals in their hygiene campaigns. For example, brands such as Dettol, Savlon, Lifebuoy, Dove and Nivea have joined the mass awareness campaigns to showcase their social responsibility and to fulfil the demand created by the need of the hour. Marketing strategy is also targeted at grabbing the rising demand of the market. Word-of-mouth publicity is actively participating in these health and hygiene-oriented campaigns. The trend is visible when celebrities, actors, sportspersons, politicians, media personalities and social media influencers have been pushing the need for health and hygiene in all campaigns.

Word-of-Mouth in the Present Times

Word-of-mouth creates new customers, with shorter sales cycles, provides detailed information and strategies of branding for the marketers (Subramanian, 2018). Word-of-mouth is happening everywhere, but it has strong links with social media marketing. The main motivators for people in creating a social media presence is in presenting their views on social media platforms. They voice their opinions in order to become powerful social media influencers.

Word-of-mouth publicity is happening when your friend visits a restaurant and shares the positive experience that they had, in terms of service, food, hygiene, quality or staff. Similarly, when your friend watches a good movie and recommends it to everyone through their social media page, it is also termed word-of-mouth publicity.

On the same lines the Travel Industry Association in the United States has accepted that friends and family members play an important role in influencing the travel destinations of individuals. Most travel plans, rental plans, car rentals, hotel bookings, sight-seeing, adventure trips or flight bookings are undertaken based on advice by friends or family members.

Event management businesses and wedding planners, for example, consider every guest as a potential customer or someone who may recommend them to others. Thus, every possible effort is made to satisfy the guests and provide an experience for customers to remember in order to lure them back. Similarly, when people attend a wedding, a positive experience will lead them to consider the venue and service for their family weddings. Likewise, when children are invited to theme-based birthday party memories, they carry the same expectation to their parents to provide them with similar experiences.

Word-of-mouth publicity has been used as a recruitment resource, as mentioned in a study conducted among 612 potential applicants to the Belgian Defense Forces (Hoye and Lievens, 2009).

The internet is a platform where consumers communicate and influence each other. Word-of-mouth publicity is a social communication strategy. It is also known as opinion leadership or 'buzz', a platform where opinion leaders share their views about products or services (Goldsmith, 2008).

Word-of-mouth publicity is popular in the hospitality sector. The views and opinions concerning a holiday trip, a tour or a resort not only count as memories, but also communicate experience, which consumers use to inform their future trips as well. Similarly, in restaurants where the motivating factors have created memorable experiences for consumers, in terms of food, ambience, service, hygiene, quality, food or other parameters, consumers like to relive such wonderful moments. In fact, they tend to share their travel memories with their friends or acquaintances, which lay the path for a word-of-mouth publicity. Moreover, due to social media, the trends of sharing posts of their lavish holidays or delicacies have become popular, which is a non-verbal way of promoting a restaurant or a resort experience through social media posts. A research study conducted among 400 respondents in Hong Kong, involving the influencing factors in travel decisions, depicted that tour leaders' services, food quality and management of the trip each play a significant role in a travel agency's reputation (Heung, 2008).

Word-of-mouth publicity is an outcome of consumer perception of equitable recovery programmes by online brand communities. This study depicts the role of word-of-mouth in a successful recovery programme (Awa et al., 2016). According to a study by Nielsen (2021), 92 per cent of the people trust recommendations from friends and family over any other type of advertising. 'Trust, encouraged by social media, significantly affects the intention to buy. Therefore, trust has a significant role in ecommerce by directly influencing to buy and indirectly influencing perceived usefulness' (Hajli et al., 2014).

Traditional word-of-mouth has transformed into reviews. Reviews play a dynamic role in the prospective buyer's research before making buying decisions. This platform is ever expanding, as an increasing number of consumers are taking part due to the monetary incentives. Texas Tech Research has indicated that 83 per cent of satisfied customers are willing to refer to a product or service, but only 29 per cent actually do. Therefore, referral rewards play a larger role by motivating customers to refer products or services either to their contacts or on social media pages. In the earlier days of many startups such as Zomato, Swiggy, Uber, Ola, Paypal, Grofers, Google Pay, and many other e-commerce brands, they offered cash back or reward points to consumers for their recommendations to their contacts (Slater, Top Rank Marketing).

Companies and their marketing teams know very well that it is worth rewarding their customers for referrals, as this brings down the cost of advertising and is much more cost-effective compared to advertising expenses. Further, if the customer recommends the product or service to ten friends or family members, and out of those ten, five may end up buying the product.

Research from Twitter claimed that 49 per cent of people agreed that they rely on recommendations from influencers while making their purchase decisions. Netflix is a brand known for its word-of-mouth marketing. Viewers post their opinions on a series, which they have binge-watched within the first few hours of launching. These recommendations build curiosity among many, and encourage them to indulging themselves in the fun and excitement. Similarly, Facebook challenges posed amongst friends lead to huge word-of-mouth publicity on social media pages. In addition, the gaming industry is also using enormous word-of-mouth publicity strategies to reach out to similar age groups and to spread the word across the networks. The gamers complete a particular level in these games, and then share the results on social media pages, which pose a challenge for their friends to compete and outshine their peers. Thus, the chain of challenges and the sharing on the social media pages continue from one person to another, and the companies capitalize on the broad network chains.

Digitization of Word-of-Mouth Publicity

Emerging changes in word-of-mouth advertising are visible in their scope and reach. The difference is the penetration of word of mouth publicity from one family member to another or from one friend to another, to social media platforms. Also, the change is in the commercialization of social media, due to demand and the changing times. The revenues are attractive to the influencers, thus giving social media an edge over the earlier scope of word-of-mouth. People initially adopted social media as a hobby and shared their views on social media pages, but as the traffic increased, this turned out to be a profitable venture.

The commercialization of word-of-mouth led to the spread of its wings on all the social media platforms or to the gaming portals leading to challenges and recommendations. Nowadays, this is also known as gamification, a source of engaging your community members. These platforms host discussions, develop forums and enhance brainstorming sessions where people from different backgrounds participate in active dialogues.

COVID-19 has introduced the Indian masses to online education, which would otherwise have taken a long time to develop. Every other school, college and educational platform has initiated online education to engage learners in these challenging times. The trend has further expanded among the enterprises offering online courses to professionals. Several young professionals have been making the best of the lockdown period by upskilling and training themselves through a range of certification programmes. The word-of-mouth publicity has been visible in the professional platforms and virtual communities, where people share their certifications among friends and across groups with a sense of achievement, as well to encourage their counterparts in enrolling in these courses. The certifications provide information on the one hand, and on the other hand they create a zeal and passion for many others to upskill themselves.

CONCLUSION

Word-of-mouth publicity is the new active trend for advertising and promoting product and services. It has enormous scope to be carried forward in the future. Word-of-mouth publicity has high popularity due to its reach and exposure, and can be used to earn more profits.

Further, it is a comprehensive approach and it is pervasive. It encompasses in its scope numerous media platforms and audiences. Moreover, this platform bears a large amount of trust, faith and is considerd to be genuine when compared to other platforms which are considered as only profit-making forums.

It can be concluded that word-of-mouth publicity should be further explored and innovated. The trust, lack of bias, and fairness of this approach can be creatively analysed and further enhanced. The increased scope of this platform would be a great venture for companies, consumers and prospective buyers.

REFERENCES

Awa, H.O., Ukoha, O., and Ogwo., E. (2016). Correlates of justice encounter in service recovery and word of mouth publicity. *Cogent Business and Management, 3*(1). https://doi.org/10.1080/23311975 .2016.1179613.

Campbell, C., Cohen, J., and Ma, J. (2014). Advertisements just aren't advertisements anymore: a new typology for evolving forms of online 'advertising'. *Journal of Advertising Research, 54*(1), 7–10. https://doi.org/10.2501/JAR-54-1-007-010.

Goldsmith, R.E. (2008), *Electronic Word of Mouth, Electronic Commerce: Concepts, Methodologies, Tools, and Applications*. IGI Global.

Hajli, N., Lin, X., Featherman, M., and Wang, Y. (2014). Social word of mouth: how trust develops in the market. *International Journal of Market Research, 56*(5), 673–689. https://doi.org/10.2501%2FIJMR -2014-045.

Heung, V.C.S. (2008), Effect of tour leaders service quality on agency's reputation and customer's word of mouth, *Journal of Vacation Marketing, 14*(4), 305–315. https://doi.org/10.1177 %2F1356766708094752.

Hoye, G.V., and Lievens, F. (2009), Tapping the grapevine: a closer look at word of mouth as a recruitment source, *Journal of Applied Psychology, 94*(2), 341. https://psycnet.apa.org/doi/10.1037/ a0014066.

Nielsen (2021). Consumer trust in online, social and mobile advertising grows. Nielsen.com. Retrieved 7 March 2021, from https://www.nielsen.com/in/en/insights/article/2012/consumer-trust-in-online -social-and-mobile-advertising-grows/.

Royo-Vela, M., and Casamassima, P. (2011). The influence of belonging to virtual brand communities on consumers' affective commitment, satisfaction and word-of-mouth advertising. *Online Information Review, 35*(4), 517–542. https://doi.org/10.1108/14684521111161918.

Subramanian, K.R. (2018). Social media and the word of mouth publicity. *International Research Journal of Advanced Engineering and Science, 3*(2), 95–100.

21. Digital content marketing practices and implementation in the tourism industry

Pramita Gurjar, Rahul Pratap Singh Kaurav and K.S. Thakur

INTRODUCTION

The emergence of information technology has made it easy to deliver information at a faster rate, which ultimately speeds up the marketing practices in the business world. Today, the organisation that can provide the right information at the right time to its consumers has an edge over the others. Content has always been the central point around which all marketing strategies revolve. Everyone is marketing content directly or indirectly, and information technology works as a stimulant in this process. State-of-the-art technology enhances the chances of success in content marketing.

When information technology came into existence, it revolutionised the way businesses were run; and most importantly, when the internet came, it opened up new opportunities for organisations. The internet gave them speed and made it possible to reach anywhere on the globe without being there. Although many organisations made online appearances through websites, at that time these websites were not much more than online brochures (Li and Wang, 2010; Özturan and Roney, 2004; Wang and Russo, 2007). Then came another revolution, called Web 2.0. It put the creation and dissemination of content within everyone's reach. This resulted in the rise of social media, user-generated content and the other various internet-aided developments. Social media engenders the concept of digital content marketing, which is still developing. Although technological advancements have always contributed to web developments, an increase in digital literacy among people is also contributing to such development (Amaral et al., 2014). The timeline in Figure 21.1 shows the evolution of information technology and the emergence of digital content marketing.

Digital Content Marketing

Content marketing simply means providing consumers with valuable content blended with product information. When it is done digitally, it is called digital content marketing (DCM). Content marketing is focused on storytelling; it does not persuade consumers to buy the product directly. For example, if a company wants to tell the consumers that it is the best, it is advertising; but when it describes the reason behind why it is the best, then it is content marketing (Kee and Yazdanifard, 2015). One of the views on digital content marketing is that it is the marketing of digital content, and some refer to it as the digital goods business (Holliman and Rowley, 2014;). Further, content marketing focuses on helping rather than selling (Holliman and Rowley, 2014). Content marketing is considered ideal as it unobtrusively attracts consumers towards the brand (Du Plessis, 2017). It is based on authentic brand

Figure 21.1   *Evolution of digital content marketing*

Table 21.1   *DCM features*

Digital content marketing (DCM)	Authors
It is a digital goods business	Holliman and Rowley, 2014; Rowley, 2008
It focuses on helping instead of selling	Holliman and Rowley, 2014
Unobtrusive	Du Plessis, 2017
Based on authentic brand stories	Du Plessis, 2017

stories, and social media platforms serve as the facilitators in this process (Du Plessis, 2017). Table 21.1 summarises the features of DCM.

What is Content?

Content is the main subject or the idea of something that can be produced in written or verbal form. It can be in the form of a picture, video or audio. When content is uploaded on a digital platform, it becomes digital content (Holliman and Rowley, 2014). Hence, whatever we market is ultimately the content (Holliman and Rowley, 2014). Organisations need to provide appropriate and engaging content that can pull consumers towards the brand (Holliman and Rowley, 2014). Content must be useful to the audience, as it is likely that the content may have minimal mention of the product but focus more on what the consumers are looking for (Holliman and Rowley, 2014). Content that has visual effects such as photos and videos, and is task-oriented rather than self-oriented, is most likely to receive consumer engagement (Barger et al., 2016). In some studies, it has been found that consumers can ignore the quality of content if they find it amusing and educational (Barger et al., 2016). Sometimes consumers determine whether the content is interesting or not by looking at the opinion of others. Consumers hardly share content that they find by themselves, but if they receive it from others they share it more frequently (Barger et al., 2016). Figure 21.2 illustrates the desirable features of content.

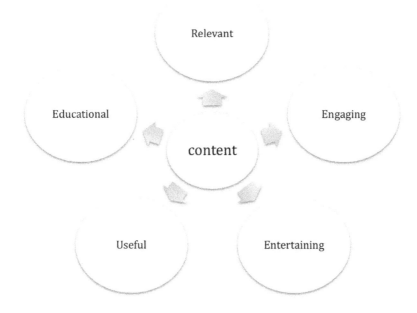

Figure 21.2   Content features

DIGITAL CONTENT MARKETING PRACTICES THROUGH SOCIAL MEDIA

Social media plays a key role in the facilitation of digital content marketing. It provides a platform that is easy to use, and where not only marketers but also consumers are involved in the creation and dissemination of content. One of the benefits of social media is its flexibility in the way content is shared. It allows the content to be shared in various formats such as audio, video and text. Social media and content marketing are different concepts, although it has been seen many times that the terms are used interchangeably (Du Plessis, 2017). Hence, more clarity is needed on what content marketing is and how it is different from social media marketing. One of the differences between social media marketing and content marketing is that social media marketing is more propagative and intrusive than content marketing (Du Plessis, 2017). Instead of only informing about the new products, content marketing is used to make connections with consumers (Du Plessis, 2017). Marketing through social media provides a much larger community to promote products and services online, which was not possible in traditional channels (Du Plessis, 2017). Content marketing through social media improves brand awareness, increases customer loyalty and also help in market research, idea generation and reputation management (Amaral et al., 2014). Hence, adopting social media has become necessary for tourism organisations; and not only adoption, but also correctly using them is equally essential. The following are the steps in digital content marketing practices (see also Figure 21.3).

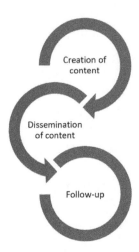

Figure 21.3   Digital content marketing process

Creation of Content

Good-quality content is essential for an influential content marketing. So, the creation of content is the first step in the digital content marketing process. In order to provide relevant and useful content, it is necessary to understand the target audience (Du Plessis, 2017). To keep the audience engaged with the brand, consistent and interactive content has to be delivered (Du Plessis, 2017). Many social media platforms facilitate the creation of content. Social media is a tool. If used effectively, it can make the content marketing strategy successful. It has been found that if visual effects are added to the content, it is more influential on the target audience (Kee and Yazdanifard, 2015). Co-creation with consumers can provide value to the products and contributes to making an excellent relationship with the consumers.

Further, it builds trust among consumers that keeps them loyal to the brand (Kee and Yazdanifard, 2015). Review sites facilitate interaction and the opinion-sharing by tourists about a destination and the services available there, which may foster positive word-of-mouth and help in establishing goodwill for the destination (Amaral et al., 2014). Social media provides various platforms for content creation that can be used depending on what type of content we wish to create. The content creation can broadly be classified into two categories that are further divided into subcategories. These are as shown in Table 21.2.

Table 21.2   Classification of content creation

User-generated content	Organisation-generated content
Review sites	Websites
Blogs	Online advertisements
YouTube	Social media page
Facebook	
Twitter	

Dissemination of Content

On the internet, consumers look for content that is useful and gives personalised experience (Kee and Yazdanifard, 2015). Hence, to provide this personalised experience, some sites give consumers the option to respond to the content individually and privately, and to share that with other members having a common interest (Kee and Yazdanifard, 2015). In this way, companies can reach the desired target audience. There is a need to understand when to pull consumers towards the content, and when to push content towards the consumers. Compelling content can drag consumers to the website, and once they reach the website, content can be pushed to the consumers via email (Rita, 2000).

Furthermore, newsletters carrying industry news can be sent via email, which keeps the consumers in touch with the company and can build trust, develop brand awareness and bring prospective consumers (Rita, 2000). A website is an excellent medium for an organisation to disseminate content. So, it should be done in such a way that it provides content which appeals to the numerous motivations of the visitors and could result in more visitor-to-consumer conversions (Rita, 2000). The following are some methods that help in the dissemination of content.

Viral marketing

Content in any form, whether audio, video or written, can be disseminated through viral marketing. Viral marketing influences consumer perception, attitude and behaviour, and can be a crucial element in an organisation's promotional mix (Woerdl et al., 2008). Any message going viral indicates the success of content marketing. Content that triggers emotion has a high possibility to become viral. The more people relate to it, the more it is shared with others (Kee and Yazdanifard, 2015). One of the advantages of viral marketing is that it is relatively less expensive and can reach a large number of viewers in a short period (Woerdl et al., 2008).

Online word-of-mouth

Word-of-mouth, whether positive or negative, has a significant influence on the behaviour of consumers, but it has been seen that a negative word-of-mouth has a greater tendency to influence the consumer's decision in comparison to positive word-of-mouth (Woerdl et al., 2008). Online or elecronic word-of-mouth (eWOM), also called viral marketing, is considered more compelling, penetrating and faster as compared to traditional word-of-mouth communication. Where in the traditional word-of-mouth there are chances of bias and manipulation of the information, in eWOM the content remains the same no matter how many times it gets transferred (Woerdl et al., 2008).

Search engine optimisation

Search engine optimisation (SEO) is a technique that brings a website to the top of the search results presented by a search engine, upon entering particular keywords (Yalçın and Köse, 2010). The steps taken by an organisation to improve its position on the search engine result list are search engine optimisation (Berman and Katona, 2013). The technique of search engine optimisation works on the keywords that describe the website and its content (Yalçın and Köse, 2010). Search engines are the websites that classify and present other websites based on their relevant keywords and content. It is data-collecting software that collects data from other sites (Yalçın and Köse, 2010). Search engine optimisation is less expensive in com-

Table 21.3   DCM practices through social media

Creation		Dissemination	Follow-up
User-generated content (UGC)	Organisation-generated content (OGC)	Viral marketing Online word-of-mouth (eWOM)	Content reaching the desired audience or not
Review sites	Websites	Search engine optimisation (SEO)	Measuring the quality of content
Blogs	Online advertisement		Reaching market segments to foresee
YouTube	Social media pages		strength and weaknesses
Facebook			
Twitter			

parison to that of internet advertising. For effective SEO implementation, straightforward and precise content is preferable. Also, the flash animations, frames and unnecessary keywords that are on the website but are irrelevant to the users should be avoided. New, useful and original content is the key to successful search engine optimisation (Yalçın and Köse, 2010). In terms of trustworthiness, consumers trust the websites that appear in the search results more than paid advertisements. There are enormous opportunities for organisations to present their content to the audience when they search for the specific keywords, and for that they need to use the technique of search engine optimisation.

Follow-Up

Only creating and disseminating the content does not get the desired results; it is also necessary to know whether the content is reaching the target audience or not. Hence, follow-up is an essential step in the content marketing process (Table 21.3). Some websites such as YouTube give the viewers an option to rate and comment that helps to measure the quality of the content (Woerdl et al., 2008) To know the performance of the website of an organisation, evaluation is necessary (Li and Wang, 2010). It must be ensured that the website is being updated and is providing accurate information about the destination (Li and Wang, 2010). Blogs also help organisations to reach market segments and anticipate the strengths and shortcomings of a destination (Akehurst, 2009).

Much user-generated content is available online, and it depends on the intelligence of the organisations how they make it useful for themselves (Akehurst, 2009). The information shared on social media is considered more reliable in comparison to the information provided by the organisations themselves. Therefore, they need to strategise wisely on using social media as it can impact upon their market value (Alves et al., 2016).

Whether it is user-generated content or organisation-generated content, it should be created by keeping in mind the platform on which it will be uploaded, as for each platform the requirement of content is different. For example, funny, beautiful and inspiring content can be uploaded on Facebook and Twitter; but the content should be more informative in the case of a newsletter or an email (Barger et al., 2016; Holliman and Rowley, 2014).

Table 21.4   DCM implementation in the tourism industry

Techniques	Authors
Experimenting with new techniques	Aspasia and Ourania, 2014
Community-building	
The authenticity of the content	
Tracking and monitoring the interactions on social media	Aspasia and Ourania, 2014
Be a publisher	Holliman and Rowley, 2014
Building trust	Holliman and Rowley, 2014
Making content culturally relevant to consumers	Kee and Yazdanifard, 2015
Localisation and translation of content	
Appropriate and accurate content	
Incentivising people who are influential and interested in the brand	Kumar and Mirchandani, 2012
Marketing through blogs	Akehurst, 2009
Using search engine optimisation (SEO)	Berman and Katona, 2013

IMPLEMENTING DIGITAL CONTENT MARKETING IN THE TOURISM INDUSTRY

Organisations should not hesitate to experiment with new techniques when the opportunity arises. Marketers need to learn the role of a publisher to be an efficient content marketer. They need to tell a different, better brand story compared to their competitors (Holliman and Rowley, 2014). The content marketing strategy should focus on community-building by allowing consumers to participate in the creation of content; and at the same time the authenticity of the content should be kept in mind (Aspasia and Ourania, 2014). Building trust among consumers is the key to the success of content marketing, and their participation can help in building this trust (Holliman and Rowley, 2014). Further, while implementing content marketing, it should be kept in mind that the content is culturally relevant to consumers. In order to do this, localisation and translation of content is essential to make it more understandable to the consumers. Also, it has to be appropriate and accurate to maintain the consumers' interest in the brand (Kee and Yazdanifard, 2015). Research supports that companies adopt culturally bound content marketing strategies instead being neutral for all cultures, as it helps consumers to better understand the brand (Zotos et al., 2014). Another thing that can be done for effective content marketing is incentivising people who are both famous and impressed with the product. In order to know how much influence a person has among the audience, an important value can be calculated through metrics (Kumar and Mirchandani, 2012). Content can be marketed through blogs which, along with the information, provide excellent networking opportunities. Blogging needs continuous updating and new and exciting content every time (Akehurst, 2009). Organisations can track and monitor the interactions among consumers on social media that can help them in understanding the likes and dislikes of the consumers, which ultimately help organisations to take anticipatory actions accordingly (Aspasia and Ourania, 2014). In a study conducted with tripadvisor.com, it was found that viewing other tourists' comments and reading travel blogs was the most prominent activity (Akehurst, 2009). Hence, content provided by the consumers about a product or service in the form of online reviews can be beneficial for the company. Table 21.4 summarises DCM implementation in the tourism industry.

Table 21.5   Problems in DCM implementation

Problems	Authors
Lesser familiarity and opportunity to learn new technologies	Buhalis, 1998; Sigala et al., 2001; Lee and Wicks, 2010
The negative perception of employees towards technology	Lee and Wicks, 2010; Sigala et al., 2001
Need for proper training	Lee and Wicks, 2010
Traditional mindset focuses on selling	Holliman and Rowley, 2014
Difficulty in tracking and coordinating a large number of social media platforms	Barger et al., 2016
Poor implementation of DCM	Aspasia and Ourania, 2014

Problems in Digital Content Marketing Implementation

Keeping up with the new and updated technology is necessary in order to be successful in every industry, and especially in the tourism industry as it is information-based. Still, there are many DMOs that are neither familiar with the new technologies, and nor do they have the opportunities to learn about them (Lee and Wicks, 2010; Buhalis, 1998; Sigala et al., 2001). One of the problems in digital content marketing implementation is the perception of DMO employees that learning new technologies is complicated, and so it should be done by the technology professionals. Also, they find it costly, especially the small and medium-sized DMOs (Lee and Wicks, 2010; Sigala et al., 2001). Hence, there is a need for proper training of the employees on web-based technologies and hardware-based technologies (Lee and Wicks, 2010). Also, particular content can be developed in order to educate DMOs.

Further, the marketing personnel with a traditional marketing mindset still focus on selling (Holliman and Rowley, 2014). It has been found that despite a dramatic increase in the usage of social media platforms, there has been less corresponding increase in consumer–brand engagement. One of the reasons for this can be the vast and varied number of social media platforms that make it hard to trace and coordinate the efforts put in by the organisation (Barger et al., 2016). In many organisations, marketing personnel are not accustomed to social media technology, and hence they either ignore or poorly apply the content marketing strategies in their organisation (Aspasia and Ourania, 2014). Table 21.5 summarises problems in digital content marketing implementation.

CONCLUSIONS

Content is the basis of all marketing practices. Ultimately, all organisations are executing content marketing, either online or offline. In this chapter, we have shed light on digital content marketing practices and how they are being implemented in the tourism industry. This chapter has focused on the three necessary steps that make the digital content marketing process complete: the first being the creation of content; and then secondly, disseminating it; and in the third step, it is ensured that the strategy which has been adopted or the platform that has been chosen is reaching its target audience, and the response of the audience and what corrective measures to be taken are taken into account.

Social media is being used as a digital content marketing tool. Consumer-generated content is widely available on social media, which plays a vital role in the decision-making process of travellers regarding a destination (Hays et al., 2013). Social media provides a platform where people can have conversations in the form of text, images, videos and audios (Hays et al., 2013). It has also been found that marketers do not find social media sites useful in the case of business-to-business (B2B) marketing (Lacka and Chong, 2016; Michaelidou et al., 2011).

For a successful digital content marketing strategy, first of all, content should be appropriate, accurate and authentic. It must build trust among consumers. Further, the content should be culturally relevant to the consumers so that they can better understand it. Blogs and SEO are other techniques that can help implement digital content marketing strategies. However, there are several problems in the implementation process, such as sometimes employees are not familiar with these technology-based marketing practices, and hence they either ignore or resist them. There is a need for proper training because, at times, poor implementation of digital content marketing creates problems.

Although this chapter contributes to the theoretical aspects of digital content marketing practices and provides a base for future researches, there are various aspects that need to be addressed. First of all, there is a confusion between the terms 'content marketing' and 'social media marketing' which future research may focus on, to give more clarity on these concepts. Another issue is about the credibility of online content, where more research needs to be done. There is a need to develop some criteria to measure the credibility of online content so that consumers could find out what content to believe and could recognise authentic sources.

REFERENCES

Akehurst, G. (2009). User-generated content: the use of blogs for tourism organisations and tourism consumers. *Service Business*, *3*(1), 51.

Alves, H., Fernandes, C., and Raposo, M. (2016). Social media marketing: a literature review and implications. *Psychology and Marketing*, *33*(12), 1029–1038.

Amaral, F., Tiago, T., and Tiago, F. (2014). User-generated content: tourists' profiles on Tripadvisor. *International Journal of Strategic Innovative Marketing*, *1*(3), 137–145.

Aspasia, V., and Ourania, N. (2014). Social media adoption and managers' perceptions. *International Journal on Strategic Innovative Marketing*, *1*, 61–73.

Barger, V., Peltier, J.W., and Schultz, D.E. (2016). Social media and consumer engagement: a review and research agenda. *Journal of Research in Interactive Marketing*, *10*(4), 268–287.

Berman, R., and Katona, Z. (2013). The role of search engine optimization in search marketing. *Marketing Science*, *32*(4), 644–651.

Buhalis, D. (1998). Strategic use of information technologies in the tourism industry. *Tourism Management*, *19*(5), 409–421.

Du Plessis, C. (2017). The role of content marketing in social media content communities. *South African Journal of Information Management*, *19*(1), 1–7.

Hays, S., Page, S.J., and Buhalis, D. (2013). Social media as a destination marketing tool: its use by national tourism organisations. *Current Issues in Tourism*, *16*(3), 211–239.

Holliman, G., and Rowley, J. (2014). Business to business digital content marketing: marketers' perceptions of best practice. *Journal of Research in Interactive Marketing*, *8*(4), 269–293.

Kee, A.W.A., and Yazdanifard, R. (2015). The review of content marketing as a new trend in marketing practices. *International Journal of Management, Accounting and Economics*, *2*(9), 1055–1064.

Kumar, V., and Mirchandani, R. (2012). Increasing the ROI of social media marketing. *MIT Sloan Management Review*, *54*(1), 55.

Lacka, E., and Chong, A. (2016). Usability perspective on social media sites' adoption in the B2B context. *Industrial Marketing Management*, *54*, 80–91.

Lee, B.C., and Wicks, B. (2010). Tourism technology training for destination marketing organisations (DMOs): need-based content development. *Journal of Hospitality, Leisure, Sports and Tourism Education (Pre-2012)*, *9*(1), 39.

Li, X., and Wang, Y. (2010). Evaluating the effectiveness of destination marketing organisations' websites: evidence from China. *International Journal of Tourism Research, 12*(5), 536–549.

Michaelidou, N., Siamagka, N.T., and Christodoulides, G. (2011). Usage, barriers and measurement of social media marketing: an exploratory investigation of small and medium B2B brands. *Industrial Marketing Management, 40*(7), 1153–1159.

Özturan, M., and Roney, S.A. (2004). Internet use among travel agencies in Turkey: an exploratory study. *Tourism Management, 25*(2), 259–266.

Rita, P. (2000). Web marketing tourism destinations. *ECIS 2000 Proceedings*, 120.

Rowley, J. (2008). Understanding digital content marketing. *Journal of Marketing Management, 24*(5–6), 517–540.

Sigala, M., Airey, D., Jones, P., and Lockwood, A. (2001). Multimedia use in the UK tourism and hospitality sector: training on skills and competencies. *Information Technology and Tourism, 4*(1), 31–39.

Wang, Y., and Russo, S.M. (2007). Conceptualizing and evaluating the functions of destination marketing systems. *Journal of Vacation Marketing, 13*(3), 187–203.

Woerdl, M., Papagiannidis, S., Bourlakis, M.A., and Li, F. (2008). Internet-induced marketing techniques: critical factors in viral marketing campaigns. *Journal of Business Science and Applied Management, 3*(1), 35–45.

Yalçın, N., and Köse, U. (2010). What is search engine optimization: SEO? *Procedia – Social and Behavioral Sciences, 9*, 487–493.

Zotos, Y., Chatzithomas, N., Boutsouki, C., and Hatzithomas, L. (2014). Social media advertising platforms: a cross-cultural study. *International Journal on Strategic Innovative Marketing, 1*(2), 74–90.

22. The influence of e-WOM via social media platforms on e-Reputation and the selection of tourist destinations

Prerana Baber, Robert L. Williams Jr and Helena A. Williams

INTRODUCTION

Word-of-mouth (WOM) has traditionally been understood as oral communication from and between users (consumers) regarding attributes of the services or products that a company offers. The term 'word-of-mouth' was defined in early literature as 'the act of exchanging marketing information among consumers' (Katz and Lazarsfeld, 1955, p. 180). Customers disseminate WOM information for two specific reasons: (1) their purchase expectations are met or exceeded and they in turn are motivated to influence others by spreading positive WOM (Maxham and Netemeyer, 2002; Sweeney et al., 2005); or (2) their purchase expectations were not fully met and they experienced anger or frustration, which in turn motivated them to engage in negative word-of-mouth among family members, relatives and peer groups (Oliver, 2014; Sweeney et. al., 2005). Word-of-mouth is generated on personal experiences and is considered the most reliable and trustworthy information (Murray, 1991).

As the internet permeates our societies, the use of social communication has increased and WOM marketing has grown exponentially (Hennig-Thurau et al., 2004). Unlike mass communication that is focused on the company distributing a message to their perceived overall market, social communication via the internet has the power to directly connect current and potential consumers as they share views, experiences and opinions (Schiffman and Kanuk, 2000). Additionally, social communication also provides the company with valuable information directly from their consumers, which contributes to rapid and responsible policy making and product and service improvement (Kiecker and Cowles, 2001).

The revolutionary evolution of WOM is attributed to the worldwide adoption of digital platforms and internet technologies (Zhang et al., 2013; Goldenberg et al., 2001). The internet has become a basic tool for e-commerce and also a reliable source to generate information directly from consumers, which can be used as an opportunity to attract potential customers (Donation, 2003; Baker and Green, 2005). Internet shopping has become an essential part of today's e-generation lifestyle and is being integrated into new paradigms for boosting the economy. It also allows potential customers to easily acquire the information they need before buying a product or service; a most important factor of online buying behaviour (Bellman et al., 1999). Digital markets play crucial roles in contemporary consumer buying behaviour (Kozinets, 1999).

Elecronic word-of-mouth (e-WOM) is a broader concept with a wider range than traditional WOM, and can be defined as: 'Any positive or negative statement made by potential, actual or former customers about a product or company, which is made available to a multitude of people and institutions via the Internet' (Hennig-Thurau et al., 2004, p. 39). It generates information from and between friends, families and peer groups, magnified by their social media activities. E-WOM is not limited to circulating only between people who know each other; e-WOM collects and transmits information across the world between strangers as well (Chu and Kim, 2011). Thus, e-WOM collected from social media platforms has become critical (not incidental) data for marketers (Flynn et al., 1996; Williams et al., 2014). Successful companies create brand promises that are strongly influenced by consumer e-WOM; these brand promises that are co-created in partnership with e-WOM contributors and eventually co-marketed (via new e-WOM messages) are clearly linked to the company's reputation and are drivers for strategic marketing plans (Williams et al., 2014).

Researchers have begun to investigate the reputation of an organisation based upon the impact of e-WOM and digital transformation (Shamma, 2012). Castellano and Dutot (2013) suggest that the excess use of internet and social media involvement transforms reputation to 'e-Reputation', and customers' perceptions created via digital platforms directly affect the image of an organisation. Social media influences the Millennial travellers' decision-making and it has become an important element in choosing the tourist destination (Kasim et al., 2019). When any traveller posts their pictures on social media, not for self-actualisation, but to influence others through reviews, articles, and blogs regarding a tourist destination and their visit or visit intention, other users of social media are influenced as they impulsively choose their own tourist destinations (Malik et al., 2016). Specifically, online information generated from others' experiences was reported as more trustworthy for the purpose of selecting a holiday destination in comparison to official websites and travel agents' information (Fotis et al., 2011).

CONCEPTUAL FRAMEWORK OF VARIABLES AND HYPOTHESIS DEVELOPMENT

e-WOM and Tourist Destination Visit Intention

Information gathered by online reviews regarding hotels, destinations, activities and local cuisine has become important for travellers (Pan et al., 2007); with the help of electronic platforms, individuals share their opinions and experiences which can affect (influence) others' decisions (Xiang and Gretzel, 2010). According to one study, approximately 84 per cent of travellers were affected by online reviews when they were planning to travel (Travelindustrywire.com, 2007). Millions of travellers consult online reviews, and WOM has positively and negatively affected tourism products (Tripadvisor.com, 2011). Online reviews strongly influence decisions regarding online sales (Govers et al., 2007). Online reviews help travellers make decisions when they choose a tourist destination, and are a good source of information for travellers as well as travel service providers (Vermeulen and Seegers, 2009). Researchers confirm that e-WOM is considered a significant tool that gathers online information, and also influences travellers in their choice of destination and their visit intention (Chung et al., 2015; Yun and Good, 2007; Jalilvand and Samiei, 2012b). Another study indicates that e-WOM positively influences the attitude of travellers in their choice of destination (Jalilvand and Samiei, 2012a). The impact of e-WOM on choice of destination is significant; this customer-driven information can help destination managers create positive images by publicising destination-specific attributes to enhance the travellers' visit intentions (Lewis and Chambers, 1989). Likewise, e-WOM can help tourism business operators quickly identify and ameliorate any negative qualities that tourists mention about the destination (Morgan et al., 2003). Yet, despite acknowledgement of the prevalence and the importance of e-WOM, studies which isolate and confirm e-WOM attributes that impact upon actual tourists' destination selection are sparce. Hence, the first research goal of this study is to identify the level of impact e-WOM has on tourists' visit intention to specific tourist destinations. The hypothesis is as follows:

H1: e-WOM significantly affects tourist destination selection.

E-WOM and e-Reputation

E-Reputation has multiple components and is derived from many sources. Importantly, in the digital world, the image of an organisation that is projected via one or multiple digital platforms equates to the company's e-Reputation: 'reputation as a state of awareness, reputation as an assessment and reputation as an asset' (Barnett et al., 2006, p. 32). E-Reputation is the strategic upgradation of reputation in the field of marketing and tourism. Reputation is influenced by the excessive use of social media platforms (Douyère and Sosthé, 2014). At the present time, any organisation can develop its own website providing a wide range of information about the products and services offered and other job-related information. These websites can also provide Information relevant to potential investors, as well as a great deal of general information. The internet and social media have offered a plethora of communication opportunities. Most of the companies using a virtual platform for their trading and for presenting themselves on the web help to create their own e-Reputation (Chun and Davies, 2001). To maintain their e-Reputation, companies adopt reputation management systems which are helpful to answer customers' complaints and reviews. Companies adopt social media platforms and rapidly react to the customers' queries. Companies actively monitor all the activities and analyse all the reviews and comments, to create a good e-Reputation. It has become a dynamic concept and also an interactive process where customers give their feedback publicly on the digital platform (Brennan and Merkl-Davies, 2018). In the tourism industry specifically, it can be difficult for a company to satisfy its customer's expectations regarding intangible products. When any customer posts a negative or positive review of a hotel, restaurant, or the services of a travel company, the comment directly targets the reputation or image of the company (Eisend, 2004).

In many instances the customer's perceptions of the organisation's image or reputation is based almost exclusively on e-WOM (Shamma, 2012). In such instances, reputation might be considered an antecedent of e-WOM (Castellano and Dutot, 2017). One empirical study suggested a link between e-WOM and e-Reputation, and identified eight separate components of e-WOM that positively affect e-Reputation (Castellano and Dutot, 2017). However, studies that examine the relationship that exists between e-WOM and e-Reputation are limited. Hence, the second goal of this study is to measure the affect that e-WOM has on e-Reputation. The second hypothesis of this study is:

H2: e-WOM significantly affects the e-Reputation of a destination.

RESEARCH METHODOLOGY

Data Collection and Sampling Design

Quantitative methods were used for the research. The sample was selected using a non-probability judgemental sampling technique. The population was selected from India. Primary data was obtained by distributing an online survey questionnaire to respondents who indicated that they actively participated on social media platforms such as Instagram, Facebook, Snapchat, YouTube and Twitter. Tourism-related activities were the prime items under investigation. In total, the instrument was shared with 250 respondents, out of which 216 valid responses were collected. The response rate was 86 per cent. The basic aim of the research is to identify the impact e-WOM had on the respondents' visit intention to a specific tourist destination, and their impression of the e-Reputation of the destination. All of the measurement items were adapted from scales used in similar studies which were proven reliable and valid for confirming the content validity of this study (Dutot and Castellano, 2015; Van Der Veen and Song, 2014; Bambauer-Sachse and Mangold, 2011; Baber et al., 2020). Figure 22.1 summarises the proposed research model.

Measurement Scales

The objective of this study is to determine the relationship between e-WOM and tourist destination visit intention, and e-WOM and e-Reputation. The questionnaire of 25 questions was prepared in two sections: (1) demographic information on the respondents; and (2) questions related to e-WOM, e-Reputation and visit intention. The format of the questionnaire utilised a seven-point Likert-type scale, ranging between 1 for strongly disagree and 7 for strongly agree. The survey consisted of three demographic questions and 22 Likert-style questions related to the research goals.

Table 22.1 presents the constructs and the measurement items that were used in this study. The e-Reputation construct was divided into four subsets each with three or five items (see appendix for the full survey questionnaire).

Completed questionnaires were received from the 216 respondents, of which 68.5 per cent were male and 31.5 per cent were female (Table 22.2). Regarding age, 74.1 per cent were

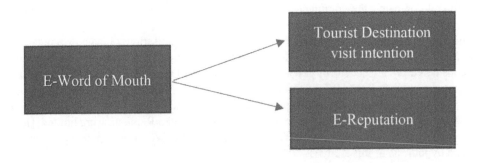

Figure 22.1   The proposed research model

Table 22.1   Source of instrument

S. No	Construct	Items	Reference
1	e-WOM	5	Bambauer-Sachse and Mangold (2011)
2	e-Reputation	3	Dutot and Castellano (2015)
	Online brand characteristics	3	
	Quality of website	5	
	Quality of online service	3	
	Social media		
3	Intention to visit	3	Van Der Veen and Song (2014)

Table 22.2   Sample profile

		N	%
Gender	Male	68	31.5
	Female	148	68.5
Education	Undergraduate	83	38.4
	Postgraduate	111	51.4
	Others	22	10.2
Age group	18–25 years	160	74.1
	26–35 years	36	16.7
	36–45 years	14	6.5
	46 years and above	5	2.7
N = 216			

between 18 and 25 years old, indicating that the majority were Generation Z respondents. A large number of respondents (51.4 per cent), were in the postgraduate category in terms of their educational level.

DATA ANALYSIS AND RESULTS DISCUSSION

The SmartPLS (partial least square) research tool was used to analyse the data within structural equation modelling. This technique was adopted because it is appropriate for small sample sizes, and is suitable for exploratory nature research (Ringle et al., 2015). Furthermore, the SmartPLS is known for its simplicity, and restricted data normality (Chin et al., 2003). SmartPLS analyses the model in two ways: firstly, it calculates reliability and vadility of the model, and secondly, it identifies the structural model (Anderson and Gerbing, 1988). A bootstrap resampling procedure (500 samples) measured the stability of estimates (Roldán and Sánchez-Franco, 2012).

The basic indexes for central tendency (mean, median and standard deviation) and variability are shown in Table 22.3. In this table convergent validity is also presented. Convergent validity includes composite reliability, item reliability (based on the factor loading of the respective constructs) and average variance extracted (AVE). The threshold value is 0.6, and all the factor loadings exceeded the threshold value, thus supporting the convergent validity. Construct validity was determined with the help of Cronbach's Alpha coefficients and composite reliability. The acceptable threshold value is 0.6, and all the values of composite reliability (CR) and Cronbach's Alpha were reported at more than 0.6, thus the convergent

Table 22.3   Item descriptive and convergent validity

Construct	Item	Mean	SD	Loadings	Cronbach's Alpha	CR	AVE
E-REPU	EREPU_OC1	0.703	0.049	0.703	0.934	0.942	0.536
	EREPU_OC2	0.714	0.055	0.713			
	EREPU_OC3	0.675	0.057	0.676			
	EREPU_QOS1	0.778	0.037	0.781			
	EREPU_QOS2	0.633	0.064	0.638			
	EREPU_QOS3	0.664	0.055	0.669			
	EREPU_QOS4	0.716	0.051	0.721			
	EREPU_QOS5	0.754	0.039	0.756			
	EREPU_QW1	0.795	0.034	0.794			
	EREPU_QW2	0.713	0.061	0.718			
	EREPU_QW3	0.747	0.052	0.750			
	EREPU_SM1	0.762	0.039	0.763			
	EREPU_SM2	0.793	0.029	0.794			
	EREPU_SM3	0.755	0.041	0.755			
E-WOM	E-WOM_1	0.764	0.034	0.765	0.801	0.862	0.557
	E-WOM_2	0.830	0.023	0.832			
	E-WOM_3	0.693	0.059	0.696			
	E-WOM_5	0.701	0.057	0.705			
	E-WOM_6	0.724	0.055	0.726			
VISITIN	VISITIN_3	0.728	0.069	0.734	0.740	0.850	0.656
	VISITIN_4	0.877	0.021	0.878			
	VISITIN_5	0.811	0.041	0.810			

Source: Extracted from SmartPLS software and computed by the authors.

validity was supported. Lastly, AVE was measured and values were also reported above the threshold value of 0.5.

Table 22.4 displays how convergent validity was supported. Cross-loading analysis indicated that the items load more on the construct that they measure than on the other constructs, further supporting convergent validity. The indicators which showed the factors cross-loading values (in bold) were >0.5 as recommended by Bagozzi and Yi (1988). Additionally, the AVE value for all variables was more than 0.5, which is also acceptable (see Table 22.1).

Table 22.5 depicts discriminate validity of variables using the Fornell–Larcker criterion, where the values for all the variables should be 0.7 or greater. As all the values for the reported variables were more than 0.7, the model has discriminant validity.

Table 22.6 depicts the direct and significant relationship between the variables which were examined in the research study. e-WOM with e-Reputation and Tourist Destination Visit Intention were directly related. E-WOM has a significant and positive effect on the e-Reputation ($r^2 = 0.336$, $\beta = 0.318$, p= 0.000). Social media marketing efforts have significant and positive effect on the Tourist Destination Visit Intention ($r^2 = 0.309$, $\beta = 0.580$, p = 0.000). Thus, both hypotheses were accepted.

Table 22.4   *Convergent validity: cross-loading analysis*

	E_REPU	E_WOM	Visit intention
EREPU_OC1	0.703	0.466	0.518
EREPU_OC2	0.713	0.436	0.486
EREPU_OC3	0.676	0.405	0.427
EREPU_QOS1	0.781	0.372	0.313
EREPU_QOS2	0.638	0.269	0.162
EREPU_QOS3	0.669	0.210	0.307
EREPU_QOS4	0.721	0.387	0.211
EREPU_QOS5	0.756	0.435	0.330
EREPU_QW1	0.794	0.478	0.395
EREPU_QW2	0.718	0.361	0.266
EREPU_QW3	0.750	0.427	0.318
EREPU_SM1	0.763	0.472	0.348
EREPU_SM2	0.794	0.530	0.394
EREPU_SM3	0.755	0.503	0.392
E-WOM_1	0.461	0.765	0.451
E-WOM_2	0.482	0.832	0.442
E-WOM_3	0.353	0.696	0.322
E-WOM_5	0.441	0.705	0.313
E-WOM_6	0.412	0.726	0.273
VISITIN_3	0.274	0.311	0.734
VISITIN_4	0.422	0.466	0.878
VISITIN_5	0.476	0.398	0.810

Source: Extracted from SmartPLS software and computed by the authors.

Table 22.5   *Discriminant validity*

	E_REPU	E_WOM	Tourist Destination Visit Intention
E_REPU	0.732		
E_WOM	0.580	0.746	
Tourist Destination Visit Intention	0.496	0.492	0.810

Source: Extracted from SmartPLS software and computed by the authors.

Table 22.6   *Path coefficients results*

Direct effects	Estimate coefficients	R^2	p-value	Result
H1: EWOM_EREPU	0.580	0.242	0.000	Supported
H2: EWOM_TDVI	0.492	0.337	0.000	Supported

Source: Extracted from SmartPLS software and computed by the authors.

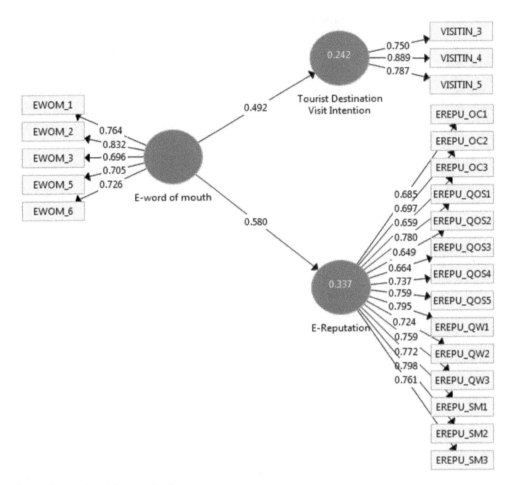

Source: Extracted from SmartPLS software.

Figure 22.2   *The final research model*

Figure 22.2 presents the final research model from the PLS algorithm and includes the values from the entire analysis. It depicts the overall measurement analysis model, the structural analysis, and the R^2 values as they relate to both the outer and inner model. This model explains that the positive relationship between e-WOM, Tourist Destination Visit Intention and e-Reputation. It will determine the extent to which tourists engage in online communication to acquire and analyze information via social media platforms.

DISCUSSION

It seems to be accepted knowledge that digital platforms help tourism organisations to directly interact with their customers using technology. Yet, prior research that investigated the relationship between e-WOM and tourists' visitor intent, or e-WOM and e-Reputation, has been limited. This study closes this gap by generating empirical evidence that solidly links e-WOM within the context of social media users to both tourist visitation intention and travel companies' e-Reputation.

The main objective of the study was to identify the influence of e-WOM on tourist visit intention and e-Reputation. The results of this research indicate a significant relationship between e-WOM and e-Reputation, and between e-WOM and tourist visit intention, in the context of social media (Jalilvand and Samiei, 2012b; Malik et al., 2016; Castellano and Dutot, 2017). Findings of the study reveal that tourists engage in online communication to acquire and analyse information via social media platforms. The study reveals that information exchanged (comments, blogs, reviews) on social media platforms accurately reflects consumers' views and practices regarding selection of destination and its e-Reputation. Online reviews affect tourists' perspectives and impact upon the choice of a destination (Kasim et al., 2019; Fotis et al., 2011). The findings of this study further confirm that e-WOM contributes to e-Reputation across online brand characteristics, quality of website, quality of online service and social media with e-WOM (Castellano and Dutot, 2017).

An organisation's success depends upon the growing relationship of consumers' peer-to-peer communications, and that between consumers and the organisation's digital platforms (Chu and Kim, 2011). This research confirms that online reviews influence visits to specific tourist destinations as well as the overall e-Reputation of an area's tourism industry. The partial least squares structural equation modelling (PLS-SEM) results of this study verify that the visit intention of tourists is positively affected by e-WOM, and that the available online reviews influence the attitude of the tourist. Such e-comments also directly influence the actions of potential consumers (Malik et al., 2016). Hence, the findings of this study could be effectively utilised by the tourism industry to improve competitive advantage.

LIMITATIONS OF THE STUDY AND FUTURE RESEARCH POTENTIAL

Even though the data was collected from Tier II cities, the geographical area was restricted. A large number of respondents from the sample size are the younger social media users between the ages of 18 and 25, so it is probable that they may have different attitudes, and travel practices, than older users of social media. Also, the sample size was limited. The result would be stronger with a larger sample size.

The study has created insights for further research. Future researchers are encouraged to conduct studies that examine e-WOM using different constructs and variables such as brand image, brand promises, and online communication between consumers and the business. Further studies are suggested to determine the effect of negative e-WOM on tourist visit intention and e-Reputation. Studies should also be conducted to better understand the risk of using social media platforms, and the risk and rewards of using social media platforms in marketing strategies.

CONCLUSION

The results of this research confirm the impact of social media on tourist visit intention and its influence on their decision-making process. Potential travellers take advantage of all available online information as a basis to make their decisions to visit particular destinations. With the help of online reviews, travellers can collect an abundance of relevant information to help them select their next travel destination. Companies which routinely monitor their own and their competitors' social media presence will be better positioned to incorporate the types of amenities and activities that attract prospective travellers to their consumer-informed (co-created) brand promise through consequential strategic cyber-marketing, and paying attention to e-Reputation based upon individual e-messages regarding consumers' intent to travel. These are critical markers for travel and tourism businesses as they craft authentic brand promises and strategic marketing plans aimed at retaining existing consumers and attracting new customers. Maintaining a strong, positive social media presence is no longer just an option, it is the communication key to sustainable and responsible tourism.

REFERENCES

Anderson, J.C., and Gerbing, D.W. (1988). Structural equation modeling in practice: A review and recommended two-step approach. *Psychological Bulletin*, *103*(3), 411.

Baber, R., Upadhyay, Y., Kaurav, R.P.S., and Baber, P. (2020). Application of 'masstige' theory and approaches for the marketing of smartphone brands in India. *International Journal of Business and Emerging Markets*, *12*(3), 296–312.

Bagozzi, R.P., and Yi, Y. (1988). On the evaluation of structural equation models. *Journal of the Academy of Marketing Science*, *16*(1), 74–94.

Baker, S., and Green, H. (2005). Blogs will change your business. *Business Week*, *3931*(5), 56–67.

Bambauer-Sachse, S., and Mangold, S. (2011). Brand equity dilution through negative online word-of-mouth communication. *Journal of Retailing and Consumer Services*, *18*(1), 38–45.

Barnett, M.L., Jermier, J.M., and Lafferty, B.A. (2006). Corporate reputation: The definitional landscape. *Corporate Reputation Review*, *9*(1), 26–38.

Bellman, S., Lohse, G.L., and Johnson, E.J. (1999). Predictors of online buying behavior. *Communications of the ACM*, *42*(12), 32–38.

Brennan, N.M., and Merkl-Davies, D.M. (2018). Do firms effectively communicate with financial stakeholders? A conceptual model of corporate communication in a capital market context. *Accounting and Business Research*, *48*(5), 553–577.

Castellano, S., and Dutot, V. (2013). Analogies and contrasts between e-Reputation and reputation: A social media perspective. *Revue Française du Marketing*, *243*, 35–51.

Castellano, S., and Dutot, V. (2017). Investigating the Influence of e-Word-of-Mouth on e-Reputation. *International Studies of Management and Organization*, *47*(1), 42–60.

Chin, W.W., Marcolin, B.L., and Newsted, P.R. (2003). A partial least squares latent variable modeling approach for measuring interaction effects: Results from a Monte Carlo simulation study and an electronic-mail emotion/adoption study. *Information Systems Research*, *14*(2), 189–217.

Chu, S.C., and Kim, Y. (2011). Determinants of consumer engagement in electronic word-of-mouth (eWOM) in social networking sites. *International Journal of Advertising*, *30*(1), 47–75.

Chun, R., and Davies, G. (2001). E-reputation: The role of mission and vision statements in positioning strategy. *Journal of Brand Management*, *8*(4), 315–333.

Chung, N., Han, H., and Joun, Y. (2015). Tourists' intention to visit a destination: The role of augmented reality (AR) application for a heritage site. *Computers in Human Behavior*, *50*, 588–599.

Donation, S. (2003). Marketing's new fascination: Figuring out word of mouth. *Advertising Age*, *74*(46), 18.

Douyère, C., and Sosthé, F. (2014). e-Reputation management and strategic business development using web 2.0 tools: The case of the hotel industry. In M.M. Mariani, R. Baggio, D. Buhalis, and C. Longhi (eds), *Tourism Management, Marketing, and Development* (pp. 99–112). New York: Palgrave Macmillan.

Dutot, V., and Castellano, S. (2015). Designing a measurement scale for e-reputation. *Corporate Reputation Review, 18*(4), 294–313.

Eisend, M. (2004). Is it still worth it to be credible? A meta-analysis of temporal patterns of source. *Advances in Consumer Research, 31*(5), 352–357.

Flynn, L.R., Goldsmith, R.E., and Eastman, J.K. (1996). Opinion leaders and opinion seekers: Two new measurement scales. *Journal of the Academy of Marketing Science, 24*(2), 137–147.

Fotis, J.N., Buhalis, D., and Rossides, N. (2011). Social media impact on holiday travel planning: The case of the Russian and the FSU markets. *International Journal of Online Marketing, 1*(4), 1–19.

Goldenberg, J., Libai, B., and Muller, E. (2001). Talk of the network: A complex systems look at the underlying process of word-of-mouth. *Marketing Letters, 12*(3), 211–223.

Govers , R., Go, F.M., and Kumar, K. (2007). Promoting tourism destination image. *Journal of travel research, 46*(1), 15–23.

Hennig-Thurau, T., Gwinner, K.P., Walsh, G., and Gremler, D.D. (2004). Electronic word-of-mouth via consumer-opinion platforms: What motivates consumers to articulate themselves on the internet? *Journal of Interactive Marketing, 18*(1), 38–52.

Jalilvand, M.R., and Samiei, N. (2012a). The effect of word of mouth on inbound tourists' decision for traveling to Islamic destinations (the case of Isfahan as a tourist destination in Iran). *Journal of Islamic Marketing, 3,* 330–334.

Jalilvand, M.R., and Samiei, N. (2012b). The impact of electronic word of mouth on a tourism destination choice: Testing the theory of planned behavior (TPB). *Internet Research, 22*(5), 591–612.

Kasim, H., Abdurachman, E., Furinto, A., and Kosasih, W. (2019). Social network for the choice of tourist destination: Attitude and behavioral intention. *Management Science Letters, 9*(13), 2415–2420.

Katz, E., and Lazarsfeld, P. (1955). *Personal Influence.* Glencoe, IL: Free Press.

Kiecker, P., and Cowles, D. (2001). Interpersonal communication and personal influence on the internet: A framework for examining. *Internet Applications in Euro Marketing, 25*(8), 65–71.

Kozinets, R.V. (1999). E-tribalized marketing? The strategic implications of virtual communities of consumption. *European Management Journal, 17*(3), 252–264.

Lewis, R.C., and Chambers, R.E. (1989). *Marketing Leadership in Hospitality. Foundations and Practices.* New York: Van Nostrand Reinhold.

Malik, A., Dhir, A., and Nieminen, M. (2016). Uses and gratifications of digital photo sharing on Facebook. *Telematics and Informatics, 33*(1), 129–138.

Maxham III, J.G., and Netemeyer, R.G. (2002). Modeling customer perceptions of complaint handling over time: The effects of perceived justice on satisfaction and intent. *Journal of Retailing, 78*(4), 239–252.

Morgan, N.J., Pritchard, A., and Piggott, R. (2003). Destination branding and the role of the stakeholders: The case of New Zealand. *Journal of Vacation Marketing, 9*(3), 285–299.

Murray, K.B. (1991). A test of services marketing theory: Consumer information acquisition. *Journal of Marketing, 55*(1), 10–25.

Oliver, R.L. (2014). *Satisfaction: A Behavioral Perspective on the Consumer.* Routledge. https://doi.org/10.4324/9781315700892.

Pan, B., MacLaurin, T., and Crotts, J.C. (2007). Travel blogs and the implications for destination marketing. *Journal of Travel Research, 46*(1), 35–45.

Ringle, C., Da Silva, D., and Bido, D. (2015). Structural equation modeling with the SmartPLS. *Brazilian Journal of Marketing, 13*(2). https://ssrn.com/abstract=2676422.

Roldán, J.L., and Sánchez-Franco, M.J. (2012). Variance-based structural equation modeling: Guidelines for using partial least squares in information systems research. In M. Mora, O. Gelman, A. Steenkamp, and M. Raisinghani (eds), *Research Methodologies, Innovations and Philosophies in Software Systems Engineering and Information Systems.* IGI Global, pp. 193–221.

Schiffman, L.G., and Kanuk, L.L. (2000). *Consumer Behavior,* 7th edn. New York: Prentice Hall.

Shamma, H.M. (2012). Toward a comprehensive understanding of corporate reputation: Concept, measurement and implication. *International Journal of Business and Management, 7*(16), 151–169.

Sweeney, J.C., Soutar, G.N., and Mazzarol, T. (2005). The difference between positive and negative word-of-mouth – Emotion as a differentiator. In *Proceedings of the ANZMAC 2005 Conference: Broadening the Boundaries*, pp. 331–337.

Travelindustrywire.com (2007). Consumers are changing your brand and reputation. Retrieved from: / http://www.travelindustrywire.com/arti

Tripadvisor.com (2011). Retrieved from: /http://tripadvisor.comS.

Van der Veen, R., and Song, H. (2014). Impact of the perceived image of celebrity endorsers on tourists' intentions to visit. *Journal of Travel Research*, 53(2), 211–224.

Vermeulen, I.E., and Seegers, D. (2009). Tried and tested: The impact of online hotel reviews on consumer consideration. *Tourism Management*, 30(1), 123–127.

Williams, H., Williams, R., and Omar, M. (2014). Gastro-tourism as destination branding in emerging markets. *International Journal of Leisure and Tourism Marketing*, 4(1), 1–18.

Xiang, Z., and Gretzel, U. (2010). Role of social media in online travel information search. *Tourism management*, 31(2), 179–188.

Yun, Z.S., and Good, L.K. (2007). Developing customer loyalty from e-tailstore. *Managing Service Quality*, 17(1), 4–22.

Zhang, Z., Guo, C., and Goes, P. (2013). Product comparison networks for competitive analysis of online word-of-mouth. *ACM Transactions on Management Information Systems (TMIS)*, 3(4), 1–22.

APPENDIX

Table 22A.1   Full survey questionnaire

Construct name	Items
E-Word of mouth	I often read other tourists' online travel reviews to know what destinations make good impressions on others.
E-Word of mouth	To make sure I choose the right destination, I often read other tourists' online travel reviews
E-Word of mouth	I often consult other tourists' online travel reviews to help choose an attractive destination.
E-Word of mouth	I frequently gather information from tourists' online travel reviews before I travel to certain destination.
E-Word of mouth	When I travel to a destination tourists' online travel reviews make me confident in travelling to the destination.
E-Reputation	Based on the social media messages my perception of the tourist destination is good.
E-Reputation	Based on the social media messages the interaction of the tourist destination on social media is good.
E-Reputation	I have a positive view on the online representation of the tourist destination.
E-Reputation	I expect the quality of the tourist destination website to be good.
E-Reputation	I expect the quality of the tourist destination website is user-friendly.
E-Reputation	I expect that the design of the tourist destination website satisfies my requirements.
E-Reputation	I expect that the online experience (information and photographs) will be improved.
E-Reputation	I expect that the tourist destination website will be user-friendly without defaults and blockades.
E-Reputation	I expect the service of tourist destination website to be safe and reliable.
E-Reputation	I expect that the users' interest are central to the tourist destination website.
E-Reputation	I expect that employees will handle customers with care after purchasing a package from tourist destination website.
E-Reputation	I expect that the interactions with the desired tourist destination website are high on social media.
E-Reputation	I expect that the desired tourist destination is present on social media.
E-Reputation	I expect that the number of likes, reactions on social media channels/messages of this tourist destination are high.
Intention to Visit	I would choose desired tourist destination as the destination from my next holidays.
Intention to Visit	I intend to visit desired tourist destination in the near future.
Intention to Visit	I would prefer to visit desired tourist destination as opposed to other similar destinations.

23. Do you believe? Online reviews and dark tourism: a sentiment analysis approach

Brent McKenzie

INTRODUCTION

'Research suggests that people heed negative reviews more than positive ones – despite their questionable credibility' (Beaton, 2018); 'When and how managers' responses to online reviews affect subsequent reviews' (Wang and Chaudhry, 2018). The growing influence of online reviews have been demonstrated to be an opportunity and/or a challenge. This is particularly true for service-oriented businesses, such as tourism and hospitality (Schuckert et al., 2015). But what is the impact of online reviews for specific types of tourism? The focus of this chapter is to analyse the impact of online reviews to the emerging sector of dark tourism. Dark tourism, as defined by Sharpley and Stone (2009), is 'the act of travel to sites associated with death, suffering and the seemingly macabre'. Dark tourism is growing in both supply and demand, while also receiving mixed support in terms of issues such as its authenticity, morality, ethics and marketability (Stone et al., 2018). Unlike more traditional leisure tourism, dark tourism sites and attractions are often successful due to people's morbid curiosity, but often experience a lack of support from traditional tourism boards, and local governmental groups (McKenzie, 2013). Thus, this chapter examines the impact of online reviews of dark tourism, as they pertain to two groups. The first is the provider/operator of such sites, and the second is the local stakeholders such as the aforementioned tourism boards and destination marketing groups.

In order to explore the impact of online reviews on these two groups, this chapter takes a sentiment analysis approach. Sentiment analysis, or the process of understanding the sentiment or opinion of a given text (Liu, 2012), has been utilized from a number of perspectives, particularly in the fields of product development and testing (Mirtalaie et al., 2017), and customer experience management (Bilro et al., 2019). This chapter extends this area of study to the field of dark tourism. The context for this analysis is dark tourism sites and attractions in the Baltic states of Estonia, Latvia and Lithuania. The reasons for the selection of these three countries are twofold. The first is that each country has a number of sites and attractions relating to dark tourism, such as Soviet atrocity museums, for example the Museum of Occupations and Freedom Fighters in Vilnius, Lithuania (http://genocid.lt/muziejus/en/); as well as 'irreverent' ones such as Communist kitsch tours, for example the KGB Shooting Package in Tallinn, Estonia (http://www.funintallinn.com/tour/kgb-shooting-package/). The second reason is that each country has had to make extensive use of destination branding activities since their joint independence from the Soviet Union in 1991, and to develop of country brand identities (Hall et al., 2006).

This chapter aims to contribute to the growing field of dark tourism literature by offering critical insights on the economic and political impact of online reviews as they relate to the growth of the Estonian, Latvian and Lithuanian brands. This chapter will also advance the understanding of the value of online reviews as they relate to more controversial aspects of tourism. The findings would be of interest to tourism operators, tourism boards and other governmental tourism stakeholders regarding the value of tracking online reviews and the resulting action plans to benefit from them, or to challenge them.

The format of the chapter is as follows. It first provides a high-level review of the dark tourism literature and how dark tourism continues to represent a growing field of tourism interest. Next, it looks at the increasing importance and relevance of social media and online reviews to the success (and challenges) of tourism sites and attractions in general, and then for dark tourism sites and attractions specifically. The main portion of the chapter follows with an in-depth analysis of dark tourism sites in the Baltic States of Estonia, Latvia and Lithuania, and the impact of how their joint, forced incorporation into the Soviet Union during the second half of the 20th century has had a lasting effect on both the tourism industry and country branding activities in each of the countries. In addition, the effect that dark tourism has had on the cultural values and orientation of the people living in these countries with respect to the role of reviews, both historically and in the present, is discussed.

The dark tourism sites and attractions selected for the individual countries are reviewed within the context of Stone's (2006) dark tourism spectrum. As noted by Stone, the 'darkest' sites relate to actual death, authenticity and education; while the 'lighter' sites focus on kitsch and entertainment. The chapter concludes with a discussion of how online reviews can be utilized by tourism operators, governmental agencies and individual consumers in terms of the potential success or failure of these ventures. There is also a discussion of how dark tourism positively and negatively impacts upon country branding and image for each of the three countries, and the relevance of taking a sentiment analysis approach for this and other forms of tourism research in this region.

THE GROWTH OF DARK TOURISM

There has been a steady growth in the type of travel which is labelled dark tourism. The term was coined in 2000 in a book by Lennon and Foley (2000) of the same name. This type of tourism has continued to grow, as reflected in the increasing number of academic and popular press books and articles on the subject (White and Frew, 2013; Light, 2017; Stone et al., 2018), and the growth in other types of media relating to dark tourism such as movies, television programmes, YouTube sites and video games (Sampson, 2019).

There exists a growing extant literature on the operational aspects of dark tourism, as well as varied positions on the classification of the 'darkness' of sites and attractions (Strange and Kempa, 2003; Stone, 2006). In 2018 the highly respected publisher Palgrave, released its *Handbook of Dark Tourism Studies* (Stone et al., 2018) which includes 30 chapters classified within six sections covering the topic. One of the most highly supported classification perspectives for what sites or attractions would fall into the category of dark tourism is the work of Sharpley and Stone (2009). They define dark tourism as sites or attractions that focus on tourism related to death, destruction and the seemingly macabre. Although this is a somewhat arbitrary definition, it nonetheless provides a context for what types of sites and attractions could be examined to better understand both the demand and supply of this phenomenon.

This definition was used as the basis for the selection of dark tourism sites and attractions for further analysis. The discussion that follows moves the research ahead in terms of the role and impact of sentiment analysis of reviews on these sites, as found in online review websites and other relevant social media settings.

Relevance of Social Media and Online Reviews to Dark Tourism Visitation

The vast growth and influence of online reviews in the area of tourism has coincided with the continual increase in online users of such information (Gretzel and Yoo, 2008). Replacing traditional travel companies in terms of expertise and influence, online sites such as Tripadvisor (www.tripadvisor.com) have seen an increase not only in their use, but also in levels of trust (Sparks and Browning, 2011; Chatterjee, 2001). Although there are a number of studies that have questioned the legitimacy and, more importantly, the independence of these reviews (Kusumasondjaja et al., 2012), there has been a constant focus on reassuring users as to the validity and accuracy of their reviews (Blal and Sturman, 2014).

The aforementioned Tripadvisor, since its inception in 2000, has seen a number of direct competitors, such as www.virtualtourist.com, go out of business. Related sites such as Expedia provide potential tourists with user reviews of organized tours and tourism companies, while the breadth of choice for city and country reviews beyond Tripadvisor has returned to more traditional forms of tourism and travel promotions, travel guides and magazines. Additional sources of information have grown, such as videos on YouTube, and Google's travel site (www.google.com/travel). 'Compensation' is given for those who post reviews: in the case of Google, it provides 'Guide' levels, while Tripadvisor provides 'Badges'. Tripadvisor states that these Badges indicate 'knowledge and expertise', which is objectively highly questionable.

Research has also examined why consumers/travellers trust or do not trust social media reviews of sites and attractions (de Laat, 2005). Research has shown that users of the information from these sites are more likely to trust, and thus utilize, information that relates to leisure sites and attractions (Schuckert et al., 2015). This has been attributed to the fact that online reviews have a greater upside in terms of enjoyment and pleasure in visiting such sites, compared to online reviews of a dark tourism site. The latter attractions may have a higher financial risk trade-off in terms of enjoyment versus cost, as well as sites and attractions from lesser-known geographic locations, be they countries or specific cities.

The use of Tripadvisor-type reviews has been studied from a number of perspectives. For example, Vásquez (2012) utilized an examination of Tripadvisor reviews to improve the understanding of the construct of involvement, while Xie et al. (2016) examined the impact of Tripadvisor reviews on hotel popularity. For sites and attractions that would fall within the realm of dark tourism, the literature focused on Tripadvisor reviews is limited. Çakar (2018) reviewed the posted experiences of people visiting the World War I battlefield of Gallipoli, while Lupu et al. (2017) researched Tripadvisor reviews related to Dracula in Romania. Thus, the field of dark tourism research will benefit from additional studies employing such data sources.

Dark Tourism Sites and Attractions in the Baltic States

The choice of the former Soviet Republics of Estonia, Latvia and Lithuania was based on them being exemplars of nations that have had similar pasts, particularly during the 20th and early 21st centuries, and also countries that have experienced a great deal of hardship, terror, war and suffering (see Misiunas and Taagepera, 1993; Anušauskas, 1999; Kasekamp, 2018). These nations have also had to meet the challenge of redeveloping tourism markets since their joint independence in 1991 (Cottrell and Cottrell, 2015). Although each had a healthy tourism sector during the initial years of independence and freedom in the years between the two World Wars, and each had a non-trivial diaspora tourism market even during the Soviet period, they nonetheless had to develop a tourist infrastructure from scratch in terms of both viable tourist sites and attractions; but often more challenging was the development of a tourism service-focused workforce (Renfors, 2018). Added to these difficulties was the frequent challenge for the three nations in terms of positioning themselves as independent, and unique, travel destinations. This difficulty was driven by the common view by international tourists that there was little difference between the three countries, and they are jointly the Baltic states (Banaszkiewicz et al., 2017).

In terms of dark tourism sites and attractions, the most prevalent examples relate to the Soviet period, and to a lesser extent to the occupation under Nazi Germany that existed between the two periods of forced annexation into the Soviet Union. Thus, of the dark tourism sites and attractions selected for analysis, almost all related to events from these two periods. As noted, there are different shades of dark tourism (Stone, 2006; Strange and Kempa, 2003), and to be able to make the greatest comparisons and contrasts across the three countries, sites were selected that would generally be considered to cover the breadth of dark tourism from darkest to lightest.

The darkest sites, as noted by Stone (2006), would be considered to have the greatest degree of authenticity, in terms of place or educational value. The 'mid-darkness' sites would have lesser degrees of existence of these variables than the 'darkest'; while the third category, the 'lightest', would be best defined by the lack of authenticity and educational focus of the site/ attraction, and more on the level of kitsch, or entertainment, that would be presented to tourists visiting and experiencing these sites.

There is no definitive way to classify a site within Stone's (2006) dark tourism spectrum, but as the author had visited each of these countries on numerous occasions, a breadth of dark tourism examples were selected to best be able to provide the insights and address the aforementioned research question relating to the impact of online reviews of dark tourism as well as country/city branding. The support for this convenience sample selection of the dark tourism sites has been shown to be effective in this form of qualitative research, because the self-selection ensures that the objects of interest can provide a level of insight and analysis based on the research questions of interest (Carson et al., 2001; Marshall and Rossman, 1995).

As noted, the reviews selected for these dark tourism sites and attractions were drawn from their respective Tripadvisor web pages, and were all downloaded for analysis within one hour on the same date, thus allowing for both individual site analysis, within-country site analysis, and cross-country site analysis. For each country, the three capital cities of Tallinn in Estonia, Riga in Latvia and Vilnius in Lithuania are both the most populous and the most visited cities by tourists in their countries. As noted in Maitland and Ritchie (2009), capital cities present themselves as an often difficult market for tourism analysis, due to their presence and impor- tance in terms of governmental focus, but also due to non-tourism visitation (commercial and business tourism). The fact that all three capital cities represented the most visited tourist destination in each of the three countries supports the greatest percentage of dark tourism sites being from each respective capital city.

In total, three dark tourism sites and attractions were selected for each of the three countries. The sites selected are all strong exemplars of dark tourism, as supported by the fact that all have been the focus of, or noted within dark tourism industry, academic or third-party (that is, not country-based) tourism firm literature. The dark tourism sites/attractions are reviewed in the order of Estonia, Latvia and Lithuania, alphabetically by country name, but also going from smallest to largest in terms of both overall country population and geographic size. A selection of the most positive and most critical reviews about each site are reviewed.

Estonia

Due to its location as the most northern Baltic state, Estonia had some advantages over the other two countries in terms of greater access to the West during the Soviet period. Finnish television and radio could be received within the greater Tallinn region, and due to the fact that Finnish and Estonian are related languages, Estonians had a more accurate view of the non-Soviet world during this period. But, as a Soviet Republic, as was generally the case for all Republics of the USSR, Estonian culture was subsumed within the dominant Russian culture and language. This fact can be seen as an additional motivation for the creation of monuments and attractions that focused on this harsh period of oppression, and is reflected in the selection of the three dark tourism sites.

Vabamu Museum of Occupations and Freedom (www.vabamu.ee), which opened in 2003 as the Museum of Occupations, focuses on the two major periods of occupation in Estonia: by the Nazis in 1941–44, and the Soviet Union in 1939–41 and 1944–91. The Museum of Occupations was founded with a large donation from an Estonian diaspora (Haven, 2011). Although privately run, there was official support for the museum from the Estonian government (Tamm, 2013). The museum has represented a source of irritation to the press of the Russian Federation, which views the museum as a propaganda tool of the Estonian government (Burch and Zander, 2010).

In terms of the degree of darkness of the museum, it would be considered on the darker side of Stone's (2006) scale. The museum's displays include photographs, videos and ephemera from the periods of occupation. There is an expectation of education and learning from those that visit. What lessens the degree of darkness is the fact that the physical location of the museum, other than the fact it is in the country of occupation, has no real significance. An additional factor in lessening of the darkness of the museum is the fact that the shop and café sell items that are not purely educational, and can arguably be considered more as kitschy souvenirs (Marcoux, 2017).

The museum was ranked on Tripadvisor in the top 15 per cent of tourist attractions in Tallinn, and over 650 reviews had been posted. What was of interest about the reviews of the museum were those written in the Russian language. A translated Russian example of a positive review acknowledged that Russians may be wary of the content of the museum, but that the way in which it was presented was not from a propaganda perspective:

> very informative place that introduces the hardships that the Estonian people suffered on the way to independence. It is possible that some compatriots from Russia (in particular, connoisseurs of the Soviet regime) could be distorted by some of the highlights, but, in my opinion, we need to think more broadly – even at the beginning of the exposition we were warned that the facts presented were in no way intended to sow any enmity. (Posted August 2019)

In contrast, an example of a critical review did touch on concerns that the museum was overtly biased and designed to criticize Russia and Russians:

> The infamous place for moral reasons, but to someone it may seem interesting. For those who do not know history, it may seem that this is a museum. But in fact, this is another point of anti-Russian and anti-Soviet propaganda. But we must pay tribute, the exhibits may seem interesting, both nostalgic for the older generation, and for young people who can see objects from the life of their fathers and grandfathers. (Posted March 2018)

The second attraction for review is the KGB Museum (https://viru.ee/en/Kgb), which is housed on the top floor of the Viru Hotel, located in Tallinn. The Viru Hotel was the first foreign-built hotel in the Soviet Union (it was built by a Finnish firm), and opened in 1972. The darkness of this site can be attributed to the fact that the floor where the museum is located in the hotel was the actual location where the KGB monitored activity within the hotel during the Soviet period (McKenzie, 2011). The museum can only be visited as part of a guided tour. In a similar vein to the previous museum, the KGB museum has been praised in terms of its authentic setting, based on the inclusion of actual spying devices, furnishings, and so on, from the Soviet period; but again, concern was raised as a fixation on both the oppression as well as the absurdity of the Soviet/Russian actions (McKenzie, 2011). The Tripadvisor ratings rank was similar to that of the Vabamu Museum, but with almost twice as many reviews. Again, the Russian language reviews provide an interesting insight as to how the museum is positioned, versus how Russian speakers interpret the attraction. An example of a negative review was: 'Not a positive experience, a painful, controversial place, I do not even want to call it a museum' (Posted October 2018).

Conversely, in terms of a visitor's expectation of what the museum was to provide, this positive review highlights the degree of authenticity of the attraction: 'It turned out to be somewhat unexpected for me to go back to the USSR. This is a story and everything corresponds to the spirit of that time' (Posted February 2017).

The final dark tourism site reviewed is located in Estonian city of Pärnu. The CCCP Pogenemistoad (Escape Room) (https://pogenemistoad.ee/en/), represented the most irreverent view of the Soviet period, as the Escape Room, although aligning itself with how one could not escape the Soviet Union, is positioned as an entertaining experience, with no focus on authenticity: that is, one could not readily escape from Soviet Estonia, and there were actual consequences of making those attempts. The fact the attraction was located in Pärnu, Estonia's third-largest city, meant that it had fewer reviews, but it was ranked as the second most popular thing to do in Pärnu. There were no negative reviews, and the following represents a typical evaluation:

> If you are passing Pärnu this is for sure one of the places u must pay a visit. Very authentic. We went into the KGB cells and escaped. Nevertheless we all were also little scared we had a great time, working on all the things we had to work out while escaping. (Posted March 2019)

The fact that the location of the Escape Rooms are in Pärnu prison, which closed in 2017, does make the location authentic; but the fact that the visitors are engaged in activities that do not focus on any atrocities or tragic events that may have occurred in the prison results in an example of the lightest form of dark tourism.

Overall, the three dark tourism examples from Estonia provide an insight into how the tragic period of Soviet occupation has been used for both educational, but also entertainment purposes. The fact that the Soviet period ended in the immediate past raises questions as to how the period will continue to be represented in terms of remembrance and its impact on present-day Estonian country branding.

Latvia

The central country of the Baltic States is Latvia. Latvia was the most 'Russified' country of the three during the Soviet period (Purs, 2012), because the greatest number of ethnic Russians were brought into Latvia. This was due to the fact that of the three Baltic nations, Latvia had the greatest amount of manufacturing, particularly military manufacturing (Prikulis, 1996). The lasting result of this action is that over one-third of those living in Latvia consider their first language to be Russian (Kim, 2018). There was a referendum conducted in 2012 to consider Russian as the second state language. The referendum was defeated, but the eastern region of Latvia that bordered Russia and Belarus supported the referendum. The capital city Riga still has a greater percentage of Russian speakers than Latvian speakers. With these facts as a background to dark tourism sites and attractions in Latvia, the three selected tourist attractions mirrored, to a degree, those from Estonia.

The Museum of Occupation of Latvia (http://okupacijasmuzejs.lv/lv/), as does the Vabamu Museum of Occupations and Freedom, mainly focuses on the Soviet period in Latvia. This museum, which opened in 1993, covers the Soviet occupation period from 1940 to 1991, and unlike the Estonian museum, is operated by a governmental agency, the Occupation Museum Association. The original building of the museum was built in 1971, and housed a museum related to the Red Latvian Rifleman, a group that aimed at supporting Latvian Bolshevism. The museum includes collections of items from the occupation period, as well as video testimonials of deportees, refugees and those who suffered under the Soviet period. The museum has also commissioned films and educational programmes about the occupation period. A temporary museum, located in the building of the former American Embassy in Riga, was opened in 2012 as the main museum is being renovated (http://okupacijasmuzejs.lv/lv/).

In terms of the level of darkness of the museum, it would fall on the darker side, as the artifacts and testimonies are authentic, with an aim of education. The site of the museum building seems somewhat ironic, or in fact a political provocation, in terms of overtly conveying the fact that a museum originally built to celebrate Bolshevism and Communism became a museum focused on the exact opposite. The museum, as ranked by Tripadvisor, falls within the top 10 per cent of attractions in Riga, and similarly to the Vabamu museum, the second-largest number of reviews were in Russian. Positive reviews were reflected by examples such as:

> A very sombre place but one with very important knowledge of the grim Soviet past. Some of the stories are very personal and it us worth remembering all those who disappeared. A letter box at entrance for relatives asking about missing loved ones is a pertinent reminder. (Posted February 2020)

In contrast, a negative review focused less on the content, and more on the comparative nature of these types of museums:

> While I have no doubt that the time period from 1939 to 1990 was a horribly difficult one for Latvians owing to the actions of the Germans and the Soviets, this museum does painfully little to persuade the visitor of that fact. Though there is a lot of verbiage and a few photographs posted to the walls of the

museum there is no really graphic evidence displayed of the otherwise well-documented misdeeds of the Soviets and the Germans. For an example of a much higher quality museum with similar objectives see The Warsaw Uprising Museum with its high quality physical displays and graphical videos. (Posted August, 2017)

In terms of a Russian language review, critical comments were focused on the purpose of the museum:

Speculation on history for the sake of political conjuncture. A pathetic attempt to prove something that never happened. My opinion does not pretend to be absolute, but this is the opinion of a person born and raised in Latvia. (Posted July 2019)

A positive Russian review reflected the sentiment of staying true to the history: 'try to stay away from politics. The ambitions of individual wayward personalities, the deceit of them and the media. The museum visited, was upset ... but thanks for the tolerance' (Posted July 2018).

The second Latvian dark tourism attraction, also in Riga, is the Riga Ghetto and Latvian Holocaust Museum (http://www.rgm.lv/). Over 70 000 of the Jewish population in Latvia died, as well as others experiencing interior deportation and tragedy during the Nazi occupation period (Gluckstein, 2012). This museum, which opened in 2010, mainly consists of an open-air museum that represents events that fall on the darkest side of the dark tourism scale due to the immense loss of life through violent means, as well as providing educational opportunities to visitors. A number of the exhibits focus on authenticity, as the entry to the Museum consists of cobblestones from Ludzas Iela, which was the main street of the Riga Ghetto during Nazi occupation (Zisere, 2005). Also, a restored house that existed in the Riga Ghetto has been reconstructed. Although there is debate on the role of reconstructions and authenticity and tourism (Bold et al., 2017), these examples, nonetheless, by utilizing actual materials from the original sites, help to temper those discussions.

The ranking of this museum was similar to that of the Occupation Museum in terms of things to do in Riga, and selected reviews compared this museum to other Holocaust-focused sites:

Much smaller than some holocaust museums, but still a poignant reminder of what happened. This mostly outdoor museum has a lot of info about other ghettos too, and an amazing indoor exhibition of lights which tell the story of lots of people who lost their lives here. (Posted March 2020)

Not on the scale of a concentration camp but still plenty to take in and to hit hard how we treat others so bad ... It shows how much Latvia was involved in the war and how the ghetto in Riga was controlled and how the Jews were treated in the country. (Posted November 2019)

As for critical reviews, the same comparison of the museum to others was found: 'having been to many museums/monuments/memorials with the same theme, this was just slightly disappointing both due to the small size of the museum and also due to the very basic exhibitions' (Posted April 2019).

The final dark tourism attraction in Latvia examined is the Secret Soviet Bunker (http://www.bunkurs.lv/en/) located in city of Ligatne, approximately 70 km northeast from Riga. The site was built as a fallout shelter in the event of a nuclear war. This bunker was similar to others built in the USSR, and this site was still considered a classified location until 2003. It was turned into a tourist attraction where the bunker, which is 9 metres underground, can be visited and Soviet era ephemera including books and maps, and a restaurant from the period, are on display. The facility has also hosted 'Holiday Party-Soviet Style' (http://www .bunkurs.lv/en/slepenie-piedavajumi/), where attendees would experience 1970 Soviet era entertainment including music and food. The facility has also offered other entertainment-type attractions.

This site, with respect to dark tourism, would be classified as authentic in terms of the location and reality of the facility, but the great number of amenities provided to visitors would fall within the lighter side of dark tourism due to the recreation of kitschy artifacts and experiences. The website for the attraction offers the ability to purchase 'authentic Soviet-era gas masks' (http://www.bunkurs.lv/en/gazmaskas/), further limiting the gravity of the site in exchange for commerce. The popularity of the site was evident, as it was the number one attraction in Ligatne, but that was interpreted as more due to the fact that only seven other things to do were recommended in Ligatne.

In terms of the Tripadvisor reviews, examples of positive reviews tended to limit the focus on the gravity to the original reason for the facility, and focus more on the entertainment value:

> A fascinating, thought provoking and (strangely) fun place to visit … one of those places that you feel a bit macabre to visit but is informative and makes us face our past, try to understand what others have endured and laugh a little at the madness of human evil. (Posted August 2019)

Critical reviews were limited, as the lowest-rated postings were still ranking the attraction as 'Average', and focused on the cost or physical nature of the exhibit itself:

> I had an interest in going on an excursion there, but for 200 euros the desire disappeared. (Posted November 2019)

> The idea is interesting, but practically not strange. The rooms you could access included 80's technology and chalky blank walls … not much difference for a person accustomed to the basement corridors of a Finnish apartment building. (Posted June 2017)

The Latvian dark tourism sites and attractions reviewed highlight the continued existence of the joint dark past in comparison to Estonia, and one could suggest that there is nothing wrong with that, as both countries experienced similar historical events. The question that can be asked would be how these similar events, if depicted in a similar fashion, limit the visitors' learning as to what would be considered Latvian or Estonian, and not just post-Soviet. This position was examined for the third collection of dark tourism attractions, in Lithuania.

Lithuania

The final, and largest Baltic state in both size and population, is Lithuania. Lithuania was the first of the Baltic states to pass a resolution leaving the Soviet Union in 1990 (Purs, 2012). This declaration was met with force, and of the three Baltic states, it experienced the most violence and death, with 13 Lithuanians being killed by Soviet troops at the TV Tower in January 1991 (Anušauskas, 2015). A further difference between Lithuania and the other two nations was the percentage of population of ethnic Russians. As Lithuania was, and remains, a heavily agricultural-based country, there was a lesser degree of Russification, with the result being that the Russian minority became the third-largest ethnic group in Lithuania at about 5 per cent, after the ethnic Poles (Davoliūtė, 2016). That being the case, in terms of dark tourism sites and attractions, Lithuania's reflect those in Estonia and Latvia.

The most visited, and reviewed, dark tourism site in Lithuania is the Museum of Occupations and Freedom Fights (Genocido Auku Muziejus). The museum is located in the former KGB building in the capital city, Vinlius (http://genocid.lt/muziejus/). The name of the museum has raised controversy as it is also been known as the Museum of Genocide Victims, and focuses on the plight of the Lithuanian resistance members who were murdered, imprisoned or deported by the Soviet Union; while not until 2011 was there a room that presented artifacts and discussed the genocide of Jewish people in Lithuania (Nordland, 2018).

The museum, which is listed as the 'KGB Museum' in Tripadvisor, has been consistently ranked as one of the top museums in Lithuania. The museum reviews have been overwhelmingly positive, with comments that highlight the content and focus of the exhibits:

> the exhibition provides excellent documentary evidence of Lithuania's history and, in particular, the genocide inflicted by the Nazis and USSR ... highly impactive, the exhibition is extremely informative, thought provoking and provides a fitting tribute to the brave people of this beautiful nation. (Posted December 2019)

The other spotlight of the comments was the horror of the events depicted in the displays: 'A chilling place to visit. To stand where hundreds of victims of Soviet oppression where tortured and executed is very disturbing' (Posted October 2019).

The percentage of negative reviews reflected a lack of attention to atrocities committed against the Jewish population in Lithuania:

> A place that rewrites history, and which honours Nazi-collaborators such as the 'forest brothers' ... not one plaque mentions how Lithuanian collaborators took part in Holocaust activities. (Posted May 2018)

> The Soviet murder of 20 000 Lithuanians for political resistance is a ghastly, horrific crime. But to almost entirely blank out 200 000 deaths in a genocide where people were murdered not for political acts, but simply because they were Jews, is highly offensive, racist, and simply wrong. (Posted September 2017)

This museum would be classified on the darker end of the dark tourism spectrum, as it depicts and presents collections of materials and recollections of atrocities that occurred both within and outside of the actual building. The criticism of the lack of content in the museum can be judged to lessen the authenticity of the site because of a political agenda.

The second dark tourism attraction selected, and the tallest structure in Lithuania, is the TV Tower and Freedom Museum (https://tvbokstas.lt/en/). The TV Tower was completed in 1980 and was the site of the aforementioned killings of Lithuanians trying to protect the tower from Soviet forces. There is an observation tower, and a museum on the ground floor that depicts the events of 1991:

> I remember visiting the TV tower in 1991 after the independence demonstration and Lithuania's declaration of independence; there were huge chunks of concrete to defend against Russian tanks. Now, it is a place to visit and to celebrate Lithuania's independence. (Posted December 2018)

Interestingly, the vast majority of the reviews, both positive and negative, related to the view from the Tower and the food at the restaurant. For those reviews that did focus on the events of 1991, there was a general conflation of the poor experience of visiting the attraction with the Soviet period: 'Unless you want to experience soviet times, soviet quality food and superb rude waiters – avoid this place at all costs' (Posted June 2018).

The TV tower represents a mid-spectrum example of dark tourism. Although the site is authentic in terms of the tragic events that occurred there, the limited focus on those events at the expense of providing tourists with a view of the Vilnius countryside, and a dining experience, represents an example of taking a tourist attraction that was most famous as a site of death and violence, and repositioning it as a more generic form of tourism attraction.

The final attraction is located in the second-largest city in Lithuania, Kaunas. The dark tourism attraction selected is the unique Devil's Museum. The museum, opened during the Soviet period in 1966, contains thousands of different works that depict the Devil, and the website refers to the Museum by a more formal name, Žmuidzinavičius Memorial Museum (https://ciurlionis.lt/en/), as Antanas Žmuidzinavičius's collection of Devil-themed sculptures makes the museum more well-known. The museum was rated as a top ten attraction in Kaunas, and very well reviewed. There was a dearth of reviews that related the museum to Lithuania in general, or Kaunas specifically, and reviews tended to concentrate on the unique aspects of the museum:

a wonderful, unusual museum featuring a wide variety of collections of devil statues and other devils and devils, drawings, clay and more. A great choice for a visit. (Posted August 2019)

I say this is not to be missed though I was very creeped out surrounded by devils of every kind of material and theme. 3 floors of Devils, the only museum of its kind. (Posted February 2017)

Critics of the Museum also did not relate the attraction to Kaunas or Lithuania: 'Devil statues (some of interest) and lots of very ugly paintings. A little bit of interaction in the exhibition would have been nice. It was just an exhibition of statues and nothing else, no history' (Posted October 2013).

This Museum would be an exemplar of a lighter type of dark tourism attraction, due to the fictional nature of the presentation of death and the macabre, as well as a lack of tying in of the location (Kaunas) to dark events. The inclusion of an extensive gift shop that markets kitschy Devil-related souvenirs further lessens the darkness of the site.

DISCUSSION, RESEARCH CONTRIBUTION AND FUTURE STUDY

The aim of this research was to present a comparative study of sites and attractions that would be classified in the growing field of dark tourism. Presenting multiple examples of dark tourist sites provides a breadth of examples of the categorization of such tourism-related enterprises in order to better understand the benefit of such classifications. The value to both the site providers and the visitors was also discussed.

The greater contribution of such research lies in the fact that dark tourism, as a controversial form of tourism (Wright, 2006), may have a positive, negative or even neutral impact on the brand image and identity of the city or country of the attractions' locations (Miller et al., 2017). The choice of the three Baltic states results in the ability to compare and contrast the implications of such sites and attractions with respect to the branding of countries that have emerged in the recent past from being forcefully incorporated into a greater entity, in this case the Soviet Union.

Each of these three countries, and by extension other countries that have had to create and develop a unique and interesting image to attract tourists – primarily foreign tourists – provide visitors with attractions related to their dark history. The attractions discussed both reflect and differentiate their respective dark pasts through these dark tourism sites. The arbitrary selection of the sites, and the focused selection of visitor comments, can be questioned in terms of the extension of these findings to other countries, but they nonetheless provide examples for using such information in terms of brand and brand identity development.

Finally, this chapter takes the position that dark tourism will continue to represent a small but growing tourism sector, one that can aid in the development of a cohesive brand identity and image for countries such as these. Additionally, the findings from research based on the study of small countries such as Estonia, Latvia and Lithuania can lead to an increased understanding of complex regional phenomena by isolating the number of confounding variables more prevalent in larger countries and regions (Hackmann, 2002). Thus, it is supposed that specific findings derived from the Baltic state nations will result in research findings that can also be extrapolated to other countries and regions of similar history. Examples could include countries of the Balkan region, other countries of the former Soviet Union, as well as emerging markets of Southeast Asia.

REFERENCES

Anušauskas, A. (ed.) (1999). *The Anti-Soviet Resistance in the Baltic States*. Vilnius: Genocide and Resistance Research Centre of Lithuania.

Anušauskas, A. (ed.) (2015). *Lithuania in 1940–1991: The History of Occupied Lithuania*. Vilnius: Genocide and Resistance Research Centre of Lithuania.

Banaszkiewicz, M., Graburn, N., and Owsianowska, S. (2017). Tourism in (post)socialist Eastern Europe. *Journal of Tourism and Cultural Change*, 15(2), 109–121.

Beaton, C. (2018, 13 June). Why you can't really trust negative online reviews. *New York Times*. Retrieved from https://www.nytimes.com/2018/06/13/smarter-living/trust-negative-product-reviews.html.

Bilro, R.G., Loureiro, S., and Guerreiro, J. (2019). Exploring online customer engagement with hospitality products and its relationship with involvement, emotional states, experience and brand advocacy. *Journal of Hospitality Marketing and Management*, 28(2), 147–171.

Blal., I, and Sturman, M. (2014). The differential effects of the quality and quantity of online reviews on hotel room sales. *Cornell Hospitality Quarterly*, 55(4), 365–375.

Bold, J., Larkham, P., and Pickard, R. (eds) (2017). *Authentic Reconstruction*. London: Bloomsbury Academic.

Burch, S., and Zander, U. (2010). Preoccupied by the past – the case of Estonia's Museum of Occupations. *Scandia*, 74(2), 53–73.

Çakar, K. (2018). Experiences of visitors to Gallipoli, a nostalgia-themed dark tourism destination: an insight from TripAdvisor. *International Journal of Tourism Cities*, 4(1), 98–109.

Carson, D., Gilmore, A., Perry, C., and Gronhaug, K. (2001). *Qualitative Marketing Research*. London: SAGE Publications.

Chatterjee, G. (2001). Online reviews. Do consumers use them? *Advances in Consumer Research*, 28, 129–133.

Cottrell, J., and Cottrell, S.P. (2015). Sense-of-place influences on perceived environmental change effects on future holiday experiences to Saaremaa, Estonia. *Scandinavian Journal of Hospitality and Tourism*, 15(4), 425–446.

Davoliūtė, V. (2016). The Sovietization of Lithuania after WWII: modernization, transculturation, and the lettered city. *Journal of Baltic Studies*, 47(1), 49–63.

de Laat, P.B. (2005). Trusting virtual trust. *Ethics and Information Technology*, 7(3), 167–180.

Gluckstein, D. (2012). *A People's History of the Second World War: Resistance Versus Empire*. London: Pluto Press.

Gretzel, U., and Yoo, K.H. (2008). Use and impact of online travel reviews. In P. O'Connor, W. Hopken and U. Gretzel (eds), *Information and Communication Technologies in Tourism* (pp. 35–46). New York: Springer.

Hackmann, J. (2002). 'From 'object' to 'subject': the contribution of small nations to regional-building in North Eastern Europe. *Journal of Baltic Studies, 33*, 412–430.

Hall, D., Smith, M., and Marciszewska, B. (2006). *Tourism in the New Europe*. London: CAB International.

Haven, C . (2011). Stanford takes Estonia's 'Museum of Occupations' under its wings. Stanford News Service. Retrieved from https://news.stanford.edu/pr/2011/pr-library-estonia-museum-092111.html.

Kasekamp, A. (2018). *A History of the Baltic States* (2nd edition). London: Macmillan.

Kim, L. (2018, October 18). A new law in Latvia aims to preserve national language by limiting Russian in schools. Retrieved from https://www.npr.org/2018/10/28/654142363/a-new-law-in-latvia-aims-to-preserve-national-language-by-limiting-russian-in-sc.

Kusumasondjaja, S., Shanka, T,, and Marchegiani, C (2012). Credibility of online reviews and initial trust: the roles of reviewer's identity and review valence. *Journal of Vacation Marketing, 18*(3), 185–195.

Lennon, J., and Foley, M. (2000). *Dark tourism: The Attraction of Death and Disaster*. London: International Thomson Business Press.

Light, D. (2017). Progress in dark tourism and thanatourism research: an uneasy relationship with heritage tourism. *Tourism Management, 61*, 275–301.

Liu, B. (2012). *Sentiment Analysis and Opinion Mining*. San Rafael, CA: Morgan & Claypool Publishers.

Lupu, C., Brochado, A., and Stoleriu, O.M. (2017). Experiencing Dracula's homeland. *Tourism Geographies, 19*(5), 756–779.

Maitland, R., and Ritchie, B.W. (2009). *City Tourism: National Capital Perspectives*. Egham, UK: CABI Publishing.

Marcoux, J. (2017). Souvenirs to forget. *Journal of Consumer Research, 43*(6), 950–969.

Marshall, C., and Rossman, G.B. (1995). *Designing Qualitative Research*. Thousand Oaks, CA: SAGE Publications.

McKenzie, B. (2011, 25 March). Hotel's top floor was a spy post. *Guelph Mercury*. Retrieved from https://www.guelphmercury.com/living-story/2758374-travel-hotel-s-top-floor-was a-spy-post/.

McKenzie, B. (2013). Soviet tourism in the Baltic States: remembrance versus nostalgia – just different shades of dark? In L. White and E. Frew (eds), *Dark Tourism and Place Identity* (pp. 115–128). New York: Routledge Publishing.

Miller, S.A., Gonzalex, C., and Hutter, M. (2017). Phoenix tourism within dark tourism. *Worldwide Hospitality and Tourism Themes, 9*(2), 196–215.

Mirtalaie, M.A., Hussain, O.K., Chang, E., and Hussain, F.K. (2017). A decision support framework for identifying novel ideas in new product development from cross domain analysis. *Information Systems, 69*, 59–80.

Misiunas, R.J., and Taagepera, R. (1993). *The Baltic States: The Years of Dependence, 1940–90*. Berkeley, CA: University of California Press.

Nordland, R. (2018, 30 March). Where the Genocide Museum is (mostly) mum on the fate of Jews. *New York Times*, Retrieved from https://www.nytimes.com/2018/03/30/world/europe/lithuania-genocide-museum-jews.html.

Prikulis J. (1996). Conversion of military industry and other military facilities in Latvia. In K. Prunskienė, and E. Altvater (eds), *Transformation, Co-operation, and Conversion.* NATO ASI Series (Series 4: Science and Technology Policy), 7. Dordrecht: Springer.

Purs, A. (2012). *Baltic Facades: Estonia, Latvia and Lithuania Since 1945*. London: Reaktion Books.

Renfors, S. (2018). Internationalising higher tourism education: the case of curriculum design in the Central Baltic Area. *Journal of Teaching in Travel and Tourism, 18*(4), 315–331.

Sampson, H. (2019, 13 November). Dark tourism, explained. *Washington Post*. Retrieved from https://www.washingtonpost.com/graphics/2019/travel/dark-tourism-explainer/.

Schuckert, M., Liu, X., and Law, R. (2015). Hospitality and tourism online reviews: recent trends and future directions. *Journal of Travel and Tourism Marketing, 32*(5), 608–621.

Sharpley, R., and Stone, P. (eds) (2009). *The Darker Side of Travel: The Theory and Practice of Dark Tourism*. Salisbury: Short Run Press.

Sparks, B., and Browning, V. (2011). The impact of online reviews on hotel booking intentions and perception of trust. *Tourism Management*, *32*(6), 1310–1323.

Stone, P. (2006). A dark tourism spectrum: towards a typology of death and macabre related tourist sites, attractions and exhibitions. *Tourism: An Interdisciplinary International Journal*, *54*(2), 145–160.

Stone, P., Hartmann, R., Seaton, A.V., Sharpley, R., and White, L. (eds) (2018). *The Palgrave Handbook of Dark Tourism Studies*. London: Palgrave Macmillan.

Strange, C., and Kempa, M. (2003). Shades of dark tourism at Alcatraz and Robben Island. *Annals of Tourism Research*, *30*(2), 386–405.

Tamm, M. (2013). In search of lost time: memory politics in Estonia, 1991–2011. *Nationalities Papers*, *41*(4), 651–674.

Vásquez, C. (2012). Narrativity and involvement in online consumer reviews: the case of TripAdvisor. *Narrative Inquiry*, *22*(1), 105–121.

Wang, Y., and Chaudhry, A. (2018). When and how managers' responses to online reviews affect subsequent reviews. *Journal of Marketing Research*, *55*(2), 163–177.

White, L., and Frew, E. (eds) (2013). *Dark Tourism and Place Identity*. New York: Routledge Publishing.

Wright, A.C. (2006). Philosophical and methodological praxes in dark tourism: controversy, contention and the evolving paradigm. *Journal of Vacation Marketing*, *12*(2), 119–129.

Xie, K, Chen, C., and Wu, S. (2016). Online consumer review factors affecting offline hotel popularity: evidence from Tripadvisor. *Journal of Travel and Tourism Marketing*, *33*(2), 1–13.

Zisere, B. (2005). The memory of the Shoah in the post-Soviet Latvia. *East European Jewish Affairs*, *35*(2), 155–165.

24. Exploring how travel blogs influence Chinese tourists to visit Japan: a netnographic study of Chinese tourists' travel blogs

Kaede Sano and João Romão

INTRODUCTION

The intense development of digital technologies, tools and infrastructures over the last decades has strongly impacted on tourism activities, particularly in the distribution sector (Buhalis and Law, 2008). Large quantities of information about diverse aspects of tourism destinations worldwide are now available and easily accessible. This contributes to the increasing autonomy of tourists, allowing for better-informed decisions and choices, while enhancing the opportunities for interaction with service providers and other users, thus generating various processes of co-creation (Binkhorst and Dekker, 2009; Rihova et al., 2018). These quick technological developments generate new opportunities and uses for the tourism sector (Boes et al., 2016), creating new areas for research in this field.

Recent trends demonstrate growing concerns with cultural and emotional aspects of consumption patterns and tourism demand. The focus of travel and tourism has gradually shifted from the passive utilization of resources to active engagement with local communities and a search for unique and authentic experiences based on the local characteristics of destinations (Tussyadiah, 2014). Thus, the mediatization of tourism arising from different media distributed through digital platforms (Mansson, 2011) contributes to a fuller perception of and knowledge about how destinations can be differently experienced by visitors, enhancing opportunities for meaningful and personalized experiences (Tussyadiah and Fesenmaier, 2009; Kim and Fesenmaier, 2017).

In this context, a clear understanding of how different users perceive and present destinations on digital platforms appears to be a crucial precondition and powerful tool for destination and service marketing in contemporary tourism (Sigala, 2012; Sabiote-Ortiz et al., 2016). Framed by relevant literature, this study analyzes and discusses the interactive relations between the characteristics of different types of travel blogs and tourists' preferences, as well as how these aspects have evolved over time. In particular, our analysis demonstrates how different contributions from "informative blogs" (which provide information about the characteristics of local resources or services) and "literature blogs" (which offer insights about how the destination is experienced) influence travelers' decisions and tourist behavior. Moreover, by analyzing these aspects over time, this study identifies changes in travel behaviors and in the relationship between tourists and travel blogs, emphasizing the dynamic character of these interactions.

Using a netnographic methodology, this empirical analysis is based on an extensive survey of the behavior of Chinese tourists visiting Japan. The Japanese government has actively promoted the inbound tourism market since the launch of the Visit Japan Campaign in 2003. To attract more international tourists to Japan, this campaign includes various events (for example, "YOKOSO! JAPAN WEEKS"), tourism goodwill ambassadors, and relationships with particular countries and regions (for example, Korea, Taiwan, the United States, China, Hong Kong and the United Kingdom). This campaign has greatly promoted Japan's inbound tourism market, with the number of international tourists increasing to 31 882 100 in 2019, compared with 5 211 725 in 2003, according to the Japan National Tourism Organization (JNTO, 2020). The Japan Tourism Agency (JTA, 2017) reports that the consumption of international tourists reached 4.1 trillion yen in 2017, comprising 15.3 percent of total consumption in Japan's tourism industry.

China is one of the main target markets for Japan's inbound tourism industry. To attract more Chinese tourists to Japan and stimulate tourism consumption, the Japanese government has implemented several policies, such as the relaxation of tourist visas in 2010, and changes to the consumption tax for foreigners in 2013. As a result, the number of Chinese tourists has continued to increase, except in 2011 and 2013 due to the Great East Japan Earthquake and political issues (see Figure 24.1), and Chinese tourists occupy the largest market share of Japan's inbound tourism industry (see Figure 24.2). Chinese tourists' great power of consumption has had a significant economic effect on the tourism industry. According to the JTA (2019), Chinese tourists' consumption in Japan was approximately 154 billion yen in 2018, constituting 34.2 percent of the total consumption by international tourists and making them the leading consumers among Japan's international tourists.

The visa relaxation in 2010 has encouraged more Chinese tourists to visit Japan individually rather than with tour groups. In 2017, the JTA reported that 47.7 percent of Chinese tourists were free individual travelers (FITs), 16.4 percent purchased individual tour packages, and 35.9 percent were part of tour groups. The increasing number of FITs has resulted in tourists

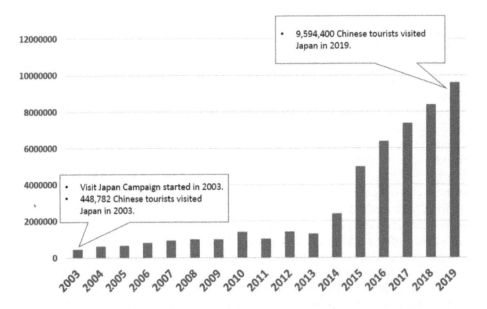

Source: Data from Japan National Tourism Organization (JNTO, 2020).

Figure 24.1   Number of international tourists to Japan, 2003–2019

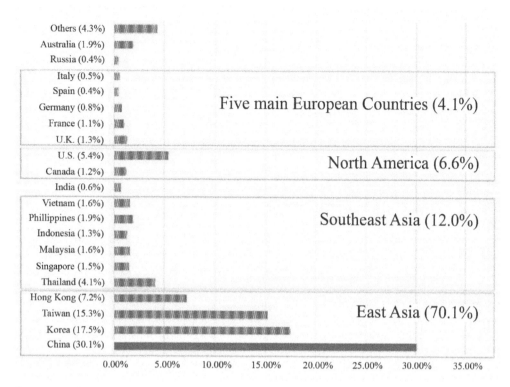

Sources: Data from Japan Tourism Agency (JTA, 2020).

Figure 24.2   Percentages of international tourists in Japan's inbound market, 2019

searching for more information, which occurs less with tour groups. The JNTO provides information about travel to Japan on its official website (http://www.welcome2japan.cn/), as well as links to Weibo and WeChat, which are the most widely used social media platforms in mainland China. However, according to the survey results of the Japan Tourist Bureau (JTB inbound solution, 2018), the official website seemed not to be used as an essential information source, as only 25.8 percent of Chinese tourists mentioned it. Instead, 66.9 percent reported using online tourism communities to collect information before travelling to Japan, which was ranked as the top information-searching method (JTB inbound solution, 2018). Japanese travel experiences have accumulated over the past decade, as more Chinese tourists visit Japan. Furthermore, because tourism is characterized as an "experience good," whose quality is difficult to judge without experiencing it, travel blogs posted in online communities by tourists who have visited Japan have become an essential information source.

Against this background, this chapter focuses on individual travel blogs posted in online tourism communities after 2011 and proposes to examine the following research questions:

1. What type of travel blogs are more attractive to potential Chinese tourists who are interested in Japan?
2. Have Chinese tourists' travel preferences changed over the past decade? If so, how?

THEORETICAL BACKGROUND

Social Media in the Tourism Industry

Over the past decade, we have witnessed a huge growth in social media, which is born of Web 2.0 technology and believed to be one of the most powerful online networking tools in various fields (Zeng and Gerritsen, 2014). Social media is defined as "user-generated content" (Leung et al., 2013), and was originally used as a communication tool to connect internet users to the world and people they care about (Hansen et al., 2011). Besides these personal practices, businesses have increasingly recognized the essential role of social media in building and maintaining long-term relationships with customers. Many have created their own social communities on Facebook, blogs and Twitter to communicate with customers, replacing traditional customer relationship management that relies on information technology (Heller Baird and Parasnis, 2011).

In tourism, internet-based social communities have greatly expanded recently as a result of evolving Web 2.0 technology. As in other industries, businesses (for example, airline companies, hotels and travel agencies) in the tourism industry use social media to attract potential customers and build emotional bonds with existing customers through online communities. For example, as of April 2020, the official Facebook page of Japan Airlines had over 2 million followers, and the official Instagram page of the JTB corporation, the largest travel agency in Japan, had over 35 000 followers. The practice of using social media to attract customers is not limited to businesses. Tourism-related government agencies and destination marketing organizations (DMOs) also use social media to promote destination images and attract tourists. For instance, the JTA has used Twitter to promote tourism in Japan since June 2014. The Wakayama Tourism Federation, the DOM in Wakayama prefecture, publicizes tourism spots in English through Facebook to attract more international tourists to the region.

Rather than being used for business-to-consumer (B2C) and government-to-consumer (G2C) communication channels, social media was originally used as a consumer-to-consumer (C2C) channel. The tourism industry is pioneering in tourists' wide use of social media to obtain information about trips and to share experiences related to trips before, during and after their vacations (Parra-López et al., 2011). Such behaviors are becoming generalized (Chung and Buhalis, 2008) into what has been called Travel 2.0 (Adam et al., 2007). Compared to companies or DMOs that market via social media, tourists believe that C2C-based online communities offer more reliable information without any business benefits (Ayeh et al., 2013). As tourism is an experienced good, whose quality is difficult to judge until people experience it themselves (Pan et al., 2016), online tourism-related communities (for example, Tripadvisor) have become important information sources (Tham et al., 2013), playing an increasingly essential role in tourist decision-making process (Öz, 2015). More importantly, electronic word-of-mouth (e-WOM) in such online communities helps to form destination images (Sun et al., 2014).

The Effect of Social Media on Tourist Information-Searching and Sharing Behaviors

Social media has significantly changed tourists' information-searching behaviors before, during and after vacations (Leung et al., 2013). Previous studies, as discussed below, have explored how tourists use social media to search for and share information, how they are affected by and react to information posted on social media, and how their decision-making processes are influenced by social media. Other studies have approached tourists' information-searching behavior on social media from the perspectives of cultural background, demographic factors, and different roles that users play on social media platforms. Regarding the relationship between social media and tourists' information-searching and sharing behaviors, past studies can be categorized into the following three main topics: intentions for using social media, tourists' attitudes toward social media, and tourists' characteristics.

Intentions for using social media

According to past studies, tourists' intentions for using social media are influenced by its perceived usefulness (Shu and Scott, 2014), the perceived benefits of the relationship between the individual and online communities (Munar and Jacobsen, 2014), perceived homophily (Ayeh et al., 2013), extraversion, social benefits, dissonance reduction (Yen and Tang, 2015), altruism and common identity (Kim et al., 2016). Some studies also suggested that tourists' willingness to self-present is another essential motivation for using social media (Dinhopl and Gretzel, 2016; Lyu, 2016).

Tourist attitudes toward social media in the tourism industry

Tourists' attitudes toward social media have received significant scholarly attention, with social media being applied to B2C, G2C and C2C communication channels in the tourism industry. Previous studies focus mainly on the perceived credibility of information sources. For example, Kusumasondjaja et al. (2012) found that negative online reviews are believed to be more credible than positive reviews. Positive attitudes toward social media can also influence tourists' purchasing behavior (Amaro and Duarte, 2015; Bynum Boley et al., 2013), hotel reservation intentions (Ladhari and Michaud, 2015), and willingness to visit (Fu et al., 2016).

The effects of tourists' characteristics on their social media behavior

For the last decade, tourists' characteristics have been discussed as a crucial factor affecting their behavior on social media. For example, Chiappa (2013) found that tourists' online purchasing of tourism products was significantly influenced by demographic factors and the frequency of their social media use. Bilgihan et al. (2014) found that online reviews and reviewers' opinions play an essential role in the information-searching behaviors of Generation Y, born between 1977 and 1997, on social media.

Travel Blogs as an Information Source for Destinations

In online communities, tourists gain information and exchange travel experiences with other online users (Zeng and Gerritsen, 2014). Therefore, social media has become a crucial information source in tourists' decision-making processes, making it an innovation in the tourism industry, especially in destination image-building (Hjalager, 2013).

Travel blogs are a type of social media characterized by a few writers and numerous consumers (Hansen et al., 2011). Sharda and Ponnada (2007, p. 2, cited in Volo, 2010, p. 2) define blogs as "virtual diaries created by individuals and stored on the web for anyone to access." With the development of social media, blogs are believed to be an ideal resource when searching for information about travel destinations (Crotts, 1999). Previous studies have discussed travel blogs from the perspectives of destination image formation (Banyai and Glover, 2011;

Llodrà-Riera et al., 2015; Sun et al., 2014; Tham et al., 2013; Tseng et al., 2015), usefulness (Chen et al., 2014; Huang et al., 2010; Schmallegger and Carson, 2008; Volo, 2010; Wang, 2012), and bloggers' motivation (Bosangit et al., 2015; Lee and Gretzel, 2014; Wenger, 2008; Wu and Pearce, 2014b, 2017).

Destination image formation: personal travel blogs as touristic looking
The emotional component of an image is essential in destination evaluation and formation (Tseng et al., 2015). As tourism products are difficult to assess without direct experience, potential tourists tend to actively seek information from past tourists. Unlike with other types of social media (for example, Facebook and Twitter), bloggers can post longer articles to online social communities, allowing travel blogs to be more informative, attractive and persuasive. Personal travel blogs not only describe the bloggers' travel experiences but also assist in forming the destination image. Tseng et al. (2015), for example, explored the image of China as a tourist destination by analyzing 630 blogs posted on TravelBlog.org and TravelPod.com and identified nine textual themes, consisting of place, Chinese, people, food, train, city, hotel, China and students. Examining the blogs of Chinese tourists to New Zealand, Sun et al. (2014) found that the perceived image of New Zealand included a protected ecological environment, a variety of activities, and a highly developed society with a "Pakeha" culture. Because travel blogs reflect touristic looking, they can be a cost-effective method for destination marketing (Banyai and Glover, 2011; Çakmak and Isaac, 2012; Pan et al., 2016).

Readers' motivation: personal travel blogs as information or entertainment
People use social media for usefulness and enjoyment (Lin and Lu, 2011). Like most social media, travel blogs can also be divided into B2C, G2C and C2C types (Schmalleger and Carson, 2008). However, personal blogs are believed to be more credible than business or government-led commercial blogs (Mack et al., 2008). Although travel blogs may include too much information and consequently confuse tourists (Lu and Gursoy, 2015), they still provide useful assistance for tourists' decision-making and have become an online community for information exchange (Schmallegger and Carson, 2008). Following this logic, Huang et al. (2010) approached blog usage as an information-searching process and highlighted the relationship between travel bloggers' involvement levels and intention to purchase tourism products. Taking the opposite approach, Chen et al. (2014) examined the effect of different types of travel on tourists' behavioral intention and found that blogs characterized as novel, understandable and interesting are more influential.

Bloggers' motivation: personal travel blogs as self-presentation
Compared with posts on Facebook, Twitter and Tripadvisor, travel blogs require bloggers to invest considerable time, mostly without any reward. What, therefore, motivates bloggers? Wu and Pearce (2014a) assessed Chinese bloggers' demographic characteristics, features of their blogging behavior, and their motives for blogging. Their study identifies six key motivations for blogging: positive self-enhancement, altruism, social status, personal status and achievement, self-documentation and sharing, and hedonic enjoyment of blogging. Bosangit et al. (2015) similarly found that bloggers' motivations closely relate to self-reflection and emotions. Approaching blogging motivation from the perspective of cultural differences, Lee and Gretzel (2014) emphasized blogging behavior as a means of forming and presenting personal and social identity. They examined the differences between Korean (Eastern collec-

tivistic culture) and American bloggers (Western collectivistic culture), and found that Korean bloggers tend to provide personal information to benefit others, whereas American bloggers simply record their own travel experiences.

RESEARCH METHODOLOGY

As its research methodology, this study employed netnography, which adapts traditional ethnography to the internet as a virtual fieldwork site (Kozinets, 2002). Netnography was originally used to analyze online communities from an insider's perspective in marketing studies (Kozinets et al., 2010), and has now been extended into tourism studies to understand consumer behaviors in online tourism communities (Björk and Kauppinen-Räisänen, 2012; Wu and Pearce, 2014a). This research method suits the current study because it provides an in-depth understanding of bloggers' and followers' motivations.

Mafengwo as the Online Research Platform

According to Kozinets (2002, p. 63), suitable online communities for netnography should be identified with the following five criteria: (1) a focused and research question-relevant segment, topic or group; (2) high "traffic" of postings; (3) numerous discrete message posters; (4) detailed or descriptively rich data; and (5) numerous between-member interactions of the type required by the research questions.

As this study aims to understand Chinese tourists' preferences and behaviors during their visit to Japan by analyzing travel blogs, an online Chinese community with a large number of travel blogs is required (criterion 1). Among China's main travel-related online communities, such as Ctrip, Qyer, Tripadvisor and Weibo, Mafengwo is the largest and most active, with 130 million users and more than 21 million eWOM posts. Approximately 80 percent of Chinese tourists to Japan reported using Mafengwo as an important information resource (criteria 2 and 3). Recently, Mafengwo has displayed information about over 60 000 tourist spots around the world, as well as travel recommendations, maps, and information about popular spots, hotels, cuisine, community and discounts (criterion 4). Mafengwo reached 8000 active users per month in 2016 and is updated daily (criterion 5). Based on the criteria suggested by Kozinets (2002), Mafengwo was selected as the online platform for this study.

Data Collection

Like the target online community, posters of online messages must also be categorized (Kozinets, 2002). Kozinets (2002, p. 64) outlines four types of posters – tourists, minglers, devotees and insiders – based on their levels of interest in activity and social ties. According to Kozinets (2002), "tourists" are posters who lack both strong social ties and deep interest in the activities; whereas "insiders" have strong social ties and deep interest in activities. "Minglers" refers to posters with strong social ties but a low interest in activities; while "devotees" show deep interest in activities but weak social ties with others. As "devoted," enthusiastic and sophisticated posts in online communities contain the richest information for research, "insiders" and "devotees" are the most influential bloggers (Kozinets, 1999, 2002, 2015).

Using this theoretical foundation, this study selected blogs based on the following criteria. First, the blog must have been viewed more than 10 000 times, because the higher attention a blog receives, the more active are the interactions within it (Kozinets, 1999, 2002, 2015). Readers' impressions of the content can also be evaluated by the number of "nice" indications (Sterne, 2011). Second, the poster of the selected blog should be an "insider" or "devotee," who responds enthusiastically to users' questions and comments. As this study aims to explore changes in Chinese tourists' preferences and behaviors over the past decade, the data collection was conducted twice. Jennings (2005) suggests that the recruitment of interviewees should end when information saturation is reached. Following this theory for sample size and data collection, the research objectives of this study comprised 110 rich blogs: one in 2011, three in 2013, 11 in 2014, 24 in 2015, 23 in 2016, 22 in 2017, 14 in 2018, 11 in 2019, and one in 2020.

Data Analysis

This study adopted a manual approach, as suggested by Wu and Pearce (2014a). First, the blogs were identified and checked; second, NVivo 12 Plus was employed as a research tool to code the blogs' content; third, the codes were transformed into different themes; and fourth, materials were sorted according to these themes. Moreover, as netnography is based primarily on observation of textual discourse and the netnographer needs to determine the importance of fixed demographic markers (Kozinets, 2002), this study analyzed the 110 blogs from the following aspects: (1) blog style (informative blogs and literature blogs); (2) blog influence in the online community (views, "nice," comment, bookmark and share); and (3) word frequency.

In this study, content style refers to how posters share their travel experiences with others in ways that closely relate to the posters' motivation. Informative blogs mainly reflect the motivation to help other tourists and facilitate their travel. Literature blogs, however, show posters' willingness to share their travel stories and feelings with others. The selected blogs were also analyzed by the number of reviews (interest from readers), comments (willingness of readers to engage), bookmarks (perceived usefulness for readers), and shares (recommendation by others), to examine their influence. Finally, this study explored Chinese tourists' preferences and travel behaviors by analyzing word frequency, as highly frequent words are supposed to reflect tourists' interests during their visits to Japan.

INTERPRETING THE RESEARCH RESULTS

Blog Style: Informative versus Literature Blogs

The authors carefully read all 110 selected blogs and categorized them as informative or literature blogs. Based on the results of the data analysis, 50 blogs were identified as informative blogs, and the other 60 blogs as literature blogs. To explore the motivations of the posters and readers, both the informative and the literature blogs were further categorized according to the year. As a result, the current study's database includes the following: no informative blogs and one literature blog in 2011, no informative and literature blogs in 2012, two informative and one literature blogs in 2013, six informative and five literature blogs in 2014, 16 informative and eight literature blogs in 2015, nine informative and 14 literature blogs in 2016, nine informative and 13 literature blogs in 2017, four informative and ten literature blogs in 2018, four informative and seven literature blogs in 2019, and one literature blog in 2020 (see Figure 24.3). Interestingly, the number of informative blogs exceeded that of literature blogs between 2013 and 2015, but literature blogs tended to outnumber informative blogs after 2016. The results reflect not only the motivation of posters, but also the potential interest of blog readers.

To understand Chinese tourists' travel style, days of travel, average total travel, average travel expense per day, average number of characters per blog, and average number of photos per blog were analyzed in both the informative and the literature blog categories. The analysis results show that posters of informative blogs tended to spend longer in Japan, and that their expenses during their visit were higher than those of posters of literature blogs in general. Moreover, the average numbers of characters and photos in each informative blog are greater than those in literature blogs. Nevertheless, regardless of the different averages, there were no significant differences between the two types of blogs (see Table 24.1).

To explore Chinese tourists' detailed expenses, the authors carefully examined the content of each blog, and found that while posters of informative blogs tended to spend on shopping, posters of literature blogs tended to spend on cultural experiences. Moreover, the informative blogs included large amounts of very detailed information concerning, for example, shopping lists, transportation, hotels, visa applications, airline tickets, and business hours of tourist spots. The posters shared the information and their recommendations not only in written articles but also through numerous photos. Literature blog posters, on the other hand, shared their feelings and thoughts during their visit to Japan, rather than primarily providing travel information. The literature blogs, therefore, were more like essays or stories, including numerous personal photos and photos of Japanese life and scenery.

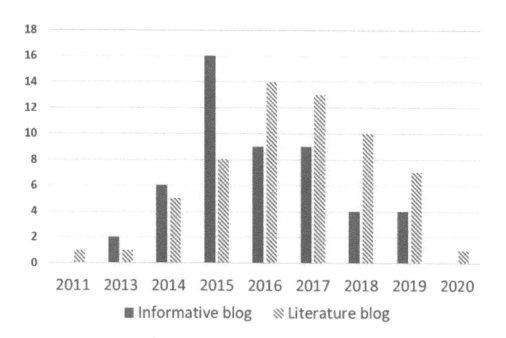

Figure 24.3   *The distribution of blog style from 2011 to 2020 (except 2012)*

Table 24.1   Characteristics of informative and literature blogs

Year	Days of travel		Average total travel expense (RMB)		Average travel expense per day		Average number of characters in each blog		Average number of photos in each blog	
	Informative	Literature	Informative	Literature	Informative	Literature	Informative	Literature	Informative	Literature
2011		4		3 000		750		10 554		240
2013	6.5	5	12 500	6 000	2 024	1 200	10 135	2 679	418	11
2014	5.8	5.6	12 833	5 738	2 253	1 019	12 007	9 915	235	221
2015	7.1	5.6	9 351	6 550	1 492	1 171	17 404	13 834	363	270
2016	6.8	7.5	9 978	9 607	1 467	1 297	12 119	16 252	240	330
2017	8.7	8.7	10 722	13 145	1 371	1 472	13 439	16 446	340	232
2018	10.2	8.9	15 500	10 600	1 516	1 303	19 342	18 480	297	351
2019	5.8	6.5	9 625	11 571	1 807	1 771	22 500	10 281	426	224
2020		10		15 000		1 500		20 504		718
Average	7.3	6.9	11 501	9 023	1 704	1 276	15 278	13 216	331	288

Note: The average total travel expense and the average expense per day were shown in Chinese yuan (RMB).

Blog Influence: Review, "Nice," Comment, Bookmark and Share

According to Sterne (2011), a post's influence on social media cannot be evaluated only by the number of "nice" clicks, as click behavior is too easy to be meaningful. However, as mentioned above, the number of reviews and "nice" clicks can still indicate the post's level of attractiveness to users in the online community. Accordingly, this study totaled the average number of reviews, "nice" clicks, comments, bookmarks and shares to explore the travel blogs' influence from various perspectives.

Based on the analysis results, although informative blogs received more readers' reaction than literature blogs, no statistical differences were found between the two blog types (see Table 24.2). However, from the perspective of average results only, informative blogs seemed to be more attractive. As the number of reviews and "nice" clicks reflect readers' interest, informative blogs seemed more attractive to potential tourists. In this study, both the review and "nice" numbers of the informative blogs greatly exceeded those of the literature blogs, indicating that the readers reviewed the travel blogs for useful information rather than purely for entertainment. This result closely relates to the numbers of bookmarks and shares; if readers perceive information as useful and are willing to introduce it to others, they will bookmark and share it. Accordingly, highly attractive informative blogs also received more bookmarks and shares than literature blogs. Interestingly, the average number of comments on literature blogs was higher than on informative blogs. Because the number of comments demonstrates the extent of interaction between readers and posters, it suggests that the literature blogs' personal stories and essays evoked empathy in the readers.

Profiles of Popular Blogs

To profile the popular blogs, the correlation coefficients among days of travel, average total travel expense, average travel expense per day, average number of characters per blog, average number of photos per blog, reviews, "nice" clocks, comments, bookmarks and shares, regardless of the blog style, was calculated (see Table 24.3). As the number of these reactions reflects the blog's influence, this study focuses on how the independent variables – days of travel, average total/per day travel expense, and average number of characters/photos in each blog – affect the blog's influence.

The study of these variables shows that compared with expenses during travel, the "travel days" significantly relate to the number of "nice" clicks and bookmarks. This result indicates that readers were not concerned about the posters' travel styles, whether luxury or budget, but about the posters' itineraries and the blogs' content. The longer tourists stayed in Japan, the richer their blog content was. Therefore, blogs by longer-stay visitors tended to be book-marked for reference. Moreover, the length of the blog, in terms of its number of characters, closely related to bookmarking, which may be because the more information that is provided, or the longer the story is, the more readers are willing to save it as a reference. The correlations between reviews, bookmarks and "nice" clicks were also strong, reflecting the readers' information-searching behavior.

Table 24.2   *The number of blog reviews, "nice" clicks, comments, bookmarks and shares from 2011 to 2020 (except 2012)*

Year	Review		"Nice"		Comment		Bookmark		Share	
	Informative	Literature	Informative	Literature	Informative	Literature	Informative	Literature	Informative	Literature
2011		47 346		361		487		177		15
2013	29 803	14 498	651	93	149	1	919	89	150	3
2014	42 654	63 535	1 356	1 186	231	228	1 205	1 028	47	55
2015	98 636	46 318	6 393	1 184	337	448	1 937	691	84	140
2016	35 391	41 439	3 753	2041	193	351	1 216	1 162	92	132
2017	50 399	35 711	3 957	1 517	147	91	2 005	947	26	32
2018	54 922	69 495	4 464	4 529	250	230	3 431	3 458	19	72
2019	19 122	49 477	410	464	76	48	191	185	6	11
2020		28 789		3 092		206		2 034		55
Average	47 275	44 068	2 998	1 607	198	232	1 558	1 086	61	57

Table 24.3 The correlation among the variables related to travel information and blog influences

	Days of travel	Average total travel expense	Average travel expense per day	Average number of characters in each blog	Average number of photos in each blog	Review	Nice	Comment	Bookmark	Share
Days of travel	1									
Average total travel expense	0.798***	1								
Average travel expense per day	0.164 (0.545)	0.692***	1							
Average number of characters in each blog	0.623 (0.010)	0.506 (0.045)	0.176 (0.515)	1						
Average number of photos in each blog	0.535 (0.033)	0.501 (0.048)	0.239 (0.372)	0.717 (0.002)	1					
Review	0.169 (0.532)	-0.073 (0.789)	-0.198 (0.461)	0.202 (0.453)	0.022 (0.934)	1				
Nice	0.650*** (0.169)	0.361 (0.169)	-0.029 (0.915)	0.489 (0.055)	0.328 (0.216)	0.679***	1			
Comment	-0.161 (0.552)	-0.375 (0.153)	-0.458 (0.075)	0.169 (0.531)	0.130 (0.631)	0.463 (0.071)	0.219 (0.415)	1		
Bookmark	0.803***	0.536 (0.032)	0.029 (0.914)	0.527 (0.036)	0.374 (0.154)	0.505 (0.046)	0.823***	0.152 (0.573)	1	
Share	0.006 (0.982)	0.009 (0.975)	0.073 (0.788)	0.040 (0.883)	0.247 (0.357)	0.151 (0.576)	0.150 (0.579)	0.445 (0.084)	0.100 (0.713)	1

Note: *** $p < 0.000$.

Table 24.4a　Word frequency query results (noun phrases)

	Informative blogs	Literature blogs
2011		Station, Park, Building, Oyster, Time, Memory, Paradise, Place, Peace, War
2013	JR (Japan Railway), Rainy season, Airplane tickets, Skyline, Cheapness, Reasons, Subway, Cherry blossom, Hotels, Position	Cherry blossom, Architecture, Church, Inn, Kabuki [Japanese classical drama], Teacher, Ando [a famous Japanese architect], Building, Meiji era, tourist spot
2014	Bus, Markets, JR [Japan Railway], Travel blogs, Hotel room, Place, Subway, Luggage, Express	Hotel, Subway, Itinerary, Photo, Gourmet, Wifi, Hometown, Travel, Time, Friends
2015	Hotel, Time, Airline, Subway, Cherry blossom, Price, Visa, Company, Travel, Skin care	Travel blog, Airport, Public transport, Price, Hotel, Hot spring, Itinerary, Transportation, Accommodation, Cities
2016	Hotel, Time, Places, Bus, Itinerary, Cherry blossom, Hour, Tour, Airport, Forest	Travel blog, Travel, Photos, Download, Snow, Story, Fresh, Hotel, Photograph, Friends
2017	Itinerary, Time, Hotel, Transportation, Comparison, JR [Japan Railway], Preparation, Convenience, Luggage, Entrance ticket	Hot spring, Hotel, Airport, Cities, Market, World, Travel, Place, Peninsula, Feelings
2018	Recommendation, Cherry blossom, Preparation, Round trip, Transportation, Travel blogs, Route, Places, Free, Tourist spot	Hotel, Place, JR [Japan Railway], Airport, Transportation, Travel, Regions, Subway, Convenience, Travel blogs
2019	Bus, Japanese Yen, Visa, Hotel, Travel, Tour, Needs, JR [Japan Railway], Subway, Airport	Kimono, Hotel, Preference, Time, Airport, Experience, Travel, Reservation, Place, Feelings
2020		Earth, Public transport, Experience, Place, Cape, Secret, Time, Travel blogs, Freedom, JR [Japan Railway]
Total	Hotel, Time, Transport, Airport, Subway, Bus, Japanese Yen exchange [currency], Visa, Itinerary, JR [Japan Railway]	Airport, JR [Japan Railway], Time, Hotel, Itinerary, Kimono, Hot spring, Travel, Travel blog, Cherry blossom

High-Frequency Words: Chinese Tourists' Preferences and Behavior in Japan

This study employed NVivo 12 Plus to code the 110 selected blogs. As noted previously, besides the use of qualitative analysis software, the content of all the blogs was carefully read by the authors, confirming consistency of content. The context analysis was conducted by running a word frequency query, as highly frequent words suggest Chinese tourists' preferences and travel behaviors. This study approached word frequency from two aspects – noun phrases and destinations – and analyzed them based on time series, which aim to identify changes over the past decade. All the selected words were listed based on the frequency in each year. Noun phrases, such as "places," "price," "hotel," and "subway," can be used to explore Chinese tourists' areas of particular attention during their visits to Japan, while destinations, such as "Tokyo," "Kyoto," "Osaka," and "Kansai region," can be used to understand Chinese tourists' itineraries (see Tables 24.4a and 24.4b).

The results of the word frequency query for noun phrases showed the most significant differences between the two blog types. Literature blogs tended to contain more phrases related to cultural experiences, such as "kimono" and "hot spring." High-frequency words in informative blogs, however, included "visa application," "transportation information" and "currency exchange," which might be very useful to potential tourists. In informative blogs, the results of the destinations' word frequency query focused on famous destinations, such as Tokyo, Osaka and Kyoto. While the high-frequency words of literature blogs included the same famous destinations as informative blogs, they also presented the Tohoku region (northeastern Japan)

Table 24.4b   Word frequency query results (destination names)

Year	Informative blogs	Literature blogs
2011		Hiroshima, Okayama, Kyoto
2013	Tokyo, Hokkaido, Ueno	Tokyo
2014	Kyoto, Nagoya, Osaka, Ohara, Tokyo, Chugoku region	Osaka, Kyoto, Nara, Kiyomizu, Todaiji temple, Kansai region, Arashiyama
2015	Osaka, Tokyo, Kyoto, Kawaguchi, Kansai region, Nara, Hokkaido, Ginza, Mt Fuji, Yokohama	Kyoto, Osaka, Tokyo, Kansai region, Nagoya, Takayama, Nara, Todaiji temple
2016	Tokyo, Mt Fuji, Osaka, Kyoto, Kansai region, Nara, Kichijoji, Kiyomizu, Kyusyu, Yamaguchi, Arashiyama	Tokyo, Tohoku region, Osaka, Kyoto, Akita, Aomori
2017	Osaka, Tokyo, Kyoto, Nara, Hokkaido, Kansai region, Mt Fuji, Arashiyama, Kiyomizu	Tokyo, Kyoto, Kansai, Nara, Tohoku region, Kanto region, Osaka
2018	Osaka, Tokyo, Kyoto, Nagoya, Hakone, Kansai region, Nara	Tokyo, Kyoto, Osaka, Tohoku region, Okayama, Nagoya, Takayama, Shiragawago, Kanazawa, Okinawa, Nara
2019	Osaka, Kyoto, Kansai, Tokyo, Kyushu, Nara, Kobe, Fukuoka, Takayama, Nagoya	Kyoto, Tokyo, Ginza, Osaka, Tohoku region, Hokkaido, Nara, Yokohama
2020		Hokkaido, Tokyo, Kyushu región
Total	Osaka, Tokyo, Kansai region, Nara, Kawaguchi, Kiyomizu, Hokkaido, Nagoya, Mt Fuji, Arashiyama, Kyushu, Kanto region	Tokyo, Kyoto, Osaka, Kansai region, Nagoya, Takayama, Tohoku region, Akita, Hokkaido, Kanto region, Nara, Aomori, Shiragawago, Kanazawa, Mt Fuji

as an attractive destination. Furthermore, with increasing travel experience, Chinese tourists have changed their travel behavior from focusing on famous destinations to exploring regions.

DISCUSSION

As well as being an increasingly important information source for potential tourists, travel blogs also mirror existing tourists' preferences and behaviors. In this section, both potential tourists' information-searching behavior and existing tourists' travel behavior are discussed.

Both Usefulness and Enjoyment Drive Reading Motivation

Lin and Lu (2011) have explored the reasons why people use social networking sites using motivation theory from as early as the beginning of social media. They found that enjoyment was more important than perceived usefulness in interpreting consumers' use of social media. Many later researchers have examined motivations for using social media in the tourism field, but have emphasized only one reason: usefulness or enjoyment.

This study took up this topic of motivations for using social media by comparing different blog types and analyzing the correlations among key variables on 110 highly attractive blogs, including 50 informative and 60 literature blogs. However, even though the average numbers of reviews, "nice" clicks, bookmarks and shares of informative blogs were higher than for literature blogs, there were no statistical differences between the two blog types. This result contrasts with previous studies (e.g., Chen et al., 2014; Huang et al., 2010) that explained potential tourists' motivations by only one reason: enjoyment or usefulness. By deeply analyzing the detailed context and comments of both informative and literature blogs, this study found that most comments on informative blogs sought information about transportation, visa applications and recommendations for souvenirs. The comments on literature blogs, however, frequently evaluated the poster's photos and showed empathy. The push–pull model has been applied to many tourism studies to explore tourist behavior (e.g., Caber and Albayrak, 2016; Wong et al., 2017; Wu and Pearce, 2014a). In this study, push factors relate to motivations for reading the blog, and pull factors relate to the blog's attractions. People read informative blogs for information that can benefit their travel, but they read literature blogs for pleasure and to seek a desirable lifestyle that they can gain from travel. Hence, as both types of travel blog attract readers, people use social media for usefulness and for enjoyment.

Changes in Chinese Tourists' Travel Behavior

From shopping to cultural experiences

Since the visa relaxation for Chinese tourists in 2010, more Chinese tourists are visiting Japan. The tax-free policy, initiated in 2013, has also greatly stimulated Chinese tourists' shopping behavior in Japan. *Bakugai*, used to describe Chinese tourists' shopping sprees, was selected as the most popular buzzword in Japan in 2015. In 2015, the authors found 16 informative blogs, compared with only eight literature blogs (see Figure 24.3); in accordance with the contemporary emphasis on shopping, most of the informative blogs discussed popular products in Japan or recommended souvenirs. For example, one of the most attractive informative blogs in 2015 was "Shopping recommendations in Japan: 80 most recommended goods," which received 736 556 reviews, 10 469 "nice" clicks, 9899 bookmarks, 257 shares, and 360 comments. In this blog, the poster provided very detailed information regarding recommended goods in Japan, such as where they could be bought, how much they cost, and why she recommended them. This blog included extremely rich information, with 16 900 words and 43 photos. Another blog titled "What should you buy in Japan – the shopping list in Hokkaido," which has been reviewed 21 526 times and has 110 "nice" clicks and 102 bookmarks, provides another example of Chinese tourists' shopping boom in Japan. Shopping recommendation blogs received high attention from potential tourists in 2015.

However, over time, this type of blog has lost its popularity. More Chinese tourists are showing interest in cultural experiences, and shopping has become a secondary rather than primary purpose for visiting Japan. Hence, literature blogs have received increasing attention. For example, the blog titled "Exploring craftsmanship – my travel in Japan" introduced the poster's cultural experience, culture shock and personal reflections during his travel in 2017. This blog had 17 496 reviews, 526 "nice" clicks, and 343 bookmarks. In addition to traditional Japanese culture, Chinese tourists turned their attention to Japanese subcultures in normal life and on the streets. A typical blog, "Lens of Japan – my travel to Kansai, Hokuriku and Chubu areas" posted in 2017, is a good example. While this literature blog was not long, with only 4472 characters and 109 photos, it received 10 326 reviews, 1298 "nice" clicks, and 198 bookmarks. Most photos in the blog were of mundane items rather than famous tourist spots, providing an accurate portrayal of Japan rather than tourism promotion. After 2016, the preferred blog photos changed to capture normal life in Japan, such as narrow streets, old buildings, people resting outside convenience stores, and commuter trains. A shift away from an interest in shopping to an interest in culture and daily life is also reflected in the results of the word frequency query (see Table 24.4a).

From big cities to local places

With increasing travel experience in Japan, Chinese tourists' preferences have changed from big cities, such as Tokyo, Osaka and Kyoto, to less famous local places (see Table 24.4b). This tendency also affected preferences in blog styles. As shown in Figure 24.3, informative blogs outnumbered literature blogs until 2015, but the opposite has occurred since 2016. When travel experience is not enough for people to plan their travel, the informative blogs are perceived to be very useful. Two informative blogs from 2015 demonstrate the type of blog popular at the time: "Our travel to Japan – Osaka, Nara, Kyoto Tokyo" was reviewed 162 186 times, with 6196 "nice" clicks, and 5223 bookmarks; and "Happy tour in Kansai area, even cannot speak in Japanese" was reviewed 99 126 times, with 26 372 "nice" clicks, and 4271 bookmarks. Both provide very detailed itineraries to be used by potential tourists as guidebooks. Additionally, the destinations these blogs include tend to be famous cities.

Currently, Chinese tourists are increasingly willing to visit less famous places, such as northeastern Japan, eager to find something new in the country. Aomori, a northeastern prefecture, is attracting a growing number of Chinese tourists who want to avoid the crowds in Hokkaido. A literature blog, "Aomori's celebration, Akita's snow festival – a five-day tour in Northeast Japan" posted in 2019, that described the poster's experience in Akita and Aomori, attracted significant attention from readers. This blog has been reviewed 17 886 times, with 539 "nice" clicks, and 249 bookmarks. Besides Aomori and Akita, numerous blogs mention Shirakawa village, a small village in the middle of Japan, which appeals to many Chinese people due to its romantic charm and fairytale-like scenery. Finally, Chinese tourists' travel behaviors are also influenced by popular Japanese anime. Numerous posters reported on their travel to Kamakura, a small city in Kanagawa, which was used as the location of a popular Japanese comic.

SUMMARY

This study explored Chinese tourists' behaviors and preferences during their travel in Japan by analyzing 110 blogs posted in Mafengwo. Travel blogs are a very useful tool to deeply understand the motivations of potential tourists and why they are willing to read blogs. This analysis has highlighted the relevance of netnographic methods in tourism studies, providing clear, original and relevant results with potential implications for policy and management related to tourism. These results relate to preferences both for different types of travel blogs and for travel behaviors. The dynamic relations between these two types of preference and their evolving interactions over time were also examined.

Whereas past studies have explained people's motivations for reading blogs in terms of perceived usefulness or enjoyment only (e.g., Chen et al., 2014; Huang et al., 2010), this study found that people browse blogs for both reasons, depending on their purpose. Some tourists read blogs to seek information that can help them arrange their travel plans, whereas others read them to learn about a different lifestyle. Moreover, travel blogs reflect potential tourists' preferences and travel behaviors. Until 2015, informative blogs received more attention from potential tourists than literature blogs; however, literature blogs seem to be increasingly popular as a result of Chinese tourists' growing travel experience. In particular, Chinese tourists appear to be shifting their travel behavior from shopping to cultural experiences.

As many previous studies have shown, destination images contain an emotional component (e.g., Sun et al., 2014; Tseng et al., 2015) that is formed by external influences. Travel blogs, which are widely used as an important source of travel information, play a crucial role in forming destination images. Travel blogs depict the feelings and experiences of existing tourists, while assisting potential tourists in their travel decision-making. This study opens up important opportunities for further research and support for policy-making, as its results can be integrated into the definition of principles and guidelines for marketing, promotion and communication strategies.

REFERENCES

Adam, J., Cobos, X., and Liu, S. (2007). *Travel 2.0: Trends in industry awareness and adoption*. New York: New York University and PhoCusWright.

Amaro, S., and Duarte, P. (2015). An integrative model of consumers' intentions to purchase travel online. *Tourism Management, 46*, 64–79. doi:10.1016/j.tourman.2014.06.006.

Ayeh, J.K., Au, N., and Law, R. (2013). "Do we believe in TripAdvisor?" Examining credibility perceptions and online travelers' attitude toward using user-generated content. *Journal of Travel Research, 52*(4), 437–452. doi:10.1177/0047287512475217.

Banyai, M., and Glover, T.D. (2011). Evaluating research methods on travel blogs. *Journal of Travel Research, 51*(3), 267–277. doi:10.1177/0047287511410323.

Bilgihan, A., Peng, C., and Kandampully, J. (2014). Generation Y's dining information seeking and sharing behavior on social networking sites. *International Journal of Contemporary Hospitality Management, 26*(3), 349–366. doi:10.1108/ijchm-11-2012-0220.

Binkhorst, E., and Dekker, T. (2009). Agenda for co-creation tourism experience research. *Journal of Hospitality Marketing and Management, 18*(2–3), 311–327. doi:10.1080/19368620802594193.

Björk, P., and Kauppinen-Räisänen, H. (2012). A netnographic examination of travelers' online discussions of risks. *Tourism Management Perspectives, 2–3*, 65–71. doi:10.1016/j.tmp.2012.03.003.

Boes, K., Buhalis, D., and Inversini, A. (2016). Smart tourism destinations: Ecosystems for tourism destination competitiveness. *International Journal of Tourism Cities, 2*(2), 108–124. doi:10.1108/IJTC-12-2015-0032.

Bosangit, C., Hibbert, S., and McCabe, S. (2015). "If I was going to die I should at least be having fun": Travel blogs, meaning and tourist experience. *Annals of Tourism Research, 55*, 1–14. doi:10.1016/j.annals.2015.08.001.

Buhalis, D., and Law, R. (2008). Progress in information technology and tourism management. *Tourism Management, 29*, 609–623. doi:10.1016/j.tourman.2008.01.005.

Bynum Boley, B., Magnini, V.P., and Tuten, T.L. (2013). Social media picture posting and souvenir purchasing behavior: Some initial findings. *Tourism Management, 37*, 27–30. doi:10.1016/j.tourman.2012.11.020.

Caber, M., and Albayrak, T. (2016). Push or pull? Identifying rock climbing tourists' motivations. *Tourism Management, 55*, 74–84. doi:10.1016/j.tourman.2016.02.003.

Çakmak, E., and Isaac, R.K. (2012). What destination marketers can learn from their visitors' blogs: An image analysis of Bethlehem, Palestine. *Journal of Destination Marketing and Management, 1*(1–2), 124–133. doi:10.1016/j.jdmm.2012.09.004.

Chen, Y.-C., Shang, R.-A., and Li, M.-J. (2014). The effects of perceived relevance of travel blogs' content on the behavioral intention to visit a tourist destination. *Computers in Human Behavior, 30*, 787–799. doi:10.1016/j.chb.2013.05.019.

Chiappa, G.D. (2013). Internet versus travel agencies: The perception of different groups of Italian online buyers. *Journal of Vacation Marketing, 19*(1), 55–66. doi:10.1177/1356766712466613.

Chung, J.Y., and Buhalis, D. (2008). Information needs in online social networks. *Information Technology and Tourism, 10*, 267–281.

Crotts, J.C. (1999). Consumer decision making and prepurchase information search. In A. Pizam and Y. Mansfeld (eds), *Consumer behavior in travel and tourism* (pp. 149–168). Binghamton, NY: Haworth Hospitality Press.

Dinhopl, A., and Gretzel, U. (2016). Selfie-taking as touristic looking. *Annals of Tourism Research, 57*, 126–139. doi:10.1016/j.annals.2015.12.015.

Fu, H., Ye, B.H., and Xiang, J. (2016). Reality TV, audience travel intentions, and destination image. *Tourism Management, 55*, 37–48. doi:10.1016/j.tourman.2016.01.009.

Hansen, D.L., Shneiderman, B., and Smith, M. (2011). *Analyzing social media networks with NodeXL*. Cambridge: Elsevier.

Heller Baird, C., and Parasnis, G. (2011). From social media to social customer relationship management. *Strategy and Leadership, 39*(5), 30–37. doi:10.1108/10878571111161507.

Hjalager, A.M. (2013). 100 innovations that transformed tourism. *Journal of Travel Research, 54*(1), 3–21. doi:10.1177/0047287513516390.

Huang, C.-Y., Chou, C.-J., and Lin, P.-C. (2010). Involvement theory in constructing bloggers' intention to purchase travel products. *Tourism Management, 31*(4), 513–526. doi:10.1016/j.tourman.2009.06.003.

Japan National Tourism Organization (JNTO) (2020). Kokuseki/Tsukibetsu Hōnichi Gaikyakusū (2003nen~2019nen) [The number of international tourists to Japan from 2003 to 2019]. Retrieved from https://www.jnto.go.jp/jpn/statistics/visitor_trends/index.html.

Japan Tourism Agency (JTA) (2017). Keizai Hakyū Kōka [Economic ripple effect]. Retrieved from https://www.mlit.go.jp/kankocho/siryou/toukei/kouka.html.

Japan Tourism Agency (JTA) (2019). Hōnichi Gaikokujin Shōhidōkō Chōsa: 2019nen nenkanchi no suikei [International tourists' consumption in Japan: The results of 2019 FY]. Retrieved from http://www.mlit.go.jp/kankocho/siryou/toukei/syouhityousa.html.

Japan Tourism Agency (JTA) (2020). *Reiwa Gan'nen Kankō Hakusho* (*Tourism White Paper of 2020*).

Japan Tourist Bureau (JTB) inbound solution (2018). Imbaundo Shijō dōkō 2019, Hōnichi Chūgokujin no Jōhō shūshū shudan towa? Chūgoku Imbaundo Shijo niokeru Dejitaru Puromōshon wo Kangaeru [The market trend in 2019: How do Chinese tourists search for information? Thinking about the digital promotion method for Chinese tourist market]. Retrieved from https://www.jtb.co.jp/inbound/market/2019/china-digital-promotion-report-2019/.

Jennings, G.R. (2005). Interviewing: A focus on qualitative techniques. In B.W. Ritchie, P. Burns and C. Palmer (eds), *Tourism research methods: Integrating theory with practice* (pp. 99–117). Wallingford: CABI.

Kim, J., and Fesenmaier, D.R. (2017). Sharing tourism experiences: The posttrip experience. *Journal of Travel Research, 56*(1), 28–40. doi:10.1177/0047287515620491.

Kim, M.J., Lee, C.-K., and Bonn, M. (2016). The effect of social capital and altruism on seniors' revisit intention to social network sites for tourism-related purposes. *Tourism Management, 53*, 96–107. doi:10.1016/j.tourman.2015.09.007.

Kozinets, R.V. (1999). E-tribalized marketing? The strategic implications. *European Management Journal, 17*(3), 252–264.

Kozinets, R.V. (2002). The field behind the screen: Using netnography for marketing research in online communities. *Journal of Marketing Research, 39*(1), 61–72.

Kozinets, R.V. (2015). *Netnography: Redefined* (2nd edn). London: SAGE Publications.

Kozinets, R.V., Valck, K.D., Wojnicki, A.C., and Wilner, S.J.S. (2010). Networked narratives: Understanding word-of-mouth marketing in online communities. *Journal of Marketing, 74*(March), 71–89.

Kusumasondjaja, S., Shanka, T., and Marchegiani, C. (2012). Credibility of online reviews and initial trust: The roles of reviewer's identity and review valence. *Journal of Vacation Marketing, 18*(3), 185–195. doi:10.1177/1356766712449365.

Ladhari, R., and Michaud, M. (2015). eWOM effects on hotel booking intentions, attitudes, trust, and website perceptions. *International Journal of Hospitality Management, 46*, 36–45. doi:10.1016/j.ijhm.2015.01.010.

Lee, Y.J., and Gretzel, U. (2014). Cross-cultural differences in social identity formation through travel blogging. *Journal of Travel and Tourism Marketing, 31*(1), 37–54. doi:10.1080/10548408.2014.861701.

Leung, D., Law, R., van Hoof, H., and Buhalis, D. (2013). Social media in tourism and hospitality: A literature review. *Journal of Travel and Tourism Marketing, 30*(1–2), 3–22. doi:10.1080/10548408 .2013.750919.

Lin, K.-Y., and Lu, H.-P. (2011). Why people use social networking sites: An empirical study integrating network externalities and motivation theory. *Computers in Human Behavior, 27*(3), 1152–1161. doi: 10.1016/j.chb.2010.12.009.

Llodrà-Riera, I., Martínez-Ruiz, M.P., Jiménez-Zarco, A.I., and Izquierdo-Yusta, A. (2015). A multidimensional analysis of the information sources construct and its relevance for destination image formation. *Tourism Management, 48*, 319–328. doi:10.1016/j.tourman.2014.11.012.

Lu, A.C.C., and Gursoy, D. (2015). A conceptual model of consumers' online tourism confusion. *International Journal of Contemporary Hospitality Management, 27*(6), 1320–1342. doi:10.1108/ ijchm-04-2014-0171.

Lyu, S.O. (2016). Travel selfies on social media as objectified self-presentation. *Tourism Management, 54*, 185–195. doi:10.1016/j.tourman.2015.11.001.

Mack, R.W., Blose, J.E., and Bing, P. (2008). Believe it or not: Credibility of blogs in tourism. *Journal of Vacation Marketing, 14*(2), 133–144. doi:10.1177/1356766707087521.

Mansson, M. (2011). Mediatized tourism. *Annals of Tourism Research, 38*(4), 1634–1652. doi:10.1016/ j.annals.2011.02.008.

Munar, A.M., and Jacobsen, J.K.S. (2014). Motivations for sharing tourism experiences through social media. *Tourism Management, 43*, 46–54. doi:10.1016/j.tourman.2014.01.012.

Öz, M. (2015). Social media utilization of tourists for travel-related purposes. *International Journal of Contemporary Hospitality Management, 27*(5), 1003–1023. doi:10.1108/ijchm-01-2014-0034.

Pan, B., MacLaurin, T., and Crotts, J.C. (2016). Travel blogs and the implications for destination marketing. *Journal of Travel Research, 46*(1), 35–45. doi:10.1177/0047287507302378.

Parra-López, E., Bulchand-Gidumal, J., Gutiérrez-Taño, D., and Díaz-Armas, R. (2011). Intentions to use social media in organizing and taking vacation trips. *Computers in Human Behavior, 27*(2), 640–654. doi:10.1016/j.chb.2010.05.022.

Rihova, I., Buhalis, B., Gouthro, M.B., and Moital, M. (2018). Customer-to-customer co-creation practices in tourism: Lessons from customer-dominant logic. *Tourism Management, 67*, 362–375. doi:10 .1016/j.tourman.2018.02.010.

Sabiote-Ortiz, C.M., Frías-Jamilena, D.M. and Castañeda-García, J.A. (2016). Overall perceived value of a tourism service delivered via different media: A cross-cultural perspective. *Journal of Travel Research, 55*(1), 34–51. doi:10.1177/0047287514535844.

Schmallegger, D., and Carson, D. (2008). Blogs in tourism: Changing approaches to information exchange. *Journal of Vacation Marketing, 14*(2), 99–110. doi:10.1177/1356766707087519.

Sharda, N., and Ponnada, M. (2007). Tourism blog visualizer for better tour planning. *First Annual Conference on Blogs in Tourism*, Kitzbuhel, Austria, July 12.

Shu, M., and Scott, N. (2014). Influence of social media on Chinese students' choice of an overseas study destination: An information adoption model perspective. *Journal of Travel and Tourism Marketing, 31*(2), 286–302. doi:10.1080/10548408.2014.873318.

Sigala, M. (2012) Exploiting Web 2.0 for new service development: Findings and implications from the Greek tourism industry. *International Journal of Tourism Research, 14*, 551–566. doi:10.1002/ jtr.1914.

Sterne, J. (2011). *Social media metrics*. Transl. Taisukei Sakai. *Jissen Sōsharumedia Māketingu Senryaku, Senjutsu*, Kōka Sokutei Shinhōsoku. Tokyo: Asahishinbun Press.

Sun, M., Ryan, C., and Pan, S. (2014). Using Chinese travel blogs to examine perceived destination image: The case of New Zealand. *Journal of Travel Research, 54*(4), 543–555. doi:10.1177/ 0047287514522882.

Tham, A., Croy, G., and Mair, J. (2013). Social media in destination choice: Distinctive electronic word-of-mouth dimensions. *Journal of Travel and Tourism Marketing, 30*(1–2), 144–155. doi:10 .1080/10548408.2013.751272.

Tseng, C., Wu, B., Morrison, A.M., Zhang, J., and Chen, Y.-C. (2015). Travel blogs on China as a destination image formation agent: A qualitative analysis using Leximancer. *Tourism Management, 46*, 347–358. doi:10.1016/j.tourman.2014.07.012.

Tussyadiah, I. (2014) Toward a theoretical foundation for experience design in tourism. *Journal of Travel Research, 53*(5), 543–564. doi:10.1177/0047287513513172.

Tussyadiah, I., and Fesenmaier, D. (2009) Mediating tourist experiences. *Annals of Tourism Research, 36*(1), 24–40. doi:10.1016/j.annals.2008.10.001.

Volo, S. (2010). Bloggers' reported tourist experiences: Their utility as a tourism data source and their effect on prospective tourists. *Journal of Vacation Marketing, 16*(4), 297–311. doi:10.1177/1356766710380884.

Wang, H.-Y. (2012). Investigating the determinants of travel blogs influencing readers' intention to travel. *Service Industries Journal, 32*(2), 231–255. doi:10.1080/02642069.2011.559225.

Wenger, A. (2008). Analysis of travel bloggers' characteristics and their communication about Austria as a tourism destination. *Journal of Vacation Marketing, 14*(2), 169–176. doi:10.1177/1356766707087525.

Wong, B.K.M., Musa, G., and Taha, A.Z. (2017). Malaysia my second home: The influence of push and pull motivations on satisfaction. *Tourism Management, 61*, 394–410. doi:10.1016/j.tourman.2017.03.003.

Wu, M.Y., and Pearce, P.L. (2014a). Chinese recreational vehicle users in Australia: A netnographic study of tourist motivation. *Tourism Management, 43*, 22–35. doi:10.1016/j.tourman.2014.01.010.

Wu, M.Y., and Pearce, P.L. (2014b). Tourism blogging motivations: Why do Chinese tourists create little "Lonely Planets"? *Journal of Travel Research, 55*(4), 537–549. doi:10.1177/0047287514553057.

Wu, M.Y., and Pearce, P.L. (2017). Understanding Chinese overseas recreational vehicle tourists: A netnographic and comparative approach. *Journal of Hospitality and Tourism Research, 41*(6), 698–718. doi:10.1177/1096348014550869.

Yen, C.-L., and Tang, C.-H. (2015). Hotel attribute performance, eWOM motivations, and media choice. *International Journal of Hospitality Management, 46*, 79–88. doi:10.1016/j.ijhm.2015.01.003.

Zeng, B., and Gerritsen, R. (2014). What do we know about social media in tourism? A review. *Tourism Management Perspectives, 10*, 27–36. doi:10.1016/j.tmp.2014.01.001.

25. Exploring antecedents of electronic word-of-mouth in tourism: a case of Tripadvisor

Farah S. Choudhary and Alka Sharma

INTRODUCTION

The Indian tourism industry is one major sector that has contributed to the growth and development of the service sector. The rich cultural diversity and heritage of India have helped in the fast growth of tourism market, leading India to be ranked third in terms of travel and tourism's total contribution to the country's gross domestic product (GDP) (WTTC, 2018). This growing trend in the tourism sector is also evident in the report published by the Ministry of Tourism, Government of India in 2019, which suggest that the share of India in the International Tourism Receipts (US$) stood at 1.97 percent, ranking 13th in the World Tourism Receipts. According to this report, the total earning from this sector stood at the US$28.6 billion in 2018 and is expected to reach the US$50 billion by 2022, thus suggesting that the tourism sector in India is an integral part of growth for the country's economy and holds immense relevance to today's global environment.

The major factors that contribute to the growth of Indian tourism sector include various government interventions, a rise in household incomes, changing consumption patterns of global as well as Indian customers, and fast-growing internet and smartphone penetration. There has been a major revolution in the tourism and travel industry with the upgrading of data services to 3G and 4G along with decreasing data tariffs. People are now consuming more data to support their decision-making.

The Indian travelers have become more technology-savvy and the internet has become an integral source of information as they plan their trips. They can book tickets online, check in to hotels, and can even exchange opinions about their trip and hotels. The internet and technological advancements have given a new capability to how people communicate and share their opinions. Thus, the internet has transformed and facilitated the tourism and hospitality industry and given a new perspective to word-of-mouth (WOM). Fox et al. (2016) have conceptualized WOM as information transferred from one customer to another to exchange their experiences. In addition, when consumers interact with each other and share their experiences online, it is called electronic word-of-mouth (e-WOM) (Hennig-Thurau and Walsh, 2004).

There are numerous researchers who have suggested the importance of e-WOM in influencing potential travellers (Ricci and Wietsma, 2006; Gretzel et al., 2007; Arsal, 2008; Hulisi and Bedri, 2012). The present research helps in understanding the perspective of e-WOM in travel decisions, and explores various antecedents of e-WOM which apply to the Indian travel industry. Thus, the present chapter will contribute to existing literature and provide useful insights into practitioners for using e-WOM strategically to attract customers/travelers towards their websites.

LITERATURE REVIEW

E-WOM is a form of communication that has proven to be one of the most effective ways of marketing (Gupta and Harris, 2010). According to Brown et al. (2007), the growing importance of online and social media has given a new meaning to WOM, as it has emerged as a fast way to share opinions. Further, Chen and Huang (2013) suggested that online reviews affect the level of contribution in both frequency and continuity.

Various researchers have found that travelers are highly influenced by e-WOM when they are traveling (Vermeulen and Seegers, 2009; Ye et al., 2009; Albarq, 2013). Further outlining the relevance of customer reviews, Vermeulen and Seegers (2009) highlighted that in the travel industry, online views increase the awareness of hotels, and positive comments improve the tourists' attitudes about a hotel. Ye et al. (2009) stated that positive e-WOM increases the number of hotel bookings. Furthermore, Abubakar and Ilkan (2016) suggested that prospective visitors consult online reviews until the moment of consumption. In a recent study conducted by Putu and I Made (2018), it was proposed that e-WOM has a direct positive and significant influence on the image of a destination and intention to visit. Thus, e-WOM is an effective consumption decision tool for travelers.

MOTIVES FOR ELECTRONIC WORD-OF-MOUTH

Numerous researchers highlight the factors or antecedents of e-WOM. In another study conducted by Hennig-Thurau and Walsh (2004), it was proposed that the social benefit to a consumer for being identified and integrated with an online community is one of the main factors that influence them to write a review. Customers enjoy communicating with other people, exchanging opinions and sharing their experiences. Various studies have underlined the relevance of social benefits and bonding, which customers recognize while giving an online review (Venketash et al., 2003; Kwon and Wen, 2010; Watjatrakul, 2013). Another significant factor identified by the literature as influencing reviewers is economic incentives. Often, customers receive economic benefits in the form of rewards and compensation for giving a review and writing comments (Stöckl et al., 2007; Hennig-Thurau and Walsh, 2004; Roumani et al., 2014). At times, consumers even collaborate for some incentives with companies to create a positive WOM about its brand before the actual launch of product/service. This is also referred to as "co-creation" (Christodoulides et al., 2012). In addition, a distinct factor considered by the reviewers is sharing experience about a product/service. An experience can be negative or positive (Chatterjee, 2001). Customers vent about their negative experience and create negative content about a product/service to reduce their anxiety and frustration (Yap et al., 2013; Yoo and Gretzel, 2011; Hennig-Thurau and Walsh, 2004). As stated by Yang and Mai (2010), consumers recognize negative e-WOM messages more than positive messages while evaluating experiential services. Customers also share their positive experiences through reviews to support other customers by means of their recommendations (Stöckl et al., 2007; Ho and Dempsey, 2010). Often, customers or travelers give reviews to help the service providers as well (Hennig-Thurau and Walsh, 2004). In addition, a distinct factor for reviewing is a concern for others. E-WOM communication may be made to help other consumers with their buying decisions, to save others from negative experiences, or both (Hennig-Thurau and Walsh, 2004; Yoo and Gretzel, 2011; Bronner and de Hoog, 2010; Cheung and Lee, 2012; Ho and Dempsey, 2010; Yap et al., 2013; Yoo et al., 2013). Concern can even be for the company or the service provider. A consumer, when satisfied with a product or service, feels the desire to support the company (Bronner and de Hoog, 2010; Jang and Jeong, 2011; Yap et al., 2013). Hence, such a message can include both positive and negative consumer experiences. Another significant factor highlighted by researchers is hedonism. Reviewers often give reviews for intrinsic fun and enjoyment (Dholakia et al., 2004; Okazaki, 2009). Often, reviewers engage in e-WOM due to hedonism motives (Toubia and Stephen, 2013; Ryan and Deci, 2000). Another factor stated by most studies is self-enhancement. Often, consumers are satisfied and contented when other consumers read their reviews. This response from others makes consumers feel they are valuable to others, giving them a sense of social status (Hennig-Thurau and Walsh, 2004; Doma et al., 2015). Many studies have suggested the importance of the desire for positive recognition from others; this is also known as self-concept (Christodoulides et al., 2012) or egoism (Cheung and Lee, 2012), and is a critical component considered by the content creators (Gretzel et al., 2007; Yoo et al., 2013; Yap et al., 2013). The sense of power to control and change perceptions of others is also a key motivator for consumers/travelers to be more involved in creating user-generated content (Bronner and de Hoog, 2010).

RESEARCH GAP

On the whole, prior studies on e-WOM have suggested various aspects of reviews (Hennig-Thurau and Walsh, 2004; Jansen et al., 2009; Isabelle et al., 2010; Lkhaasuren and Nam, 2018). Furthermore, it has been proposed by Cheema and Kaikati (2010) that every reviewer is distinct from others, and this feeling of distinctiveness can be the main reason for online reviewers to share their opinions. However, most of the studies have focused on the outcome effects of e-WOM. There are very few researcheswhich analyze the antecedents persuading the customers to write online reviews. Thus, studying these antecedents and exploring these factors could help academics narrow the gap that exists in the literature, put together the building blocks to understand Indian consumers' e-WOM behavior, and improve the travel marketers' efforts with their customers. The present chapter also examines and expands the heterogeneous behavior of reviewers and attempts to comprehend and validate those attributes which shape this behavior, along with the manner in which it affects product/ service evaluation.

In the travel industry, travelers are unsure about the quality of the experiential services that they will encounter. Due to this intangible aspect of the tourism industry, travelers have to depend on reviews and WOM on various travel websites as a reference for a good experience (Kwok et al., 2017; Kim and Kim, 2018; Narangajavana Kaosiri et al., 2019). Owing to this characteristic of the travel industry and the fast-growing adoption of technology in this industry, the impact of online reviews is even more important in tourism, as they facilitate the decision-making process (Yoo and Gretzel, 2011; Vermeulen and Seegers, 2009; Jang and Moutinho, 2019).

Hence, the main objective of this study is to identify the relative importance of the various antecedents of e-WOM in the travel industry and develop a conceptual framework that will help the industry to gain an insight into using e-WOM as a strategic tool to create a competitive advantage for long-term sustainability.

RESEARCH METHODOLOGY

This chapter has used mixed research methodology, including qualitative and quantitative research, to determine the important antecedents that influence e-WOM and the reasons as to why travelers give online reviews in the tourism industry. The study has adopted certain focus groups, supported by an introductory semi-structured questionnaire for better triangulation of data. A focus group analysis of travelers who have given reviews online was conducted to understand their reasons for writing the reviews. Three focus groups of 12 members each were conducted. All focus groups were audiotaped, translated and analyzed using content analysis. On the basis of content analysis, a list of keywords was prepared. Based on these keywords and past studies, the questionnaire was prepared, which was further modified to fit the context. Data was collected from travelers who had given their reviews on the travel website Tripadvisor. A total of 140 questionnaires were collected.

ANALYSIS

All the data collected through the questionnaire was entered into the Statistical Package for the Social Sciences (SPSS). Statistical techniques including Cronbach's alpha coefficient and exploratory factor analysis were applied to validate the results. Later, analysis of variance (ANOVA) was used to investigate the variation in antecedents of online customer reviews with respect to frequency of writing and demographic factors (gender and age).

Focus Groups

Three focus groups were conducted (n1 = 15 participants; n2 = 15 participants; n3 = 15 participants) and were guided by a moderator and an observer. Three groups varying in age and occupation were selected. There were 21 men and 24 women, a total of 45 participants.

Group 1 was mainly formed by a cluster of postgraduate students younger than 30 years old; comprising males and females. Group 2 was a mix of the male and female clusters, between 30 and 45 years old. Finally, group 3 was a group of participants older than 45.

The discussion was focused on key motives to write a review.

Each focus group discussion lasted 45 to 60 minutes and was tape-recorded. First, some generic questions related to demographics and pattern of reviewing were asked. The participants were asked about their frequency of writing. They were asked whether they write after every purchase or only after a positive or negative experience. Furthermore, the focus groups were inquired about the length of the reviews they write.

Also, the moderator asked participants about the following broad topics: (1) traveling; (2) experience of traveling; and (3) reviewing online. More specific questions included: Why do you review? What do you like/dislike about your travel experience? Do you write a review when you have a positive travel experience, a negative travel experience, or both? Do you get any economic incentives for reviewing? Do you feel any social bond or benefit while giving reviews? Do you write a review to warn or help other customers? Do you write a review to help/harm service providers? Do you engage in e-WOM for fun and enjoyment? Do you feel motivated by the sense that you can change other customer's perception? What do you feel when other consumers read your reviews?

Several different texts about writing a review were submitted by participants. The data collected was analyzed and a content analysis of the keywords received from the participants was performed.

Based on the literature and focus group analysis, a total of seven different motivations were summarized, as follows:

1. Self-enhancement.
2. Social benefits.
3. Economic incentive.
4. Concern for others.
5. Positive experience.
6. Negative experience.
7. Hedonism.

Questionnaire Design and Development

Based on the keywords and variables obtained from the focus group analysis, a structured questionnaire was framed. An extensive literature was reviewed to develop an appropriate scale for this research.

The following measures of e-WOM have been adopted for the study: the self-enhancement scale proposed by Doma et al. (2015) and Christodoulides et al. (2012); and the social benefits scale by Hennig-Thurau and Walsh (2004), Kwon and Wen (2010) and Watjatrakul (2013). Further, for measuring economic incentive, the scale proposed by Stöckl et al. (2007), Hennig-Thurau and Walsh (2004) and Roumani et al. (2014) was used. For hedonism, the scale proposed by Ryan and Deci (2000), Okazaki (2009) and Toubia and Stephen (2013) was adapted. Additionally, for measuring the "concern for others" variables, the scale proposed by Bronner and de Hoog (2010), Cheung and Lee (2012), Ho and Dempsey (2010), Yap et al. (2013) and Yoo et al. (2013) was considered. Also, the positive experience scale has been adopted from the study of Stöckl et al. (2007) and Ho and Dempsey (2010); and finally, the scale of negative experience has been taken from Yap et al. (2013) and Yoo and Gretzel (2011).

The initial questionnaire contained seven Likert-scale items adopted from past studies; however, these were modified to fit the context of the research topic. The initial questionnaire contains 33 items for measuring various variables (see the Appendix).

Sampling

The data was collected using purposive sampling from travelers who had given their reviews on the travel website Tripadvisor. A total of 150 questionnaires were distributed among the respondents. After removing the outliers, a total of 140 questionnaires were retained for final analysis.

The optimal ratio approach of five observations for each item was used. Since the number of measuring variables for the present instrument is around 33, the appropriateness of the sample size of minimum 165 (33 x 5 = 165) respondents was verified to use for the multivariate analysis (Barlett et al., 2001).

Table 25.1   *Gender and age characteristics of the respondents*

	Characteristics	Frequency	%
Gender	Male	73	52.14
	Female	67	47.86
Age	Up to 25 years	32	22.85
	26–35 years	22	15.71
	36–45 years	59	42.14
	46–55 years	16	11.42
	55 years and older	11	7.85

Table 25.2   *Kaiser–Meyer–Olkin measure of sampling adequacy*

Kaiser–Meyer–Olkin measure of sampling adequacy		0.789
Bartlett's test of sphericity	Approx. Chi-square	6754.552
	Df	21
	Sig.	0.000

It was also noted during the literature survey that the majority of past research regarding online reviews has been conducted using a sample size of 100 to 150 respondents (Hennig-Thurau and Walsh, 2004; Jansen et al., 2009; Isabelle et al., 2010; Lkhaasuren and Nam, 2018). Thus, a final sample of 140 was taken. The demographic representation of the sample is presented in Table 25.1.

Factor Analysis

Factor analysis was used in the study to simplify and reduce the data. Cronbach's alpha test for the reliability of the scale was used to test the scale. Factor analysis was carried out using principal component analysis along with a varimax rotation procedure for summarizing the original data with minimum and most important factors. The statements with factor loading less than 0.5 and Eigen value less than 1.0 were ignored for further data analysis.

First, Kaiser–Meyer–Olkin (KMO) and Barlett's test were conducted. Bartlett's test of sphericity indicated a high Chi-square value of 6754.552 with 21 degrees of freedom at a significance level of 0.000, thereby confirming that the population correlation matrix is not an identity matrix (Table 25.2). Further, the acceptable value for KMO is 0.7 and for this study, it was 0.789. Thus, the instrument was accepted. After that, Barlett's test was conducted and the value was 0.000, which is again acceptable to perform factor analysis. Table 25.2 presents detailed KMO and Barlett's test results.

The detailed pattern matrix of the various e-WOM items is given in Table 25.3. After performing factor analysis, it was configured so that the 33 items can be grouped into seven factors. Out of the 33 items, two items had loading in more than one factor and two had a factor loading less than 0.5, and so were ignored. In conclusion, 29 items were left under seven factors. The factors were grouped and named accordingly:

1. Self-enhancement: 5 items.
2. Social benefits: 4 items.
3. Economic incentive: 3 items.
4. Concern for others: 3 items.

5. Positive experience: 6 items.
6. Negative experience: 4 items.
7. Hedonism: 4 items.

Table 25.3　Pattern matrix

	Components						
	1	2	3	4	5	6	7
Negative Experience 3	0.865						
Negative Experience 2	0.814						
Negative Experience 1	0.696						
Negative Experience 4	0.779						
Incentives 2		0.753					
Incentives 3		0.682					
Incentives 1		0.672					
Concern for Others 2			0.432				
Concern for Others 1			0.554		0.342		
Concern for Others 3	0.230		0.653				
Concern for Others 4			0.765				
Concern for Others 5			0.771				
Social Benefit 2				0.857			
Social Benefit 3				0.791			
Social Benefit 1				0.743			
Social Benefit 4				0.669			
Positive Experience 1					0.978		
Positive Experience 6					0.680		
Positive Experience 3					0.637		
Positive Experience 2					0.576		
Positive Experience 5					0.879		
Positive Experience 4					0.830		
Hedonism 3						0.771	
Hedonism 4						0.845	
Hedonism 2						0.222	
Hedonism 5						0.682	
Hedonism 1						0.539	
Hedonism 6						0.311	
Self-enhancement 5							0.854
Self-enhancement 4							0.844
Self-enhancement 1							0.801
Self-enhancement 3							0.879
Self-enhancement 2							0.830

Extraction method: principal component analysis

Rotation method: Promax with Kaiser normalization

Rotation converged in two iterations

Table 25.4   *Discriminant validity among e-word-of-mouth factors*

	Self-enhancement	Social benefits	Economic incentive	Concern for others	Positive experience	Negative experience	Hedonism
Self-Enhancement	1.000						
Social benefits	0.308(**)	1.000					
Economic incentive	0.411(**)	0.443(**)	1.000				
Concern for others	0.382(**)	0.417(**)	0.324(**)	1.000			
Positive experience	0.324(**)	0.428(**)	0.431(**)	0.353(**)	1.000		
Negative experience	0.391(**)	0.315(**)	0.299(**)	0.326(**)	0.381(**)	1.000	
Hedonism	0.403(**)	0.354(**)	0.372(**)	0.438(**)	0.376(**)	0.351(**)	1.000

Note: ** Correlation is statistically significant at the 0.01 level (two-tailed).

Discriminant Validity

It can be seen in Table 25.4 that there is a very low correlation among all the factors of e-WOM, that is, $R < 0.5$. Hence, the factorial design is validated.

Analysis of Variance for Electronic Word-of-Mouth

Analysis of variance (ANOVA) is a statistical tool that is used to compare the means of more than two populations. In the present research, the data was subjected to an ANOVA test to investigate the variation in e-WOM with respect to the frequency of writing and demographic factors (gender and age) of the respondents.

Electronic Word-of-Mouth with Respect to the Frequency of Writing

Electronic-WOM antecedents include self-enhancement, social benefits, economic incentive, concern for others, positive experience, negative experience and hedonism. A detailed analysis of variance was conducted with respect to the frequency of writing.

It is clear from the significance column of Table 25.5 that in terms of the factors related to e-WOM, there is a significant difference between groups, as the p-value of all the factors is 0.000, which is less than 0.005. Hence, post hoc testing was applied to identify the homogeneous subsets of means of factors of e-WOM.

Post Hoc Test

Once it was determined from ANOVA table that differences exist among the means, Tukey's "honestly significant difference" (HSD) test, which is a post hoc test, was used to determine which means differ. This test recognizes homogeneous subsets of means that are not different from each other at an alpha value of 0.05. Table 25.6 depicts that customers give online reviews more after a negative experience. Also, very few customers give a review after every purchase.

Table 25.5   ANOVA: electronic word-of-mouth with respect to the frequency of writing

		Sum of squares	df	Mean square	F	Sig.
Self-enhancement	Between groups	24.146	2	9.117	7.761	0.000
	Within groups	1054.442	137	1.312		
	Total	1078.588	139			
Social benefits	Between groups	18.232	2	11.653	9.905	0.000
	Within groups	1113.569	137	1.321		
	Total	1131.801	139			
Economic incentive	Between groups	15.432	2	18.654	8.187	0.000
	Within groups	1087.119	137	1.338		
	Total	1102.551	139			
Concern for others	Between groups	76.895	2	15.103	9.227	0.000
	Within groups	1262.547	137	1.256		
	Total	1339.442	139			
Positive experience	Between groups	21.235	2	13.946	8.932	0.000
	Within groups	1232.343	137	1.581		
	Total	1253.578	139			
Negative experience	Between groups	72.432	2	11.677	9.766	0.000
	Within groups	1489.643	137	1.235		
	Total	1562.075	139			
Hedonism	Between groups	11.214	2	15.375	8.287	0.000
	Within groups	1186.321	137	1.456		
	Total	1197.535	139			

Table 25.6   ANOVA: Tukey's HSD homogeneous subsets for the frequency of writing

Frequency of writing	N	Subset for alpha = 0.05	
		1	2
After every purchase	29	4.875	
After positive experiences	43	5.121	
After negative experiences	68		5.745
Sig.		0.976	0.791

ANALYSIS OF ELECTRONIC WORD-OF-MOUTH WITH RESPECT TO DEMOGRAPHIC FACTORS

Data was collected for various demographic factors including age and gender. Therefore, in data analysis, analysis was undertaken to understand the relationship between these demographic variables and e-WOM.

Electronic Word-of-Mouth with Respect to Gender

Table 25.7 represents the response of gender towards e-WOM. The mean value for the response of males towards e-WOM is higher than that of females, clearly showing that males tend to give more online reviews than females. In addition, Table 25.8 indicates the results of the analysis of variance among females and males with regard to online reviews. It can be

Table 25.7   *Descriptive for gender response to electronic word-of-mouth*

Gender	N	Mean	Std. deviation	Std. error	95% Confidence interval for mean		Minimum	Maximum
					Lower bound	Upper bound		
Male	73	5.142	0.811	0.028	5.032	5.342	1.87	7.00
Female	67	5.231	0.858	0.047	5.115	5.872	2.23	7.00
Total	140	5.427	0.837	0.016	5.153	5.811	1.87	7.00

Table 25.8   *ANOVA: electronic word-of-mouth with respect to gender*

	Sum of squares	Df	Mean square	F	Sig.
Between groups	3.598	1	3.752	5.608	0.002
Within groups	118.927	138	0.591		
Total	122.525	139			

Table 25.9   *ANOVA: electronic word-of-mouth with respect to age*

	Sum of squares	Df	Mean square	F	Sig.
Between groups	13.764	4	7.381	2.666	0.000
Within groups	173.575	135	1.256		
Total	187.339	139			

comprehended from the significance column of Table 25.8 that there is a significant difference between males and females pertaining to e-WOM, as the p-value is less than 0.05. Post hoc testing was not performed for the analysis as there were fewer than three groups.

Electronic Word-of-Mouth with Respect to Age

Table 25.9 represents the response of customers of various age groups towards e-WOM. It indicates the results of the analysis of variance among customers of various age groups with regard to e-WOM. It can be comprehended from the significance column that there is a significant difference between customers of various age groups related to e-WOM, as the p-value is less than 0.05. Post hoc testing has been applied to identify the homogeneous subsets of means of various age groups.

Post Hoc Test

Table 25.10 depicts that customers of age groups 36–45 years, 46–55 years, and 55 years and above have a similar inclination towards e-WOM. However, customers in the age group of 36–45 years tend to give more reviews in comparison with other age groups.

DISCUSSION

In accordance with previous studies, the key antecedents identified in the research for giving customers' reviews are experience, concern for others, social benefits, incentives given by the website, hedonism and self-enhancement. Furthermore, the study provides insights into the

Table 25.10   ANOVA: Tukey's HSD homogeneous subsets for age groups

Websites	N	Subset for alpha = 0.05	
		1	2
Up to 25 years	32	4.621	
26–35 years	22	4.769	
36–45 years	59		5.394
46–55 years	16		5.214
55 years and older	11		5.034
Sig.		1.000	0.812

antecedents motivating different e-WOM. Hence, it is important to mention that e-WOM plays an important role in affecting tourists' travel intentions, so marketers and organizations should try to focus on the kind of reviews they are receiving through e-WOM and try to change the negative thoughts of the travelers by solving and responding to their problems.

Furthermore, the analysis of demographic factors such as gender and age group has been undertaken to analyze the relationship of demographic factors with online reviews. The results of the gender analysis exhibit that males write more frequently than females. Also, it is distinctly evident that individuals within the age group of 36–45 years tend to provide more e-WOM than other age groups. Therefore, marketers and retailers need to devise e-WOM strategies keeping in mind this particular target group for encouraging customers towards a product/service. Furthermore, the analysis of the frequency of writing depicts that individuals tends to write more after a negative purchase experience. Thus, marketers and service providers should develop a mechanism for handling customers' complaints and grievances promptly.

On the whole, the present study provides useful insight into online retailers about the driving motives of online reviewers. Understanding these antecedents can be valuable for the tourism industry also, as it can help companies to strategize their services/products to make them high in experience and reduce the uncertainty of expectations of the customers.

LIMITATIONS AND FUTURE RESEARCH

The present research investigates only the antecedents that affect online reviewers. Future research with other outcome variables of online reviews can be explored to understand the whole concept of e-WOM in an online format. Furthermore, the role of customer outcomes such as customer behavior, behavior intention, destination image, satisfaction, and so on, can be deliberated in relation to online reviews in future studies. e-WOM also enables an understanding of the behavior of reviewers; therefore, research may be undertaken to understand their psychology and analyze the relevance of emotions.

REFERENCES

Abubakar, A.M., and Ilkan, M. (2016). Impact of online WOM on destination trust and intention to travel: A medical tourism perspective. *Journal of Destination Marketing and Management*. Retrieved (June 4, 2020) from http://dx.doi.org/10.1016/j.jdmm.2015.12.005.

Abubakar, A.M., Ilkan, M., and Sahin, P. (2016). eWOM, eReferral and gender in the virtual community. *Marketing Intelligence and Planning.* Retrieved (May 18, 2020) from http://dx.doi.org/10.1108/MIP-05-2015-0090.

Albarq, A.N. (2013). Measuring the impacts of online word-of-mouth on tourists' attitude and intentions to visit Jordan: An empirical study. *International Business Research, 7*(1), 14–22.

Arsal, I. (2008). The influence of electronic word of mouth in an online travel community on travel decisions: A case study. *All Dissertations, 273.* Retrieved (June 5, 2020) from https://tigerprints.clemson.edu/all_dissertations/273.

Barlett, J.E., Kotrlik, J.W., and Higgins, C.C. (2001). Organizational research: Determining appropriate sample size in survey research. *Information Technology, Learning, and Performance Journal, 19*(1), 43.

Bronner, F., and de Hoog, R. (2010). Vacationers and eWOM: Who posting, and why, where, and what? *Journal of Travel Research, 50*(1), 15–26.

Brown, J., Brodering, A., and Lee, N. (2007). Word of mouth communication within online communities: Conceptualizing the online social network. *Journal of Interactive Marketing, 21*(3), 2–20.

Chatterjee, P. (2001). Online reviews: Do consumers use them? *Advances in Consumer Research, 28*(1), 129–133.

Cheema, A., and Kaikati, A.M. (2010). The effect of need for uniqueness on word of mouth. *Journal of Marketing Research, 47*(3), 553–563.

Chen, H.N., and Huang, C.Y. (2013). An investigation into online reviewers' behavior. *European Journal of Marketing, 47*(10), 1758–1773.

Cheung, C.M., and Lee, M.K. (2012). What drives consumers to spread electronic word of mouth in online consumer-opinion platforms? *Decision Support Systems, 53*(1), 218–225.

Christodoulides, G., Jevons, C., and Bonhomme, J. (2012). Memo to marketers: Quantitative evidence for change – How user-generated content really affects brands. *Journal of Advertising Research, 52*(1), 53–65.

Dholakia, U.M., Bagozzi, R.P., and Pearo, L.K. (2004). A social influence model of consumerparticipation in network- and small-group-based virtual communities. *International Journal of Research in Marketing, 21*(3), 241–263.

Doma, S.S., N.A. Elaref and M.A. Abo Elnaga (2015). Factors affecting electronic word-of-mouth on social networking websites in Egypt – An application of the technology acceptance model. *Journal of Internet Social Networking and Virtual Communities,* Vol. 2015 Article ID 280025. DOI: 10.5171/2015.280025.

Fox, Gavin and Longart, Pedro (2016). Electronic word-of-mouth: Successful communication strategies for restaurants. *Tourism and Hospitality Management, 22*(2), 211–223.

Gretzel, U., Yoo, K.Y., and Purifoy, M. (2007). Online travel reviews study: Role and impact of online travel reviews: Laboratory for intelligent systems in tourism. Texas A&M University, Retrieved (December 2020) from http://www.tripadvisor.com/pdfs/OnlineTravelReviewReport.pdf.

Gupta, P. and Harris, J. (2010). How e-WOM recommendations influence product consideration and quality of choice: A motivation to process information perspective. *Journal of Business Research, 63,* 1041–1049.

Hennig-Thurau, T., and Walsh, G. (2004). Electronic word-of-mouth: Motives for and consequences of reading customer articulations on the internet. *International Journal of Electronic Commerce, 8*(2), 51–74.

Ho, J.Y., and Dempsey, M. (2010). Viral marketing: Motivations to forward online content. *Journal of Business Research, 63*(9-10), 1000–1006.

Hulisi, O., and Bedri, K.O.T. (2012). The influence of internet customer reviews on the online sales and prices in hotel industry. *Service Industries Journal, 32*(2), 197–214.

Isabelle, G., Jasmin, B., and François, M. (2010). e-WOM scale: Word-of-mouth measurement scale for e-services context. *Canadian Journal of Administrative Sciences, 27,* 5–23.

Jang, S.C., and Jeong, E.H. (2011). Restaurant experiences triggering positive electronic word-of-mouth (eWOM) motivations. *International Journal of Hospitality Management, 30*(2), 356–366.

Jang, S., and Moutinho, L. (2019). Do price promotions drive consumer spending on luxury hotel services? The moderating roles of room price and user-generated content. *International Journal of Hospitality Management, 78,* 27–35.

Jansen, B.J., Zhang, M., Sobel, K., and Chowdury, A. (2009). Twitter power: Tweets as electronic word of mouth. *Journal of the American Society for Information Science and Technology*, *60*(11), 2169–2188.

Kim, M.S., and Kim, J. (2018). Linking marketing mix elements to passion-driven behavior toward a brand: Evidence from the foodservice industry. *International Journal of Contemporary Hospitality Management*, *30*(10), 3040–3058.

Kwok, L., Xie, K.L., and Richards, T. (2017). Thematic framework of online review research: A systematic analysis of contemporary literature on seven major hospitality and tourism journals. *International Journal of Contemporary Hospitality Management*, *29*(1), 307–354.

Kwon, O., and Wen, Y. (2010). An empirical study of the factors affecting social network service use. *Journal of Computers in Human Behavior*, 26, 254–263.

Lkhaasuren, Mendbayar and Nam, Kyung-Doo (2018). The effect of electronic word of mouth (eWOM) on purchase intention on Korean cosmetic products in the Mongolian market. *Journal of International Trade and Commerce*, *14*(4), 161–175. Retrieved (May 11, 2020) from http://dx.doi.org/10.16980/jitc .14.4.201808.161.

Ministry of Tourism, Government of India (2019). India tourism statistics at a glance 2019. Retrieved (June 1, 2020) from http://tourism.gov.in/sites/default/files/Other/India%20Tourism%20Statistics %20at%20a%20Glance%202019.pdf.

Narangajavana Kaosiri, Y., Callarisa Fiol, L.J., Moliner Tena, M.Á., Rodríguez Artola, R.M., and Sánchez García, J. (2019). User-generated content sources in social media: A new approach to explore tourist satisfaction. *Journal of Travel Research*, *58*(2), 253–265.

Okazaki, S. (2009). Social influence model and electronic word of mouth. *International Journal of Advertising*, *28*(3), 439–472.

Putu, Y.S., and I Made, A.W. (2018). The effect of eWOM on intention to visit and the mediating role of destination image. *IOSR Journal of Business and Management*, *20*(9), 21–27.

Ricci, F., and Wietsma, R.T.A. (2006). Product reviews in travel decision making. Paper presented at Information and Communication Technologies in Tourism 2006, Lausanne, Switzerland.

Roumani, Y., Nwankpa, J.K., and Roumani, Y.F. (2014). The impact of incentives on the intention to try a new technology. *Technology Analysis and Strategic Management*, *27*(2), 126–141.

Ryan, R.M., and Deci, E.L. (2000). Self-determination theory and the facilitation of intrinsic motivation, social development, and well-being. *American Psychologist*, *55*, 68–78.

Stöckl, R., Rohrmeier, P., and Hess, T. (2007). Why customers produce user generated content. In Hass, B.H., Walsh, G., and Kilian, T. (eds), *Web 2.0: Neue Perspektivenfür Marketing und Medien*, Springer, Heidelberg, pp. 272–287.

Toubia, O., and Stephen, A.T. (2013). Intrinsic versus image-related utility in social media: whydo people contribute content to Twitter? *Marketing Science*, *32*(3), 368–392.

Venkatesh, V., Morris, M.G., Davis, G.B., and Davis, F.D. (2003). User acceptance of information technology: Toward a unified view. *MIS Quarterly*, *27*(3), 425–478.

Vermeulen, I.E., and Seegers, D. (2009). Tried and tested: The impact of online hotel reviews on consumer consideration. *Tourism Management*, *30*, 23-127.

Watjatrakul, B. (2013). Intention to use a free voluntary service: The effects of social influence, knowledge and perceptions. *Journal of Systems and Information Technology*, *15*(2), 202–220.

World Travel and Tourism Council (WTTC) (2018). *Economic Impact Report (2018)*. Retrieved (June 1, 2020) from https://wttc.org/Research/Economic-Impact.

Yang, J., and Mai, E. (2010). Experiential goods with network externalities effects: An empirical study of online rating system. *Journal of Business Research*, *63*, 1050–1057.

Yap, K.B., Soetarto, B., and Sweeney, J.C. (2013). The relationship between electronic word-of-mouth motivations and message characteristics: The sender's perspective. *Australasian Marketing Journal*, *21*, 66–74.

Ye, Q., Law, R., and Gu, B. (2009). The impact of online user reviews on hotelroom sales. *International Journal of Hospitality Management*, *28*(1), 180–182.

Yoo, C.W., Sanders, G.L., and Moon, J. (2013). Exploring the effect of e-WOM participation on e-loyalty in e-commerce. *Decision Support Systems*, *55*(3), 669–678.

Yoo, K.H., and Gretzel, U. (2011). Influence of personality on travel-related consumer-generated media creation. *Computers in Human Behavior*, *27*(2), 609–621.

APPENDIX: QUESTIONNAIRE

Please respond to the following questions based on how you write *Online Reviews* on a scale of 1 to 7 with the following:
(1) = Strongly Disagree, (2) = Disagree, (3) = Somewhat Disagree, (4) = Neither Agree Nor Disagree, (5) = Somewhat Agree, (6) = Agree, (7) = Strongly Agree

Serial No.	Parameters	1	2	3	4	5	6	7
	POSITIVE EXPERIENCES							
	I write only when I have to express my positive experience.							
	I mostly share my positive experiences about the service.							
	In my review, I recommend service to others.							
	I write to help others with my own positive experiences.							
	I write about the good aspects of the service.							
	I recommend people to buy service from a particular online platform.							
	NEGATIVE EXPERIENCES							
	I mostly share my negative experience of the service.							
	I want to save others from having a similar negative experience.							
	In my review, I voice my complaint.							
	I write to warn others of bad services.							
	CONCERN FOR OTHERS							
	I want hotels I like to be successful.							
	I want to retaliate against the hotel for a bad experience.							
	I want good companies should be supported.							
	I want others to use the same service.							
	I want others to use better service.							
	INCENTIVES							
	I comment only when it is a sponsored review.							
	I generally receive incentives for writing comments.							
	I receive reward points for writing reviews.							
	HEDONISM							
	Writing reviews is an exciting activity.							
	Writing reviews is an enjoyable activity.							
	I think writing reviews is an interesting activity.							
	I think providing comments on websites are a pleasant activity.							
	Writing reviews is a fun activity.							
	I feel good when I write a review on the Internet.							
	SOCIAL BENEFIT							
	I can communicate with various people sharing similar interests.							
	I can develop a bond/association with other people.							
	I enjoy sharing knowledge with other people.							
	I meet nice people this way.							
	SELF-ENHANCEMENT							
	Writing reviews is a status symbol.							
	Writing reviews present me as an influencer.							
	I think writing reviews helps me become an opinion leader.							
	I feel good when I can tell others about my service.							
	My review shows others that I am a clever customer.							

Number of Sentences Written in a Review	
Very Short (0–2 lines)	
Short (3–5 lines)	
Lengthy (above 5 lines)	

Frequency of writing	
After every purchase	
After positive experiences	
After negative experiences	

Gender	
Male	
Female	

Age	
Up to 25 years	
26–35 years	
36–45 years	
46–55 years	
55 and older	

PART V

SOCIAL MEDIA AND DECISION-MAKING

26. Impacts of social media on travelers' decision-making process

Hasan Kilic, Ali Ozturen, Cathrine Banga and Ruth Bamidele

INTRODUCTION

Empirical findings indicate that the travel and tourism industry is currently the fastest-growing sector in the world. The advent of social media nearly 20 years ago following the expansion of internet services and the World Wide Web access to the masses from the near-exclusive preserve of the broadcasting industry, as well as a few high-tech private and public companies and institutions such as banks and stock exchanges, has added a new dimension to the dynamic sector of the global economy. In particular, social media (SOMED) has drastically transformed the way people communicate and interact among themselves and with companies. It has changed the means of sharing ideas and opinions as well as the process of receiving and reviewing products and services (Mariani et al., 2019). This is predominantly the case in the hospitality and tourism sector. Tourism and hospitality organizations' usage of social media to communicate with potential travelers or customers is also expanding (Mariani et al., 2014). According to Gohil (2015), SOMED platforms have become a central feature of tourism. Such platforms have enabled travelers to view, receive, evaluate, rank, buy and use tourism products and services on the internet.

The extant literature abounds on the use, role and impact of SOMED in tourism, particularly on travelers' decision-making process (Mariani et al., 2019; Gupta, 2019; Paul et al., 2019). Empirical evidence suggests that SOMED plays a crucial role in the pre-travel stage, during which travelers use social media for data search, reviewing, planning and decision-making about where, when and how to travel (Verma et al., 2012; Lange-Faria and Elliot, 2012). However, SOMED can either positively or negatively influence a potential customer's decision to travel to a certain destination (Gros, 2012; Lange-Faria and Elliot, 2012), take a specific mode of transportation, and/or select a particular hotel or other type of accommodation even before finalizing the decision to take a trip. Although most prior investigations focused on the positive impact of SOMED on travelers' decision-making process, they neglected the negative effect of travel to a destination and other interrelated issues stated above. Similarly, the literature on this topic in the context of developing countries is lacking, particularly on destinations in Africa.

In the light of the preceding discussion, this chapter presents an evaluation of the impacts of social media on tourists' travel decisions. The chapter mainly focuses on Zimbabwe, one of Africa's world-renowned tourist destinations. It features Victoria Falls, a world-class resort town in the country and continent at large, as a case study. From the perspectives of consumer behavior theory and the theory of travel buying behavior, as well as the usage of information on social media (Dwityas and Braiandana, 2017), this chapter explores the effects of SOMED on travelers' decision-making process. The chapter initially defines SOMED and briefly describes the various social media platforms. It further broadens the knowledge on the negative and positive effects of social media on travelers' decision-making process. It particularly focuses on travelers to destinations in developing economies, especially Africa, and the case study of Victoria Falls, Zimbabwe.

DEFINITION OF SOCIAL MEDIA

Social media (SOMED) is a communication platform for promoting and cultivating networks that enable individuals, organizations and potential customers to interact and communicate using internet connectivity. Several authors agree that social media pertains to a group of Web 2.0 online applications, media and platforms operating on the internet, which allow different users to exchange information (Colomo-Palacois et al., 2013; Kaplan and Haenlein, 2010; Zeng and Gerritsen, 2014). In other words, as an interactive medium, SOMED enables the establishment and cultivation of relationships that allow users to exchange ideas, information, experiences and opinions on products or services (Dwityas and Briandana, 2017). In the tourism sector, SOMED provides users with channels for communicating with travel communities, thereby enabling them to acquire information on desired products or services through the sharing of views and reviews via audio, video and still pictures, that potentially affect travel decisions (Kietzmann et al., 2011; Kim and Fesenmaier, 2017; Lange-Faria and Elliot, 2012; Mariani et al., 2019).

SOCIAL MEDIA PLATFORMS

Several types of SOMED platforms are available on the World Wide Web, including general or non-travel-specific ones such as Facebook, Twitter, Instagram, YouTube, SnapChat, WeChat and MySpace; and travel-specific ones such as Tripadvisor, Expedia, Travelocity, Skyscanner and Wikitravel (Gupta, 2019; Leung et al., 2013; Mariani et al., 2019; Paul et al., 2019). In the tourism and hospitality sector, these platforms are similarly categorized in diverse ways, including social networks and microblogging sites (for example, Facebook and Twitter), social sharing sites (for example, YouTube), tourist review sites (for example, Tripadvisor and Yelp) and purchase review sites (for example, Amazon, Travelocity and Expedia) (Jones and Fox, 2009). Constantinides and Fountain (2008) classify SOMED platforms into five main categories, namely: blogs, forums, social networks, bulletin boards, and content communities and content aggregators.

Given that the tourism industry thrives on intensive information, SOMED functions as an ideal tool of communication in the sector through its capacity to disseminate significant amounts of information within a brief span of time (Ráthonyi, 2013). Social media is advantageous to the sector in that it creates peer-to-peer communication channels and makes available multiple consumer review and social networking sites to online communities, and other types of information and communication technology tools, regardless of time and geographical location (Kaplan and Haenlein, 2010; Zeng and Gerristen, 2014). Hence, tourism and hospitality organizations can post information and customer testimonials on their products and services. Travelers can also post their opinions and experiences on a particular product or service (that is, comments on destination quality, hotel food quality, customer service and general hotel or restaurant cleanliness), which are also referred to as user-generated content (Lange-Faria and

Elliot, 2012). In other words, SOMED creates a communication platform where online comments and reviews can be exchanged among tourism and hospitality actors, which may affect potential customers' decision-making (Gautam and Sharma, 2017; Gros, 2012; Lange-Faria and Elliot, 2012). For example, a service that obtains high and positive ratings online and shows pleasing images of a resort or a product has a higher chance of stimulating prospective online customers' positive notions, which may lead to a purchase. By contrast, services or products with low or negative ratings and poor online reviews reduce their chances of being purchased.

Therefore, SOMED is a space for interaction and conversation among all the tourism actors and stakeholders. Customers refer to SOMED for product reviews, whereas businesses may use it for marketing purposes (Lange-Faria and Elliot, 2012). Moreover, Kaplan and Haenlein (2010) and Zeng and Gerristen (2014) suggest that SOMED can be utilized for drawing inspiration for long-term strategies to promote product or service brands.

IMPORTANCE OF SOCIAL MEDIA

According to Leung et al. (2013), a myriad of academic studies and findings underscore the role and importance of SOMED in tourism and hospitality management in general, as well as in travel decision-making in particular, and most of these studies and findings are documented in the many refereed journals relevant to the field. First, social media networks constitute an essential source of information for travelers (Gros, 2012) and play an essential role during holiday planning processes. These social networks on SOMED generate a massive amount of information that is useful for travelers. However, the generation and presentation of this information on social networks makes a difference to end users or customers. In this context, upon providing information, the writing of reviews and sharing of opinions and ideas, images and experiences are sometimes the factors that mostly sell the idea or concept. According to Fotis et al. (2012), online content interest is generated by the manner of presenting the information. Online content would be most impactful if the information was presented in the form of images, and feedback was given as experiences. This postulation indicates that SOMED platforms provide people with opportunities to read and see information on a particular product or service, as well as potential customers with a chance to view other tourists' experiences that can also influence their own decision.

Social media platforms are relevant to both the demand side, consisting of potential travelers or customers, and the supply side, comprising tourism and hospitality service providers. The social networking aspect of the platforms creates a podium for dual communication among tourism and hospitality stakeholders. Additionally, it allows tourism organizations and destinations to directly communicate with tourists or potential customers, and among themselves as suppliers. Thus, organizations build product awareness and participate in brand marketing and many other forms of promotional work (Chan and Guillet, 2011; Kim and Hardin, 2010; Pantelidis, 2010; Lee and Wicks, 2010). Organizations can also communicate among themselves, share ideas and even establish business collaborations. The tourism and hospitality sector is not self-reliant; business collaborations are prerequisites, such that several supply chains are formed in this industry. For example, to maintain product quality, hotels sometimes collaborate with other tourism services operators. The emergence of tour operators in the industry brings multiple service providers together to create a complete holiday package. Communication is made more accessible with the aid of social media.

Some authors highlight that tourism organizations use social media platforms for product distribution (Leung et al., 2013), which, in a way, is a means of building product awareness and ensuring competitiveness. Popesku (2015) concludes that social media helps tourism destinations to remain competitive through its capacity to inspire, inform and engage customers on their products and services. Tourism organizations and destinations generally use SOMED for building and maintaining communities, the clientele of interest, or those customers who prefer their products and services. Organizations and destination marketers through social media primarily keep in touch with their customers at three time points: before, during and after travel. Before travel, communication on these platforms aims to inform, inspire and engage customers. During travel, communication is conducted to ensure proper facilitation at the destination. After travel, communication on SOMED platforms is largely to share memories, help customers to remember, and engage them once more.

In summary, social media is advantageous to the tourism and hospitality industry in that it permits organizations and destinations to interact with customers at low cost, and increases the level of efficiency, which are hardly possible through traditional communication channels (for example, use of brochures) (Kaplan and Haenlein, 2010). Furthermore, these online platforms enable destinations and tourism organizations to monitor what the viewers and or customers say about their products and services and view how they are evaluated. Familiarization with the type of SOMED commonly used by most of their customers is likewise crucial for tourism businesses (Matikiti-Manyevere and Kruger, 2019). Although SOMED is mostly positive, and often used for a good cause, it also has disadvantages for both the travelers and hospitality organizations, as explained in the next section.

NEGATIVE EFFECTS OF SOCIAL MEDIA

In business, social media may be harmful to organizations because companies lack control over user-generated content (UGC) (Lange-Faria and Elliot, 2012). Destination managers essentially do not have a say on who posts and what is posted on the platforms. Companies decide and control the content they post and send on social media platforms, but they cannot control customer feedback, ideas and opinions, especially in cases where customers post their experiences on other SOMED platforms that are different from the ones to which tourism companies are accustomed. Such negative reviews on a service or product are detrimental to business. Social media is the new word-of-mouth; in the literature, word-of-mouth is one of the strongest and most sensitive methods of communication and promotion.

Operating the platforms is also quite time-consuming for businesses. Tourism organizations need to ensure that content is accurate before posting, and that the platforms are continuously updated (Matikiti-Manyevere and Kruger, 2019). Accuracy in entering content is of the essence, as mistakes on SOMED are mostly tricky and laborious to rectify. The quality of a service or product can be depicted in the way content is presented on SOMED platforms. Therefore, users need to ensure that information is accurate, and any other artifacts (for example, images) used to attract clientele are up to standard and appealing. Content sometimes lacks authenticity, or some organizations tend to overmarket a product, which again can be harmful to a business in the near future.

Issues of trust in the online environment are another concern, mostly on the part of customers. Hence, customers rely on and trust their families and friends' UGC on SOMED before consuming products and services (Lange-Faria and Elliot, 2012; Matikiti-Manyevere and Kruger, 2019; Milano et al., 2011). Although other customers do not need to say anything negative about a company and its products or services, some customers may overexaggerate a poor experience that would certainly affect the travel decisions of prospective customers, while reducing a potential sale for the organization. There are also barriers of perceived risk, web design and content, and privacy concerns (Lange-Faria and Elliot, 2012; Leenes et al., 2008). Privacy concerns are the most crucial issue, because the internet does not give provisions for determining who communicates with whom, except one-on-one social media platforms such as WhatsApp and WeChat, in contrast to other types of SOMED social networking sites or communities such as social sharing sites (for example, YouTube) and tourist review sites (for example, Tripadvisor) that are open to everybody. Compared to traditional means of communication, given a business set-up, damage control on social media may be difficult. Despite what a service provider has access to, it has no control whatsoever over the UGC that is posted on the platforms and timelines, or the information sent to or circulated on other social media platforms within the reach of customers only, not service providers. For instance, most service organizations in Zimbabwe use Facebook and Instagram for their businesses, which is not necessarily the case with all their customers on other platforms, based on what is commonly used in their region. For example, a Chinese traveler is accustomed to the use of WeChat, which is barely known or utilized in Zimbabwe. Making an open statement to correct a wrong and show sincerity in response to a poor review on the common platforms that these service organizations are accustomed to may constitute a simple solution, but the organizations cannot do the same on other platforms within the reach of customers only.

Other matters of concern include the negative aspects of SOMED, including the credibility of information, privacy intrusion, identity theft, forgery and financial scams (Milano et al., 2011). Findings generally reveal that unscrupulous elements pose as tourism providers to dupe individuals out of their hard-earned resources; and at times they pose as customers, posting false information or exaggerating an unsatisfactory destination experience and thus defaming a particular supplier (Yazdanifard and Yee, 2014). Unscrupulous competitors sometimes engage in the fake identities of their fellow suppliers for personal gain (Milano et al., 2011). Another concern is the challenge of some travelers overloading the platforms with needless details, which can make searching cumbersome for other users and sometimes cause confusion and loss of interest in seeking out the real information. Finally, other issues pertain to the shortage of, or failure by tourism suppliers to hire, a competent information and communications technology (ICT) workforce to manage this crucial part of the business (Milano et al., 2011).

SOCIAL MEDIA DECISION-MAKING

Although social media has some shortfalls, it certainly represents a welcome development in the tourism and hospitality industry. The literature affirms that travelers seek travel information on social media and use it for decision-making despite the aforementioned concerns (Leung et al., 2013). Furthermore, the literature findings on studies conducted between 2007 and 2011 indicate that travelers mostly use social media platforms during the pre-travel and post-travel stages of their travel plan (Burgess et al., 2011; Cox et al., 2009; Fotis et al., 2011;

Huang et al., 2010; Lee, 2011; Lo et al., 2011; Scott and Orlikowski, 2012; Yoo and Gretzel, 2011; Papathanassis and Knolle, 2011; Parra-López et al., 2011; Sparks and Browning, 2011; Xiang and Gretzel, 2010; Yoo and Gretzel, 2010, 2011). Customers can hardly review tourism products before the actual consumption, due to the absence of an opportunity to directly interact with the product to assess its value and benefit before making a decision; thus, the advent of the internet, particularly social media, constitutes a welcome development in the industry (Paul et al., 2019; Leung et al., 2013).

The trajectory of tourism industry indicates that in the pre-internet and pre-Web 2.0 era, word-of-mouth (WOM), print media in the form of pamphlets, handbills and brochures, as well as broadcast media such as TV and radio stations, were among the resources commonly used by travel agents, hoteliers and airlines for providing and circulating information about tourism products and influencing consumption (Andereck, 2005; Heung, 2008; Santos, 1998). However, the advent of SOMED has transformed the space and granted additional power to customers and would-be consumers of tourism products in the value chain. The dynamism of SOMED enables tourism consumers and suppliers to shape and reshape communication, connection, product packaging, delivery, information sharing and the entire travel experience before, during and after travel.

Dwityas and Briandana (2017) conclude that at every stage of the travel experience, travelers usually seek and use the information on SOMED platforms for carrying out all their decision-making activities, ranging from the selection of destinations, transportation modes, accommodation and leisure activities to staying touch with families and friends during the trips. Varkaris and Neuhofer (2017) concur that all these aspects underscore the critical function of SOMED as a source of information in this age of connectivity and interactivity with the use of Web 2.0, in assisting travelers at every stage of the travel decision-making process and other stakeholders in the tourism industry in general (Dwityas and Briandana, 2017). Figure 26.1 illustrates the three levels in which travelers use social media.

The figure shows that travelers are connected to SOMED before the trip, while on the trip, and after the trip. However, Matikiti-Manyevere and Kruger (2019) note that travelers predominantly use SOMED in the pre-trip and post-trip stages. In the pre-trip phase, travelers seek information on possible destinations. As potential travelers or customers evaluate products and services at this stage, organizations need to ensure that their online content is accurate and that visuals edify a product. The inclusion of testimonials from past customer travel experience is also an additional advantage, as this step helps potential customers to make decisions on their travel. Extending reviews to other non-biased social networks would also be an added benefit for organizations in terms of enhancing their credibility. For example, platforms such as Tripadvisor and Yelp, which function independently of organizations and generate content for multiple service providers, allow customers to review a service or product without any filtrations. Content from such platforms is trustworthy because the organizations have no access to alter reviews for a low-rated service, for example. The first stage of decision-making is critical, as potential customers are limited to the information provided by service providers on the platforms to which the latter are accustomed. At the same time, considerable evaluation transpires, such that customers seek information from other sources. Customers usually try to search for information on reviews by other travelers who have used a product or traveled to their destination of interest.

In the second stage (the trip information phase), customers seek the specific aspects or features of a destination (for example, activities and agencies to use). Relating this stage to the

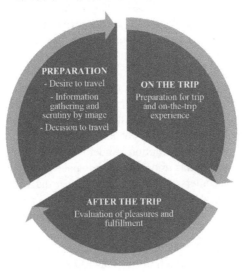

Figure 26.1   *Travel decision-making through use of social media*

case study and helping travelers to make informed decisions, tour operators in Victoria Falls often post tour activities with guests on their social networking platforms. The online posting of daily entries of exciting features or activities on Facebook or Instagram is quite reasonable, because it is another means of advertising products and services and enticing other guests during the trip, or individuals who are still engaged in pre-trip evaluations.

In the final stage, customers share their post-travel experiences, whereas organizations or service providers share the travelers' testimonials. From the viewpoint of service providers, as would be noted in most hotels in Zimbabwe, they have a guest book in the main hotel lobby or at the guest services desk where customers are free to make comments on their stay in the hotel. When the reviews are favorable, some hotels or service providers use them as testimonials on their social media platforms. In some instances, Zimbabwean operators, hotels or service providers simply ask guests to provide reviews and share their opinions and experiences on their self-operated platforms such as Facebook and Instagram. To enhance service ratings on social networking platforms such as Tripadvisor, on which most hotels and service providers are registered, hoteliers and tour operators encourage their guests to make sure that they rate their services on the platforms.

Furthermore, findings indicate many areas where travelers use SOMED in the decision-making process, and these usages are principally categorized as pre-trip, during-trip and post-trip. Examples abound as depicted in Figure 26.2 and Table 26.1, from travelers' and tour operators' perspectives in Zimbabwe.

Matikiti's (2015) work, which constitutes a shift from most previous studies, shared Page and Connell's (2009) model that highlights the five-stage decision-making process in

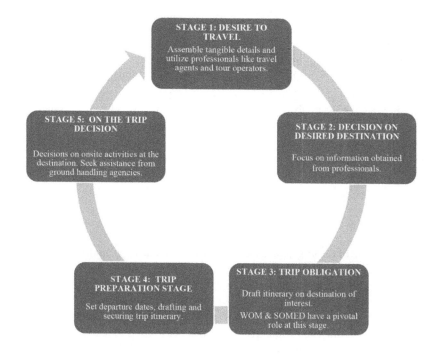

Figure 26.2   The decision-making process stages by travelers

Table 26.1   Travel decision-making process by tour operators in Zimbabwe

Travelers' decision-making process	Use of information on social media
Before travel	
1. Travel intentions	Reaction to social media information about travel. Guests seek detailed information on destination (e.g., suggested itineraries and request of videos, pictures and any other helpful information).
2. Information processing	Assessing information retrieved from social media and industry professionals and WOM (friends and relatives).
3. Decision to travel	Resolve to travel and securing trip.
	Confirm travel itinerary.
During travel	
4. Supplementary preparation and on the trip activities	Decide on extra on-site activities through the help of handling agents, tour guides and/or other travel companions.
After travel	
5. Travel experience and quality appraisal	Overall trip assessment and experience sharing.

the pre-trip segment. This model is not only peculiar to tourism and travelers in particular regardless of space and time, but is also distinct from other forms of decision-making for other life endeavors. Furthermore, the model is supported by Dwityas and Briandana (2017), who explain their findings in the Indonesian context, which also briefly reflects the post-trip segment to balance the process. Table 26.1 shows the travel decision-making process as perceived by tour operators and travel agencies in the context of Zimbabwe.

In 2018, Africa recorded a 7 percent growth in tourist arrivals, which is on a par with Asia and the Pacific; additionally, the Middle East recorded 5 percent (UNWTO, 2019), which is a confirmation that tourism in Africa is gradually experiencing growth and popularity among tourists, especially from other parts of the globe. The sector also contributed 7.1 percent to the total gross domestic product (GDP) in Africa in 2019 (WTTC, 2020).

Among the famous destinations in Africa are Morocco, South Africa and Tunisia. Others are Côte d'Ivoire, Kenya, Zimbabwe, Namibia and Botswana (WTTC, 2020). Many of these countries are a tourist's delight due to distinct features such as their favorable climate or moderate weather conditions all year round, wildlife and safari parks, exotic resorts and historical sites of international repute. The focus of this chapter is on Zimbabwe, a picturesque country in the southern part of Africa.

CASE STUDY: ZIMBABWE TOURISM

The tourism sector, one of the largest and fastest-growing industries globally, is arguably a significant source of employment and means of support for many people, most notably in developing nations. This is true for Africa as a continent, including Zimbabwe as an independent, developing nation. Although other industries are operating within Zimbabwe and providing sources of livelihood, Zimbabwe has mostly focused on tourism as a source of growth and diversification. The tourism and hospitality sector has been among the top five highest GDP contributors to the macroeconomic development of the country. It has developed into one of the key sectors, providing more benefits to the country than other sectors such as agriculture, manufacturing and the tobacco industry. The Zimbabwe tourism industry employs more than 90 000 people, while providing numerous business opportunities for both local and international investors. Small and medium-sized enterprises (SMEs) are benefiting from the sector, and the micro local enterprises within the resort towns also benefit from the sale of their local artifacts, not to mention other subsidiary industries.

Zimbabwe is a landlocked country in the southern region of Africa. Although Zimbabwe lacks the famous 3S's (sun, sea and sand), it is one of the world's top travel destinations. As a tourist destination, Zimbabwe is sometimes denoted as a "world of wonders." It has innumerable attractions, ranging from natural, cultural and historical attractions to wildlife. Zimbabwe has generally been known as the breadbasket of Africa within the continent, but its tourism and hospitality sector has become one of the fastest-growing sectors following the independence of the country.

Zimbabwe is endowed with an exotic scenery and a natural heritage. The country features numerous tourist attractions, some of which have been conferred World Heritage status by the United Nations Educational, Scientific and Cultural Organization (UNESCO). These attractions include the Matopos National Park and Great Zimbabwe Ruins, which are both historical monuments; Kariba Dam, a man-made lake within a national park; the Eastern Highlands; and Mana Pools. In essence, Zimbabwe features extraordinary attractions that tourists would indeed love to experience and enjoy. Zimbabwe is home to about 26 game parks and safari destinations with various game and bird species. It is also home to one of the seven natural wonders of the world: the mighty Victoria Falls, locally referred to as Mosi-oa-Tunya, or "the smoke that thunders." Victoria Falls is a UNESCO World Heritage Site. Although Zimbabwe's manifold attractions generally draw multiple tourists, Victoria Falls is a significant tourist pull factor in the country and the region (UNWTO, 2019).

Tourism and Hospitality, Zimbabwe: Adoption of ICT

The advent and diffusion of ICT over the past decades has considerably transformed the tourism and hospitality industry in Zimbabwe. The tourism sector as a whole thrives on voluminous information. Its growth is exponential when fully supported by the development of communication technologies and information systems. Tourism suppliers in Zimbabwe typically use the internet or Web 2.0 for marketing and effective communication with customers and potential consumers.

Information and communications technology has been in use since the 1970s, but most developing nations became aware of it in the early 1990s, and some nations on the continent are yet to grasp and utilize the service to its fullest potential. Nonetheless, ICT has come in handy for industries that have adopted this means of communication, including the tourism and hospitality sector. As a developing nation with a thriving tourism industry, Zimbabwe adopted the use of ICT way behind its global introduction; most organizations have massively benefited.

For hotels and tourism services, their adoption of ICT initially involved changing manual booking systems to enable these systems' hosting and management on the internet. Marketing strategies shifted from the use of traditional marketing tools (for example, brochures) to marketing products, hosting services and products on the internet. The technological undertaking began with the World Wide Web, which remains useful. The World Wide Web, which is used as the primary marketing page, provides a general outline of an organization's products and services. Other communication and information systems are simultaneously created from smaller communication platforms.

Social Media: Zimbabwe Tourism and Hospitality

As a result of ICT, social networks have been enabled such that small yet effective platforms (SOMED) have emerged. Furthermore, these platforms have helped organizations to further communicate with their customers, while also creating possibilities for customer-to-customer communication. The use of SOMED platforms in Zimbabwe has significantly influenced tourism organizations, thereby enabling their targeted customers to become strongly connected to and highly affiliated with such platforms. Marketing efforts have been launched through websites, and Zimbabwean organizations have attended international travel markets. Nonetheless, the key to Zimbabwe's fame as a destination largely lies in the ratings it has received on various SOMED platforms.

Most touring companies and hotels in Victoria Falls, Zimbabwe, use Facebook and Instagram more than any other platform on the internet. They not only post content online but also prompt their customers to post content on these pages. Customers' sharing of their experiences with a product on a service provider's page is thus commonplace. Organizations use the World Wide Web as their primary platform for general information on their products and services, and then filter more detailed information in terms of experiences and day-to-day occurrences on smaller networks such as Facebook and Instagram. In most cases, safari operators post daily pictures of game animals that are seen on safari. Such information forms part of the content that travelers evaluate and consider in travel decision-making.

Linking the three stages of the decision-making process to how tourism providers in Zimbabwe engage their customers, past guests' travel experiences are posted as testimonials on the accustomed platforms usually shown on the organizations' web pages. Hence, at the pre-trip stage, instead of simply being given information on the web page for evaluation, potential customers are provided with links to further review the opinions on these other platforms. During the trip, guests are encouraged to visit the accustomed platforms for additional reviews and to make new entries that, in turn, assist potential tourists. Moreover, instead of filling in the traditional guest book, the guests are reminded once more to add their reviews to networking platforms such as Tripadvisor, Facebook and Instagram.

From a Customer Perspective

Most people traveling to Zimbabwe are mainly from the Americas and Europe, and partly from Asia. A thorough assessment of the customer base indicates that inbound tourists to Zimbabwe largely come from developed nations, thus confirming that the hype surrounding the use of technology and social media platforms is high and at an advanced stage. As a destination, Zimbabwe subscribes to a specific platform, but its customer base uses varied platforms. Thus, organization-to-customer communication is determined by the hosting operator, while the customer determines customer-to-customer podiums; as such, further destination marketing is enhanced on these other platforms between customers. The literature denotes that word-of-mouth (WOM) is a strong influence on customers' decision-making processes. Organizations may undertake efforts to upsell products or services, no matter how appealing these products or services may be. However, once a customer has given a low rating to these products or services, the effect on potential customers is severe; in most cases, these customers decide to forgo the experience or refuse to purchase the product or service, to the detriment of the organization.

Tourism operators and hotels are normally interested in determining how their customers learned about their products and services. According to these tourism service providers, prior to traveling, most travelers initially learned about the destination on TV broadcasts (for example, television programs such as those on the National Geographic channel; news broadcasts by the BBC, CNN and Sky News), whereas some travelers obtained their information by attending international travel shows (for example, the World Travel Market and INDABA). A large number of such travelers acknowledged that they benefited from the WOM of friends or relatives who had been to the destination before. Following the awareness, mostly stimulated by friends and family, travelers would seek further information on the destination and a specific organization on the internet. The data collected would be further filtered down to other social media platforms indicated by the organizations; these platforms are generally podiums which tourism destinations are accustomed to. Content on these platforms is primarily entered and managed by the organizations themselves; however, organizations sometimes encourage and allow their customers or past travelers to post content on their platforms. Customers conduct further research on their own: for instance, as they search for independent reviews on other networking platforms, they visit review sites such as Tripadvisor, Booking. com, Yelp, Expedia, and many others that customers believe to be specific to their countries.

As previously noted, travelers whose background and exposure to ICT is advanced, compared to the destination experts in developing countries (Zimbabwe in this case), are limited to a specific platform, while there are also chances that information may be circulating on other platforms unknown to and not reachable by the service providers. The probability of harmful and useful content is 50 percent, which ultimately positively or negatively affects business, depending on the content shared on social media.

A typical example from the past would be unfavorable publicity on Zimbabwe during the 2000–2008 period. Despite a global economic recession in the latter part of this period, Zimbabwe as a destination generally obtained adverse publicity on almost all forms of media. At the time, Zimbabwe was confronted by underlying political issues; however, its problems were exaggerated in the media. This incident affected its crucial supply destinations at the time, such as the United States and Germany, which imposed a travel ban on Zimbabwe, even though traveling to the country was deemed generally safe. Furthermore, hardly any issues transpired in Zimbabwe's resort areas; in fact, Victoria Falls was considered as safe to visit. Based on their tourist testimonials on arrival, travelers expressed surprise at being informed that it was not safe to travel to Victoria Falls, only to realize the contrary case. A few tourists defied the travel warning issued by their respective countries and proceeded to travel to Zimbabwe; their move inspired hope and provided encouragement (through their testimonials on social media) to others, which eventually prompted others to travel to the destination in the following year despite the travel ban. However, a large number of travelers heeded the warnings on media and withdrew their plans to travel to the destination, causing a revenue loss for several tour operators due to the cancellation of bookings.

Business was low in the resort town; a city once booming with many tourists was nearly at a standstill, with less tourist traffic and many operators shutting down their businesses. Despite the efforts by local businesses and the local tourist board to revive business and assure supply destinations that Victoria Falls was safe for travel, several SOMED platforms and networks had nothing positive to say. Revival and normality only occurred in 2013 after the 20th Session of the United Nations World Tourism Organization (UNWTO) General Assembly was held in Victoria Falls, Zimbabwe. As soon as Zimbabwe was nominated as the host destination of this event, word quickly spread on social media and networking platforms, and business gradually flourished immediately after the session. In a way, the UN's hosting of the assembly partially indicated that traveling to Zimbabwe was safe. Indeed, upon completing the meeting, all the negative publicity on the state of affairs in the country and the resort ceased, making tourists free to travel to the country. Testimonials, reviews and feedback about how great a destination Zimbabwe is once again intensified on social media, thus resulting in a business boom. This situation confirms the power of social media to positively or negatively affect people's decision to travel.

During late 2019 and the writing of this chapter (in March 2020), an old picture of Victoria Falls during a drought year circulated on social media and networking platforms; the photo depicts a group of tourists sharing a false report of their experience at the destination. The unsatisfactory and overblown information circulated far and wide, such that the destination began to instantly experience a negative impact. Several business associates and stakeholders, including travelers, sought feedback on the resort's status. In some instances, signs of cancellations emerged, and requests to withhold booking reservations and or amend dates of travel occurred. The adverse development prompted an international TV broadcast network, the BBC, to launch an investigation into the matter by sending a team of reporters to visit the destination. Following the findings of the investigation, a sort of counter-report was aired on the channel for a period to eliminate the impact of the tourists' false information. The intervention of this reputable global broadcast organization was instrumental in gradually rebuilding the trust and confidence of potential travelers, who probably read via SOMED the BBC version shared by other users, before the Falls began to witness a gradual surge of visitors to the resort. Local tour operators in the town likewise took video footage and pictures of their staff at the site and posted their opinions on various SOMED platforms. In one instance, to counteract the circulated image's negative effects on the attraction, a group of hotel and touring organizations' representatives gathered and took a picture of themselves in front of a viewing point of Victoria Falls, which was circulated on Instagram. And in another scenario, also on Instagram, a customer who had traveled to Victoria Falls around the time of the incident, posted a picture of themselves swimming at the edge of the Falls, assuring viewers that the Falls were not dry. A thorough examination of other viewers' comments revealed the potential guests' inquiries about the date of the new picture and their concerns about the false information circulated earlier on social media.

The example in this case study underscores the influence and role of SOMED in travel decision-making, with its attendant drawbacks and the damage that SOMED poses to destinations if left unmonitored. The reason is that at the pre-trip stage, travelers typically search for information on various platforms, and any destinations with negative reviews are automatically discounted from those to be shortlisted for further research before travelers make their final decision on whether to visit a destination. Nevertheless, the results of the rescue mission or fact-finding exercise embarked upon by the BBC were further disseminated on travel-specific SOMED, which helped to restore the image of Victoria Falls and aid the subsequent recovery from the incident.

CONCLUSION

Empirical findings reveal that the diffusion of ICT and internet access triggered the emergence of the Travel 2.0 concept, with travel communities both online and offline present on different social media (SOMED) platforms, including Facebook, blogs and other social forums. Social media is a space where everyone with a common interest (for example, traveling) can meet, write and read self-generated information and posts, including still and motion pictures, images, and sights and sounds about their travel experiences for others to learn from and admire (Milano et al., 2011; Goeldner and Ritchie, 2012). WhatsApp, Twitter, Instagram, YouTube and LinkedIn are among the other SOMED platforms that are commonly used by travel communities (Chigora and Mutambara, 2019). Compared to traditional means of communication, SOMED use is more advantageous to both customers and organizations. Despite the adverse effects associated with social media, these are outweighed by the positive benefits, which explains its continual usage by all stakeholders.

REFERENCES

Andereck, K.L. (2005). Evaluation of a tourist brochure. *Journal of Travel and Tourism Marketing*, 18(2), 1–13.

Burgess, S., Sellitto, C., Cox, C., and Buultjens, J. (2011). Trust perceptions of online travel information by different content creators: some social and legal implications. *Information Systems Frontiers*, 13(2), 221–235.

Chan, N.L., and Guillet, B.D. (2011). Investigation of social media marketing: how does the hotel industry in Hong Kong perform in marketing on social media websites? *Journal of Travel and Tourism Marketing*, 28(4), 345–368.

Chigora, F., and Mutambara, E. (2019). Branding in the post-truth news era: a social media hegemony in Zimbabwe tourism brand equity modelling.

Colomo-Palacios, R., Soto-Acosta, P., Ramayah, T., and Russ, M. (2013). Electronic markets and the future internet: from clouds to semantics. *Electronic Markets*, 23(2), 89–91.

Constantinides, E., and Fountain, S.J. (2008). Web 2.0: conceptual foundations and marketing issues. *Journal of Direct, Data and Digital Marketing Practice*, 9(3), 231–244.

Cox, C., Burgess, S., Sellitto, C., and Buultjens, J. (2009). The role of user-generated content in tourists' travel planning behavior. *Journal of Hospitality Marketing and Management*, 18(8), 743–764.

Dwityas, N.A., and Briandana, R. (2017). Social media in travel decision-making process. *International Journal of Humanities and Social Science*, 7(7), 291–292.

Fotis, J., Buhalis, D., and Rossides, N. (2011). Social media impact on holiday travel planning: The case of the Russian and the FSU markets. *International Journal of Online Marketing*, 1(4), 1–19.

Fotis, J.N., Buhalis, D., and Rossides, N. (2012). Social media use and impact during the holiday travel planning process. In Fuchs, M., Ricci, F., and Cantoni, L. (eds), *Information and Communication Technologies in Tourism 2012* (pp. 13–24). Vienna: Springer-Verlag.

Gautam, V., and Sharma, V. (2017). The mediating role of customer relationship on social media marketing and purchase intention relationship with particular reference to luxury fashion brands. *Journal of Promotion Management*, 23(6), 872–888.

Goeldner, C.R., and Ritchie, J.R.B. (2012). *Tourism: Principles, Practices, Philosophies*. Hoboken, NJ: John Wiley & Sons.

Gohil, N. (2015), Role and impact of social media in tourism: a case study on the initiatives of Madhya Pradesh state tourism. *International Journal of Research in Economics and Social Sciences*, 5(4), 8–15.

Gros, C.H. (2012). The influence of social media on consumers during their purchase decision-making process and the implications for the marketer. Doctoral dissertation, Dublin Business School.

Gupta, V. (2019). The influencing role of social media in the consumer's hotel decision-making process. *Worldwide Hospitality and Tourism Themes*, 11(4), 378–391.

Huang, Y., Basu, C., and Hsu, M. K. (2010). Exploring motivations of travel knowledge sharing on social network sites: an empirical investigation of US college students. *Journal of Hospitality Marketing and Management*, 19(7), 717–734.

Heung, V.C. (2008). Effects of tour leader's service quality on the agency's reputation and customers' word-of-mouth. *Journal of Vacation Marketing*, 14(4), 305–315.

Jones, S., and Fox, S. (2009). Generations Online in 2009. Pew Research Center. 28 January.

Kaplan, A.M., and Haenlein, M. (2010). Users of the world, unite! The challenges and opportunities of Social Media. *Business Horizons*, 53(1), 59–68.

Kietzmann, J.H., Hermkens, K., McCarthy, I.P., and Silvestre, B.S. (2011). Social media? Get serious! Understanding the functional building blocks of social media. *Business Horizons*, 54(3), 241–251.

Kim, J., and Fesenmaier, D.R. (2017). Sharing tourism experiences: the posttrip experience. *Journal of Travel Research*, 56(1), 28–40.

Kim, J., and Hardin, A. (2010). The impact of virtual worlds on word-of-mouth: improving social networking and servicescape in the hospitality industry. *Journal of Hospitality Marketing and Management*, 19(7), 735–753.

Lange-Faria, W., and Elliot, S. (2012). Understanding the role of social media in destination marketing. *Tourism*, 7(1). DOI: 10.15240/tul/001/2018-4-015.

Lee, B.C., and Wicks, B. (2010). Tourism technology training for destination marketing organisations (DMOs): need-based content development. *Journal of Hospitality, Leisure, Sports and Tourism Education* (Pre-2012), 9(1), 39.

Lee, S. (2011, October). To tweet or not to tweet: an exploratory study of meeting professionals' attitudes toward applying social media for meeting sessions. *Journal of Convention and Event Tourism*, 12(4), 271–289).

Leenes, R., Schallabock, J., and Hansen, M. (2008). PRIME White Paper, third and final version. PRIME (Privacy and Identity Management for Europe). http://www. mendeley.com/research/prime -whitepaper-v2/.

Leung, D., Law, R., Van Hoof, H., and Buhalis, D. (2013). Social media in tourism and hospitality: a literature review. *Journal of Travel and Tourism Marketing*, 30(1–2), 3–22.

Lo, I. S., McKercher, B., Lo, A., Cheung, C., and Law, R. (2011). Tourism and online photography. *Tourism Management*, 32(4), 725–731.

Mariani, M.M., Baggio, R., Buhalis, D., and Longhi, C. (eds) (2014), *Tourism Management, Marketing, and Development: Volume I: The Importance of Networks and ICTs*. New York: Palgrave.

Mariani, M., Styven, M.E., and Ayeh, J.K. (2019). Using Facebook for travel decision-making: an international study of antecedents. *International Journal of Contemporary Hospitality Management*.

Matikiti, R. (2015). The efficacy of social networks as marketing tools in the South African and Zimbabwean accommodation sector. Doctoral dissertation.

Matikiti-Manyevere, R., and Kruger, M. (2019). The role of social media sites in trip planning and destination decision-making processes. *African Journal of Hospitality, Tourism and Leisure*, 8(5), 1–10.

Milano, R., Baggio, R., and Piattelli, R. (2011, January). The effects of online social media on tourism websites. In *ENTER* (pp. 471–483). https://link-springer.com/chapter/10.1007/978-3-7091-0503-0_38

Page, S. and Connell, J. (2009). *Trade and Tourism: A Modern Synthesis*, 2nd edn. Amazon: Cangage Learning EMEA.

Pantelidis, I.S. (2010). Electronic meal experience: a content analysis of online restaurant comments. *Cornell Hospitality Quarterly*, 51(4), 483–491.

Papathanassis, A., and Knolle, F. (2011). Exploring the adoption and processing of online holiday reviews: a grounded theory approach. *Tourism Management*, 32(2), 215–224.

Parra-López, E., Bulchand-Gidumal, J., Gutiérrez-Taño, D., and Díaz-Armas, R. (2011). Intentions to use social media in organizing and taking vacation trips. *Computers in Human Behavior*, 27(2), 640–654.

Paul, H.S., Roy, D., and Mia, R. (2019). Influence of social media on tourists' destination selection decision. *Sch. Bull*, 5(11), 658–664.

Popesku, M. (2015). Clarifying value in use and value creation process. Doctoral dissertation, University of Nottingham.

Ráthonyi, G. (2013). Influence of social media on tourism – especially among students of the University of Debrecen. *Applied Studies in Agribusiness and Commerce*, 7(1), 105–112.

Santos, J. (1998). The role of tour operators' promotional material in the formation of destination image and consumer expectations: the case of the People's Republic of China. *Journal of Vacation Marketing*, 4(3), 282–297.

Scott, S.V., and Orlikowski, W.J. (2012). Reconfiguring relations of accountability: materialization of social media in the travel sector. *Accounting, Organizations and Society*, 37(1), 26–40.

Sparks, B.A., and Browning, V. (2011). The impact of online reviews on hotel booking intentions and perception of trust. *Tourism Management*, 32(6), 1310–1323.

United Nations World Tourism Organization (UNWTO) (2013). UNWTO General Assembly Opens in Victoria Falls. https://www.unwto.org/archive/global/press-release/2013-08-25/unwto-general -assembly-opens-victoria-falls.

United Nations World Tourism Organization (UNWTO) (2019). International Tourism Highlights. https://www.e-unwto.org/doi/pdf/10.18111/9789284421152.

Varkaris, E., and Neuhofer, B. (2017). The influence of social media on the consumers' hotel decision journey. *Journal of Hospitality and Tourism Technology*, 8(1), 101–118.

Verma, R., Stock, D., and McCarthy, L. (2012). Customer preferences for online, social media, and mobile innovations in the hospitality industry. *Cornell Hospitality Quarterly*, 53(3), 183–186.

World Travel and Tourism Council (WTTC) (2020, April 5). Economic Impacts Report. https://wttc.org/ Research/Economic-Impact.

Xiang, Z., and Gretzel, U. (2010). Role of social media in online travel information search. *Tourism Management*, 31(2), 179–188.

Yazdanifard, R., and Yee, L.T. (2014). Impact of social networking sites on hospitality and tourism industries. *Global Journal of Human–Social Science: Economics*, 14(8), 1–5.

Yoo, K.H., and Gretzel, U. (2010). Antecedents and impacts of trust in travel-related consumer-generated media. *Information Technology and Tourism*, 12(2), 139–152.

Yoo, K.H., and Gretzel, U. (2011). Influence of personality on travel-related consumer-generated media creation. *Computers in Human Behavior*, 27(2), 609–621.

Zeng, B., and Gerritsen, R. (2014). What do we know about social media in tourism? A review. *Tourism Management Perspectives*, 10, 27–36.

27. Impact of social media on millennials' destination choice behavior: a study of Delhi NCR

Pramendra Singh and Heena Chauhan

INTRODUCTION

The internet and smartphones have brought a revolution around the world by making information easily accessible to all. People from all walks of life now have access to the internet. The internet has penetrated hugely into both urban and rural areas. The internet is helping the people in every aspect of their lives: education, training, employment, business, entertainment, shopping, travel, and so on. It has simplified the lives of people, and nothing is far from their reach now. It has made the world globalized in a real sense, where everyone is connected with one another. It has also made business processes easy, by connecting with customers and designing customized services for them.

As the internet grew, so did the usage of social media. There are different purposes for which social media is used, such as sharing information, seeking opinions and giving feedback online. A huge amount of content is uploaded and shared everyday on the social media platforms. India is one of the largest markets of social media users. According to recent reports by Google, there are more than 500 million internet users in India, out of which more than 300 million are on social media. India is considered to have the largest population of young people in the world. And the millennials make up a fair proportion of the population of India.

Millennials are not only present in large numbers in India, but they are also the prime market segment for many companies. They are targeted by business competitors through various means including customized services, specific marketing strategies, enticing product usage, retaining customer base or sales promotion. As this generation is very tech-savvy and has a good presence on social media, millennials take many decisions on the basis of social media reviews, feedback and opinions, and experience sharing. As traveling has become a common phenomenon among the youth, they share their holiday experiences through their photos, clips and full videos on social media, which also influence many others. Social media has an impact on millennials' destination choice behavior as well.

MILLENNIALS

The entire population can be divided on the basis of their age or year of birth, and thus it can be categorized into different generations. The generations known to us are the baby boomers, Generation X, millennials and Generation Z. These generations belong to different time periods and different conditions, so their choices, liking and consumption, and usage patterns are different. They were also born with different gadgets and technological systems around them.

Stein (2013) said that millennials consist of people born from 1980 to 2000 in an era of computers and technology. Information technology tools have empowered them so much that they are capable of making their own decisions in varied fields. Millennials are one of the biggest chunks of today's population who enjoy the free flow of ideas and suggestions, and therefore they are adept in using the internet and social media for sharing their opinions, and thus influence their peers (Smith, 2012).

The definition of millennials in terms of the time frame for date of birth has been debated and is still unresolved, but the United States Census Bureau and Pew Research Center have considered it to be between 1981 and 1995 (Stewart et al., 2016). Some other research works define the time period differently. But it can be construed that millennials are those people who were born in the last 20 years of the 20th century, and they are more inclined towards usage of technological gadgets and social media tools (McDonald, 2015). According to Mangold and Smith (2011), millennials are also called Generation Y, and are identified by their use of computers and mobiles to a large extent, especially social media, for various purposes to make their lives easier and more comfortable. Millennials are influenced by digital marketing tools, and companies nowadays target this segment of customers through social media as well (Smith, 2011).

SOCIAL MEDIA

As globalization has brought many changes in the day-to-day lives of all human beings across the globe, people like to be connected to one another for various purposes. This has been made possible by internet technology. Social media is one of the technological means by which people can also achieve digital social networking. There are various social media websites and applications which are available on digital platforms. The basic purpose of social media is to connect people, and its provides many other services.

In today's era, social media as a medium of communication is successful because it can transmit messages to many people in the shortest possible period of time. Social media has the ability to work as mass media, through which messages can be transported quickly (Dijck and Poell, 2013). Internet technology has brought disruptive changes in all areas, including information and technology. Internet technology has helped the social media platforms to penetrate all corners of the world.

Kaplan and Haenlein (2010) stated that social media can be classified on the basis of many dimensions, such as social media and media richness, which may include social networking (for example, Facebook), content communities (for example, YouTube), social worlds (for example, interactive games), collaborative projects (for example, Wikipedia), and so on. Social media also provides multiple options to communicate messages. Social media allows people to share experiences in different ways, such as stories, pictures, clips, blogs and vlogs (Xiang and Gretzel, 2010). Social media is powerful tool with which individuals or communities can generate content, discuss and share it with the help of mobile or web-based platforms (Kietzmann et al., 2011). Kietzmann et al. further elaborated its role in conversations, relationship building, enhancing reputation and forming groups. The flexibility which has been extended by technology also enables these social media tools to be used via websites or applications through computers or mobile phones.

Companies provide many forums on social media which may be used by different people for different purposes (Mangold and Faulds, 2009). They can be used for gaining knowledge, sharing information, giving opinions and feedback, suggesting products and services, and seeking information. Social media has the ability not only to share the information, but also to influence the users in terms of purchase behavior, attitude, decision-making process, and so on (Mangold and Faulds, 2009; Kaurav et al., 2020). Social media is now not only a platform to provide information, but it has also become a platform to influence people and their decision-making (Hanna et al., 2011).

Social media has a wide reach, and its users form a huge part of the population. And millennials constitute a good proportion of this population. As times have changed, so have the needs of the millennials changed. To keep themselves updated with recent developments, to have wide reachability and a strong network, millennials tend to use social media more than their predecessors.

LITERATURE REVIEW

Tourism is a service-based industry which does not produce the same kind of product every time; rather, it banks heavily on quality services to enhance visitor experiences. To match the expectations of the visitors and to sustain the competitiveness in the industry, service providers need to be quick in adapting to changes, and delivering customized services. In today's internet and computer era where consumer needs and wants change so frequently, service providers should look for all possible options to lead the sector.

Social media has become one of the strongest elements of the service marketing mix. Companies and service providers have now recognized its dominance by the fact that every prospective customer is using some social media platform or other, and being influenced by other users when they post, share or give feedback about any product, service or company. So companies are also using this tool to follow and tap into their customers. In the tourism industry also, social media plays very important role for both the travelers and the service providers.

Rashidi et al. (2017) stated that the use of social media is growing tremendously because of the increase in usage of smartphones and tablets, which providing users with all the information that they require. The use of the internet through mobile devices enhances tourists' experience, and they readily use it to access quick updates and information about others' experiences (Prayag et al., 2012). Siddiqui and Singh (2016) state that social media helps youngsters to get connected, exchange information, and find online support, for advice and information sharing. The young generation tends to have a higher level of positive perception towards the trustworthiness of social media information (Berhanu and Raj, 2020).

With the information technology trends in recent times, a new consumer profile has emerged known as digital users, who are more flexible and adaptive in terms of social media usage (Buhalis and Jun, 2011). Social media provides different types of information, and at every stage it influences the user in some way or another (Pabel and Prideaux, 2016). Social media also helps tourists in their decision-making by providing up-to-date information (Paul et al., 2019). Social media has changed the way people think and make decisions in tourism, and it has enabled travelers to analyze and decide on a destination (Nezakati et al., 2015).

Pan et al. (2010) stated that social media sites appears at the top and above of other sites on search engines because they cover enormous amounts of information and real-time experiences of the travelers. Pabel and Prideaux (2016) stated that the ability of social media to generate frequent updates easily and promptly captures the attention of users, and they develop a likelihood of getting motivated to visit that destination or use that service. Rathonyi (n.d.) said that social media may have a huge impact on prospective tourists when they come across the experiences and opinions of other travelers on social media platforms. This influence of social media reviews may even compel tourists to change their original plans.

The use of social media by travelers can be divided into three phases: before the trip, during and after the trip (Amaro et al., 2016). Before the trip they use social media to plan and gather information about the where to go, accommodation information, leisure activities, and so on. During the trip they use social media for gathering visit related information and sharing their own experiences. And post-trip use of social media includes experience sharing and feedback about the destination and other services.

Leung et al. (2013) also discussed the use of social media in different perspectives such as research, product distribution, management and promotion. They found that travelers predominantly use social media specifically before the trip for planning and purchasing process. Social media has a huge impact on decisions taken by the travelers from the travel planning phase to the post-travel advocacy stage (Jadhav et al., 2018).

Tourism is a part of service-based industries which needs enhanced marketing tools such as social media for better connectivity with the public (Gulbahar and Yildirim, 2015). The businesses and destinations need to alter their marketing strategies from conventional marketing to digital or social media marketing, to tap into the growing opportunities there (Pabel and Prideaux, 2016). Jamaludin et al. (2017) also mentioned the importance of social media as it is being used by e-commerce networks to promote their products extensively, and it highly influences travelers to visit and revisit the destination.

Naidu (2019) stated that social media is a landmark internet-based technology which has opened up many horizons for businesses as well as their clients, through which the businesses try to analyze the tourists' psychology and market their products accordingly. Nowadays social media can also refine the usage pattern of the users based on their likes and dislikes, which can be used by companies to target their specific markets. Companies can carry out marketing strategies for their customers by customizing their products, which they can do by identifying their differential needs (Dwityas and Briandana, 2017).

Hamid et al. (2016) stated that there is relationship between the virtual tour information provided through social media, and travelers' decision to use social media for travelling. Social media works as an effective tool in promoting various pull and push factors (Negm, 2018). It can help destinations to lead the competition by providing interesting content, using creativity or innovation and supporting interactive means of communication, because tourists look for a personal approach, and creative, interactive and informative communications (Kiralova and Pavliceka, 2015).

RESEARCH METHODOLOGY

The study was carried out in Delhi National Capital Region (NCR) on millennials with the aim of investigating the impact of social media on their destination selection behavior. The objectives were to identify the importance of social media, and its usage, reliability and impact on destination selection through information sharing, reviews and feedback. The study was also aimed at knowing about the elements that have a higher impact on social media than others. The data was collected through primary as well as secondary sources. For secondary data, various previous research papers were reviewed, on social media, social media platforms and its impact on destination selection. The literature was also reviewed on millennials and their travel behavior.

To collect the primary data, a questionnaire was prepared through Google doc. It was divided into different sections. One section was created to collect the demographic information; and in another section there were some dichotomous questions, and some questions based on a five-point Likert scale, to measure the impact of social media on destination selection. More than 500 questionnaires were sent through email and social media messages, but only 193 were completed in response. Some were found to be wrongly filled in, so they were omitted, and only 180 properly answered questionnaires were used for the final analysis. The analysis, which was done with the help of the statistical tool SPSS 18, brought many important facts to the fore.

The study is descriptive in nature. The outcome of the study is to highlight the importance of social media in to identify the important social media platforms, the usage and reliability of their content, their influence, and so on.

DATA ANALYSIS

The data was analyzed with the help of the statistical tool SPSS 18. The demographic information of the respondents (Table 27.1) was analyzed on parameters such as gender, marital status, age and occupation. Then the data was analyzed for usage of social media or not. Some questions were asked related to social media usage, planning, social media search, and so on, on a three-level scale. The respondents were also asked questions on a five-point Likert scale about what elements of social media influence their decisions.

Table 27.1 presents the demographic information about the respondents. A total of 180 respondents who filled in the questionnaire were analyzed for their gender, marital status, age and occupation to help understand the different aspects of millennials and their decision-making for holidays with respect to the usage of social media. Fifty-five percent of the total respondents were male and 45 percent were female. The majority of the millennial respondents were unmarried and belong to the age category of 21–25 years of age. Around half of the respondents are students, followed by employed people as the next-largest group.

Table 27.2 presents the opinions of the millennials about their usage of social media for their tour planning phase. When they were asked as to how they book their tour, around 68 percent of the respondents said they book their tour through travel agencies, and only around 18 percent said they book their own tour elements. This high majority of the response may be attributed to the growing use of technology and easy access to the travel agencies online, which make it easy for them to compare the rates of tour elements and then comfortably book the tour. Almost all the respondents said that they use various social media tools, irrespective of the purpose or objective of use. The respondents were also asked if they read the destination blogs which are purposely written or put on social media regarding a destination; around 38 percent said they read them, and around 39 percent said they read them sometimes. And when

Table 27.1 Demographic information of the respondents

	Frequency	%
Gender		
Male	99	55.0
Female	81	45.0
Marital status		
Unmarried	117	65.0
Married	63	35.0
Age		
21–25 years	83	46.1
26–30 years	41	22.7
31–35 years	37	20.5
36–39 years	19	10.5
Occupation		
student	86	47.7
employed	49	27.2
self-employed	12	6.6
business	18	10.0
housewife	15	8.3

they were asked if these blogs portray the correct picture of a destination, only 7 percent of them said 'no'; all others affirmed 'yes' or 'sometimes'.

When the respondents were asked if they go through different social media elements and their content before deciding to visit a particular destination, a huge majority of the respondents, 77 percent, said 'yes'; while 16 percent said 'sometimes'. Half of the respondents, about 52 percent, said that they make an alternative list of destinations to be visited on the basis of reviews or feedback on social media. This can be understood as that social media is largely used by the millennials in their destination selection planning phase, and its content creates an impact in their minds while selecting the destination to visit.

Social media is present in different forms, which gives users access to various types of content, such as photos, videos, blogs, vlogs, comments, opinions and feedback. Due to heavy internet and mobile technology penetration in the market, it has reached people from all walks of life. Tourism has become a common phenomenon nowadays and people like to post about their experiences and memories on their social networking setups. This may be for various reasons, such as gaining people's attention, recognition, showing off, information sharing, or other reasons. But it has a significant impact on the psyche of other social media users, who may either like or dislike any specific destination on the basis of the experiences of other users.

The respondents were asked about the five factors in social media which influence their decision process – photos, videos, reading, blogs and feedback – on a five-point Likert scale (Table 27.3). With a 4.18 mean value, respondents gave the highest weighting to the feedback and comments from other users about any specific destination. It appears that the users perceive feedback and comments or conversations on social media as the first-hand experiences and reviews of the destinations. There is more probability of relying on this factor compared to other factors. Then comes the next factor which influences the users' decision-making process

Table 27.2   *Social media usage and tour planning*

	Frequency	%	
How do you plan your trip?			
By travel agencies	122	67.8	
By oneself	32	17.8	
By others	26	14.4	
Do you use social media?			
Yes	176	97.8	
No	4	2.2	
Do you read destination blogs?			
Yes	68	37.8	
No	42	23.3	
Sometimes	70	38.9	
Do you think blogs give you correct picture of a destination?			
Yes	64	35.6	
No	13	7.2	
Sometimes	103	57.2	
Do you search about the destination on social media before visiting it?			
Yes	139	77.2	
No	12	6.7	
Sometimes	29	16.1	
Do you make alternative list of destinations to visit due to social media reviews?			
Yes	94	52.2	
No	37	20.6	
Sometimes	49	27.2	

to visit, which is watching videos about the destination, with a mean value of 4.05. Videos capture the attention of the users and give them the feeling that they are witnessing the destination themselves. Other than these two strongest factors which had an influence on visitors, the other factors are reading about the destination on social media, pictures of the destination and blogs about the destination.

The respondents were also asked about some other parameters related to usefulness and their dependency on social media for destination information (Table 27.4). For almost all the items related to usefulness of information, impact of advertisements, rescheduling the trip, content satisfaction and reviews/feedback, the respondents were neutral. This may be because

Table 27.3   *What influences your decision on social media?*

	N	Mean	Std. deviation
Reading about destination	180	3.92	0.724
Watching destination videos	180	4.05	0.719
Pictures of the destination	180	3.87	0.798
Blogs about destination	180	3.81	0.761
Written communication / feedback	180	4.18	0.741

Table 27.4   *Usefulness of social media for users related to destination selection*

	N	Mean	Std. deviation
Social media information more useful than other sources	180	2.33	0.812
Advertisement on social media changed perception about a destination	180	2.11	0.862
Because of social media, can reschedule the trip	180	3.07	1.112
Satisfaction with social media content related to destination information	180	3.26	0.987
Reviews / feedback are reliable	180	3.12	0.955

of the many unauthorized, fake and unauthenticated accounts and pages which are generally found on social media. So the users have to take decisions very judiciously to identify, recognize and verify these accounts and their sources of information. Sometimes it baffles the users what to rely on or what not to, for exact and correct information.

Lastly, the respondents were asked about their preferences for and usage of different social media platforms (Figure 27.1). Some of the most famous social media platforms were used for analysis. Instagram was found to be the most popular social media platform among the millennials, with 82 percent of them using it; closely followed by WhatsApp (80 percent). The other social media platforms which are used by millennials are YouTube (71 percent), Facebook (61 percent), Snapchat (40 percent) and Twitter (20 percent).

CONCLUSION

India is considered a young nation, because of its young population, which also has huge diversity. And this young generation today is very much inclined towards traveling and experiencing different things, whether natural wonders or cultural manifestations of human genius. Traveling has become a regular and normal phenomenon. In 2018, around 1.4 billion travelers traveled around the world, and if the number of domestic tourists is counted as well, the total will go beyond many more billions. Technology has been pivotal in making the whole process of tourism activities more easy and comfortable. With technology came new forms of applications and websites which have made it possible to connect people virtually.

This study was carried out to investigate the usage, importance, reliability and impact of social media on millennials' destination choice behavior; specifically, in reference to Delhi NCR. The study had a sample size of 180 respondents. The demographic information of the respondents included gender, marital status, age and occupation. It sample was somewhat

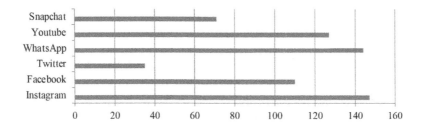

Figure 27.1   *Important social media platforms and their usage*

gender-equal, and represented more unmarried respondents than married. Around half of the respondents were in the age bracket of 21–25 years, and almost same proportion of respondents were students.

Almost all the respondents were found to be using social media platforms. Nearly two-thirds of the respondents book their tours through travel agencies. Almost same percentage of people affirmed 'yes' or 'sometimes' that they read destination blogs, and that these represent the correct image of the destination. Around half of the respondents said that they can reschedule their tours on the basis of social media reviews. A majority of respondents, 77 percent, said that they refer to social media before deciding and finalizing a destination to visit.

The millennials seem to be influenced most by the social media reviews and feedback presented by other social media users about any destination or its services. Videos about the destinations to a large extent also influence their decision-making process; followed by reading material about the destination, then by pictures and blogs. When it comes to reliability of the content, it seems that the millennials are of the view that they search the social media for information gathering, but they do not rely on social media alone. They think that the reviews or feedbacks available on social media are useful, but not totally reliable compared to other sources of information. The study also analyzed which were the most preferred social media handles or platforms used by the millennials. Instagram was found to be most-used by millennials, followed by WhatsApp, YouTube, Facebook, Snapchat and Twitter.

The millennials spend good amount of their time on social media every day, and they see, watch, read and share a lot of information on social media. It has now become a very important and common source of information. Companies, irrespective of their products and services, are now targeting their prospective clients using social media marketing tools. Now they have dedicated social media marketing teams which are responsible for identifying the customer needs, their likings and preferences, through social media activities, and for targeting these clients accordingly. Advertisements, promotions and sponsoring tools are also being used to market the products, services and destinations.

LIMITATIONS AND FUTURE RESEARCH

No study is free from limitations and there are always chances for improvements and modifications in all existing studies. Likewise, this study also has some limitations. The study is descriptive in nature and used a frequency distribution method. If causal or empirical study is conducted with millennials concerning other social media aspects, then it may shed new light on the subject. Future studies may be carried out with different sets of parameters and items in the questionnaire, at different geographical locations, for more insights about the importance and usability of social media in influencing the millennials in their destination choice behavior.

REFERENCES

Amaro, S., Duarte, P., and Henriques, C. (2016). Travelers' use of social media: A clustering approach. *Annals of tourism research*, 59, 1–5. http://dx.doi.org/10.1016/j.annals.2016.03.007.
Berhanu, K., and Raj, Sahil (2020). The trustworthiness of travel and tourism information sources of social media: Perspectives of international tourists visiting Ethiopia. *Heliyon*, 6(3), e03439. doi: 10.1016/j.heliyon.2020.e03439. https://doi.org/10.1016/j.heliyon.2020.e03439.

Buhalis, D. and Jun, H.S. (2011). *E-tourism, contemporary tourism reviews*. Goodfellow Publishers Limited, Oxford.

Dijck, J.V., and Poell, T. (2013). Understanding social media logic. *Media and communication, 1*(1), 2–14. https://doi.org/10.12924/mac2013.01010002.

Dwityas, N.A., and Briandana, R. (2017). Social media in travel decision making process. *International journal of humanities and social science, 7*(7), 193–201. https://www.researchgate.net/publication/322749479

Gulbahar, M.O., and Yildirim, F. (2015). Marketing efforts related to social media channels and mobile application usage in tourism: Case study in Istanbul. *Procedia – Social and behavioral sciences, 195*, 453–462. https://doi.org/10.1016/j.sbspro.2015.06.489.

Hamid, Z.A., Wee, H., Hanafiah, M.H., and Asri, N.A.A. (2016). The effect of social media on tourists' decision to travel to Islamic destination: A Case of Malaysia. In Radzi et al. (eds), *Heritage, culture and society*. Taylor and Francis Group, London, 501–505.

Hanna, R., Rohm, A., and Crittenden, V.L. (2011). We're all connected: The power of the social media ecosystem. *Business Horizons*. https://doi.org/10.1016/j.bushor.2011.01.007.

Jadhav, V., Raman, S., Patwa, N., Moorthy, K., and Pathrose, J. (2018). Impact of Facebook on leisure travel behavior of Singapore residents. *International journal of tourism studies, 4*(2), 157–178. https://doi.org/10.1108/IJTC-06-2017-0032.

Jamaludin, M., Aziz, A., Maripan, M., Lim, E., and Lin, A. (2017). Trust on social media content among travelers. *International journal of academic research in business and social sciences, 7*(12), 214–221. https://doi.org/10.6007/IJARBSS/v7-i12/3606.

Kaplan, A.M., and Haenlein, M. (2010). Users of the world, unite! The challenges and opportunities of social media. *Business horizons, 53*, 59–68. https://doi.org/10.1016/j.bushor.2009.09.003.

Kaurav, R.P.S., Baber, R., and Rajput, S. (2020). Technology-driven tourism and hospitality industry as a tool for economic development: a bibliometric analysis. In *The Emerald handbook of ICT in tourism and hospitality*. Emerald Publishing Limited.

Kietzmann, J.H., Hermkens, K., McCarthy, I.P., and Silvestre, B.S. (2011). Social media? Get serious! Understanding the functional building blocks of social media. *Business horizons, 54*, 241–251.

Kiralova, A., and Pavliceka, A. (2015). Development of social media strategies in tourism destination. *Procedia – Social and behavioral sciences, 175*, 358–366. https://doi.org/10.1016/j.sbspro.2015.01.1211.

Leung, D., Law, R., Hoof, H.V., and Buhalis, D. (2013). Social media in tourism and hospitality: A literature review. *Journal of travel and tourism marketing, 30*(1–2), 3–22. https://doi.org/10.1080/10548408.2013.750919.

Mangold, W.G., and Faulds, D.J. (2009). Social media: The new hybrid element of the promotion mix. *Business horizons, 52*, 357–365.

Mangold, W.G. and Smith, K.T. (2011). Selling to Millennials with online reviews. *Business horizons, 55*(2), 141–153.

McDonald, N.C. (2015) Are millennials really the "go-nowhere" generation? *Journal of the American Planning Association, 81(*2), 90–103. https://doi.org/10.1080/01944363.2015.1057196.

Naidu, S. (2019). A study on the influence of social media on tourist psychology. *International journal of management, technology and engineering, 9*(1), 537–545.

Negm, E.M. (2018). Investigating the power of social media in stimulating push and pull factors, encouraging students' intents to study abroad. *International journal of learning and teaching, 4*(3). https://doi.org/10.18178/ijlt.4.3.216-223.

Nezakati, H., Amidi, A., Jusoh, Y.Y., Moghadas, S., Aziz, Y.A., and Sohrabinezhadtalemi, R. (2015). Review of social media potential on knowledge sharing and collaboration in tourism industry. *Procedia – Social and behavioral sciences, 172*, 120–125. https://doi.org/10.1016/j.sbspro.2015.01.344.

Pabel, A., and Prideaux, B. (2016). Social media use in pre-trip planning by tourists visiting a small regional leisure destination. *Journal of vacation marketing, 22*(4), 335–348. https://doi.org/10.1177/1356766715618998.

Pan, B., Xiang, Z., Law, R., and Fesenmaier, D.R. et al. (2010). The dynamics of search engine marketing for tourist destinations. *Journal of travel research, 20*(10), 1–13. https://doi.org/10.1177/0047287510369558.

Paul, H.S., Roy, D., and Mia, R. (2019). Influence of social media on tourists' destination selection decision. *Scholars Bulletin*, 5(11), 658–664. https://doi.org/10.36348/SB.2019.v05i11.009.

Prayag, G., Dimanche, F., and Keup, M. (2012). The tourism experience. In M. Stickdorn and B. Frischhut (eds), *Service design in tourism: Case studies of applied research projects on mobile ethnography for tourism destinations*. Books on Demand GmbH, Cologne, 36–47.

Rashidi, T.H., Abbasi, A., Maghrebi, M., Hasan, S., and Waller, T.S. (2017). Exploring the capacity of social media data for modelling travel behaviour: Opportunities and challenges. *Transportation research, Part C*, 197–211. http://dx.doi.org/10.1016/j.trc.2016.12.008.

Rathonyi, G. (n.d.). *Influence of social media on tourism – Especially among students of the university of Debrecen*. Agroinform Publishing House, Budapest.

Siddiqui, S. and Singh, T. (2016). Social media: Its impact with positive and negative aspects. *International journal of computer applications technology and research*, 5(2), 71–75.

Smith, K.T. (2011). Digital marketing strategies that millennials find appealing, motivating, or just annoying. *Journal of strategic marketing*, 19(6), 489–499. http://dx.doi.org/10.1080/0965254X.2011.581383.

Smith, K.T. (2012). Longitudinal study of digital marketing strategies targeting millennials. *Journal of consumer marketing*, 29(2), 86–92.

Stein, J. (2013). Millennials: The me me me generation. *TIME*, August 14. www.time.com/time/subscriber/printout/0,8816,2143001,00.html#.

Stewart, J.S., Oliver, E.G., Cravens, K.S., and Oishi, S. (2016). Managing millennials: Embracing general differences. *Business horizons*, 60(1), 45–54. http://dx.doi.org/10.1016/j.bushor.2016.08.011.

Xiang, Z. and Gretzel, U. (2010). Role of social media in online travel search. *Tourism management*, 31, 179–188. https://doi.org/10.1016/j.tourman.2009.02.016.

28. Travel influencers and influencer marketing in tourism

Kubra Asan and Medet Yolal

INTRODUCTION

Social media, which rose with the transformation of mass media as a result of technological advances, has become an indispensable characteristic of present-day societies. Social media, which gives people an opportunity to create content and communicate with others, has also brought about distinct concepts, life practices and communication norms. One of these concepts is the social media influencer. Influencers, who have impacts on consumers, are frequently encountered in topics related to tourism as well. They can become important tourism marketing actors and stakeholders, especially in niche tourism fields, with their specialization and credibility characteristics. This chapter examines travel influencers, influencer marketing, and the effects of traveling cyclists on their followers, as a part of niche tourism, in order to present a number of implications about the functions of travel influencers.

INFLUENCERS

The term "influencer" is defined in various ways. The Interactive Advertising Bureau (IAB, 2018) defines social media influencers as those who "have the potential to create engagement, drive conversation and/or sell products/services with the intended target audience." According to another definition, influencers are "individuals who can influence the actions/decisions of a loyal group of local online followers with regard to their particular area of expertise" (Backaler, 2018, p. 1). Lou and Yuan (2019) emphasize that influencers are regular content generators, and explain them as follows: "A social media influencer is first and foremost a content-generator; one who has a status of expertise in a specific area, who has cultivated a sizable number of captive followers – those are of marketing value to brands – by regularly producing valuable content via social media" (p. 65)

As can be understood from the definitions, the term "influencer" is used to define individuals who influence and change the behaviors and/or preferences of people on online media. Alternative terms such as "content creator," "talent," "YouTuber," "blogger," "vlogger," "instagrammer," or "phenomenon" may be used instead of "influencer" (Backaler, 2018; Brown and Hayes, 2008; De Veirman et al., 2017). Influencers are examined in three categories based on their number of followers (Christodoulaki, 2018, p. 78):

- Micro influencers are social media users whose number of followers is between 1000 and 100 000 and who have an average 25–50 percent engagement rate per post.
- Macro influencers are users who have between 100 000 and 1 million followers and an average 5–25 percent engagement rate per post.

● Mega influencers are celebrities who have more than 1 million followers and an average 2–5 percent engagement rate per post.

Influencers, who have the power to influence consumer behavior, are referred to in the marketing literature and applications under the "influencer marketing" approach (Brown and Hayes, 2008; Ge and Gretzel, 2018; Gretzel and Yoo, 2013; De Veirman et al., 2017). According to this approach, influencers are considered opinion leaders with regard to their function (Martensen et al., 2018). Opinion leadership, on the basis of a two-step flow model (Katz and Lazarsfeld, 1995), describes individuals who have strong influence over society in terms of communication. Opinion leaders are reference individuals (or a communication element) who take on the task of stimulating and directing people in terms of social issues and consumer preferences (Nisbet and Kotcher, 2009, p. 329).

Advances in technology and the increasing effects of communication technologies on everyday life have led to the digitalization of opinion leaders. This development process was strongly influenced by Web 2.0 technology, which spread in the 2000s and propelled users from a receptive position in terms of information to a transmitting position. This communication technology enables its users to easily create content in the new media. These new online media can easily reach the masses; thus, opinion leaders can quickly become prominent in online platforms. Martensen et al. (2018) define influencers in online media as the new generation of opinion leaders. However, Ong and Ito (2019) remark that influencers are more than opinion leaders. According to the researchers, influencers not only give information about products from a consumption point of view, but also experience these products themselves (Ong and Ito, 2019, p. 134).

Influencers create contents out from different motivations . The basic motivations of bloggers, who are among the first examples of influencers, were observed to be "self-expression, life documenting, commenting, community forum participation and information seeking" (Huang et al., 2007, p. 474). In addition to these, social media influencers share posts with motivations such as garnering positive reactions, inspiring their followers, having precedence over other users, and benefiting themselves with respect to exploring new places, making friends and cultural change (Yılmaz et al., 2020). Moreover, influencers' inner need for self-entertainment and yearning for self-esteem are intricately intertwined with interactions, compliments from their fans (viewers), or even materialistic desires, such as virtual gifts (Scheibe et al., 2016).

The influencer offers certain experiences to followers based on social interaction. Influencers inform and also reduce complexity, which means that they prepare content in a comprehensible way (Merz, 2019). Influencers basically serve their followers as a source of information (Ay et al., 2019). Accordingly, it can be thought that followers go through a learning experience. Beyond this, Lou and Yuan (2019) state that influencers also generate entertainment value; influencers stamp their posts with personal aesthetic touches and personality twists, which usually create an enjoyable experience. In this context, it is observed that influencers can offer entertainment and aesthetic experiences to their followers in addition to education experiences.

Influencers build identities for both themselves and their followers (Locher and Bolander, 2017). Social media applications have turned into a medium through which users willingly and openly share their names, photos, videos and world views. Individuals share their moment-to-moment actions with other people through status updates. In general, it appears that individuals share a considerable amount of information about themselves; they perform creative identity construction by positioning this information in the way that they desire (Locher and Bolander, 2017, p. 407). There is a tangible presentation of personal identities here, together with lifestyles; which can be defined as all life practices (Giddens and Sutton, 2018, p. 110). Personal identity includes individuals' differences from others, specific properties, and their unique relationships regarding these (Hogg, 1992, p. 93). Influencers create indicators of certain interests, hobbies, activities or even lifestyles, and share them. In this way, influencers create identity values not only for themselves, but also for their followers, who receive these indicators willingly. Connecting with influencers who point to certain lifestyle indicators may also serve the creative identity construction of followers.

The social interactions between influencers and their followers are explained with the terms "cyber-social environment" and "para-social interaction" (De Veirman et al., 2017; Deng et al., 2019; Wang, 2012). Para-social interaction has been described as the illusion of a face-to-face relationship with a media performer (Colliander and Dahlen, 2011).

Culture theorist Byung-Chul Han (2015) points out that the individual is exposed to too much information in the information age. This gigantic pool of information does not make people happy. However, individuals can choose which information they are exposed to, thanks to the democratization effect of social media. By way of personalized applications, individuals can reach information specifically on the subjects and fields in which they are interested. For instance, someone who is interested in a certain hobby searches for information about it on the internet and social media. In time, the software that stores these searches starts to offer advertisements and posts only based on the hobby in question. Byunh-Chul Han (2015) suggests that individuals create closed areas that are tailored for themselves with these applications of personalized search engines. These areas can be explained with the "filter bubble" term by Pariser (2011). Filter bubbles define isolated spaces that include certain points of view or content created by online personalization applications for people. The individual only meets those who are similar to themself in this area. People personalize their worlds in this area, named the "digital neighborhood" by Han (2015). Individuals can design these areas by affirming the facts the way they desire, and can become neighbors with influencers in their digital neighborhood by their own volition. Each individual can have their own truth, and is interested in sharing content that will support and affirm this truth. As a result, influencers can settle in these digital neighborhoods that conventional media tools cannot reach.

According to another sociological approach, influencers can also create new public areas (Deng et al., 2019; Turner, 2010). Internet-based social networks enable ordinary individuals to find a place and even become "phenomena" themselves, just like celebrities. Turner (2010) sees this as "The Demotic Turn." According to this, media is no longer monopolized by the elite, but is expanding to the masses. People can turn themselves into media content with the demotic turn, making live broadcasts or posting photos or videos thanks to social media technology. Deng et al. (2019) point out that influencers who make live broadcasts create new realities via self-expression and self-presentation, for both themselves and their followers. Initially, live-streaming was used as a tool for sharing exciting or contentious events, but in its current form it enables the public broadcast of life through a shared channel (Deng et al., 2019, p. 214).

Consumers who are suspicious of traditional marketing methods can more easily embrace, care about and pay attention to influencers, who they can communicate with over social networks. As influencers' endorsements are highly personal and interwoven with the constant stream of textual and visual narration of their personal lives, they are perceived as the influencers' unbiased opinions (De Vierman et al., 2018, p. 801).

The characteristics of influencers can be summarized as:

- Their most significant characteristic is that they are content creators.
- They can simultaneously create content on different social media platforms, such as Instagram, Twitter or Facebook, or on more than one channel.
- They are perceived as credible and attractive.
- They can emerge from among ordinary people.
- They can specialize in a certain area.
- They can be classified based on their follower counts or the size of the content they create.
- They assume the role of an information source for their followers.
- They can offer entertainment and esthetic experiences to their followers in addition to educational experiences.
- They serve creative identity creation.
- They create para-social interactions.
- They can create new public areas.
- They can become efficient marketing partners to reach consumers outside traditional marketing approaches.

INFLUENCER MARKETING

Social media influencer marketing is a viral marketing approach in which an online personality shapes consumers' attitudes through tweets, posts, blogs, or any other format of communication on social media (Xiao et al., 2018, p. 190). Influencers are utilized in influencer marketing as opinion leaders to reach consumers. Because of their dual role as consumers and marketers, influencers play an active role in encouraging engagement (Ge and Gretzel, 2018). Furthermore, a recent report (eMarketer, 2017) shows that 90 percent of the social media marketing impact comes from message creation by influencers, rather than distribution; moreover, influencer content has been found to be more accountable and effective than firm-generated content in terms of influencing consumer purchase decisions.

Influencer marketing is not only applied in business-to-consumer (B2C) markets, but also in business-to-business (B2B) markets (Backaler, 2018; Brown and Hayes, 2008). Influencer marketing is seen as a rapid method for businesses to connect with local elements to develop international strategies (Backaler, 2018).

Consumers' distrust in brands appears to be the primary factor that led to the emergence of influencer marketing. In addition, advertisements that are frequently encountered in accordance with traditional marketing methods have started to become boring for consumers. A similar message is perceived as more authentic and credible when it is communicated by a fellow consumer rather than an advertiser (De Veirman et al., 2017, p. 800). Based on this, it is suggested that marketers focus more on positive mouth-to-mouth marketing approaches (Backaler, 2018).

Social media has become a staple in the everyday lives of consumers with the advancements in internet-based technologies (Xiao et al., 2018). In this context, electronic word-of-mouth (eWOM) has become an emerging marketing approach. eWOM is defined as "any positive or negative statement made by potential, actual, or former customers about a product or company, which is made available to a multitude of people and institutions via the Internet" (Hennig-Thurau et al., 2004, p. 39). While traditional WOM (face-to-face "verbal" communication) has a momentary nature, eWOM exists in a "written" form in cyberspace which can be retrieved, linked and searched, so its effects last much longer (Wang, 2012, p. 234). Influencers, who are regarded as digital opinion leaders, are utilized within the frame of the eWOM marketing approach (Backaler, 2018; De Veirman et al., 2017).

Contrary to traditional marketing methods, influencers can convey messages regarding brands to target audiences in their own way (Childers et al., 2019). The messages they convey are found to be much more meaningful by their followers since there is a connection between them. Influencers also make up communities called decision-maker ecosystems, which revolve around a decision-maker (Brown and Hayes, 2008).

Credibility and attractiveness are the two basic characteristics of influencers that affect consumers (Xiao et al., 2018). The information or source credibility perceived by their followers is very important for influencers (Lou and Yuan, 2019; Xiao et al., 2018). Considering that creating and spreading false information is quite easy on digital media, credibility has become one of the most important properties sought in influencers.

There are several models explaining credibility. For example, Hovland et al. (1953) propose a source credibility model that explains credibility with competence and trustworthiness. A more recent study on YouTube influencers by Xiao et al. (2018) revealed that trustworthiness, social influence, argument quality and information involvement are influential factors affecting consumers' perceptions of information credibility on YouTube. Trustworthiness especially comes to the fore in this context. Trust is a strong value that constantly needs to be manifested (Merz, 2019). Furthermore, trustworthiness as a predictor variable of credibility is more important than expertise when individuals evaluate the credibility of eWOM communications (Brown et al., 2007; Reichelt et al., 2014). Lou and Yuan (2019) proposed a four-dimensional model which includes trustworthiness, expertise, similarity and attractiveness to explain resource reliability. This study also shows that source credibility positively affects followers' trust in influencers' branded posts, which subsequently influences brand awareness and purchase intentions.

Influencers can become brands themselves. In this context, a corporate brand can collaborate with a brand influencer to generate much more diverse values and reach their target audiences in many different ways (Backaler, 2018, p. 67). From another viewpoint, influencers are multipliers who spread products, messages and brands over particular digital channels (Merz, 2019, p. 119).

Backaler (2018) explains influencers in three levels in terms of marketing. The first are celebrity influencers, such as actors, sportspeople or artists who have vast fanbases. The second, category influencers, are people who are experts in specific areas such as lifestyle design, beauty or entrepreneurship, and have earned the trust of their followers. Lastly, micro-influencers are individuals who are willing to create content about a certain product, location, experience or brand. In another classification, McQuarrie et al. (2013) distinguish between grassroots influencers (that is, ordinary consumers lacking professional experience and not holding an institutional position) and designated celebrities (that is, professionals with institutional positions). These classifications developed for influencer marketing propose that the marketing campaign should employ influencers of appropriate types and levels for the campaign goals; it is possible to collaborate with influencers of all levels in accordance with the aims and goals of marketing.

There are several points to consider to conduct an effective influencer marketing campaign. First, when developing an influencer marketing campaign, the social media platform that will host the campaign (Instagram, Twitter, YouTube, and so on) should be planned well (Droesch, 2020). The target audience and the characteristics of the audience should be taken as a basis when choosing the social media platform. Similarly, businesses should ensure that the influencer is the right person to increase the value of their brands or products and to carry the brand to the desired goals of the campaign (Abo, 2018). For instance, influencers who work with various brands or businesses and do not have many followers may not always be a good choice. Working with such an influencer decreases a brand's perceived uniqueness and consequently brand attitudes (De Veirman et al., 2017). Businesses may also prefer to scout a new influencer on the basis of their target audiences (Backaler, 2018).

Social network analyses and data mining modeling are utilized in defining influencers (Tsugawa and Kimura, 2018; More and Lingam, 2016). Moreover, businesses can apply to influencer marketing agencies that generally have exclusive talent or pre-existing relationships with an extensive network of tested influencers.

The key to a successful influencer marketing campaign is research (Abo, 2018). The research process starts with finding the appropriate social media platform and influencer, but it should continue throughout the whole campaign. Influencer marketing includes a number of phases involving influencer discovery, influencer outreach, design of influencer campaigns, influencer tracking/measurement and influencer relations (Inkybee, 2016). Since influencers run campaigns within their own areas of freedom, the control area of brands or businesses is quite narrow. Because of this, influencers should be followed closely during the whole campaign and their effects should be examined.

Marketing professionals warn that influencers should be set free in terms of content creation and should not be controlled. Although this is seen as a risky action, influencer marketing works best when the content coming from the influencer is natural, genuine and realistic (Childers et al., 2019). "Genuineness" is the primary characteristic sought in a good influencer (Abo, 2018). Influencers can create genuine content when they are set free.

Backaler (2018, p. 34) proposes that influencers should collaborate with brands with an eye towards their own points of view, and underlines these four elements:

- Authenticity. An authentic, trusted relationship with a community is at the heart of what makes an influencer successful. When collaborating with brands, influencers' top concern is how to maintain this authentic connection, without being viewed as a "sell-out."
- Brand fit. A consistent personal brand is critical for an influencer to gain increasing influence, but the influencer needs to balance their personal brand with those of the company brands they want to collaborate with, which are sometimes at odds.
- Community. A targeted, engaged and growing community is the ultimate measure of success for an influencer.
- Content. Content is how an influencer adds value to and builds a relationship with their community.

Collaborations must be well planned for a successful influencer campaign. In this context, the role of the influencer and the messages that the influencer is responsible for creating must be clearly defined and bound by contract (Abo, 2018). Moreover, establishing strategic collaborations that create long-term relationships between the influencer and the brand, rather than short-term campaigns, increases success (Droesch, 2020). There is no clear limitation for influencer marketing applications; they are quite open to creativity. Businesses can invite influencers to help with product development, or create an advisory board to help improve their customer experience in this context (Backaler, 2018, p. 134).

However, influencer marketing carries some risks. First, businesses take the risk of potential consequences that may damage their brand reputation by collaborating with an influencer that they cannot fully control. Also, businesses can be deceived by some influencers who resort to tricks such as creating fake followers, follower counts, clicks or impressions. However, both social media software companies and legal authorities are developing their systems to stay ahead of fraudulent acts such as these (Childers et al., 2019). In any case, businesses should protect themselves by researching and monitoring the influencer that they collaborate with (Backaler, 2018).

TRAVEL INFLUENCER

Tourism is also intensely affected by communication technologies. The advances in Web 2.0 technology have increased content creation in the tourism area. Individuals can now create content about their travel experiences or plans and share it with the masses; thus, it is possible to see social media influencers in many areas such as gastronomy, travel, tourism and recreation.

In the case of tourism, it is observed that travelers who share their travels on social media have a number of followers. These travelers create content that provides information and images about destinations, routes, tour packages, events and the services provided by tourism businesses. More importantly, their followers learn about travel formalities such as transport services or currency exchange, in addition to leaning about unknown destinations, landscapes and cultures, thanks to the social media content created by these travelers. They are defined as travel influencers for their ability to influence consumer behaviors of prospective travelers and followers (Kaur, 2018; Hanifah, 2019). They act as information sources about destinations and tourism products.

Studies about travel influencers are increasing, and most of these focus on the functions of influencers with the marketing approach (Li et al., 2015; Ong and Ito, 2019; Wang, 2012). The next section discusses these functions. However, contrary to the marketing point of view, Yılmaz et al. (2020) focused on the experiences of Turkish instagrammer influencers. The study observed that the motivations driving influencers are positive reactions, inspiring their followers, having precedence over other users, and the fact that the work they do benefits themselves with respect to exploring new places, making friends and cultural change. The participants, who define being an influencer as an occupation, also stated that the job contains difficulties such as a heavy workload, the need for approval, and impression management.

Tourism is a practice with a rich product diversity. In this regard, influencers can also become diversified depending on the theme of tourism. Influencers who are experts in their fields mostly distinguish themselves in niche tourism; examples include backpacker influencers, gastronomy influencers, and mountaineer influencers in the adventure tourism area. Influencers' target audiences and their effects on these audiences may differ based on the theme of tourism. On this point, a case study on influencer effects on followers in the niche of cycling travel is presented in this chapter.

INFLUENCER MARKETING IN TOURISM

Tourism marketing professionals are aware of travel influencers' potential effects on target audiences. Travel influencers are utilized in tourism marketing campaigns as a form of eWOM. Destination marketing organizations (DMOs), tour operators, and accommodation, catering and transportation companies collaborate with influencers to promote their products (Yılmaz et al., 2020; Gretzel, 2017). For example, Tourism New Zealand's collaboration with Chinese micro-blogger Yao Chen is a prominent and well-documented example of early influencer marketing in tourism (Gretzel, 2017, p. 151). Furthermore, the travel equipment used by influencers, such as backpacks, climbing gear or camping supplies, is also promoted to their followers (Yılmaz et al., 2020).

Backaler (2018) emphasizes that Airbnb has reached the right balance of global strategy and local implementation by utilizing local influencers. The company began by utilizing local influencers with authenticity and authority in order to globally increase its brand recognition, instead of directly reaching consumers, and has succeeded. This example shows that local influencers can be a reference guide for global strategies.

Social media influencers (in this case, travel bloggers) affect their followers' travel-related intentions (Magno and Cassia, 2018). When examined as marketing actors, travel influencers affect the traveling decision-making process as reliable sources of information (Ay et al., 2019; Book and Tanford, 2019; Gretzel, 2017, p. 151). People take heed of bloggers' advice and solutions because they think that they are competent in their area (Ay et al., 2019). In this context, travel bloggers who convey their experiences and ideas to thousands of people have the power to influence individuals in the pre-purchase process (Wang, 2012).

Community structures can be seen within the frame of tourism and travel-themed blogs. Wang (2012) claims that people gather in travel blog communities as a cybercommunity and exchange social interactions. A travel blog community is advantageous for the blogger to discuss, share and exchange perspectives with other bloggers on travel-related issues, offers them a chance to meet people with common interests, and provides them with a channel to comment on personal feelings concerning a specific destination or tourism product (Wang, 2012, p. 240). These constructs are examples of the decision-maker ecosystems proposed by Brown and Hayes (2008). Opinion leaders who come forth within these communities take the role of influencers. Wang (2012) has empirically proven that cybercommunity interactions affect a destination's image and travel behavior tendencies.

Ong and Ito (2019) conducted a study to evaluate the effectiveness of influencer marketing campaigns executed by DMOs for consumers in Singapore. They found that influencer campaigns have direct, positive effects on the behavior intentions of consumers. Moreover, the study proved that the influencer marketing campaigns' engagement with target audiences also has positive effects on a destination's image. Li et al. (2015) also suggest that travel influencers can shape a destination's image with the content they create, in both the cognitive and affective dimensions.

It is important to find the right social media platform and the right influencer, to constantly examine the process, and to create well-planned, long-term collaborations in order to achieve success with influencer marketing in tourism. Travel influencers are free-spirited people who chase after their dreams, so it is necessary to be mindful of the freedom area of the influencer in projects (Ay et al., 2019). Influencers, in turn, are expected to see genuine local values and reflect them in their work. Influencers who can create content on a global scale have a very large area of effect, so it would be beneficial to think globally and act locally based on the continuity of this effect.

CASE STUDY: THE EFFECTS OF TRAVEL INFLUENCERS ON FOLLOWERS – A SCALE DEVELOPMENT STUDY ON BICYCLE TRAVELERS' SOCIAL MEDIA FOLLOWERS

People use bicycles to have fun in open spaces in their daily lives. These activities generally take the form of short excursions as an example of recreational cycling. In terms of tourism, however, riding a bicycle is sometimes a means of transportation and sometimes an activity. Independent cycling tourists come to the fore in this regard (Lamont and Buultjens, 2011). These tourists use bicycles as their primary vehicle to reach their destinations, and spend their whole vacations cycling. The activities of independent cycling tourists correspond to bicycle touring in the field.

Bicycle touring is continually increasing. Travelers can take their bicycles to foreign countries and continue their tours thanks to the smoothing of visa and passport applications, increasing means of transport such as trains or planes, and ticket offers. Advancements in the bicycle and equipment sector also play an encouraging role since people can easily access the equipment they need.

Bicycle travelers are seen as opinion leaders by independent tour cyclists or recreational cyclists. The followers of these travelers on online media are thought to consist of potential (or current) bicycle tourists, and individuals who actively use bicycles recreationally, or at least sympathize with cycling activities. In this context, bicycle tourists who gather many followers by sharing their experiences on social media, blogs and websites provide an example of travel influencers.

Cyclist travel influencers can become important actors in marketing and destination image development activities towards cycling as special-interest tourism; however, the specific effects of these influencers on their followers should be examined closely. On this basis, this case study includes a scale development study on the followers of Turkish bicycle travelers.

First, in-depth interviews were conducted with followers who actively perform tour cycling. The themes and codes from these interviews were used for the scale draft. Later, the scale draft was given its final form after being submitted to experts for review. The data were gathered via online surveys, which were shared on social media platforms by the 15 Turkish cycling travelers with the highest follower counts, determined through purposive sampling. Finally, 915 usable surveys were gathered at the end of the data gathering process, which ended in February 2020.

The survey study included participants from all of Turkey's different regions. These participants were asked questions about their demographics and some supplemental questions about bicycle tours. The answers generally shed light on the characteristics of Turkey's bicycle market behavior. Some significant results are as follows:

- The followers' average age is 39, although individual ages differ considerably (min. 17, max. 73).
- Most of the followers are male (76.9 percent male, 23.1 percent female).
- Education levels are quite high. Nearly 80 percent of the followers have bachelor's or postgraduate degrees.
- Nearly half of the followers (49 percent) consist of middle-class public officials or white-collar employees.
- 48.5 percent of the followers participate in touristic cycling events (bicycle tours or festivals that are longer than 24 hours and include overnight stays).
- Camping is the preferred type of accommodation for the majority (73 percent), while 18 percent prefer hotels.
- 60 percent of the cycling followers cook their own meals during tours, while roughly 34 percent prefer restaurants.
- Most tours of cycling followers are three nights long.
- 33 percent of the followers attend bicycle festivals.
- 57.9 percent of the followers participate in recreational cycling events (entertainment, travel or exercise tours that are shorter than 24 hours).
- The followers who participate in recreational tours join at least one tour per month; 50 percent of the followers join in recreational tours for more than four days per month.

After the exploratory and confirmatory factor analyses, it was observed that bicycle travelers' effects on their followers can be explained with four factors. These are motivation, information, role model and communal effects (Table 28.1).

According to the analysis, the most apparent effect of influencers on their followers is in motivating them. Influencers create excitement about cycling in their followers, and drive them to do tours. Following this is the informative effect of influencers. Traveling influencers inform their followers about destinations, travel arrangements, routes, bicycles, cycling and equipment. Furthermore, influencers are observed to be role models for their travelers due to their successfully completing difficult activities and their alternative, out-of-the-ordinary lifestyles. Finally, followers perceive that travelers serve their cycling socialities. Travelers were found to especially support social responsibility projects and cyclist organizations.

As explained above, in addition to the informative function of travel influencers emphasized by the literature, this case study shows that travel influencers have other positive effects, such as motivation, role model and communal effects. Thus, it is understood that influencers can be an important resource in the field of marketing. The examined case reveals that followers actively do bicycle tours and are part of the cycling market. As a result, we predict that influencers can be a good reference guide in marketing studies on niche areas such as cycling tourism.

CONCLUSION

Travel influencers are important actors who can be collaborated with in the field of tourism marketing. In addition to the informative function of travel influencers emphasized by the

Table 28.1   *Factor analysis results: the effects of travel influencers on followers*

Factors and items (n = 915)	Explained Variance	Mean	Standard Deviation	Factor Loads	Standard Loads
Motivation (α = 0.89)	40.51	4.63			
They make you dream of doing a bicycle tour.		4.62	0.64	-0.67	0.69
They encourage you to do a bicycle tour.		4.65	0.60	-0.90	0.78
They inspire you to do a bicycle tour.		4.72	0.56	-0.76	0.75
They make people excited about bicycle tours.		4.67	0.59	-0.68	0.80
They give you self-confidence in cycling.		4.58	0.68	-0.75	0.80
They encourage you to do a bicycle tour.		4.52	0.73	-0.63	0.74
Information (α = 0.88)	10.71	4.45			
They inform you about traveling abroad (visa, transfer, foreign exchange transactions, etc.).		4.19	0.92	0.70	0.67
They set an example with the bicycles and equipment they use.		4.48	0.74	0.65	0.70
They show new destinations.		4.70	0.56	0.64	0.68
They inform you about destinations (cultural, geographical, socioeconomic info, etc.).		4.57	0.64	0.70	0.73
They offer practical solutions to the difficulties that can be encountered during tours.		4.45	0.74	0.69	0.77
They give technical information about bicycles and cycling.		4.09	0.96	0.57	0.73
They inform you about routes (driving routes, camping facilities, food and beverage facilities, etc.).		4.39	0.78	0.67	0.78
Role model (α = 0.80)	6.06	4.53			
They carry out tours that are not thought to be possible.		4.49	0.80	0.39	0.60
They become icons/models for their followers.		4.42	0.79	0.57	0.70
They are indicators of the development of tour cycling.		4.47	0.76	0.50	0.65
They expand new horizons for their followers.		4.65	0.58	0.72	0.79
They exhibit an alternative/outside the system lifestyle.		4.60	0.69	0.62	0.67
Communal (α = 0.84)	5.01	3.90			
They are useful for cycling-related civil society organizations (associations, clubs, communities).		4.09	0.97	0.62	0.77
They draw attention to social responsibility issues.		4.06	0.98	0.78	0.70
They increase the demand for bicycle festivals.		3.76	1.13	0.66	0.71
Mutual communication (online, face to face, etc.) can be established.		4.13	0.93	0.42	0.66
They become references for sponsors.		3.45	1.18	0.56	0.63
Total (α = 0.93)	54.49				

Note: X^2 /df = 4.75 (p = 0.000); RMSEA = 0.064; NFI = 0.90; CFI = 0.92; GFI = 0.90. The model has acceptable values on goodness of fit indices (Schumacker and Lomax, 2016; Hair et al., 2010).

literature, this case study shows that travel influencers have other positive effects, such as motivation, role model and communal effects. This has several implications.

The examined case reveals that followers actively do bicycle tours and are part of the cycling market. As a result, influencers can be a good reference guide in marketing studies on niche areas such as cycling tourism.

The most significant effect of bicycle travelers on their followers is creating motivation. This function can increase the participation of followers in tourist activities and enables followers to open up to new and different experiences. In this regard, bicycle travelers can be an important reference in promotional activities for new touristic products and destinations.

Bicycle travelers inform their followers about new destinations and cultures in addition to important travel information. Bicycle activities also have unique technical characteristics; influencers are important actors in marketing new bicycles and equipment as well.

Influencers' function of affecting a destination's image is also emphasized in the literature (Li et al., 2015; Ong and Ito, 2019). Bicycle traveler influencers are seen to discover new destinations, create routes and generate demand for these routes with the content they share online. As a result, influencers have the function of not only affecting a destination's image, but also developing the destination. Based on this, influencers can be collaborated with when developing destinations and new touristic products.

Bicycle travelers are role models for their followers, who think that they can join activities similar to the influencers' and imitate them. The influencers' role model effect can steer their followers' behavior: the influencers' shared experiences about touristic products and destinations determine their followers' attitudes as well.

Bicycle travelers can be influential in social movements about cycling as opinion leaders. Travelers feed the bicycle community culture. These effects increase the attendance of bicycle events, and also create new public spheres in the field of cycling. These spheres can be a very rich resource for the cycling tourism market. Influencers know and can direct these public spheres very well, so they can be collaborated with to create micro-niche markets.

The bicycle travelers examined in the study are seen mostly as bicycle users by their followers. Their marketing role is not yet dominant, so they are "grassroots influencers" rather than "designated" in terms of McQuarrie et al.'s (2013) classification. Their primary characteristic in this regard is that they create unique and genuine content. Thus, it is quite important in bicycle tourism marketing that traveling influencers are given free areas where they can continue their uniqueness when establishing collaborations.

We predict that influencer marketing will also come to the fore in tourism, given the already expanding influence of social media on everyday life. Influencers help to generate new niche markets with the content they create (Li et al., 2015). They are significant new actors who can substantially affect the trajectories of tourism consumption (Yılmaz et al., 2020); so much so that businesses and brands may have to follow travel influencers and trends even if they have no collaboration. Ultimately, understanding travel influencers well, and inviting them into marketing endeavors as partners, would significantly benefit businesses and brands.

REFERENCES

Abo, J. (2018). *Unfiltered: How to be as Happy as You Look on Social Media*. Irvine, CA: Entrepreneur Media, Inc.

Ay, E., İpek, K., Özdağ, N.B, Özekici, E., and Alvare, D. (2019). Travel bloggers as influencers: What compels them to blog. In N. Kozak and M. Kozak (eds), *Tourist Destination Management* (pp. 159–177). Cham: Springer.

Backaler, J. (2018). *Digital Influence: Unleash the Power of Influencer Marketing to Accelerate your Global Business*. Cham: Palgrave Macmillan.

Book, L.A., and Tanford, S. (2019). Measuring social influence from online traveler reviews. *Journal of Hospitality and Tourism Insights*, 3(1), 54–72.

Brown, D., and Hayes, N. (2008). *Influencer Marketing: Who Really Influences Your Customers?* London: Routledge, Taylor & Francis Group.

Brown, J., Broderick, A.J., and Lee, N. (2007). Word of mouth communication within online communities: Conceptualizing the online social network. *Journal of Interactive Marketing*, 21(3), 2–20.

Childers, C. C., Lemon, L.L., and Hoy, M.G. (2019). #Sponsored #Ad: Agency perspective on influencer marketing campaigns. *Journal of Current Issues and Research in Advertising*, *40*(3), 258–274.

Christodoulaki, A. (2018). The effects of micro vs macro influencers on brand awareness, brand attitude, and purchase intention, and the moderating role of advertising appeals. Master's thesis, University of Amsterdam. UvA Scripties Online Document Archive. http://www.scriptiesonline.uba.uva.nl/document/662510.

Colliander, J., and Dahlen, M. (2011). Following the fashionable friend: The power of social media. Weighing publicity effectiveness of blogs versus online magazines. *Journal of Advertising Research*, *51*, 313–320.

Deng, Z., Benckendorff, P., and Wang, J. (2019). Blended tourism experiencescape: A conceptualisation of live-streaming tourism. In *Information and Communication Technologies in Tourism 2019: Proceedings of the International Conference in Nicosia, Cyprus, January 30–February 1 2019* (pp. 212–225). Cham: Springer.

De Veirman, M., Cauberghe, V., and Hudders, L. (2017). Marketing through Instagram influencers: The impact of number of followers and product divergence on brand attitude. *International Journal of Advertising*, *36*(5), 798–828.

Droesch, B. (2020). Six influencers on collaborating with brands. Retrieved May 28, 2020, from https://www.emarketer.com/content/six-influencers-on-collaborating-with-brands?ecid=NL1001.

eMarketer (2017). Influencer marketing roundup. Retrieved from https://www.emarketer.com/public_media/docs/eMarketer_Roundup_Influencer_Marketing_2017_5.pd.

Ge, J., and Gretzel, U. (2018). A taxonomy of value co-creation on Weibo – A communication perspective. *International Journal of Contemporary Hospitality Management*, *30*, 2075–2092.

Giddens, A., and Sutton, P.W. (2018). *Essential Concepts in Sociology*. London: Polity Press.

Gretzel, U. (2017). Advances in social media for travel, tourism and hospitality new perspectives, practice and cases travel and tourism. In M. Sigala and U. Gretzel (eds), *Advances in Social Media for Travel, Tourism and Hospitality: New Perspectives, Practice and Cases* (pp. 147–156). Abingdon: Routledge.

Gretzel, U., and Yoo, K.H. (2013). Premises and promises of social media marketing in tourism. In S. McCabe (ed.), *The Routledge Handbook of Tourism Marketing* (pp. 491–504). New York: Routledge.

Hair, J.F., Black, W.B., Babin, B.J., and Anderson, R.E. (2010). *Multivariate Data Analysis: A Global Perspective*. Upper Saddle River, NJ: Pearson Education.

Han, B. (2015). *Transparency Society*. Stanford, CA: Stanford University Press.

Hanifah, R.D. (2019). The influence of Instagram travel influencer on visiting decision of tourist destinations for Generation Y. *Proceedings of CATEA 2019* (pp. 235–247). Jakarta: Sekolah Tinggi Pariwisata Triasakti.

Hennig-Thurau, T., Gwinner, K.P., Walsh, G., and Gremler, D.D. (2004). Electronic word-of-mouth via consumer-opinion platforms: What motivates consumers to articulate themselves on the internet? *Journal of Interactive Marketing*, *18*(1), 38–52.

Hogg, M.A. (1992). *The Social Psychology of Group Cohesiveness: From Attraction to Social Identity*. New York: New York University Press.

Hovland, C.I., Janis, I., and Kelley, H.H. (1953). *Communication and Persuasion: Psychological Studies and Opinion Change*. New Haven, CT: Yale University Press.

Huang, C., Shen, Y., Lin, H., and Chang, S. (2007). Bloggers' motivations and behaviors: A model. *Journal of Advertising Research*, *47*(4), 472–484.

Inkybee (2016). *The Best Practice Guide for Effective Blogger Outreach*. Retrieved May 28, 2020, from https://www.inkybee.com/blogger-outreach-a-best-practice-guide/#.WKejBzsrKUl.

Interactive Advertising Bureau (IAB) (2018). Inside influence. Accessed June 3, 2020. https://www.iab.com/wpcontent/uploads/2018/01/IAB_Influencer_Marketing_for_Publishers_2018-01-25.pdf.

Katz, E., and Lazarsfeld, P.F. (1995). *Personal Influence*. New York and London: Routledge.

Kaur, H. (2018). Social media as a travel influencer: A review of recent studies. *International Journal of Academic Research and Development*, *4*(2), 81–85.

Lamont, M., and Buultjens, J. (2011). Putting the brakes on: Impediments to the development of independent cycle tourism in Australia, *Current Issues in Tourism*, *14*(1), 57–78.

Li, Y. R., Lin, Y.C., Tsai, P.H., and Wang, Y.Y. (2015). Traveller-generated contents for destination image formation: Mainland China travellers to Taiwan as a case study. *Journal of Travel and Tourism Marketing*, *32*(5), 518–533.

Locher, A., and Bolander, B. (2017). Facework and identity. In C. Hoffmann and W. Bublitz (eds), *Pragmatics of Social Media*. Berlin: De Gruyter.

Lou, C., and Yuan, S. (2019). Influencer marketing: How message value and credibility affect consumer trust of branded content on social media. *Journal of Interactive Advertising*, *19*(1), 58–73.

Magno, F., and Cassia, F. (2018). The impact of social media influencers in tourism. *Anatolia*, *29*(2), 288–290. doi:10.1080/13032917.2018.1476981.

Martensen, A., Brockenhuus-Schack, S., and Zahid, A.L. (2018). How citizen influencers persuade their followers. *Journal of Fashion Marketing and Management*, *22*(3), 335–353.

McQuarrie, E.F., Miller, J., and Phillips, B.J. (2013). The megaphone effect: Taste and audience in fashion blogging. *Journal of Consumer Research*, *40*(1), 136–158.

Merz, J. (2019). From trusted friend to trusted brand? Influencer marketing between trust and mistrust. In T. Osburg and S. Heinecke (eds), *Media Trust in a Digital World* (pp. 117–126). Cham: Springer. https://doi.org/10.1007/978-3-030-30774-5.

More, J., and Lingam, C. (2016). A scalable data mining model for social media influencer identification. In A. Unal, M. Nayak, D.K. Mishra, D. Singh and A. Joshi (eds), *Smart Trends in Information Technology and Computer Communications First International Conference, SmartCom 2016, Jaipur, India, August 6–7, 2016, Revised Selected Papers* (pp. 625–632). Singapore: Springer.

Nisbet, M.C., and Kotcher, J.E. (2009). A two-step flow of influence? Opinion leader campaigns on climate change. *Science Communication*, *30*(3), 328–354.

Ong, Y.X., and Ito, N. (2019). "I want to go there too!" Evaluating social media influencer marketing effectiveness: A case study of Hokkaido's DMO. In *Information and Communication Technologies in Tourism 2019: Proceedings of the International Conference in Nicosia, Cyprus, January 30–February 1 2019* (pp. 132–145). Cham: Springer.

Pariser, E. (2011) *The Filter Bubble: What the Internet is Hiding From You*. New York: Penguin.

Reichelt, J., Sievert, J., and Jacob, F. (2014). How credibility affects eWOM reading: The influences of expertise, trustworthiness, and similarity on utilitarian and social functions. *Journal of Marketing Communications*, *20*(1–2), 65–81.

Scheibe, K., Fietkiewicz, K.J., and Stock, W.G. (2016). Information behavior on social live streaming services. *Journal of Information Science Theory and Practice*, *4*(2), 6–20.

Schumacker, R.E., and Lomax, R.G. (2016). *A Beginners Guide to Structural Equation Modeling*. New York: Routledge.

Tsugawa, S., and Kimura, K. (2018). Identifying influencers from sampled social networks. *Physica A: Statistical Mechanics and Its Applications*, *507*, 294–303.

Turner, G. (2010). *Ordinary People and the Media: The Demotic Turn*. Los Angeles, CA: SAGE.

Wang, H.Y. (2012). Investigating the determinants of travel blogs influencing readers' intention to travel. *Service Industries Journal*, *32*(2), 231–255.

Xiao, M., Wang, R., and Chan-Olmsted, S. (2018). Factors affecting YouTube influencer marketing credibility: A heuristic-systematic model. *Journal of Media Business Studies*, *15*(3), 188–213.

Yılmaz, M., Sezerel, H., and Uzuner, Y. (2020). Sharing experiences and interpretation of experiences: A phenomenological research on Instagram influencers. *Current Issues in Tourism*, 1–8. doi:10.1080/13683500.2020.1763270.

FURTHER READING

Abo, J. (2018). *Unfiltered: How to be as Happy as You Look on Social Media*. Irvine, CA: Entrepreneur Media, Inc.

Award-winning journalist and sought-after speaker Jessica Abo addresses the relationship between psychology technologies and provides practical insights from experts.

Ay, E., İpek, K., Özdağ, N. B, Özekici, E. and Alvare, D. (2019). Travel bloggers as Influencers: What compels them to blog. InN. Kozak and M. Kozak (eds), *Tourist Destination Management* (pp. 159–177). Cham: Springer.

This study, which is based on interviews with Turkish travel bloggers, covered issues concerning motivations of bloggers, existence of collaboration and bloggers' perceptions concerning their role as influencers.

Backaler, J. (2018). *Digital Influence: Unleash the Power of Influencer Marketing to Accelerate your Global Business*. Cham: Palgrave Macmillan.

Written for marketing professionals working in both domestic and international markets, this book provides readers with context, frameworks, and best practices about influencer marketing.

Book, L.A., and Tanford, S. (2019). Measuring social influence from online traveler reviews. *Journal of Hospitality and Tourism Insights*, *3*(1), 54–72.

This study provides a scale for researchers to investigate the process whereby different characteristics of online reviews influence travel decisions.

Emarketer. (n.d.). Retrieved June 23, 2020, from https://www.emarketer.com/

Data and research source on digital for business professionals.

Hoffmann, C.R., and Bublitz, W. (2017). *Pragmatics of Social Media*. Berlin: De Gruyter Mouton.

This handbook provides a comprehensive overview of the pragmatics of social media and includes chapters related to identity building and socialities of social media.

Ong, Y.X., and Ito, N. (2019). "I want to go there too!" Evaluating social media influencer marketing effectiveness: A case study of Hokkaido's DMO. In *Information and Communication Technologies in Tourism 2019: Proceedings of the International Conference in Nicosia, Cyprus, January 30–February 1 2019* (pp. 132–145). Cham: Springer.

This study evaluates the effectiveness of the influencers marketing campaign executed by Hokkaido Tourism Organization in Singapore.

Wang, H.Y. (2012). Investigating the determinants of travel blogs influencing readers' intention to travel. *Service Industries Journal*, *32*(2), 231–255.

The study proposes a model that can explore travel blogs influencing readers' intention to travel.

Xiao, M., Wang, R., and Chan-Olmsted, S. (2018). Factors affecting YouTube influencer marketing credibility: A heuristic-systematic model. *Journal of Media Business Studies*, *15*(3), 188–213.

This study offers heuristic-systematic model to investigate influence credibility evaluations of information posted by YouTube influencers.

Yılmaz, M., Sezerel, H., and Uzuner, Y. (2020). Sharing experiences and interpretation of experiences: A phenomenological research on Instagram influencers. *Current Issues in Tourism*, 1–8. doi:10.1080/13683500.2020.1763270.

This research examines Instagram travel influencers' views on their experiences using phenomeno-logical approach.

PART VI

SOCIAL MEDIA AND FOOD

29. Gastronomy on Twitter: drawing representations from a food event

Francesc Fusté-Forné and Pere Masip

INTRODUCTION

Social media networks can be a significant communicational and promotional tool (Carson, 2005), since social media allows the easy dissemination of cultural heritage (Khalid and Chowdhury, 2018) and cultural expressions (Van House, 2007). In particular, social media and social networking have become a central agent for cultural heritage communication (Stuedahl, 2009). Solo-Anaeto and Jacobs (2015, p. 40) supported this view that 'culture and values are passed and kept alive from generation to generation through communication and socialization'. Furthermore, Ginzarly et al. (2019) mentioned the benefits of use of social media for cultural heritage.

In this sense, media and social media influence on how sites are perceived by tourists (Jansson, 2018; Månsson, 2011; Trant, 2009; Tribe and Mkono, 2017; Van der Hoeven, 2017), and also influence the construction of food narratives. As a consequence, they contribute to the promotion of food tourism (Ranteallo and Andilolo, 2017). In this context, this chapter understands food-based social media-generated contents as a form of cultural communication and a food (media) tourism practice. Drawing from the analysis of Twitter content produced around a food event, the objective of this chapter is to analyse Twitter representations of actors and practices derived from the study of The World's 50 Best Restaurants Awards. In particular, the research explores what actors and practices are represented and, in consequence, what Twitter activity is derived from a food-based event as a pathway to communicate food tourism.

FOOD, TOURISM AND SOCIAL MEDIA

This section is focused on the use of social media analysis for (food) tourism purposes. Online social networking sites (SNSs) are increasingly used for travel research and information gathering (Fotis et al., 2012; Xiang and Gretzel, 2010). Also, online social networks help in creating competitive advantage (Mozas et al., 2016) and trust among consumers (Laroche et al., 2013). Added to traditional marketing communication tools, social media 'exerts an important impact on a brand's success' (Bruhn et al., 2012, p. 771). The impact of incorporating social media in tourism brand strategies is clear (Moro and Rita, 2018).

Leung et al. (2013, p. 7) differentiate social media applications from the consumers' and the suppliers' perspectives. From the suppliers' perspective, they highlight social media applications for promotion and communication, for product distribution, for management and for market research. All of them contribute to future engagement with visitors and tourists. In this sense, previous studies have reviewed the effect of social media communication on consumer perceptions of brands (Moore et al., 2013; Schivinski and Dabrowski, 2014), and they found that firm-created social media communication affects brand attitude, which has a positive influence on purchase intention, and affects brand image and trust (Jeacle and Carter, 2011). However, 'since social media offers an opportunity for consumers to talk to hundreds or even thousands of other consumers around the world, companies are no longer the sole source of brand communication' (Bruhn et al., 2012, p. 771). This same idea is supported by other researchers such as Hays et al. (2013) and Thevenot (2007) who advocate that as a consequence, companies have lost the ultimate control over their image. The benefits of social media refer to not only many-to-many but also many-to-one communication (Bruhn Jensen and Helles, 2017).

The Promotion of Food Tourism in Social Media

Tourism marketing representations of social media have been widely reviewed in the literature. Dellarocas (2003) affirmed that social media provide tourism companies with a range of opportunities to communicate and interact with consumers. Also, De Bernardi (2019) adds to the discussion on authenticity in tourism marketing by analysing the promotional tourism websites of Sámi tourism companies, and builds a critical discourse analysis on the production of marketing material in the context of tourism. On the destination management organizations level, the relationships between social media, tourism marketing and DMOs were also reviewed by authors such as Hays et al. (2013) and Lasarte (2014). In particular, Hays et al. (2013) analysed how top national tourism authorities use social media to market destinations and to engage with consumers through Twitter and Facebook.

Since Twitter is the largest microblogging platform (Park et al., 2016), previous research has largely focused on its analysis. Wilson and Quinton affirm that:

> in an era when marketing is required to be more accountable the researchers suggest that embedding Twitter within the marketing strategy would be a practical approach to measuring social media's effectiveness. Early findings from this research have indicated that soft value is created via Twitter and that hard value may follow as the medium matures. (Wilson and Quinton, 2012, p. 283)

Further studies have reviewed the use of Twitter by national tourism organizations (Dwivedi et al., 2012; Ćurlin et al., 2019a).

Researches based on social media, focuses towards the sources of data, and reflect the reality about society itself (Boyd and Crawford, 2012; Mayer-Schönberger and Cukier, 2013). Specifically, previous investigations analysed both websites and social networking sites, for example Pinterest, Facebook or Twitter, as interactive SNSs. On one hand, Campillo-Alhama and Martínez-Sala (2019) studied the strategy of online tourism marketing of DMOs in World Heritage Sites. In particular, they reviewed the impact of online events in Facebook and Twitter, and analysed how events promote the brand, from a comparative perspective between 40 different World Heritage Sites. On the other hand, McMullen (2020) carried a visual analysis to examine Pinterest photographs of four heritage tourist destinations in the United States. Her research approached what types of photographs are shared on Pinterest to visually represent heritage tourist destinations, which is important for destination marketing and promotion.

In a similar approach, Villena (2019) dealt with the promotion of cultural tourism through social media during the celebration of the tenth edition of La Noche en Blanco festival. He reviewed the official social media profiles (Facebook, Twitter and Instagram) of the Cultural and Tourism departments of Malaga town hall. They have low levels of use, indicating that they may derive a huge potential for social media presence development. This also confirms the difficulties observed in the use of social media in small and medium-sized organizations, from the managers' perspective (Amboage et al., 2019). With regard to how gastronomy is featured in digital environments, previous research revealed that most studies are focused on wine, and they have identified social media as a major factor of influence for both wine tourists and wine suppliers (Bonn et al., 2018; Sigala and Haller, 2019; Thach et al., 2016). In this sense, 'food represents one of the key themes discussed on Twitter' (Platania and Spadoni, 2018, p. 151), where this platform is crucial as a source of information, also for tourists.

Co-Creation and Co-Sharing of Digital Tourism

Liu et al. (2018) researched on how travel experience sharing on SNSs has a great influence on consumers' travel decision-making processes. As seen above, travellers heavily rely on user-generated content for travel information searching and travel planning (Ayeh et al., 2013; Xiang and Gretzel, 2010), and digital media platforms and practices have a direct effect on the way people engage with 'real' issues (Bruns and Burgess, 2015). Within this context, Litvin et al. (2008, p. 461) suggest that electronic word-of-mouth (eWOM) can be defined as 'all informal communications directed at consumers through Internet-based technology related to the usage or characteristics of particular good and services, or their sellers'. This brings us back to the concept of multiple communications between producers and consumers, and between consumers themselves. Here, Williams et al. (2015) explored the structure and content of online word-of-mouth on Twitter during the development of a festival at a tourist destination such as Bournemouth. Results demonstrate that festivals as tourism venues are both generators and animators of eWOM. This confirms that the analysis of the narratives created on social media around events and destinations (Neuhofer et al., 2012) serve to understand the scale, extent and content of eWOM about a tourism event or destination (Cleave et al., 2017; Zaglia, 2013). This chapter contributes to expand this conversation.

To this extent, previous research also analysed online consumer reviews. Kim et al. (2016) focused on the study of online reviews on Tripadvisor, while Sashi et al. (2019) reviewed the use of social media (in their case, Twitter) to provide opinion on restaurant services. From the supplier's perspective, others have compared online review platforms such as Tripadvisor, Expedia and Yelp, with regard to the case of how Manhattan hotels are represented on these platforms (Xiang et al., 2017). In this context, online conversations are regarded as trusted eWOM (Gligorijevic, 2016; Ye et al., 2011; Sotiriadis and Van Zyl, 2013). Thus, eWOM on social media is a critical ingredient of customer engagement with tourism companies or destinations (Leung et al., 2015; So et al., 2014), which is expected to be independent of commercial influence (Litvin et al., 2008).

Previous research also highlighted the importance of user-generated content on social media, especially on Twitter (Sotiriadis and Van Zyl, 2013). Ćurlin et al. (2019b) reviewed the Twitter usage in tourism and the importance of Twitter in business strategies and planning. They:

> confirmed the relationship of Twitter posts and tourist's decision making, hotel branding, e-WoM, and booking intentions so the hotels and touristic destinations can create business and marketing strategies and more distinguished and personalized supply. Personalized supply is singled out as a critical factor in gaining competitive advantage and marketing spread. (Ćurlin et al., 2019b, p. 113)

Thus 'the appeal of Twitter messages lies in the information they contain beyond photo attachments and spatial coordinates, such as textual information contained in the tweet's body and hashtags, as well as insights on social links expressed through likes and retweets' (Brandt et al., 2017, p. 704). These variables helped Brandt et al. to determine appealing attractions and events in San Francisco, and to provide guidelines to further develop tourist destination from social media data. This also matches with the study conducted by Shimada et al. (2011), where they highlighted the importance of tourist information available on Twitter for local cities, regarding their feelings about sightseeing areas.

This can also boost city marketing (Yoon and Chung, 2018) and contribute to the enhancement of innovation in product and experience development (Jovicic, 2017). In addition, recent research has tried to determine the attractiveness of tourism sites by investigating the behaviour of users through social media (Giglio et al., 2019). Added to destinations, Kim and Chae (2018) analysed the use of social networking sites by hotels and the role of social media presence in hotel management, marketing and industry performance (Kim and Park, 2017; Taylor et al., 2015). Also, other studies, such as that carried out by Park et al. (2016), showcased how Twitter data may serve for tourism marketing in specialist tourism companies, destinations and tourism typologies, such as the case of cruise tourism. Applied to this chapter, Twitter data can also be useful to promote special interest tourisms, such as food tourism.

OBJECTIVE AND METHODOLOGY

This chapter aims to analyse Twitter representations of actors and practices, departing from the case of a food event. To achieve this, the study focuses on the celebration of The World's 50 Best Restaurants Awards, which took place in Singapore on 25 June 2019. The World's 50 Best Restaurants Awards are the Oscars of gastronomy, and they started to award the best eateries in the world in 2002. Since then, it:

> has reflected the diversity of the world's culinary landscape. Thanks to its panel of more than 1,000 culinary experts, as well as its structured and audited voting procedure, the annual list of the world's finest restaurants provides a snapshot of some of the best destinations for unique culinary experiences, in addition to being a barometer for global gastronomic trends. (William Reed, 2020)

As of June 2020, only eight restaurants have been acknowledged as the best of the best: El Bulli and El Celler de Can Roca in Girona (Catalonia, Spain), The French Laundry and Eleven Madison Park in the United States, The Fat Duck in the United Kingdom, Noma in Denmark, Osteria Francescana in Italy, and in 2019, Mirazur in France.

For this research, we analysed a total of 10 500 tweets generated from 23 June to 27 June 2019. The messages were collected with NodeXL using four samples taken in the period 23–27 June, under the hashtag #TheWorlds50Best, and analysed later using NodeXL and Atlas.ti. For the analysis of the sample, we took as our starting point the approach of researchers at the Queensland University of Technology (Bruns and Burgess, 2011), which, like other similar work, is based on the assumption that replies indicate interactions between users, a form of public conversation; and that retweets and mentions indicate authority, and point to the influence of the various actors. Based on that assumption, we took a combined quantitative and qualitative approach for the analysis of the tweets. The quantitative approach enabled us, from the number of tweets, but in particular the retweets and replies made, to identify the

Table 29.1   Twitter activity

Number of tweets	N	%	Tweets	% tweets
1 tweet	719	29.5	719	6.8
2–5 tweets	1 334	54.7	3 954	37.7
6–15 tweets	312	12.8	2 759	26.3
16–25 tweets	36	1.5	680	6.5
26–49 tweets	22	0.9	756	7.2
More than 50 tweets	15	0.6	1 632	15.5
Total	2 438	100.0	10 500	100.0

Table 29.2   Type of activity

Action	N	%
Mentions	5 803	55.3
Replies to	71	0.7
Retweet	4 076	38.8
Tweet	550	5.2
Total	10 500	100.0

central and peripheral users in the 'Twittersphere' on the subject being analysed. The second approach was carried out through the analysis of the content of the tweets (Russell et al., 2015). First, we computed the most frequently used words, which enabled us to identify the most discussed subjects in the tweets studied.

RESULTS

This section is divided into two subsections. First, the most relevant actors are presented according to their profiles. Second, the most significant tweets are described. From the total number of messages analysed (10 500), there were 550 original tweets (5.2 per cent), 4076 retweets (38.8 per cent), 71 replies (0.7 per cent), and 5803 mentions (55.3 per cent).

Actors' Presence and Profiles: Who Are They?

The 10 500 Twitter messages were posted by a total of 2438 different profiles, which means an average of 4.3 tweets per user. Tables 29.1 and 29.2 show the Twitter activity. A total of 385 actors published more than five tweets, representing 55.5 per cent of the tweets analysed. Interestingly, results show a solid community of users with a certain degree of activity around the event. These figures contrast those obtained in other kind of events, such as breaking news, where there is a greater spread of users: very numerous quantitatively, but with low activity (Bruns and Stieglitz, 2012; Masip et al., 2019).

As displayed in Table 29.1, and later developed in Table 29.3, there is a very small group of 15 users that tweeted at least 50 times during the event. They produced 1632 tweets (15.5 per cent). On the other hand, there is a long tail of users, a total of 2053, that posted only between 1 and 5 tweets, and represent 4673 tweets (44.5 per cent). In this sense, added to the users highlighted in this section, it is observed that there is a range of participants that contributed to the conversation with less than five tweets, and are not analysed in this study – which, in order

Table 29.3   *Most active contributors*

User	Mentions	Replies to	Retweet	Tweet	Total
theworlds50best	337		5	98	440
gastroeconomy	89	16	7	64	176
7canibales	152		10		162
sebastrios	48		61	2	111
foodandwinees	41		53		94
filiplanghoff	40		53		93
finedininglover	45		4	31	80
agoisfoto	33		42		75
eltrinchecom	30		38		68
jayjayti	33		26		59
ssgastronomika	39		20		59
elsllepaplats	29		28		57
ana_captures	27		29		56
spiritedsg	50			2	52
aitanaandreu	32		18		50
Total	5 803	71	4 076	550	10 500

to build a picture of gastronomy on social media, is focused on its most impactful users and, later, messages. As previously outlined, there is a prevalence of retweets and mentions, which are very significant resources for the dissemination of the information (Table 29.2). Most users tend to concentrate their activity on a single type of action, especially on mentioning and retweeting third-party content. Replies are, as we have acknowledged, testimonial. In addition, mentions are the most popular activity and are directly linked to retweets. The type of actors, according to their participation in the online conversation, is observed in Table 29.3, which shows the most active contributors (N = 15). The official account of the event, The World's 50 Best Restaurants Awards (@theworlds50best), generated the highest number of tweets, where @gastroeconomy and @finedininglover are also highlighted, and whose profiles are described below. With regard to the mentions and retweets, we observe again a relevant weight of the official account (337 mentions), which is the actor that generated a major volume of conversation. Also, among the most mentioned and retweeted users, there are @7canibales, @foodandwinees and @sebastrios. All of them are professional users. While the first two profiles are media outlets, which are described below, the third is an individual journalist. In addition, chef @filiplanghoff also joined in the propagation of the food event. As displayed in Table 29.3, the majority of contributors only participated by disseminating information, and very few of them were also generating original tweets.

The actors that contributed to the online discussion about the food event are both individuals and corporations, which are featured by their interest on food. This section only approaches the most relevant users. First of all, it is obvious that the official Twitter account of the event (@theworlds50best) generated the highest contribution linked to a solo account. With regard to the individuals, a diverse range of actors is observed: a journalist from Argentina (@sebastrios), a chef from Finland (@filiplanghoff), a photographer from Peru (@agoisfoto), and three food influencers, from Ecuador (@Jayjayti), the United Kingdom (@ana_captures) and Spain (@aitanaandreu). Half of these users come from the Latin America context, which shows the growing importance of the event in this geographical region. The presence of Latin America chefs in the top lists of the world's best restaurants also results in the configuration of the online conversation.

On the other hand, data analysis showed that @gastroeconomy, @7canibales and @foodandwinees emerged as the media outlets with the highest participation in the conversation. All of them are Spanish. *Food and Wine* refers to the Spanish edition of the renowned publication. In this sense, several Spanish restaurants have been acknowledged every year as the best in the world since the first edition of the event, in 2002. Each edition has witnessed a Spanish restaurant in the top three. In particular, all these top-three restaurants are located in the culinary regions of the Basque Country and Catalonia, from where @ssgastronomika and @elsllepaplats also contributed to the Twitter discussion. International food portals such as @fineithinglover and @spiritedsg are also highlighted, the latter based in Singapore, the city where the event took place. In addition, a portal from Peru (@eltrinchecom) again showcased the role of Peruvian chefs, such as Virgilio Martinez, whose restaurant in Lima reached number 6 in the ranking of the The World's 50 Best Restaurants Awards in 2019.

The Tweets' Content: What Do They Say?

After an analysis of the most frequent words (Table 29.4), it is observed that 21 words were mentioned more than 500 times. The total number of words analysed is 102 583. The concepts which are critical to the conversation around the food event and which inform the highlights of the information are, first of all, the key words related to the organisers and sponsors of the event, San Pellegrino and Acqua Panna; and second, the names of awarded chefs and restaurants. In this sense, the places where the eateries are located also take an important portion of the conversation, mostly from a national perspective.

Particularly, the most relevant messages (considering mentions and retweets) are congratulatory tweets to the newly proclaimed restaurants; not only to the best restaurants in the top category, but also to the best according to specific geographical contexts, as explained below, and The World's Best Female Chef. In this context, most of the tweets are inevitably setting a clear relationship between the celebrity restaurant, the star chef and the place where the eatery is located, both the city and the country.

Mirazur, in France, was acknowledged as the new best restaurant in the world. Despite the long French culinary tradition and its influence in the history of gastronomy, this was the first time a French restaurant reached the first position in the ranking. This is reflected in Table 29.4, where Mirazur (by Mauro Colagreco) is placed at the centre of the online conversation. Not only Mirazur, but also Menton, the city where it is located, and France. In addition, the Twitter media scenario is mostly focused on American restaurants: first, Pujol (by Enrique Olvera) in Mexico as the best restaurant in North America; later, Central (by Virgilio Martínez) in Peru, the best in Latin America. The tweets specifically congratulated the establishments, and they mentioned the 'best' in their geographical contexts. The gastronomical relevance of both countries is also transferred to other restaurants included in the highest positions of the list, and as a result in the subsequent tweets. This is the case of Quintonil (Mexico) and Maido (in Lima, Peru). This geographical component is relevant as a factor of tourist attraction. It is obvious that restaurants prepare starred menus by using both local and global ingredients. While there is a diverse landscape of tasting menus, restaurants are identified as a place to visit in a specific destination. Furthermore, chefs are regarded as culinary ambassadors of national

Table 29.4   *Most frequent words*

	Word	N	%
1	restaurant / restaurants / restaurantes	4371	4.26
2	sanpellegrino / spellegrino	4326	4.22
3	acqua /panna	3505	3.42
4	worlds	2714	2.65
5	mexico / #mexico / #mexicocity	2556	2.49
6	mirazur / #mirazur	2328	2.27
7	pujol / pujolrestaurant	2067	2.01
8	sponsored	1883	1.84
9	virgiliocentral / central / centralrest	1783	1.74
10	maurocolagreco	1539	1.50
11	congratulations	1405	1.37
12	enriqueolvera	1179	1.15
13	menton	1065	1.04
14	#france	1049	1.02
15	america	922	0.90
16	chef	865	0.84
17	danisotoinnes	833	0.81
18	mundo	804	0.78
19	#singapore	710	0.69
20	cosmenyc	508	0.50
21	quintonil	505	0.49

cuisines, who communicate the cultural and natural heritages of a region, and contribute to the promotion of tourism.

For example, the DNA of Mexican cuisine, which was inscribed by the United Nations Educational, Scientific and Cultural Organization (UNESCO) on the list of Intangible Cultural Heritage of Humanity in 2010, is presented in the current Twitter discourse. To talk about Cosme is to talk about a Mexican restaurant led by the Mexican star chef Enrique Olvera and the World's Best Female Chef, also Mexican, Daniela Soto-Innes. This confirms the central role of Central and South American chefs in contemporary gastronomy (see also Boragó, in Santiago, Chile). However, this does not mean that restaurants from other regions are not taking part in the conversation. This is for example the case of Noma, in Copenhagen. The Danish restaurant, which was previously acknowledged as the best in world four times, now classified as the runner-up. In parallel, several Catalan and Basque restaurants are also contributing to the online discussion. While they do not appear in Table 29.4 as the most frequent words, a series of messages commented on restaurants such as Asador Etxebarri, Mugaritz and Disfrutar, the last of these led by three chefs who belonged to the team of the legendary restaurant El Bulli.

DISCUSSION AND CONCLUSION

This chapter has innovatively discussed the role of social media in the promotion of food-based tourism. In particular, the research has critically approached gastronomy on Twitter. Drawing from a network analysis, the chapter has studied the most relevant users and tweets. Events such as The World's 50 Best Restaurants Awards have been leading global gastronomy since the beginning of the twenty-first century. They have created a culinary discourse which is focused on celebrity chefs and their restaurants, and they have defined the pathways and trends of food worldwide. This is also transferred to online media, and social networks. Results of this research have revealed a certainty: the new World's Best Restaurants are at the centre of social media conversation. This is accentuated by the growing number of awards, with specific lists attached to geographical contexts (for example, Latin America's 50 Best Restaurants). In particular, Central and Latin America took the most significant role. The World's Best Restaurant, Mirazur, is led by an Argentinian chef, and the two best restaurants in North and South America are in Mexico and Peru. In addition, the World's Best Female Chef is also Mexican, as discussed above. In this context, it is obvious that the gastronomical prominence of Central and Latin American gastronomies is increasing. They are expected to rapidly join culinary traditions with longer journeys in gastronomy star systems, such as Spain, which is still the most influential nation, according to The World's 50 Best Restaurants Awards.

The study has also offered an approach to the users and the narratives. The Twitter storytelling derived from a food-based event, in this case, The World's 50 Best Restaurants Awards, is based on the gala winners, not only the restaurants, but also the chef's name. Restaurants and chefs make an indissoluble bond, in a similar vein to a film and its director. Chefs have emerged as the new rock stars (see, e.g., Lewis and Huber, 2015), with an extraordinary media presence (Fusté-Forné, 2017), whose art is acknowledged by the Michelin Guides or, as in this case, The World's 50 Best Restaurants Awards. The connection between a chef and a restaurant happens in a place (a city, a nation), which also gathers social media attention.

This research contributes to food tourism, social media and marketing research. First, it delivers a new approach to the analysis and promotion of food-based tourism activities and experiences, drawing from the online conversation on a topic: a food event. Virtual experiences fit well with the notion of 'armchair tourism' (Damkjœr and Waade, 2014) and provide food-based knowledge about chefs, restaurants and places. Furthermore, data reveals that this information also encapsulates multiple concepts such as the globalization of gastronomy – The World's 50 Best Restaurants Awards; the importance of local culinary traditions to create a meaningful narrative – food products and recipes elaborated in each of the restaurants, and the food service; and cultural and social processes such as the migration of a Mexican chef, Daniela Soto-Innes, to become a star chef in a New York City restaurant. Implications for the further study of the narratives attached to food by social media are indisputable. In particular, Leung et al. (2013, p. 18) mention that 'drawing on the research findings, social media appear to be a strategic tool that plays an important role in tourism and hospitality management – particularly in promotion, business management, and research function'.

In line with the importance of user-generated content on social media and, especially, on Twitter (Sotiriadis and Van Zyl, 2013), this chapter has reviewed the use of SNSs by a food (tourism) event, which also reveals a strategy for destination marketing and promotion based on a threefold identity: the chef, the restaurant and the location. In this sense, recent research has determined the attractiveness of various tourism sites by investigating the behaviour of users on social media (Giglio et al., 2019). This emerged as the main limitation of the current study, which is descriptive in nature, and it is only focused on who are the actors and what is the content; which can lead to upcoming research on the motivations for sharing tourism experiences through social media (Munar and Jacobsen, 2014), particularly related to food (Ranteallo and Andilolo, 2017), and comparative research with other culinary activities and gastronomy destinations. Marketing implications of social media, from a business perspective, according to Leung et al. (2019, p. 14), 'represent an under-researched area and should be a major focus in the future. How to use social media in pricing, promotion, and even distribution should draw more attention in academia to better guide industry practices'; and, potentially, attract more visitors (Fukui and Ohe, 2020; Kim et al., 2017). Since social media provides an added value, for example, to smart urban tourism (Brandt et al., 2017), this chapter concludes that food events, and their attached online conversation, contribute to the development of a food tourism based on the co-creation and co-sharing of tasting experiences.

REFERENCES

Amboage, E.S., Fernández, V.A.M., Boga, O.J. and Fernández, M.M.R. (2019). Redes sociales y promoción de destinos turísticos termales de la Eurorregión Galicia-Norte de Portugal. *Observatorio*, 13(1), 137–152.

Ayeh, J.K., Au, N. and Law, R. (2013). Predicting the intention to use consumer-generated media for travel planning. *Tourism Management*, 35, 132–143.

Bonn, M.A., Cho, M. and Um, H. (2018). The evolution of wine research: A 26-year historical examination of topics, trends and future direction. *International Journal of Contemporary Hospitality Management*, 30(1), 286–312.

Boyd, D. and Crawford, K. (2012). Critical questions for big data: Provocations for a cultural, technological, and scholarly phenomenon. *Information, Communication and Society*, 15(5), 662–679.

Brandt, T., Bendler, J. and Neumann, D. (2017). Social media analytics and value creation in urban smart tourism ecosystems. *Information and Management*, 54, 703–713.

Bruhn, M., Schoenmueller, V. and Schäfer, D.B. (2012). Are social media replacing traditional media in terms of brand equity creation? *Management Research Review*, 35(9), 770–790.

Bruhn Jensen, K. and Helles, R. (2017). Speaking into the system: Social media and many-to-one communication. *European Journal of Communication*, 32(1), 16–25.

Bruns, A. and Burgess, J. (2011). #ausvotes: How Twitter covered the 2010 Australian federal election. *Communication, Politics and Culture*, 44(2), 37–56.

Bruns, A. and Burgess, J. (2015). Twitter hashtags from ad hoc to calculated publics. In N. Rambukkana (ed.), *Hashtag Publics* (pp. 13–28). New York: Peter Lang.

Bruns, A. and Stieglitz, S. (2012). Quantitative approaches to comparing communication patterns on Twitter. *Journal of Technology in Human Services*, 30(3–4), 160–185.

Campillo-Alhama, C. and Martínez-Sala, A.-M. (2019). La estrategia de marketing turístico de los Sitios Patrimonio Mundial a través de los eventos 2.0. *PASOS. Revista de Turismo y Patrimonio Cultural*, 17(2), 425–452.

Carson, D. (2005). An overview of developing regional tourism using information communications technology. In S. Marshall, W. Taylor and X. Yu (eds), *Encyclopaedia of Developing Regional Communities with Information and Communication Technology* (pp. 176–181). Hershey, PA: Idea Group.

Cleave, E., Arku, G., Sadler, R. and Kyeremeh, E. (2017). Place marketing, place branding, and social media: Perspectives of municipal practitioners. *Growth and Change*, 48, 1012–1033.

Ćurlin, T., Bach, M.P. and Miloloža, I. (2019a). Use of Twitter by national tourism organizations of European countries. *Interdisciplinary Description of Complex Systems*, 17(1–B), 226–241.

Ćurlin, T., Jaković, B. and Miloloža, I. (2019b). Twitter usage in tourism: Literature review. *Business Systems Research*, 10(1), 102–119.

Damkjær, M.S. and Waade, A.M. (2014). Armchair tourism: The travel series as a hybrid genre. In F. Hanusch and E. Fürsich (eds), *Travel Journalism: Exploring Production, Impact and Culture* (pp. 39–59). Basingstoke: Palgrave Macmillan.

De Bernardi, C. (2019). Authenticity as a compromise: A critical discourse analysis of Sámi tourism websites. *Journal of Heritage Tourism*, 14(3), 249–262.

Dellarocas, C. (2003). The digitization of word of mouth: Promise and challenges of online feedback mechanisms. *Management Science*, 29(10), 1407–1424.

Dwivedi, M., Yadav, A. and Venkatesh, U. (2012). Use of social media by national tourism organizations: A preliminary analysis. *Information Technology and Tourism*, 13, 93–103.

Fotis, J., Buhalis, D. and Rossides, N. (2012). Social media use and impact during the holiday travel planning process. In M. Fuchs, F. Ricci and L. Cantoni (eds), *Information and Communication Technologies in Tourism* (pp. 13–24). Vienna: Springer-Verlag.

Fukui, M. and Ohe, Y. (2020). Assessing the role of social media in tourism recovery in tsunami-hit coastal areas in Tohoku, Japan. *Tourism Economics*, 26(5), 776–791.

Fusté-Forné, F. (2017). *Food Journalism: Building the Discourse on the Popularization of Gastronomy in the Twenty-First Century*. Barcelona: Universitat Ramon Llull.

Giglio, S., Bertacchini, F., Bilotta, E. and Pantano, P. (2019). Using social media to identify tourism attractiveness in six Italian cities. *Tourism Management*, 72, 306–312.

Ginzarly, M., Roders, A.P. and Teller, J. (2019). Mapping historic urban landscape values through social media. *Journal of Cultural Heritage*, 36, 1–11.

Gligorijevic, B. (2016). Review platforms in destinations and hospitality. In R. Egger, M.A. Gula and D. Walcher (eds), *Open Tourism* (pp. 215–228). Berlin: Springer.

Hays, S., Page, S.J. and Buhalis, D. (2013). Social media as a destination marketing tool: Its use by national tourism organisations. *Current Issues in Tourism*, 16(3), 211–239.

Jansson, A. (2018). Rethinking post-tourism in the age of social media. *Annals of Tourism Research*, 69, 101–110.

Jeacle, I. and Carter, C. (2011). In TripAdvisor we trust: Rankings, calculative regimes and abstract systems. *Accounting, Organizations and Society*, 36(4), 293–309.

Jovicic, D.Z. (2017). From the traditional understanding of tourism destination to the smart tourism destination. *Current Issues in Tourism*, 22(3), 276–282.

Khalid, S. and Chowdhury, S.A. (2018). Representation of intangible cultural heritage of Bangladesh through social media. *Anatolia*, 29(2), 194–203.

Kim, B., Kim, S. and Heo, C.Y. (2016). Analysis of satisfiers and dissatisfiers in online hotel reviews on social media. *International Journal of Contemporary Hospitality Management*, 28(9), 1915–1936.

Kim, S.-E., Lee, K.Y., Shin, S.I. and Yang, S.-B. (2017). Effects of tourism information quality in social media on destination image formation: The case of Sina Weibo. *Information and Management*, 54, 687–702.

Kim, W. and Park, S. (2017). Social media review rating versus traditional customer satisfaction: Which one has more incremental predictive power in explaining hotel performance? *International Journal of Contemporary Hospitality Management*, 29(2), 784–802.

Kim, W.-H. and Chae, B.K. (2018). Understanding the relationship among resources, social media use and hotel performance: The case of Twitter use by hotels. *International Journal of Contemporary Hospitality Management*, 30(9), 2888–2907.

Laroche, M., Habibi, M.R. and Richard, M.O. (2013). To be or not to be in social media: How brand loyalty is affected by social media? *International Journal of Information Management*, 33(1), 76–82.

Lasarte, M.P. (2014). The presence and importance of tourist destinations on Twitter. *Journal of Urban Regeneration and Renewal*, 8(1), 16–30.

Leung, X.Y., Bai, B. and Stahura, K.A. (2015). The marketing effectiveness of social media in the hotel industry: A comparison of Facebook and Twitter. *Journal of Hospitality and Tourism Research*, 39(2), 147–169.

Leung, D., Law, R., Van Hoof, H. and Buhalis, D. (2013). Social media in tourism and hospitality: a literature review. *Journal of Travel and Tourism Marketing*, 30(1–2), 3–22.

Leung, X.Y., Sun, J. and Bai, B. (2019). Thematic framework of social media research: State of the art. *Tourism Review*, 74(3), 517–531.

Lewis, T. and Huber, A. (2015). A revolution in an eggcup? Supermarket wars, celebrity chefs and ethical consumption. *Food, Culture and Society*, 18(2), 289–307.

Litvin, W.S., Goldsmith, E.R. and Pan, B. (2008). Electronic word-of-mouth in hospitality and tourism management. *Tourism Management*, 29(3), 458–468.

Liu, H., Wu, L. and Li, X.(R.) (2018). Social media envy: How experience sharing on social networking sites drives millennials' aspirational tourism consumption. *Journal of Travel Research*, 58(3), 355–369.

Månsson, M. (2011). Mediatized tourism. *Annals of Tourism Research*, 38(4), 1634–1652.

Masip, P., Ruiz, C. and Suau, J. (2019). Contesting professional procedures of journalists: Public conversation on Twitter after Germanwings accident. *Digital Journalism*, 7(6), 762–782.

Mayer-Schönberger, V. and Cukier, K. (2013). *Big Data: A Revolution that will Transform How We Live, Work, and Think*. Houghton Mifflin Harcourt.

McMullen, M. (2020). 'Pinning' tourist photographs: Analyzing the photographs shared on Pinterest of heritage tourist destinations. *Current Issues in Tourism*, 23(3), 376–387.

Moore, J.N., Hopkins, C.D. and Raymond, M.A. (2013). Utilization of relationship-oriented social media in the selling process: A comparison of consumer (B2C) and industrial (B2B) salespeople. *Journal of Internet Commerce*, 12(1), 48–75.

Moro, S. and Rita, P. (2018). Brand strategies in social media in hospitality and tourism. *International Journal of Contemporary Hospitality Management*, 30(1), 343–364.

Mozas, A., Bernal, E., Medina, M.J. and Fernández, D. (2016). Factors for success in online social networks: An fsQCA approach. *Journal of Business Research*, 69(11), 5261–5264.

Munar, A.M. and Jacobsen, J.K.S. (2014). Motivations for sharing tourism experiences through social media. *Tourism Management*, 43, 46–54.

Neuhofer, B., Buhalis, D. and Ladkin, A. (2012). Conceptualising technology enhanced destination experiences. *Journal of Destination Marketing and Management*, 1(1–2), 36–46.

Park, S.B., Ok, C.M. and Chae, B.K. (2016). Using Twitter data for cruise tourism marketing and research. *Journal of Travel and Tourism Marketing*, 33(6), 885–898.

Platania, M. and Spadoni, R. (2018). How people share information about food: Insights from tweets regarding two Italian regions. *International Journal of Food System Dynamics*, 9(2), 149–165.

Ranteallo, I.C. and Andilolo, I.R. (2017). Food representation and media: Experiencing culinary tourism through foodgasm and foodporn. In A. Saufi, I.R. Andilolo, N. Othman and A.A. Lew (eds), *Balancing Development and Sustainability in Tourism Destinations* (pp. 117–127). Singapore: Springer.

Russell, F.M., Hendricks, M.A., Choi, H. and Stephens, E.C. (2015). Who sets the news agenda on Twitter? Journalists' posts during the 2013 US government shutdown. *Digital Journalism*, 3(6), 925–943.

Sashi, C.M., Brynildsen, G. and Bilgihan, A. (2019). Social media, customer engagement and advocacy: An empirical investigation using Twitter data for quick service restaurants. *International Journal of Contemporary Hospitality Management*, 31(3), 1247–1272.

Schivinski, B. and Dabrowski, D. (2014). The effect of social media communication on consumer perceptions of brands. *Journal of Marketing Communications*, 22(2), 189–214.

Shimada, K., Inoue, S., Maeda, H. and Endo, T. (2011). Analyzing tourism information on twitter for a local city. In *2011 First ACIS International Symposium on Software and Network Engineering* (pp. 61–66). Washington, DC: IEEE Computer Society.

Sigala, M. and Haller, C. (2019). The impact of social media on the behavior of wine tourists: A typology of power sources. In M. Sigala and R. Robinson (eds), *Management and Marketing of Wine Tourism Business* (pp. 139–154). Basingstoke: Palgrave Macmillan.

So, K.K.F., King, C., Sparks, B.A. and Wang, Y. (2014). The role of customer engagement in building consumer loyalty to tourism brands. *Journal of Travel Research*, 55(1), 64–78.

Solo-Anaeto, M. and Jacobs, B. (2015). Exploring social media as channels for sustaining African culture. *International Journal of Humanities and Social Science*, 5(4– 1), 37–42.

Sotiriadis, M.D. and Van Zyl, C. (2013). Electronic word-of-mouth and online reviews in tourism services: The use of Twitter by tourists. *Electronic Commerce Research*, 13(1), 103–124.

Stuedahl, D. (2009). Digital cultural heritage engagement – A new research field for ethnology. *Ethnologia Scandinavica*, 39, 67–81.

Taylor, D., Barber, N. and Deale, C. (2015). To tweet or not to tweet: That is the question for hoteliers: A preliminary study. *Information Technology and Tourism*, 15(1), 71–99.

Thach, E., Lease, T. and Barton, M. (2016). Exploring the impact of social media practices on wine sales in US wineries. *Journal of Direct, Data and Digital Marketing Practice*, 17(4), 272–283.

Thevenot, G. (2007). Blogging as a social media. *Tourism and Hospitality Research*, 7(3/4), 282–289.

Trant, J. (2009). Studying social tagging and folksonomy: A review and framework. *Journal of Digital Information*, 10(1), 1–44.

Tribe, J. and Mkono, M. (2017). Not such smart tourism? The concept of e-lienation. *Annals of Tourism Research*, 66, 105–115.

Van der Hoeven, A. (2017). The mediatization of urban cultural heritage: Participatory approaches to narrating the urban past. In O. Driessens, G. Bolin, A. Hepp and S. Hjarvard (eds), *Dynamics of Mediatization: Understanding Cultural and Social Change* (pp. 293–312). Basingstoke: Palgrave Macmillan.

Van House, N. (2007). Flickr and public image-sharing: Distant closeness and photo exhibition. In *CHI' 07 Extended Abstracts on Human Factors in Computing Systems* (pp. 2717–2722). New York: ACM Press.

Villena, E. (2019). (2018). Promoción del turismo cultural en redes sociales: El caso de la ciudad de Málaga en la Noche en Blanco. *International Journal of Scientific Management and Tourism*, 4(2), 563–570.

William Reed (2020). The World's 50 Best Restaurants. https://www.theworlds50best.com.

Williams, N.L., Inversini, A., Buhalis, D. and Ferdinand, N. (2015) Community crosstalk: an exploratory analysis of destination and festival eWOM on Twitter. *Journal of Marketing Management*, 31(9–10), 1113–1140.

Wilson, D. and Quinton, S. (2012). Let's talk about wine: does Twitter have value? *International Journal of Wine Business Research*, 24(4), 271–286.

Xiang, Z., Du, Q., Ma, Y. and Fan, W. (2017). A comparative analysis of major online review platforms: Implications for social media analytics in hospitality and tourism. *Tourism Management*, 58, 51–65.

Xiang, Z. and Gretzel, U. (2010). Role of social media in online travel information search. *Tourism Management*, 31(2), 179–188.

Ye, Q., Law, R., Gu, B. and Chen, W. (2011). The influence of user-generated content on traveler behavior: An empirical investigation on the effects of e-word-of-mouth to hotel online bookings. *Computers in Human Behavior*, 27(2), 634–639.

Yoon, S.-W. and Chung, S.W. (2018). Promoting a World Heritage Site through social media: Suwon City's Facebook promotion strategy on Hwaseong Fortress (in South Korea). *Sustainability*, 10, 1–21.

Zaglia, M.E. (2013). Brand communities embedded in social networks. *Journal of Business Research*, 66(2), 216–223.

30. Components of gastro-tourists' experiences in culinary destinations: evidence from sharing economy platforms

Ibrahim Cifci and Ozan Atsiz

INTRODUCTION

While the sharing economy has become common in all industries (Belk, 2014), it seems to be more prevalent in the realm of tourism and hospitality (Priporas et al., 2017). This is not surprising given the nature of tourism and hospitality services and the fact that the sharing economy is more related to the supply of services (Abrate and Viglia, 2019). Nevertheless, tourism also has a considerable impact on demand in a destination (Okumus and Cetin, 2018). For instance, consuming local food and beverages in a destination creates culinary experiences for travelers (Agyeiwaah et al., 2019). It thus generates a reciprocal benefit while travelers provide a market for these products (Boyne et al., 2003). This supply and the demand-oriented process adds value to the destination's core attributions and provide a congruence to make a connection between travelers and the destination's way of life (Cetin and Bilgihan, 2016). Thus, participation in the sharing economy is not only driven by economics but is also more about sustainability and interacting with new people in the visited destinations (Lampinen and Cheshire, 2016). The growing popularity of sharing economy platforms has already enabled individuals to engage in a sort of dining experience by being hosted in a local's home (Williams et al., 2019). However, while there has been considerable research on the tourism sharing economy users, little is known about components of gastro-tourists' experiences in culinary destinations.

Overall, despite some valuable efforts to investigate tourists' experiences in the informal economy and, to a lesser extent, within the context of the sharing economy, little work has been done to thoroughly explore the component of gastro-tourists' experiences in the Eatwith platform in culinary destinations. In response to this gap, this study involved online comments of gastro-tourists about their Eatwith experience in Istanbul, to identify the key themes for the components of gastro-tourists' experiences in culinary destinations, to identify existing limitations, and to guide future research directions. The chapter also discusses several practical implications for sharing economy users and service providers.

CONCEPTUAL FRAMEWORK

Gastro-Tourists' Experience in the Culinary Destination

Gastronomy generally refers to food and beverages produced in a particular destination, or "the art of science of cooking or eating well" and is an emerging new tourism product that attracts high-spending gastro-tourists (Ozdemir and Seyitoglu, 2017; Kumar, 2019). Therefore, gastronomy experiences in culinary destinations have become essential to travelers, and have gained importance among tourism scholars and destination planners in the past decade (Williams et al., 2019; Yu and Sun, 2019). According to the United Nations World Tourism Organization (UNWTO), gastronomy is commonly referred to as "a type of tourism activity which is characterized by the visitor's experience linked with food and related products and activities while traveling."

Gastro-tourists are mainly pushed by intrinsic motivational factors such as tasting new foods, socializing, learning, and exploring different local food cultures. Furthermore, they are pulled by some destination attributes related to food and beverages (Williams et al., 2019). During their visit, they are motivated wholly or partially to taste local foods and beverages to have an authentic experience (Tudorache et al., 2014). The motivation to savor local foods in an unfamiliar destination refers to the psychological needs attached to the emotional or epistemic benefits (Choe and Kim, 2018, 2019), because the primary purpose of travelers is to seek gastronomic experiences when traveling or planning to visit destinations (Kivela and Crotts, 2006a). Gastro-tourists also have a higher level of destination attachment due to having a memorable culinary experience and experiencing locality (Lin and Mao, 2015). Besides satisfying their appetite, consuming traditional foods offers opportunities to encounter authenticity and thus enhances the memorability of travel (Tung and Ritchie, 2011; Correia et al., 2020).

Also, gastro-tourists are among the high-spending travelers and contribute to the destinations in terms of providing an economic benefit, and sustaining the development of rural destinations (Pérez Gálvez et al., 2017) by consuming the local gastronomic product (López-Guzmán and Sánchez-Cañizares, 2012). Therefore, gastronomy elements and the characteristics of gastro-tourists are central interests in tourism destination planning and destination marketing (du Rand and Heath, 2006; Okumus et al., 2007). The majority of studies advocate that gastronomy is an essential value in the economic development of a destination (Kivela and Crotts, 2006b), destination image formation (Marine-Roig et al., 2019), destination attractiveness (Hillel et al., 2013) and tourists' behavioral intentions (Leong et al., 2017; Levitt et al., 2017). Correia et al. (2008) have thus suggested that a destination should give importance to satisfying gastro-tourists' experiences and their motivations.

Gastronomy studies have constituted an essential area in the tourism literature for decades. These studies focused on gastronomy product development, consumer product evaluation, or tourist experiences in culinary destinations and the dimensions that probably impact tourists' decision-making process. A wide range of studies that have focused on gastro-tourists from different disciplines, including social psychology, sociology, cultural anthropology, management and marketing fields, which have provided significant knowledge (du Rand and Heath, 2006; Mak et al., 2012; Ellis et al., 2018; Okumus and Cetin, 2018). For instance, gastronomy products assist in increasing the quality of gastro-tourists' experiences and provide some benefits to them, as follows (Kivela and Crotts, 2006b):

- The culinary destination offers them pleasurable, pristine and extraordinary gastronomy products and services.
- Gastro-tourists are expected to experience and learn about local cultural elements through food.
- Gastro-tourists try to taste local foods on-site and have an opportunity to buy these foods, such as Turkish coffee or Chinese tea, when returning to their own countries.

- Gastronomy products and services allow gastro-tourists to explore new taste sensations through distinctive ways.
- Gastro-tourists have an opportunity to experience integrated gastronomy products and services in the culinary destination.

Authenticity is regarded as an essential component of the food experience, and the authenticity of local food plays a significant role in enhancing tourist experiences in the culinary destination (Ozdemir and Seyitoglu, 2017). Gastro-tourists seek a unique, pristine and pleasurable food experience. To achieve this, they visit various destinations to taste something unique, or foods that are new to them (Antón et al., 2019). Authentic clues of the destination culture are associated with encouraging tourists to experience locals' lives (Chang et al., 2010), which plays a significant role in tourist satisfaction (Ramkissoon and Uysal, 2011). Numerous studies (e.g., Liu and Jang, 2009; Jang et al., 2011) addressed the importance of the authentic dining atmosphere in tourists' behavioral intention. Therefore, local foods are now deemed to be a vital authentic experience resource for tourist motivation (Antón et al., 2019).

In tourism, individual recognition or prestige derived from the travel experience is associated with social value (Williams and Soutar, 2000). Social requirements have become consumers' common consumption psychology. Today, many people are trying to make friends by consuming services. Goolaup and Mossberg (2016) state that a critical travel experience for tourists is to socialize while enjoying eating local foods. Socialization or social interaction is one of the main motivational factors for gastro-tourists as well (Björk and Kauppinen-Räisänen, 2014; Babolian Hendijani, 2016), which lies in the connection between tourists and locals (Reisinger and Turner, 1998). Gastro-tourists desire to come together with other travelers and their friends or families for various reasons, including being given advice related to foods, tasting local food to increase friendship, transmitting their experience through local foods, and experiencing a memorable moment with others (Pérez Gálvez et al., 2017). Besides, food tourists travel to the culinary destinations to increase their culinary knowledge and knowledge of a destination's culture (Ridvan Yurtseven and Kaya, 2011) by enhancing their dining experience (Kivela and Crotts, 2006a). During their travel, tourists increase their knowledge based on local or regional cuisine by participating in food-related activities (Poria et al., 2004). Many activities, such as taking cooking lessons, culinary workshops, farm and vineyard visits and harvest festivals, fit well in today's gastronomy trends.

Moreover, local foods have diverse cognitive values, including cooking methods, variety of foods and beverages, types of eating behaviors, as well as customs and table manners, which offer in-depth knowledge about the local cuisine and destination (Kim et al., 2009). Along with this, Ignatov and Smith (2006) emphasized that gastro-tourists purchase or consume regional foods (including beverages) or observe and participate in food production (from agriculture to cooking schools). Furthermore, gastro-tourists particularly seek the stories pertinent to the local food and culture, as well as develop their knowledge and their palate by delighting in local cuisines (Choe and Kim, 2018). Attributes of service providers such as tour guides on gastronomic tours, waiters in restaurants, and hosts in the sharing economy may increase the positive feelings of tourists toward services, thus resulting in behavioral consequences (repurchase or recommendation) and tourist satisfaction (Seyitoglu, 2020, 2021). Gastro-tourists also expect the service providers to behave with professionalism, friendliness and politeness, and to have knowledge about the foods. It is emphasized that these features would enhance the service (Reisinger and Waryszak, 1996).

The Meal-Sharing Economy Platforms in Culinary Destinations

The sharing economy (SE) is generally known as 'the collaborative economy, collaborative consumption, access economy, platform economy, and community-based economy' (Hossain, 2020). This new economic model has been defined in several ways. According to Muñoz and Cohen (2017, p. 21), the SE is defined as "a socioeconomic system enabling an intermediated set of exchanges of goods and services between individuals and organizations which aim to increase efficiency and optimization of under-utilized resources in society." The SE is widely used in the tourism and hospitality industry by modern tourists. SE platforms allow tourists and locals to share accommodation places, transportation tools, food and beverages, and destination knowledge through local tour guides (Sigala, 2015). The SE enables the tourist to encounter and interact with locals very profoundly. For example, Uber is real-time ridesharing for arriving at a place with a local driver, Eatwith allows tourists to eat their dinner or lunch in a local's home, and Airbnb enables visitors to be accommodated in a local's apartment (Ketter, 2019).

The meal-sharing economy, known as a collaborative economy or as peer-to-peer dining, is a platform widely used in destinations by tourists. Meal-sharing platforms encourage the tourist to be a guest/customer in a local's home. Locals cook a meal for them or can prepare some cooking practice to provide knowledge about local ingredients and cooking methods. This encounter can happen anywhere the local people wish, such as at home, in a restaurant or classroom (Zurek, 2016). Some examples of meal-sharing platforms are presented in Table 30.1 (Hotrec, 2018). Of these platforms, Eatwith is the most commonly used and preferred meal sharing economy platform, with its 260 000 guests and 25 000 hosts, operating in 130 or more countries. According to Zurek (2016), dining in locals' homes with them provides a unique and deeply local food experience. Thus, tourists would rather meet their food needs in a local's home than in a tourist restaurant. For these reasons, Eatwith was chosen for this study.

The modern tourist wishes to experience the daily life of locals (Maitland, 2010) and sharing economy areas, especially home restaurants, are considerable platforms for tourists who desire to get to know this food culture and interact with locals (Demir, 2020). Ketter (2019) emphasized that Eatwith guests use meal-sharing platforms from motivations of their ideals (values, principles), achievement, and self-expression. Privitera and Abushena (2019) stated that meal-sharing platforms in tourism destinations provide cultural exchanges, more affordable prices, and real encounters between hosts and guests. Furthermore, these platforms contribute to regional economies, such as generating local employment and locals' income. It is also highlighted that these platforms could reduce the employment rates in the tourism industry, ignore several laws, and cause hygiene issues to emerge in the following years.

These sharing economy platforms enable the production, distribution and sharing of foods or tourists or visitors via the internet. These platforms are also increasingly becoming a critical consumption area in the hospitality industry, and tourists are intensely using them when planning to visit destinations (Privitera and Abushena, 2019). On these platforms there are mainly two sides: a host, referred to as "An individual or a business who or which supplies food and drink to guests in their own home or a non-registered venue, through contact with the guest arranged via an online platform"; and a guest, referred to as "an individual who consumes the food and drink supplied by the host" (Hotrec, 2018). Hosts offer a service that brings tourists together with other international tourists and locals. By doing so, locals provide tourists with an opportunity to create social connections and enhance friendships, as well as providing

Table 30.1   *Some examples of meal-sharing platforms*

Meal-sharing economy platforms	Year	Country of origin	Countries	Hosts	Guests	About
Eatwith	2012	France	130+ countries	25 000	265 000	"Eatwith is a community for authentic culinary experiences with locals, available in over 130 countries. We connect people who are seeking unique and immersive experiences with our hand-selected local hosts, in private homes and exclusive venues."
Meal Sharing	2012	USA	150+ countries	N.A.	N.A.	"Meal Sharing is building a community based on the real-world experience of sharing a home-cooked meal. To do this, we are getting people from around the world to sit down and eat with each other."
Withlocals	2013	The Netherlands	50+ cities	N.A.	N.A.	"Withlocals' mission is to connect people with cultures by breaking down barriers between travelers and locals worldwide. With this in mind, the Withlocals platform was created as a marketplace which facilitates the connection between travellers and local hosts all around the world!"
LetsLunch	2010	California	6 countries worldwide	100 000	N.A.	"Get connected with other professionals and build a strong professional network."
BonAppetour	2013	Singapore	80 cities worldwide	15 000+	N.A.	"BonAppetour is a community marketplace that connects travelers with local home chefs for a unique home-dining experience, anywhere around the world."
YeatUp	2015	Turkey	15 cities	80	N.A.	"YeatUp gives access to a unique culinary experience. We will provide exciting social dining opportunities by connecting amateur or professional chefs, who love to hold dining events at their private places, with adventurous food-lovers and travelers who would like to discover the unknowns of local lives."

Sources: Compiled from various sources. See: https://www.eatwith.com/about-us; https://www.llworldtour.com/eat-with-locals-meal-sharing/; https://www.withlocals.com/info/about-withlocals/; https://letslunch.com/; https://www.bonappetour.com/e/about; https://yeatup.com/).

authentic values and information for the food culture of the destination through dinner events. The quest for authentic foods is an essential motivation factor for gastro-tourists, and this search enhances tourist experience in a cultural context (Beer, 2008). With these platforms providing unique and memorable food experiences, tourists are thought to experience authenticity in a broad sense, and home-restaurants are known to be branded as authentic (Mhlanga, 2020).

METHODOLOGY

This study aims to explore the components of the gastro-tourists' experiences in a culinary destination within the context of the meal-sharing economy based on 145 online reviews posted to Eatwith for Istanbul, Turkey. A qualitative research approach was taken through employing simultaneously both inductive analysis (categorized themes derived from data) and deductive analysis (a literature review) (Gummersson, 2000). Istanbul was chosen as the research context because the city attracts almost 15 million international tourists according to the latest indicators (Turkish Statistical Institute, 2020), and offers various products and services for the tourism industry, such as culture, heritage, natural beauties, shopping opportunities and culinary attractions.

In total, there were 36 Eatwith service providers for Istanbul, and among these, only nine had been reviewed by users , between the years 2014 to 2020. Between 20 and 25 March 2020, all reviews were gathered by the authors. Apart for five reviews (four in French and one in Portuguese), 140 reviews were available in English, and filled a total of 49 pages on digital media. The authors examined only reviews written in English. Considering the suggestion of other studies (e.g., Dincer and Alrawadieh, 2017) on including online reviews written in all languages, the authors decided to use web-based dictionaries and online translation services to translate the remaining reviews into English, so as to include these five reviews for data analysis. The authors examined the translated reviews after using the translation services, and there was no ambiguity or disagreement on the translations. The translated versions were then included in the analysis.

By employing the content analysis method, firstly, the authors conducted an extensive literature review to become familiar with the categories and themes identified in the previous literature. Secondly, each author independently read all the reviews several times (Braun and Clarke, 2006) and employed a color-coding technique systematically, based on creating a pool of themes by extracting all commonalities and irrelevant descriptions from the data (Neuman, 2011). The coding process was carried out manually rather than using a software program. Numerous studies have suggested that manual coding is more efficient than coding supported by software programs (Krippendor, 2004), which also ensures creativity in qualitative analysis (Patton, 1990). Then, the authors came together several times to discuss all the themes and codes that emerged from their separate coding process and reached a consensus on the main themes that were grouped under higher-order clusters after distillation (Patton, 2002; Creswell, 2007; Lune and Berg, 2016). Lastly, the determined main themes were examined by a third researcher who had a solid background in qualitative research and the content analysis method. In this way, the trustworthiness of the study findings enhanced and contributed to the reliability and validity of the results (Sikolia et al., 2013).

By using this technique, the data was explained and categorized to obtain a better understanding of gastro-tourists' experiences. At the end of this analysis process, six interconnected components emerged: knowledge, authenticity, socio-cultural integration, memorable, hospitality and service attributes. These components were discussed, with original quotations from reviewers (Elo and Kyngas, 2008), as well as reinforcement from previous studies' findings (Gummersson, 2000). The outcomes of the data analysis are presented in Figure 30.1.

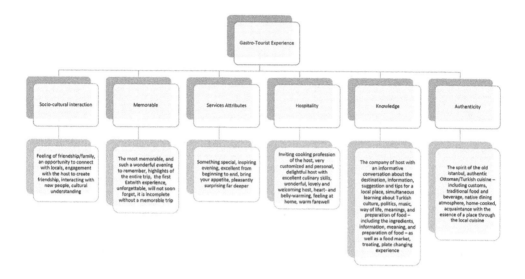

Figure 30.1   Overall representatives of gastro-experience in culinary destination

FINDINGS

Demographic Profile of Eatwith Reviewers

Eatwith allows limited public sharing of its users' personal information. Users are able to share only their gender information and whether they participated as singles or as a couple, country of origin and the points they give to their service providers. As illustrated in Figure 30.2, the reviewers are 64 percent men, 25 percent women, and 11 percent participated as a couple. More than one-third of the users were from Europe, and almost all users evaluated the services of their providers with the highest score.

Main Findings

Based on previous studies and coding of the underlying themes that relate to gastro-tourists' experience of the sharing economy platform in a culinary destination, six main dimensions emerged as interconnected, vital constructs. Concerning the coding process, the frequencies for each related theme, and the number of reviews with each related theme is presented in Table 30.2.

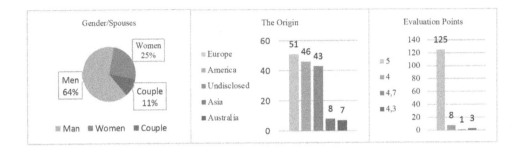

Figure 30.2   *Reviewers' profile*

Table 30.2   *Text breakdown*

Dimensions	Frequencies for each related theme	# of reviews with each related theme
Knowledge	139	136
Authenticity	84	73
Socio-cultural interaction	29	29
Memorable	25	24
Hospitality	87	66
Service attributes	81	57

It is also worth noting that almost all reviewers were delighted with their Eatwith experience and often commented with either a recommendation for others or to state their revisit intentions. For instance, R60 stated as follows: "I wish I could eat with Esra again, and I feel sure that you will be satisfied if you choose to dine with her in fabulous Istanbul."

Knowledge
The findings implied that knowing the destination through the eyes and impressions of locals (for example, the way of life, history, politics, culinary culture) during Eatwith was a pivotal experience. R20: "We enjoyed our over dinner and after dinner conversation, which gave us a local's perspective of Turkey, Istanbul, and different aspects of culture, politics, and all sorts of topics." The qualitative data revealed that reviewers were surprised to receive specialized care from the locals. It underlined that they were pleased to have an informative talk about the destination with the locals, and described this feeling as a service that would never have been experienced outside of the hosts' homes in the touristic facilities of the same destination. R86 posted:

> To all those who are interested in expanding their understanding and seeing beyond what is merely on the streets for tourists to experience. Consider that for the amount you are paying, you are welcomed into a home, given everything you could eat, and have an opportunity to learn about a culture and life that is often inaccessible to most.

Numerous studies have mentioned that gastro-tourists have a motivation to seek an educational travel experience to improve their culinary expertise and learn about the specific destination (Hjalager and Richards, 2002; Poria et al., 2004; Choe and Kim, 2018; Williams et al., 2019).

The qualitative data of this study hence contributes to a better understanding of the travelers' knowledge-seeking motivation in the tourism field. The findings particularly also highlighted that tourists obtained value from almost everything unique that is an essential part of the local cuisine. This finding supports the study of Choe and Kim (2018) in which gastro-tourists mentioned seeking out local food which has a story behind it. For instance, a woman reviewer (R93) expressed this idea as follows: "Not only was the food delicious, but she shared stories about the origin of each dish and some personal stories about how the food was prepared in her family." Confirming this, R103 reviewed: "Having a story behind each dish along with her touches gave the whole meal a delicate balance of homeliness and sophistication." Under the knowledge dimension, reviewers expressed some of their benefits from local cuisine such as ingredients information, meanings, and preparation of food, culinary experimentation, discovering new flavors, as well as changing their palate. R71: "Our market tour, cooking, and Meza with her were all that I had hoped it would be. A trip to the Saturday market, with tastes and a lesson in market etiquette, shopping for our ingredients, home with her to prepare them (great cooking lesson), and then the reward...."

Authenticity
The majority of the reviewers discussed many factors related to their authenticity experience perceptions that distinctively characterize the Eatwith service. An authenticity experience is generally attributed to the uniqueness and originality of local attributes of a destination that cannot be found back home (Cetin and Bilgihan, 2016). Beyond that, the context of the Eatwith service is described as a unique experience that could not even be found at any restaurant in the same destination. For instance, R100, described the authenticity of the Eatwith service as follows: "It was a great treat to try her homemade dishes, something we would never have experienced at any restaurant." R58 elaborated on this issue as follows: "Before coming for dinner to her, we have visited many Turkish restaurants in Istanbul and were sure that we know a lot about local cuisine. However, that evening when we came for dinner to her, we reopened Turkish cuisine for all of us again."

As a core component of the food experience, authentic foods play a cornerstone role in the overall tourism experience (Ozdemir and Seyitoglu, 2017). Escaping from daily dietary habits in culinary destinations adds value for a holiday (Ramkissoon and Uysal, 2011). The qualitative data of this study support this phenomenon by the fact that gastro-tourist frequently related their authentic experiences to local foods, provided by local people. In this study, the authentic experience was mainly emphasized with the characteristics of local foods (for example, family recipes, homemade, personal touch, traditional, the abundance of flavors, well-seasoned) and also some authentic attributes were mentioned about the visited destination, such as the spirit of old Istanbul, and the authentic Ottoman/Turkish cuisine, including customs, traditional food and beverages, native dining atmosphere, home-cooked food, and acquaintance with the essence of a place through the local cuisine were given as examples things that constructed the authentic experience. The studies of both Liu and Jang (2009) and Jang et al. (2011) suggested that the authentic dining atmosphere has an influence on tourists' behavioral intention. This study also supports their notions. For instance, R1 described her authentic experience attached to the local atmosphere as follows: "A gourmet dinner accompanied by a relaxed aristocratic atmosphere in the spirit of the old Istanbul ... fulfilling our desire for authentic Turkish cuisine done with an eye for the details and professionalism, and the stories behind these high-end dishes."

Some examples of reviews related to the same category are the following. R76: "The Turkish music on the radio, the entertaining cross-cultural conversations, drinking Rakı – Turkish national drink – all set for a great night." R110: "one of the surest ways to acquaint yourself with the essence of a place is through the local cuisine."

The findings also implied that gastro-tourists value the local customs as well, which is one of the ways to experience authenticity (Sims, 2009). For instance, sharing leftovers after hosting a guest is one of the original Turkish customs, and the qualitative data of this study revealed that reviewers also benefited from the local customs. For instance, in their review R87 mentioned that: "After we enjoyed a delicious variety of dishes, a divine dessert, and the requisite Turkish tea, she even insisted on sending us home with leftovers."

Socio-cultural interaction

The desire to be involved in the social life of the visiting destination is one of the primary motivations for gastro-tourism (Björk and Kauppinen-Räisänen, 2014; Babolian Hendijani, 2016; Pérez Gálvez et al., 2017), which provides interaction with locals and their culture (Reisinger and Turner, 1998). By their nature, sharing-economy platforms provide opportunities for the interaction of tourists and local people (Demir, 2020); hence the Eatwith experience provides this opportunity as well (Ketter, 2019; Privitera and Abushena, 2019), because being a guest in a local's home to share a dining atmosphere offers socio-cultural interaction (Lampinen and Cheshire, 2016). This interaction is driven by the characteristics of the Eatwith experience, such as connection with locals, engagement with a host to create friendship, interacting with new people, and the feeling of friendship/family, as well as experiencing cultural understanding (Ketter, 2019). The qualitative data of this study support this notion and also further highlight the importance of social and cultural interaction in the sharing economy platforms. For instance, R110: "From the moment of arrival until the time I left, I felt not simply that I ate a meal with someone, but rather that I had spent the evening with an old friend." Confirming this, R139: "It is great to make friends in a new city, and I hope to meet with … again."

Socializing, while eating local foods, is one of the main requirements of gastro-tourists, which provides social value (Williams and Soutar, 2000; Goolaup and Mossberg, 2016). The Eatwith service is occasionally offered in the company of several other guests at the same time. This situation has been seen as beneficial by gastro-tourists as a way to make new friends from different nationalities and to attain a cultural understanding. R72: "A gentleman from Switzerland joined us for our dinner, and it was a wonderful evening of lively conversation with new friends." Confirming this, R98 mentioned: "Excellent and typical diner and meaningful thoughts to help different cultures understanding each other!"

The qualitative data of this study also revealed that reviewers agreed that the characteristics of the host were particularly influential on their socio-cultural integration experience, and observed that reviewers perceive these locals to have such personal characteristics as: warm, polite, patient, friendly, open-minded, attentive, an intriguing speaker, a food enthusiast, and a culinary expert. R58: "Esra is a very open-minded and interesting person, and it was really interesting to have a conversation with her."

Memorable

The native dining experience during Eatwith prolonged the memorability of the trip because the value of the varied foods to gastro-tourists lies in its being the genuine cuisine of the locals (Tung and Ritchie, 2011; Lin and Mao, 2015; Pérez Gálvez et al., 2017; Correia et al., 2020;

Mhlanga, 2020). The findings revealed that gastro-tourists had gained a memorable culinary experience from the Eatwith service, offered by locals from the destination. Under the memorable experience dimension, reviewers mentioned that it was unforgettable, will not soon be forgotten, a completely memorable trip, and so on. This is highlighted by a review given by a woman from the United States. R88 commented: "Our meal with Asude was a once in a lifetime, priceless experience with incredibly divine food, culture sharing, and newly created friendships. I will never forget it! She has hosted many before us, but you would think we were the only guests + were treated like royalty!"

Hospitality

Hospitality is mainly explored as a consequence of the tourists' encounter with the host, examined under two different settings: the local (traditional) hospitality and the commercial (managerial) hospitality (Cetin and Okumus, 2018). When considering Eatwith in the context of the sharing economy, it might be perceived as both traditional and commercial hospitality, because the locals also provide this service as a way of making money. However, the qualitative findings of this study pointed out that gastro-tourists perceived the Eatwith service as traditional hospitality. The majority of reviewers mentioned that they felt at home, just because their hosts provided special attention and care for them. The following are two examples of the reviews related to this experience. R86: "Istanbul was a bit challenging for me due to both cultural and physical reasons, but Asude made me feel welcomed and well cared for her in-home [*sic*]." R102: "There is never a dull moment at the dining table, and Asude pays special attention to her guests' interests, which means that every experience is very customized and personal."

Service attributes

The findings also revealed that the service attributes dimension was mostly associated with the quality of the service that locals provided at their homes, linked to hospitality (for example, it was special, the abundance of food, inspiring, excellent, appetited, surprising, and touching). R2 mentioned: "Dinner at Ata's was like having a gourmet experience at home." Moreover, reviewers mentioned the plentifulness of traditional foods and flavors, which is precisely what the gastro-tourists demand for a culinary destination:

> There was plenty of food, and even a couple more guests would have had enough to eat. The food was delicious, and we were able to taste everything the Istanbul kitchen has to offer: a variation of starters, salad, lamb stew, and a tasty dessert with Turkish coffee to round up the dinner. (R43)

CONCLUSION

Theoretical Contributions

Addressing gastro-tourism and the body of agenda on the tourism experience, the study provided a deep insight into a neglected topic. Therefore, this chapter provides an essential framework to contribute to a better understanding of international tourists' experience in culinary destinations. Considering the study's originality, no such research has currently been encountered in the existing literature on identifying the representatives of gastro-tourists' experience in culinary destinations on meal-sharing economy platforms. Therefore, this recent study is most likely one of the first attempts to examine the components of gastro-tourists' experience in culinary destinations based on a meal-sharing economy platform, namely from the perspective of international tourists' online reviews.

Unlike previous research, this study has identified that knowledge experience is the most significant factor of gastro-tourists' experience in the meal-sharing economy. The experience of understanding the real life of locals as a consequence of meal-sharing at a local's home constituted the vital aspect of knowledge experience. The cognitive elements, such as information about the destination (history, politics, culture, music, and genuinely local places) and the inclusion of local culinary information (ingredients, meanings, stories, preparation, and tasting) were mostly provided by locals. A variety of studies indicate that gastro-tourists have a motivation to learn more about the visited destination and to explore its local cuisine (Tudorache et al., 2014; Cetin and Bilgihan, 2016; Choe and Kim, 2018, 2019; Williams et al., 2019). Besides, the desire to improve the culinary experience by tasting new food combinations and buying some of them to consume back home is generally attributed as one of the most sought-after tourism experiences (Hjalager and Richards, 2002; Poria et al., 2004; Kivela and Crotts, 2006a, 2006b; Correia et al., 2008; Kim et al., 2009; Ridvan Yurtseven and Kaya, 2011; Tung and Ritchie, 2011; Choe and Kim, 2018, 2019; Williams et al., 2019).

In addition, authenticity is identified as another essential dimension of the gastro-tourist experience for the meal sharing platform, which refers to a feeling of originality or genuineness of the food attractions of the destination. Rather than only satisfying their appetite, gastro-tourists seek an opportunity to encounter authenticity (Tung and Ritchie, 2011; Correia et al., 2020). The authentic foods in a destination reflect the spirit of the destination (Sims, 2009). Therefore, tourists use sharing economy platforms to get a feeling for any authenticity attributes and thus broaden their overall travel experiences in visiting destinations (Privitera and Abushena, 2019; Mhlanga, 2020). The findings revealed that acquaintance with the spirit of a destination through home-cooked traditional food in a native dining atmosphere offers diverse authenticity elements for the gastro-tourists' experience. The authentic experience dimension in the meal-sharing economy notably shows similarity with the dimensions identified in the previous investigations of food experiences in destinations (e.g., Correia et al., 2008; Liu and Jang, 2009; Jang et al., 2011; Tudorache et al., 2014; Cetin and Bilgihan, 2016; Ozdemir and Seyitoglu, 2017; Antón et al., 2019). However, beyond the previous studies' findings, the qualitative analysis of this chapter also reveals that the authentic experience of meal-sharing economy platforms is deeply insightful in the tourist experience phenomenon, and is described as something genuine that cannot be found elsewhere in the touristic service areas of the same destination.

Based on the nature of sharing economy platforms, these platforms provide positive guest and host interactions (Reisinger and Turner, 1998; Björk and Kauppinen-Räisänen, 2014; Hendijani, 2016; Pérez Gálvez et al., 2017). Especially on meal-sharing economy platforms, tourists also feel that they broaden the sense of their travel's memorability with authentic food experiences by dining in locals' homes (Mhlanga, 2020). Privitera and Abushena (2019) suggest that meal-sharing platforms provide cultural exchange, more affordable prices, and real encounters between hosts and guests. The findings also revealed that tourists and hosts have a conversational ambiance through the meal-sharing economy platforms, which enables them to create close friendships and to share some culinary advice as well as accurate destination information. This relationship is proven by the hospitality of the hosts and their special care for their guests. Therefore, the chapter suggests that a meal-sharing economy experience in a culinary destination offers more socio-cultural interaction between parties, which has a close relationship with the hospitality and the service experience that prolongs the memorability of the travel. This result also supports Williams et al.'s (2019) study findings, which pointed out the importance of encounters between host and guest in providing crucial co-creation relationships.

Practical Applications

The study findings also have some practical implications for sharing economy service providers. In light of the identified dimensions, service providers can develop their services and shape their strategies to ensure that all their guests are satisfied, as well as get their guests to recommend their service to others. According to Ketter (2019), Eatwith guests use these platforms for motivations of their ideals (values, principles), achievements and self-expression. According to the present study's findings, knowledge experience is an essential factor for gastro-tourists to use meal-sharing economy platforms in a culinary destination. Therefore, service providers should be aware that the cognitive elements they offer about their homeland and authentic foods have to be both convincing and satisfying for their guests. The authentic experience is also another essential factor that meal-sharing economy users seek, particularly in terms of originality or genuineness. This finding also means that meal-sharing economy service providers should mainly focus on providing more authentic clues about their destinations and local foods. For instance, service providers can improve by learning more about their destination and its national cuisine. Providing more information about the destination and more recipes from the local culinary tradition will enhance the gastro-tourist meal-sharing experience and increase the memorability of the travel as well.

On the other hand, the qualitative findings of this study reveal that the service attributions have an attachment with the hospitality experience. When the hosts are more hospitable and pay special attention to their guests by creating a friendly and comfortable atmosphere, they can enhance their guests' overall experience. Lastly, sharing economy platforms provide more socio-cultural interaction as a consequence of their nature, which is also one of the main reasons why these applications are referred to as a peer-to-peer economy. For this reason, meal-sharing economy applications can also be a way for both their services providers and users to increase their international friendship network and, in this way, contribute to cultural understanding.

This study also provides some suggestions for destination authorities. It observes that gastro-tourists utilize and value almost everything regarding the local cuisine in the destination. No tourists faced any challenges or complained about their meal-sharing economy experience. Considering also that the gastro-tourists spend more compared to the other types of tourists (Pérez Gálvez et al., 2017), positioning Istanbul as a culinary destination may be essential for enhancing overall tourism revenues. Furthermore, Okumus and Cetin (2018) suggested that understanding the gastro-tourist experience and motivations would provide an effective marketing strategy for destination planners and service providers. For a culinary destination to thrive, it is imperative to introduce new marketing strategies. These strategies will enhance tourism demand because they will attract the gastro-tourist cluster. Therefore, responsible authorities should pay special attention to developing some specific marketing and promotional materials immediately.

Limitations and Future Research

Like many other academic studies, this study also has some limitations. For instance, the study was based on qualitative data from only one meal-sharing economy platform, Eatwith, and used the reviews for only one destination, Istanbul. Therefore, further research should consider more diverse samples, including reviews from different cities for qualitative studies, or they should consider adopting quantitative data to verify and raise the generalizability of the qualitative studies on the same topics. To shed light on this study, all these limitations and suggestions for future research need to be addressed.

REFERENCES

Abrate, G., and Viglia, G. (2019). Personal or product reputation? Optimizing revenues in the sharing economy. *Journal of Travel Research, 58*(1), 136–148.

Agyeiwaah, E., Otoo, F.E., Suntikul, W., and Huang, W.J. (2019). Understanding culinary tourist motivation, experience, satisfaction, and loyalty using a structural approach. *Journal of Travel and Tourism Marketing, 36*(3), 295–313.

Antón, C., Camarero, C., Laguna, M., and Buhalis, D. (2019). Impacts of authenticity, degree of adaptation and cultural contrast on travellers' memorable gastronomy experiences. *Journal of Hospitality Marketing and Management, 28*(7), 743–764.

Babolian Hendijani, R. (2016). Effect of food experience on tourist satisfaction: the case of Indonesia. *International Journal of Culture, Tourism, and Hospitality Research, 10*(3), 272–282.

Beer, S. (2008). Authenticity and food experience – commercial and academic perspectives. *Journal of Foodservice, 19*(3), 153–163.

Belk, R. (2014). You are what you can access: sharing and collaborative consumption online. *Journal of Business Research, 67*(8), 1595–1600.

Björk, P., and Kauppinen-Räisänen, H. (2014). Culinary-gastronomic tourism – a search for local food experiences. *Nutrition and Food Science, 44*(4), 294–309.

Boyne, S., Hall, D., and Williams, F. (2003). Policy, support and promotion for food-related tourism initiatives. *Journal of Travel and Tourism Marketing, 14*(3–4), 131–154.

Braun, V., and Clarke, V. (2006). Using thematic analysis in psychology. *Qualitative Research in Psychology, 3*(2), 77–101.

Cetin, G., and Bilgihan, A. (2016). Components of cultural tourists' experiences in destinations. *Current Issues in Tourism, 19*(2), 137–154.

Cetin, G., and Okumus, F. (2018). Experiencing local Turkish hospitality in Istanbul, Turkey. *International Journal of Culture, Tourism and Hospitality Research, 12*(2), 223–237.

Chang, R.C.Y., Kivela, J., and Mak, A.H.N. (2010). Food preferences of Chinese tourists. *Annals of Tourism Research, 37*(4), 989–1011.

Choe, J., and Kim, S. (2018). Effects of tourists' local food consumption value on attitude, food destination image, and behavioural intention. *International Journal of Hospitality Management, 71*, 1–10.

Choe, J., and Kim, S. (2019). Development and validation of a multidimensional tourist's local food consumption value (TLFCV) scale. *International Journal of Hospitality Management, 77*, 245–259.

Correia, A., Kim, S., and Kozak, M. (2020). Gastronomy experiential traits and their effects on intentions for recommendation: a fuzzy set approach. *International Journal of Tourism Research, 22*(3), 351–363.

Correia, A., Moital, M., Da Costa, C.F., and Peres, R. (2008). The determinants of gastronomic tourists' satisfaction: a second-order factor analysis. *Journal of Foodservice, 19*(3), 164–176.

Creswell, J.W. (2007). *Qualitative Inquiry and Research Design: Choosing Among Five Approaches.* SAGE.

Demir, Y. (2020). Paylaşım Ekonomisi Kapsamında Yemek Paylaşma Sitelerinin Analizi. *Güncel Turizm Araştırmaları Dergisi, 4*(1), 54–69.

Dincer, M.Z., and Alrawadieh, Z. (2017). Negative word of mouse in the hotel industry: a content analysis of online reviews on luxury hotels in Jordan. *Journal of Hospitality Marketing and Management*, *26*(8), 785–804.

Du Rand, G.E., and Heath, E. (2006). Towards a framework for food tourism as an element of destination marketing. *Current Issues in Tourism*, *9*(3), 206–234.

Ellis, A., Park, E., Kim, S., and Yeoman, I. (2018). What is food tourism? *Tourism Management*, *68*, 250–263.

Elo, S., and Kyngas, H. (2008). The qualitative content analysis process. *Journal of Advanced Nursing*, *62*(1), 107–115.

Goolaup, S., and Mossberg, L. (2016). Exploring the concept of extraordinary related to food tourists' nature-based experience, *Scandinavian Journal of Hospitality and Tourism*, 17(1), 27–43.

Gummersson, E. (2000). *Qualitative Methods in Research Management*. SAGE.

Hillel, D., Belhassen, Y., and Shani, A. (2013). What makes a gastronomic destination attractive? Evidence from the Israeli Negev. *Tourism Management*, *36*, 200–209.

Hjalager, A.M., and Richards, G. (2002). Still undigested: research issues in tourism and gastronomy. In A.M. Hjalager and G. Richards (eds), *Tourism and Gastronomy* (pp. 224–234). London: Routledge.

Hossain, M. (2020). Sharing economy: a comprehensive literature review. *International Journal of Hospitality Management*, *87*.

Hotrec (2018). Shedding light on the 'meal-sharing' platform economy: proposals to level the playing field with the food sector. https://www.hotrec.eu/wp-content/customer-area/storage/1cc3b896f3369 eecf2568229a1c11a23/Final-meal-sharing-report.pdf.

Ignatov, E., and Smith, S.L.J. (2006). Segmenting Canadian culinary tourists. *Current Issues in Tourism*, *9*(3), 235–255.

Jang, S., Liu, Y., and Namkung, Y. (2011). Effects of authentic atmospherics in ethnic restaurants: investigating Chinese restaurants. *International Journal of Contemporary Hospitality Management*, *23*(5), 662–680.

Ketter, E. (2019). Eating with EatWith: analyzing tourism-sharing economy consumers. *Current Issues in Tourism*, *22*(9), 1062–1075.

Kim, Y.G., Eves, A., and Scarles, C. (2009). Building a model of local food consumption on trips and holidays: a grounded theory approach. *International Journal of Hospitality Management*, *28*(3), 423–431.

Kivela, J., and Crotts, J.C. (2006a). Gastronomy tourism: a meaningful travel market segment. *Journal of Culinary Science and Technology*, *4*(2–3), 39–55.

Kivela, J., and Crotts, J.C. (2006b). Tourism and gastronomy: gastronomy's influence on how tourists experience a destination. *Journal of Hospitality and Tourism Research*, *30*(3), 354–377.

Krippendor, K. (2004). *Content Analysis: An Introduction to Its Methodology*, 2nd edition. SAGE Publications.

Kumar, G.M.K. (2019). Gastronomic tourism – a way of supplementing tourism in the Andaman and Nicobar Islands. *International Journal of Gastronomy and Food Science*, *16*, 100139.

Lampinen, A., and Cheshire, C. (2016). Hosting via Airbnb: motivations and financial assurances in monetized network hospitality. *CHI '16: CHI Conference on Human Factors in Computing Systems*, (pp. 1669–1680). San Jose, CA.

Leong, Q.L., Ab Karim, S., Awang, K.W., and Abu Bakar, A.Z. (2017). An integrated structural model of gastronomy tourists' behaviour. *International Journal of Culture, Tourism, and Hospitality Research*, 11(4), 573–592.

Levitt, J.A., Zhang, P., DiPietro, R.B., and Meng, F. (2017). Food tourist segmentation: attitude, behavioral intentions and travel planning behavior based on food involvement and motivation. *International Journal of Hospitality and Tourism Administration*, 20(2), 129–155.

Lin, L., and Mao, P.C. (2015). Food for memories and culture – a content analysis study of food specialties and souvenirs. *Journal of Hospitality and Tourism Management*, *22*, 19–29.

Liu, Y., and Jang, S. (2009). The effects of dining atmospherics: an extended Mehrabian–Russell model. *International Journal of Hospitality Management*, *28*(4), 494–503.

López-Guzmán, T., and Sánchez-Cañizares, S. (2012). Gastronomy, tourism and destination differentiation: a case study in Spain. *Review of Economics and Finance*, 63–72.

Lune, H., and Berg, B.L. (2016). *Qualitative Research Methods for the Social Sciences*. Pearson Higher Education.

Maitland, R. (2010). Everyday life as a creative experience in cities. *International Journal of Culture, Tourism and Hospitality Research, 4*(3), 176–185.

Mak, A.H.N., Lumbers, M., Eves, A., and Chang, R.C.Y. (2012). Factors influencing tourist food consumption. *International Journal of Hospitality Management, 31*(3), 928–936.

Marine-Roig, E., Ferrer-Rosell, B., Daries, N., and Cristobal-Fransi, E. (2019). Measuring gastronomic image online. *International Journal of Environmental Research and Public Health*, 4631. https://doi .org/10.3390/ijerph16234631.

Mhlanga, O. (2020). 'Meal-sharing' platforms: a boon or bane for restaurants? *Current Issues in Tourism*, 1–18.

Muñoz, P., and Cohen, B. (2017). Mapping out the sharing economy: a configurational approach to sharing business modeling. *Technological Forecasting and Social Change, 125*, 21–37.

Neuman, W.L. (2011). *Social Research Methods: Qualitative and Quantitative Approaches*. Pearson Education.

Okumus, B., and Cetin, G. (2018). Marketing Istanbul as a culinary destination. *Journal of Destination Marketing and Management, 9*, 340–346.

Okumus, B., Okumus, F., and McKercher, B. (2007). Incorporating local and international cuisines in the marketing of tourism destinations: the cases of Hong Kong and Turkey. *Tourism Management, 28*(1), 253–261.

Ozdemir, B., and Seyitoglu, F. (2017). A conceptual study of gastronomical quests of tourists: authenticity or safety and comfort? *Tourism Management Perspectives, 23*, 1–7.

Patton, M.Q. (1990). *Qualitative Evaluation and Research Methods* (2nd edn). SAGE.

Patton, M.Q. (2002). Two decades of developments in qualitative inquiry: a personal, experiential perspective. *Qualitative Social Work, 1*(3), 261–283.

Pérez Gálvez, J.C., López-Guzmán, T., Cordova Buiza, F., and Medina-Viruel, M.J. (2017). Gastronomy as an element of attraction in a tourist destination: the case of Lima, Peru. *Journal of Ethnic Foods, 4*(4), 254–261.

Poria, Y., Butler, R., and Airey, D. (2004). Links between tourists, heritage, and reasons for visiting heritage sites. *Journal of Travel Research, 4*, 19–28.

Priporas, C.V., Stylos, N., Rahimi, R., and Vedanthachari, L.N. (2017). Unraveling the diverse nature of service quality in a sharing economy: a social exchange theory perspective of Airbnb accommodation. *International Journal of Contemporary Hospitality Management, 29*(9), 2279–2301.

Privitera, D., and Abushena, R. (2019). The home as a consumption space: promoting social eating. In John Byrom and Dominic Medway (eds), *Case Studies in Food Retailing and Distribution* (pp. 69–86). Woodhead Publishing.

Ramkissoon, H., and Uysal, M.S. (2011). The effects of perceived authenticity, information search behaviour, motivation and destination imagery on cultural behavioural intentions of tourists. *Current Issues in Tourism, 14*(6), 537–562.

Reisinger, Y., and Turner, L. (1998). A cultural analysis of Japanese tourists: challenges for tourism marketers. *European Journal of Marketing, 33*, 1203–1227.

Reisinger, Y., and Waryszak, R. (1996). Catering to Japanese tourists. *Journal of Restaurant and Foodservice Marketing, 1*(3–4), 53–72.

Ridvan Yurtseven, H., and Kaya, O. (2011). Local food in local menus: the case of Gokceada. *Tourismos, 6*(2), 263–275.

Seyitoglu, F. (2020). Tourists' perceptions of the tour guides: the case of gastronomic tours in Istanbul. *Anatolia*, 1–13.

Seyitoglu, F. (2021). Tourist experiences of guided culinary tours: the case of Istanbul. *Journal of Culinary Science and Technology, 19*(2), 93–114.

Sigala, M. (2015). Collaborative commerce in tourism: implications for research and industry. *Current Issues in Tourism, 20*(4), 346–355.

Sikolia, D., Biros, D., Mason, M., and Weiser, M. (2013). Trustworthiness of grounded theory methodology research in information systems. *MWAIS 2013 Proceedings, 16*

Sims, R. (2009). Food, place and authenticity: local food and the sustainable tourism experience. *Journal of Sustainable Tourism, 17*(3), 321–336.

Tudorache, P., Nistoreanu, P., and Faculty, T. (2014). Gastronomic tourism, a new trend for contemporary tourism? *Cactus Tourism Journal, 9*(1), 12–21

Tung, V., and Ritchie, J. (2011). Exploring the essence of memorable tourism experiences. *Annals of Tourism Research, 38*, 1367–1386.

Turkish Statistical Institute (TUIK) (2020). Statistical indicators: province indicators. Turkish Statistical Institute. https://biruni.tuik.gov.tr/ilgosterge/?locale=tr (accessed 1 May 2020).

Williams, H.A., Yuan, J., and Williams Jr, R.L. (2019). Attributes of memorable gastro-tourists' experiences. *Journal of Hospitality and Tourism Research, 43*(3), 327–348.

Williams, P., and Soutar, G.N. (2000). Dimensions of customer value and the tourism experience: an exploratory study. In *Australian and New Zealand Marketing Academy Conference* (Vol. 28, pp. 1415–1421).

Yu, C.E., and Sun, R. (2019). The role of Instagram in the UNESCO's creative city of gastronomy: a case study of Macau. *Tourism Management, 75*, 257–268.

Zurek, K. (2016). Food sharing in Europe: between regulating risks and the risks of regulating. *European Journal of Risk Regulation, 7*(4), 675–687.

31. The effects of social media on the food preferences of Generation Z within the scope of gastronomy tourism

Özlem Altun, Mehmet Necati Cizrelioğulları and Mehmet Veysi Babayiğit

INTRODUCTION

The greatest need for survival is the need to eat and drink. This need has started to diversify due to all the developments and changes in the world. While people previously were preparing and consuming their meals according to their own means, the rate of eating out or purchasing takeaway meals has increased greatly today. People's travel demands have increased in order to discover new tastes, to experience them on-site (Kahvecioğlu et al., 2019). As a result of this demand, the concept of gastronomy tourism has been to our lives. In the past, when tourism was mentioned, the first things that came to mind were sea, sand and sun. Eating and drinking activities were defined as products supporting tourism and since they was not a reason for travel, they were not very important for tourism. Today, food and drink are a source of attraction for the destinations they belong to, and they play a big role as a reason for tourists preferring a travel region (Okumus et al., 2007; Dilsiz, 2010; Albayrak, 2013; Pullphothong and Sopha, 2013; Aslan et al., 2014; Bekar and Kılıç, 2014).

In this context, gastronomy tourism has become one of the most popular and preferred tourism types today. It is possible to define gastronomy tourism as follows: tourists travel and visit restaurants, food festivals, and production destinations in order to understand the different chefs, to taste the dishes, to see the preparation processes and the places where they are prepared (Hall et al., 2004; Tang et al., 2019). The technological developments in the world, the increase in the use of the internet and the use of different social media tools, have created awareness in the field of gastronomy as well as in other fields, and have brought a different dimension. Through the internet and social media, all developments and activities in the field of gastronomy can be followed, and information and awareness are increasing. In addition, conferences, festivals and competitions in the field of gastronomy are effective in providing an international dimension and are the most preferred type of gastronomy tourism (Dilsiz, 2010; Blakey, 2012). Academic studies reveal that gastronomic elements have a great importance for tourists, and when planning to travel, most tourists consider the variety of gastronomic facilities at the destination (Kivela and Crotts, 2005a, 2006; Du Rand and Heath, 2006; Fox, 2007; Harrington and Ottenbacher, 2010; Karim and Chi, 2010; Lin et al., 2011). People take videos and pictures of traditional foods, drinks, recipes, food presentations of the region, and they deliver them to hundreds and thousands of people all over the world at the same time, and share their experiences. In addition, they purchase products for their loved ones as gifts or souvenirs, and take them back to their countries. Therefore, the tourists share the region they visit during their gastronomic trips both socially and concretely, and these shares contribute greatly to the promotion of the region or the country (Ab Karim and Chi, 2010; Blakey, 2012). Social media, as a result of technological developments, is effective in every aspect of our lives, such as education, trade, finance, communication and tourism (Edosomwan et al., 2011). Social media has become an indispensable part of our lives. Social media, which has reached the level of addiction, affects people's lifestyles and is the biggest focus in decision-making (Lange-Faria and Elliot, 2012). People share what they eat, drink, travel and wear, and create positive or negative examples on social media; hence, by shaping the lives of people, a different and new culture consisting of their actions, ideas and preferences emerges (Karaduman, 2017). In recent years, social media has become one of the ways in which people most interact with each other. The users of social media actively participate in this interaction through conversation, instant announcements and photo sharing, or their reactions to the posts other than being informed or watching. In addition, they create their own icons and become known and followed by a large community by presenting themselves to their followers and increasing the number of likes and followers (Özdemir and Celebi, 2015). Through social media, many people have gained fame and formed a fan base. Everything that these people who are famous or have a large fan base do and share is being followed and imitated, including the places they go and their lifestyle, and these conversations and behaviors reach hundreds, thousands and even millions of curious followers (Ozkan and Solmaz, 2015). Advertising is inevitable where there is consumption, so developments in social media provided a new dimension in the advertising industry (Knoll, 2016). All these developments in social media have been proven by scientific studies to cause changes in consumption habits, but also to affect local cultures. Social media, which has begun to affect all areas of human life, has a huge impact on nutrition, which is the most important need of human life (Zeng and Gerritsen, 2014). In addition, shares on social media affect eating and drinking preferences of the followers. For instance, if the person they admire shares about their food and drinks, and allows the followers to order or buy that product, the followers will directly act on this. In addition, there is a desire to follow the social media pages not only of famous people, but also of companies producing the products they use (Rambe and Jafeta, 2017). On the other hand, the products being sent to the followers of the company webpage hold a crucial role in increasing the number of the followers. Accordingly, companies' knowledge of followers' age, gender and marital status information, and updating of this information, helps them to recognize their potential customers. In addition, it enables businesses to reach their target customers and to market effectively and intensively (Kara and Coşkun, 2012; Battallar and Cömert, 2015). With the latest developments in the world, many things have changed in our lives, and new innovations and concepts are added day by day. It is argued that the year in which people are born affects the emergence of many features and habits of these people. One of these concepts is the "generation" concept, defined as those born and living around the same the time and who experience a similar collective destiny (Kahvecioğlu et al., 2019). Generations are heavily emphasized as a feature of the global market, and dividing people into homogeneous groups and partitioning this market has had a huge impact. In academic research, generations are classified and named as follows: the Silent Generation, Baby Boomers, Generation X, Generation Y and Generation Z (Euromonitor International, 2011; Singh, 2014; Schroer, 2015). The younger generations are Generations X, Y and Z. Researchers have not yet made a clear judgment about the years when Generation Z, the youngest generation, were born; they are also known as the 'Crystal generation' (Çetin and Karalar, 2016). Many studies consider Generation Z to be those born in 2000 or later (Altuntuğ, 2012; Akdemir et al., 2013; Adıgüzel et al., 2014; Demirkaya et al., 2015). Other studies argue that this generation were born between the mid-1990s and 2012, and therefore the oldest of this generation are currently attending undergraduate and graduate-level studies at university (Puiu, 2016; Zorn, 2017).

Generation Z is described as the most material, technological, upgraded, globally connected and officially trained generation the world has ever seen. Generation Z students are expected to be better equipped and educated than previous generations because they prefer interactive, participation-oriented learning environments (McCrindle and Wolfinger, 2009). Additionally, they are materialists, characterized as realists, pragmatics and well-educated (Freidrich et al. 2010; Lanier, 2017). It is very important to know the significant impact of social media on the food preferences of Generation Z. From this point of view, this study is designed as a conceptual review study aiming to evaluate the social media usage of the youngest generation, Generation Z: specifically, their opinions, attitudes and food preferences within the scope of gastronomic tourism; as well as the effects of social media on food preferences of this generation. In the literature review, there is not much research on the effect on food preferences of social media usage of Generation Z. The results of the research will determine the factors affecting the eating and drinking preferences of Generation Z, which will shape the future and provide an insight for the food and beverage sector about Generation Z; and it will make a great contribution to the literature in determining the impact of social media on the most important nutritional habits in their lives.

CONCEPTUAL FRAMEWORK

Social Media Development Process

Social media is important to human beings as it is a basic component of human communication and interaction. Since it came into existence, social media has been affecting people in various communication styles, which have evolved into social networks currently. In recent times, the use of social media has become a main daily practice in many people's lives (Edosomwan et al., 2011). Social media has impacts in many areas, such as education and tourism. In order to define social media, it may be useful to check the definitions of "social" and "media." "Social" is sharing information or interaction among people, and "media" means to be a communication tool such as the internet or online web-based applications; hence, it can be claimed that social media is the future of communication and interaction, as it has many tools and platforms enhancing the spread of information worldwide. People generally share or transfer text, photos, audio, video and information via social media applications such as Facebook, Twitter, Instagram, Snapchat, YouTube, WhatsApp, Flixster and LinkedIn.

There have been many claims for and definitions of social media. To exemplify, the Merriam-Webster dictionary attempts to define it as "forms of electronic communication (as websites for social networking and blogging) through which users create online communities to share information, ideas, personal messages, and other content (as videos)." The Merriam-Webster dictionary also claims that social media networking includes the exchange of information or services among individuals, institutions or groups in terms of managing ongoing interactions. It is also stated that social media utilizes technologies such as mobile and web-based ones. The purpose of these technologies is to come up with highly interactive areas, enabling humans to have more virtual and accurate interaction and communication in the form of collaboration or sharing (Kaplan and Haenlein, 2010; Kietzmann et al., 2011). In addition, the utilization of social media has been highlighted positively by many scholars. Carton (2009) stated that, "Throughout much of human history, we've developed technologies that make it easier for us to communicate with each other"; hence, it can be claimed that social media technology is developed for the sake of human interaction and communication, via many web-based tools (Kirakosyan, 2014, p. 226).

It may be useful to look at the traces of social communication and interaction in the emergence of much earlier tools, such as paintings on cave walls, the abacus, writing slates, blackboard, and so on, which helped interaction among people many years ago. In terms of transferring information, the first traces can be dated back to 1792, which is the year of starting to use the telegraph to send and receive messages over long distances (Winston, 1998; Ritholz, 2010). The popularity of radio and TV was gained in the late 1800s in terms of social interaction among places (Rimskii, 2011). Social networks are related to the digital tools that we use currently; however, social media is not just based on digital tools, which is why it cannot be claimed that social media is a current innovation. The base of social media may have started in the 1950s, which was the time of the first telephone-based hackings. Since the networking system was actually able to conduct various telephone conversations during one conversation, Borders (2009) claimed that it was possible to hack into former voice mailboxes via network theft, which indicates the first podcasts and blogs. In the 1960s emails, which were used to send messages online just from one personal computer to another, became quite widespread (Borders, 2009). Via computer technology, social media was further developed in the 1970s, and MUD (originally known as multi-user dungeon, multi-user dimension, or multi-user domain) for role-playing games, interactive fiction, and online chat; and the BBS or bulletin board system (to upload and download software, read news, or exchange messages with others) were developed (Crystal, 2011). WELL, GEnie, Listserv, and IRC were introduced for private messages, chat, and data transfers in the 1980s; and many social networking sites, such as Six Degrees, BlackPlanet, Asian Avenue, move on, Blogger, Epinions, Third Voice and Napster, were created for entertainment and interaction (Ritholz, 2010). And since 2000, social media has boomed, as many online applications such as LunarStorm, six degrees, cyworld, ryze, Wikipedia, fotolog, sky blog and Friendster were launched; and in 2003, MySpace, LinkedIn, lastFM, tribe.net, Hi5, Facebook Harvard, Dogster, Mixi, Yahoo!360, YouTube, cyword, Black planet and Instagram, whose general aims are to develop communication, interaction, friendship and entertainment, have emerged (Junco et al., 2011).

In our modern-day lives, the benefits of social media are multiple, but these are generally intangible benefits (Hollier, 2009). Social media has also boosted the reputations and advertisement topics of various brands. It is clear that it develops friendship, entertainment, interaction and engagement among human beings. It is also claimed that if a company is approachable and people-friendly, then the company can make itself famous on the web (Carraher et al., 2009). Apart from these benefits, Edosomwan et al. (2011), claimed the benefits of social media as the following:

- Promote open communication between employees and management.
- Enable employees to share project ideas and work in teams effectively, which helps in sharing knowledge and experiences.
- Social media also promotes better content, such as webcast and videos, than just simple text.
- Helps to communicate collaboratively between current and potential customers, in receiving feedback, product definition, product development, or any forms of customer service and support.

- Encourage members, or part of the company's employees, to become members of a well-recognized community.
- Social media becomes a good venue for discussions and becomes a classic goal of marketing and communications, but the companies must ensure that the employees are adhering to the rules and etiquettes of social media.

Based on these benefits, it is clear that social media is transparent, realistic, comprehensive and interactive. For companies, social media can promote their reputation; for tourism, it can make facilities visible; for the best outcomes in education, both students and teachers should be actively engaged. Cankül et al. (2018), claims that the most preferred social media application of food and beverage businesses is Instagram. In addition, it has been observed that the majority of businesses operating within the scope of gastronomic tourism have been using social media applications more efficiently in the past few years, and the purpose of social media usage of businesses is to create product and brand awareness.

Generation Z and Social Media

Generation X, the first of the younger generations, consists of those born between 1965 and 1980. As of 2021, the oldest of this generation is 56 years old and the youngest is 41 years old. Generation X are law-abiding, have a sense of belonging, respect authority, are loyal to their workplaces, hardworking, compatible with flexible working hours, patient, and have high motivation. Members of this generation have experienced many transformations, and are especially trying to adapt to what technology brings and changes. Generation Y, the second generation of younger generations, were born between 1981 and 1996. As of 2021, the oldest is 40 years old, and the youngest is 25 years old. This generation are impatient for promotion in their working lives, and prefer working to spending money. Generation Y members who do not give up their rights do not prefer to interfere in the business of others, preferring to play games on their tablets or laptops instead of playing with others on the street. They are the generation in which the conflict between generations is seen most, and they are fond of freedom and love independence. Compared to Generation X, they can change jobs often since the sense of attachment of Generation Y is weak. While the rebellious and unknown Generation Y have difficulty in adapting, they are cruelly critical of those who are not like them. Generation Z use technology rather intensively, and have a great love for the internet and technology. Generation Z consists of individuals preferring to socialize over the internet rather than face to face, and all the benefits offered by technology shape their lifestyles (Levickaite, 2010; McCrindle and Wolfinger, 2009; Schroer, 2015; Bağcı and İçöz, 2019).

When the studies on Generation Z are reviewed, it is seen that each study investigates people born at different time intervals, although the these are close to each other. Schroer (2015) and Singh (2014), classified Generation Z as being born between 1995 and 2012. Another study that examined Generation Z assumed they were born in 1995 and later (Fister-Gale, 2015), and a further study defined Generation Z as consisting of people born between 1994 and 2010 (Schawabel, 2014). In Kuran's research conducted in 2013, Generation Z are the generation born after 2000 (Kuran, 2013). In a report prepared by Euromonitor International in 2011, Generation Z covers those born between 1991 and 2002 (Euromonitor International, 2011). Generation Z, given the latest technology, access information very easily and in a short time; also, they prefer to write instead of speaking (Berkup, 2014). Generation Z, who are distracted, speed-loving, impatient and unhappy, and seeking trust, are defined as the "New

Silent Generation" because they prefer to be individual (Akdemir et al., 2013; Berkup, 2014). In terms of the consumption habits of Generation Z, quality is very important for them. They are passionate about innovation, supportive of creativity, have an interest in different cultures, have multiple decision-making and attention skills, and exhibit brand loyalty (Altuntuğ, 2012; Berkup, 2014; Yiğit Seyfi, 2016). Young individuals of Generation Z read other people's recommendations on social media before travelling for gastronomy purposes; through mobile applications, they share during their travel; and after their experience, they convey their comments, evaluations and feelings about their experiences on social media (Prakash Yadav and Rai, 2017; Desai and Lele, 2017). The widespread use of internet access, which is one of the social media tools, and the increase in the use of social media, enable Generation Z to learn about gastronomic tourism (Levickaite, 2010; Kapil and Roy, 2014; Curtis et al., 2019). Since social media tools are a source of information about products and services, they are increasingly important (Goyal, 2013). Businesses also enhance the use of social media and related marketing strategies to create brand awareness, interact and publicize gastronomy products to existing and potential customers. Social media also heavily affects gastronomic tourism (Evans, 2010; Horng and Tsai, 2012).

Tourism enterprises have shown the importance to gastronomy destination marketing of the widespread use of the internet, which is the basis of social media, and the use of social media by Generation Z (Zengin and Arıcı, 2017; Haddouche and Salomone, 2018). Because of the changes in communication technologies, Generation Z is one of the generations using communication technologies the most (Curtis et al., 2019). The internet, which emerged in the mid-1990s, was to to be an important development for this generation, and it is claimed that this generation was influenced by the internet (Hargittai, 2010; Desai and Lele, 2017). When Generation Z are evaluated in terms of consumption habits, we can assert that they are individuals who care about quality, enjoy creativity and innovation, are interested in different cultures, consume instantly and have low brand loyalty; they use virtual platforms and technology efficiently, and are affected by these environments (Kapıl and Roy, 2014; Berkup, 2014; Haddouche and Salomone, 2018). Therefore, the fact that this generation is dominant in technology and uses social media efficiently plays a significant role in the development and marketing of gastronomic tourism (Ozkan and Solmaz, 2015; Kahvecioğlu et al., 2019). It can be claimed that the attitude of Generation Z towards gastronomic tourism is evaluated within the scope of their search for innovation. Eighty-two percent of Generation Z use social media to express their interests (Cone Communication, 2017). Also, social media plays an important role for Generation Z to satisfy the culinary delights of the destinations, in terms of their gastronomic values, their innovation, adventure and cultural pursuit, and to make them interested in local purchases and local places (Kahvecioğlu et al., 2019). Businesses wish to advertise their products; as Generation Z are in search of innovation, looking for excitement and dominate the technology, these business markets put importance on advertising targeted to Generation Z consumers, who were born and grew up in a digital age, to sell local products through social media tools (Levickaite, 2010; Wood, 2013; Kapil and Roy, 2014).

Gastronomy Tourism and Generation Z

Today, tourism is the sector that generates the highest income in the world, and makes the greatest contribution to the economy of each country. Tourism is the whole journey that people make from one place to another in order to see the cities, countries they plan to visit for a holiday or business purposes. Tourism has diversified and and now takes place all year round, not just based on seasonality. One of the contributions of tourism to a country's economy is that it affects many subsectors directly or indirectly (Cohen, 2004; Kivela and Crotts, 2006). One of these sectors is gastronomy. Altınel (2014), describes gastronomy as follows: "gastronomy" is formed by combining the Greek words *gaster* meaning stomach, and *nomas* which means law, but it is more useful and important to interpret what it means, rather than just the dictionary meaning. The concept of gastronomy is defined by various people as the art of eating and drinking. However, it is a branch of arts and sciences that embodies many different disciplines and is directly related to these disciplines. The disciplines that gastronomy is related to are biology, chemistry, literature, geology, music, philosophy, history, sociology, agriculture, psychology, nutrition and medicine (Santich, 2004; Kivela and Crotts, 2006; Gacnik, 2012). The aim of gastronomy is to provide nutrition that will keep human health at the highest level while enjoying life and eating. The fields of work of gastronomy are ready-to-eat foods and beverages which are tasty and hygienically produced (Sormaz et al., 2016).

Gastronomy integrates with tourism, and increases the importance of both domestic and foreign tourism, thereby contributing to the country's economy as a source of income (Sánchez-Cañizares and López-Guzmán, 2012). In this context, gastronomy, which emerged as a field in which nutrition-related professions developed in the 19th century, is among the constantly developing and rising tourism trends, creating awareness in a wide and effective way (Richards, 2002; Guzman and Canizares, 2011). Gastronomy tourism is a phenomenon including significant and strategically effective activities in the promotion of countries and regions in the realization of the activities of the local people, and makes a significant contribution to the development and image of any region of a country (Kivela and Crotts, 2005b). Therefore, while all definitions related to the concept of gastronomy emphasize certain aspects of gastronomy, it would be better to consider gastronomy in many different areas. It may be asserted that gastronomy encompasses gastronomy tourism, gastronomic identity, attitudes and behaviors of tourists, local tourism and gastronomy, gastronomy experiences of domestic and foreign tourists, and destination and local cuisine (Özdemir and Altıner, 2019).

It is also a part of the local culture, and effective in promoting regional tourism consumed by tourists, and is a part of regional agricultural and economic development. In addition, it is considered as a product and service form by tourists with certain preferences and consumption models, with competitive target marketing as a key point (Hall et al., 2004). When analysed from another point of view, although the tourism promotion of countries is in the social and cultural area, food and beverage promotion has started to be seen as a type of gastronomy tourism in itself (de Albuquerque Meneguel et al., 2019). From this perspective, it is possible to expand the area of interest of gastronomy into advice and guidance on where, when, how and what to eat and drink, since it reflects cultural values, rules and norms related to eating and drinking (Nestle, 2013; Okumus et al., 2018). In fact, food and beverage consumption is one of the most important elements of experience of tourism (Sidali et al., 2011). Thus, many researchers have mentioned the social importance of food and beverages culture and the role of gastronomy in tourism, as an important factor affecting the preferences of individuals (Cohen and Avieli, 2004; Harrington, 2005; Sánchez-Cañizares and López-Guzmán, 2012; Gajic, 2015). Activities for the development of gastronomic tourism contribute to cultural interaction with other people in the world by providing individuals with unique experiences, and the development of the regions and brand city image within the scope of gastronomy tourism (Gacnik, 2012; Gheorghe et al., 2014).

The factor affecting the development of gastronomy tourism significantly is the social media factor (Rodríguez-Fernández et al., 2017). Social media contributes positively to the tourism destination because knowledge, experiences and interests are shared through the internet (Correa et al., 2010; Alalwan et al., 2017). Social media is an important source of information for individuals, especially for Generation Z, born after 2000, and is critical in the travel planning process (Turner, 2015; Belhadjali et al., 2016). Since the competitiveness in the tourism sector over social media has a strategic importance, it focuses on the applications of many destination marketing organizations primarily targeting Generation Z, and social media applications, which are increasingly appropriate as destination marketing tools (Khang et al., 2012; Curtis et al., 2019). For this reason, many destination marketing organizations implement media strategies to inform the pre- or post-travel young generations, as their current or potential customers, to introduce their destinations, to interact with them to facilitate and inspire them, and to encourage the young generations to share during or after their travel (Lange-Faria and Elliot, 2012; Hassan, 2013; Hays et al., 2013). On the other hand, in the gastronomy culture of destinations, the importance of social media in the promotion and marketing of different food and beverage products of businesses operating in different destinations for Generation Z also draws attention (Haddouche and Salomone, 2018; Tavares et al., 2018). Social media tools affect the ability of gastronomy culture to evaluate opportunities in the marketing destination and to examine the sales strategies comprehensively (Hay, 2017; Rodríguez-Fernández et al., 2017). Furthermore, determining the users of social media tools and which social media tools users prefer, their frequency of use, and knowing the consumption characteristics of each generation, especially Generation Z, are extremely important factors for successfully implementing marketing strategies (Özdemir and Celebi, 2015). In this context, the use of social media is an important factor in stating the unique gastronomic culture characteristics of each country, as each region provides an advantage in the intense competition environment for the marketing of the destination, since it has an attraction in the marketing of the gastronomy culture that is specific to the local destination (Lange-Faria and Elliot, 2012; Hassan, 2013).

METHOD

This conceptual chapter is based on the review and interpretation of studies in the literature. Different methods have been used to collect and interpret the literature. First of all, the key terms related to Generation Z, social media, gastronomy and gastronomy tourism were researched in the Google Scholar database. Then, the relationship between Generation Z and social media, the relationship between Generation Z and gastronomy tourism, and the relationship between social media and gastronomy tourism were investigated based on articles from between 2002 and 2019. Articles published after 2010 were collected from over different databases, and journals with a high impact factor: from Science Direct, JSTOR, SAGE journals and Emerald journals, (*Annals of Tourism Research*: impact factor, 5.49; *International Journal of Tourism Research*: impact factor, 2.27; *Journal of Hospitality Marketing and Management*: impact factor, 3.73; *Journal of Hospitality and Tourism Research*: impact factor, 2.84; *International Journal of Hospitality Management*: impact factor, 4.46; *Current Issues in Tourism*: impact factor, 3.39). The articles found as the search results of the keywords are shown in detail in Table 31.1. A total of 95 sources related to our research. Within the

Table 31.1   *Journal resources*

	JSTOR	Emerald	SAGE	Google Scholar
Generation Z	298 897	27 187	716 999	5 460 000
Social media	735 803	98 130	315 063	4 600 000
Gastronomy	4 142	840	1362	71 800
Gastronomy tourism	600	567	490	18 400
Generation Z and social media	37 508	12 372	165 004	2 610 000
Generation Z and gastronomy tourism	58	115	358	6 460
Social media and gastronomy tourism	303	368	278	15 700

scope of the works collected from articles, books and websites, first of all their summaries and entries were listed in order of importance. Then, within the scope of the study, the effect of social media on the food preferences of Generation Z for gastronomy tourism was examined.

CONCLUSION

As a result of the literature review conducted within the scope of this study, research evaluating the social media usage of the youngest Generation Z, their opinions and attitudes regarding food preferences within the scope of gastronomic tourism, as well as the effects of social media on the food preferences of this generation, were examined. Smartphones and technology are at the forefront in the consumption life of Generation Z (those born after 2000). Technology is an indispensable element for Generation Z, who actively use social media through the internet for friendship, communication and information; visit online stores instead of physical stores to shop; by considering various foods and beverages that come from different cultures. Previous studies mentioned in the literature have shown that Generation Z are the most effective users of social media, able to use all the benefits of the digital world. Today's university students, Generation Z, are a talented generation, gifted with the ability to reveal previously unknown facts, and to produce solutions, with high levels of autonomy. Also, social media plays a part in every moment of their lives, and has a great impact on their nutrition. Generation Z, the most intense social media users, prefer brands having strong interactions with researchers and other consumers in order to make them feel special. In addition, they have a consumer profile of using traditional and digital media applications frequently, and preferring to purchase products via an online shopping method. Generation Z read the recommendations and complaints shared on social media before deciding on their travels for gastronomic purposes. During their travels, they share simultaneously via mobile applications. Due to the fact that Generation Z are curious and innovative, they love non-traditional information and they are affected by the advertisements on social media. As a result, companies advertising on social media applications receive positive feedback on sales. Companies produce their own products and services by marketing them in a social media environment to increase their visibility. People come across many ads during their daily use of social media, and their sense of being influenced for shopping is triggered. There is no doubt that these shares and advertisements have an impact on young people's food and beverage preferences, as the advertisements and shares made on social media draw attention to the cuisine, the dishes of different cultures, and increase the interest in gastronomy tourism. Although the preferences of Generation Z in their daily lives are generally for fast food and easy-to-prepare food, they also care about pleasure and satisfaction. On the other hand, due to their innovative and curious nature, they travel or visit various places in order to taste foods that differ from those of their own culture, to learn how to make them, or to learn about their preparation. In addition, the presence of food bloggers on social media, and restaurant sharing by celebrities, affects people's desire to eat out and what places they go to. In short, the sharing on social media affects the preference of eating in the restaurant and at home.

From a different perspective, Generation Z, called the Millennium generation, prefer ethnic, local organic dishes, as they are willing to try different culinary cultures. In addition, menus with dishes created for visual awareness attract their attention. In this context, Generation Z prefer to take a picture of a meal and share it on social media before eating it. From another point of view, since the visual richness and variety of food is an important factor for Generation Z, it turns out that it is an important concept in the impact of gastronomy tourism on social media. Studies on Generation Z's features and the impact on gastronomic tourism are still new, but they are rapidly increasing in different disciplines and using different methods.

In this study, the effect of social media on the food preferences of Generation Z in gastronomy tourism was investigated. Evaluations of Generation Z related to gastronomy tourism, the effect of social media on Generation Z, and relations between social media and gastronomic tourism, were examined. The problem in the study is that there were few national and international literature reviews. Consequently, the current study indicates areas for future studies. In later studies, the curiosity of Generation Z and the effect of the search for innovation on other types of tourism can be understood. In addition, the effects of internet use and social media on e-commerce and its economic implications can be investigated within the scope of online transactions. Considering the consumption habits of Generation Z and other generations in the digitalized world, studies can be conducted to evaluate the dimensions of the use of social media in terms of gastronomic tourism.

REFERENCES

Ab Karim, S., and Chi, C.G.Q. (2010). Culinary tourism as a destination attraction: an empirical examination of destinations' food image. *Journal of Hospitality Marketing and Management*, *19*(6), 531–555.

Adıgüzel, O., Batur, H.Z., and Ekşili, N. (2014). Kuşakların değişen yüzü ve y kuşağı ile ortaya çıkan yeni çalışma tarzı: mobil yakalılar. *Süleyman Demirel Üniversitesi Sosyal Bilimler Enstitüsü Dergisi*, *1*(19), 165–182.

Akdemir, A., Konakay, G., and Demirkaya H. (2013). Y kuşağının kariyer algısı, kariyer değişimi ve liderlik tarzı beklentilerinin araştırılması. *Ekonomi ve Yönetim Araştırmaları Dergisi*, *2*(2), 11–42.

Alalwan, A.A., Rana, N.P., Dwivedi, Y.K., and Algharabat, R. (2017). Social media in marketing: a review and analysis of the existing literature. *Telematics and Informatics*, *34*(7), 1177–1190.

Albayrak, A. (2013). Farklı Milletlerden Turistlerin Türk Mutfağına İlişkin Görüşlerinin Saptanması Üzerine Bir Çalışma. *Journal of Yasar University*, *3*(8), 5049–5063.

Altınel, H. (2014). *Menu Yönetimi ve Menu Planlama*. Detay Publishing.

Altuntuğ, N. (2012). Kuşaktan kuşağa tüketim olgusu ve geleceğin tüketici profili, *Organizasyon ve Yönetim Bilimleri Dergisi*, *4*(1), 203–212.

Aslan, Z., Güneren, E., and Çoban, G. (2014). Destinasyon Markalaşma Sürecinde Yöresel Mutfağın Rolü: Nevşehir Örneği. *Journal of Tourism and Gastronomy Studies*, *2*(4), 3–13.

Bağçı, E. and İçöz, O. (2019). Z ve Alfa Kuşağı ile Dijitalleşen Turizm. *Güncel Turizm Araştırmaları Dergisi*, *3*(2), 232–256.

Battallar, Z., and Cömert, M. (2015). Tüketicilerin tercihlerinde sosyal medyadaki reklamların etkisi. *Turizm Akademik Dergisi*, *2*(1), 39–48.

Bekar, A., and Kılıç, B. (2014). Turistlerin Gelir Düzeylerine Göre Destinasyondaki Gastronomi Turizmi Etkinliklerine Katılımları. *Uluslararası Sosyal ve Ekonomik Bilimler Dergisi*, *4*(1), 19–26.

Belhadjali, M., Abbasi, S.M., and Whaley, G.L. (2016). Social media applications preference by generation and gender: an exploratory study. *Competition Forum*, *14*(1), 103). Accessed March 30, 2020 at https://www.questia.com/library/journal/1P3-4244273201/socialmedia-applications-preference-by-generation.

Berkup, S.B. (2014). Working with generations X and Y in generation Z period: management of different generations in business life. *Mediterranean Journal of Social Sciences*, *5*(19), 218–218.

Blakey, C. (2012). Consuming place: tourism's gastronomy connection. *University of Hawai'i at Hilo: Hawai'i College of HOHONU*, *10*(1), 51–54.

Borders, B. (2009). A brief history of social media. Web log post, Copy Brighter Marketing. http://copybrighter.com/history-of-social-media.

Cankül, D., Metin, M., and Özvatan, D. (2018). Yiyecek İçecek İşletmeleri ve Sosyal Medya Kullanimi (Food and beverage business and social media usage). *Journal of Gastronomy Hospitality and Travel*, *1*(1), 29–37.

Carraher, S.M., Parnell, J., and Spillan, J. (2009). Customer service-orientation of small retail business owners in Austria, the Czech Republic, Hungary, Latvia, Slovakia, and Slovenia. *Baltic Journal of Management*, *4*(3), 251–268.

Carton, S. (2009). Defining social media. Click Z. Retrieved from http://www.clickz.com/clickz/column/1711156/what-do-people-want-online.

Çetin, C., and Karalar, S. (2016). X, Y ve Z kuşağı öğrencilerin çok yönlü ve sınırsız kariyer algıları üzerine bir araştırma, *Yönetim Bilimleri Dergisi*, *14*(28), 157–197.

Cohen, E. (2004). Tourism and gastronomy. *Annals of Tourism Research*, *3*(31), 731–733.

Cohen, E., and Avieli, N. (2004). Food in tourism: attraction and impediment. *Annals of Tourism Research*, *31*(4), 755–778.

Cone Communication (2017). 2017 Cone Gen Z CSR Study: How to Speak Z. Accessed April 1, 2020, at http://www.conecomm.com/2017-cone-gen-z-csr-study-pdf.

Correa, T., Hinsley, A.W., and De Zuniga, H.G. (2010). Who interacts on the Web? The intersection of users' personality and social media use. *Computers in Human Behavior*, *26*(2), 247–253.

Crystal, D. (2011). *Language and the Internet*. Cambridge University Press.

Curtis, B.L., Ashford, R.D., Magnuson, K.I., and Ryan-Pettes, S.R. (2019). Comparison of smartphone ownership, social media use, and willingness to use digital interventions between Generation Z and Millennials in the treatment of substance use: cross-sectional questionnaire study. *Journal of Medical Internet Research*, *21*(4), e13050.

de Albuquerque Meneguel, C.R., Mundet, L., and Aulet, S. (2019). The role of a high-quality restaurant in stimulating the creation and development of gastronomy tourism. *International Journal of Hospitality Management*, *83*, 220–228.

Demirkaya, H., Akdemir, A., Karaman, E., and Atan, Ö. (2015). Kuşakların yönetim politikası beklentilerinin araştırılması. *İşletme Araştırmaları Dergisi*, *7*(1), 186–204.

Desai, S.P., and Lele, V. (2017). Correlating internet, social networks and workplace – a case of Generation Z students. *Journal of Commerce and Management Thought*, *8*(4), 802–815.

Dilsiz, B. (2010). Türkiye'de Gastronomi ve Turizm (İstanbul Örneği). İstanbul Üniversitesi, Sosyal Bilimler Enstitüsü, Turizm İşletmeciliği Anabilim Dalı, Yayımlanmamış Yüksek Lisans Tezi, İstanbul.

Du Rand, G., and Heath, E. (2006). Towards a framework for food tourism as an element of destination marketing. *Current Issues in Tourism*, *9*(3), 206–234.

Edosomwan, S., Prakasan, S.K., Kouame, D., Watson, J., and Seymour, T. (2011). The history of social media and its impact on business. *Journal of Applied Management and Entrepreneurship*, *16*(3), 79–91.

Euromonitor International (2011). Make way for Generation Z: marketing to today's tweens and teens. Accessed March 20, 2020 at https://oaltabo2012.files.wordpress.com/2012/03/make-way-for-generation-z1.pdf.

Evans, D. (2010). *Social Media Marketing: The Next Generation of Business Engagement*. John Wiley & Sons.

Fister-Gale, S. (2015). Forget millennials: are you ready for Generation Z. *Chief Learning Officer, 14*(7), 38–48.

Fox, R. (2007). Reinventing the gastronomic identity of Croatian tourist destinations. *International Journal of Hospitality Management, 26*(3), 546–559.

Friedrich, R., Peterson, M. Koster, A., and Blum, S. (2010). The rise of Generation C: implications for the world of 2020. Booz & Company. Accessed March 20, 2020 at http://www.strategyand.pwc.com/media/file/Strategyand_Rise-of-Generation-C.pdf.

Gacnik, A. (2012). Gastronomy heritage as a source of development for gastronomy tourism and as a means of increasing Slovenia's tourism visibility. *Academia Turistica, 5*(2), 39–60.

Gajic, M. (2015). Gastronomic tourism – a way of tourism in growth. *Quaestus, 6,* 155–166.

Gheorghe, G., Tudorache, P., and Nistoreanu, P. (2014). Gastronomic tourism, a new trend for contemporary tourism. *Cactus Tourism Journal, 9*(1), 12–21.

Goyal, S. (2013). Advertising on social media. *Scientific Journal of Pure and Applied Sciences, 2*(5), 220–223.

Guzman, L.T., and Canizares, S.S. (2011). Gastronomy, tourism and differentiation: a case study in Spain. *Review of Economics and Finance, 2*(1), 63–72.

Haddouche, H., and Salomone, C. (2018). Generation Z and the tourist experience: tourist stories and use of social networks. *Journal of Tourism Futures, 4*(1), 66–79.

Hall, C.M., Sharples, L., Mitchell, R., Macionis, N., and Cambourne, B. (2004). *Food Tourism around the World.* Routledge.

Hargittai, E. (2010). Digital na(t)ives? variation in ınternet skills and uses among members of the net generation. *Sociological Inquiry, 80*(1), 92–113.

Harrington, R.J. (2005). Defining gastronomic identity: the impact of environment and culture on prevailing components, texture and flavors in wine and food. *Journal of Culinary Science and Technology, 4*(2–3), 129–152.

Harrington, R.J., and Ottenbacher, M.C. (2010). Culinary tourism: a case study of the gastronomic capital. *Journal of Culinary Science and Technology, 8,* 14–32.

Hassan, S.B. (2013). Social media and destination positioning: Egypt as a case study. *European Journal of Tourism, Hospitality and Recreation, 4*(1), 98–103.

Hay, B. (2017). Gastronomy, tourism and the media. *Journal of Tourism Futures, 3*(2), 184–185.

Hays, S., Page, S.J., and Buhalis, D. (2013). Social media as a destination marketing tool: its use by national tourism organisations. *Current İssues in Tourism, 16*(3), 211–239.

Hollier, P. (2009). The "intangible" benefits of social media. Accessed April 1, 2020 at http://seowizardry.ca/The_Wizards_Blog/the%E2%80%9Cintangible%E2%80%9D-benefits-of-social-media/.

Horng, J.S., and Tsai, C.T. (2012). Culinary tourism strategic development: an Asia-Pacific perspective. *International Journal of Tourism Research, 14*(1), 40–55.

Junco, R., Heiberger, G., and Loken, E. (2011). The effect of Twitter on college student engagement and grades. *Journal of Computer Assisted Learning, 27*(2), 119–132.

Kahvecioğlu, J., Bekar, A., and Kılıç, B. (2019). Z Kuşağının Gastronomi Turizmine İlişkin Tutumlarının Yenilik Arayışı Kapsamında Değerlendirilmesi. *Journal of Tourism and Gastronomy Studies, 7*(4), 2855–2872.

Kapil, Y., and Roy, A. (2014). Critical evaluation of generation Z at workplaces. *International Journal of Social Relevance and Concern, 2*(1), 10–14.

Kaplan, A.M., and Haenlein, M. (2010). Users of the world, unite! The challenges and opportunities of social media. *Business Horizons, 53*(1), 59–68.

Kara, Y., and Coşkun, A. (2012). Sosyal Ağlarin Pazarlama Araci Olarak Kullanimi: Türkiye'deki Hazir Giyim Firmalari Örneği. *Journal of Economics and Administrative Sciences / Afyon Kocatepe Üniversitesi Iktisadi ve Idari Bilimler Fakültesi Dergisi, 14*(2).

Karaduman, N. (2017). Popüler Kültürün Oluşmasında ve Aktarılmasında Sosyal Medyanın Rolü. *Erciyes Üniversitesi Sosyal Bilimler Enstitüsü Dergisi, 31*(43), 113–133.

Karim, S.A.B., and Chi, C.G.Q. (2010). culinary tourism as a destination attraction: an empiricial examination of destinations food image. *Journal of Hospitality Marketing and Management, 19*(6), 531–555.

Khang, H., Ki, E., and Ye, L. (2012). Social media research in advertising, communication, marketing, and public relations 1997–2010. *Journalism and Mass Communication Quarterly, 89*(2), 279–298.

Kietzmann, J.H., Hermkens, K., McCarthy, I.P., and Silvestre, B.S. (2011). Social media? Get serious! Understanding the functional building blocks of social media. *Business Horizons*, *54*(3), 241–251.

Kirakosyan, K. (2014). The managerial view of social media usage in banking industry: case study for Romanian banking system. *Proceedings of the International Management Conference, Faculty of Management, Academy of Economic Studies, Bucharest, Romania*, 8(1), 225–241.

Kivela, J., and Crotts, C.J. (2005a). Gastronomy Tourism. *Journal of Culinary Science and Technology*, *4*(2–3), 29–55.

Kivela, J., and Crotts, J.C. (2005b). Gastronomy tourism: a meaningful travel market segment. *Journal of Culinary Science and Technology*, *4*(2–3), 39–55.

Kivela, J.J., and Crotts, J.C. (2006). Tourism and gastronomy: gastronomy's influence on how tourists experience a destination. *Journal of Hospitality and Tourism Research*, *30*(3), 354–377.

Knoll, J. (2016). Advertising in social media: a review of empirical evidence. *International Journal of Advertising*, *35*(2), 266–300.

Kuran, E. (2013). Yaşasın Y Kuşağı!. Röportaj: Ayşe Arman, Hürriyet, June 9 and 11, 2013. Access ed April 5, 2020 at https://www.hurriyet.com.tr/yasasin-y-kusagi-23465715.

Lange-Faria, W., and Elliot, S. (2012). Understanding the role of social media in destination marketing. *Tourismos*, *7*(1), 193–211.

Lanier, K. (2017). 5 things HR professionals need to know about Generation Z. *Strategic HR Review*, *16*(6), 288–290.

Levickaite, R. (2010). Generations X, Y, Z: how social networks form the concept of the world without borders (the case of Lithuania). *LIMES: Cultural Regionalistics*, *3*(2), 170–183.

Lin, Y.C., Pearson, E.T., and Liping, A. (2011). Food As a form of destination identity: a tourism destination brand perspective. *Tourism and Hospitality Research*, *11*(1), 30–48.

McCrindle, M., and Wolfinger, E. (2009), *The ABC of XYZ: Understanding the Global Generations*. UNSW Press.

Nestle, M. (2013). *Food Politics: How the Food İndustry İnfluences Nutrition and Health* (Vol. 3). University of California Press.

Okumus, B., Koseoglu, M.A., and Ma, F. (2018). Food and gastronomy research in tourism and hospitality: a bibliometric analysis. *International Journal of Hospitality Management*, *73*, 64–74.

Okumus, B., Okumus, F., and McKercher, B. (2007). Incorporating local and international cuisines in the marketing of tourism destinations: the cases of Hong Kong and Turkey. *Tourism Management*, *28*(1), 253–261.

Özdemir, G., and Altıner, D.D. (2019). Gastronomi Kavramları ve Gastronomi Turizmi Üzerine Bir İnceleme. *Erzincan Üniversitesi Sosyal Bilimler Enstitüsü Dergisi*, *12*(1), 1–14.

Özdemir, G., and Celebi, D. (2015). Reflections of destinations on social media. In Katsoni, V. (ed.), *Cultural Tourism in a Digital Era* (pp. 243–249). Springer.

Ozkan, M., and Solmaz, B. (2015). Mobile addiction of Generation Z and its effects on their social lifes (an application among university students in the 18–23 age group). *Procedia – Social and Behavioral Sciences*, *205*, 92–98.

Prakash Yadav, G., and Rai, J. (2017). The Generation Z and their social media usage: a review and a research outline. *Global Journal of Enterprise İnformation System*, *9*(2),110–116.

Puiu, S. (2016). Generation Z – A new type of consumer. *Young Economists Journal*, *13*(27), 67–79.

Pullphothong, L., and Sopha, C. (2013, February). Gastronomic tourism in Ayutthaya, Thailand. In *Proceedings of the International Conference on Tourism, Transport, and Logistics* (Vol. 1416).

Rambe, P., and Jafeta, R.J. (2017). Impact of social media advertising on high energy drink preferences and consumption. *Journal of Applied Business Research (JABR)*, *33*(4), 653–668.

Richards, G. (2002). Gastronomy: an essential ingredient in tourism production and consumption. *Tourism and Gastronomy*, *11*, 2–20.

Rimskii, V. (2011). The influence of the Internet on active social involvement and the formation and development of identities. *Russian Social Science Review*, *52*(1), 79–101.

Ritholz, B. (2010). History of social media. Accessed March 10, 2020 at http://www.ritholtz.com/blog/2010/12/history-of-social-media/.

Rodríguez-Fernández, M.M., Artieda-Ponce, P.M., Chango-Cañaveral, P.M., and Gaibor-Monar, F.M. (2017). Gastronomy as a part of the Ecuadorian identity: positioning on the internet and social networks. In Freire, F., Rúas Araújo, X., Martínez Fernández, V., and García, X. (eds), *Media and Metamedia Management* (pp. 335–341). Cham: Springer.

Sánchez-Cañizares, S.M., and López-Guzmán, T. (2012). Gastronomy as a tourism resource: profile of the culinary tourist. *Current İssues in Tourism, 15*(3), 229–245.

Santich, B. (2004). The study of gastronomy and its relevance to hospitality education and training. *International Journal of Hospitality Management, 23*(1), 15–24.

Schroer, W.J. (2015). Generations X, Y, Z and the others. Accessed April 2, 2020 at http://socialmarketing .org/archives/generations-xy-z-and-the-others/.

Schwabel, D. (2014). Gen Y and Gen Z Global Workplace Expectations Study. Accessed March 25, 2020 at http://millennialbranding.com/2014/geny-genz-global-workplace-expectations-study/.

Sidali, K.L., Spiller, A., and Schulze, B. (eds) (2011). *Food, Agri-Culture and Tourism: Linking Local Gastronomy and Rural Tourism: Interdisciplinary Perspectives*. Springer Science & Business Media.

Singh, A. (2014). Challenges and issues of Generation Z. *IOSR Journal of Business and Management, 16*(7), 59–63.

Sormaz, U., Akmese, H., Gunes, E., and Aras, S. (2016). Gastronomy in tourism. *Procedia Economics and Finance, 39*, 725–730.

Tang, J., Williams, A.M., Makkonen, T., and Jiang, J. (2019). Are different types of interfirm linkages conducive to different types of tourism innovation?. *International Journal of Tourism Research, 21*(6), 901–913.

Tavares, J.M., Sawant, M., and Ban, O. (2018). A study of the travel preferences of generation Z located in Belo Horizonte (Minas Gerais-Brazil). *E-Review of Tourism Research, 15(2–3)*, 223–241.

Turner, A. (2015). Generation Z: Technology and social interest. *Journal of Individual Psychology, 71*(2), 103–113.

Winston, B. (1998). *Media Technology and Society: A History: From the Telegraph to the Internet*. Psychology Press.

Wood, S. (2013). *Generation Z as consumers: trends and innovation*. Institute for Emerging Issues, NC State University.

Yiğit Seyfi, Ü. (2016). X ve Y kuşaklarının ruhsal zeka özellikleri ile çalışma algıları üzerine bir analiz. Yayınlanmamış Doktora Tezi, Manisa: Celal Bayar Üniversitesi Sosyal Bilimler Enstitüsü.

Zeng, B., and Gerritsen, R. (2014). What do we know about social media in tourism? A review. *Tourism Management Perspectives, 10*, 27–36.

Zengin, B., and Arıcı, S. (2017). Konaklama İşletmelerinin Sosyal Medya Kullanım Şekillerinin Tüketici Satın Alma Niyeti Üzerindeki Etkisi. *İşletme Araştırmaları Dergisi, 9*(4), 375–399.

Zorn, B.R.L. (2017). Coming in 2017: a new generation of graduate students – the Z generation. *College and University, 92*(1), 61–64.

32. Uncovering food experience from social media

Kuan-Huei Lee, Zhengkui Wang and Nur Syazreema Binte Sazari

INTRODUCTION

Singapore is one of the cities well known for its diversity of food; the island is positioned as one of the most attractive food tourism destinations in Asia (Brien, 2014). Singapore is a multi-racial country consisting of Chinese, Malay, Indian and Eurasian ethnic groups. Visitors encounter a large variety in the choice of food, from hawker centers to high-end Michelin star restaurants. Being a heavily urbanized country, Singapore sees new eateries launching almost every month to satisfy customers' demand, even though it is a small city-state.

Singapore is also known to be one of the most digitally connected nations. According to *The Global Information Technology Report 2010–2011* (Soumitra and Irene, 2011) published by the World Economic Forum, Singapore came out second in the rankings and topped Asia for advancement in technologies. A local news article reported that the country was also ranked the highest internationally for smartphone penetration, and a survey by Deloitte in 2015 showed that nine out of ten respondents in Singapore own a smartphone.

With the introduction of smartphones, social media was the main application used and it became the main source of communication. Singaporeans spend an average of 45 hours per week on social media channels, namely Facebook, Instagram and Twitter (Hashmeta, 2015). These mediums are used to share opinions and reviews about products and to interact with other users. Netizens have the habit of sharing their own experiences and opinions about travels, food and service; this sharing is known as electronic word-of-mouth (eWOM). These micro-blogging sites could be the best platforms to obtain instant feedback within a few clicks.

Using big data analytics, the present study investigates consumers' dining experiences and satisfaction based on online reviews. The two main strands of this study are social media platforms and selected eateries in Singapore. The two social media platforms Twitter and Instagram were used to compare the findings on 20 chosen eateries – ten hawker centers and ten cafés – in Singapore.

FOOD CONSUMPTION IN SINGAPORE

Singapore became an independent country after separating from Malaysia in 1965. After more than five decades, it has developed from a third world to a first world country, and the island has an abundance of food service providers of all varieties. The country is home to mainly Chinese, Malay and Indian races, which means visitors have a broad range of cuisines to choose from. According to the Food & Beverage Services Index (Statistics Singapore, 2017), Singapore has approximately 7000 food outlets and the expenditure on food and beverages (F&B) was SG$748 million in 2017.

The gross domestic product (GDP) per capita at nominal value in Singapore reached US$56 319 (SG$75 700), rating at number 9 in the world, in 2014 (World Bank, 2015). The economic growth and stability in Singapore and its openness to international visitors have enabled Singapore to position itself globally as a well-known gourmet city. Every year, there are about 15 million tourists visiting Singapore, and F&B can account for as much as one-third of their total expenditure (STB, 2016). The average check per customer in a full-service restaurant is SG$56, compared to SG$9 in a quick-service restaurant, and SG$15 in kiosks (Centre, 2014).

Unique and memorable gastronomic experiences in a destination will have positive impacts on WOM advertising and intention to revisit a place (Kivela and Crotts, 2005). Positive food experiences might become peak experiences for visitors in their overall travel experience (Quan and Wang, 2004). It is therefore important to understand consumers' overall food experiences in Singapore and their satisfaction level with these food encounters. From a destination marketing organization (DMO) point of view, food can be a theme to be exploited in promoting local tourism and in expressing local identity.

Food enthusiasts can be segmented into culinary, gastronomic, cuisine or gourmet tourists, reflecting the view of consumers who consider their interest in food and wine to be "serious leisure." One motivating factor for food tourists to travel is the opportunity to visit food-related institutions and events (Hall and Sharples, 2008). For instance, gourmet tourists may travel to France or Italy in search of elite Western cuisine experiences, while gourmet package trips from Asian countries to Europe may include Michelin star restaurants in their itineraries (Hjalager and Richards, 2002). Food is a representation of the historical experience of a society, and Singapore is known as a city with a diverse world of flavours, providing a range of cuisines including Chinese, Malay, Indian and Peranakan (Chua and Rajah, 2001).

Hawker stalls have a long history in Singapore that can be traced back to before the country's independence. Hawkers had long been selling different kinds of food on the street but in the 1970s the government implemented hygiene regulations and prevented illegal trading (Kong, 2007). Currently, every Singaporean eats out on average four times a week, and the most frequent dining places include hawker centers and coffee shops (Centre, 2014).

SOCIAL MEDIA

Social media or social networking is very popular amongst all generations in Singapore. It is widely used on a daily basis, with users creating and sharing content to interact with other users on the internet. Some of the prominent applications used are Facebook, Instagram, Twitter, YouTube, Pinterest, WhatsApp and LinkedIn. Each of these platforms has its own specialty of usage. For instance, Facebook is commonly used to reconnect with friends and to share articles such as news, gossip, blogs, and much more. It also allows users to preserve memorable events that have occurred by allowing them to share photo albums and videos. Instagram, on the other hand, specializes in photo-sharing. Users usually post well-taken pictures on their account to share with their followers as a record. Twitter is used to create short texts (also known as micro-blogging) that are visible to users' followers. Other than texts, images and clips can also be shared. Other users are able to re-tweet the tweets if they find them interesting.

Through social media, netizens are able to garner information about any subject, including reviews on a certain eatery or its food. On Instagram, for instance, users have the habit of posting photos of the food whenever they try out a new cuisine. Together with that photo,

Table 32.1   *Eateries in Singapore selected in this project*

No.	Café name	District	No.	Hawker center name	District
1	Artistry	Central	1	Adam Road Food Center	Central
2	Bodoque Café	East	2	Bugis Street	Central
3	Crossroads Café SG	Central	3	Chinatown Hawker Centre	Central
4	Fluff Bakery	Central	4	East Coast Park	East
5	Paddy Hills	West	5	Geylang Serai	East
6	Prive Café	South	6	Holland Village	Central
7	Riders Café	West	7	Jalan Kayu	North
8	The Lab	Central	8	Lao Pa Sat	Central
9	The Lokal	Central	9	Satay by the Bay	South
10	Wild Honey	Central	10	Simpang Bedok	East

a short caption will be included, which normally describes what they think about the food. These are considered as food reviews reaped from social media (Kim et al., 2016).

Another source to obtain food reviews is via blogs. Food bloggers occasionally share their reviews on the cuisines they had in restaurants so that netizens would have a rough idea about a certain dish. That way, a trip to the restaurant would be worthwhile because consumers would already have a suitable pick in their mind. This will increase customers' satisfaction and improve the eatery's reputation. However, the idea of relying on food bloggers only is not recommended, as they are normally paid a huge sum for their reviews. It might be worrying to discover that the good reviews given are not genuine, but based on the incentives given. It was reported in the *Business Times* that a food blogger by the name of Ladyironchef was paid up to SG$3800 for a single advertisement on his blog. Some of the netizens felt disgusted by this, and argued that food bloggers should pay for their meals anonymously in order to give purposeful reviews (FoodDiary.com, 2013).

Social media is one of the most efficient ways to spread messages, as it is free and reachable within a few clicks. Four out of five brands now utilize Twitter as a marketing tool, while 65 percent of small business owners claimed that social media has helped them stay connected with their customers. Since social media has succeeded in attracting and holding users, it is assuredly one of the most powerful tools for giving and getting reviews (Leung et al., 2013).

METHODOLOGY

For this study, ten cafés and ten hawker centers in Singapore were selected for analysis purposes. Two crawlers to scrape information from Twitter and Instagram were performed in early 2017. All the information gathered was then converted into meaningful stories to benefit the end users. A list of the 20 selected eateries is shown in Table 32.1. These two types of eateries (hawker center and café) were chosen due to their popularity, based on a pre-study survey conducted for this project. Comparisons were established between consumers' experiences and satisfaction when they dine in a hawker center and a café.

A website was created to feature tweets and Instagram posts related to the 20 cafés and hawker centers studied in this project. This provides genuine information, as consumers usually share the posts right after experiencing the food. This website was called FoodSpread as it gave users a spread of information about food. The posts were updated regularly and presented using interesting charts for a better understanding. Through the charts, users were able to make comparisons and correlations between the eateries and social media platforms.

Data Collection using Web Scraping

Social media has become one of the most critical platforms for Singaporeans and tourists to share their dining experiences in Singapore. For this study, the team collected the dining experience data from social media platforms for the selected Singapore eateries, which enabled large-scale data collection and timely updates. In particular, all the tweets and Instagram posts related to the selected eateries from Twitter and Instagram were collected by developing automated data crawlers (Castillo, 2005). Data crawlers are computer programs that can browse the World Wide Web in a systematic and automated manner. Note that FoodSpread can easily be extended to support other social media datasets.

The abundant information on Twitter and Instagram might not have direct relevance to the eateries the team were interested in. The team first investigated what feeds (for example, hashtags, official web pages for those eateries) could be used to crawl the data related to the relevant eateries. Then, the team developed scripting programs to collect all the information automatically. The crawled data was stored in a secured local database for analysis purposes.

SENTIMENT ANALYSIS

With the collected data, the study aimed to analyze the consumers' experiences and satisfaction after dining in a hawker center or a café. A sentiment analysis was performed based on the collected data. Sentiment analysis has been widely used in different applications to discover people's opinions expressed in a written text. By identifying the sentiment from the text, questions such as "What does a person feel about their dining experience?" or "What is the attitude of the customer towards a particular eatery?" can be answered. Sentiment analysis brings together various research areas of natural language processing, text mining and data mining. Intuitively, a positive sentiment of commenting on a dining experience indicates a consumer's satisfaction, while a negative one indicates their dissatisfaction. Therefore, sentiment analysis enabled our system to discover the customers' opinions over a huge number of tweets and posts about various eateries in Singapore.

Data Pre-processing

To perform the sentiment analysis, the first thing is to pre-process the data. The Tweets and Instagram comments are short messages. Due to the nature of short and quick messages, people may use acronyms, emoticons and other characters that express special meanings. For example, emoticons are the facial expressions pictorially represented using punctuation and letters; the target @ symbol refers to other users on the message; and hashtags are used to mark topics. The message may contain information that may not contribute to the sentiment discovery. The data pre-processing allows the algorithm to remove this information.

Two different dictionaries were adopted to pre-process the data: the emoticon dictionary and an acronym dictionary. The emotion dictionary includes the popular emotions people commonly use in social media platforms, for example :) for happy and :(for unhappy. The acronym dictionary includes the acronyms that people typically use, such as gr8t for "great."

The data pre-processing consisted of different steps. First, the emotion symbols were changed to their sentiment polarity based on the emotion dictionary. Second, all the URLs and targets were removed from messages as they do not have any sentiment meaning. Third, all the acronyms were converted into their interpretation. Finally, all the text written in other languages was translated into English or removed to improve the performance of the sentiment analysis.

Sentiment Classification

After the data pre-processing, the team further developed the model to classify the messages into different sentiment categories, namely positive, neutral and negative. A positive message indicates a good experience in the text, while a negative message indicates a bad experience. Neutral messages are those ones without any emotions.

For sentiment classification, there are three major approaches: (1) the machine learning-based approach (Jin et al., 2009); (2) the lexicon-based approach (Colbaugh and Glass, 2013; Taboada et al., 2011); and (3) the hybrid approach (Ahmad et al., 2017). The machine learning-based approach is to steer a set of labeled datasets towards a classification model by choosing different word features. The lexicon-based approach is to assign the sentiment scores to each word based on positive and negative lexicon dictionaries. As its name suggests, the hybrid approach tries to integrate these two models together. The main disadvantage of the machine learning models is their reliance on the labeled data. It is extremely challenging to ensure that sufficient and correctly labeled data can be obtained from the social media datasets. Therefore, in this study, the team decided to apply a lexicon-based approach to avoid the need to generate a labeled training dataset.

The basic idea of the lexicon-based sentiment analysis approach is to adopt the sentiment lexicon to derive a sentiment score for all the messages. There are different available sentiment lexicons that can be applied, such as the SentiWordNet (Esuli and Sebastiani, 2006). Typically, each word in the lexicon is associated with a sentiment score. For example, a positive word is represented with a positive value, and a negative word is represented with a negative value. To better classify a message, the team further cleaned the message by removing all the words that may not contribute to the sentiment scoring, such as the function words (a, the, these). Then, the team combined all the evidence and sentiment values of the message to decide a final sentiment score for the message. Based on the final score derived, the message could finally be given one of the labels: positive, negative or neutral. These messages classified into sentiment categories provided the insights about the dining experience. For the 20 selected eateries, the team completed the sentiment analysis of their own data and aggregated the findings towards a better decision-making process.

Website Design

The FoodSpread website takes these following three components very seriously: usability, intuitiveness and visual design. The information was presented in a concise and unambiguous manner. The placement of items was easy to use and understand at one glance. To reduce overcrowding, fewer words were used. Attractive graphics were used to describe a feature instead. This leads to a good visual design, with neutral colours being employed so that the website stays professional.

The website was categorized into two categories: core pages and peripheral pages. Core pages refer to the main pages, which contain food information presented in a form of visualization. Peripheral pages refer to the non-dynamic pages where stories from the findings and the media are placed. The following are the pages of FoodSpread website. The Homepage, Twitter page and Instagram page were the core pages for collection of data.

Homepage

Previously, the look of FoodSpread page was rather plain and uninteresting as there was no graphical display. After adding the image carousel, the purpose of the website becomes clearer as users are able to identify what the website is about at a glance. Colour-wise, the theme of the website is monochrome with a splash of pink to match the logo. It is recommended to use a maximum of five different colours (plus or minus two) in a website design (Helander, 2014). This protocol makes the website look neater and not too chaotic. Users' main purpose in coming to a website is to perform a specific task, hence simplicity is key.

Another essential feature of every website is the navigation menu whereby users can cross from one page to another. For this website, the team implemented a vertical menu bar as it gives a better user experience. A vertical menu bar provides an easy navigation on a single page and is suitable for any screen size. In addition, sub-menus would not disrupt the content of the website, unlike with a horizontal menu bar. This navigation style gives the website a more compact look and helps to keep attention focused on the core pages.

Twitter Page

The next page on the list of the navigation bar is the Twitter page. There are two sub-pages for Twitter, namely "Twitter Information" and "Twitter Posts." Twitter Information consists of information that is visualized in the form of charts. Twitter Posts shows a table of tweets, displaying useful information such as the username, date, time, tweet, location, satisfaction level and also topic.

Twitter Information page

A column graph and a donut chart were used to display the information, as they are easy to understand and have the data displayed clearly when toggled. Column graphs summarize a huge amount of data in a visually interpretable form. This will improve user experience as the insight of the results can be grasped quickly.

Twitter Posts page

This page displays in a table all the tweets that have been collected. Table view improves readability and allows users to see the information clearly as it is well organized according to the types of information. Other than summarizing a large dataset in a visual form, a bar chart is good for displaying relative numbers or percentages of multiple categories. It also highlights key values at a glance and does not look too cluttered. A donut chart, on the other hand, is one of the less commonly used charts, chosen because the team wants to display something fresh and different. It is similar to a pie chart, but a donut chart allows data labels and values to be displayed in the hole of the chart. This helps to save some space on the website as legends are not required. Another attractive element is the toggle effect. Different information is displayed when a mouse hovers over other parts of the chart. This feature will instantly attract users' attention and make them stay longer on the website.

Instagram Page

The third page on the navigation bar is the Instagram page. There are three sub-pages for Instagram, namely "Instagram Information," "Instagram Posts" and "Instagram Photos." Instagram Information consists of information that is visualized in the form of charts. Instagram Posts, on the other hand, shows a table of posts, displaying the username, date, time, caption, link to the image posted, satisfaction level and also topic. Lastly, Instagram Photos consists of all the images collected which are related to the 20 eateries mentioned in Table 32.1.

Instagram Information page

Similar to the Twitter Information page, a column graph and donut charts are used to display the findings from Instagram. When one part of the donut chart is clicked on (for example, "Fun"), all posts related to the topic will be displayed underneath the chart.

Instagram Posts page

This page displays all the Instagram posts in a table. A table view improves readability and allows users to see the information clearly, as it is well organized according to the types of information.

Instagram Photos page

Additional information that has been collected from Instagram is in the form of images. Users have the habit of sharing aesthetic photos on their accounts; these photos are displayed on this page using the grid view to give users a better idea about what the food looks like. A table is used to display all tweets, as it is the most constructive way to display a chunk of information with multiple fields. Users can read the information easily if it is displayed in a table. To make their tasks easier, a drop-down filter is also included above the table so that they can choose which eatery to focus on. For the images, a grid view is chosen for easier viewing as it allows bigger thumbnails, hence the images will be clearer. Since the information displayed is not lengthy (only the caption and date are displayed), it is not necessary to use a list view for image display.

Information Integration on FoodSpread

One purpose of this case study is to do a comparison or correlation between the reviews on the 20 selected eateries gathered on Twitter and Instagram. The FoodSpread webpage was designed to display the integrated information from both the Twitter database and the Instagram database.

A stacked bar chart was used to display combined information from both databases. For instance, if a user wants to know in which area hawker centers have the most positive reviews from both social media, they should be looking at the north, as it has the highest positive portion on the bar chart. The web page presents the data about the 20 eateries extracted from both databases (Twitter and Instagram) and integrates all the information together, separating only the type of eatery, that is, hawker center or café. Users can filter the type of eatery they wish to look at by using the radio button above the chart. This page gives users the flexibility to toggle between information based on what they require.

After the crawling process, classification of sentiments and topic detention phases were completed, the project was left with one remaining component to be completed, which was the web application. The web application is the most important component as it serves as the "face" of the project. No matter how efficiently the program works, users would not be interested in engaging with the system without an interesting user interface.

The main idea of the website is to show all the information that has been crawled from both social media platforms. However, it is different from other food portals in the sense that all data is presented in the form of charts. Existing websites commonly have the contents displayed in plain words, and that may actually bore users as the site is either too simple or too wordy. Other than seeing the data using charts, users are also able to read the full tweets and Instagram posts on our website. They also have the choice to filter what they wish to see. This helps when users are already aware of what they want and do not wish to confuse themselves with too much information. For Instagram specifically, since its main element is images, the images were displayed in a grid view. This not only helps users in deciding which cuisine to choose, but also gives them a real insight into what the dishes look in real life.

CONCLUSION AND LIMITATIONS

This study investigated consumers' satisfaction based on the micro-blog posts available online after they have experienced the food, services and surroundings of a particular eatery. The findings were collated and presented on a website in visual form for easier understanding and neater presentation. This particular way of presentation could be an alternative to analyze the standard and quality of the food and other related information that might be obtained online. This method would help netizens in choosing a preferred place to eat at, especially when they are dining there for the first time.

The following is a summary of views extracted from the Twitter Information page:

1. 55 percent of the positive reviews gathered from the Twitter users are directed to the cafés.
2. The reviews on hawker centers gathered from Twitter have a balanced spread of satisfaction level, that is, positive, neutral and negative.
3. However, at the beginning of the year 2017, hawker centers seemed to receive more positive feedbacks from Twitter users.
4. Of the hawker centers, Jalan Kayu received the most (61 percent) positive reviews.
5. Of the cafés, Prive Café received the most (72 percent) positive reviews.
6. Looking into the negative reviews received on Twitter, Laopasat has the highest number (77 percent). The most frequently recurring topic for Laopasat is "CBD," which stands for the central business district in Singapore.
7. Badoque Café received the most negative ratings (48 percent), with "crying" appearing as the most frequently recurring topic.

The following is a summary of the views extracted from the Instagram Information Page:

1. It seemed that the frequency of negative reviews found on Instagram is less compared to Twitter. This appears to show that consumers have the habit of sharing only good things on Instagram, because of the app's culture.
2. Of the hawker centers, Bugis Street received the highest number of positive reviews (60 percent). The most frequently recurring topic is "Food."
3. Of the cafés, Paddy Hill SG Café received the most positive reviews (66 percent), with "Fun" appearing as the most frequently recurring topic.

For Hawker centers:

1. The hawker centers located in the north of Singapore received the most positive comments (61 percent).
2. Based on location, hawker centers located in the east and central districts of Singapore have about the same results.
3. Looking at the top ten recurring topics, the top topics that received positive comments are "ayam" (chicken) and "Canning" (referring to Fort Canning, one of Singapore's attractions).
4. The hawker centers with the most positive reviews are Jalan Kayu, Adam Road Food Center and Satay by the Bay.

For cafés:

1. Cafés located in the eastern district of Singapore have the highest percentage (47 percent) of negative reviews.
2. The most common topic for cafés is "FoodHealth."
3. Paddy Hills has the most (69 percent) positive reviews.

All these findings could help future diners in making the right decision before they dine at an unknown eatery, with the hope of encountering a good experience. The government and stall owners can also benefit from this case study. With proper study of the findings, they are able to analyze consumers' eating behaviour and work towards achieving better decision-making.

Limitations of this study include the fact that the targeted audience might be confined to a certain population that use Twitter and Instagram as a medium to express their opinions. The time of conducting the data collection might also be influenced by seasonality and might extend the length of data collection. However, the team presented a promising approach to study food consumers. The ordinary way of collating food reviews is normally through interviews and user observation, which might be costly and time-consuming. Differently, in our study, the team adopted a technology-enhanced solution to tackle the limitation of traditional food consumer studies. In particular, crawling social media data for food experience enables us to collect more feedback data from a large number of customers automatically and quickly, which is likely to provide more accurate insight. Furthermore, adopting artificial intelligence techniques such as sentiment analysis and natural language processing enabled us to discover the customers' satisfaction and interest intelligently by analyzing text data written by customers. The FoodSpread system provides users with an intuitive way to examine the findings using informative visualizations.

This study has opened up various research opportunities in the domain. As our future research work, the team will study more eateries and collect data from more social media platforms and food review websites. It is interesting to study the user behaviour pattern difference among different platforms and eateries. In addition, the team will also investigate the food experience difference among various groups of customers with differences in age, gender or ethnicity.

REFERENCES

Ahmad, M., Aftab, S., Ali, I., and Hameed, N. (2017). Hybrid tools and techniques for sentiment analysis: A review. *International Journal of Multidisciplinary Sciences and Engineering*, *8*, 31–38.

Brien, D.L. (2014). A taste of Singapore: Singapore food writing and culinary tourism. *M/C Journal*, *17*(1), 3–13.

Castillo C. (2005). Effective web crawling. *ACM SIGIR Forum*, *39*(1), 55–56.

Centre, S.P. (2014). Productivity benchmarking report (Food service). Retrieved from https://www.sgpc .sg/resources/benchmarking-portal-2/.

Chua, B.H., and Rajah, A. (2001). Hybridity, ethnicity and food in Singapore. In David Y.H. Wu and C.B. Tan (eds), *Changing Chinese Foodways in Asia*. Hong Kong: Chinese University Press.

Colbaugh, R., and Glass, K. (2013). Analyzing social media content for security informatics. Paper presented at the 2013 European Intelligence and Security Informatics Conference.

Deloitte (2015). Global mobile consumer survey. Retrieved from https://www2.deloitte.com/gu/en/ pages/technology-media-and-telecommunications/articles/2015-mobile-consumer-sea.html.

Esuli, A., and Sebastiani, F. (2006). Sentiwordnet: A publicly available lexical resource for opinion mining. Paper presented at the Fifth International Conference on Language Resources and Evaluation (LREC'06).

FoodDiary.com (2013). There is no such thing as a free meal. This is the cost of food blogging. Retrieved from https://danielfooddiary.com/2013/11/14/costoffoodblogging/.

Hall, C.M., and Sharples, L. (2008). Food events, festivals and farmers' markets: An introduction. In C.M. Hall and L. Sharples (eds), *Food and Wine Festivals and Events around the World: Development, Management and Markets* (pp. 3–22). Amsterdam: Elsevier/Butterworth-Heinemann.

Hashmeta (2015). Social media in Singapore. Retrieved from https://hashmeta.com/blog/social-media -singapore-2015/.

Helander, M.G. (2014). *Handbook of Human–Computer Interaction*. Amsterdam: Elsevier.

Hjalager, A.-M., and Richards, G. (2002). *Tourism and Gastronomy* (Vol. 11). London: Routledge.

Jin, W., Ho, H.H., and Srihari, R.K. (2009). OpinionMiner: A novel machine learning system for web opinion mining and extraction. Paper presented at the 15th ACM SIGKDD International Conference on Knowledge Discovery and Data Mining.

Kim, W.G., Li, J., and Brymer, R.A. (2016). The impact of social media reviews on restaurant performance: The moderating role of excellence certificate. *International Journal of Hospitality Management*, *55*, 41–51. doi:10.1016/j.ijhm.2016.03.001.

Kivela, J., and Crotts, J.C. (2005). Gastronomy tourism: A meaningful travel market segment. *Journal of Culinary Science and Technology*, *4*(2–3), 39–55.

Kong, L. (2007). *Singapore Hawker Centres: People, Places, Food*. Singapore: National Environment Agency.

Leung, D., Law, R., van Hoof, H., and Buhalis, D. (2013). Social media in tourism and hospitality: A literature review. *Journal of Travel and Tourism Marketing*, *30*(1–2), 3–22.

Quan, S., and Wang, N. (2004). Towards a structural model of the tourist experience: An illustration from food experiences in tourism. *Tourism Management*, *25*(3), 297–305.

Statistics Singapore (2017). F&B Service Index. Retrieved from https://www.singstat.gov.sg/find-data/ search-by-theme/industry/services/latest-data.

Soumitra, D., and Irene, M. (2011). *The Global Information Technology Report 2010–2011*. World Economic Forum. Retrieved from http://reports.weforum.org/wp-content/pdf/gitr-2011/wef-gitr-2010 -2011.pdf.

STB (2016). *Singapore Annual Report*. Retrieved from https://www.stb.gov.sg/content/stb/en/media -centre/corporate-publications/annual-reports.html.

Taboada M., Brooke J., Tofiloski M., Voll K., and Stede, M. (2011). Lexicon-based methods for sentiment analysis. *Computational Linguistics*, *37*, 267–307.

World Bank (2015). The World Bank in Singapore. Retrieved from https://www.worldbank.org/en/ country/singapore/overview.

33. Sharing photos of food traveler experiences: a case study of foodstagramming

Sevinc Goktepe, Merve Aydogan Cifci and Mehmet Altug Sahin

Today, the impact of social media on people is too great to be ignored. With social media, people can find ways to show aspects of their lives which are different from the ordinary, in terms of sociability, networking, and so on (Andersen and Pold, 2015). For this purpose, millions of posts are generated on social media platforms every day. People share pieces from their own lives and support them with short captions. In addition, they can create interactions by opening these posts to everyone. These posts come with hashtags that link posts about the same topic (Dhingra et al., 2016).

The growing popularity of the internet and social media makes it faster, cheaper and more efficient to distribute information than traditional methods (Lafreniere and Basil, 2019). Email, e-marketing, mobile marketing and or social media are potentially powerful tools, and they are inexpensive (Noam, 2019). By posting images on social media people are creating an uplifting virtual sharing economy (Hall, 2016).

Food has become one of many travel motives and may influence travelers' preferences for food and their travel outcomes (Ji et al., 2016). Experiences from food-related tourism movements arise with people's curiosity for new tastes and different cultural forms of food and beverages (Harun et al., 2019). Different motives for sharing these experiences and making them accessible to other individuals on social media platforms have led to a new social media term: foodstagramming.

The mentality of eating and the food itself is not just for filling the stomach any more. It has now transformed into a sign or symbol that people want to show on social media via foodstagramming (Destriana et al., 2020). Despite the popularity of foodstagramming, the studies about this social phenomenon are rare, with little if any academic literature reporting on it to date (Wong et al., 2019).

In this study, the subject of sharing food experience is examined by addressing the related social media platforms. It focuses on foodstagramming as a prominent subject and its possible effects in terms of user-generated content (UGC) and electronic word-of-mouth (e-WOM). Then a foodstagrammer, Yemek Müptelası, is presented and analyzed as a case study within the framework of these topics.

SOCIAL MEDIA AND FOOD EXPERIENCES

Social platforms are media tools, which allow people to communicate with each other, share music, photos, ideas, and so on (Papadopoulou et al., 2017). Social media platforms consist of blogs, collaborative projects (for example, Wikipedia), social networking sites (for example, Facebook), content communities (for example, YouTube), virtual social worlds (for example,

Second Life) and virtual gaming worlds (for example, World of Warcraft) (Kaplan and Haenlein, 2010).

Some social media platforms – such as social networking sites and content communities – allow users to upload and share their videos, photos, and so on (Tan and Loo, 2014) with a network of contacts (Minazzi, 2015). They also enable users to take photographs, apply digital photographic filters and upload the image, together with a short caption (Zappavigna, 2016). On these platforms, not only photos taken from special moments such as trips or parties, but also photos taken from everyday life – such as food – can be shared (Yanai et al., 2019). Briefly, social media platforms provide different ways for users to express their opinions online (Scott, 2011).

Social media platforms do what food does best: they bring people together. Therefore, if there is one area that has been reformed by social media, it is the world of food (Rousseau, 2012). Food is one of the most fundamental components of our daily life (Sheng et al., 2018). But in today's world, it has become more than this. People are showing the world what they eat by photographing everyday meals and expressing themselves, probably even more clearly than they might have, by only mentioning the names of the meals (Murphy, 2010). The things shared are shaping communities and people. Therefore, the types of images that have been chosen to share online reveals much about people. As people share more and more images of food online, they are sending the message of "we are what we eat" (Bouvier, 2018).

Experience Sharing Through Social Media: UGC and e-WOM

UGC refers to media content created or produced by regular people who voluntarily contribute data (Krumm et al., 2008) and primarily distribute it on the web (Daugherty et al., 2008). UGC sites create new viewing patterns and social interactions, empower users to be more creative, and develop new business opportunities (Cha et al., 2007). These platforms help to establish viable business models based on lively forums, blogs and personalized social network sites where users can publish their own diaries on their own websites, post photos or videos, express opinions, meet other users and establish communities based on shared interests (Leung, 2009).

Nowadays, hundreds of internet users are not only consumers, but also publishers of content (Cha et al., 2009). Most UGC across various media is brand-related and has the potential to shape consumer brand perceptions (Smith et al., 2012) and influence viewers' decisions (Cox et al., 2009). Customers' likes and dislikes, positive or negative reviews, can also be viewed by other potential customers (Tiago et al., 2017). Most commercial sites can convert surfers into buyers with this interaction. For example, retailing sites such as Amazon.com and Ebay.com encourage their consumers to write reviews about products they have purchased on their sites, and use these reviews as promotional tools (O'Connor, 2008). Briefly, UGC has the power to serve as a new form of word of mouth for products/services or their providers (Ye et al., 2011).

Word-of-mouth (WOM) is known for providing the most reliable information from actual consumers to potential ones (Chi and Qu, 2008). E-WOM as an electronic version of WOM is defined as "any positive or negative statement made by potential, actual, or former customers about a product or company which is made available to multitude of the people and institutes via the Internet" (Hennig-Thurau et al., 2004, p. 39). E-WOM has a complex process which includes incomprehensible motivations of customers to share their experience with others that service producers cannot actually manage (Jalilvand and Samiei, 2012). However, it has greater credibility and greater ability to evoke empathy for marketing activities compared to commercial corporate efforts (Bickart and Schindler, 2001). Furthermore, the information shared by a trustworthy person (famous blogger, gourmet, and so on), without any compulsion of the producer, is considered as a more reliable source for a stronger marketing activity. E-WOM also enables reaching wider specific groups to encourage purchasing behavior (Setiawan, 2014), while providing product information visibility for a long period of time without any costs.

Social media is a very commonly known tool for e-WOM. One of the sources of the UGC is social media, which shows some different characteristics for both sender/narrator and receiver of the marketing message. While the sender/narrator can create rich content, the receiver can also be interactive. The sender/narrator generally is willing to share elements of satisfaction, pleasure or sadness, due to different motivation factors (Sotiriadis and Van Zyl, 2013). The receivers evaluate these elements with various expectations such as honesty, credibility, encouragement, inspiration, guidance, and so on. Therefore, the recommendations of prior customers are seen as crucial for purchasing decisions, where e-WOM plays a central role.

Particularly Instagram, which is known for UGC, is also one of the social media tools for e-WOM. Instagram earned its reputation by focusing on photo and video content created by its users. This is seen as an advantage for visualizing experiences, to create targeted images. Reviews and recommendations are not imaginary and supported with photos and short videos. UGC of food, restaurants, and so on, on Instagram is considered a very convenient way of e-WOM.

Motivations of Sharing Photos of Food Travel Experiences in Social Media

The camera is seen as a traveler's "identity badge" (Chalfen, 1979), and photography has been intrinsically linked with tourism, as if one cannot travel without being engaged in some forms of photography (Lo and McKercher, 2015). Therefore, photo taking and its motivations have become notable research topics in tourism and travel experiences (Albers and James, 1983; Kim and Stepchenkova, 2015; Lo and McKercher, 2015; Lyu, 2016). Travelers take photos during their visit to "consume them with their eyes" (Dinhopl and Gretzel, 2016). They also may want to make other people comment on their photos. They share the photos with family and friends to show their feelings and experiences. Since photos capture the moment while traveling or experiencing, they also expose the individuals' point of view, behaviors, and so on.

In sharing the photos and travel experiences, relationships have been transformed by new communication technologies. The photos shared with audiences are not only limited to family members and friends as before, but can also be shared with followers who posters are not acquainted with (Lo and McKercher, 2015). People do not even have to wait until returning home to share these experiences (Prideaux and Coghlan, 2010). As a result, methods and motivations for sharing photos have changed much more since the development of communication technologies such as social media or blogging.

Food experience seekers – just like other experience-seeking travelers – have various motivations for sharing photos on social media. They take photos and share on social media not only to let people know what they do, but also to share their experiences, such as paying attention to togetherness, friendship, social presence, self-identification, self-presentation and so on (Wong et al., 2019). Capturing the moment is particularly meaningful to satisfy the need to remembering it. Yet, the photo taking motivations are not concerned only with recall.

As a relatively new phenomenon, motivations of sharing food experience photos on social media can be classified as functional and psychological motivations towards oneself or other people. For the self, functional motivations are concerned with recording experiences and information, and digital convenience; while psychological motivations are more concerned with social approval, and emotions while creating content and interacting with others, managing one's self-image and showing off. Functional motivations towards other people focus on sharing information about destination and experience, influencing the decision-making of others and reassuring family/friends about their food experiences. Psychological motivations are more focused on making others feel a certain way, social interaction, reminiscing with a companion and representing oneself through food (Wang et al., 2017).

Some psychological motivations for sharing content on social media are also explained with psychological ownership theory. This theory is defined with the needs of efficacy, having a place and self-identity. Social media users mostly feel a need to learn about and express themselves (Karahanna et al., 2015). In this manner particularly, self-identity is related to people's endeavor to define, express and maintain their identity, shown by means of their belongings (Wang et al., 2017). Consumer behavior is strongly supported by the statement "we are what we have" (Tuan, 1980), and social media is a remarkable tool for observing individuals' behaviors.

On the other hand, a food experience is very tough to understand and share. Smell, aromas and flavors can be described, but are helpful to understand the taste. However, they are not enough for sharing a food experience that includes feelings of taste and atmosphere. Taste experience is subjective and cannot be exactly described and psychologically shared (Trubek, 2008). Therefore, a food traveler's photo taking and sharing motivations can also be related to making people understand food taste characteristics and feelings about their own experience (Chi and Qu, 2008).

FOODSTAGRAMMING: A MEETING POINT OF INSTAGRAM AND BLOGGING

Blogs used to contain long articles. When people realized that after their long hours spent writing them, their blogs were not read as they once were, they no longer wanted to devote their time to blogs. Yet, blogs are not completely dead. They have started to evolve into something better and more useful. Today, blogs are shared on different social media platforms, such as Instagram. Thus, the term "Instablogging" emerged (Turner and Shah, 2010). Briefly, Instablogging is a way of combining people's desires to write to blogs and share photos. This means using Instagram as a blog, experiencing and sharing things such as products or services via different themes with audiences. Food is one of these Instablog themes, and "foodstagramming" is the sharing of experience on Instagram using food photos.

Food Blogging

Blogs are personal websites written by people who are passionate about a topic and share that passion with the world (Scott, 2011), and are the best-known form of invitation that writers use to initiate conversations with readers online (Thurman, 2008). Blogs function as personal diaries, but as publicly accessible ones (Koh, 2017). Hence, bloggers disclose their lives to the readers, in an attempt to foster connections, promote interactivity and involvement on their blogs (Lepkowska-White and Kortright, 2018). They encourage, even require, engagement and production from users, as opposed to passive consumption (Pennell, 2018).

David Meerman Scott, the author of *The New Rules of Marketing and PR*, expresses his feelings about social phenomena by saying, "How amazing is it that something you create has the potential to keep spreading from one person to the next and, in the process, expose your ideas to people you don't even know?" (Scott, 2011). Therefore, blogs are important social networks for two reasons. First, a considerable amount of effort goes into writing good blogs. Second, some bloggers have a reputation that helps them attract followers influenced by their content (Dhar and Chang, 2009).

Food blogging is one of the UGC platforms for the internet-savvy generation to communicate and express their sense of identity. Blogging removes the borders between the professional and amateur, the private and the public (Koh, 2017). Food blogging, moreover, has the potential to become even more close, as it deals with something so mundane and necessary (Rousseau, 2012). Just as food blogs offer individuals opportunities for entry into food-related media professions, they also offer media and other industries some opportunities to promote their own services and products (Lepkowska-White and Kortright, 2018), reach broader audiences and source new talents (Lofgren, 2013). They do this via influencers, "who create leads with product information or purchasing a product or a service online" (Van Looy, 2016).

There are many blog platforms (BlogSpot, YouTube, and so on) where influencers share their articles, videos and photos. Therefore, users can easily get plenty of information about a food and beverage business from these blog platforms (Chang et al., 2017). However, blogging is not a platform where bloggers only interact with followers; they also refer to and link to one another's blogs, and state their desire to try a certain food or meal after seeing it on another blog (Lynch, 2010). It is also a grassroots and widespread activity that is not exclusively the domain of professionals or bloggers (Kozinets et al., 2017). This makes the food photo sharing more attractive for all segments.

Food Photos, Instagram and Hashtags

Instagram, which has over 1 billion monthly active users, allows people to edit and share photos with the public or with pre-approved followers. In 2018, there were approximately 3.7 million sponsored influencer posts on the platform. The most popular worldwide content type of Instagram posts by influencers were photos and videos, which accounted for just 13.56 percent of influencer posts (Clement, 2020a). A significant feature of Instagram is that, instead of simply browsing through the content, users can also add comments to the images they see, and see others' comments, and like them as well (Zimmerman and Brown-Schmidt, 2020).

Hashtags can be encountered on multiple social media platforms. In general, they play the role of a keyword that explains the topic and aids the users in finding related results (Small, 2011). They are also being used as an important function on Instagram. Instagram allows its users to add hashtags to their captions, stories, and so on, while sharing photos or videos (Hu et al., 2014), which can also act as a filter (Schlesselman-Tarango, 2013).

Food is no longer something that people share simply around a table, and recipes are not only shared with neighbors (Petit et al., 2016). With the development of social media, a new class-based eating phenomenon has emerged: "food porn" (Koh, 2017). "Food porn" is a combination of the words of "food" and "pornography." This phenomenon refers to the current ubiquity of food as a topic of conversation, a field of research, and the engine of imaginative literature and art practice (Carruth, 2013), and also attracts people to ask for the virtual while complicating the relationship with real (Chan, 2003). Briefly, the line between fiction and reality is often blurred in the visual representation of food (Koh, 2017).

"Food porn" is a term for photos and videos of food that are extremely glorified (Arumsari and Agung, 2019), and which are associated with cultural distinction and elevated tastes (Donnar, 2017). The world is now experiencing a phenomenon called "eat and tweet" or "first camera then fork" (Murphy, 2010), or "camera eats first" (Koh, 2015), where an increasing number of people are sharing photos of the food that they cook or eat through various social platforms such as Instagram, Twitter and Facebook (Amato et al., 2017). Also, many bloggers and food celebrities (Johnston and Goodman, 2015) who share their photographs on Tumblr, Instagram and Pinterest refer to their blogs as "food porn," or sometimes, alternatively, "gastro porn" (Lavis, 2017). Regardless of the many names of this social media stream, "food porn" term has been accepted by the vast majority of social media users.

Food travelers use hashtags to reach people interested in reviewing food experiences. In addition to narcissistic reasons, the motivation for sharing photos with these tags is seen as more related to people's wish for acknowledgement of social economic status in a specific group (Ranteallo and Andilolo, 2017). Sharing these photographs with hashtags, consumer experience embodies the user's judgment of taste, feeding into their mediated self-presentation on social media (Peng, 2019).

The hashtag #foodporn refers to any visual or written representation (Majors, 2012) of food that people use to glamorize their cooking or eating by posting beautiful and attractive pictures (Amato et al., 2017) across various social media platforms. The hashtag #foodporn is one of the most popular hashtags on social media, often accompanied by a close-up of a tantalizing dish (Mejova et al., 2016). This hashtag is the best friend of internet users, who display media-worthy culinary brands, famous burger joints, and exquisitely prepared meals from great restaurants on social media (Marti and Berthelot-Guiet, 2019). Thus, #foodporn can be interpreted as a positive attribute, expressing consumers' enthusiasm for food products (Klostermann et al., 2018).

People share #foodporn to derive satisfaction by demonstrating conspicuous consumption (Narumi, 2016). The magnitude of this phenomenon is suggested by the number of pictures accompanied by the corresponding hashtag on social networks: over 228 million images can be found on Instagram with the hashtag of #foodporn (Cavazza et al., 2020). Yet, nowadays, it is very common to see an Instagram post associated with multiple hashtags (Zhang, 2019). For instance, according to current data, #food on Instagram has more than 394 million results, usually being followed by #foodporn with 231 million, #instafood with 173 million, #yummy with 156 million, #foodie with 155 million, #delicious with 112 million results – and the list goes on (Yan and Corino, 2019).

Foodstagramming

Foodstagramming is a phenomenon whereby people take photos of their food and post them on Instagram (Behm-Morawitz et al., 2017). The reason for the occurrence of this phenomenon is due to many culinary lovers' intentions of taking photos of food and posting them on Instagram (Wardhani and Putri, 2018) to share with other users and let others see, give likes and comment on the photos uploaded (King and Paramita, 2016). Foodstagram was born out of Instagram and probably started from a simple act, such as sharing food with friends or showing off fancy foods to show people that you are rich, and eventually this activity has become a global trend (Arumsari and Agung, 2019). The logic is simple: cook or order a nice dish, feel good about yourself, share it with others on social media, watch the likes flood in, and feel even better (Hall, 2016). In fact, for foodstagrammers who get so accustomed to photographing their supper, abstaining from this ritual can make them feel as if an important ingredient is missing (Bogomilova, 2016).

Instagram has a great potential to motivate people for food traveling. Foodstagrammers' photos or video content are criticized by other followers. Furthermore, they also encourage or discourage shared food content. Therefore, the follower is also able to evaluate recommendations voted on by other interested people.

Foodstagrammers also (some of them mostly) share barely known cultural food, regional gastronomy or creative lifestyles, which are significant for them. E-WOM via foodstagramming could be an easy, efficient and cheap way for marketing less-known touristic products, to transform them to be a part of unique touristic experiences. Foodstagrammers have the potential for becoming mediators between experience seekers and local gastronomy.

A CASE STUDY OF FOODSTAGRAMMING

Food experience and tourism are closely related. Today, gastronomy is becoming one of the most important travel objectives of tourists, with the desire of tourists to discover new, unique experiences and alternative forms of tourism (Akın, 2018). Present-day tourists who are active internet users come from different backgrounds and have different intentions. They can be food travelers, food bloggers, chef bloggers, food photographers and even extreme food travelers (Ranteallo and Andilolo, 2017). As a result, many people participate in travel especially to try local dishes. Foodstagrammers play a big role in this environment.

This study chooses the case study approach, focusing on the aforementioned issues. The foodstagrammer called Yemek Müptelası, who is the focus of our case study, has been generating food-oriented content since 2016. The founder of this page with over 194 000 followers is an ordinary person who is not an expert in the field of food or tourism, loves food, and enjoys taking pictures of food and beverages (King and Paramita, 2016). He also has a YouTube page which promotes local gastronomic products of Gaziantep, a region in Turkey. Like many foodstagrammers, the primary motivation for him to take food photographs is the love of food. It is a great pleasure for him to visit different cities, find previously unexplored flavor points, meet new people, chat with chefs and gourmets and listen to their stories. Briefly, the foodstagrammer experiences and then directs his followers in this sense.

Foodstagramming is one of the examples of experience marketing. Intentionally or not, the content about food on Instagram focuses on showing people how food is consumed, and which senses food appeals to. Therefore, sharing food photos on Instagram is seen as a way to create a platform which pushes people to be willing to pay more to engage the total of those senses. As Pine and Gilmore (1999) stated, experience or experiential marketing is related to transforming products in consumer's perception through creating added value. Since Yemek Müptelası and other foodstagrammers not only share the product but also share their experiences, they evoke marketers to find a new way to create added value.

Yemek Müptelası shows his followers where and which local dishes can be consumed in many destinations, while also promoting Gaziantep dishes and places. While he prefers to make food-based travel from time to time; he has recently been planning long trips of 20–30 days, aiming to find and visit places where he can taste local food and beverages. At this point, while determining the places to travel by first researching the food culture of that destination, he makes choices that will suit his own taste and also analyzes whether they will appeal to his followers.

Since food is both an essential necessity and a pleasure for people, it is important for foodstagrammers to check carefully before sharing their food photos. A good food photo is related to the color of the food and the right light. Yemek Müptelası prefers not to present any photographs he does not like to his followers. He chooses to share mouth-watering ("food porn") food photos and videos that appeal to the senses of his followers. Although the number of followers is of great importance for content generators, it is more important how actively interested the followers are in the page. At this point, Yemek Müptelası and other foodstagrammers provide confidence to their followers by analyzing them correctly. Many followers return to him after trying the dishes shared and experienced in his page. In this sense, the speed of social media in getting feedback is important for both foodstagrammers and businesses.

Gaziantep, which was entitled to join the United Nations Educational, Scientific and Cultural Organization (UNESCO) Creative Cities Network in Gastronomy branch in 2015, is a city where cultural interaction is high, and this is reflected in its food culture. Product variety has an impact on this, as well as the texture it has. Cooking meat and vegetable dishes with different spices in the region makes the dishes attractive for content generators (Aksoy and Sezgi, 2015). Domestic tourists traveling to this city only for food purposes think that they understand the culture of Gaziantep by consuming local gastronomic products (Sert, 2019). Researchers show that the passion for local food leads local tourists to visit Gaziantep again (Bayrakcı and Akdağ, 2016). At this point, foodstagrammers such as Yemek Müptelası can be a guide for followers who are curious about local foods. According to Yemek Müptelası, the effect of food sharing is an important issue. This is also valid for many cities leading in the field of gastronomy.

In addition, social media affects food preferences and restaurant choices in Gaziantep (Tuç and Özkanlı, 2017). Food and beverage business owners may be timid about foodstagrammers promoting their businesses. However, as the positive feedback comes in, more and more business owners want to cooperate with foodstagrammers. It is even possible to say that this has become a kind of industry. From time to time, businesses benefit from word-of-mouth communication by making agreements with bloggers. Thus, many destinations such as Gaziantep have the opportunity to promote both food culture and food and beverage businesses, thanks to bloggers.

UGC, created by foodstagrammers, plays an important role as e-WOM that acts as a meeting point for both businesses and followers. While promoting the food of a business or destination, it also triggers the followers' inclination to share these experiences. As a result of this process, the purchasing behavior is being encouraged. Yemek Müptelası plays the role of mediator between his followers and the businesses and destinations he experiences. As he shares his content with his followers, which acts as e-WOM, he intends to influence them in a positive way and try to evoke the urge to experience it themselves. If the follower decides to experience the food and share it on social media, it causes a loop of shared experiences, and the follower becomes the content generator. This never-ending process shows us the power of UGC and e-WOM.

CONCLUSION

Social media is constantly developing and becoming a daily activity of our lives. The increase in usage cannot be ignored, as there is a 3.81 billion active global social media population worldwide in 2020 (Clement, 2020b). They provide a massive amount of UGC data for research in tourism and related areas. Therefore, the persuasive power of UGC as e-WOM has become an important research topic in recent years (Lu and Stepchenkova, 2015).

Food takes up a lot of space in social media posts, as the most important part of our daily lives. In social media, there are not only people who generate content by focusing on food, but also ordinary people who share food which they cook or order in a restaurant. Briefly, food is one of the most common topics to be shared on social media. Because everyone eats.

Sharing memorable experiences about a destination which involve food can have an influence on the decision-making process of others (Wang et al., 2017). Food acts as a medium and an image (Ibrahim, 2015), that can create motives for traveling. Users can share their travel and food experiences with their followers and other social media users through various social media platforms such as blogs and Instagram.

Food experiences shared on various social media platforms have an effect on consumers. Information and suggestions provided from food blogs have an effect on the food consumption of others (Ho and Chang Chien, 2010), while Instagram plays a major role in advertising the food and the related experience (Kusumasondjaja and Tjiptono, 2019). The role of Instagram has transformed from being just a communication tool, to a more complex role which provides an economic, business and social configuration (Fatanti and Suyadnya, 2015). UGC, shared content on Instagram, plays an important role in the travel planning process (Cox et al., 2009) and offers each user the role of a marketer (Fatanti and Suyadnya, 2015). As a result of this trend, the "foodstagramming" term has emerged and is used for the sharing of food travel experience.

Yemek Müptelası was analyzed as a case study of foodstagramming. He plays the role of intermediary between his followers and the businesses and destinations. While making food experience-based shares, he becomes the sender/narrator of this marketing message and provides detailed information of his experience, which is referred to as UGC that acts as e-WOM.

Foodstagramming helps to promote the businesses and destinations through various social media platforms and acts as cues that help to elicit heuristic choices (Wong et al., 2019). It also becomes a new image that symbolizes a social class of the community (Destriana et al., 2020). As a result, as shown in Figure 33.1, UGC on social media about food, as mentioned for the case of foodstagramming, supplies one of the motivations for travel.

As a result, UGC on social media about food, as mentioned for the case of foodstagramming, is one of the examples of travel motivators. With different motivations, social media users share photos and they create a wide e-WOM platform. Consequently, e-WOM is likely to encourage food traveling and the circle repeats over and over again as it attracts and gathers more interested people. They are also motivated to take and share food photos and help to promote a destination. As also mentioned by (Gyimóthy and Mykletun, 2009) encouraging

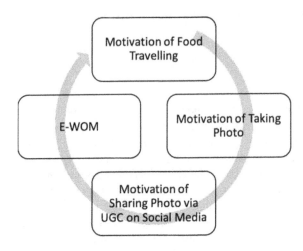

*Figure 33.1   Motivation circle of food traveling through e-WOM by sharing photo on
social media*

people to travel for food experiences and food media sharing is becoming an important factor
to attract potential consumers to a particular destination.

REFERENCES

Akın, A. (2018). Gaziantep in gastronomi şehri olarak belirlenmesinde demografik değişkenlerin etkisi
(The effect of demographic factors on determination of Gaziantep as a gastronomy city). *Journal of
Tourism and Gastronomy Studies*, *6*(2), 299–316.

Aksoy, M., and Sezgi, G. (2015). Gastronomi turizmi ve Güneydoğu Anadolu Bölgesi gastronomik
unsurları (Gastronomy tourism and Southeastern Anatolia Region gastronomic elements). *Journal of
Tourism and Gastronomy Studies*, *3*(3), 79–89.

Albers, P.C., and James, W.R. (1983). Tourism and the changing photographic image of the Great Lakes
Indians. *Annals of Tourism Research*, *10*(1), 123–148. https://doi.org/10.1016/0160-7383(83)90119
-6.

Amato, G., Bolettieri, P., Monteiro de Lira, V., Muntean, C.I., Perego, R., and Renso, C. (2017). Social
media image recognition for food trend analysis. *Proceedings of the 40th International ACM SIGIR
Conference on Research and Development in Information Retrieval* (pp. 1333–1336).

Andersen, C.U., and Pold, S.B. (2015). Aesthetics of the banal – "new aesthetics" in an era of diverted
digital revolutions. In Berry, D.M., and Dieter. M. (eds), *Postdigital Aesthetics* (pp. 271–288).
Palgrave Macmillan.

Arumsari, R.Y., and Agung, L. (2019). Constructing deliciousness through instagram: the aesthetics of
foodstagram. *6th Bandung Creative Movement 2019* (pp. 351–355). Telkom University.

Bayrakcı, S., and Akdağ, G. (2016). Yerel yemek tüketim motivasyonlarının turistlerin tekrar ziyaret
eğilimlerine etkisi: Gaziantep'i ziyaret eden yerli turistler üzerine bir araştırma. *Anatolia: Turizm
Araştırmaları Dergisi*, *27*(1), 96–110.

Behm-Morawitz, E., Choi, G., and Miller, B. (2017). Psychological perspectives on the impact of marketing and media on ethnic groups. In Blume, A.W. (ed.), *Social Issues in Living Color: Challenges
and Solutions from the Perspective of Ethnic Minority Psychology: Overview and Interpersonal Issues*
(pp. 283–304). Praeger/ABC-CLIO.

Bickart, B., and Schindler, R.M. (2001). Internet forums as influential sources of consumer information.
Journal of Interactive Marketing, *15*(3), 31–40.

Bogomilova, A. (2016, October 16). The psychology of foodstagramming. Socialmediapsychology.eu. http://socialmediapsychology.eu/2016/10/16/psychology-of-foodstagramming/.

Bouvier, E. (2018). Breaking bread online: social media, photography and the virtual experience of food. In Namaste, N., and Nadales, M. (eds), *Who Decides?* (pp. 157–172). Brill Rodopi.

Carruth, A. (2013). Culturing food: bioart and in vitro mea. *Parallax*, *19*(1), 88–100.

Cavazza, N., Graziani, A.R., and Guidetti, M. (2020). Impression formation via# foodporn: effects of posting gender-stereotyped food pictures on instagram profiles. *Appetite*, *147*. DOI: https://doi.org/10.1016/j.appet.2019.104565.

Cha, M., Kwak, H., Rodriguez, P., Ahn, Y.Y., and Moon, S. (2007). I tube, you tube, everybody tubes: analyzing the world's largest user generated content video system. *Proceedings of the 7th ACM SIGCOMM Conference on Internet Measurement* (pp. 1–14).

Cha, M., Kwak, H., Rodriguez, P., Ahn, Y.-Y., and Moon, S. (2009). Analyzing the video popularity characteristics of large-scale user generated content systems. *IEEE/ACM Transactions on Networking*, *17*(5), 1357–1370.

Chalfen, R.M. (1979). Photograph's role in tourism: some unexplored relationships. *Annals of Tourism Research*, *6*(4), 435–447.

Chan, A. (2003). "La grande bouffe" cooking shows as pornography. *Gastronomica*, *3*(4), 46–53.

Chang, S., Ciampo, M., and Mitchell, H. (2017). Creating images with impact: food photography tips from MyPlate. *Journal of the Academy of Nutrition and Dietetics*, *117*(8), 1171–1173.

Chi, C.-Q., and Qu, H. (2008). Examining the structural relationships of destination image, touristsatisfaction and destination loyalty: an integrated approach. *Tourism Management*, *29*, 624–636.

Clement, J. (2020a, May 14). Number of daily active Instagram Stories users from October 2016 to January 2019. Statista. https://www.statista.com/statistics/730315/instagram-stories-dau/.

Clement, J. (2020b, May 18). Social media – statistics and facts. Statista. https://www.statista.com/topics/1164/social-networks/#dossierSummary__chapter7.

Cox, C., Burgess, S., Sellitto, C., and Buultjens, J. (2009). The role of user-generated content in tourists' travel planning behavior. *Journal of Hospitality Marketing and Management*, *18*(8), 743–764.

Daugherty, T., Eastin, M.S., and Bright, L. (2008). Exploring consumer motivations for creating user-generated content. *Journal of Interactive Advertising*, *8*(2), 16–25.

Destriana, N.M., Pranawa, S., and Nurhadi, N. (2020). Foodstagramming hyperreality in consumption behavior in Indonesia. *Harmoni Sosial: Jurnal Pendidikan IPS*, *7*(1), 85–95.

Dhar, V., and Chang, E.A. (2009). Does chatter matter? The impact of user-generated content on music sales. *Journal of Interactive Marketing*, *23*, 300–307.

Dhingra, B., Zhou, Z., Fitzpatrick, D., Muehl, M., and Cohen, W.W. (2016). Tweet2vec: character-based distributed representations for social media. *Proceedings of the 54th Annual Meeting of the Association for Computational Linguistics* (pp. 269–274). Association for Computational Linguistics, Berlin.

Dinhopl, A., and Gretzel, U. (2016). Selfie-taking as touristic looking. *Annals of Tourism Research*, *57*, 126–139.

Donnar, G. (2017). "Food porn" or intimate sociality: committed celebrity and cultural performances of overeating in Meokbang. *Celebrity Studies*, *8*(1), 122–127.

Fatanti, M.N., and Suyadnya, I.W. (2015). Beyond user gaze: how Instagram creates tourism destination brand? *2nd Global Conference on Business and Social Science* (pp. 1089–1095). Procedia – Social and Behavioral Sciences, Bali.

Gyimóthy, S., and Mykletun, R. (2009). Scary food: commodifying culinary heritage as meal adventures in tourism. *Journal of Vacation Marketing*, *15*(3), 259–273.

Hall, J.P. (2016, November 30). "Foodstagramming" has changed the way we eat. Gulfnews. https://gulfnews.com/food/foodstagramming-has-changed-the-way-we-eat-1.1937767.

Harun, A.F., Ruslan, N., Suliman, S.I., Ismail, J., Baharin, H., and Noor, N.L. (2019). We who eats: understanding food perception upon first sight. *Journal of Image and Graphics*, *7*(2), 39–44.

Hennig-Thurau, T., Gwinner, K., Walsh, G., and Gremler, D.D. (2004). Electronic word-of-mouth via consumer-opinion platforms: what motivates consumers to articulate themselves on the Internet? *Journal of Interactive Marketing*, *18*(1), 38–52.

Ho, H.-Y., and Chang Chien, P.-H. (2010). Influence of message trust in online word-of-mouth on consumer behavior – by the example of food blog. *International Conference on Electronics and Information Engineering (ICEIE 2010)* (pp. 395–399).

Hu, Y., Manikonda, L., and Kambhampati, S. (2014). What we Instagram: a first analysis of Instagram photo content and user types. *Proceedings of the Eighth International AAAI Conference on Weblogs and Social Media* (pp. 595–598). Association for the Advancement of Artificial Intelligence.

Ibrahim, Y. (2015). Food porn and the invitation to gaze: ephemeral consumption and the digital specta-cle. *International Journal of E-Politics, 6*(3), 1–12.

Jalilvand, M.R., and Samiei, N. (2012). The impact of electronic word of mouth on a tourism destination choice: testing the theory of planned behavior (TPB). *Internet Research, 22*(5), 591–612.

Ji, M., Wong, I.A., Eves, A., and Scarles, C. (2016). Food-related personality traits and the moderating role of novelty-seeking in food satisfaction and travel outcome. *Tourism Management, 57*, 387–396.

Johnston, J., and Goodman, M.K. (2015). Spectacular foodscapes: food celebrities and the politics of lifestyle mediation in an age of inequality. *Food, Culture and Society, 18*(2), 205–222.

Kaplan, A.M., and Haenlein, M. (2010). Users of the world, unite! The challenges and opportunities of social media. *Business Horizons, 53*, 59–68.

Karahanna, E., Xu, S., and Zhang, N. (2015). Psychological ownership motivation and use of social media. *Journal of Marketing Theory and Practice, 23*(2), 185–207.

Kim, H., and Stepchenkova, S. (2015). Effect of tourist photographs on attitudes towards destination: manifest and latent content. *Tourism Management, 49*, 29–41.

King, K.N., and Paramita, E.L. (2016). Foodstagram endorsement and buying interest in café/restaurant. *Jurnal Manajemen dan Kewirausahaan, 18*(2), 100–110.

Klostermann, J., Plumeyer, A., Böger, D., and Decker, R. (2018). Extracting brand information from social networks: integrating image, text, and social tagging data. *International Journal of Research in Marketing, 35*(4), 538–556.

Koh, G. (2017). Food porn as visual narrative: food blogging and identity construction. *SARE: Southeast Asian Review of English, 52*(1), 122–142.

Koh, J. (2015, December). Camera eats first: Is Instagram changing the way we eat? ... and is it for the better? Timeout. https://www.timeout.com/kuala-lumpur/restaurants/camera-eats-first-is-instagram -changing-the-way-we-eat.

Kozinets, R., Patterson, A., and Ashman, R. (2017). Networks of desire: how technology increases our passion to consume. *Journal of Consumer Research, 43*(5), 659–682.

Krumm, J., Davies, N., and Narayanaswami, C. (2008). User-generated content. *IEEE Pervasive Computing, 7*(4), 10–11.

Kusumasondjaja, S., and Tjiptono, F. (2019). Endorsement and visual complexity in food advertising on Instagram. *Internet Research, 29*(4), 659–687.

Lafreniere, K.C., and Basil, M.D. (2019). Vancouver Aquarium and World Wildlife Foundation's Great Canadian Shoreline Cleanup: increasing volunteerism by targeting social networks. In Basil, D., Diaz-Meneses, G., and Basil, M. (eds), *Social Marketing in Action* (pp. 327–338). Springer.

Lavis, A. (2017). Food porn, pro-anorexia and the viscerality of virtual affect: exploring eating in cyber-space. *Geoforum, 84*, 198–205.

Lepkowska-White, E., and Kortright, E. (2018). The business of blogging: effective approaches of women food bloggers. *Journal of Foodservice Business Research, 21*(3), 257–279.

Leung, L. (2009). User-generated content on the internet: an examination of gratifications, civic engage-ment and psychological empowerment. *New Media and Society, 11*(8), 1327–1347.

Lo, I.S., and McKercher, B. (2015). Ideal image in process: online tourist photography and impression management. *Annals of Tourism Research, 52*, 104–116.

Lofgren, J. (2013). Food blogging and food-related media convergence. *M/C Journal, 16*(3). http://www .journal.media-culture.org.au/index.php/mcjournal/article/view/638.

Lu, W., and Stepchenkova, S. (2015). User-generated content as a research mode in tourism and hospi-tality applications: topics, methods, and software. *Journal of Hospitality Marketing and Management, 24*(2), 119–154.

Lynch, M. (2010). Healthy habits or damaging diets: an exploratory study of a food blogging community. *Ecology of Food and Nutrition, 49*(4), 316–335.

Lyu, S.O. (2016). Travel selfies on social media as objectified self-presentation. *Tourism Management, 54*, 185–195.

Majors, K. (2012). Out of the frying pan: food in fiction. *Midwest Quarterly, 54*(1), 67–81.

Marti, C., and Berthelot-Guiet, K. (2019). Advertising or not advertising: representations and expressions of advertising digital literacy on social media. *International Conference on Human–Computer Interaction* (pp. 417–433). Springer.

Mejova, Y., Abbar, S., and Haddadi, H. (2016). Fetishizing food in digital age: #foodporn around the world. *Tenth International AAAI Conference on Web and Social Media.*

Minazzi, R. (2015). *Social Media Marketing in Tourism and Hospitality.* Springer International Publishing.

Murphy, K. (2010, April 6). First camera, then fork. *New York Times.* https://www.nytimes.com/2010/04/07/dining/07camera.html.

Narumi, T. (2016). Multi-sensorial virtual reality and augmented human food interaction. *Proceedings of the 1st Workshop on Multi-sensorial Approaches to Human–Food Interaction* (pp. 1–6).

Noam, E.M. (2019). *Managing Media and Digital Organizations.* Palgrave Macmillan.

O'Connor, P. (2008). User-generated content and travel: a case study on tripadvisor.com. In O'Connor, P., Höpken, W., and Gretzel, U. (eds), *Information and Communication Technologies in Tourism 2008* (pp. 47–58). Springer.

Papadopoulou, T., Nasiopoulos, D.K., and Vlachos, D. (2017). Merchandizing IT products via social networks. Modeling and simulation of the procedures. In Kavoura, A., Sakas, D., and Tomaras, P. (eds), *Strategic Innovative Marketing* (pp. 507–513). Springer.

Peng, A.Y. (2019). Sharing food photographs on social media: performative Xiaozi lifestyle in young, middle-class chinese urbanites' WeChat "moments." *Social Identities, 25*(2), 269–287.

Pennell, M. (2018). (Dis)comfort food: connecting food, social media, and first-year college undergraduates. *Food, Culture and Society, 21*(2), 255–270.

Petit, O., Cheok, A.D., and Oullier, O. (2016). Can food porn make us slim? How brains of consumers react to food in digital environments. *Integrative Food, Nutrition and Metabolism, 3,* 251–255.

Pine, J., and Gilmore, J. (1999). *The Experience Economy: Work is Theatre and Every Business a Stage.* Harvard Business School.

Prideaux, B., and Coghlan, A. (2010). Digital cameras and photo taking behaviour on the Great Barrier Reef – marketing opportunities for Reef tour operators. *Journal of Vacation Marketing, 16*(3), 171–183.

Ranteallo, I.C., and Andilolo, I.R. (2017). Food representation and media: experiencing culinary tourism through foodgasm and foodporn. In Saufi, A., Andilolo, I., Othman, N., and Lew A. (eds), *Balancing Development and Sustainability in Tourism Destinations* (pp. 117–127). Springer.

Rousseau, S. (2012). *Food and Social Media: You Are What You Tweet.* Altamira Press.

Schlesselman-Tarango, G. (2013). Searchable signatures: context and the struggle for recognition. *Information Technology and Libraries, 32*(3), 5–19.

Scott, D.M. (2011). *The New Rules of Marketing and PR: How to Use Social Media, New Releases, Online Video, and Viral Marketing to Reach Buyers Directly* (3rd edition). Wiley.

Sert, A.N. (2019). The effect of local food on tourism: Gaziantep case. *Gaziantep University Journal of Social Sciences, 18*(4), 1611–1625.

Setiawan, P.Y. (2014). The effect of e-WOM on destination image, satisfaction and loyalty. *International Journal of Business and Management Invention, 3*(1), 22–29.

Sheng, K., Dong, W., Huang, H., Ma, C., and Hu, B.-G. (2018). Gourmet photography dataset for aesthetic assessment. *SIGGRAPH Asia 2018 Technical Briefs* (pp. 1–4). Tokyo, Japan.

Small, T.A. (2011). What the hashtag? *Information, Communication and Society, 14*(6), 872–895.

Smith, A., Fischer, E., and Yongjan, C. (2012). How does brand-related user-generated content differ across YouTube, Facebook, and Twitter? *Journal of Interactive Marketing, 26,* 102–113.

Sotiriadis, M.D., and Van Zyl, C. (2013). Electronic word-of-mouth and online reviews in tourism services: the use of twitter by tourists. *Electronic Commerce Research, 13*(1), 103–124.

Tan, A., and Loo, P. (2014). Impact of food advertising in social media among local university students in Malaysia. *Proceedings of the Australian Academy of Business and Social Sciences* (pp. 1–12). Adelaide, Australia.

Thurman, N. (2008). Forums for citizen journalists? Adoption of user generated content initiatives by online news media. *New media and society, 10*(1), 139–157.

Tiago, T., Amaral, F., and Tiago, F. (2017). Food experiences: the oldest social network ... In Kavoura, A., Sakas, D.P., and Tomaras, P. (eds), *Strategic Innovative Marketing* (pp. 435–444). Springer.

Trubek, A.B. (2008). *The Taste of Place: A Cultural Journey into Terroir (Vol. 20)*. University of California Press.

Tuç, Z., and Özkanlı, O. (2017). Resource about reshaping of food and beverage culture by social media: Sample Gaziantep City. *Journal of Urban Culture and Management, 10*(2), 216–239.

Tuan, Y.F. (1980). The significance of the artifact. *Geographical Review, 70*(4), 462–472.

Turner, J., and Shah, R. (2010). *How to Make Money with Social Media: An Insider's Guide on Using New and Emerging Media to Grow Your Business*. Pearson Education.

Van Looy, A. (2016). *Social Media Management: Technologies and Strategies for Creating Business Value*. Springer Texts in Business and Economics.

Wang, S., Kirillova, K., and Lehto, X. (2017). Travelers' food experience sharing on social network sites. *Journal of Travel and Tourism Marketing, 5*, 680–693.

Wardhani, A.C., and Putri, A.W. (2018). Experience of communication and self-concept in foodstagrammer in Bandar Lampung City in phenomenology perspective. *Proceedings of International Indonesia Conference on Interdisciplinary Studies* (pp. 30–36). Lampung University, Bandar Lampung.

Wong, I.A., Liu, D., Li, N., Wu, S., Lu, L., and Law, R. (2019). Foodstagramming in the travel encounter. *Tourism Management, 71*, 99–115.

Yan, J., and Corino, G. (2019). Digital foraging: how social media is changing our relationship with food and nutrition? *DigitCult – Scientific Journal on Digital Cultures, 4*(3), 39–46.

Yanai, K., Okamoto, K., Nagano, T., and Horita, D. (2019). Large-scale Twitter food photo mining and its applications. *2019 IEEE Fifth International Conference on Multimedia Big Data (BigMM)* (pp. 77–85). IEEE.

Ye, Q., Law, R., Gu , B., and Chen, W. (2011). The influence of user-generated content on traveler behavior: an empirical investigation on the effects of e-word-of-mouth to hotel online bookings. *Computers in Human Behavior, 27*, 634–639.

Zappavigna, M. (2016). Social media photography: construing subjectivity in Instagram images. *Visual Communication, 15*(3), 271–292.

Zhang, Y. (2019). Language in our time: an empirical analysis of hashtags. *The World Wide Web Conference*, pp. 2378–2389.

Zimmerman, J., and Brown-Schmidt, S. (2020). #foodie: implications of interacting with social media for memory. *Cognitive Research: Principles and Implications, 5*, 1–16.

PART VII

BUSINESS PERFORMANCE-RELATED CHALLENGES

34. The effect of social media on business performance: a case study of a Turkish travel agency

Oya Yildirim

INTRODUCTION

The Internet has brought people closer than ever before by connecting those with similar interests, even if they are thousands of miles apart (Eley and Tilley, 2009). The Internet plays a vital role in ensuring social interaction between individuals and communities (Zolkepli and Kamarulzaman, 2015). Internet-based social media platforms have become an important element of daily life. Social media constitute an effective cyberspace in which individuals are able to access reliable and updated information continually and with ease (Tajvidi and Karami, 2017). Commercial advertisements, groups and/or personal pages on social media have a significant effect on people's purchasing behaviours. Individuals using social media can easily acquire information from others, including their experience of products and recommendations. This creates an environment of trust, and it influences what they buy (Chen et al., 2011).

Experience, information and photos shared through social media have a tremendous impact on customers, especially in the tourism sector where one cannot trial the product. Photos of the destinations to be visited, comments about accommodation or travel agencies, may affect the decisions that tourists make. Tourism enterprises that want to survive in an intensely competitive environment and increase their profitability must adapt to these developments. The business performance of companies that have managed to use social media effectively usually improves. Social media are seen as an influential billboard for business objectives and performance (Tajvidi and Karami, 2017). Therefore, firms keep in touch with their consumers through social media and work towards creating a good image through them. This is why tourist companies should not be indifferent to the use of social media.

The present chapter aims to explain the effect of social media usage on the performance of accommodation businesses and travel agencies, both of which occupy an important place in the tourism industry. It employs a case study methodology and looks at the performance of a travel agency based in Adana in Turkey to better analyse the possible effects of social media.

SOCIAL MEDIA AND MARKETING

'Social media' is a broad term that defines different types of content, for example blogs and forums, videos, photos, audio recordings, links, profile pages on social networking sites, and more (Eley and Tilley, 2009). Westbrook (1987) evaluated social media as an effective means of electronic word-of-mouth (eWOM) communication and described it as an unofficial communication space where consumers share knowledge about the use, features or sellers of products or services. In other words, social media are a group of Internet-based applications which, using Web 2.0 technology, allow the creation of user-generated content and the swapping of knowledge between users (Kaplan and Haenlein, 2010). Web 2.0 technology has made social media popular because it makes information more accessible. It also enables users to comment on content and express their opinions more generally. Thus, they can enjoy the benefits of mutual communication (Poynter, 2010). Today, social networks are expanding much faster than the Internet itself (Eley and Tilley, 2009).

Internet users interact with others using various social media devices, and share their experiences and opinions (Xiang and Gretzel, 2010). They use different social media components such as forums, blogs, micro-blogs, social networks, social marketing, photo and video sharing platforms, online publications and customer reviews to share their experiences (Wilson, 2010). Social media networks such as Wikipedia, Scribd, YouTube, Facebook, Twitter, Instagram, Google+ and Myspace have billions of users around the world, and often they are at the centre of people's lives. Digital 2020's report for January (WeareSocial, 2020) showed that digital, mobile and social media have become an indispensable part of daily life for many people around the world. More than 5.19 billion people use mobile phones worldwide. The number of people using the Internet increased by 7 per cent (298 million new users, and 4.54 billion users in total) between January 2020 and January 2019. There were 3.8 billion social media users worldwide in January 2020 (321 million of whom were new users), an increase of 9 per cent compared with the previous year. An Internet user spends an average of six hours and 43 minutes a day online, and uses social media for more than a third of this time. The most-used social media platforms are Facebook, YouTube, WhatsApp, Messenger, WeChat and Instagram (WeareSocial, 2020). They attract many tourism entrepreneurs.

The Internet has evolved from a platform for information to a platform for interaction (mostly via social media). This has made communication between firm and consumer highly interactive, to the point where the latter has a say in the nature, scope and context of marketing exchanges (Hanna et al., 2011). Consumers are no longer just passive buyers in the marketing process, but active agents in the co-creation with the company of everything from product design to promotional messages (Berthon et al., 2007). These developments in interactive digital media have revolutionised marketing and have radically changed the ecosystem of social media marketing (Walmsley, 2010). Many social media platforms have started to transform their understanding of marketing, advertising and promotion. Social media have become an integral part of the marketing mix. Businesses have started to market their products and services actively, drawing on the feedback they receive from Facebook, Instagram, YouTube, Twitter, and so on (Mangold and Faulds, 2009).

Social media marketing is described as a process that allows individuals or organisations to promote their own products by way of social media tools, and to communicate and interact with a large audience that conventional advertising channels cannot reach (Weinberg, 2009). Social media marketing covers various channels in which content marketing is implemented on the digital platform (Järvinen and Taiminen, 2016). This is what is known as non-traditional online marketing. Traditional marketing is referred to as interruptive marketing, because traditional marketing channels, such as television, radio and billboards, are designed to interrupt people's work and behaviour and disrupt their concentration. People have learnt to live with full-page advertisements in the middle of articles, with commercials before, during and after television programmes, and with hoardings at the side of roads with spectacular views (or not). Most use this kind of interruption as an opportunity to have something to eat, or absorb what is being presented to them. However, social media allow businesses to talk directly to their customers. Businesses create content, and actual or potential customers find, read and discuss it (Eley and Tilley, 2009). While it takes weeks to create brand awareness with traditional marketing, and months to become a brand in great demand, social media have the power to do it overnight (Scott, 2010). One of the key roles of social media is to spread information electronically through word-of-mouth, which has more transfer impact than traditional marketing methods and causes faster reactions (Kim et al., 2015). For example, marketers can reach millions of users in a very short time by preparing videos, with very little expertise, and uploading them to YouTube (Zarrella, 2009). Customer testimonials are extremely powerful, and word-of-mouth marketing has long been the most effective, cheapest and most successful form. When people meet online on social networks, they discuss whether they like products and services, and what is said spreads very quickly (Eley and Tilley, 2009). Therefore, ease of use, low cost and speed of transmission are the biggest attractions of social media marketing.

Social media marketing for promotion has two important and interrelated functions. The first is that companies can communicate with consumers. The second is that consumers can communicate with each other. This is what makes social media unique (Mangold and Faulds, 2009). Social media marketing is used to promote products, to increase brand awareness, and to enable businesses to keep track of what they are doing, in addition to communicating with consumers (Jason, 2010). Moreover, businesses use social media to create their own business plans by reviewing and trying to understand the successes of other businesses. Therefore, businesses should participate in organisations and activities where they meet with other companies and share their message. Thus, it is possible to have close contact with competitors, and at the same time have the opportunity to develop their businesses (Zarrella, 2009). Social media marketing is a way to achieve various business goals: creating brand awareness, examining consumer behaviour and customer groups, identifying opinion leaders, developing new marketing strategies and viral spreading private messages, increasing brand reputation, image and product sales, and initiating and maintaining lines of communication (Weinberg, 2009).

As with other platforms, it is important to adapt to innovations in social media and to be creative and sustainable. For this reason, the key methods to be applied to achieve success in social media marketing have been determined (Halligan and Shah, 2010). They are as follows:

1. Tell your story: people react most to stories.
2. Participate: it is necessary to follow and respond to comments. It is especially important to respond to adverse comments and to offer solutions to gain the trust of consumers who have judged the business negatively.
3. Be clear: social media provide the easiest platforms to build relationships on. You should treat people they way you want to be treated.
4. Be a listener: this will give you access to a great deal of information about your business.
5. Use social media for building long-term relationships before short-term campaigns. Continuous investment and organisational participation are required. They will not be reflected in the sales figures at the beginning, but if social media are used correctly, the business will be able to reach the target audience.

SOCIAL MEDIA AND BUSINESS PERFORMANCE

The role of marketing in explaining the business performance of companies has always been a topic of interest for scholars and practitioners of the discipline. Today, its role is clearer than previously (Morgan, 2012). Continuous changes in the market and in technology cause businesses to focus on entrepreneurial and innovative behaviours. These are a significant factor in improving the performance of companies. Therefore, developments in social media marketing and their effect on business performance of the enterprises have become increasingly important. Dynamic market conditions require businesses to continually review their goals and performance to remain competitive. The concept of performance is associated with the carrying out of a particular task, or reaching a goal. It also refers to the effective and efficient use by of resources by the business (Daft, 2000). It expresses the degree of success of a strategy at the end of a defined period (Porter, 1991).

The best way to monitor an enterprise's status, growth and progress in the market is to measure its performance against its intended goals. Businesses that regularly check their performance can avoid financial or organisational problems and thereby increase their productivity. Businesses need to track relevant metrics. Performance measurement involves finding the right key performance indicators (KPIs) and putting them to use. Income and profit indicators will ultimately determine the performance of businesses, but there are a number of other KPIs that should be prioritised. Unique website visitors, sample product downloads, volume of sales, revenue per visitor and page views per visitor are examples (Eley and Tilley, 2009).

Key performance indicators provide information about business performance and so, as has been noted, it is important to choose KPIs that are meaningful for the business and that help it to achieve positive results. These include marketing indicators, sales indicators, financial indicators and online indicators. Both financial and non-financial data are used to measure business performance. Marketing performance provides non-financial data and concerns factors such as sales, growth and market share, while financial performance refers to data on profitability and return on investment (Merrilees et al., 2011). In the 1960s and 1970s, performance measurements were based entirely on financial criteria. In the 1980s, financial criteria were seen to be focused on short-term goals; they offered a narrow perspective and were not a sufficient guide for success. In the 1990s, it was possible to adopt and digitise non-financial performance criteria and connect them seamlessly to the performance measurement system (Swamy, 2002). Researchers and managers became concerned with two distinctive aspects of business performance: product–market and financial (Morgan, 2012). Recently, innovation performance has been added (Eibe Sørensen, 2009).

Businesses may not want to disclose their financial data. One of the recommended methods for the confidentiality or objectivity of financial data is to compare business performance with competitors or past performance. Questions that are used to evaluate managers (for example, relating to the previous three years) can be developed to reduce the likelihood that information obtained from primary sources will be biased (He and Wong, 2004). Today, social media has a wide influence on all areas of business performance: financial, operational and corporate. Financial performance indicators usually contain details about profitability, stock price, and sales levels and growth. They focus on operational performance, product quality, new product introduction, operational efficiency, customer satisfaction and share position. Corporate social performance (CSP) is largely based on the company's ability to build relationships with the community with regard to its brand and reputation. Social media comprise seven functional sources (identity, chats, content sharing, reputation, presence, relationships and groups), and affect business performance through four channels. These are conceptualised as social capital, customers' revealed preferences, social marketing and corporate networks. The 'followers' and 'likes' increase the share value of a company (Paniagua and Sapena, 2014).

As has been stated, the wide use of smartphones and fast Internet connections have become widespread, and social media have become an integral part of people's lives. Visually oriented platforms are becoming an important component of social media, and more and more people are using them (Gretzel, 2017). As a result, businesses are obliged to use social media, because they enable rapid and transglobal communication (Aichner and Jacob, 2015). Businesses aiming to reach potential customers have to develop robust marketing strategies on social media and carry out more effective marketing activities in this field. Social media facilitate communication and content creation without the need for the physical presence of users, and they are thus effective platforms for achieving commercial goals (Tajvidi and Karami, 2017). Facebook, Instagram and Twitter are now more feasible for business use. Once managers understand how to represent their businesses effectively on social media, they are ready to enter a larger market, and they will be able to establish a strong and personal bond with their potential customers (Eley and Tilley, 2009). The power of social media lies in their capacity to generate eWOM, a very effective marketing technique to attract consumers and influence their purchase intentions (Xie et al., 2016). While word-of-mouth marketing previously consisted mostly of one-off scenarios, social media platforms and email offer constant interactions between consumers (Mohr, 2007). Litvin et al. (2008) stated that interpersonal impact, or eWOM, is one of the most potent sources of information for customers in the hospitality and tourism industry. It is essential that businesses try to exploit it to increase their performance.

Today, the successful use of social media has become one of the most important objectives of marketers. Customer relationship management (CRM) departments base their strategies on social media and use them to provide more satisfying experiences. They develop participatory activities for the enterprise and interact with social media platforms to increase their connections with consumers (Trainor et al., 2014). This is known as social CRM, and it enhances the bond with customers and ultimately increases performance (Wang and Kim, 2017).

Business performance is essentially driven by the degree of competition in the markets in which the business chooses to operate (Morgan, 2012). It is a given that companies which want to survive in an intensely competitive environment must keep up with technological change. Therefore, using cyber and web technology has become widespread practice (Zhang et al., 2017). Many businesses use social media networks to promote their products, increase brand awareness by emphasising their image, gather feedback from their customers, and resolve customer complaints (Civelek and Dalgın, 2013). Companies have to use all available platforms to compete (Weinberg, 2009), and when they do they reap the benefits. Those that cannot incorporate social media into their marketing will probably fall behind (Cormany and Erdem, 2010). While the larger brands can maintain their superiority without investing hugely in social media, small brands can use them to take big steps. A good example of this is Blendtec, a small company that sells high-performance blenders. The chief executive officer of the company has prepared videos in which he mixes different objects such as a Rubik's cube and a television remote control in the blender, and has uploaded them to different video sharing sites such as YouTube. More than 100 million people have watched them. This was for Blendtec a unique marketing strategy (Zarrella, 2009).

American Express designed and promoted the Small Business Saturday advertising campaign in 2010 mainly through social media. The campaign received more than 1 million 'likes' on Facebook and generated approximately 30 000 tweets. After the campaign, 40 per cent of the public were aware of Small Business Saturday, and revenues from small businesses increased by 28 per cent (Markowitz, 2013). Afterwards, American Express share prices increased by 74 per cent (Paniagua and Sapena, 2014).

THE IMPORTANCE OF SOCIAL MEDIA FOR ACCOMMODATION BUSINESSES AND TRAVEL AGENCIES

The tourism industry relies heavily on service delivery. It has grown rapidly and steadily and has become a global industry that contributes significantly to the economic growth of many countries, especially developing ones (Tajvidi and Karami, 2017). Accommodation businesses and travel agencies are the two most important pillars of the tourism industry. Information and communication technologies are actively used by accommodation and travel companies to reach the target audiences in areas such as corporate communication, human resources management, public relations, and marketing itself (Cascio, 2014). Developments in information technology have stimulated online communication between consumers through various media such as travel websites (for example, Expedia, TripAdvisor, Orbitz and Hotels.com) and social networking platforms (for example, Instagram, Twitter and Facebook) (Kim et al., 2015). The impact of Travel 2.0, the tourist version of Web 2.0, has meant that the image and business performance of companies, organisations and destinations are very important. Tourism has long been one of the most signficant constituents of online trade, and has been instrumental in changing the structure of trade generally (Milano et al., 2011). Competition is intense in this sector, and the success of businesses depends on their effective use of information and communication technologies. At this stage, the power of social media platforms in terms of information and communication is at its height, so tourism companies have to exploit them to the full.

Accommodation businesses and travel agencies are information-intensive enterprises, and it is not possible for a customer to try the product and service before purchase. Consumption can only take place in a geographical area that has tourist supply opportunities (Park and Oh, 2012; Xiang and Gretzel, 2010). The annual Country Brand Index (CBI) measures the attractiveness of countries in various regions, and it has been confirmed that the Web is the channel that most people use to access it (67 per cent) (Milano et al., 2011). Potential tourists are likely to obtain information and comments from tourists who have used the same product before. Therefore, the rapidly developing social media have created a new distribution channel and market research source for businesses (Matikiti et al., 2012). It has become the most widely used tool in the tourism industry, and it is highly effective in many areas of the marketing mix, such as direct email marketing for accommodation and travel businesses, customer service, advertising, information provision, marketing relations, distribution and sales (Goeldner and Ritchie, 2009). Social media tools are used effectively in travel research (Xiang and Gretzel, 2010). Today, many hotels and travel agencies are developing social media. They encourage their customers to like, interpret, share and rate their businesses on various social networking platforms, and this increases brand awareness amongst users (Gensler et al., 2013). However, while the sharing of tourists' positive and negative experiences may present opportunities for firms, it can also be problematic: businesses that do not grasp this and act accordingly may lose their competitive advantage (Hays et al., 2013).

Accommodation businesses and travel agencies use social media relatively more than other tourism enterprises. Social media can have a profound effect on all of them, by increasing the interaction between these businesses and customers, enabling them to announce their services more effectively and to evaluate customer requests, suggestions and complaints more quickly. A customer who has benefited from the service of an accommodation business or travel agency can make a significant contribution to the recognition and image of the company by sharing their experiences, photos, videos and comments through social media. Tourists mostly use social media tools such as Facebook, Instagram, Twitter and Myspace to express their opinions. There has been a considerable increase in the number of tourists sharing their travel experiences through travel social media sites (Xiang and Gretzel, 2010). In this way, it is not so much the businesses that promote themselves, but their customers, and this has a stronger impact on others. In addition, consumers acquire information and follow company advertising campaigns through social media. It has been estimated that 80 per cent of tourists benefit from the evaluations and recommendations of other tourists before they purchase their holiday (Tourism Talks, 2011). Social media are increasing their effectiveness in the selection of tourist products because they can convey opinions to large masses of people. Sharing images of locations of historical or natural beauty and touristic attractions on social media also encourages consumption. Thus, social media have become an essential means for tourists to exchange information about destinations and facilities (Jacobsen and Munar, 2012). Tourists can access all the information they need about their holiday plans, and choose their destinations, travel agencies or accommodation accordingly (Aymankuy et al., 2013). In a case study of Kars Eastern Express, social media played a significant role in the holiday decisions of customers. Those who use social media actively to assist in their travel choices are mostly university graduates, young people and singles (Doğan et al., 2018).

Social media have many advantages for accommodation and travel agencies. For example, they help to reduce their costs and increase their income (Morrison et al., 2001). They also raise awareness about new products and services and business brands (Kim et al., 2015), and reduce the need for expenditure on traditional offline publicity channels and public relations (Trusov et al., 2009). They therefore offer an effective and inexpensive alternative for small and medium-sized accommodation businesses with limited advertising and publicity budgets (Heinonen, 2011). They also offer an effective tool for businesses that want to reach individuals from other countries who are making vacation plans with limited resources (Hays et al., 2013). Another advantage of the social media is that they can be used as a reservation portal for accommodation and travel companies. Today, most customers are encouraged to book online, either directly through social media or through reservation websites. This option has encouraged greater sales (and thus increased profitability), and has contributed to the further internationalisation of tourism (Tajvidi and Karami, 2017).

Information from online reviews has a critical impact on customer purchasing decisions. This usually takes two forms. The first is the overall product assessment, and the second is the detailed description. For example, Tripadvisor allows customers to give a general rating for a hotel service using the five-star rating system, and also provides the opportunity for in-depth comments on their experience (Kim et al., 2015). The evaluations of customers are very valuable because they provide information about the performance of companies both for potential customers and the businesses themselves (for example, for purposes of advertising and assessment of performance). Highly rated hotels receive more online reservations (Ye et al., 2009). Tripadvisor functions as a free market research tool; it focuses on customer reviews and comments from several social networking sites, and it gives hotel and agency managers an idea of their overall business performance (Jeong and Mindy Jeon, 2008). It is very important that consumers come together on social media to share their knowledge and experience, and to address the positive features or shortcomings of accommodation and travel businesses, thereby increase customer satisfaction (Curkan, 2013). Companies have to regard social media not only as an advertising space, but also as a platform they can use to explore consumer trends and catch the right demand. Those that do so have the chance to influence the buying and decision-making behaviour of potential customers, and to improve their own performance (Hajli, 2015). Research has shown that the use of social media and online networks has a positive impact on performance (Güzel et al., 2018). Therefore, accommodation companies and travel agencies should understand how tourists use social media in the purchasing process and otherwise (McCarthy et al., 2010).

It has been pointed out that consumers can post negative comments about the performance or experiences of the businesses from which they purchase services on social media, and so it is important that those who come under such criticism respond promptly and constructively. Therefore, online reviews (particularly overall assessments) and response to negative comments should be managed as a critical element in company marketing (Kim et al., 2015). Responding to negative online comments conveys the message that the business is listening to guests' complaints and that it is willing to compensate for failures in service. This will ultimately lead to better financial outcomes for all (Chen and Xie, 2008). The significance of the relationship between company and consumer is such that it has arguably come to constitute the basic function of social media (Chan and Guillet, 2011).

TATILPEREST TOURISM: A CASE STUDY

The present study has examined the effect of social media on business performance by using a case study of a travel agency. This was carried out using a qualitative research method involving a questionnaire survey and interviews with senior managers in the business, in May 2020. An interview protocol was prepared in advance, and questions on the demographic characteristics of the participants, the general features of the business, the use of online and offline networks (13 items), and business performance over the past three years (six items) were included in the survey. They were adapted from the work of Tajvidi and Karami (2017).

The performance of Tatilperest Tourism, a Group A travel agency, was analysed. Group A travel agencies are authorised to access and monitor all travel agency services (Law No. 1618 on Travel Agencies and Travel Agencies Association, 1972). This travel agency is a commercial institution authorised to provide tourism-related information for tourists; to create package tours; to organise accommodation, transportation and travel; to offer sports and entertainment services for tourism purposes; and to market the products. Tatilperest Tourism organises domestic tours, cultural tours and school trips, and has been operating for 15 years. It was sold in 2018, and the new owners started to use Facebook and Instagram actively. The business has 1557 followers, 598 posts and 1524 likes on Facebook (TATİL PEREST; Facebook.com, 2020) and 3147 followers and 708 posts on Instagram (@tatilperestadana; Instagram.com, 2020). It is followed on Google+ and LinkedIn. Official tour photos and tour

Table 34.1   *Social media usage and business performance of Tatilperest Tourism*

Using online networks		
Facebook	Yes	
LinkedIn	Yes	
Twitter		No
YouTube		No
Instagram	Yes	
Pinterest		No
Google+	Yes	
Tripadvisor		No
Using offline networks		
Face-to-face meetings	Yes	
Tv/Radio		No
Magazines		No
Exhibitions/events/festivals	Yes	
Print advertisement	Yes	
Business performance		
Increase in market share over the past 3 years	Yes	
Increase in annual turnover over the past 3 years	Yes	
Number of employees over the past 3 years	Yes	
Achieving firm profit goals over the past 3 years	Yes	
Having a better return on investment over the past 3 years	Yes	
Increase in total income over the past 3 years	Yes	

programmes are shared on social media platforms, and there are also pictures of historical places and selfies taken by customers (some of whom have tagged the company). Social media are often used for advertisement and promotion purposes. At the same time, face-to-face interviews are held for offline advertising and promotion purposes, and the company participates in events such as exhibitions and festivals. Businesses naturally tend to be sensitive about sharing financial data, and this was so in the present instance. Subjective information can be used in cases where objective information cannot be accessed, and in fact can produce similar results (Dess and Robinson, 1984).

The interview responses of senior managers are presented in Table 34.1. Although the company is now being run by different managers, it has been promoted very effectively through social media, and its profits have increased.

RESULTS

Social media networks have billions of users, and consequently have become an important force in the sharing of information and the raising of awareness. Users' evaluations, thoughts and attitudes play an indispensable role in customers' decision-making and purchasing behaviour (Mangold and Faulds, 2009). Hospitality and travel industry businesses are significantly impacted upon by the comments (positive, negative or neutral) from the tourists they serve.

Social media are a reliable and effective way for tourism consumers to share their experiences, to post images, and to recommend the products they have enjoyed to other users. Travel photos shared on platforms such as Instagram, Twitter and Facebook, and comments on various tourism portals, provide primary information for tourists. They help people to make their own travel decisions and to choose the right provider. Therefore, it is vital that businesses use social media appropriately to improve their performance and attract more customers. Social media coverage is growing by the day, and innovative accommodation and travel businesses know this. As a result, they are usually the most competitive in the sector. They maintain close communication with their customers via multiple platforms, and closely follow changes and expectations in demand. They provide solutions to problems in short time frames, and attempt to reach more consumers by using the Internet to transcend national borders. This results in better business performance and greater profitability.

The success of travel agencies lies with offering tourists holidays that meet their expectations. Selling holidays involves selling a dream experience. Evidence is needed to make dreams come true. For tourists, such evidence can take the form of images and the real experience of others. Tatilperest Tourism, conscious of the might of social media, has oriented its marketing towards platforms such as Facebook and Instagram. It has received many positive comments from users, and it has improved its performance markedly within the past two years (2018 and 2019).

REFERENCES

Aichner, T., and Jacob, F. (2015). Measuring the degree of corporate social media use. *International Journal of Market Research*, *57*(2), 257–275.

Aymankuy, Y., Soydaş, E.M., and Saçlı, Ç. (2013). The effect of social media utilization on holiday decision of tourists: A study on academic staff. *International Human Science*, *10*(1), 376–397.

Berthon, P.R., Pitt, L.F., McCarthy, I., and Kates, S. (2007). When customers get clever: Managerial approaches to dealing with creative consumers. *Business Horizons*, *50*(1), 39–48.

Cascio, W.F. (2014). Leveranging employer branding, performance management and human resource development to enhance employee retention. *Human Resource Development International*, *17*(2), 121–128, DOI: 10.1080/13678868.2014.886443.

Chan, N.L., and Guillet, B.D. (2011). Investigation of social media marketing: How does the hotel industry in Hong Kong perform in marketing on social media websites. *Journal of Travel and Tourism Marketing*, *28*(4), 345–368.

Chen, Y., Fay, S., and Wang, Q. (2011). The role of marketing in social media: How online consumer reviews evolve. *Journal of Interactive Marketing*, *25*, 85–94.

Chen, Y., and Xie, J., (2008). Online consumer review: Word-of-mouth as a new element of marketing communication mix. *Management Science*, *54*(3), 477–491. DOI: 10.1287/mnsc.1070.0810.

Civelek, M., and Dalgın, T. (2013). Turizm pazarlamasında sosyal medya, turizm işletmeleri üzerine bir araştırma: Muğla örneği. In Karamustafa, K. (ed.), *14. Ulusal Turizm Kongresi Bildiriler Kitabı* (pp. 266-282). Kayseri: Erciyes Üniversitesi Turizm Fakültesi Yayınları.

Cormany, D., and Erdem, M. (2010). Shift to an experience economy: Online communities are center to new marketing approach. *Bottomline*, *25*(3), 39–44.

Curkan, S.C. (2013). Sosyal medya ve turizm: Türkiye'deki turistik destinasyonların değerlendirilmesi. Unpublished master's thesis, University of Balıkesir, Balıkesir, Turkey.

Daft, R.L. (2000) *Organization Theory and Design*. Cincinnati, OH: South-Western Publishing.

Dess, G.G., and Robinson Jr, R.B. (1984). Measuring organizational performance in the absence of objective measures: The case of the privately-held firm and conglomerate business unit. *Strategic Management Journal*, *5*(3), 265–273.

Doğan, M., Pekiner, A.B., and Karaca, E. (2018). The effect of social media on tourism and tourist choices: Case of Kars-Doğu Express. *Journal of Travel and Hospitality Management, 15*(3), 669–683.

Eibe Sørensen, H. (2009). Why competitors matter for market orientation. *European Journal of Marketing, 43*(5/6), 735–761.

Eley, B., and Tilley, S. (2009). *Online Marketing Inside Out*. Collingwood, Vic.: Sitepoint.

Facebook.com (2020). Retrieved 28 May 2020 from https://www.facebook.com/press/info.php?statistics.

Gensler, S., Völckner, F., Liu-Thompkins, Y., and Wiertz, C. (2013). Managing brands in the social media environment. *Journal Of İnteractive Marketing, 27*(4), 242–256.

Goeldner C., and Ritchie J.R.B. (2009). *Tourism: Principles, Practices, Philosophies.* New York: John Wiley & Sons.

Gretzel, U. (2017). #travelselfie: A netnographic study of travel identity communicated via Instagram. In Carson, S. and Pennings, M. (eds), *Performing Cultural Tourism: Communities, Tourists and Creative Practices* (pp. 115–128). New York: Routledge.

Güzel, D., Korkmaz, G., and Yazıcılar, F. G. (2018). Sosyal medyanın firma performansı üzerindeki etkisi. *Atatürk Üniversitesi Sosyal Bilimler Enstitüsü Dergisi, 22*(4), 2237–2247.

Hajli, N. (2015). Social commerce constructs and consumer's intention to buy. *International Journal of Information Management, 35*(2), 183–191.

Halligan, B., and Shah, D. (2010). *Inbound Marketing*. Hoboken, NJ: John Wiley & Sons.

Hanna, R., Rohm, A., and Crittenden, V. L. (2011). We're all connected: The power of the social media ecosystem. *Business Horizons, 54*(3), 265–273.

Hays, S., Page, S.J., and Buhalis, D. (2013). Social media as a destination marketing tool: Its use by national tourism organisations. *Current Issues in Tourism, 16*(3), 211–239. http://dx.doi.org/10.1080/13683500.2012.662215.

He, Z.L., and Wong, P.K. (2004). Exploration vs. exploitation: An empirical test of the ambidexterity hypothesis. *Organization Science 15*(4), 481–494.

Heinonen, J. (2011). Social media perceptions on Finnish tourism sector. *Interdisciplinary Studies Journal, 1*(3), 53–66.

Instagram.com (2020). Tatilperest tourism. Retrieved 15 June 2020 from https://www.instagram.com/tatilperestadana/?hl=tr.

Jacobsen, J.K.S., and Munar, A.M. (2012). Tourist information search and destination choice in a digital age. *Tourism Management Perspectives, 1*, 39–47.

Jason, K. (2010). How do I learn more about social media? *Aba Bank Marketing, 42*(3), 40.

Järvinen, J., and Taiminen, H. (2016). Harnessing marketing automation for B2B content marketing. *Industrial Marketing Management, 54*, 164–175.

Jeong, M., and Mindy Jeon, M. (2008). Customer reviews of hotel experiences through consumer generated media (CGM). *Journal of Hospitality and Leisure Marketing, 17*(1–2), 121–138.

Kaplan, A.M., and Haenlein, M. (2010). Users of the world, unite! The challanges and opportunities of social media. *Business Horizons* (53), 59–68.

Kim, W.G., Lim, H., and Brymer, R.A. (2015). The effectiveness of managing social media on hotel performance. *International Journal of Hospitality Management, 44*, 165–171.

Law No. 1618 on Travel Agencies and Travel Agencies Association (1972). *T. C. Resmi Gazete,* 14320, 28 September 1972.

Litvin, S.W., Goldsmith, R.E., and Pan, B. (2008). Electronic word-of-mouth in hospitality and tourism management. *Tourism Management, 29*, 458–468.

Mangold, G.W., and Faulds, J.D. (2009). Social media: The new hybrid element of the promotion mix. *Business Horizons, 52*(4), 357–365.

Matikiti, R., Bola A., and Wilhelmina, S. (2012). An empirical evidence on the usage of internet marketing in the hospitality sector in an emerging economy and its relationship to profitability. *International Review of Social Sciences and Humanities, 4*(1), 181–197.

Markowitz, E. (2013). Small Business Saturday by the numbers. CNBC.com. Retrieved 12 September 2013 from http://www.cnbc.com/id/49968762.

McCarthy, L., Stock, D., and Verma., R. (2010). How travelers use online and social media channels to make hotel-choice decisions. *Cornell Hospitality Report, 10*(18). https://www.researchgate.net/publication/265520868_How_Travelers_Use_Online_and_Social_Media_Channels_to_Make_Hotel-choice_Decisions.

Merrilees, B., Thiele, S.R., and Lye, A. (2011). Marketing capabilities: Antecedents and implications for B2B SME performance. *Industrial Marketing Management, 40*, 368–375.

Milano, R., Baggio, R., and Piattelli, R. (2011). The effects of online social media on tourism websites. 18th International Conference on Information Technology and Travel and Tourism, Austria.

Mohr, I. (2007). Buzz marketing for movies. *Business Horizons, 50*(5), 395–403.

Morgan, A.N. (2012). Marketing and business performance. *Journal of the Academy of Marketing Science, 40*(1), 102–119. DOI 10.1007/s11747-011-0279-9

Morrison, A.M., Jing, S., O'Leary, J.T., and Cai, L.A. (2001). Prediction usage of the internet for travel bookings: An exploratory study. *Information Technology and Tourism, 4*(1), 15–30.

Paniagua, J., and Sapena, J. (2014). Business performance and social media: Love or hate? *Business Horizons, 57*(6), 719–728.

Park, J., and Oh, I.K. (2012). A case study of social media marketing by travel agency: The salience of social media marketing in tourism industry. *International Journal of Tourism Sciences, 12*(1), 93–106. DOI: 10.1080/15980634.2012.11434654.

Porter, M.E. (1991). Towards a dynamic theory of strategy. *Strategic Management Journal, 12*(S2), 95–117.

Poynter, R. (2010). *The Handbook of Online and Social Media Researh: Tools and Techniques for Market Researchers.* Chichester: John Wiley & Sons.

Scott, M.D. (2010). *The New Rules of Marketing and PR.* Hoboken, NJ: John Wiley & Sons.

Swamy, R. (2002). Information technology strategic performance measurement in the new millennium. *CMA Management, 76*(3), 44–47.

Tajvidi, R., and Karami, A. (2017). The effect of social media on firm performance. *Computers in Human Behavior*, 1–10. https://doi.org/10.1016/j.chb.2017.09.026.

Tourism Talks (2011, October). Retrieved 20 May 2014 from http://svc065.bookeasy.com/images/latrobe/TOURISM%20TALKS%20October%202011%20SK.pdf.

Trainor, K.J., Andzulis, J.M., Rapp, A., and Agnihotri, R. (2014). Social media technology usage and customer relationship performance: A capabilities-based examination of social CRM. *Journal of Business Research, 67*(6), 1201–1208.

Trusov, M., Bucklin, R.E., and Pauwels, K. (2009). Effects of word-of-mouth versus traditional marketing: Findings from an internet social networking site. *Journal of Marketing, 73*(5), 90–102.

Walmsley, A. (2010). New media needs new PR. Retrieved 28 September 2010 from http://www.marketingmagazine.co.uk.

Wang, Z., and Kim, H.G. (2017). Can social media marketing improve customer relationship capabilities and firm performance? Dynamic capability perspective. *Journal of Interactive Marketing, 39*, 15–26.

WeareSocial (2020). Digital in 2020. Retrieved 28 May 2020 from https://wearesocial.com/blog/2020/01/digital-2020-3-8-billion-people-use-social-media.

Weinberg, T. (2009). *The New Community Rules: Marketing on the Social Web.* Sebastopol: O'Reilly Media.

Westbrook, R.A. (1987). Product/consumption-based affective responses and post purchase processes. *Journal of Marketing Research, 24*(3), ss. 258–270.

Wilson, S. (2010). *Social Media and Small Business Marketing.* New York: University Business Printing and Press.

Xiang, Z., and Gretzel, U. (2010). Role of social media in online travel information search. *Tourism Management, 31*(2), 179–188.

Xie, K.L., Zhang, Z., Zhang, Z., Singh, A., and Lee, S.K. (2016). Effects of managerial response on consumer eWOM and hotel performance: evidence from TripAdvisor. *International Journal of Contemporary Hospitality Management, 28*(9), 2013–2034.

Ye, Q., Law, R., and Gu, B. (2009). The impact of online user reviews on hotel room sales. *International Journal of Hospitality Management, 28*(1), 180–182.

Zarrella, D. (2009). *The Social Media Marketing Book.* Sebastopol: O'Reilly Media.

Zhang, M., Guo, L., Hu, M., and Liu, W. (2017). Influence of customer engagement with company social networks on stickiness: Mediating effect of customer value creation. *International Journal of Information Management, 37*(3), 229–240.

Zolkepli, I.A., Kamarulzaman Y. (2015). Social media adoption: The role of media needs and innovation characteristics. *Computers in Human Behavior, 43*, 189–209.

35. Social media and tourism development in Africa: an empirical investigation

Sheereen Fauzel and Verena Tandrayen-Ragoobur

INTRODUCTION

More and more Africans are using technologies to access social media especially Facebook. Facebook represents the largest cyberspace, accommodating 2 224 726 721 subscribers around the world.[1] Many companies use Facebook to market their services and products.

Businesses operating in the tourism sector need to stay relevant through social media marketing as it is relatively a cheaper way to promote their activities. Tourism in Africa represents a significant business activity and is projected to grow further. According to the estimates of the WTTC (2020), by 2028, tourism will add \$275 billion to African economies, up from less than \$150 billion in 2011. Famous sites such as Tastemakers Africa, Everyday Africa and Visiter L'Afrique use social media widely to showcase the new possibilities for Africans, the African diaspora and international travellers.[2] Enabling its users to market their products and services, the platforms also connect with others having similar interests.

Facebook has been identified by Kasavana et al. (2010) as a platform assisting travel companies to pursue international electronic marketing. It allows companies to create their own page on the site and provide all information related to the tourism product or service they are offering (Leung et al., 2013). Facebook is widely used to inform and attract international travellers. This platform has enabled the tourism sector to better market its products. Asongu and Odhiambo (2019) discuss how social media platforms allow people and organisations to communicate beyond their geographical locations, bringing rivals together, whilst giving a voice to different stakeholders. Moreover, social media platforms improve the overall development of various businesses including the tourism industry.

Referring to the literature on the determinants of tourism, we observed that studies investigating the impact of social media, in particular Facebook, on tourism development is rather sparse. Most studies undertaken adopt case studies of particular countries, hence ignoring the use of rigorous methodological approaches. This can be explained by the lack of available data on Facebook users, especially those companies operating in the tourism industry. To the best of our knowledge, studies relating to African countries are missing. The present chapter thus attempts to address this gap in the literature. The analysis builds on recent literature analysing the determinants of tourism, and those which have used mainly a qualitative method. The study adopts an in-depth quantitative and econometric approach for selected African countries. A static as well as a dynamic analysis have been used. The structure of the chapter is as follows: it first reviews the literature, and then describes the methodology adopted. The following section analyses the findings, and the final section concludes.

LITERATURE REVIEW

The impact of social media on tourism decisions to visit a particular destination can be explained by the theory of reasoned action (TRA), the theory of planned behaviour (TPB) and the technology acceptance model (TAM) (Nikiforova, 2013; Cusick, 2014; Lee et al., 2015). The TRA and TPB analyse the psycho-social variables that predict people's use of platforms such as Facebook. The TRA is based on the concept whereby the voluntary behaviour of an individual is examined based on their motivation to do an action. Hence, a person's behaviour is influenced by their intention to perform that behaviour. In addition, behaviour is influenced by social factors such as the social circle surrounding that person and social media. This concept was developed by Bagozzi (1982), Ajzen and Fishbein (1980) and Fishbein and Ajzen (1975). By applying the TRA to the present study, the information sharing behaviour on social media is determined by the individual's attitude and subjective norms. Ajzen (1991) later extends the TRA to the TPB. This theory emphasises the fact that intentions are based on attitudes, subjective norms and perceived behavioural control. Scholars such as Brown and Venkatesh (2005) and Tseng and Teng (2014) have used the TPB in a number of technology adoption contexts. Another theory that can be applied is the TAM, developed by Davis (1989). This theory is based on the fact that the adoption of a particular technology by customers depend on the voluntary intention of that customer to accept and use the technology.

The factors discussed in these three theories motivate the use of social media by both tourists and those engaged in tourism marketing and management (Asongu and Odhiambo, 2019). Scholars noted that social media sites are a growing imperative in the tourism sector. For instance, Xiang and Gretzel (2010) observe that there is an increased use on social media to search for information related to tourism activities, and these include blog sites (e.g., TravelPost and BlogSpot) and social networking sites. Several social media websites such as Tripadvisor, VirtualTourist and other travel-specific sites are becoming more popular and are evolving into primary online travel information sources. The tagging system is another factor influencing travellers' choice of destination. This tagging system is more likely to influence domestic tourism. Alemneh et al. (2016) point out that Twitter is offering new platforms to countries to showcase their resources with customers and visitors in a more personalised way. For instance, tourists tweeting about their experiences can positively or negatively affect the destinations' image, reputation and attractiveness.

Chung and Buhalis (2008) and Leung et al. (2011) write that there are still improvements that need to be made in the field of managing social media by both tourism customers and suppliers. They identify that the manipulation and management of social media still remains unknown to key stakeholders.

Referring to research on social media and travellers' travel planning process, Torres (2010) found that a large proportion of leisure travellers use the internet to plan their travel. Xiang and Gretzel (2010) also reveal that one-tenth of travellers use social media while searching for information on prospective future travel destinations. Furthermore, Huang et al. (2010) show that the main factor influencing travelling choice is the search of travel information on the internet and social media. Information on social media comes in the form of text, image, audio and video, which gives travellers a better idea of a particular destination (Thevenot, 2007). Based on these characteristics, various scholars have pointed out that social media is more effective than traditional methods in assisting travellers with the necessary facts on a tourism-related product or service.

Social media plays an important role in influencing travellers' choice of destination (see Cox et al., 2009; Lo et al., 2011; Tussyadiah et al., 2011; Yoo and Gretzel, 2010). The reason why travellers search for information prior to visiting a location is identified by the fact that mostly all products and services related to the tourism sector are highly priced and require high involvement. They prefer to be well informed on the location by collecting information on experiences of previous travellers on social media sites. This prior information becomes an important determinant in their decision-making process (Schmallegger and Carson, 2008; Jeng and Fesenmaier, 2002). Likewise, Casaló et al. (2011) and Litvin et al. (2008) identify that travellers prefer to base their decision on customers' reviews rather than the information provided by the tourism suppliers. Traditionally travellers relied on the experience of previous travellers through word-of-mouth. With the emergence of technology, their decisions are influenced by other peoples' experiences via the electronic word-of-mouth through reviews and tweets, amongst others. Hence, electronic word-of-mouth has enlarged the access of information beyond friends, relatives and social circles (Yoo and Gretzel, 2010). Travellers now have the opportunity to access wider information on different destinations, which facilitates their choice of travel destination.

In addition to consumers widely using the social media for making decisions about their travel, tourism suppliers have recognised the importance of this platform to market their tourism products and services. Social media is an important tourism marketing tool (Chan and Denizci Guillet, 2011; Huang, 2011; Inversini et al., 2009; Munar, 2010; Xiang and Gretzel, 2010). Research has shown that countries are likely to lag behind in attracting tourists if they do not use social media to market their services (Stepchenkova and Morrison, 2006). As discussed previously, reviews of customers are widely used information by travellers in their decision-making process. Hence, such reviews and blogs have been recognised by scholars to be important evidence which reflect travellers' opinions on a particular destination (Sparks and Browning, 2011). Hence, tourism product and service suppliers and destination management organisations can make use of this information to improve their products and services (Akehurst, 2009; Leung et al., 2011; Pan et al., 2007). Hence, online tools and platforms can be used to further improve the online image of tourism destinations, and offer innovative ways of attracting consumers (Pantelidis, 2010; Schmallegger and Carson, 2008). Blogs represent a vital and cheaper marketing tool when compared to traditional advertising methods. There are company blogs and business-to-customer blogs that provide animated and attractive content on the suppliers' website which ease the contact with customers (Ellion, 2007). In several high-income countries, blogs are provided on the official websites of several destinations. Destination management organisations thus contribute to these blogs and provide useful information to customers on the features and uniqueness of several destinations (Schmollgruber, 2007). Moreover, blogs are able to connect companies and customers through the development of a brand voice that boosts customers' trust.

However, it has been noted that even though social media contributes widely as an e-marketing platform, some firms still do not innovate and make wide use of these technologies (Chan and Denizci Guillet, 2011). This can be explained by the fact that some tourism suppliers are unsure about the potential returns of social media marketing. In addition, given that there is a lack of research on the potential advantages of such new marketing media, some organisations are reluctant to use it extensively.

The review of the existing literature indicates an absence of a rigorous methodology to assess the impact of social media on the tourism industry. Existing studies have adopted mainly case study methods or surveys. Hence, the aim of this chapter is to apply innovative econometric methods to investigate the link between social media and the tourism sector, with additional information on the other determinants of tourism such as the use of the internet, amongst others. This chapter addresses an important gap in the theoretical literature and adds to the existing empirical work by investigating into the link between social media and the tourism sector in the case of African countries.

METHODOLOGY

The objective of this study is to investigate the impact of social media and internet penetration on tourism development in African countries[3] from 1995 to 2017. As per Asongu and Odhiambo (2019) and Garín-Muñoz and Pérez-Amaral (2011), the tourism demand model is augmented to include the social media and internet penetration variables, as follows:

$$TOU = f(SM, INT, WGDP, CPI) \tag{35.1}$$

Because of the variance stabilising properties of log transformation, the log values of the variables are used. In fact, logged variables yield a more clear-cut interpretation of the coefficients in terms of percentage change.

Converting all the variables in logarithmic terms (except the dummy variable) yields:

$$lnlnTOU_{it} = \alpha_0 + \beta_1 SM_{it} + \beta_2 lnINT_{it} + \beta_3 lnWGDP_{it} + \beta_4 lnCPI_{it} + \varepsilon_{it} \tag{35.2}$$

With the exception of the dummy variables, all variables are expressed in log form. This log model has been adopted to account for the elasticity of the dependent variable with respect to the different explanatory variables.

Variables Definition

The variable tourism receipts as a measure of tourism development in the different countries is used as dependent variable in the present model. To capture tourism development, various studies such as Sönmez (1998) have used tourism receipts as the proxy. Data has been extracted from the World Bank Development Indicators 2020 database.

Independent Variables

The internet plays an important role in the travel and tourism industry. Travel suppliers and tourism authorities are using marketing strategies through the internet as an innovative means of communication to fully exploit this market (Garín-Muñoz and Pérez-Amaral, 2011). Hence, the present study uses the internet penetration rate, which represents the percentage of the total population of a given country that uses the internet. A similar proxy was used by Garín-Muñoz and Pérez-Amaral (2011).

Moreover, social media is another variable used by tourism authorities and suppliers to market their products and services. Since the launch of Facebook, various tourism suppliers have been using this platform to inform prospective tourists and influence their choices regarding tourist destinations and the type of touristic products they purchase. Due to lack of data on yearly Facebook users by country, a dummy variable is used for social media, taking a value of 0 prior to the launch of Facebook and a value of 1 as from 2004, marking the launch of this social networking site.

WGDP is a proxy used for world gross domestic product (GDP) per capita. This variable is included as it represents the income of tourists and their spending capacity. A similar proxy was used by various scholars in the tourism demand model, such as Buigut and Amendah (2016), Seetanah and Fauzel (2019) and Fauzel (2020). A positive relationship is expected between tourism demand and world income.

Another proxy included is the level of inflation in the African country, as measured by the consumer price index. This variable affects tourism demand, as higher prices in the tourist receiving countries may discourage the flow of international tourism. Hence, a negative relationship may hold between tourism demand in African countries and prices. Therefore, the lower the cost of living in the host countries, the higher is the expected tourism demand (Boojhawon and Seetanah, 2016). Apart from the dummy variable, other data was collected from the World Bank Development Indicators 2020 database.

Panel Data Estimates

Before proceeding with the estimation of the model, it is important to investigate the time series properties of the panel series. Applying regression on time series data may generate spurious results due to the possibility of non-stationarity data. For this purpose, a panel unit root test is performed to find the order of integration of the various variables under consideration. Im et al. (2003) panel unit root tests are used.

For investigation purposes, firstly the static technique is employed to analyse the impact of social media on tourism development in the selected African countries. By using panel data, we control for unobserved cross-country heterogeneity and investigate into the dynamic relations. The Hausman test has been conducted to choose between the random or fixed effect estimation.

Many important modelling issues for static panel model can be discussed with reference to:

$$y_{it} = \alpha_i + x_{it}\beta_i + \varepsilon_{it}, i = 1, 2, \ldots, N. \ t = 1, 2, \ldots, T \ \mu_{it} \sim IID\left(0, \sigma^2\right), \alpha_i \beta_i unknown constants$$

Variables in the equation are as follows: y_{it} is the dependent variable; x_{it} is a K-dimensional vector of explanatory variables; α_i is the intercept term; β is a (K × 1) vector representing the slopes; μ_{it}, the error, varies over i and t (t is the time period and i represents the countries); IID represents independent, identically distributed random variables.

The individual effects model can be further divided into fixed effects models and random effects models. In both cases, the starting point is that the individual effects are unobservable. In the fixed effects model it is assumed that the individual effects are correlated with x_{it}. The opposite of fixed effects are random effects. These variables are, as the name suggests, random and unpredictable; they are literally random effects.

Table 35.1   Panel data estimates

	Panel data estimates: (1995–2017) Dependent variable: LTOU			
Variable	Coefficient	Standard error	T-ratio	Probability
Constant	-82.08821	9.356618	-8.773278	0.0000
SM	0.282219	0.080100	3.523356	0.0005
LINT	0.218870	0.066741	3.279417	0.0011
LWINC	3.180129	0.291651	10.90387	0.0000
LCPI	-0.173587	0.031680	-5.479457	0.0000
R^2	0.93			
Hausman test	Recommend RE estimates			

The Hausman Test

The Hausman test is sometimes described as a test for model misspecification. In panel data analysis, the Hausman test helps to choose between a fixed effects model and a random effects model. The null hypothesis is that the preferred model is random effects; the alternate hypothesis is that the model is fixed effects. Essentially, the tests probe into whether there is a correlation between the unique errors and the regressors in the model. The null hypothesis is that there is no correlation between the two.

EMPIRICAL RESULTS

Test for Stationarity and Cointegration

The stationarity of the variables is tested using the augmented Dickey–Fuller and Phillips–Perron unit root tests. Lag length selection is based on the Schwarz information criterion (SIC). From the results obtained it can be concluded that the variables follow an I(1) process. The next step is to test for the existence of a long-run equilibrium relationship between the variables. Actually, non-stationary variables may deviate from each other in the short run. However, the existence of cointegration will cause them to be associated in the long run as they share the same stochastic trends. If the series are cointegrated, the above equation will depict a long-run relationship. A heterogeneous panel cointegration test developed by Pedroni (1999) is used. Pedroni panel cointegration uses a residual-based ADF test. Seven different statistics are included in the Pedroni test for cointegration. The first set of tests includes Panel V-stat, Panel Rho-stat panel, Panel PP-stat and Panel ADF-stat. The second group includes Group Rho-stat, Group PP-stat and Group ADF-stat. The results show that the null hypothesis of no cointegration is rejected, and it can be confirmed that there exists a long-run cointegration relationship between the variables. The Hausman test recommends the use of the random effects model, and Table 35.1 reports the relevant estimates.

The results are in line with the existing literature review discussed above. The main variable of interest is the social media one. This variable has a positive and significant coefficient, implying that an increase in social media has led to a rise in tourism demand in the sample of countries studied. This result is in coherence with Asongu and Odhiambo (2019), who argue that social media and more specifically the use of Facebook, has improved the ways tourism companies communicate and market their services. Moreover, this social media platform is widely used by tourists to decide on their holiday destinations. More importantly, the hospitality and travel sectors have innovated their marketing strategies with Facebook. The more tourism companies can use Facebook in order to market their tourism services, the higher will be tourism demand. For the African continent, in particular, we can argue that even though the traditional marketing campaigns still exist, the internet and social media have provided new opportunities for the tourism companies to market their services practically free (Alemneh et al., 2016).

The results for internet penetration are also positive and significant. This result can be explained by the fact the tourism sector has been adopting and developing information and communication technology (ICT) applications, and scholars have discussed that tourism services are rated as the top service purchased through the internet (Garín-Muñoz and Pérez-Amaral, 2009, 2011). Moreover, it has been discussed that travel products represent high-involvement products and are less tangible and more differentiated than many other consumer goods, which makes them appropriate for sale through the Internet (Bonn et al., 1998; Lewis et al., 1998).

Referring to the coefficient of world income, it is observed that when it increases by 1 per cent, tourism revenue increases by 3.15 per cent in the long run. World income is a crucial factor determining tourism demand, and this result validates those of Seetanah and Fauzel (2019), Fauzel (2020), Chi (2015) and Martins et al. (2017).

Further analysing the results, we can observe that an increase in inflation discourages tourism flow in the countries. This supports the view that consumers are conscious of prices while choosing their travel destinations. This result can be explained by the various crises that the world has suffered which has resulted in depreciating currencies. Economic recessions suffered by various countries as a result of the Asian currency crisis in 1997–98, the 1998 Russian financial crisis, and even the recession in the United States and other countries in late 2008 (Boojhawon and Seetanah, 2016) may also explain the result obtained here. More so, this finding is in line with Martins et al. (2017), who argued that prices are an important variable determining tourism demand mainly when the study is using tourism receipts as the dependent variable. This result is also consistent with Içöz (1991), discussing that international tourism is highly susceptible to internal changes (for example, prices) and external changes (for example, global economic trends) to the industry.

Dynamic Panel Data Regression

It should be noted that there is still the possibility of endogeneity of the explanatory variables and the loss of dynamic information even in a panel data framework. Since the series are cointegrated, an error correction model is used (Table 35.2). Engel and Granger (Granger, 1983; Engel and Granger, 1987) argue that the presence of cointegration eliminates the likelihood of the estimates being spurious as a result of omitted variable bias and endogeneity. The short run properties of the series are observed using a panel vector error correction model (PVECM), which is specified as follows:

$$\Delta(Z_{xt}) = \varphi + \rho\Delta(Z_{xt-1}) + \theta_{xt} \tag{35.3}$$

Table 35.2   PVECM

		Panel data estimates: (1995–2017) Dependent variable: LTOU			
Long-run result	Variable	CointEq	Standard Error	T-ratio	Probability
	SM	0.963650	0.08376	11.5054	0.0000
	LINT	0.764046	0.06094	12.5381	0.0000
	LWINC	7.353643	0.30243	24.3152	0.0000
	LCPI	0.715583	0.02709	26.4188	0.0000
Short-run result	Error correction	D(LTOU)	Standard error	T-ratio	Probability
	CointEq	-0.239326	0.02862	-8.36248	0.000
	D(LTOU(-1))	0.233216	0.05693	4.09635	0.000
	D(SM(-1))	-0.107188	0.07706	-1.39097	0.1651
	D(LINT(-1))	0.262467	0.05415	4.84661	0.000
	D(LWINC(-1))	1.898519	1.03673	1.83126	0.000
	D(LCPI(-1))	0.556850	0.08651	6.43696	0.000
	Constant	-0.304195	0.06443	4.72155	0.0000

where: Δ is the first difference operator, Z_{xt} represents a vector of the 5 variables used in this study; φ is a vector constant term; ρ symbolises a (5 x 5) matrix of parameters; Zxt-1 is a vector of the five variables lagged by 1; and θ is the vector error term.

The long-run result from the dynamic panel analysis that is the impact of social media on tourism revenue is positive and significant. In addition, world income and internet penetration play an important role in attracting tourists to these destinations. Referring to the short-run results, we observe a positive and significant coefficient of tou_{it-1}, showing that the lagged of tourist revenue has contributed positively towards the current level of tourist revenue. This shows that there is a self-reinforcing effect and proves the concept of repeat tourism. The value of the coefficient of the lagged of tourist revenue is 0.23, implying a coefficient of partial adjustment of 0.23. It means that tourist revenue in one year is 23 per cent of the difference between the optimal and its current level. This confirms the existence of dynamism and endogeneity in the tourism demand model.

In the short, similar to the results obtained for the long run, world income and internet penetration are positive and significant. However, the social media variable is insignificant, and this can be explained by the fact that in the dynamic framework, we are dealing with difference variables which are short-term parameters. Some variables take time to have their full effect on tourism demand.

CONCLUSION

This chapter has investigated the impact of social media on tourism development in Africa from 1995 to 2017. Both the static and dynamic framework have been used. The empirical evidence is based on the random effect estimation and panel vector error correction model. In the end, both models confirm that social media has contributed to tourism demand. Other determinants of tourism demand are internet penetration and world income. Further, the dynamic results show that the lagged of tourist revenue has contributed positively towards the current level of tourist revenue. Hence, this confirms the existence of a self-reinforcing effect and proves the concept of repeat tourism in the short run.

Based on the findings, travel agencies, tourism companies and policy-makers must develop appropriate schemes to improve and boost electronic commerce. By further increasing the internet penetration rate, authorities can promote the use of the Internet for the sector. It can be postulated that social media has transformed the whole tourism industry in Africa. Tourists use social media to choose their holiday destinations and accommodation. Online reviews on past travellers' experiences, videos and photos impact upon their travel decisions.

Travel and tourism organisations also use social media to improve their services, mainly based on online reviews and recommendations from past travellers. These operators use their Facebook pages to increase awareness of their products and communicate with unsatisfied clients to find ways to improve their services. Hence, tourist service providers must use their social media pages effectively to improve their services. For instance, an immediate response to online comments in a constructive way is highly recommended.

NOTES

1.   https://www.internetworldstats.com/stats1.htm.
2.   https://yali.state.gov/african-tourism-thrives-social-media/.
3.   Algeria, Angola, Djibouti, Guinea, Kenya, Lesotho, Madagascar, Malawi, Mali, Mozambique, Namibia, Niger, Nigeria, Rwanda, Senegal, Tanzania, Togo, Uganda, Zambia.

REFERENCES

Ajzen, I. (1991). The theory of planned behavior. *Organizational Behavior and Human Decision Processes*, *50*(2), 179–211.
Ajzen, I. and Fishbein, M. (1980). *Understanding Attitudes and Predicting Social Behaviour*. Englewood Cliffs NJ: Prentice Hall.
Akehurst, G. (2009). User generated content: The use of blogs for tourism organisations and tourism consumers. *Service Business*, *3*(1), 51–61.
Alemneh, D.G., Rorissa, A. and Assefa, S. (2016). Harnessing social media for promoting tourism in Africa: An exploratory analysis of tweets. *IConference 2016 Proceedings*.
Asongu, S. and Odhiambo, N.M. (2019). Tourism and social media in the world: An empirical investigation. *Journal of Economic Studies*, *46*(7), 1319–1331.
Bagozzi, R., (1982). A field investigation of causal relations among cognitions, affect, intentions, and behaviour. *Journal of Marketing Research*, *19*(4), 562–584.
Bonn, M.A., Furr, H.L. and Susskind, A.M. (1998). Using the Internet as a pleasure travel planning tool: An examination of the sociodemographic and behavioral characteristics among Internet users and nonusers. *Journal of Hospitality and Tourism Research*, *22*(3), 303–317.
Boojhawon, D., and Seetanah, B. (2016). The impact of terrorism on tourism demand in Mauritius. http://wtochairs.org/sites/default/files/5%20paper%20terrorism%20and %20tourism.pdf.
Brown, S.A. and Venkatesh, V. (2005). Model of adoption of technology in households: A baseline model test and extension incorporating household life cycle. *MIS Quarterly*, *29*(3), 399–426.
Buigut, S. and Amendah, D.D. (2016). Effect of terrorism on demand for tourism in Kenya. *Tourism Economics*, *22*(5), 928–938.
Casaló, L.V., Flavián, C. and Guinalíu, M. (2011). Understanding the intention to follow the advice obtained in an online travel community. *Computers in Human Behavior*, *27*(2), 622–633.

Chan, N.L., and Denizci Guillet, B. (2011). Investigation of social media marketing: How does the hotel industry in Hong Kong perform in marketing on social media websites? *Journal of Travel and Tourism Marketing*, *28*(4), 345–368.

Chi, J. (2015). Dynamic impacts of income and the exchange rate on US tourism, 1960–2011. *Tourism Economics*, *21*(5), 1047–1060.

Chung, J.Y., and Buhalis, D. (2008). Web 2.0: A study of online travel community. In P. O'Connor, W. Höpken, and U. Gretzel (eds), *Information and Communication Technologies in Tourism 2008* (pp. 70–81). New York: Springer-Wien.

Cox, C., Burgess, S., Sellitto, C., and Buultjens, J. (2009). The role of user-generated content in tourists' travel planning behavior. *Journal of Hospitality Marketing and Management*, *18*(8), 743–764.

Cusick, J. (2014). A review of: "Social media in travel, tourism and hospitality: theory, practice and cases." *Tourism Geographies*, *16*(1), 161–162.

Davis, F. (1989). Perceived usefulness, perceived ease of use, and user acceptance of information technology. *MIS Quarterly*, *13*(3), 319–340.

Ellion (2007). *Web 2.0 and the Travel Industry: Practical Strategies for Exploiting the Social Media Revolution*. ICT-Technical Reports. http://www.elliontravel.com/pdfs/41.pdf.

Engel, R. and Granger, C. (1987). Co-integration and error-correction: Representation, estimation and testing. *Econometrica, Journal of the Econometric Society*, *55*(2), 251–276.

Fauzel, S. (2020). FDI and tourism futures: a dynamic investigation for a panel of small island economies. *Journal of Tourism Futures*, *7*(1), 98–110.

Fishbein, M. and Ajzen, I. (1975). *Belief, Attitude, Intention, and Behavior: An Introduction to Theory and Research*. Reading, MA: Addison-Wesley.

Garín Muñoz, T. and Perez Amaral, T. (2009). Internet purchases of specific products in Spain. Available at SSRN 1367063.

Garín-Muñoz, T. and Pérez-Amaral, T. (2011). Internet usage for travel and tourism: The case of Spain. *Tourism Economics*, *17*(5), 1071–1085.

Granger, C.W. (1983). Co-integrated variables and error-correcting models. Doctoral dissertation, Discussion Paper 83-13. Department of Economics, University of California at San Diego.

Huang, L. (2011). Social media as a new play in a marketing channel strategy: Evidence from Taiwan travel agencies' blogs. *Asia Pacific Journal of Tourism Research*, *17*, 615–634. doi:10.1080/10941665.2011.635664.

Huang, Y.H., Basu, C. and Hsu, M.K. (2010). Exploring motivations of travel knowledge sharing on social network sites: An empirical investigation of U.S. college students. *Journal of Hospitality Marketing and Management*, *19*(7), 717–734.

Içöz, O. (1991). The impacts of inflation on the tourism sector. *Anatolia*, *2*(13–14), 19–21.

Im, K.S., Pesaran, M.H. and Shin, Y. (2003). Testing for unit roots in heterogeneous panels. *Journal of Econometrics*, *115*(1), 53–74.

Inversini, A., Cantoni, L. and Buhalis, D. (2009). Destinations' information competition and web reputation. *Information Technology and Tourism*, *11*(3), 221–234.

Jeng, J. and Fesenmaier, D. (2002). Conceptualizing the travel decision-making hierarchy: A review of recent developments. *Tourism Analysis*, *7*(1), 15–32.

Kasavana, M.L., Nusair, K. and Teodosic, K. (2010). Online social networking: Redefining the human web. *Journal of Hospitality and Tourism Technology*, *1*(1), 68–82.

Lee, M., Lowry, L.L. and Delconte, J.D. (2015). Social media in tourism research: A literature review. *Proceedings of Tourism Travel and Research Association: Advancing Tourism Research Globally*. Paper 21.

Leung, D., Law, R. and Lee, H.A. (2011). The perceived destination image of Hong Kong on Ctrip.com. *International Journal of Tourism Research*, *13*(2), 124–140.

Leung, D., Law, R., Van Hoof, H. and Buhalis, D. (2013). Social media in tourism and hospitality: A literature review. *Journal of Travel and Tourism Marketing*, *30*(1–2), 3–22.

Lewis, I., Semeijn, J. and Talalayevsky, A. (1998), The impact of information technology on travel agents. *Transportation Journal*, *37*(4), 20–25.

Litvin, S.W., Goldsmith, R.E. and Pan, B. (2008). Electronic word-of-mouth in hospitality and tourism management. *Tourism Management*, *29*(3), 458–468.

Lo, I.S., McKercher, B., Lo, A., Cheung, C. and Law, R. (2011). Tourism and online photography. *Tourism Management, 32*(4), 725–731.

Martins, L., Gan, Y. and Ferreira-Lopes, A. (2017). An empirical analysis of the influence of macroeconomic determinants on world tourism demand. *Tourism Management, 61*, 248–260.

Munar, A.M. (2010). Digital exhibitionism: The age of exposure. *Culture Unbound, 2*(3), 401–422.

Nikiforova, B. (2013). Social media in travel, tourism and hospitality: Theory, practice and cases. *Journal of Tourism History, 5*(1), 99–101.

Pan, B., MacLaurin, T. and Crotts, J.C. (2007). Travel blogs and the implications for destination marketing. *Journal of Travel Research, 46*(1), 35–45.

Pantelidis, I.S. (2010). Electronic meal experience: A content analysis of online restaurant comments. *Cornell Hospitality Quarterly, 51*(4), 483–491.

Pedroni, P. (1999). Critical values for cointegration tests in heterogeneous panels with multiple regressors. *Oxford Bulletin of Economics and Statistics, 61*(S1), 653–670.

Schmallegger, D., and Carson, D. (2008). Blogs in tourism: Changing approaches to information exchange. *Journal of Vacation Marketing, 14*(2), 99–110.

Schmollgruber, K. (2007). The social web in destination marketing – Canada and New Zealand relaunch. http://passionpr.typepad.com/tourism/2007/06/index.html.

Seetanah, B. and Fauzel, S. (2019). Investigating the impact of climate change on the tourism sector: Evidence from a sample of island economies. *Tourism Review, 74*(2), 194–203.

Sönmez, S.F. (1998). Tourism, terrorism, and political instability. *Annals of Tourism Research, 25*(2), 416–456.

Sparks, B.A. and Browning, V. (2011). The impact of online reviews on hotel booking intentions and perception of trust. *Tourism Management, 32*(6), 1310–1323.

Stepchenkova, S. and Morrison, A.M. (2006). The destination image of Russia: From the online induced perspective. *Tourism Management, 27*(5), 943–956.

Thevenot, G. (2007). Blogging as a social media. *Tourism and Hospitality Review, 7*(3–4), 287–289.

Torres, R. (2010, October). Today's traveler online: 5 consumer trends to guide your marketing strategy. Paper presented at the Eye for Travel, Travel Distribution Summit, Chicago, IL.

Tseng, F.C. and Teng, C.I. (2014). Antecedents for user intention to adopt another auction site. *Internet Research: Electronic Networking Applications and Policy, 24*(2), 205–222.

Tussyadiah, I., Park, S. and Fesenmaier, D.R. (2011). Assessing the effectiveness of consumer narratives for destination marketing. *Journal of Hospitality and Tourism Research, 35*(1), 64–78.

World Bank (2020). *World Development Indicators 2020.* World Bank.

WTTC (2020). *Travel & Tourism: Global Economics Impact & Trends 2020.* WTTC: London. https://wttc.org/Portals/0/Documents/Reports/2020/Global%20Economic%20Impact%20Trends%202020.pdf?ver=2021-02-25-183118-360.

Xiang, Z. and Gretzel, U. (2010). Role of social media in online travel information search. *Tourism Management, 31*(2), 179–188.

Yoo, K.H. and Gretzel, U. (2010). Antecedents and impacts of trust in travel-related consumer-generated media. *Information Technology and Tourism, 12*(2), 139–152.

36. Impact of social media on tourism, hospitality and events

Gulcin Bilgin Turna

INTRODUCTION

As we start a new decade in 2020, it is clear that social media have become an indispensable part of everyday life: 7.5 billion people live in our world, and 4.5 billion people (53 percent) use the Internet, while social media users have passed the 3.8 billion mark. Nearly 60 percent of the world's population is already online, and the latest trends suggest that more than half of the world's total population have social media accounts.

Tourism management mainly relies on social media in order to develop a good relationship with both existing and prospective customers. A tourist usually chooses a destination by checking social media, where people share photos, videos and stories about their travel experiences. People check their friends', celebrities' and companies' social media profiles before making a touristic choice. By encouraging positive reviews, hospitality managers can take advantage of social media to increase brand awareness and loyalty.

Internet users spend an average of 6 hours and 43 minutes online each day. The typical user now spends more than 40 percent of the time when they are awake using the Internet. It is expected that mobile devices will account for more than half of all the time we spend online this year, but most Internet users still use a combination of mobiles and computers to access it. When it comes to mobile activities, apps now account for more than 90 percent of our total time spent. Social media still account for half of all the time we spend using mobile devices. On average, all the Internet users in the world spend 2 hours and 24 minutes using social media across all devices each day, accounting for more than one-third of our total Internet time (Kemp, 2020, p. 3).

Tourism is an important sector for many countries in terms of providing peace between countries, contributing positively to the balance of external payments, employment opportunities, and contributions to the region where it is promoted. Social media also give institutions great tips on measuring the response of the target audience. Institutions can direct their work by taking into account the complaints, suggestions, and positive or negative comments of the target audience. People who follow the reviews of the holiday resorts and hotels on social media make their decisions based on the comments they read and the ratings of the hotels.

Tourism includes activities aimed at providing a social, psychological, cultural and economic interest that facilitates the purchase of tourist goods and services. Thanks to the Internet, the target audience can be reached in a short period of time at a low cost (Biber, 2000; Alonso et al., 2013). Social media, which change the communication of businesses and brands with consumers, affect the way business is done in many ways. Enterprises use social media to reach their existing customers, gain new customers, build trust, increase their awareness, and to protect their brand image (Mills, 2012). Social media can create information exchange among social units such as people, groups and organizations, and provide users with the opportunity to share information, thoughts, interests and information, and individuals can create content in social media (Scott, 2010, p. 38). Social media include blogs, chat rooms, inter-consumer email, product and service evaluation websites, social sharing sites, and forums. From politics and sportsmanship to activism, from cultural activities to voting behavior and political information process, social media direct many activities and business styles and affect many behaviors in social life (Pelenk, 2011).

People who want to choose a place as a destination can realize their holiday planning through social media, access the information they need, and obtain opportunities such as searching, finding and sharing the information they need for the selection of tourism-related products and destinations (Dina and Sabou, 2012; Zeng and Gerritsen, 2014; Pabel and Prideaux, 2016). People share their travel experiences, photos, videos taken during their travels, comments for their travels on social networking sites. Tourists who show a great interest in shared experience and information make decisions by being influenced by this shared content when making travel decisions (Atadil, 2011, p. 2). Of the participants, 47.5 percent stated that they would share their positive or negative experiences about their preferred accommodation on social networks (Turkcan, 2017). People find the information about holiday travel on social media more reliable than advertisements on traditional media, travel agencies and official tourism sites (Esitti and Isik, 2015). Social media represent 26 percent of academicians' behaviors related to the choice of vacation place (Aymankuy et al., 2013); and 32.3 percent of the youth are affected by social media (Erol and Hassan, 2014). The tourism sector, which is a labor-intensive sector, has two important elements that constantly change and are becoming more important: human and technology. Due to the fact that touristic products appeal to the emotions and are subjectively evaluated, sharing experiences by users and making recommendations can be found more reliable by consumers (Eroz and Dogdubay, 2012).

DESTINATION MARKETING ORGANIZATIONS (DMOs)

How is your organization perceived? Do people trust you? Are they emotionally connected to you? How do they describe your company to friends? These questions make up an intangible and invaluable part of your business: your brand reputation. By using social media to proactively strengthen and protect your organization's reputation, you can increase your target, establish credibility, grow your community, and build the kind of brand loyalty that will separate you from your competitors.

Thanks to the proliferation of online reviews and social media, consumers are now in charge of a brand's reputation just as much as the organization itself. Nearly half of digital buyers worldwide say that reading reviews, comments and feedback on social media influences their shopping behavior (emarketer, 2017). And with more than 2.1 million negative mentions about brands shared on social media every day in the United States alone, the importance of managing your brand reputation on social media is clear (VentureBeat, 2015). Your reputation on social media revolves around the community you build and the content you publish. Social data are an often untapped resource for better understanding your community and your competitors, which can help you make smarter decisions about the content you produce and publish. Here is how to use social data to your advantage, along with tips for building trust and credibility through social content (Newberry, 2021):

First, gain a deeper understanding of your audience using social data, Social listening – monitoring social media networks for mentions of your product or brand name – is an important way to gauge how people perceive your brand. But this is a reactive tactic that only scratches the surface of what is possible with social data. Use these social insights to deliver a better customer experience. Social insights give you a way to quantify and address customer frustrations, common complaints or gaps in the purchase journey. Create content that is more relevant and valuable to your target audience. Keep your finger on the pulse of public sentiment. This will help you avoid putting out campaigns or messages that might damage your reputation.

Second, earn trust through high-quality content, Brands with strong reputations often excel at the same thing on social media by producing content that people actually want to consume and share. Tips for creating high-quality social content: Create content with a purpose. Before posting any piece of content on social media, ask: "How will this benefit our followers?" To build your brand reputation on social media, you need to be a constant source of useful and valuable content, whether it is educational, entertaining, or inspiring. No matter what purpose your content serves, make it sound human and keep it relevant to your brand. Use social listening as a gut check. Spend as much time listening as you do talking on social media, and you will be better able to tell whether or not your content will resonate or be appropriate. Invest in social ads to compensate for declining organic reach. As more people and businesses compete for attention on social media, and networks such as Facebook continue to tweak their algorithms, brands are struggling to reach the majority of their followers through organic posts alone.

Third, build credibility through employee advocacy. The voices of employees on social media can greatly influence your brand reputation. Create social media guidelines and communicate them to all staff. These guidelines should clearly outline how employees are expected to conduct themselves online when associating themselves with the organization. This will help safeguard your brand reputation while also encouraging employees to share. Educate employees on social media best practices. In addition to company-wide social media guidelines, your employee advocacy program will benefit from formal social media training. Bring everyone up to speed on social media best practices, across all departments and seniority levels. Appoint employee advocacy leaders. Before you begin scaling social media use throughout the organization, identify who is responsible for communicating employee advocacy initiatives and creating appropriate incentives. This is especially important for large organizations, where it is difficult to ensure participation across all departments. Make it easy for employees to share your brand's content.

Here are three ways to proactively protect your brand on social media:

1. Secure your accounts and shut down threats. Account hijacking and fraud are two of the most prevalent risks on social media.
2. Track brand sentiment to prevent crises. Social media allows anyone to openly criticize your brand. Handling this criticism appropriately can lead to healthy dialogue. It can even turn vocal critics into brand advocates. When it is not handled well – or, worse, it is not handled at all – it can spiral into a public relations (PR) crisis on social media.
3. Ensure compliance with regulatory standards. If your organization operates in a regulated industry such as health care, financial services or government, you are familiar with the compliance requirements that your marketing and communication efforts must follow.

Social media compliance is still a relatively new area, however, and failing to comply has serious consequences.

From compliance breaches and fake accounts to account hijacking and fraud, your brand faces many different risks on social media. Using social media to strengthen your reputation can both increase the value of your brand and protect it against these risks. But a strong brand reputation cannot be created overnight. Your entire organization needs to think about reputation as a competitive advantage, a driver of growth, and a strategic asset that can be harnessed through social media.

"Destination managers and marketers should understand that different tourists have different types of information needs. Destination managers and marketers can use tourists' level of prior product knowledge (familiarity and expertise) as a segmentation tool to develop communication strategies that are most appropriate for each segment" (Gursoy and McCleary, 2003). Therefore, DMOs might address a different type of tourist segments by implementing different techniques on social networking services. Some tourism organizations such as VisitBritain, Disney, Vail Resorts, Virgin and KLM are embracing social media to good effect (Hudson and Thal, 2013).

Hotel operators in Malaysia have challenges in maintaining the level of engagement with their customers, and they do not have good knowledge on how to measure their level of engagement with the customers. Selecting multilingual and professional employees with good interpersonal skills provides the key characteristics to ensure that a hotel's social media platform is managed effectively (Hashim and Fadhil, 2017). Local chain hotels in Turkey provide social media operation with their marketing staff located inside their hotels, and they are act less professionally and create personal dependency on marketing persons. International hotels have central social media operation centers with more enhanced social media tools, but they cannot reach all of the events worldwide (Gulbahar and Yildirim, 2015). According to a survey of 50 hotels of Madhya Pradesh in India, it was proven that the concept of internal marketing (the combined discipline of marketing, human resources and operations) could be applied to the hotels in all locations regardless of the country. "Hotel managers and policymakers must open their minds to new ideas such as internal marketing and apply this concept in a more focused and thorough manner" (Kaurav et al., 2015).

Business managers increasingly understand the importance of social media in gaining new customers and establishing loyal customers. DMOs can expand their activities, such as customer relations, sales development and advertisement, to large audiences at low cost.

While there are hundreds of different online threats that may affect your organization, risks on social media fall into six main categories of common social media risks and threats which you need to know about.

The first is account neglect. If your organization has social media accounts, but you do not actively monitor or respond to conversations, that is account neglect. This leaves your brand vulnerable to unaddressed customer complaints, product issues or spam, which can be extremely damaging to your brand. Whether you are active on social or not, people will engage with your brand. When customers ask questions on social media, they expect a response within a few hours; and 82 percent of customers say that having a fast response time is essential for a positive brand experience.

Second is human error. When security processes break down, we may be tempted to blame faulty systems and networks, but people are often responsible. When someone accidentally uploads the wrong image for a social post, shares information from the wrong account, or unknowingly shares sensitive data, that is human error. According to a Forbes Insights Report, human error is the threat with the highest economic impact. It is behind one-third of information technology disruptions, and it is the leading cause of those disruptions. If you do not have tools and processes in place to catch these errors, a single error can have disastrous consequences for your brand. For example, a copy and paste error by US Airlines' Twitter account has been dubbed one of the biggest brand fails of all time. In response to a customer complaint, they accidentally posted a pornographic link in their tweet. With a proper approval system, this incident could have been avoided altogether.

Third is compliance violation. A compliance violation occurs when you break the rules laid out by your company or regulatory body. There are regulatory bodies such as FINRA (see FINRA, n.d.). It has defined rules around what businesses can do on social media. For instance:

> Regulatory Notice 10-06 states that, as a general matter, posts by customers or other third parties on social media sites established by a firm or its personnel do not constitute communications with the public by the firm or its associated persons under Rule 2210; therefore, the pre-use principal approval, content and filing requirements of the rule do not apply to these posts. The same principle is generally true of posts by customers or other third parties on any website established by a firm or its associated persons, regardless of whether the site is part of a social network.

Your team needs to understand what these policies are and how they affect your social activity. Without an approval process to safeguard social media interactions and catch violations, you are subject to hefty fines and lengthy investigations.

Fourth is phishing. It is "the activity of defrauding an online account holder of financial information by posing as a legitimate company" (Davis, 2014, p. 247). Phishing scams are a way for cybercriminals to steal sensitive information such as banking details. There are hundreds of phishing ploys on social media; in fact, the number rose by 150 percent in 2019. A common phishing scam on social media is the fake social media customer service account, which is designed to get people to click a fraudulent link and enter banking information. When someone tweets at your brand, for example, the imposter account will intercept and reply with a link for that person to enter their personal information.

Fifth is account hacks. An account hack happens when a cybercriminal takes over your social media account and sends out messages that are nasty, inappropriate or otherwise off-brand. When branded accounts get hacked, it is a costly PR nightmare, as the response from customers can be swift and severe. According to a report by ZeroFOX, the 2016 hack of NFL (American football) player Laremy Tunsil's social accounts caused around $21 million in damage. Account hacks happen to big brands every day, as McDonald's learned when a hacker used its Twitter account to post about American politics.

Sixth is malware. Malware (short for "malicious software") is designed to gain access to your computer systems and data through malicious software code. It can lead to temporary or permanent loss of your brand's proprietary data. Ransomware – malware that locks or encrypts your computer data and prevents entry until you pay a ransom demanded by the criminal – is also becoming increasingly common. According to a report by the United States Justice Department, there were over 4000 ransomware attacks every day in 2016. That is a 300 percent increase since 2015.

You need strategies to protect your brand on social media. By understanding the risks that face your organization on social media, you can better prepare your team to implement strategies in a safe and secure way. The following six strategies will help you to reduce the risk of human error and will allow you to identify and diffuse issues before they become a problem.

First, identify and remove neglected social accounts. If you do not understand what social accounts are associated with your brand or how they are being perceived, you are at high risk for brand-damaging incidents. By identifying and shutting down accounts that do not add value to your business, you can ensure a consistent brand voice across all your social channels. For example, a multibillion-dollar hospitality organization Delaware North unified its social presence by identifying and dealing with over 40 rogue accounts. By doing a basic inventory, they were able to remove inactive and low-value accounts, and invest more in high-value ones.

Second, update your password policy. A password policy is an important but often overlooked aspect of protecting your brand. Implementing a strong password policy makes it harder for people to hack your company's accounts and impersonate your brand. Everyone using your organization's social accounts should be subject to this policy, which should include at least the following minimum requirements. Complex passwords: passwords should be between eight and 20 characters, and should include uppercase, lowercase and special characters. Two-factor authentication: a two-factor authentication system adds a second level of authentication when you sign in. For example, after signing in with your password, you may be required to enter a code sent to your mobile phone. This adds an extra layer of security to your sign-in process. Single sign-on (SSO) reduces the number of passwords floating around by allowing you to sign in to multiple systems using a single set of credentials. Passwords should be updated regularly and managed by a single administrator or group within your organization. You should limit access strictly to ensure that passwords remain confidential.

Third, create a social media policy. By creating a social media policy, you establish a set of processes and protocols for your brand channels. Most importantly, you make all employees accountable for protecting your brand from malicious behavior. While social media policies will vary depending on the company, your policy should clearly emphasize the importance of protecting your brand's integrity, reputation and values.

Fourth, train your employees. The new reality of bringing your own device (BYOD) policies significantly increases security risk. That is why all employees should undergo basic social media awareness training, regardless of whether they use your organizational accounts or not. Without employee training and education on social media, you will struggle to implement your company policies successfully across your organization. Employee training should include best practices and appropriate use of social networks, an overview of your company's social media policy, a list of common risks involved with using social media, and how to comply with company guidelines, and mitigate risk.

Fifth, set up an approval hierarchy for social media outreach. All of your company's branded social accounts should be protected by a clear approval system to ensure nothing goes on social media without the right approval. You can control who has full access to social content, who can post content, who can submit draft content for approval, and who has limited, read-only access. If you are using third-party apps or integrations, you can also set up systems to flag potentially sensitive content and automatically stop it from being published.

Sixth, use social listening. Social listening is a technique you can use to "hear" the unfiltered conversations happening on social media around your business. It is an excellent way to uncover new opportunities, but also an important aspect of protecting your brand on social media. Social listening sets you up to address complaints, negative brand sentiment, or spam messages before they escalate. Using your social media management software, set up streams or alerts to listen to conversations that include the following:

- Company name (and common misspellings). Start by listening for direct mentions of your brand, and for customers trying to contact you directly. This is a first step toward gauging general sentiment around your brand and addressing any immediate issues. Be sure to include variations of your brand name (for example, for Coca-Cola, include Coca Cola, Coke, Cola, and so on), along with common misspellings.
- Industry keywords and hashtags. Monitoring industry-specific terms and hashtags lets you engage with broader conversations and trends happening in your space. For example, if there is a discussion on social media around a competitor's product recall, people may be wondering whether your product has similar issues, or they may be asking questions about switching to a different product. By following conversations outside your direct brand circle, you can catch these issues, offer facts and build trust with your community.
- Campaign keywords and hashtags. It is important to monitor campaign keywords so you can understand how people engage with your campaign. For example, Dove's Real Beauty Bottles campaign quickly snowballed into a negative commentary on social media. Many of the tweets responding to Dove's ad (that have been featured in articles) have no response from Dove. Without actively listening to your campaign's keywords and hashtags, you risk letting the conversation get away from you and damage your brand reputation.
- Sentiment. Using social media sentiment analysis tools allows you to monitor sentiment around your brand across the globe and in multiple languages. You can get real-time feedback on how your social content is perceived, allowing you to adjust your messaging accordingly.

EVENT PLANNING ON SOCIAL MEDIA FOR TOURISM COMPANIES

Social media has been affecting event organizations more than ever, and any other businesses, by allowing companies to target specific demographics. Promoting events on social media drives attendance. There are millions of people on Facebook, Twitter and LinkedIn, so it is most likely for some of those people to be interested in attending the event. Planners of an event can lead registered attendees to reach out to their social network so that they can also invite their friends to the events. That way, the information can spread virally. Attendees can communicate both before and after the event on LinkedIn and Facebook. In other words, attendees might become reviewers of the events. If the reviews are affirmative, social media stands as a huge opportunity to improve the company's success.

Surveys were distributed to event organizations across Ireland through email, and two interviews were conducted with event professionals to acquire their opinions and experiences of social media in business. It was found that "social media has immensely affected event organizations in Ireland more than other businesses as it allows the company to target specific demographics and provides a medium to display their professional work" (Spillane et al., 2013).

Turkish Airlines is the national flag carrier airline of Turkey. As of August 2019, it operated scheduled services to 315 destinations in Europe, Asia, Africa and the Americas, making it the largest mainline carrier in the world by the number of passenger destinations. The airline serves more destinations non-stop from a single airport than any other airline in the world, and flies to 126 countries, more than any other airline. With an operational fleet of 24 cargo aircraft, the airline's cargo division serves 82 destinations (Wikipedia, 2020).

It all started when former Vine video apps star Jerome Jarre posted a video to Twitter calling for action. He was moved by a story about a six-year-old Somali girl who died from dehydration after having to walk 150 kilometers to find water with her mother. (The Horn of Africa is in the grip of famine, with 6.2 million Somalis in need urgent humanitarian aid; approximately half of the country's population.)

A group of online celebrities joined in, including YouTuber Juanpa Zurita, NFL star Colin Kaepernick and actor Ben Stiller, promoting the hashtag #TurkishAirlinesHelpSomalia. Turkish Airlines pledged to send a plane of supplies to Somalia on March 27, 2017. It gave the campaign organizers ten days to raise funds for the supplies, and a GoFundMe page was set up with the initial goal of $1 million. This goal was reached in less than 24 hours.

Turkish Airlines, the only commercial carrier to service Mogadishu airport in Somalia, did fly a plane of food and water to Somalia in 2017, earned the goodwill of the influencers it attracted, won the admiration of its followers and the respect of the world. "Turns out that social media is for more than selfies" (Lansdown, 2017).

CONCLUSION

People have always loved to share videos and photos taken on their travels. Social media provides an excellent opportunity to share their travel experiences and photos with larger audiences than ever before. Contests and campaigns on social media started to improve in order to take part in the social media activities of many hotel and resort guests who realized this new trend.

Some hotel chains and restaurants used wedding photos shared by guests on social media rather than sharing and marketing their own professional photos on social media. This campaign encouraged the guests who came to the wedding to take photos and share them with the private hashtag of the hotel. This revealed that user-generated content is more important within marketing channels.

Companies that respond to complaints with a sincere attitude establish a strong bond with their existing and potential customers and strengthen their reputation in their eyes. When more than half of Twitter users communicate with a brand, they are waiting for an answer. Answering incoming complaints and questions helps companies to humanize their brands. It is a great way of saying to the current and potential customers that "You are valuable to us."

Social media has a big impact on travel agencies. The fact that users have easy access to information and can book on their own has forced travel agencies to adapt to digital life. These travel agencies are not outdated, so travel reservations are still carried out thanks to these agencies. However, with the advancement of technology, agents have shifted to the digital world rather than face-to-face contact. When young people are the target audience, it is necessary to aim for them to have a good experience in general (or to inspire them to share a new photo on Instagram). It is an undeniable fact that some customers are still looking for face-to-face communication, even though travel agencies have to compensate for the time and money they have lost during the coronavirus pandemic lockdown

Attracting new customers to an establishment is always more expensive than trying to retain customers. Loyalty programs have been an indispensable strategy of travel agencies for a long time. It has been observed that social media has a huge impact on the strategies created by hotels to create regular customers. As many customers are aware, the sharing of one's own experiences with others has a major impact on the institution in question.

The possibility of hashtag tracking, which is a blessing of developing technology, makes it easy for hotels to find their loyal customers and reward them in different ways by using this method. Sharing on social media and getting feedback there can be easily integrated into the customer loyalty program run by hotels. When social media users share posts about an institution they are regular customers of, it becomes much easier for potential customers to see the opportunities offered by the institution and realize the advantages of being a regular customer.

Social media has radically changed the marketing space in the entertainment and hospitality industry. Many customers, in making choices when planning a trip, are influenced by online comments and posts. This makes it imperative for hotels to have an online customer support line to make a good impression. This rise of social media has greatly differentiated the way hotels handle customer relations. As a result, an institution both positively advertises and transfers the experience offered to potential customers by increasing the number of clicks and collecting favorable comments on social media.

The hotels, agencies and airline companies in the tourism sector are connected with each other. Therefore, they should not set up any contradictory promotions and activities. The three elements should be integrated and should work in communication with each other. Word-of-mouth marketing should be included in order to prepare the advertisements and promotions carefully and to achieve success. More efficient marketing and advertising management can be undertaken. The effective use of social media in advertising and marketing should be paid attention to, because the photos, location, website and phone number of your business are visible. In this way, business customers will be able to receive the necessary information quickly and simply. The bloggers who are very popular in this field, and especially travellers, should be followed and paid or contracted.

CASE STUDY 1: COVID-19 IMPLICATIONS FOR THE HOSPITALITY INDUSTRY

Pneumonia of unknown cause detected in Wuhan, China was first reported to the World Health Organization (WHO) Country Office in China on December 31, 2019. The outbreak was declared a Public Health Emergency of International Concern on January 30, 2020. On February 11, 2020, the WHO announced a name for the novel coronavirus disease: COVID-19. COVID-19 is an infectious disease caused by a new virus. It causes respiratory illness (like the flu) with symptoms such as a cough, fever and, in more severe cases, difficulty breathing. It affects especially the elderly and is highly contagious, spreading primarily through contact with an infected person when they cough or sneeze. It also spreads when a person touches a surface or object that has the virus on it, then touches their eyes, nose or mouth. People can protect themselves by washing their hands frequently, avoiding touching their face, and keeping a "social distance" (at least 1 meter) from other people. As of April 6,

2020, there were 1.3 million confirmed cases (the number of people diagnosed with the novel coronavirus), 70 000 deaths, and 270 000 people who had recovered from it around the world (WHO, April 6, 2020).

As of May 20, 2021, there are 250 million confirmed cases of Covid-19, 5 million deaths, 220 million recoveries. Many countries have closed their borders in response to the outbreak. Impacts of the virus are far-reaching and continue to ripple throughout the world as businesses and people in their everyday lives get acclimated to their new reality.

As the phrase "social distancing" becomes a household term, many consumers are playing it safe and staying at home, while some are attempting to continue typical day-to-day operations amidst the restrictions. Curfews, and in some cities full lockdowns, have created a precarious business climate for restaurants, bars, cafes and other businesses dependent on guests. These roadblocks are significantly impacting their bottom line.

The hospitality and leisure industry has been suffering the most immediate repercussions. The news has been featuring the postponement and cancelation of events, conferences, conventions and sports leagues, which immediately drives down travel and tourism for business and pleasure. Therefore, there are two scenarios for which the hospitality industry should prepare a response: the event that a guest, customer or employee contracts COVID-19, and the probable drop in profits.

Preparing for a Business Disruption

In the event of a significant disruption, such as the one the world is facing now, there are several steps that businesses might or should take.

Owners and management should check with their insurance provider to inquire what their policy defines as "major disasters" and business interruption

Many travel insurance companies may not consider this a coverable event. As the pandemic continues to dominate the news, the assumption is that travelers should be aware of the global implications and potential for disturbances. Lodging companies should advise their patrons and owners to review their personal insurance travel policies closely.

Plan for varying lengths of reduced revenue flow by conserving cash and considering a line of credit for the short term. Begin to evaluate your contracts and prioritize expenditures; an immediate action can be to delay or remove non-essential expenses such as travel, entertainment and marketing in the meantime. In the long term, expenditures such as major capital projects or property improvements can be put on hold until business revenue returns to normal.

Consider hosting a strategic planning session with key stakeholders to determine how the impacts might affect the business.

Keep your team's morale up. A strong and effective leader will be needed to reassure your team. As stressful as times may be, it is crucial that your guests/customers have a positive experience, as it is a reflection of your business.

Operational Recommendations

Ensuring that your business is prepared to prevent the spread of viruses is vital to protect your employees and guests. Commonsense guidance includes washing hands frequently, avoiding touching your face, and using soap and water to clean and disinfect frequently used surfaces.

Disaster Preparedness and Business Continuity

If the coronavirus outbreak has taught businesses anything, it is the practicality of having a disaster preparedness and business continuity plan. Any existing plans that enable data recovery, combat property loss and protect safety should also have action items added to protect your business from adverse effects of the pandemic.

Prepare accordingly, not only to offset the damage caused by this outbreak, but to prevent future damage in the event of another, or different, emergency. Being proactive in managing insurance policies, conserving cash and having a comprehensive preparedness plan will protect you, your team and your customers in the long run.

Never forget to look ahead and be optimistic (Combs, 2020).

CASE STUDY 2: HOTELS MUST LEARN FROM HOSPITALS ABOUT THE NEW REALITY OF TOURISM

What hotels must learn from hospitals about the new reality of tourism:

- Like hospitals, hotels must now work to assure customers that they are safe to use.
- Owners must reimagine their businesses as safety companies first, hospitality providers second.

Hotels and hospitals face a daunting and similar task by re-establishing trust with the public after the initial closures intended to stem the surge of COVID-19 cases. Worldwide, most hotels have closed, while most hospitals have been closed for non-COVID-19 elective surgeries and diagnostics.

As a result, both hospitals and hospitality face the same future: assuring the public that our facilities are safe. For both of us, trust is essential; and trust is derived from safety measures that are communicated well. Consider reimagining your business. Prior to COVID-19, you were a hotel company that had safety protocols. Today, you are a safety company that has hotels. Here are nine lessons to help ensure a successful transition to a post-COVID-19 future.

The Safety of Your Employees Comes First

We cannot emphasize this enough. This is the single most important way the hospitality industry can develop the trust of customers. There are two critical aspects here: what you do to keep them safe, and how you communicate about what you are doing. Hospitals found they could cut the rate of transmission of the virus among their own workers through universal masking, universal precautions and cleaning protocols. Some portion of the staff of all big businesses will be infected because of the high prevalence in our communities. Whether your employees attribute that infection to your business will be largely related to the efficacy of your safety measures, and how well you communicated that this was your top priority. Make safety your top priority.

Create an Incident Command Centre

This group should meet every day, and everyone should have a clear role (incident commander, operations chief, planning chief, logistics chief, staffing chief and communications chief). The incident commander should not be your chief executive. Each of your chiefs should be experts in their area, and should possess excellent communication and critical thinking skills. For a small organization, some of these roles could be assigned to the same person. For larger organizations, these roles should each be assigned to a separate individual, supported by teams. We are dealing with tremendous uncertainty and a general lack of information due to the nature of this crisis. Only a formal incident command structure puts you in a position to make good decisions and execute those decisions well. Our advice: if you already have an incident command structure, stick to it. Do not allow areas of the organization to work around that structure. The core of a good incident command process is constant communication. Any pertinent information – any possible problem – must be brought to the command level.

Universal Precautions and Training

After the HIV epidemic, healthcare workers have been relentlessly trained to avoid contact with bodily fluids of any kind from patients. That kind of retraining will be needed for everyone in the hospitality industry.

Cleaning Protocols

A hospital room is easier to clean than a hotel room, but rigorous cleaning works. Hospital protocols include waiting an hour after a patient has been moved out (where possible), the use of an anti-viral cleaning agent on all hard surfaces, and personal protective equipment for cleaning crews. It is possible that some hotels will use UV light. Consider mounting hand sanitizer dispensers outside and inside of rooms, and near high-touch areas such as elevators. Consider putting wipes inside the rooms so that wary customers can perform their own wipe-down of high-touch surfaces.

Consider placing a handout on every bed that details exactly how the room was cleaned. Consider making cleanliness part of your identity: make it visible. On your website or hotel app, give updates on when the room was cleaned, what disinfectants were used, and how air filters are tested and cleaned. Be the first to market with safety as part of who you are.

Invest in Technology

Move towards "low-touch" experiences. Invest in mobile check-in and encourage people to use it, even if they are standing in the lobby. A best-case scenario would be allowing a guest to enter your building and have no physical contact with any surface outside of their room. This is the iPhone moment for the hospitality industry. Just as healthcare rapidly adopted telehealth, so hotels will need to speed up the shift to online check-in. And the tattered plastic menus at restaurants? They have to go.

Continue Physical Distancing

For example, eliminate waiting rooms and crowded lobbies. Customers will not want to stand in crowded lines to check in. Restaurants will have to reopen with more space between tables.

Investigate the Science of Air Filtration and Aerosol Transmission

Hospitals are able to use negative air pressure rooms, which will be difficult for restaurants and hotels. But the reports of aerosol transmission at restaurants suggest investment in clean air-handling equipment.

Understand and Track Recommendations as they Develop for when Individuals are "Safe"

COVID-19 PCR (polymerase chain reaction) tests have been developed. A PCR test detects genetic material from a person's nose and throat. It is anticipated that more tests will be developed to get immediate (such as, in one minute) results by taking a simple saliva swab. By 2021, in order to travel by public transportation, people can obtain a "health pass" if they are vaccinated.

Communicate Your Commitment to a Safe Environment for Customers and Staff Alike, and Live up to those Promises

Investments in training, technology and safety will pay off for the long term. Join association ratings for cleanliness and safety. The hotels and restaurants that deliver on safety will differentiate themselves quickly (Klasko et al., 2020).

REFERENCES

Alonso, A.D., Bressan, A., O'Shea, M.M., and Krajsic, V. (2013). Website and social media usage: Implications for the further development of wine tourism, hospitality, and the wine sector. *Tourism Planning and Development*, 10 (3), 229–248.

Atadil, H.A. (2011). Otel isletmelerinde sosyal medya pazarlamasi: Turizm tuketicilerinin sosyal paylasim sitelerine iliskin algilari uzerine bir alan calismasi. Yuksek lisans tezi, Dokuz Eylul Universitesi Sosyal Bilimler Enstitusu.

Aymankuy, Y., Soydas, M.E., and Sacli, Ç. (2013). Sosyal medya kullaniminin turistlerin tatil kararlarina etkisi: Akademik personel uzerinde bir uygulama. *International Journal of Human Sciences*, 10 (1), 376–397.

Biber, A. (2000). Küresellesen dünyada gelisen Internet ve degisen halkla iliskiler. *Gazi Universitesi Iletisim Fakultesi Dergisi*, Bahar, 60–66.

Combs, L. (2020). COVID-19 implications on the hospitality industry. Global Advisory and Accounting Network. https://www.hlb.global/covid-19-implications-on-the-hospitality-industry/ (retrieved on October 20, 2021).

Davis, V. (2014). *Reinventing Writing: The 9 Tools That Are Changing Writing, Teaching, and Learning Forever*. Abingdon: Routledge.

Dina, R. and Sabou, G. (2012). Influence of social media in choice of touristic destination. *Cactus Tourism Journal*, 3 (2), 24–30.

eMarketer (2017). How social media influences shopping behavior. March 17.

Erol, G. and Hassan, A. (2014). Gençlerin sosyal medya kullanımı ve sosyal medya kullanımının tatil tercihlerine etkisi. *Uluslararası Sosyal Araştırmalar Dergisi,* 7 (31), 804–812.

Eroz, S.S. and Dogdubay, M. (2012). Turistik urun tercihinde sosyal medyanin rolu ve etik iliskisi. *Dokuz Eylul Universitesi Iktisadi ve Idari Bilimler Fakultesi Dergisi,* 27(1), 133–157.

Esitti, S. and Isik, M. (2015). Sosyal medyanin yabanci turistlerin Turkiye'yi tatil destinasyonu olarak tercih etmelerine etkisi. *Karadeniz,* 27, 11–30.

FINRA (n.d.), Regulatory Notice 17-18, Guidance on Social Networking Websites and Business Communications. https://www.finra.org/rules-guidance/notices/17-18 (retrieved on October 20, 2021).

Gulbahar, M.O. and Yildirim, F. (2015). Marketing efforts related to social media channels and mobile application usage in tourism: Case study in Istanbul. *Procedia – Social and Behavioral Sciences,* 195, 453–462.

Gursoy, D. and McCleary, K.W. (2003). An integrative model of tourists' information search behavior. *Annals of Tourism Research,* 31 (2), 353–373.

Hashim, K.F. and Fadhil, N.A. (2017). Engaging customer using social media platform: A case study of Malaysia hotels. *Procedia Computer Science,* 124, 4–11.

Hudson, S. and Thal, K. (2013). The impact of social media on the consumer decision process: Implications for tourism marketing. *Journal of Travel and Tourism Marketing,* 30 (1–2), 156–160.

Kaurav, R.P.S., Paul, J. and Chowdhary, N. (2015). Effect of internal marketing on hotels: Empirical evidence for internal customers. *International Journal of Hospitality and Tourism Administration,* 16 (4), 311–330.

Kemp, S. (2020). Global digital overview, essential insights into how people around the world use the Internet, mobile devices, social media, and ecommerce, we are social. *Hootsuite.*

Klasko, S., Gleason, J.L. and Hoad, M. (2020). What hotels must learn from hospitals for the new reality of tourism. *World Economic Forum,* May 4.

Lansdown, S. (2017). Turkish Airlines to send supplies to Somalia after social media campaign. *Huffpost,* March 20.

Mills, A. (2012). Virality in social media: The SPIN framework. *Journal of Public Affairs,* 12 (2), 162–169.

Newberry, C. (2021). What is Social Listening, Why it Matters, and 10 Tools to Make it Easier. Hootsuite.

Pabel, A. and Prideaux, B. (2016). Social media use in pre-trip planning bu tourists visiting a small regional leisure destination. *Journal of Vacation Marketing,* 22 (4), 335–348.

Pelenk, A. (2011). Sosyal medya ve guven: Hukumet, sivil toplum orgutleri ve ticari kuruluslara yonelik ampirik bir arastirma. *Academic Journal of Information Technology,* 2 (4), 1–31.

Scott, D.M. (2010). *The New Rules of Marketing and PR.* Hoboken, NJ: John Wiley & Sons.

Spillane, D., O'Leary, S. and O'Conor, N. (2013). An analysis of the impact of social media on event organizations in Ireland. *International Hospitality and Tourism Student Journal,* 5 (3), 224–233.

Turkcan, B. (2017). Yerli turistlerin turistik konaklama tesisi tercihlerinde Internet temelli sosyal aglarin rolu: Izmir ornegi. *Ege Stratejik Arastirmalar Dergisi,* 8 (1), 39–59.

VentureBeat (2015). Digital pitchforks: Turning social media complaints into brand wins. December 15.

Wikipedia (2020). Turkish Airlines.

Zeng, B. and Gerritsen, R. (2014). What do we know about social media in tourism? A review. *Tourism Management Perspectives,* 10, 27–36.

Index